WITHDRAWN
HARVARD LIBRARY
WITHDRAWN

IOWA LETTERS

THE HISTORICAL SERIES OF THE REFORMED CHURCH IN AMERICA, NO. 47

IOWA LETTERS

Dutch Immigrants on the American Frontier

JOHAN STELLINGWERFF

ROBERT P. SWIERENGA, EDITOR

WALTER LAGERWEY, TRANSLATOR

WILLIAM B. EERDMANS PUBLISHING COMPANY
Grand Rapids, MI / Cambridge, U. K.

© 2004 Reformed Church Press
All rights reserved

Wm. B. Eerdmans Publishing Co.
255 Jefferson Ave. S. E., Grand Rapids, Michigan 49503/
P.O. Box 163, Cambridge, CB3 9PU U.K.
www.eerdmans.com

Printed in the United States of America

Library of Congress Cataloging-in-Publication Data

Iowa Letters: Dutch Immigrants on the American Frontier/[compiled by Johan Stellingwerff; Robert P. Swierenga, editor; Walter Lagerwey, translator.
  p. cm. - (The historical series of the Reformed Church in America; no. 47)
Expanded ed. of the original Dutch ed. published under title: Amsterdamse emigranten. Amsterdam: Buijten & Schipperheijn, 1975/
Includes bibliographic references and index.
ISBN 0-8028-2668-7 (alk. paper)
  1. Dutch Americans—Iowa—Correspondence. 2. Immigrants—Iowa—Correspondence. 3. Pioneers—Iowa—Correspondence. 4. Frontier and pioneer life—Iowa—Sources. 5. Iowa—History—19th century—Sources. 6. Iowa—Emigration and immigration—History—19th century—Sources. 7. Netherlands—Emigration and immigration—History—19th century—Sources. I.Stellingwerf, Johannes, 1924- II. Swierenga, Robert P. III. Amsterdamse emigranten. IV. Series.

F630.D9159 2004
977.70043931dc22

2004059396

To the Dutch on the Iowa frontier
who contributed to the building of the nation

The Historical Series of the Reformed Church in America

The series was inaugurated in 1968 by the General Synod of the Reformed Church in America acting through the Commission on History to communicate the church's heritage and collective memory and to reflect on our identity and mission, encouraging historical scholarship which informs both church and academy.

General Editor,
  The Rev. Donald J. Bruggink, Ph.D, D.D.
  Western Theological Seminary
  Van Raalte Institute, Hope College

Commission on History
  James Hart Brumm, M.Div., Blooming Grove, New York
  Lynn Japinga, Ph.D., Hope College, Holland, Michigan
  Mary L. Kansfield, M.A., New Brunswick, New Jersey
  Scott M. Manetsch, Ph.D., Trinity Seminary, Deerfield, Illinois
  Melody Meeter, M.Div., Brooklyn, New York
  Jesus Serrano, B.A., Norwalk, California

Contents

Illustrations	ix
Editor's Preface	xiii
Foreword by H.A. Höweler	xxiii
Preface	xxix
1 Emigration: Background and Context	1
2 Amsterdam to Iowa (Wormser Letters 1-16, Budde Letters 1-5)	43
3 The Optimism of Jan and Hendrik Hospers (Hospers Letters 1-65)	115
4 The Disappointment of Andries N. Wormser (Wormser Letters 17-37)	219
5 The Emigrants of 1849 (Hospers Letter 66, Wormser Letters 38-49, Budde Letters 6-7)	327
6 The In-Between Years, 1853-1861	

	(Wormser Letters 50-61, Budde Letters 8-25)	383
7	The Later Years, 1861-1873 (Wormser Letters 62-88, Budde Letters 26-61)	471
8	In Memoriam: D.A. Budde, J.A. Wormser, and H.P. Scholte	625
9	Pella and Amsterdam	635
	Biography of Johan Stellingwerff	639
	List of letters	641
	Bibliography	655
	Index	665

Illustrations

Aerial view of Amsterdam, 1975	3
Johan A. Wormser, Sr. family	4
Henricus Höveker	20
Hendrik P. Scholte and Sara M. Scholte-Brandt	26
Johannes P. Hasebroek	28
Otto G. Heldring	33
Isaac Overkamp	38
G. H. Overkamp	38
Isaac N. Wyckoff	44
Netherlands Steamboat Company advertisement	44
Antonie J. Betten, Jr.	45
A. Wigny	45
Log cabin interior of Frans Le Cocq, Sr.	84
Peter Lubberden	85
Jansje Wormser	97
"Uprising on the Dam," Amsterdam, 1848	98
Map of Gorinchem region	116
Hendrik Hospers	117
Rotterdam harbor, 1847	118
Immigrant ship *Maastroom*	121
Log cabin of O.H. Viersen	127
Pella panorama, 1851	128
Lake Prairie Township map, 1848	136
Hendrik Hospers's drawing of Pella lots	138
Map of southeastern Iowa	175
Plat of Pella	176
Sketch of Hospers farm	185

Guillaume Groen van Prinsterer	220
Jan de Liefde	222
Anthony Brummelkamp	225
Simon van Velzen	226
Carl A. F. Schwartz	227
Scottish Missionary Church, Amsterdam	227
House *Postwijk*, Amsterdam	247
Map locating Budde farm, Burlington	262
Judith J. Zeelt	282
Paris Revolution of 1848	296
Pella panorama, 1849	313
Frans Le Cocq, Sr.	315
Jan Hospers	327
A.E. Dudok Bousquet, Sr.	339
Willem Lubberden	381
J.A. Wormser's booklet, *Infant Baptism*	382
Pieter J. Oggel	390
Budde letterhead, Burlington panorama	401
Scholte Church, Pella	437
Johan A. Wormser, Jr.	439
Albertus C. Van Raalte	461
Floris Adriaan van Hall	472
Hendrik P. Scholte, 1860s	474
Christina Maria Budde-Stomp	510
Diedrich A. Budde	513
Jansje Wüstenhoff-Wormser	608
Budde family gravestone	626
Johan A. Wormser, Sr.	627

'Tis True
C. Rijnsdorp

'Tis true, there is
poisonous hatred in the green hell of primitive forests,
absence of God in the mist banks of the sea,
blinding of eyes in icy snowstorms,
Wrath in avalanches thundering down the mountains.
But in midsummer,
above the endless, green prairies,
by the lightning of departing rain clouds,
there is renewal after the crushing storm,
grace recovered in millions of glimmerings upon the grasses.
And over the earth is displayed
the fragile bow,
clad in the colors of morning.
And so trekking farmers and pioneers move on
to places even more remote.
Not to return again erelong
to speak idle words in a great city,
but to let the tall prairie grasses
wave over their forgotten graves some day.
They sought God's countenance in His creation,
understood the call of the earth
and responded with the silent fidelity of their lives.
And therefore God loved them
and blessed them with a peace
that surpasses all civilization.*

---

* C. Rijnsdorp, "Balkon op de wereld" [Balcony on the World], *Christelijk Perspectief* 21 (1973): 47-48.

Editor's Preface

The Dutch American Historical Commission (DAHC), in cooperation with the Commission on History of the Reformed Church in America and the William B. Eerdmans Publishing Company, is pleased to provide this expanded English-language edition of Johan Stellingwerff's *Amsterdamse Emigranten: onbekende brieven uit de prairie van Iowa, 1846-1873*, published in 1976 by the firm of Buijten & Schipperheijn of Amsterdam. This English edition takes its place in the venerable Historical Series of the Reformed Church in America, under the editorship of the Reverend Dr. Donald J. Bruggink, and with the Eerdmans Company imprint.

The DAHC is a consortium of four West Michigan institutions—Hope College, Western Theological Seminary, Calvin College, and Calvin Theological Seminary. The purpose of the commission is to encourage, coordinate, and support the publication of crucial historical works concerning Dutch immigration to America in the nineteenth and twentieth centuries.

Early in 1999 the commission undertook its most ambitious project yet—the translation and publication of Stellingwerff's massive tome of nearly four hundred pages, together with some sixty illustrations and photographs that enhanced the text. Dr. Walter Lagerwey, professor emeritus of Dutch Language, Literature, and Culture at Calvin College, willingly undertook the task of translating the text, with the assistance of Stellingwerff himself, who cooperated fully in every aspect of the project. Lagerwey's skill at capturing the meaning of the text, even when the words are archaic or obscure, is a tribute to his mastery of both his native and adopted languages. Christina Van Regenmorter, a Hope College English major, assisted in editing the text; her care for detail made this a better book. Finishing editorial touches were from the able hand of Laurie Baron. Jan Niemeijer provided timely advice concerning publication rights, which made this book possible. Geoffrey Reynolds, director of the Joint Archives of Holland, scanned and prepared the illustrations. Cornelia B. Kennedy edited the bibliography to bring it into conformity with the *Chicago Manual of Style*. The layout and typesetting were provided by Russell L. Gasero. Dr. Elton Bruins, as treasurer of the Dutch-American Historical Commission, did much to insure the financial viability of this endeavor.

After the project was well underway, I learned of an additional cache of Wormser letters in the possession of Dr. Jan Peter Verhave, professor of parasitic diseases in the Catholic University of Nijmegen. These "Amsterdam letters," some sixty in number, are the mirror of the "America letters" in the Stellingwerff book. Dr. Verhave graciously donated an exact copy of the letters, and, after a careful review and evaluation, it was decided to have Professor Lagerwey translate them and include them in this English edition. Professor Verhave published a history on the Wormser family of Amsterdam, entitled *Afgescheiden en wedergekeerd: het leven van J.A. Wormser en zijn gezin* [Secession and Return: The Life of J.A. Wormser and his Family] (Heerenveen: Uitgeverij Groen, 2000), which complements the Iowa story told here.

Subsequently, Nico Plomp, a specialist in Dutch immigration at the Central Bureau for Genealogy in the Hague, informed me that Northwestern College in Orange City, Iowa, owned a collection of letters of Jan (John) and son Hendrik (Henry) Hospers, most of which were translated into English many years ago. All these letters relate to Pella's founding. Stellingwerff's original book contained twenty-one of these letters and a travel diary kept by Jan Hospers in the Central College Archives. Stellingwerff copied them while on a research trip to North America in 1974. Forty-five additional Hospers family letters in the Northwestern College library are published here for the first time, thanks to the cooperation of Daniel Daily. The letters are typed English translations, thought to be the work of Henry Hospers's son, Gerrit Hendrik Hospers. Since many of the original manuscripts are no longer extant and the translation cannot be reviewed, these letters are marked with an asterisk, e.g. Hospers 3*, to differentiate them from letters translated by Professor Lagerwey.

Crucial financial support for this book was provided by the Peter H. and E. Lucille Gaass Kuyper Foundation of Pella, Iowa, directed by Mary Van Zante. The foundation's $10,000 matching grant was augmented by contributions from Ralph and Elaine Jaarsma of Jaarsma Bakery in Pella, and from the Dutch-American Historical Commission. Gratitude is also due the family of Elizabeth Bovenkerk Huizenga for establishing the Van Raalte Institute, which has made it possible for me to act as editor of this important collection of letters.

The commission chose to publish *Iowa Letters* because it is one of the most important primary works dealing with the origins of the emigration of Christian seceders from the Netherlands to the American midwestern colonies. Documents relating to Pella's history have also been slighted unduly in the published works on Dutch immigration. This important collection of immigrant letters was wholly inaccessible to the grandchildren of those immigrants. Now they and all future generations can read the story of the founding and settlement of Pella in the very words of the pioneers themselves.

This expanded book contains 215 letters, which is nearly twice the 109 letters in the original Dutch-language edition. All were written during the first twenty-five years of the Pella immigration, 1846-1873; 149 letters are in the Höveker-Wormser Collection, Historical Documentation Center for Netherlands Protestantism, 1800-Present, at the Free University Library in Amsterdam; 66 letters are in the libraries of Central College, Pella, and Northwestern College, Orange City. The foreword by H. A. Höweler and Stellingwerff's preface explain the origin of the initial letter collections.

All the writers were prominent members of the Christian Seceded Church of Amsterdam, some of whom emigrated to Iowa in 1846-1848. The Seceders had left the national Hervormde Kerk beginning in 1834, in hopes of founding a purer church that warmed the hearts of believers as well as stimulated their minds. The national church, state-managed and influenced by the "new thought" of the French Enlightenment, attempted to quash the secession by force. But the effort failed, at great cost to the national social fabric, and Seceders streamed to America by the thousands for religious freedom and economic betterment.

Höweler's great grandfather was a bookseller who in 1837 became the publisher of Hendrik P. Scholte's religious journal, *De Reformatie* [*The Reformation*], the magazine of the Christian Seceded Church in the Netherlands. Johan Adam Wormser, a legal functionary, was an intimate friend of the Christian political leader Guillaume Groen van Prinsterer, the intellectual Jewish convert Isaac Da Costa, and many Seceder ministers. Wormser used his base in Amsterdam to help the immigrants in Iowa establish themselves. On request, he sent goods for the home and farm that were scarce and expensive in frontier Iowa.

The letters in the hands of Professor Verhave, which are added to the Höveker-Wormser Collection, are the "mirror letters" that Wormser sent from Amsterdam to his coreligionists in Iowa, especially his dear friends in Burlington, Diedrich and Christina Budde. The Höveker-Wormser Collection also includes several letters each from the primary immigrant leaders, H.P. Scholte and A.C. Van Raalte. Stellingwerff is a great grandson of Höveker and Wormser, and he inherited all these America letters and gave them to the Free University Library, of which he was then the director. By merging these documents from both sides of the Atlantic, this book provides, as it were, a two-way international conversation about the founding of Pella.

The letters give both American and Netherlandic perspectives on the key issue in the minds of the immigrants themselves and of their relatives in Holland; that is, was emigration a wise decision or a major mistake? In the early days this was an open question. The Buddes, for example, were positive about their decision to settle in Burlington, and their letters urged family and friends to join them. These are typical "bacon letters" [*spek brieven*].

Andries Wormser and family, however, had such a sour experience—two of their children died from scarlet fever within a month—that the family returned to Amsterdam after six months. Wormser's missives provide a rare example of anti-America letters. During his brief time in Iowa, Andries wrote strong letters home recommending that all but the very desperate stay put in the Netherlands. He condemned immigrant leaders bitterly for hoodwinking their followers, and he castigated settlers like the Buddes, who would encourage family and friends to come to an early grave in Iowa or Michigan. This was a self-serving effort, Wormser explained. "I recall that when we were still at home and we read a letter and the contents were not as favorable as we would wish, they were considered derogatory. Later, when it was apparent that a return was not possible, better news is written in order to attract family and friends" (Wormser Letter 30).

Despite his pessimistic outlook, Andries Wormser was a perceptive observer of frontier Iowa. He gave detailed descriptions of early farm implements, crops, livestock, and buildings. He was a realist, little given to the spiritual reflection and pietism that characterized most Seceders.

"Here we are in a wasteland," he wrote, "that at first made a deep impression on us but later bored us because of its sameness" (Wormser Letter 30). When difficulties befell the immigrants, Andries blamed the dominies, especially Van Raalte and Scholte, for leading them out.

The Pella bookseller, Jan Berkhout, and his wife similarly criticized Scholte and offered a jaundiced view of the immigrant experience in four letters in the collection. "One busies himself here as a mole in the earth, trying to keep one's head above water, but with few exceptions, failing to do so. And if we found on the Lord's Day what we missed in Holland for such a long time, then I believe our move to America would have been worthwhile, but . . . the calling to the ministry is denied here. Scholte will preach once in a while but no more." Berkhout's wife noted that "we dare not send truthful letters to Holland—one should be quiet about such matters." She also noted that "all women here are slaves rather than mistresses of households" (Wormser Letter 43).

The carping letters of Andries Wormser and Jan Berkhout are quite remarkable because they are so unusual. Indeed, I know of few other immigrant letter collections that convey such a negative tone as theirs. Herbert Brinks had no such letters in his book, *Dutch American Voices*. Yet, their unhappy experience was very typical; only Wormser's decision to remigrate was atypical. The best estimates are that fewer than 5 percent of Dutch immigrants remigrated in the nineteenth century. Most could not afford to return, even if they desperately wanted to do so.

The letters exchanged between father Jan Hospers in the Netherlands and son Hendrik in Pella between 1847 and 1849 provide a bright contrast to the dreary missives of Andries Wormser and Jan Berkhout. The Hospers's family correspondence, like the Buddes', is upbeat and positive, although the Reverend Hendrik Scholte receives more than his share of criticism.

Hendrik Hospers came to Pella in the first wave in 1847, and Jan Hospers arrived two years later, coming on the same ship as A.E. Dudok Bosquet, A.C. Kuyper, and Jacob Maasdam. Both father and son became leaders in the Pella church and community. Hendrik opened a real estate office and practiced law. In 1861 the father and son, with eight others, purchased Scholte's defunct *Pella Gazette* and launched the Dutch language newspaper, *Pella's Weekblad*. Hendrik served as mayor of Pella from 1867 to 1871 and then became the leader of Pella's daughter colony in Sioux County. The town of Hospers testifies to his business acumen as a real estate promoter and politician.

The second half of Stellingwerff's book contains a long series of letters exchanged between Diedrich and Christina Budde in Burlington, Iowa, and Johan Wormser and his wife in Amsterdam. The Buddes were Ost Frisians who had lived in Amsterdam for many years where they became close friends with the Wormsers in the Christian Seceded Church, before emigrating. The letters were exchanged over a span of twenty-five years, from 1847 to 1873. While the Wormsers kept the Buddes informed about their old friends and struggles in the Amsterdam congregation, the Buddes recounted the loneliness and hardships of opening a farm on the Iowa frontier and the difficulties of keeping their Dutch Reformed faith alive in an American setting. The Buddes helped establish a Reformed church in Burlington, where Diedrich frequently led the worship services and taught catechism. But most Dutch immigrants went to Pella, and the Burlington congregation had to close. The Buddes then joined a German Reformed congregation.

The Budde letters tell of ordinary day-to-day life in the nineteenth century and the struggles against physical deterioration, contagious diseases, and the death of children. Christina's letters provide a woman's view of life as an immigrant in early Iowa. Despite the difficulties, the Buddes remained unfailingly optimistic, unlike the pessimistic Andries Wormser. The Buddes had the true American spirit. Diedrich was industrious, trustworthy, and generous, and Christina knew that the children would benefit from their sacrifices. God had led them thus far and he would continue to carry them. This couple is an example of devout Christians whose faith guided and sustained them in one crisis after another.

If the Buddes were typical pietists, so were the Wormsers and almost all of the correspondents in this book. A deep and abiding faith in God's providence was a hallmark of the Seceders of 1834. Whatever the trial and loss, they saw it as a sign of God's benevolent care, even when they could not understand his purposes. The letters are replete with expressions of simple trust that modern readers will find quite astonishing. Yet, this was the idiom of religious expression among the Dutch Reformed Seceders.

Stellingwerff's book reveals the central role of the Amsterdam Seceders in nurturing the new denomination, and it sheds much light on the interrelationships among the Seceder leaders in the Netherlands and in America. The letters show that Pella pioneer families such as the Buddes, Berkhouts, Hospers, and Wormsers, were city-bred folks who had to make a sudden adjustment to the harsh conditions of the Iowa frontier. These Amsterdammers left a six hundred-year-old city of two hundred thousand inhabitants, with well established institutions, to settle in a country barely seventy years old and a state that had come into existence that very year, 1846.

Interestingly, the Wormser, Budde, and Scholte families were originally all Lutherans from Germany who had settled in Amsterdam, where they joined the Restored Evangelical Lutheran Church, a vital, free church movement. During the religious revival known as the *Rèveil*, which began in the 1820s, these families joined the Hervormde Kerk and then, following the *Afscheiding* (Secession) of 1834, they became Calvinist Seceders, subject to government persecution with the rest. Indeed, Scholte's magazine, the *Reformation,* is filled with reports of church services broken up by police or soldiers, the quartering of troops in parishioners' homes, and expulsions and sheriff's sales of property to satisfy the heavy fines.

But Scholte, Wormser, and Höveker were too independent minded to stay with the new Seceded denomination. Within a short time, Wormser and Höveker withdrew and Scholte was deposed. All became independents, worshiping in house churches apart from any denominational structure. Clearly, these thrice seceders took their religious life seriously.

The seven Scholte letters and two Van Raalte letters published by Stellingwerff are very important sources. Scholte's letter of May 1847, written from New York shortly after he arrived, outlines his thinking about the merits of Iowa over Illinois for the planned Dutch colony. Scholte here also mentions offhandedly that Van Raalte intended to link up with the Reformed Church in America, centered in New York and New Jersey. This was fully three years before Van Raalte actually took this controversial step and long before his own correspondence gives any hint of such intentions.

Scholte's August 1848 letter describes the formation of the government in Pella, his role as justice of the peace and school inspector, and the development of infant industries. In this letter Scholte takes a swipe at Van Raalte for blatantly recruiting new immigrants to Michigan at the expense of Pella. In his letter of January 1849, Scholte implores a rich widow in Amsterdam to lend him $8,000 to avoid personal bankruptcy in a land deal involving the Des Moines River lands for which the state was demanding payment (Wormser Letter 29).

Van Raalte's brief letter of January 1848 from Allegan, Michigan, to Wormser reveals a growing sense of confidence that the Holland colony would survive. Van Raalte confesses:

> When I look back on this past year, then I feel a sense of gratitude in my soul....God has heard my cries....He has helped and planted an entire people thus far for three years....I feared that I would go to the grave having accomplished nothing at all, and now I stand amazed that God has granted me my wish with such a strong arm (Wormser Letter 10).

Van Raalte's lengthy letter of March 1864 to the Reverend Johannes H. Donner in the Netherlands is eye opening (Wormser Letter 60). It was written from Pella while Van Raalte was mentoring the First Reformed Church in the calling of Donner to serve as its pastor. In the letter to Donner, Van Raalte excoriated Scholte for creating in Pella a "Babel" of religious confusion. "For years I have been deeply concerned about Pella," Van Raalte noted. "I was aware that God's people were being shamefully destroyed there, banished from the consciences of the people....For years we had to let them muddle along, and Pella was a slander on the name of God and a disgrace to the people of the Netherlands." If Donner accepted the call, all this would change for the better. And, Van Raalte added, Donner need not fear Scholte. Most people were cured of these "speculative, quaint new ideas, and people began to thirst for a spiritual, godly ministry [of the Word]....That lion of the street is dead—as dead as a worm....He has lost all esteem among Americans and Hollanders....Scholte will be leaving Pella sooner or later, if only he can succeed in disposing of his properties....May God still grant him a resurrection from the dead."

Van Raalte's assessment of Scholte's situation in Pella is confirmed in the letters of others. We learn from Diedrich Budde as early as January 1848, barely six months after Pella's founding, that Scholte refused to organize a church, believing someone else should take the initiative. Many children could not be baptized as a result. A year after the church was finally organized, Scholte was suspended from the pulpit by the congregation. He was preaching premillenial sermons about the imminent return of Jesus and allowing laymen to teach and dispense the sacraments. Said Jan Berkhout, "No father is seen or even taken into account when a child is baptized. You only see the mother, as if she were a whore. She stands there with her child, and without addressing a word to the mother either before or after [the baptismal rite], the speaker comes up to the mother and baptizes [the infant] in the name of the Father, of the Son, and of the Holy Spirit, Amen. That's it" (Wormser Letter 39). Berkhout further complained that because of Scholte's actions in church and in business life the "Hollanders are not highly regarded in America and Rev. Scholte and his gang have finally dealt them the deathblow" (Wormser Letter 27).

The colonists also criticized the lavish home Scholte built on the square in Pella, when everyone else lived in squalid huts and dugouts with roofs of straw. But the biggest cause of grumbling was Scholte's delay in giving a timely financial accounting of his land dealings on behalf of the colonists. When he did so after several years, that festering boil was finally lanced.

Some rumors that circulated in the Netherlands about Pella are laughable. In July 1849 an Amsterdammer reported that a "rumor arrived to the effect that Pella had been attacked by the Indians, that it had been plundered and burned, and that a Holland woman had perished in the flames" (Wormser Letter 37). Of course, nothing of the kind ever happened. Although not always flattering, these letters provide a firsthand picture of daily life, farming, travel, church worship, politics, and almost every aspect of pioneering among the Iowa Dutch immigrants. Since Henry Lucas's *Dutch Immigrant Memoirs* virtually ignored the Pella colony, and because other primary documents are few, Stellingwerff's book is all the more important. This rare collection of immigrant letters gives Pella its due. The letters are also the last essential primary source concerning the 1840s Seceder immigration to America that had remained inaccessable to American readers.

Robert P. Swierenga

Foreword
H.A. Höweler

The papers left by the Amsterdam process server and publicist Johan Adam Wormser (1807-1862) include at least sixty letters that were addressed to him and others in his immediate circle by Amsterdam Secessionists who had emigrated in 1846 or later, principally to Burlington and Pella in the state of Iowa. After Wormser's death on November 1, 1862, his widow, Janke van der Ven (1810-1871), maintained contact with the emigrants until her death. Her oldest daughter, Jansje, also participated in the correspondence. She was a friend of several emigrant children, including Sara Scholte, daughter of the Rev. H.P. Scholte, whose letter of December 29, 1873, concludes the collection (Wormser Letter 88). To my knowledge, none of the letters of Johan and Janke Wormser to Iowa have been located, nor are copies of the letter abstracts extant in the Wormser Archive. [Jan Peter Verhave, another descendent, has these letters in his possession, some sixty in number, and they are included in this volume. —RPS] Thanks to the initiative and sleuthing of Dr. J. Stellingwerff, who also had the opportunity to visit Iowa during a study trip to Canada and the United States in 1974, the publication of the letters was enriched by many new important collections. These include twenty letters of Hendrik Hospers and a diary of his father, Jan Hospers.

The death of Wormser was the loss of an energetic and gifted kindred spirit to the Secessionists, one who was known for his journalistic contributions in the defense of their principles and their rights. He was also highly regarded in the *Réveil* circles. Isaac Da Costa admired him for his intellect and character. For years Wormser had been a close friend and militant partner of [Guilluame] Groen van Prinsterer, who even called him his privy councilor. As his son informs us later in a publication, Wormser suffered terribly from chronic gout, beginning about 1840; especially his left hand and right foot were seriously affected by the painful malady. Having to stay in bed for weeks at a time, he would do his daily writing on a board with a pencil, until the fever returned again. A Bible always lay close at hand.

If Wormser occasionally might have considered joining the Amsterdam emigrants, the condition of his health surely was not his last reason for his decision to remain in Amsterdam. The critical letters from his brother, A.N. Wormser, who for a considerable period was an eyewitness to the hard life of the emigrants, constituted still another warning. The long sea journey on a ship packed to the hilt, under primitive conditions as far as comfort, hygiene, food, and drink were concerned, alone could have been fatal for a patient like Wormser. He was used to a quiet, comfortable life and had no reason to emigrate. After doing office work for years, he was unsuited for physical labor. However, by remaining in Amsterdam, Wormser could provide important assistance to his kindred spirits in Iowa. And that he did.

Wormser became the confidant of a number of Amsterdam emigrants. They provided him not only with detailed reports of their state of mind and what they had encountered in their difficult life as pioneers, but they also requested his assistance in the acquisition and sending of all kinds of necessities for everyday life in home, garden, barn, and business, things that they either could not purchase in Iowa or only at very high prices. In his efforts on behalf of the Amsterdam emigrants as regards money and business matters, Wormser employed the services of the famous banking house, Hope & Co.

It is likely that some letters that Wormser received from Iowa were written with the intention that he should also let others read them as circular letters within a limited circle. The only son of Wormser Sr., his namesake Johan Adam Wormser Jr. (1845-1916), inherited the collection of letters from his father and augmented it with many written documents, including letters from the estate of his father-in-law, Henricus Höveker (1807-1889), and manuscripts from Dr. Abraham Kuyper. The eldest daughter of Höveker was named Catharina Johanna; in 1869 she married Wormser Jr. The couple had ten children, four of whom died at an early age; four sons and two daughters reached the age of maturity. The oldest girl was named Catharina Johanna after her mother. Through her marriage in 1894 with Casper Andries Höweler, she became the mother of this writer in 1899. She died in 1945, a few days after the liberation, and in accordance with her last request she wore an orange ribbon [for the House of Orange] on her deathbed on May 5.

Through the estate of my mother I came into possession of the letter collection of Höveker and of Wormser Sr., my two great grandfathers, plus what my grandfather Wormser Jr. had added. I have designated this collection as the Höveker-Wormser Archive, and under that name I have made it available as a permanent loan to the Free University of Amsterdam. The archive consists of about thirteen hundred letters and other documents.

I have a lovely painted portrait of my grandmother, Catharina Johanna Höveker, which portrays her as a young girl in a light blue dress. She was a small woman with a vigorous spirit and a strong will. The maker of the painting is unknown to me. The same is true for the painting, of which a photograph is included in this book. It [The painting] was made on the occasion of the silver wedding anniversary of J.A. Wormser Sr. and Janke van der Ven, May 7, 1859. Experts who have restored and cleaned the painting have ascertained that it is not signed or identified in any way. They gave several reasons why they considered it to be a good painting; both the plan and its execution attest to the skill of the painter. He has grouped the silver wedding couple, the four daughters and the son and heir, with the little dog, about a round table upon which lies an opened Bible that is the focal point of the action. Wormser Sr. is reading and apparently reflecting with his family about a passage from the Old Testament and is questioning his then thirteen-year-old son. The little dog also shows its interest, which is one of the humorous features of the painting.

As far as I have been able to determine, the portraits of the family members are excellent. Two of them I met often and knew very well, largely through frequent stays with them in my later adolescent years. They are the oldest daughter, Jansje, who is sitting to the right of her father, and Wormser Jr., the basis for whose later solid grounding in the Bible was laid early on by his father, as is evident in the portrait. When I owned rabbits in my younger years and a pair of rabbits had been born, I asked my grandfather, who was staying with us, to give nice names to the pair. He reflected a moment and then said: "Just name them Muppin and Huppin after two sons of Benjamin." The sons of Benjamin are listed in Numbers 26:38ff. In the Dutch *Statenbijbel* [the Dutch equivalent of the King James Bible, translated between 1619 and 1637], they are Bela, Asbel, Ahiram, Sephupharn, Hupham. The name Huppin may be a playful derivative from Hupham. The Dutch word *huppelen* means to hop or skip. And so *Huppin* could be a nice name for a rabbit, with biblical antecedents even, and if you call one Huppin why not the other Muppin!

Jansje Wormser had a very attractive appearance; she was always meticulously dressed and, despite all the ironic sternness in her judgments of people and conditions, things about which she spoke in a very entertaining manner, she was friendly in her conduct. Her special attachment to her younger brother is captured movingly in her facial expression within the portrait. The accuracy of the artist in portraying his objects realistically may be evident from the following. In the painting Jansje holds her hands together in front of her on the table, the left hand with the index and middle fingers outstretched, the right hand partially visible. About fifty years later I often saw my aunt, Jans Wüstendorff-Wormser, sitting in exactly the same position when we both lived in Velp and she was about eighty years old. At the time, a glasses case was never absent from her right hand, while she sat quietly at the table talking or listening, just as in the painting.

The Amsterdam emigrants with whom Wormser Sr. corresponded addressed their letters to his home located in the old downtown street of Amsterdam known as the Oudezijds Voorburgwal near the Pijlsteeg. The painting shows the interior of the room, where in all likelihood the letters from Iowa were read and answered. I still recall the inkstand on the low chest of drawers, since I have seen it used by my grandfather.

Dr. Stellingwerff has fulfilled a long-standing wish of mine by publishing in their entirety the "American" letters that are present in the Höveker Wormser Archive. For this I am very much indebted to him, especially because it was his desire to continue and complete the work that I could no longer do because of an incurable muscle disease that rendered me an invalid.

After granting my request to assume responsibility for the publication of the letters, Stellingwerff got to work with admirable acumen and proficiency, following his own way in securing the necessary, largely new collections from Iowa and the Netherlands. As a result, the letters are now much more clearly within the purview of modern readers. In the reports of their experiences in Iowa, the letter writers repeatedly refer to American customs and practices. As sympathetic witnesses they tell about the good things that they observed in their new environment, but they also express criticism. In the letters we hear the voices of women as well as those of men, and rightly so, for their work in the home and family surely demanded no less effort and care than the men gave to their professions. It seems to me that the letters are not without importance for our knowledge of daily life around 1850 in what was then the western border area of the United States.

I hope that the appearance of his book will provide Dr. Stellingwerff lasting satisfaction and that many people will listen to the Dutch voices coming from Iowa's past.

Written in the Nursing Home of the Johannite Foundation
"Theodotion,"
Laren, Noord Holland, July 1973.

Preface

Iowa Letters consists of 150 letters written by Dutch immigrants about life on the prairies of Iowa during the years 1846-1873 and sixty letters of reply from relatives and friends in the Netherlands. The letters describe the journey, the difficult beginning of settling on still uncultivated land, their family life, and the spiritual support in their church fellowship. Of course, the immigrants took with them a large piece of their past from the Netherlands, so that past and future are woven together in these letters. The documents of the histories of these ordinary yet enterprising people were passed on in their authentic form, but they have now been translated into the language of the land where they settled.

The 150 letters, all originally published in *Amsterdamse Emigranten*, provide a description of the emigrant families of Diedrich Arnold Budde and Mrs. Christian Maria Budde-Stomp, Johannes Berkhout and Mrs. G. Berkhout-Smit, Hendrik Hospers, and Andries Nicholas Wormser and Mrs. Maria Wormser-Portengen. All, except twenty-one Hospers letters, were sent to Johan Adam Wormser and Mrs. Janke Wormser-van der Ven and their children in Amsterdam. They saved the letters and eventually, by a happy coincidence, Johan Wormser's great grandson, H. A. Höweler, director of the library in the *Vrije Universitiet* [Free University] of Amsterdam, entrusted them to me with the request to preserve and publish them. The letters inspired me to establish the *Historisch Documentatiecentrum voor het Nederlands Protestantisme*, where the originals reside today in the Höveker-Wormser Archive. Dr. Jan Peter Verhave intends to donate some sixty additional letters to the collection, mostly penned by Johan and Janke Wormser and their children to the Budde family in Iowa. These letters from the Amsterdam Wormsers are translated and published here for the first time and provide responses to the Buddes, as well as provide a picture of family and religious activities of Seceders who remained in the mother country.

The men who took the initiative as immigrant leaders were the Reverends Hendrik Pieter Scholte and Albertus Christiaan Van Raalte, the founders, respectively, in 1847 of the Pella, Iowa, and Holland, Michigan, colonies. Both were remarkably strong figures who led the *Afgescheidenen* [Seceders] in their break with the Nederlands Hervormde Kerk in 1834, believing that it had deserted the old confessions of the Synod of Dort. It was Scholte who promoted the independence movement. In contrast to Van Raalte, his unbridled urge for liberty made it difficult for him to work with others. He could lead, but to implement established rules was not easy. He labored in his own congregation in Pella, which was opposed to joining any kind of denomination. He stood alone even though he led others.

Scholte, however, is not the main character in this book. Most of the letters consist of correspondence between the Buddes, Berkhouts, and Andries Wormser in Iowa and Johan Wormser, process server in Amsterdam, and his wife, Janke. Andries was Johan's older brother, who in late 1848 immigrated to Pella but returned disappointed six months later. All the families were mutual friends and founding members of the Christian Seceded Church in Amsterdam, but none were closer in heart and mind than the Johan Wormser and Diedrich Budde families.

What struck me most in this research was the fact that the emigrants came from a large city such as Amsterdam. In connection with the Secession of 1834 and their immigration to North America, we think first of rural villages in the provinces of Zeeland, Gelderland, Overijssel, Drenthe, Friesland, and Groningen. If Amsterdam is absent from the picture, then an important link is missing. I hope that this publication will clarify the relationship between Amsterdam and the Secession and between Amsterdam and the immigration of 1847 to America.

This book is important for American immigration history. The town of Pella still maintains a Dutch character, which is also the case in some other settlements in that state. The immigration to Iowa, furthermore, cannot be seen separately from the simultaneous immigration to

Michigan, preceded by the immigration to New York and New Jersey two centuries before, and followed by the immigration to Canada, especially after 1945.

The letter series are labeled in the book according to the *recipients*. That is, the "Wormser Letters" are the letters from Iowa received by the family in Amsterdam; and conversely, the "Budde Letters" are those from the Netherlands received by the Budde family in Iowa. The third set of letters, designated the "Hospers Letters," are those of Hendrik Hospers, a native of the province of Zuid Holland, penned from Pella to his parental family to aid in their subsequent immigration. These letters are in the archives of Central College in Pella. Hospers rose to become mayor of Pella, and he later established a number of settlements in northwest Iowa, one town bearing his name. The twenty-one letters of Andries Wormser recount the disappointments of an immigrant who found life on the Iowa prairies unbearable and returned to the homeland. Remigrating was rare among the Dutch, and less than 5 percent did so in the nineteenth century.

The letters are grouped by chapters, adhering to the chronological order wherever possible. Each chapter begins with a brief explanation of the historical context of that set (or subset) of letters. The letters in the Hospers collection are divided into two parts and interspersed among the letters in the Wormser collection, as are the letters in the Budde collection, retaining, as much as possible, the chronological sequence. Each of the letters in the respective Wormser, Hospers, and Budde collections are identified by sequential numbering. Letters were added from other publications or archives when that seemed desirable either for clarification or enrichment.

I visited the province of Ontario, Canada, and the states of Michigan, Illinois, Iowa, Ohio, and New York between September 18 and October 17, 1974. The cost of this research trip for the publication of these letters was jointly underwritten by the organization for *Zuiver-Wetenschappelijk Onderzoek* at Rijswijk and the Board of Directors of the Free University of Amsterdam. Institutions that were especially helpful included Calvin College, Grand Rapids, Michigan; Hope College, Holland, Michigan; Central College, Pella, Iowa; Northwestern College, Orange City, Iowa; and Dordt College, Sioux Center, Iowa. I owe a special word of thanks to Dr. Elton J. Bruins in Holland, Michigan, and, in Pella, Iowa, to Glenn Andreas and his wife, Verna, and Hendrika Hospers. All those who gave permission to reproduce illustrations, I sincerely thank for their cooperation. In particular, I think of the pleasant responses from Albany and the Municipal Archives at

Amsterdam.

In the last century the rules for punctuation and the use of capital letters were different from what they are now. Some correspondents, especially Mrs. C.M. Budde-Stomp, made scarcely any use of periods and commas. Sentences often run together in a stream of consciousness style. To make the letters more readable, periods and commas were inserted and capital letters added to introduce new sentences. Most of the numerous capital letters within the text, many of which are lower case letters writ large, have been changed to lower case.

Johan Stellingwerff

CHAPTER 1

Emigration: Background and Context

Emigrants Forewarned

"We were spared trouble and grief." Thus Mrs. C. M. Budde-Stomp summarized the social history of her emigration. Her voice is often heard in this book. Not only the men among the emigrants but also their spouses wrote letters. The emigrants of 1846-1848 had been warned. In 1846 a "Catholic citizen" published a brochure in 's-Hertogenbosch entitled, "Verzint eer gij begint! Een hartelijik woord aan mijne landgenooten, over de in ons Vaderland heerschende ziekte genaamd: Landverhuizing" ["Look before you leap! A friendly word to my fellow countrymen, about the disease rampant in our fatherland and named: Emigration"]. He called the magic cry, Emigration, a remarkable phenomenon, a strange longing, and a sickness. "A blinded multitude heeds that cry and is led to believe that therein lies the only anchor of salvation, the only means of rescue from trouble and distress."

The prospect the writer envisions for the emigrant is a difficult ocean journey; hard work; servants who regard themselves your equals; competition; lack of unity in the midst of uncivilized, rapacious, and plundering hordes; and on top of all that, homesickness. This warning pertains not only to Catholic Netherlanders, a considerable number of whom wished to emigrate, but specifically to the so-called *Afgescheidenen* [Secessionists], also commonly called Scholtians for their principal leader [H. P. Scholte]. The author asks these followers of Scholte: "Is it really just a genuine desire for religious freedom that motivates *all* or indeed *most of you* and will piety withstand disappointment, adversity, and probably poverty? You will [be able to] worship and praise the Lord in your own way; but for this privilege are you resolutely determined and are you wholly ready to suffer hardship, hunger, thirst, and all the discomforts, unpleasant experiences, and adversities of life?"

From this book it will become evident that this warning was not overly somber. In 1847 emigration meant crossing the ocean on a sailing vessel to prairies as yet unplowed or to newly cultivated and impassable forests. One became a pioneer, even though the frontier of the settled American frontier had already moved farther west. The immigrants to Iowa came to a land where the first white settlers had driven out the Indians only a few years earlier. Many Dutch were the first to turn a spade in the forests of Michigan and in the prairies of Iowa, and their hands were the first to sow and to plant there.

The largest city between Michigan and Iowa was Chicago. Although it was newly founded in 1835, by 1848 this settlement had become a major center with the opening of the canal that linked Lake Michigan with the Illinois and Mississippi Rivers and the completion of the first railroad. Chicago, the "capital" of the Midwest, was a city of wooden houses that was destroyed in an enormous fire in 1871.

The writers of the letters came from Amsterdam, a city that had received its municipal charter already in 1275. In 1846 the United States had been independent scarcely seventy years, and Iowa was recognized as a new state in that very year. The emigrants came to unsettled areas where houses still had to be erected for the first time.

Who were these Amsterdam natives who ignored the warnings and still left, and to which people left behind did they write their letters?

The Amsterdam Background

The most important and most critical writer in the collection is Andries Nicolaas Wormser, but the largest number of letters were exchanged between Diedrich Arnold Budde and his wife Christina Maria Stomp of Burlington, Iowa, and Andries Wormser's younger brother, the Amsterdam process server Johan Adam Wormser, and his wife, Janke van der Ven.

Budde, who was born in 1800 at Leer in Ost-Friesland [Germany],

Emigration: Background and Context 3

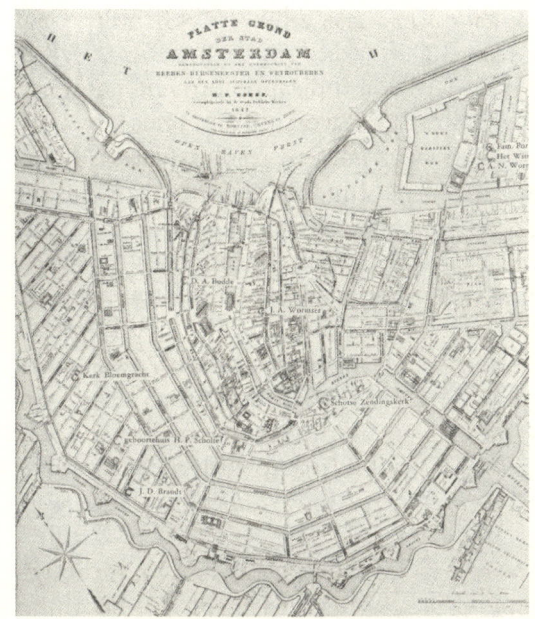

Aerial view of Amsterdam, 1975

moved to Amsterdam with his family, but I have not been able to ascertain the year. His marriage to Christina Maria Stomp, also born in Leer, November 12, 1802, took place in Amsterdam on August 4, 1824. Three surviving children accompanied them to America: Johan Georg Budde, born March 21, 1829; Diedrich Christiaan, born April 13, 1840; and Maria, born September 17, 1844. From the deeds it appears that Budde was a wheelwright and resided at 139 Nieuwe Zijds Achterburgwal in downtown Amsterdam. This is at the back of the present lot at 104 Nieuwezijds Voorburgwal, situated just behind the Nieuwe Kerk. Johann Georg Stump, grandfather of the children and a tailor, appears as a witness in several deeds. He was seventy-three years old at the time of Diedrich's birth in 1840, and he was seventy-eight when Maria was born.

The membership register of the Hervormde Gemeente [Reformed Congregation] of Amsterdam reports that Diedrich Arnold Budde, living in the Wijde Steeg, became a member by profession of faith March 20, 1833. In the margin there is also reference to a deed of secession dated April 7, 1836. Early in 1837 Budde was elected an elder in the Christian Seceded Church of Amsterdam, and his correspondence often references this secession. But on December 8, 1840, Budde became disillusioned with the infighting among the Seceders and resigned his eldership. His letter of resignation read:

Amsterdam, Dec. 8, 1840

To the Esteemed Council of the Christian Seceded Congregation in Amsterdam

Esteemed Brethren!

At the beginning of the year 1837 I was confirmed as an elder in this congregation. Given all the sins and weaknesses that cleaved to me in carrying out that office, I may, in the presence of the Lord, and to this very moment, be assured in my inmost self that I have never sought anything but the honor of his name and the true well being of the congregation. However, the circumstances that have gradually developed among the secessionists, and the sad events that are present on all sides, have shocked me to such a degree, that I must confess, at least for the present, that I am lacking in the courage and strength and clarity to continue in my office, and that I feel compelled to lay it down herewith. I request that Your Reverences to bear with me also in this; and in my prayer wishing Your Reverences the grace of our Lord Jesus Christ and the love of God the Father and the fellowship of the Holy Ghost, I remain, Your Reverend Brother in the Lord.

D.A. Budde

(In Budde Letters collection of Jan Peter Verhave.)

Johan A. Wormser, Sr. family portrait, on twenty-fifth wedding anniversary (May 7 1859) of J. A. Wormser (1807-1872) and Janke Wormser-van der Ven (1809-1862)

(Courtesy of Jan Peter Verhave © Foto Ten Haurtesen)

The Wormser family also stems from Germany. Georg Adam Wormser was born July 22, 1767, in Talbeim. On April 15, 1803, he married Catharina Korink, who had been baptized in the Lutheran church in Amsterdam in 1777. Six children are known to have been born of this marriage:

1. Johanna Christiaan Wormser, 1804-1820.
2. Andries Nicolaas Wormser, baptized a Lutheran September 1, 1805, and died in Amsterdam February 1, 1864.
3. Johan Adam Wormser, baptized a Lutheran June 17, 1807, and died in Amsterdam November 1, 1862.
4. Hendrik Wormser, baptized a Lutheran February 21, 1810, and died in Leiden March 25, 1887.
5. Catharina Wormser, born in Amsterdam June 4, 1813, lived in with the family of Hendrik Wormser in Nijverdal, where she died August 13, 1859.
6. Martinus Wormser, born in Amsterdam April 11, 1815. Like the eldest son he seems to have died at an early age.

In the letters we encounter the three sons, Andries, Johan, and Hendrik Wormser, as adult citizens; their mother, Catharina Korink, is also mentioned. She died in 1852, twenty-eight years after her husband. All three sons were office clerks. During the Belgian Revolt, Andries took military service, became a mobile marksman, and was awarded the medal of the *Militaire Willemsorde* [Military Williams Order]. Johan, after studying to become a teacher, was employed in the law office of F.A. van Hall, who later became a cabinet minister. There, Johan worked himself up to become a process server, and he resided at 205 Oude Zijds Voorburgwal by the Pijlsteeg. This parcel was later absorbed into the warehouse of Wijnand Fockink. The location was near the present monument on the Dam Square. Hendrik became an employee of the Netherlands Trading Company and moved to Noetele near Hellendoorn, the present-day Nijverdal.

On August 3, 1836, Andries married Maria Portengen. He was then thirty years old, and she was six years younger than he was. Their daughters, Anna, Maria, Lena, and Sophie, were born in 1837, 1838, 1839, and 1841, respectively. Several brothers of his wife, Willem, Leendert, and Carel Portengen, signed the birth registers as witnesses. They were all carpenters, but their father, Jacob Portengen, is designated as a ship's carpenter. They worked on Kattenberg [Island] near the White Cross wharf. Andries Wormser moved in close to them, in 1838 at 155 Hoogte van Kadijk and in 1839 at 24 Kleine Kattenburgerstraat. There is also a reference to Captain Jacob Portengen in the letters. He was captain of the *Fosca Helena* (1853-55), the *Eensgezindheid* (1855-58), the *Henriette* (1859-63), and the *Nicolaas Witsen* (1864-68) for the ship owner J. Meyes and Son of Amsterdam. Thus, we must locate Andries Wormser in the vicinity of the naval yard and the harbor of Amsterdam.

From the letters it is evident that Andries Wormser was an accurate observer of implements, products, and structures. Clearly, he was a realist who, when the emigration fell behind expectations, blamed the "advocates such as the Reverends Van Raalte, Brummelkamp, and Scholte" (Wormser Letter 24). His motto might as well have been, "As far as I am concerned you can keep your novelties if they are not better or at least as good as the old" (Wormser Letter 20). We do not find any religious motifs in him, and nature did not continue to fascinate him: "Here you enter a wasteland that can make a very deep impression on you initially, but presently it becomes wearisome and boring by its monotony" (Wormser Letter 30).

The prairie offered an overwhelming spectacle of vast fields with their tremendous thunderstorms in the summer, the blazing prairie fires in the fall, blinding snow storms in the winter, and the splendor of flowers in spring time with slopes full of blooming flowers and undulating grass where the trees cluster in the dales of brooks and rivers, and with its lonely log cabins that were called a town when there were just three to five of them standing together. Andries Wormser did have an eye for all that, but his calculating mind soon saw the reverse side of things.

Johan Adam Wormser was an entirely different kind of person. He became a process server, but he lived in the world of the knowledge of the truth. An office clerk at the age of twenty-six, he married twenty-four-year-old Janke van der Ven. When their eldest daughter, Jansje, was born August 10, 1835, the book dealer Gerrit van Peursen signed as a witness, and after the birth of Catharina October 27, 1836, the same Van Peursen appeared at the register of deeds, accompanied by the book dealer Henricus Höveker, age twenty-nine, residing at Warmoesgracht 1.

Wormser wrote the jurist G[uillaume] Groen van Prinsterer on April 6, 1849, that he had been converted at the age of twenty-three. When he married Janke, who had been baptized in the Hervormde Westerkerk [in Amsterdam] March 9, 1810, instead of joining the *Herteld Evangelisch Lutherse Kerk* [Restored Evangelical Lutheran Church], he became a member of the Hervormde Kerk. He wrote to Groen (December 1, 1843), "Since my secession from the Hervormde Kerk in 1836, I have constantly been engaged in the religious training of our children." Wormser became an elder with the Secessionists in 1837. By then Budde had already served several months as an elder.

Hendrik Wormser, living in Overijssel, married Magdalena Arends July 27, 1836, in Amsterdam. She was a maid, born in Ommen [Overijssel], living on the Heerengracht where it intersects with the Warmoesstraat. Nine children were born to them in Nijverdal in the years between 1837 and 1851. Their daughter Elizabeth later became the mother of Willem de Merode, the poet.[1] After being married seventeen years, the wife of Hendrik died. Her tombstone reads: "Magdalena Arends, housewife of Hendrik Wormser, born March 3, 1812, died March 22, 1854. A sorely tested but patient sufferer in this life, but now blessed with God through Christ."

The young age of his many children, the poor health of his wife, and a good position were reason enough for Hendrik Wormser not to emigrate when half of the Secessionist congregation of Hellendoorn left for Michigan with the Reverend Seine Bolks August 18, 1847.

Hendrik Wormser remarried with Maria Arends, a half-sister of his former wife and fourteen years his junior. Four more children were born and all four of them later emigrated to America, as well as four of the nine children by his first marriage. Hendrik Wormser was the leader of the Secessionist congregation in Hellendoorn near Nijverdal until Seine Bolks became preacher there December 19, 1841. Wormser took over again when Bolks emigrated.

The great leader of the emigration to the forests of Michigan, the Reverend A. C. Van Raalte, was the Seceder preacher in Ommen. The wife of Hendrik Wormser came from Ommen. Van Raalte preached in Ommen on more than one occasion, and it was at the suggestion of Hendrik Wormser that the congregation of Hellendoorn made it possible for the sheepherder Seine Bolks to be trained for the ministry by Van Raalte. Thus, contact between the process server Johan Adam Wormser in Amsterdam and Van Raalte could easily have came about via Hendrik Wormser. Van Raalte is one of the few letter writers who was not a native of Amsterdam. There is only one letter from him (Wormser Letter 10), and an enclosed letter to the Reverend Johannes H. Donner. Letters of Hendrik Hospers and others, which are not part of the collection, were also added. These are not letters from natives of Amsterdam. Jan Hospers was born in Amsterdam, it is true, but his son Hendrik Hospers was not.

---

1. Willem Eduard Keuning, born in Spijk, province of Groningen, on September 2, 1887, was the son of the principal of the school, Jan Keuning, and of Elisabeth Wormser from Nijverdal.

Dirk Budde and Andries and Johan Wormser were genuine natives of Amsterdam, living in the old inner city. The city then was not any larger than it had been in the seventeenth and eighteenth centuries. The Singelgracht formed the outermost circle. The twenty-six bulwarks and walls were leveled between 1840 and 1848. Two gates and five canals have been spared to the present time. Three city gates, the Leidse, the Utrechtse, and the Weesperpoort were demolished after 1848. Now the only gates still standing as lonely sentinels from an earlier age are those of Haarlem and Muiden. The census of 1840 showed over 200,000 people living within the city walls. Of these, 143,123 were Protestants, 44,858 Catholics, 23,132 Jews, and 236 "others," for a total of 211,349 persons in 24,532 houses, constituting 45,969 households.[2]

The Scholte Club

We are publishing two letters of the Reverend H. P. Scholte. Hendrik Peter Scholte was born September 25, 1805, on the Lauriergracht in Amsterdam, thus only a few weeks after Andries Wormser, and was baptized in the Hersteld Evangelisch Lutherse Kerk. His family was active in the sugar industry; his father owned a factory for the production of boxes for shipping sugar.

The sugar industry was still one of the main supports of Amsterdam. Negroes were transported as slaves to the tobacco, cotton, and sugar plantations in Central and South America; the sugar and tobacco were shipped to Amsterdam; and the sale of these supplied the means for getting new slaves in Africa. After French rule in the Netherlands came to an end [in 1814], the sugar industry continued to be an important one for Amsterdam. Initially, Scholte made his small wooden boxes for reed sugar, then also for beet sugar. But Scholte's father died October 11, 1821, and his grandfather followed a year later. Then in 1827 his mother died, followed by his only brother. H. P. Scholte was left alone with a house, a business, and a capital of about 40,000 guilders [$16,000].

Scholte decided to become a preacher. He left the Hersteld Evangelisch Lutherse Kerk and joined the Nederlandse Hervormde Kerk in Amsterdam. In 1827 he enrolled as a student in the Amsterdam

---

2. H. Brugmans, *Stilstaand getij, 1795-1848*, vol. 5 of *Geschiedenis van Amsterdam* (Utrecht: Het Spectrum, 1973), 197-98.

Athenaeum. In 1828 the student Anthony Brummelkamp joined Scholte. In 1829 Scholte left for the University of Leiden, where Brummelkamp joined him a year later. Following the Belgian Revolt in 1830, the Scholte Club at Leiden included, besides Scholte and Brummelkamp, Simon van Velzen from Amsterdam, George Frans Gezelle Meerburg, and C. D. Louis Bähler. In 1832 Albertus Van Raalte also joined the five.

Anthony Brummelkamp was born October 14, 1811, in Amsterdam. His father was a tobacco dealer forced to sell his business because of Napoleonic measures; he left Amsterdam in 1813. The family first moved to Drenthe and subsequently to Elburg. Anthony then began to study for the ministry, first at the Amsterdam Athenaeum, and then at Leiden University. At Amsterdam he was warned against the followers of [Isaac] Da Costa, of whom Scholte especially was a most dangerous individual, a proselytizer for whom you really had to be on your guard. At that time Amsterdam was the center of the Réveil movement. Scholte introduced Brummelkamp to the circle of the Réveil, people who were referred to as stuffy, Dortian, or orthodox fanatics.

Together with Scholte and van Velzen, in 1830 Brummelkamp participated as a Volunteer Rifleman of Leiden University in the Ten Day Campaign Against Belgium. Back in Leiden, the Scholte Club members realized that they would not be able to become ministers in the Nederlandse Hervormde Kerk without a struggle. A friend of Scholte's, Hermann Friedrich Kohlbrugge, a resident of Amsterdam, wished to transfer from the Hersteld Evangelisch Lutherse Kerk to the Hervormde Kerk after his graduation in 1829, but he was not admitted, not in Amsterdam, not in Utrecht, and not in Nijkerk in 1845. Even baptism was denied to his children. Scholte came from a family that had seceded from the Lutheran Church of Amsterdam to become Restored Evangelical Lutheran. He followed a practice that was occurring abroad: the secession under César Malan in Geneva in 1823 and in France under Frédéric Monod. The latter was the editor of the *Archives de Christianisme au XIXme siècle* [*Archives of XIXth Century Christianity*], a publication that was read by Scholte. So the Scholte Club's members realized that they too might be involved in a secession.

In addition to the friendly and courteous Brummelkamp with his brown curls, Simon van Velzen had also already come under the influence of Scholte in Amsterdam. Van Velzen was not only a native of Amsterdam by birth, as was Brummelkamp, but he had also grown up there. He was enrolled as a student at the Amsterdam Athenaeum at the same time as Scholte. As a student he was known for his polite manners, and for being slender, lithe, and casual. Van Velzen was born December 14, 1809, on the Bloemgracht near the Westerkerk in Amsterdam. After the Secession [of 1834], the house where he was born was to serve as a church and simultaneously as a parsonage. The owner then was Mrs. J. J. Zeelt, but van Velzen was to occupy this parsonage from 1839 to 1854.

Of the members of the Scholte Club, C.D. Louis Bähler was the only one who never joined the Secession. C.F. Gezelle Meerburg, originally from Leiden, became the minister at Almkerk, was deposed, and stayed on as a Seceder pastor. He was loved for his personal style of preaching that focused on the individual. But due to his poor health and early death in 1854, he did not become a leader like Scholte, Brummelkamp, van Velzen, or Van Raalte.

After Scholte, Bähler, and Gezelle Meerburg had already become ministers, Van Raalte, who had been studying in Leiden since 1829, made the acquaintance of van Velzen. The latter introduced him to Brummelkamp, and in turn Gezelle Meerburg introduced them to the De Moen family, which consisted of three sisters and two brothers. Because of his unusual talent, his international orientation, and his independent character, Scholte became the leader of the Scholte Club. But when he was already a minister, three members of the club developed a very special bond through their marriages with the three De Moen sisters. Anthony Brummelkamp married Maria Wilhelmina August 16, 1834, and Simon van Velzen married Johanna Christina on the same day. On March 11, 1836, the younger Albertus Christiaan Van Raalte married Christina Johanna de Moen, born in Leiden, residing on the Heerengracht [Amsterdam], no profession, twenty-one years of age. Their youngest brother, Carel Godefroi de Moen, was a medical student at Leiden and also belonged to the Scholte Club. Besides becoming a physician, he later also became a well-known Seceder preacher. Thus it was not until later that Van Raalte got to know Scholte through van Velzen and Brummelkamp. About that time, [Leiden] professors warned him against the orientation of a couple of Jews who had converted to Christianity, namely Da Costa and [Abraham] Capadose—"kindred spirits and disciples of that old grouser [Willem] Bilderdijk,"—and against Scholte, their disciple.

Van Raalte was neither a native of Amsterdam nor a true follower of Scholte. He was born October 17, 1811, in the parsonage at Wanneperveen [Overijssel]. He was a student at the grammar school in

Bergen-op-Zoom (1827-1829), after which he studied literature at Leiden (1829-1831). After getting his bachelor's degree in literature in 1831, he continued with the study of theology at Leiden, gaining his bachelor of divinity degree January 17, 1835. The son of J. A. Wormser, who met Van Raalte when he was visiting his mother in Amsterdam in 1846, described him as follows: "Van Raalte's personality made a deep impression on me. I can still see him at the table—short in stature; slightly but almost unnoticeably stooped; thin; graying hair; wide forehead; bright blue eyes; tightly closed lips; cheerful but earnest in his speech; his entire countenance that of a man who thought clearly, responding without any hesitation at all; honest and headstrong in his actions and persistent in following through."[3] The son of Brummelkamp wrote: "In his later years Van Raalte was a man short of stature, but with the look and bearing of a general."[4] He reminded one of the little Napoleon, a leader like Scholte.

The Scholte Followers in Amsterdam

When Scholte completed his studies in 1832, he soon received a call to Doeveren, Genderen, and Gansoyen in Noord Brabant. A month later he married Sara Maria Brandt in Amsterdam. She had been born January 17, 1806, and was the daughter of a sugar refiner. She lived at 172 Baangracht at the Elandsgracht, close to the Lauriergracht, where Scholte, who was four months older than she, had produced sugar boxes for her father. On December 20, 1832, he married her.

Their oldest daughter, Sara Johanna, was born in Doeveren in 1834. Then followed two daughters who were born in Amsterdam, lived only a few months, and died in infancy. On June 6, 1839, Sara Maria was born in Utrecht, and Sara Johanna Suzanna was born there June 3, 1842. The three of them immigrated to Pella as Sara, Maria, and Johanna, and there took the names of their husbands: Mrs. B. F. Keables, Mrs. P. H. Bousquet, and Mrs. J. Nollen. Their mother died in Utrecht January 23, 1844.

---

3. J. A. Wormser, 'Door kwaad gerucht en goed gerucht': het leven van Hendrik de Cock, vol 2 of *Een Schat in aarden vaten: De Afscheiding in levensbeschrijvingen geschetst* (Nijverdal: E. J. Bosch, 1915), 11.

4. A. Brummelkamp, *Levensbeschrijving van wijlen Prof. A. Brummelkamp, hoogleeraar aan de Theologische School in Kampen, door zijn jongsten zoon* (Kampen: J. H. Kok, 1910), 34.

We need not repeat here the history of the Secession of 1834, nor the persecution, the billeting of troops [in homes], the mistreatment, the many fines, and the prison sentences that H. de Cock, H. P. Scholte, A. Brummelkamp, S. van Velzen, A. C. Van Raalte, H. J. Budding, and many others endured.

The word *Afscheiding* [Secession] comes from the Royal Decree, No. 1, of January 7, 1816, whereby the *Algemeen Reglement voor het Bestuur der Hervormde Kerk in het Koninkrijk der Nederlanden* [General Regulation for the Governance of the Reformed Church in the Netherlands] was introduced by the state. Article 1 defines membership. Article 2 reads, "All the aforementioned continue to be members of the Hervormde Kerk as long as they have not freely and clearly declared that they are seceding from it, or for lawful reasons have seceded from it."

Because of the governmental regulations, many people felt that joining the Secession of 1834 was an absolute necessity, but that was not acceptable to the government. Freedom of worship was granted only to existing churches, not to new ones. Large gatherings against the Seceders were permitted, but on the basis of a provision in the Napoleonic code, the latter might not assemble in groups of more than twenty people. What particularly irked the ministers of the Hervormde Kerk, the state church, was the pretension of the Seceders that fundamentally they constituted the true continuation of the church of the Reformation.

One year after the first beginnings of the Secession, Scholte founded a Seceder congregation in Amsterdam. On October 14, 1835, a council was chosen and ordained by Scholte in the home of N. Obbes, a broker living on the Bloemgracht. Notice was given to the municipal authorities of Amsterdam. A petition to the king requesting protection, dated October 30, was enclosed. On October 29, the burgomaster and council requested the advice of the governor of Noord-Holland. The next day the governor requested that the police be called in. On November 3, there was already a report from the police, stating that the number attending [worship] had remained below twenty. And on November 9, 1835, the Classical Board of the Hervormde Kerk provided the minister [of justice] with information about the Seceders in Amsterdam: C. Deteleff, H. Middel, N. Obbes, and J. D. Brandt. Concerning the latter we need say no more than that he was a brother-in-law of the ex-preacher H. P. Scholte. Before all the commotion around Scholte occurred, Brandt was diligent in attending public worship services, as was his entire family. Of the four signatories, he was the most well-to-do, because of the fortune of his mother who also seceded. He was a sugar refiner.

Known supporters of the four signatories, who until then included only twenty-five to thirty people, successively resigned their membership in the Hervormde Kerk. These were all people of the lower class, many of whom are scarcely known to us. There was only one among them who, because of her monetary wealth, was capable of doing much. She was the widow Van Ysseldijk-Zeelt, a very narrow-minded woman of limited mental faculties, who was taken in by anyone with a pious look on his face, and who from her extensive monetary resources had given considerable sums to the congregations at Mijdrecht and Zwijndrecht.[5]

This secession was the occasion for the writing of a *Herderlijke Brief* [Pastoral Letter] by the joint ministers of the gospel in the Nederduitsche Hervormde Kerk in Amsterdam. In it, the twenty-seven preachers say: "In order to gainsay increasing rumors to the effect that the number of the Seceders in our congregation already includes many hundreds, indeed even thousands, we only say that there are scarcely seventy who have resigned their membership in the Hervormde Kerk in a written communication to the council" (p.7). Five months later, on July 8, 1835, a request was made for permission to hold Sunday church services at 42 Bloemgracht. There were then 346 persons who were Seceders. On July 14, 1836, the burgomaster and town council granted the request.

The police made a report on the church service held July 17, 1836, that included the [Bible] texts and the content of the prayers. Scholte was preaching. "Each time the flood of hearers was so great that many who were late had to be turned away. The audience consisted mostly of members of the lower class, as well as country folk and skippers, while nevertheless the more affluent and well-known members of the fellowship, such as Mr. Weimer, etc., were already also present. The one exception was Mr. A. C. van Hall, who is presently staying with one of the Bousquets and so was not in the city."[6]

The following week, the ministers and King Willem I were already concerning themselves with the permission granted. On July 24 and 25, 1836, the public prosecutor of Amsterdam informed the minister as follows: "In the gathering of the Separatists there was no one of name or rank other than Mr. A. C. van Hall, lawyer, and his wife." Scholte preached three times. "At the morning meeting there were 360 persons

---

5. F.L. Bos and A. Goslinga, eds., *Archiefstukken betreffende de Afscheiding van 1834*, 4 vols. (Kampen: J.H. Kok, 1940-1946), 2:543.

6. Bos and Goslinga, 3: 323.

in attendance, men as well as women and children, in the afternoon there were 583, and in the evening 463 persons."⁷

The following week, on July 31, Brummelkamp preached three times. He preached again August 7, in the morning to 255, in the afternoon to 154, and in the evening to 247 persons. On August 14, Van Raalte preached to respectively 315, 188, and 251 persons. On August 21, Van Raalte preached again, now to 373, 180, and 329 persons. On August 28, van Velzen preached, respectively, to 391, 209, and 298 persons. In his prayer he said, "Be thou with us, even though the authorities and those in power persecute and oppress us, and probably would like to exterminate us from the earth." At this Minister Van Maanen became so angry that he wrote the attorney general that the prosecuting attorney at the Court of Justice in Amsterdam must give scrupulous attention to this kind of offence. Van Velzen preached again September 4, to 409, 171, and 366 persons.

Meanwhile, many documents were exchanged about the permission granted, and the meetings in Amsterdam went on practically unimpeded. On October 3, 1836, the chief of police reported to the minister that J. Comprie and D. A. Budde had been appointed as elders and H. Höveker and J. C. Keer as deacons. Budde is the author of most of the emigrant letters, and Höveker is the book dealer who served as a witness when the birth of Catharina Wormser was registered three weeks later.

Between November 1835 (thirty members) and summer 1836 (between three and four hundred members) much had taken place in Amsterdam. The newspaper, *Het Algemeen Handelsblad*, published a critical article January 28, 1837, which said: "To sum it up in one word, the government does not say: I declare that I desire to protect those of the Reformed religious persuasion, but, the religious persuasion I desire to protect, I declare to be Reformed. Thus this action of the government is unconstitutional, and it is also impolitic."⁸ The king was vexed by the article, and the ministers conjectured whether the young van Hall might be the author. The attorney general wrote to the minister that the conclusion of the article was "framed in that conceited, confused, and malicious tone, which characterizes all the writings which originate in the bosom of the Scholtians and related groups, and which gives rise to the fear, that they, being incorrigible, will degenerate to madness."⁹ But the government did not dare take harsh action.

7. Ibid., 3: 339-40.
8. Ibid., 3: 150.
9. Ibid., 3: 153.

On April 21, 1836, H. P. Scholte and others were acquitted by the Court of Amsterdam. On May 17, 1836, A. Brummelkamp and W. Weimer were acquitted by other judges of the Amsterdam bench. Neither the king nor his ministers could change anything in these proceedings.

In the meanwhile, the first synod of the Seceded churches was held March 2-12, 1836. It took place in Amsterdam in the sugar refinery De Drie Fonteynen [The Three Fountains], of which Sara Koopman, the widow of J. D. Brandt, was the owner. The *Proceedings* of the synod were published by H. Höveker in Amsterdam and by J. van Golverdinge in The Hague and presented to the king. Scholte, who presided over this synod, wrote the *Voorrede aan de Inwoners van Nederland!* [Preface to the Inhabitants of the Netherlands]. Members of the Scholte Club present at this synod were Gezelle Meerburg, Brummelkamp, and van Velzen. One of the first items of business was the examination and installation of candidate A. C. Van Raalte as a minister of the gospel. Scholte, De Cock, and Brummelkamp were charged with getting out a journal.

Together with the *Proceedings*, there appeared in the shops of the book dealers mentioned above an *Adres* [Address] presented to His Majesty the King, prepared on behalf of the synod by President Scholte and Secretary de Cock, and signed by all the members, including Van Raalte. When the *Proceedings* were reprinted, the following notice was added on page 48:

> *Postscript*
> On Wednesday, the 16th of March, the *Formulieren van eenigheid* [the Forms of Unity], namely *de Geloofsbelijdenis* [the Belgic Confession], *de Catchismus* [the Heidelberg Catechism], and *de Leerregels der Synode van Dordrecht* [the Canons of the Synod of Dordrecht], and the *Liturgie* [Liturgy], together with the *Adres* [Address], was presented in the name of the Seceded Churches to His Majesty, our respected King, in regular audience. Together with those documents there was presented an *afschrift van de handelingen der Synode* [copy of the proceedings of the synod], in order that His Majesty might thereby be persuaded that the Seceded Church does not wish to undertake or to do anything that might disturb the public peace or safety.
> H. P. Scholte, Minister of the Word
> March 17, 1836
> General Correspondent of the Church

The Seceded Church of Amsterdam, basing itself on the acquittal of Scholte and Brummelkamp, on June 10, 1836, sent a letter to the municipal government in which it stated that it would be holding worship services at 42 Bloemgracht. The minister, however, demanded that the police take such action as to prevent a worship service from being held. Then, on July 5, 1836, there is a royal decree authorizing local governments to grant permission for closed religious assemblies. Already July 8 permission was requested in Amsterdam and granted on July 14, as we have seen. Thus, the Seceded church in Amsterdam got more than the royal decree wished to grant.

In the *Geschiedenis van Amsterdam* [*History of Amsterdam*] by H. Brugmans, the Réveil is seen as an Amsterdam movement, and the author says the following about the Secession: "Amsterdam did not play a leading role in this movement," and "the Amsterdam congregation was not established before 1840."[10] To the contrary, it should be noted that Amsterdam was the birthplace of the Scholtians and that Amsterdam clearly and early distanced itself from the enlightened despotism of King Willem I in religious affairs. The congregation was established October 14, 1835. Beyond that, the man who linked the Réveil to Amsterdam was a prominent citizen of Amsterdam: Anne Maurits Cornelis van Hall, who was born February 26, 1808, the son of the president of the District Court in Amsterdam. He graduated January 18, 1830, from Leiden University and was a lawyer in Amsterdam. Already on October 10, 1835, he defended the cause of the Seceders in Arnhem. At that time he said: "Judges, this persecution is driving them into a corner! We deny them the protection and recognition for which they have pleaded and asked repeatedly; and we persecute them, because we do not recognize them. Do we wish to compel these people to seek freedom of religion in other lands, in England, France, or America?"[11]

J. A. Wormser was working at the law office of the van Hall firm from 1826 to 1839. In July 1836, A. M. C. van Hall and his wife, Helena Suzanna van Schermbeek, joined the Seceders in Amsterdam. According to his son, the secession of J. A. Wormser occurred July 27, 1836.[12] The

---

10. Brugmans, Stilstaand getij, 186-87.

11. A.M.C. van Hall, *De Vrijheid van Godsdienst-Oefeningen in Nederland, verdedigd: Pleitrede* (Amsterdam: Messchert, 1835), 51.

12. J.A. Wormser, *"Door kwaad gerucht en goed gerucht": het leven van Hendrik Peter Scholte*, vol. 2, *Een Schat in aarden vaten: de Afscheiding in levensbeschrijvingen geschetst* (Nijverdal: E.J. Bosch, 1915), 139.

same day, his brother married a domestic from Ommen in Amsterdam. They soon left for Hellendoorn in order to establish a Seceded congregation there. The witnesses to this marriage were Andries and Johan Adam Wormser, the book dealer Gerrit van Peursen, and Johannes Berkhout, a thirty-year-old carpenter. The last two names appear in the letters often. But we do not find the names of either Andries Wormser or Johannes Berkhout among the signatories of the address to the king. We do find the following names: D. A. Budde with a child and his wife, C. M. Stomp; J. J. Zeelt; Jan Balke and his wife, H. C. Verheij; Trijntje van Raalte; H. Höveker, "also on behalf of my wife"; G. H. Teleman and his wife, Johanna; J. D. Brandt and his wife, W. L. Hasselman; J. A. Wormser, "also on behalf of my wife Janke van der Ven" with a child; B. J. Hoogkamer and his wife; and more than two hundred others.

However, the sunny summer of 1836 in Amsterdam came to a swift end. A consequence of van Hall's affiliation with the Seceders was that his father and brother proposed that he leave the law office and set up an independent practice in The Hague. He left September 14, 1836, and died in The Hague August 15, 1838. His friends, the Reverends H. P. Scholte, J. Bousquet Esq., Dr. A. Capadose, and G. Groen van Prinsterer, Esq., stood at the graveside with van Hall and fourteen brothers and brothers-in-law. More than a year before Groen van Prinsterer, van Hall had already examined the constitutionality of the measures against the Seceders.

The royal decree of June 5, 1836, of which Amsterdam had so quickly taken advantage, it turned out, did not make it possible to give permission for worship services or for baptism and Communion with a minister from out of town. The only permission granted was for the holding of closed religious assemblies of citizens of a given city whose names had been registered. When this became evident, the Seceders did not care to make any more use of the permission granted. Consequently, there was renewed opposition to the church services in September 1836, and again a number of petitions reached the king. The signatories to the petition of September 15, 1836 asked the burgomaster, W. D. Cramer, to certify that the signatures had been made in person. After listening to that request for two days, the burgomaster refused any further cooperation because of the content of the petition. Again there was consultation at the highest levels about these matters, and again the hard line was followed: quartering of troops, fines, and now also the public sale of property. The king agreed with the minister of justice that quartering of troops could be useful whenever the law fell short.[13]

13. Bos en Goslinga, *Archiefstukken*, 4: 56.

It appears that in Amsterdam the assembly of the Seceded congregation was connived at, until the church council, meeting January 24, 1837, sent a new memorial to the city council informing them that they wished to meet freely as a church. The public prosecutor of Amsterdam appended the following information above the signatory D. A. Budde: "born in Ost Friesland; foreman in a wheelwright shop; rather well educated, but not qualified to make a speech."[14]

On March 22, 1837, the city council wrote that on that day police were posted at 42 Bloemgracht. At 9:30 a hackney carriage appeared in which A. C. Van Raalte, J. C. Comprie, and H. Höveker rode away to the Nieuwe Zijds Achterburgwal home of D. A. Budde, opposite the savings bank. Apparently the police arrived there too late. The account goes on as follows:

> The commissioner of police in the Third District then had the house reported to him, located on the Nieuwe Zijds Achterburgwal between the Gasthuismolensteeg and Huiszittensteeg, put under surveillance to determine whether a meeting was be being held there, and he was informed that at about 12:30 [p.m.] two hundred persons left the house, and as they did there were some cheers from boys. In the afternoon there was again a religious meeting of more than a hundred persons at the same place, at which the speaker was *Albertus Christiaan Van Raalte*, who calls himself a minister of the divine Word, and by his own declaration lives in Genemuiden. The commissioner of police for the Third District, upon arriving at the house, asked this Van Raalte, as well as the occupant of the house, D. A. Budde, for the permit to hold a meeting, to which the former replied that he had a permit from the Lord, and in response to the question whom he meant by that, he said: Christ. Having been told that in this instance a permit from the secular authorities was intended, he appealed to the Constitution and refused to comply with the summons to suspend the meeting and to disband his listeners, saying that he had no power over them. Those present, also being summoned to leave the house, likewise refused, whereupon the commissioner declared that they were in violation of the law and that a warrant would be served. After this solemn declaration, Van Raalte called for the singing of a psalm, which prevented the commissioner from speaking any further. The meeting was

---

14. Ibid., 4: 145.

concluded about five o'clock, and the peace in the street was not disturbed.

At the end of the afternoon meeting, Van Raalte also told those present that anyone who wished to remain could do so; whereupon about fifty persons did stay. About six o'clock the meeting again began with a long period of singing, and Van Raalte moved in front of the table, whereupon Van Raalte and the occupant of the house were summoned by the commissioner to halt the meeting, which Van Raalte, citing many scripture passages, refused to do, saying finally "that he would not stop preaching unless he was compelled to do so by force," while Budde in a fearful tone only said, "I may not do that." Thereupon, it was declared to them that by persisting in their refusal they were placing themselves in rebellion against the law, the king, and the public authority, which declaration was again answered by Van Raalte with scriptural passages. However, in so doing he made a slip of the tongue, saying that the government itself had broken the Constitution. Hereafter the sermon began, and the meeting was concluded about eight o'clock. Although many people had assembled in front of and in the vicinity of the house, there was no disturbance of the peace.

Burgomaster and Councilmen of the city of Amsterdam
(signed) W. D. Cramer[15]

Already the next day the minister discussed the matter with the king. The minister of the interior summed up the situation: "The orders have been given; permission has been withdrawn. Notwithstanding all this, the so-called separatists are holding meetings with more than twenty persons; there is nothing to do but to enforce the revocation and to enforce the orders for the disbanding of meetings. What possesses the burgomaster, the councilmen and police to delay any longer? Go ahead, disperse them! The king commands the governor of Noord Holland to move in 'with a strong arm.'"

However, the Seceders in Amsterdam decided to meet at several different houses the next Sunday, with no more than twenty people at each address, except the inhabitants. The police report for March 27 mentioned as many as seventeen addresses, including J. D. Brandt, Baangracht at the Elandsgracht; J. A. Wormser, Lange

---

15. Ibid., 4: 150-51.

Henricus Höveker (1807-1889), Seceder book publisher and dealer, Amsterdam
(*Courtesy of Jan Peter Verhave*)

Leidschedwarsstraat at the Kruisstraat; and H. Höveker, Warmoesgracht No. 1. The police arranged for military guards at each address, in order to take action if more than twenty persons entered. At four locations, 300, 19, 115, and 17 persons, respectively, gathered, and the police drove them out. The justification for breaking up gatherings of less than twenty was "to protect these very same people from the assaults of the riotous rabble lurking about."[16] The police action thus became a rationale for persecution.

During the summer of 1837, meetings were disrupted repeatedly in Amsterdam, as well as in Amstelveen and Diemen. Alternately, the preachers Scholte, van Velzen, De Cock, Brummelkamp, and Van Raalte were involved in these meetings of from thirty to three hundred people.

Meanwhile, the monthly periodical, *De Reformatie* [*The Reformation*], made its appearance in January 1837. Scholte was the editor-in-chief and van Hall was an important fellow editor; Höveker was the publisher. *De Reformatie* was the *Tijdschrift der Christelijke Gereformeerde Kerk in Nederland* [*Periodical of the Christian Reformed Church in the Netherlands*]. After an introduction, the first issue in 1836 began with "*Het Amsterdamse adres aan de koning*" ["The Amsterdam Address to the King"]. For the most part, the annual volumes contained reports on persecution, troop quartering, court judgments, breaking up of meetings, public sale of chattels, and progress of the Seceder movement.

16. Ibid., 4: 157.

In March 1837, privy councilor G. Groen van Prinsterer, Esq., sent in a memorial that was published July 13 as *"de maatregelen tegen de afgescheidenen aan het staatsrecht getoetst"* ["the measures taken against the Seceders judged by the Constitution"]. By then Groen had already published three volumes of his famous *Archives ou Correspondance inédite de la Maison d'Orange-Nassau* [*Archives of Unedited Correspondence of the House of Orange-Nassau*] and had been the king's secretary for years. This member of the privy council wrote about religious persecution in the Netherlands!

Abroad there were also voices that began to speak this kind of language. The worst thing for the government was the fact that the persecution had unintended consequences. From the Belgian Secession and the Secession in the Netherlands, it became evident that the establishment of a single undivided state church was not possible. Trespassing could not be stopped; in many places trespassing of the law occurred week after week regardless of the penalties imposed. The court system was incapable of dealing with imprisonment on a large scale or even worse. The aged van Hall in Amsterdam was outspoken in his defense of the independence of the [local] magistrate.

In June 1837, the eldest son of van Hall proposed that a compromise be worked out. He himself had no other interest in the "unfortunate religious controversies...other than my dismay at the lot of my good, honest and beloved brother, who to my great regret, is involved therein." He contacted the Amsterdam Seceders, and, because they were peace loving, he wanted them to regulate the matters of the church order in such a way that they could be recognized. However, A.W. Appeltere, who was the head clerk charged with preparing a writ of defense against Groen, opposed the proffered mediation.[17]

The Leiden professor J.R. Thorbecke toward the end of 1837 proposed, as a matter of good will, that one separatist church be recognized somewhere. The government, weary of the struggle, on March 27, 1838, readied a draft resolution to recognize the Amsterdam Seceders, subject to six conditions. The name must be The Christian Church that seceded from the *Hervormde Kerkgenootschap* [Reformed Church]. The king hesitated and wanted a shorter document. The new recommendations were contradictory, and the admission of the Seceded Church in Amsterdam dragged on until May 28, 1839, when the recognition finally took place.

17. Ibid., 4: 165.

Willem I abdicated a year later, and the last of the enlightened despots was gone. But among the Seceders, discord had developed. The future of the Amsterdam church was at stake. When Willem I died in 1844, *De Reformatie* observed:

> The monarch who was so unexpectedly and suddenly translated to eternity by the hand of God was in his time the object of excessive flattery and hollow praises, but also of bitter and unreasonable abuse and humiliation. His reign, beginning under such auspicious circumstances, ended disastrously. Far from the land to which he had always been drawn, he gave his last gasp without a single human witness.[18]

The Wormser "Society"

Until the royal recognition occurred of the *De Christelijke Gereformeerde Gemeente* [Christian Reformed Church] of Amsterdam, Scholte had looked after this congregation. From the very beginning, each Seceder minister assumed responsibility from the church he was serving for one or more provinces. These ministers personally instructed individuals suitable for assisting in this task. They traveled a circuit, preaching everywhere, but still it was not possible to maintain unanimity. Some congregations went their own way under the leadership of a lay preacher. As it turned out, there were differences in point of view even among the leaders. H. de Cock and Budding did not belong to the Scholte Club. De Cock was Reformed in the old tradition; Budding was not consistent or clear in his policies. Among the members of the Scholte Club, Meerburg was in poor health. Brummelkamp and Van Raalte were of a Reformed type somewhere between Scholte and De Cock. Their brother-in-law van Velzen "had a natural penchant for polemics: he liked to put one over on his adversary, would never admit that he was wrong, and beyond that he was inflexible, headstrong, and domineering."[19]

Scholte was quite the contrary; he was ecumenical in his Christianity. On the one hand, he coupled a biblical freedom motif with individualism; on the other hand, he defended Reformed confessions.

---

18. Ibid., 4: 210-12.
19. H. Bouwman, *De Crisis der Jeugd: eenige bladzijden uit de geschiedenis van de kerken der Afscheiding* (Kampen: J. H. Kok, 1914), 39.

More than anyone else, he was the leader of the Secession movement, but without being wholly wrapped up in it. He really stood above individual differences within the Secessionist camp, for some of whom faith demanded placing the kingship of Christ above that of [King] Willem I.

After getting official recognition, the Separatist congregation in Amsterdam wished to have its own preacher. Scholte was called but could not come because he did not wish to give up his work in Utrecht and in Zuid Holland. Brummelkamp refused because he was needed in Gelderland. Then, by a small majority, Van Velzen received the call. He accepted, but he refused to give up Friesland. Elder J. A. Wormser protested in writing and spoke of ambiguity, insincerity, and an unlawful intrusion into the affairs of the Amsterdam congregation.[20]

Van Velzen's intent was to contest the influence of Scholte in Amsterdam. However, a segment of the Amsterdam congregation felt spiritually more akin to Scholte, who had founded and supported the congregation. Like Scholte, they believed that Van Velzen could not be exonerated from the charges of being ambiguous, disputatious, and domineering. Together with Scholte they complained that Van Velzen preached "only a skeleton of doctrinal truths, without a living Christ, without a quickening Spirit, and without a living and active faith."[21]

No wonder Van Velzen took action against these charges. By January 3, 1840, he had dismissed the elders D.A. Budde and J. A. Wormser and the deacons H. Höveker and D. Lijsen. The individuals suspended thereupon announced in the February issue of *De Reformatie* that they constituted the lawful church council of the *Christelijke Afgescheidene Gemeente* [Christian Seceded Church] of Amsterdam.

The synod did not recognize this council. Moreover, on December 19, 1840, H. Höveker returned to the Nederlands Hervormde Kerk, followed on February 25, 1841, by his brother-in-law, deacon J. Lijsen. After 1840 Höveker was no longer the publisher of *De Reformatie*.

Thereafter, Budde and Wormser [and the Secessionists] no longer appeared in public as an official ecclesiastical congregation. Their meetings, held under the name of a *Vereeniging* [Society], took place in Budde's home in downtown Amsterdam. Wormser wrote to Groen van Prinsterer:

---

20. De Reformatie 8 (1840): 189.
21. Ibid., 261.

Our Society in Amsterdam is constantly growing in numbers as Hervormden [members of the Hervormde Kerk] join us (3-23-1844).... Because of the limited space of our [meeting] room, and the very considerable burdens our brother Budde and his wife have taken upon themselves during the past few years, we have been longing for accommodations that are better and free for a long time already (8-30-1844).... My brother and friend Budde, at whose home we have been gathering for about six years, has decided, as have many of our members, to leave for America in the spring (12-19-1846).

The part that Wormser himself undertook in the work of the church is evident in what he wrote to Groen, "On Friday evenings I have a meeting at the home of Miss Abrahamsz; I lead a Bible study for the women, and also for as many men as choose to participate" (12-25-1844). Besides this, he had also been constantly engaged in the religious instruction of children since 1836 (12-18-43).

According to Wormser the purpose of the church is to gather for prayer, to sing, and to read the Word of God for the reformation of one's heart and family, and to lead a quiet and godly life; to seek to provide a godly upbringing for one's children; aiming first at inner renewal, and then letting one's light shine (6-20-1845).

J. A. Wormser took an independent stance over against Scholte. He would report church meetings to the government, but he opposed requests for recognition and authorization [of worship services]. When Scholte and his congregation at Utrecht requested recognition from the authorities in December 1838, Wormser made a pointed comment: "The Secession movement has fallen into a trap" (8-30-1844). Because of Scholte, the Secession movement had been caught in the fish net of the government; Wormser saw this as a source of disunity. Just the same, his friendship with Scholte continued, whereas his relationship with Van Velzen remained estranged. The cooperation between Scholte and Wormser came to expression best in the periodical *De Reformatie*, of which they, along with A. M. C. van Hall (until his death August 15, 1838), constituted the editorial staff.

The appearance in *De Reformatie* of articles by Wormser, Budde, Höveker, and Lijsen that were directed against van Velzen occasioned the Synod of 1840 to make a declaration against this periodical.

We already encountered the names of Budde, Wormser, and Scholte together some years earlier in connection with the publication of the "old writers." Scholte published works of R. Erskine, W. Cowper, T.

Schott, T. van der Groe, C. Ziegeurer, J. Koelman, and J. van Lodenstein, with publisher Höveker in Amsterdam between 1836 and 1839. The book included a foreword by Scholte and had the approval of the church literature commission of Noord Holland, which consisted of Scholte, Wormser, and Budde.

Another example is the booklet of the Reverend Theodorus van der Groe, entitled *Het zaligmakend geloof* [*Saving Faith*]. Typical for this booklet was the attention given to different kinds of faith [temporary, miraculous, true], instead of focusing on the one in whom faith is held. In the time of these "old writers" and later as well, many people sought the assurance of faith by asking what is the nature of saving faith, instead of focusing on faith in the Christ of the Scriptures. In these years Scholte, as well as Wormser and Budde, gave their approval to this kind of theological thinking. In later years Wormser would be most explicit in distancing himself from these views. But in his letter to the ailing Van Hall in July of 1838, he still inquired whether all is well with his soul.

In order to resolve the dispute between Wormser, Budde, Scholte, and Van Velzen, Brummelkamp called for a meeting in Amsterdam on March 6 and 7, 1840. Brummelkamp presided and wrote a report of the meeting. It was his wish that the accusations against Van Velzen be retracted and that the dismissals [of the elders and deacons] be invalidated. But the only result of this meeting was to widen the gulf between Scholte and Van Velzen.

After the fall synod of November 1840, Scholte started taking a more independent course. Even though he had been suspended, Scholte appeared at the synod of July 1843 in Amsterdam, but there he and Van Velzen continued to remain at odds. The result was that on July 27, 1843, Scholte, Brummelkamp, Gezelle Meerburg, Van Raalte, and their fellow delegates withdrew from the synod. After the emigration of Scholte and Van Raalte, the discord between Brummelkamp and van Velzen continued. Only after years of vacillation on the part of Brummelkamp was the unity between these two brothers-in-law restored. Wormser was not a party to this unity.[22] After 1892, we find Van Velzen, Brummelkamp, and Wormser united in one denomination.

De Reformatie reappeared in 1841, no longer put out by Höveker but by Hoogkamer & Co. in Amsterdam. It bore a new subtitle, *Tijdschrift ter bevordering van Gods Koninkrijk in Nederland* [*Journal for Furthering the Kingdom of God in the Netherlands*]. The first series appeared from 1836 to

---

22. De Reformatie 8 (1840): 122.

1840 and contained thirty-nine articles by Wormser. The second series ran from 1841 to 1844 and had twenty-five articles by Wormser. The last series, increasingly devoted to emigration, appeared from 1845-1846 and included one article by Wormser.

In an article about the Amsterdam question, Wormser, Budde, and Lijsen referred to Scholte, saying that they desired greater meekness, composure, and discretion in him, and that they regretted his lack of moderation and patience. But they did not wish to give up on him, because of the effects on his brothers-in-law, whose sensibilities had been aroused when in a moment of passion he attacked things that were fundamentally wrong. He had been guided less by prudence than by sincerity."[23]

When Sara Maria Brandt, Scholte's first wife, died January 23, 1844, in Utrecht, followed four days later by Helena Suzanna van Hall-van Schermbeek, Wormser had to ask Willem de Clercq for permission to publish his poem about these two departed friends in *De Reformatie*. In a letter dated July 7, 1844, from Wormser to Groen we read, "Reverend Scholte, whose three children are being cared for by my wife and me provisionally and until his household is ready, became indisposed last Monday."

In the last letter in this book, the oldest of the three daughters reminisced about these times. Scholte's household was definitely restored on June 13, 1845, by his marriage with the well-educated and artistic Maria Hendrika Elisabeth Krantz, who was from Maastricht, having been born there March 26, 1820. The Reverend A. Brummelkamp of Arnhem performed an ecclesiastical wedding ceremony in Utrecht June 16, following a sermon.

Both Brummelkamp and Scholte preached for the Wormser-Budde Society in Amsterdam, even though this society "in common parlance did not belong to any church." That is what Wormser wrote to Groen

Hendrik Pieter Scholte (1805-1868) and Sara M. Scholte-Brandt (1806-1844) wedding day 1832

23 De Reformatie 8 (1840): 122.

August 30, 1844, but he added that the church is "a spiritual matter..., we *believe* in her."

Wormser, in contrast to De Cock, clung to the baptism of the children of believing parents and later published on infant baptism. He did not have his children baptized in a church, but in this "society." Scholte wrote Groen about these matters on March 23, 1843: "Even the Amsterdam Secessionists still lack nothing that belongs to the real essence of the Christian church. They regularly hold services in which the inquiry into God's Word edifies and nurtures them; the gospel is preached within their fellowship. They enjoy baptism and [Holy] Communion without being compelled to cling to words of the sacraments in the face of the denial of Christ and his atoning death, and they practice genuine Christian discipline among themselves. The only thing they lack to be called a church in the eyes of the world is a separate building, a name, and a societal organization."

According to Wormser's account to Groen of August 30, 1844, this society is "probably the only one of its kind in the Netherlands not carefully thought out beforehand, but established by simply following the Word of God. It stands in weakness, only under the Lord Jesus, and as long as it pleases him. If it were to be disrupted by one thing or another, we have nothing, not even an archive."

Scholte, Wormser, Budde, and to a lesser degree Brummelkamp, greatly relativized the church as institution. The mighty Roman Catholic church, the national Hervormde church, and the "dominocratic" Seceded churches have not been the church for all true Christbelievers. The Constantine period with its big and small churches striving for power, influence, and institutional authority had not yet come to an end. But Wormser, Budde, and Scholte did erect a standard against the Constantinian fall of Christendom.

Groen van Prinsterer, in a letter of August 6, 1845, to Isaac da Costa, described the character of Wormser as follows: "I do hope that Wormser in particular will be invited. I lay it upon your heart; for truly I know few people who, it appears to me, combine such an upright and active faith with such great clarity of insight."

It is indeed significant that Groen van Prinsterer not only published the letters of the House of Orange-Nassau, but also the letters of Isaac Da Costa (1872-1876), of J. R. Thorbecke (1873), and of J. A. Wormser (1874-1876). Groen also republished Wormser's book, *De Kinderdoop* [Infant Baptism], published by H. Höveker in Amsterdam in 1853, two years after Wormser's death.

In 1847, Budde left for America. Andries Wormser followed during the severe winter of 1847-1848 and returned to Amsterdam. J. A. Wormser did not emigrate, and the society continued to exist until 1851. In February 1851, Wormser became seriously ill. In November of 1851, he again experienced severe rheumatic pains. Then on November 3, 1851, he wrote to Groen:

> What a lot of grief the Secession has already cost. I think that we are out of it for good now [that is to say after Brummelkamp ceased cooperating with Da Costa, via Wormser, in setting up a common seminary in Amsterdam]. I expect to discontinue our [Sunday] meetings as soon as Rev. Hasebroek arrives. They have been in existence for about twelve years. But now, because of the prospect that Rev. Br[ummelkamp] might be coming here, we have lost our little hall; and I lack the courage and the strength to lead in worship any longer and to start all over again.

The Reverend A. Brummelkamp, the man in the Scholte Club who stood closest to Scholte and Wormser, became a stumbling block to Wormser because of his actions. Thereafter, Wormser sought closer

The Rev. Johannes P. Hasebroek (1812-1896), Seceder pastor, Amsterdam, 1851-1896
(*Courtesy of Jan Peter Verhave*)

contact with the orthodox Reformed preacher, the Reverend J. P. Hasebroek. In Wormser Letter 47, Budde wrote that he also would not have returned to the Seceded congregation of the Reverend S. van Velzen on the Bloemgracht.

Finally, to round out the sketch of the background, we publish the last letter of Helena Suzanna van Schermbeek, the widow of the lawyer of the Seceders, A. M. C. van Hall, Esq. She wrote this letter in December 1843, a full month before she, Scholte's wife, and the Réveil-poet Willem de Clercq all died. The letter is directed to her children, to Maurits Cornelis (1836-1900), father of nine children and grandfather of the Amsterdam burgomaster Gijsbert van Hall [who on March 10, 1966 officiated at the wedding of Crown Princess Beatrix and Claus van Amsburg], to Johanna Justina (1837-1884), and to Floris Adriaan (1838-1929). She gave copies [of the letter] made by the old Amsterdam judge Van Hall to her children before her death. The original has been preserved in the Wormser archives, along with a letter that Wormser wrote a month before his death July 13, 1838, to A. M. C. van Hall himself. There was indeed a strong bond of friendship and faith between the Van Hall, Scholte, and Wormser families.

In the Van Hall and Van Schermbeek family, "after that there was only one fear, namely that the children might come into contact with reformed Seceders and that then they would catch cold and get tuberculosis." About 1893 in the home of Maurits Cornelis van Hall, the only reference to his parents was as follows: "There will be no talk about those people in our house! They have been in jail! They may have been drunkards or something like that." [24]

The letter reads, "Last letter of Mrs. van Hall to her children:"

> Dear children,
> I do not know whether these lines will ever reach you, and still I feel the need to write them. It may be long after the worms have eaten my flesh before your eyes will be able to read them. Dear children, I am very ill, and I believe the same illness that took your beloved father from us five years ago already will perhaps very soon bring your mother to God. Yes, my dear children, I am going to God, and I would leave this earth with joy were it not that I am leaving you behind.

---

24. M.C. Van Hall, *Drie eeuwen: de kroniek van een Nederlandse familie* (Amsterdam: W. Ten Have, 1961), 63.

My Maurits! The speaking image of your father, may you share not only his mind, but also his faith. Oh, pray to God that he may grant you faith and then use all your strength to uphold the truth. My child, how often did I see in your eyes the tears of love and tenderness when I spoke to you of our eternal Lord and King, God revealed in the flesh, of his suffering, of his death. How he bore the curse that was ours, and his blood *alone* gives us life. My son! Follow God's word, do not forget the lessons of your mother, and believe my testimony, perhaps with half-stilled lips: there is no means of salvation, save Christ alone. Choose; in him is life, outside him perdition! Oh, Almighty God! Hear my prayers, and let my son love you above all else.

Dear Johanna! Dear tender child! Alas, indeed, when you get farther along, you will miss your mother. Oh, how my heart leapt for joy when you put your little arms around my neck and buried your sweet little face when I spoke to you about the crucified savior and you said that you wished to love him. Oh, my daughter, give your heart to the Lord. He who watches over the birds of heaven and the lilies of the field, he will be more than a father and mother to you; even if a mother could forget her child, the Lord does not forget those who trust in him. My child! My prayer is for you, my dear loving little girl; oh, may God guard you from lying lips and treacherous tongues.

And you, my Floris, child of joy, child of sorrow. Oh! My consolation and joy often in deepest grief, how often I have entrusted you as a Samuel to the Lord. Oh, if only my prayer might be heard, that you become a servant of the Lord. Darling creature, with your enticing and friendly eye, oh, do forgive my weakness, Lord, the bond is so very tender. Oh, Lord, strengthen me and forsake me not.

I wrote up to this point, but then I could go no farther, and my health did not allow me to continue. Now it is two weeks later. I have been feeling much better the last few days and still what will the end be, since I continue to fluctuate like a dobber. Dearest children! As for me, I long for heaven, where your father has preceded us.

I do not fear death, because I know what I believe, and then there is no more damnation—for those who believe. If it is God's will to restore me, oh, I will gladly remain with you, if it be his will, and if it is his will to make me suffer long, oh, may no complaint then slip from my lips, and may I be patient, be patient to the very end!

Dear children, oh, pray to God daily and do not let a day pass without reading his Word! Let nothing keep you from doing that; it alone remains when all else fails. Love those who love you, pray for all people, including those of whom you think that they do not love you, and as you are able, do good to all men. Love your grandfather, your grandmother, your uncles and aunts. Be obedient to those under whose jurisdiction you will be placed after my death. Often seek out those people who love God, whether rich or poor, for with God there is no distinction. Attend to the lessons that you get from Reverend Scholte now and in the future. Children, he was the friend of your father, the friend of your mother, oh my dear children. I could add much more, but why should I, my dearest children. If only God by his grace, by his Holy Spirit, might still convert you! Oh! What a joy if after your death I also saw you in Heaven. Oh, Almighty God, hear me please, hear my dying prayer. Oh, convert, do convert my children. Dear Father, thou wilt be a father to them. Oh! Hear me! Hear my prayer! And now my dearest children, dear Maurits, Johanna, and Floris, receive my farewell kiss. My children, how hard it is for me to part from you. But it is God's will, and his will is love. Farewell, farewell, dearest, most precious creatures, my treasure and my joy, receive my last blessing, dear children! Do not forget me, you know how I always loved you. When you look up to Heaven, then your dear father and mother will be living there. Farewell, farewell, I cannot go on any longer. Almighty God, thou knowest my struggle. God bless you and be near unto you.

Utrecht, December 20, 1843.
Your Dearly Loving Mother,
H. S. van Schermbeek
Widow of A. M. C. van Hall, Esq.

The Emigration

On August 1, 1846, Isaac da Costa wrote to Groen van Prinsterer: "Have you already read the most important pamphlet by Brummelkamp and Van Raalte? It made a deep impression on me and in any case it must be one of the subjects we will be discussing."

The pamphlet, *Landverhuizing of waarom bevorderen wij de volksverhuizing wel naar Noord-Amerika en niet naar Java?* (*Emigration, or why do we promote emigration to North America and not to Java?*) was published by Hoogkamer in Amsterdam under the date May 25, 1846. The pamphlet included the letter that A. Hartgerink of Toledo, Ohio, had written May 3, 1846, with the proposal "to establish a colony with ministers, churches, schools and all." Hartgerink was the teacher from Neede who, in September 1845, came to Arnhem to take leave of the Reverend A. Brummelkamp and then acquainted him with the emigration movement in Germany and the Achterhoek [in East Gelderland, bordering on Germany]. Brummelkamp got in touch with Van Raalte; Scholte also reacted very strongly from the start, and J. A. Wormser wrote the constitution for a *Vereeniging ter regeling van de Nederlandsche Volksverhuizing naar Nooord-Amerika* [Society to regulate Dutch emigration to North America].[25]

On April 15, 1846, the *Grondslagen der Vereeniging van Christenen voor de Hollandsche Volksverhuizing naar de Vereenigde Staten in N. Amerika* [The Constitution of the Society of Christians for the Holland Emigration to the United States of N. America] was formulated and written up by Van Raalte in the *Memoriaal van de Landverhuizing* [Memorial of the Emigration]. Here we find the political and religious grounds for the emigration to Michigan.

In Amsterdam, Van Raalte and Brummelkamp discussed why no emigration to Java, Borneo, or South Africa was being proposed. In a petition to the minister, the Reverends O. G. Heldring and H. P. Scholte requested freedom of religion and education for emigrants bound for the Netherlands East Indies. That was early in May 1846. They were refused such freedom. Already in the April 1846 issue of *De Reformatie*, Scholte had written about the expulsion of a bishop and four priests from the [East] Indies as follows:

> Now if this can be viewed by the governor general as creating unrest, in consequence of which an expulsion from the colony can be ordered, then the government never need count on Christians having any interest at all in colonization in our East Indies, but their eye will rather be fixed on the United States of America, where the constitution makes anything like that impossible. This observation may also be cast to the winds; when at last all this talk turns into deeds, and we see a very large share of the Christians leaving the Netherlands in order to cross the ocean to the North

25. Brummelkamp, *Levensbeschrijving*, 203.

The Rev. Otto G. Heldring (1804-1876), Seceder editor, *De Reformatie*
(*Courtesy of Jan Peter Verhave*)

American Free States, then we shall be too late in recognizing the consequences of the neglect of not giving a decent burial to the presently existing relationship between church and state, and allowing freedom for the development of a new life.

Early in June, the aforementioned pamphlet on emigration by Brummelkamp and Van Raalte appeared in print. The May issue of *De Reformatie* carried three articles on this subject: the Reverend O. G. Heldring wrote about colonization in general, and Scholte write about America and about emigration by Christians in a group context. Persons interested in registering for emigration could write to Hoogkamer, the publisher of *De Reformatie* and the pamphlet, in Amsterdam, to H. P. Scholte in Utrecht, and to A. Brummelkamp in Arnhem.

Scholte had decided to join the emigrants a few months before Van Raalte did. The May issue of *De Reformatie* left no doubt about this. *De Reformatie* was a journal intended to further the kingdom of God in the Netherlands. Hence the question: "Does this periodical still reflect its heading today?" And the answer of Scholte was:

> When it has become clear that all attempts at reformation are frustrated by the hardness, the insensitivity, the lukewarmness of government and people, then this witness in the Netherlands will

come to an end, and the talents and energies expended here will then be moved elsewhere.

We are speaking of an emigration, whereby those who leave cease to be Netherlanders, in order to become citizens, and live in a land where they have a broader conception of constitutional liberties and rights, where worshiping God with more than twenty persons, without prior consent of the higher authorities, is not counted as a crime, where one does not run the risk of being exiled after being caught a third time for having given elementary instruction to more than five children at one time, without the approval of the representatives of [*De Maatschappij tot*] *Nut van 't Algemeen* [The Society for Public Welfare], which is a horrible crime in the Netherlands. They reject our revival because their consciences tell them that our departure is a protest against the social, moral, and religious condition of the Netherlands.

Because of the potato blight of 1845 and 1846, there was much hunger among the poor. Scholte foresaw revolution. The poverty, the measures against the Seceders, and the prevention of biblical education, were making the time ripe, "not to bring about a revolution in the Netherlands," but to leave the Netherlands. Scholte concluded by saying, "and we are ready to go along."

The article, "De roeping der rijken in betrekking tot de armen" ["The calling of the rich in relation to the poor"], called upon the well to do to assist the poor in their emigration. Another article, "Vervolging van godsdientoefening" ["Persecution of worship services"], observed that after so much witness against the government, they had the freedom to leave the country.

Then followed the articles about persecution of the printing press, and about American colonization in Africa (Liberia). The issue ends with "observations relative to the emigration to North-America." There Scholte remarked:

> Fourth, since the principles of our colonization are Christian in the fullest sense of the word, we need to inform all who might wish to participate, that, as far as the ecclesiastical fellowship and organization of the colony are concerned, the Word of God shall be the only rule, foundation, and touchstone, and that without being bound by any earlier or later [creedal] forms not commanded by God.

Fifth, there is every likelihood that in our first settlement there will be adequate provisions for divine worship and education, while at the same time there is a good prospect that a capable midwife, one adept in the healing arts also, will join us, and in addition there will be no lack of female help.

In the pamphlet on emigration by Brummelkamp and Van Raalte, we find similar observations. The Netherlands provided much benevolence "for the emaciated farm hands who should not need any benevolence, but who were forced down to this low estate because their lawful wages were being withheld.... The Netherlands does not compensate the laborer according to his work." They also berated the imperialism in the East Indies, "where the government abuses freedom of conscience, where people are prevented from educating their children in the fear of God, but where the same government that goes its opinionated way here, rules autocratically over there." To bring the Drenthe heath under cultivation is more expensive than emigrating, reclaiming the Zuider Zee does not benefit the poor but the rich, and so emigration to America is the only way out.[26]

In the same pamphlet, Milwaukee in Wisconsin was designated as the place of assembly to be reached via Albany. A letter, "To the Believers in the United States of North America," written May 26, 1846, in Arnhem by Van Raalte and Brummelkamp, was reproduced in the pamphlet. This letter was taken along by R. Sleijster and personally handed to the Reverend I. N. Wyckoff, who saw to it that the letter was translated and published in the *Christian Intelligencer*.[27] Wyckoff then formed the Protestant Evangelical Holland Emigrant Society in Albany to protect emigrants from the Netherlands, to advise them, and to offer assistance. In New York, "The Netherlands Society for the Protection of Emigrants" was established by Dr. Thomas De Witt, who had visited Scholte in Utrecht in July of 1846.

After June of 1846, there were six more issues of *De Reformatie* dealing with persecution in the Netherlands, the evangelical churches in North America, and with emigration. In September it reported that the

---

26. A. Brummelkamp and A.C. Van Raalte, *Landverhuizing, of waarom bevorderen wij deVolksverhuizing en wel naar Noord-Amerika en niet naar Java?* (Amsterdam: Hoogkamer, 1846), 9, 17, 18, 26.

27. Henry S. Lucas, *Dutch Immigrant Memoirs and Related Writings*, 2 vols. (Assen: Van Gorcum, 1955; English edition, Grand Rapids, Baker Book House, 1985), 1:14-20.

Reverend Van Raalte would soon be emigrating and that a few pioneers would be leaving for New Orleans and St. Louis October 3.

Scholte wrote that Van Raalte and the brethren from Gelderland were thinking of going to the same region as that chosen by the society formed in Holland, that is Iowa near St. Louis. In December a half issue appeared, and in it Scholte reported that Van Raalte had arrived in New York November 18 and had traveled on to Wisconsin.

The second half of the last issue of *De Reformatie* appeared in March 1847. In it is published the "Letter from North America," written in St. Louis on December 14, 1846, by Hendrik Barendregt, who preceded the main body. On the last page there was an advertisement: *Reglement der Zeeuwsche Vereeniging naar de Vereenigde Staten van Noord-Amerikaa, prijs 15 cent* [Rules and Regulations of the Zeeland Society to the United States of North America, price 15 cents].

Meanwhile, Van Raalte was in America with fifty emigrants; on December 16, 1846, he was in Detroit. That day he wrote: "I hope to travel straight across Wisconsin, and from there to proceed along the Mississippi or through Iowa to St. Louis in order to meet the Barendregt brothers there.[28]

On December 25, 1846, Van Raalte talked for the first time about establishing a colony in Michigan.[29] Van Raalte mentioned several arguments for staying in Michigan, but he did not mention the fact that the traveling funds were nearly exhausted, and that in Michigan he would be able to proceed with his plans at once without having to wait months for passage to Chicago and St. Louis. Van Raalte pressed on in Michigan and expected Scholte to join him.

Scholte had made his decision earlier, but he was more deliberate in carrying out his plans. Scholte considered emigration to other continents. He studied the history and geography of America. When *Het Handelsblad* published three lead articles against emigration November 19, 20, and 21, Scholte's answer in *De Reformatie* that very same month attested to his superior knowledge of the subject.

Scholte asked the anonymous writer in *Het Handelsblad*:

> Is he acquainted with the conditions and the development of the West? Does he know, for example, that the state of Iowa has

---

28. A. Brummelkamp, ed., *Stemmen uit Noord-Amerika* (Amsterdam: Hoogkamer, 1847), 87.

29. Albert Hyman, *Albertus C. Van Raalte and his Dutch Settlements in the United States* (Grand Rapids: Eerdmans, 1947), 71.

numerous small towns that have steam, water, and wind mills for wood and grain, that in the several small towns you will find stores with the necessities for everyday living, that you do not have to start by felling trees there in order to cultivate the land because there are adequate pasture lands? If he does know all that, then he is doing wrong by making such an unfavorable portrayal of the West (p. 363).

Scholte knew more about the churches, the laws, the mail service, and the "predatory raids of the savage tribes," than did *Het Handelslblad*. No immigrant could settle beyond the carefully designated congressional territories, and far beyond that designated land there were the military outposts to guard against the raids of the remaining uncivilized tribes (p. 305). In Iowa the Indians were already so weakened that, in exchange for money, on October 11, 1842, they concluded a treaty to leave the state to the east of the Red Rocks [just west of Pella] before May 1843 and all of Iowa before June 1846. Military outposts had already replaced most of the forts further west when Scholte arrived in Iowa in 1847. [30]

On the same day that Van Raalte decided on the spot to settle in Michigan, December 25, 1846, the rules and regulations for the "Society for Emigration to North America" were drawn up in twenty-five articles in Utrecht. The first meeting had been held in Utrecht in August 1846. The emigrants hoped to leave by the end of March 1847. In December 1847, H. P. Scholte of Utrecht was elected president, A. J. Betten of Noordeloos vice-president, I. Overkamp of Utrecht secretary, and J. F. Le Cocq of Amsterdam, A. Wigney of Dordrecht, G. H. Overkamp of Leerdam, and J. Rietveld of Noordeloos were elected directors. [31]

The Emigration Society calculated that, on average, travel costs would be between eighty and one hundred guilders [$32-$40]. Those purchasing land would pay five guilders [$2] per acre in advance. Costs for a school and a dwelling for the schoolmaster and doctor would be shared, as well as other common expenditures. Until the farmhouses were ready for occupancy, sheds would be built for initial lodging on a centrally located piece of land, which would later be sold for trade and commercial properties. The board of directors would make arrangements for the journey, land purchases, allocation of land and roads, a registry of deeds, and financial matters; they would have final

---

30. Leland L. Sage, *A History of Iowa* (Ames: Iowa State Univ. Press, 1974), 71, 72.
31. *De Reformatie* (December 1846), 339.

Isaac Overkamp (1810-1895), school teacher, Pella

G. H. Overkamp (1808-1899), furniture store owner, elder, First Reformed Church, Pella

responsibility in all matters. Church and state, in accordance with the views of Scholte, were to be entirely separate. Consequently, there were no regulations concerning the church, but membership was limited to Protestants who were not morally or civilly suspect, and there was the regulation that lands purchased could not be sold outside the society.[32]

The secretary, Isaac Overkamp, had been a student friend of Scholte at Leiden [University]. Legend has it that his father had died at sea and that he had studied under a scholarship from King Willem I. Overkamp had been born in The Hague February 26, 1810. He told the story that about 1826 the king saw him on his way to church. The following day he and his mother were invited [to the palace] by the king and queen. His mother became a seamstress at the royal court and Isaac, after his studies at Leiden, became a teacher of French, German, and English on behalf of the royal family. His brother, Gerrit H. Overkamp, who was two years older, was a paint dealer in Leerdam. On January 3, 1830, Isaac married Aafje Kruijt, and they had seven children when they emigrated.

Isaac Overkamp told his granddaughter, Marie Isaacs Scholte, that the king entrusted him with the task of teaching the sons of the royal family. When they had finished their studies with him, they left silver

---

32. Henry S. Lucas, "A Document Relating to Dutch Immigration to Iowa in 1846," *Iowa Journal of History and Politics* 21 (July 1923): 457-65.

objects bearing the royal coat of arms behind as a gratuity. The reference must be to the two oldest sons of the later king Willem II, namely Willem III and his brother Willem Alexander Frederik Constantijn Nicolaas Michael (1818-1848). But after an extensive search in the Royal Archives not a single confirmation of these reports was found.

Published documents do tell us some other things about Isaac Overkamp. In December 1836 he was staying with the Seceder minister J. van Rhee at a cheap hotel in Rotterdam. The next day the lady hotelkeeper circulated rumors about unnatural [sexual] conduct. Isaac Overkamp also accused Van Rhee of an attempt at "conduct most scandalous." Van Rhee denied it. The matter was dealt with at the first synod in Amsterdam. The day his brother was summoned, elder G. H. Overkamp did not attend the synod out of feelings of delicacy. That was March 10, 1836. Scholte took I. Overkamp under his wing. He was cleared of blame. Van Rhee remained the accused who was admonished to defend himself. He did not appear [at synod] but wrote "that the actual matter of the accusation was absolutely false and was malicious, filthy slander, but nevertheless he acknowledged that he was guilty of gross indiscretion in the matter of his affectionate friendship and communion with Isaac Overkamp." The result was that on March 12 Van Rhee was unfrocked. All of this was published in the *Proceedings of the first Synod of the Seceders*, which Scholte personally presented to the king March 16, 1836.

In the report of the minister of public worship dated October 3, 1835, the following was reported on the three brothers: "G. H. Overkamp of Leerdam is a painter by trade who earlier had a good living, but since his departure from the congregation his business has gone downhill and his financial situation has deteriorated. Concerning his moral conduct, there is nothing in the reports made that merits comment. His brother, I. Overkamp, who had been an elementary teacher in Wassenaar and who left there in the spring, is, we are told, a custodian and song leader with Scholte, often accompanying him as an assistant or secretary. [Church] meetings are held regularly at the home of G. H. Overkamp; some of these are Seceders but not all."[33] In 1840 Isaac Overkamp was secretary of the church council, and in 1846 of the emigration society, both times as Scholte's "henchman." He lived with Scholte and was the teacher of his three daughters. Later, in Pella, it was especially he who gave Christian instruction to young people.

33. Bos and Goslinga, *Archiefstukken*, 2:404.

Before they left, Scholte published still another extensive, passionate appeal: *Nieuwejaarsgeschenk aan Nederland, een ernstig woord aan Vorst en Volk* [*New Year's Present to the Netherlands, a solemn word to the King and the People*]. In it he addressed a solemn word to the king, the courts, the officials, the states general, the orthodox, and the very experiential Christians. Concerning his own history he related one more detail:

> A servant of Christ from North America, on a fund raising trip through the Netherlands and Germany, was the means in God's hand to arouse in me the desire to become a minister of the Word of God. But I rejected out of hand an invitation to accompany him to the United States and to study at a seminary that was newly being established. Though the challenge to preach the gospel touched a responsive chord in my heart as a call from God, the challenge to leave the Netherlands...remained powerless....The act of secession brought about a sense of community, but it soon became evident that there were big differences in secession principles. Many had in mind the restoration of ecclesiastical orthodoxy; I intended the sole rule of the Word of God.[34]
>
> I believe and confess that the Word of God must have the last word in all things, whether personal, domestic, societal, ecclesiastical....Kings, judges, authorities, and nations are addressed and dealt with in that Word. Those who are free and those who serve, parents and children, men and women, all will find prescribed in it the way that is well pleasing to God. Church members as well as overseers will find set forth there the will of God on how we shall conduct ourselves in his house, that is, the church.[35]

Finally, it is evident from this publication that Scholte was sending *De Reformatie* to the king every month. He asked the king for a copy of *Archives et Correspondence de la Maison d'Orange* [*Archives and Correspondence of the House of Orange*] published by Groen van Prinsterer, and received it as a gift in February 1845. Finally, Scholte took most of the subpoenas, judgments, and receipts for fines paid with him to America. The *New Year's Present to the Netherlands* of January 1, 1847, is a piece of forgotten prose writing of high quality. Historically, it is probably more important

---

34. H.P. Scholte, *Nieuwjaarsgeschenk aan Nederland, een ernstig Woord aan Vorst en Volk* (Amsterdam: Hoogkamer, 1847), 42-43.

35. Ibid., 51.

than the well-known *Bezwaren tegen den geest der eeuw* [*Scruples against the spirit of the age*] by I. Da Costa Esq. (1823).

In 1845 and 1846 the potato blight had already struck. In October of 1846 the first bread riots were occurring in Paris. There was hunger in Ireland, and the *Illustrated London News* of October 10, 1846, demanded [governmental] action, "Hunger cannot wait for reports and resolutions."

Scholte had an intuition about what was brewing in Europe. This intuition was shared by Groen van Prinsterer, who in the winter of 1845-1846 titled his Hague lectures, "*Ongeloof en Revolutie*" ["Unbelief and Revolution"]. Hunger riots were reported in May 1847 in Ireland and in all of Germany, in Stuttgart, and Stettin. However, the really great riots did not occur until a year later—the French Revolution in February 1848 and the revolution of March 1848 in Prussia and Berlin; riots in Milan and Rome, war in northern Italy, revolution in Austria, the June blood bath in Paris, the September uprisings in Germany, the October revolt in Vienna, and, in 1849, the suppression of revolutions in the Palatinate and Baden. It was the revolution to which the manifesto of the Communist Party addressed itself. But Scholte's *New Year's Present* related to it no less. Both manifestos spoke of community and of freedom, but the one concerned itself above all with money and material possessions, the other with religion and education.

What one can object to in Scholte's *New Year's Present* is the romantic multiplicity of variations on the theme: "Christians in the Netherlands! Hearken to my words, we are leaving you, but we have warned you clearly many times." But in all of this we must hear the voice of one who loved the Netherlands, and who would very much have liked to remain.

However, there was defamation also within his own inner circle. The Reverend S. van Velzen felt constrained to inform the king on January 29, 1847, that Scholte had not spoken on his behalf and that he would not be going along to America. Of Scholte he said:

> At a meeting of representatives from most of the Christian Seceded Churches, held in Amsterdam from November 17 to December 3, 1840, the said preacher H. P. Scholte was removed from office. Nevertheless, the said person has continued to exercise the office, while some of those in the Christian Seceded Congregation at Utrecht and also in other places continued their ecclesiastical affiliation with them.[36]

36. Bos and Goslinga, *Archiefstukken*, 4:482.

The [cabinet] minister then took the occasion to write the king that the Seceders were divided into several factions; foremost among these were those that had Messrs. Van Velzen and Scholte, two former Hervormde ministers, as their leaders. He also wrote that the latter was getting ready to leave for America with many of his followers and thus seemed to be yielding the field to Van Velzen.[37]

Scholte left two months later. The last issue of *De Reformatie* appeared in March 1847 and included an article on Holy Baptism and on Holy Communion, as well as the "Letter from North America" by H. Barendregt, and two book announcements, namely *Onderzoek naar den toestand der Landverhuizers in de Vereenigde Staten van Noord-Amerika* [*Inquiry into the condition of immigrants in the United States of North America*] by B. A. van Straten Pinthor, and *The Little American*, an English primer by H. Picard.

In the article dealing with baptism and Communion, Scholte opposed the Darbyites. But at the same time he testified against a so-called spirituality that imposed itself upon the congregation as a privileged group and supported and confirmed the illusion that they [the privileged ones] must be utilized. He believed that unless that be done, the activities that God had prescribed for the congregation could not be lawfully performed (p. 316). With that message, Scholte left the Netherlands. Did the Reformed Church in Amsterdam ever rehabilitate him? He would never ask for it, for in Pella he found his free city, and his hope and refuge was in God.

---

37. Ibid., 4:484.

CHAPTER 2

Amsterdam to Iowa
(Wormser Letters 1-16, Budde Letters 1-5)

The first letter is a circular one written by Mannes Mensink in Albany, the capital of New York. The Reverend Isaac Newton Wyckoff was minister of the Second Reformed Church in Albany from 1836 to 1866. He was born August 29, 1792, in New Jersey and graduated from Rutgers College in 1813. Together with the Reverends Thomas De Witt and John Garretson, both of New York, Wyckoff was most helpful to the immigrants. So it is not coincidental that the letters begin with one written from Albany. However, Mensink did not come from Amsterdam but rather from Hellendoorn. He crossed the ocean on the sailing vessel *Isabella* at the same time that Van Raalte was sailing on the *Southerner*. As a student of Van Raalte, he had led Bible classes aboard ship. Mensink arrived in New York December 19, and on the 23rd he left for Albany by train. Later he became an elder in the Alto, Wisconsin, and Preston (Greenleafton), Minnesota Reformed churches.

The vanguard of Scholte's group consisted of thirteen men, six women, and nine children. They left October 2, 1846, traveling via Rotterdam and New Orleans, and arrived in St. Louis November 19. From there Hendrik Barendregt wrote an important letter on December 14, 1846, which has been published at least three times already.[1] Except for this letter, the vanguard produced little writings of any consequence.

---

1. *De Reformatie* (1847); K. Van Stigt, *Geschiedenis van Pella, Iowa, en Omgeving*, 3 vols. (Pella: Weekblad Drukkerij, 1897), 1:76-85; Lucas, *Dutch Immigrant Memoirs*, 2: 514-21.

The Rev. Isaac N. Wyckoff (1792-1869), pastor, Second Reformed Church, Albany, New York

Netherlands Steamboat Company advertisement, Rotterdam

In the *Nieuwe Rotterdamsche Courant* of March 16, 1847, three vessels were listed that were seeking cargo for a voyage to America. The Society chartered these three vessels as well as a fourth for the ocean crossing.

Wormser Letters 2-9 tell about the journey of the Budde family, which did not take any of the above four vessels. Nor did they sail via Baltimore. The Budde family consisted of husband, wife, and three children—Jan had just turned eighteen, Diedrich was almost seven, and Maria was two and a half years old. A widow, Johanna Teleman, and her daughter Jansje also belonged to this household of seven persons. Both women were forty-four years old; D. A. Budde was two years older. They left from Purmerend March 25, 1847, and from Den Helder April 4, and they arrived in New York May 19 aboard the bark *Zeemeeuw* (gross 443 tons, net 200 tons), built in Amsterdam, and launched March 16, 1835, at Witte Kruis wharf on Kattenburgh. H. L. Kayzer was captain from 1840 to 1864, when the ship was lost at sea. Scholte had been on board the vessel while it was still in Den Helder, and when the group arrived in New York he was one of the first persons to meet them. Scholte had made his trip by steamship and train by way of England, and in Liverpool he had taken the steamer *Sarah Sand*, bound for Boston, for his family. This voyage was faster, more luxurious, and more expensive. The first sail-steamship to cross the Atlantic Ocean was the three-masted *Savannah* out of New York in 1819. The first steamship that made regular crossings was the *Sirius* in 1833. On May 31, 1847, *De Hollandsche IJzeren Spoorweg Maatschappij* [The Holland Iron Railroad Company] inaugurated the Amsterdam-Rotterdam line (1st class fl[orin] 4.20, 2nd class fl.3.40 and third class fl.2.10). The draining of the Haarlemmermeer Polder by the steam pumps Leeghwater, Cruquius, and Lynden between 1846 and 1852 was considered one of the wonders of the world. However, until about 1850, most emigrants traveled on sailing vessels.

In a private collection in Pella, I found a copy of a letter written by Scholte while in New York; it is printed here between Wormser Letters 6 and 7. After traveling from Boston to Albany, Scholte journeyed alone to Washington and Baltimore. He then brought his family over from Albany to New York. In Albany he preached in the church of the Reverend Wyckoff and attended a meeting of the state senate. He rejected the invitation of Van Raalte to come to Michigan because he preferred the prairies to the forests. When one of the four ships arrived in Baltimore, he was notified by telegraph. He then left New York with his family to welcome the colonists and to accompany them from Baltimore to Pittsburgh, and then via the Ohio and Mississippi Rivers to St. Louis, and thence to Keokuk, Iowa.

The Budde household followed the Van Raalte trek via Albany to

The Rev. Anthony J. Betten (1813-1900), immigrant leader, businessman, and early Pella religious leader

A. Wigny (18??-1869), leader of Pella settlement
(Photos from Souvenir History of Pella, Iowa, 1847-1922, *Pella: 1922)*

Buffalo. But instead of taking the lake route [Lakes Erie, Huron, and Michigan]—via Detroit—to Chicago, they went by ship to Sandusky, and then by train to Richland, by wagon to Springfield, by train to Cincinnati, and finally by boat to Burlington.

The four ships arrived in Baltimore. Emigrants on the Dutch bark *Nagasaki*, which had left Rotterdam April 11, were under the leadership of the Reverend A. J. Betten and A. Wigny. Those on the Dutch copper-clad, fast frigate *Maasstroom*, which left from Rotterdam, were under the leadership of G. H. and J. Overkamp. The sailing ship *Pieter Floris* left Amsterdam under the leadership of J. F. Le Cocq and H. J. Viersen, and the American frigate *Katherina Jackson* left Rotterdam under the leadership of J. Rietveld and J. Smeenk. The mother of G. H. and I. Overkamp was also on board the *Maasstroom*. But she was already ill by then. She died while they were en route in America, just beyond Pittsburgh, and was buried at Wheeling on the bank of the Ohio River. The household of G. H. Overkamp included a sixteen-year-old youth, Hendrik Hospers, from Hoogblokland near Gorkum.

Because the interesting letters of Hendrik Hospers present a different picture of Pella than those of Andries Wormser, a number of them are included in this publication. In a letter from Pella, dated November 20, 1847, Hendrik Hospers wrote:

> It is especially about travel costs en route that I wish to inform you, after consulting with I. Overkamp, a most reliable informant. As to the costs of the ocean voyage, you are better informed than I. The land journey from New York, Boston, and Baltimore is very tiring and is very hard on your luggage because of the constant transfers. From New Orleans it is not only much cheaper but it is also much better all around. After arriving in New Orleans and anchoring in the harbor, you take a steamboat that transports passengers and luggage up the Mississippi to the city of Keokuk. This town is located one hundred hours [upstream] beyond St. Louis. It's not hard at all to book passage; usually it costs no more than $4.50 per person and 25 cents per hundred pounds of luggage. One of these boats then comes alongside the ocean vessel, and so the goods are easily transferred, and not unloaded until you get to Keokuk. But between Baltimore and Keokuk, this happens no less than six times, and the amount of damage this causes to your goods we know from experience. It takes twenty-one days to get to Keokuk. During this journey you must provide your own provisions, but that is not

expensive, because as a rule there is something left of the ample provisions taken for the ocean voyage. It is a good idea to stock a large quantity of peas and beans for the ocean voyage, and especially of good quality; then you will arrive in Pella in good shape. When you get to Keokuk, there will undoubtedly be information available to you, but if I am alive and well, I hope to meet you there, with your own wagon, if it is available, and if not, we will rent wagons there that will take our goods to Pella for 75 cents per hundred pounds (people travel for the same price.) So now you can make a fairly accurate calculation of what the trip will cost you.

After reading the letter, Isaac Overkamp made the following correction: "The cost per person is 75 cents per hundred pounds if you sit on top of your luggage. If that is not the case and you take a separate wagon, it costs more, at least $2 per person."

On the route to Keokuk there were several transfers: at Baltimore from the ocean vessel to the train, and on to Columbus, Pennsylvania; then through Pennsylvania, first by canal boat to Harrisburg, by train again to Johnstown, and to Pittsburgh by canal boat. From there the immigrants traveled by steamboat to Cincinnati, continuing on to St. Louis, and finally upstream on the Mississippi to Keokuk or Burlington.

Budde was in St. Louis earlier than Scholte, having arrived in Burlington June 21, 1847. Scholte arrived in St. Louis with the immigrants from the four ships in July; and after a journey from July 29 to August 4 in order to buy land, they arrived in Pella August 19. Scholte's family, as well as the maids and artisans who had found work in St. Louis, stayed behind in order to make money. While the immigrants were still in St. Louis, they were visited by a committee from Nauvoo, Illinois. The committee offered to sell the Hollanders the entire town because the Mormons there had been driven out.

That same summer, on August 18, 1847, the Reverend Seine Bolks left Hellendoorn with 125 persons, 87 of whom were Seceders. Hendrik Wormser did not accompany them. From Rotterdam they went by steamship to London and from there by sailing ship to New York. At Albany, Wyckoff advised them to winter in Syracuse. They left there May 1, 1848, and arrived at Van Raalte's colony a month later. This group included the miller Gerrit Harmannus Lankheet with his wife and two children and Hendrik Klein Heksel with his wife and five children.[2]

2. A. Ponsteen, *Het kerkdorp Hellendoorn in vroeger eeuwen* (Enschede: Stichting Oald Heldern, [1972]), 284-304.

We find both names in Wormser Letter 1, Lankheet again in Letters 27 and 31, and the Reverend Seine Bolks is mentioned in Letters 1, 13, 30, 35, and 52.

The first letter to Mrs. Christina Budde from their dear friend, Mrs. Janke Wormser-van der Ven in Amsterdam is dated 24 April 1848. It was penned only weeks after the fellow congregants had left Rotterdam and opens with a lament that the "loss of your esteemed presence grieves us daily,... [yet] when there is a letter from you all then our joy is great" (Budde Letter 1). The painful rending of the bonds of love and friendship is a constant theme in the Budde-Wormser correspondence, as is the folksy news tidbits about the bane and blessing of mutual friends on both sides of the ocean. Putting the deepest thoughts and cravings of the heart on paper kept the old friends linked emotionally for decades until, one by one, they passed away, and then the adult children picked up the duty to write. Sometimes the writers testify at length in the pietist idiom of the group about their religious ups and downs. News of key life passages—births, marriages, and deaths—often triggered the spiritual tone [RPS].

Letter 10 of Van Raalte and Letter 13 of Budde refer to the burning of a steamboat [the *Phoenix*] on Lake Michigan, in which 150 immigrants perished. Scholte mentions this same accident in *Een Stem uit Pella* [*A Voice from Pella*].[3] This accident is well known, but we hear nothing about the loss of the three-master, *William and Mary*, on May 3, 1853. When approximately sixty Frisian survivors of the shipwreck, traveling from New Orleans, arrived in St. Louis, the consul of the Netherlands there, Frederik R. Toe Water, refused to offer them assistance on their further journey to Wisconsin (cf. *Handelsblad* of September 2 and 3, 1853).

In the Budde letters we read about the straw city Pella, where people lived temporarily like the peat workers in their sod huts in [the province of] Drenthe. By the end of October 1847, a church had still not been organized in Pella because Scholte took the position that others, not he, should take the initiative. At the time Scholte was just going to St. Louis to pick up his wife and three daughters. His wife was not suited for immigrant life and initially she did not wish to go along to America. To accommodate her, her sister Hubertina Krantz went along. In St. Louis Hubertina married a Mr. Hazebroek, a jurist whom she had met

---

3. J. Van Hinte, *Nederlanders in Amerika: een studie over landverhuizers en volksplanters in de 19e and 20ste eeuw in de Vereenigde Staten van Amerika*, 2 vols. (Groningen: P. Noordhoff, 1928), 2: 178. An English edition is Robert P. Swierenga, general editor, Adriaan de Wit, translator, *Netherlanders in America: A Study of Emigration and Colonization in the 19th and 20th Centuries in the United States of North America* (Grand Rapids: Baker Book House, 1985; reprint, The Archives, Calvin College, 2003), 105-106.

at sea. On the last Sunday before the departure their brother, Jan Willem Daniel Krantz, was excommunicated from the congregation by the Utrecht council, among others, because he had attempted "...to encourage Scholte's wife, his sister, not to follow her husband in what he saw as the way [God] had appointed for him to go, to North America."[4] It was in part for his wife's sake that Scholte had taken a steamboat. Because of this she had been seasick for fourteen days, instead of six weeks on a sailing vessel. She remained behind in St. Louis until Scholte's [new] house [in Pella] was ready. His [first] house was still a log cabin, but in April 1848 the new house was completed, one of the first and biggest houses in Pella, behind which the plans called for a splendid enclosed garden. Because so many people were living in sod houses, this almost inevitably became the occasion for mud slinging, to wit, when Scholte did not go ahead with the establishment of a church, and settlements on land purchases were not forthcoming.

The dramatic tale of the arrival of Mariah Krantz as Mrs. Scholte in the book, *A Stranger in a Strange Land*, by Leonora Scholte, is based on a painting in the Pella Museum. It is about her arrival on August 19, 1847. "Where is Pella?" Mariah asks before she breaks out in hysterical tears. In reality she did not arrive in Pella until several months later, in November 1847. There were then four houses in the center of Pella: one for the Reverend Post, one for Scholte, a school and church building, and the house of the schoolmaster, G. H. Overkamp.

Scholte had purchased the entire townships 76 and 77, between the Skunk and Des Moines Rivers. About thirty existing farms were sold to colonists of means. The greater part, however, consisted of prairie and some woods. This land had to be divided into sections of five, ten, twenty, and forty acres. In doing so, the immigrants had to take into account the roads, the division in prairie lands and woods, good land and bad, and who would be a neighbor to whom. First, a map was drawn up and the parcels described by Walter Clements, Esq., and H. Hospers. This mapping out and dividing of the land took place between September 1847 and winter 1848. Like every American city, Pella consisted of blocks. In the fall, nine city blocks of Pella were being readied, and, in the summer of 1848, a total of 480 acres for the development of Pella were platted.

Burlington on the Mississippi came into existence in 1834 at the site where the Indians sought stone for their tools in the higher areas. In

---

4. C. Smits, *Gorichem en "Beneden-Gelderland,"* vol. 1 of *De Afscheiding van 1834* (Oudkarspel: De Nijverheid, 1971), 56.

1838 Burlington became the temporary capital of Iowa. The road from Burlington to Pella via Mount Pleasant begins at a high point from which one has a splendid view over the Mississippi. A good two miles farther down, there is now a little side road, named Budde, that runs along an old cemetery. The site of the Budde farm is now a suburb of Burlington, and it is the fairgrounds of the city. A small creek runs along the road to it. The name is Vineyard, and there are still some very tall trees of various kinds.

Because some twenty thousand Mormons had their headquarters in Nauvoo, south of Burlington and half way to Keokuk, before they were driven out in 1846 by the State of Iowa, some people have assumed that Budde bought a farm deserted by the Mormons. The Mormons left Nauvoo in February 1846, and the last of the saints were driven out in September.[5]

The letters provide no answer to the question of the origin of the land. Wormser Letter 14 says that the owner sold Budde 80 acres. The son of this owner was selling 318 acres, which he himself had worked. Near Budde there are another 450 acres and 240 acres for sale. The fact that the father will sell a piece of his land, and that the son is only willing to sell all of his land, does not suggest that this was very newly acquired land. What is worth noting is the fact that Budde bought his land for a substantial sum immediately after he had visited Pella. He probably was reluctant to be a real pioneer. He was a city dweller and still had to learn all about farming. When a believing renter proved willing to help him, he decided to stay in Burlington.

Wormser Letter 16 is from Scholte. It shows the growing rivalry for settlers between Pella and Holland, Michigan. Scholte glowingly praises Pella and enclosed several maps to provide prospective immigrants with the "lay of the land," but he would not station an agent in New York to direct colonists to Pella, as he charged Van Raalte with doing. Scholte closed by asked his friend Wormser to send copies of his *Een Stem uit Pella* [*A Voice from Pella*], a promotional brochure of the first order.

---

5. Sage, *History of Iowa*, 72-79.

Wormser 1

M. Mensink to fellow believers in the Netherlands
[*In all likelihood a copy of a pastoral letter to H. Wormser*]
Albany, 30 December 1846

Esteemed and Dearly Beloved Brethren in Christ Jesus,

May the Lord bless you with temporal and spiritual blessings; that is the prayer of my heart. [I am writing] after having waited a few days, in order to be able to give you some positive information about our activities. However, as of now I still cannot tell you anything. Still, I do expect to find work any day now. Three or four of us hope to find it with the help of Reverend Wyckoff, who does much for the immigrants; he is a man who fears the Lord. There are many Hollanders here. Some came earlier, others more recently, and they are overjoyed that I might be preaching in the church of Reverend Wyckoff once a week; how things will work out I do not know as yet. There are many here who fear the Lord, but there are also many others. Shops are closed on Sunday. There are many cheats among the Germans; you really have to be on the alert or you will be cheated before you know it. We did not lose any of our goods, but the one lost this, and the other that. The Lord is good to us; if only we were more aware of it.

We also stayed in inns where we paid at least a shilling less per person, even though we had enjoyed food and drink in the evening, while the others had not. While we were traveling to Albany on the steam train, there were times when we rode under and through the rocky mountains [in tunnels] and it would be dark as midnight. It is all clay soil here, but mountainous, with many rocky outcroppings. The soil looks very good to me, but it is now winter and then the Americans do not like to work. They earn so much during the summer that they do not need to. Advise everyone not to start traveling in the fall, at least not later than August. Potatoes are expensive—about 3 shillings for a five-liter container, but flour is only 4 or 5 cents [a pound]; the best pork is 12½ cents [a pound], and bread is also cheaper than in Holland. There is no rye bread here.

I have nothing special to write because it is winter; I do hear good reports about this country. Van Raalte is gone, from Buffalo to Detroit and then to Michigan and Wisconsin. He intends to buy land—nine hundred acres for seven thousand dollars—on the Grand River; just check it on the map, between [Lake] Huron and [Lake] Michigan. It will be a big mistake if it actually happens; he has asked the Reverends

Wyckoff and De Witt in New York for money. I hope the Lord will direct all things. They have gotten started on the land, and there are already a few log cabins. Very likely we will be spending the winter there. Answer as soon as possible, in care of Reverend Wyckoff, 100 N. Lydius Street in Albany [New York]. We are all eager to hear from you. We have rented a room for 10 shillings a month. The Klein Heksels and we are living in one house, and the [Jan] Plaggemars are living in one house with the Kolvoorts [Jan Kolvoord]. Mrs. Plaggemars is the same old woman she ever was in Holland; [Mr.] Plaggemars himself became weak on board ship, but he is improving now that he is back on land. For the rest everyone is well, and that includes the Klein Heksels and ourselves. I have never seen H[endrik] Beltman as fat as he is now; he is healthy all right; some other time he will include a letter to his father. Do let us know how things are with you all. There's nothing for my sister this time to spare [her] postage costs, because I am sure they cannot afford it. I wrote a letter from New York; it is 540 miles from New York to Buffalo and a thousand miles from Buffalo to Wisconsin; [walking], you can cover three miles in an hour. Anyone [traveling] by ship should have 130 kilos [of food], that is in American pounds, about two of the older Dutch pounds. It does not matter what the food is as long as it is dry, and advise everyone to bake and dry bread, because the ship's bread is tasteless. Potatoes on board are very good; also pepper, vinegar, mustard, and onions, anything that is hearty. [Be sure to take] elixir, Haarlem oil, gin, and bitters; otherwise, humanly speaking, you just can't make it. Take some smoked meats, bacon, rice, beans, crushed barley, a little of everything; your food is gone before you know it. Also take beer to drink, for the water is poor. Also flour—that is still the best—to cook in a pan, to make porridge, and herring is really great, butter and salt, that goes without saying; also many sweets and pickled things.

The ocean journey is not all that far; if the wind is favorable it can easily be made in twenty days. Three children—who were ailing when they came on board—died at sea, one of Windjes from Gelre [Gelderland], one of Strabbers [Jan Rabbers], one of Strabbink [Jan Strabbing] from the Coevorden area, and three women died at Albany; one was ill when she came aboard ship, and the two others were not strong either. One was a Rabbers, [one] a Strabbink [Strabbing], the other a [Jan] Snoek; the others are well. Of 126 [passengers] there were 120 survivors.

As to religion, on the one hand I have suffered a great deal, and on the other the Lord has been good to me. We were of two factions; those from Drenthe opposed us; the gunsmith from Arnhem is to blame. At first they did not have anything against me, but the gunsmith had to get off his chest what he perceived to be the evils of Van Raalte and Brummelkamp, and he was no match for me in matters of the faith, and that was what it was all about. If I were willing to read one of the old writers [like Smijtegeld], then everything would be fine, but I cannot [and will not] do that. The Lord fired my spirit, and I really let him have it, but to no avail. Finally, I was really discouraged, and then the Lord caused me to understand that it [inner change] is not by might or by power, but only by his spirit; and then I was tender [yielding] before God, and then a change did come about. The next Sunday I was discoursing about Achan—that there was a ban on the army [of Israel] and the Lord said to Joshua: Consecrate the people! Then the hard rock was shattered to pieces.

When we arrived here, we spent a night at the inn, and the next day Bloemers and Veldhorst took us into their home. These people showed us much kindness. Bloemers is from Winterswijk and the other from Verseveld [Varsseveld]. They asked me to write you that the two of them were here together, and to ask Reverend Bolks to write some letters to Winterswijk, to the daughter of Bloemers (Christiana Bloemers of Winterswijk near the hamlet of Happel). Johanna [Bloemers] remained in Boston, and Tobias is working for a farmer, and the other older girl is also working here as a maid; do be so kind to write this. To practice our religion we are getting a large house next to Wyckoff's church, the one in which he preaches during the week. It is twice as large as the church in Hellendoorn.

I have written a letter to R. Sleyster but have not received a reply as yet. Write me back soon, for I long to hear from you, not that I am disappointed or that I am longing for Holland, far from it; I don't want to be go back to Holland again, the thought has never entered my mind. I think of you all often and in spirit I have much spiritual communion with you. I feel a bond of love [between us], placed in my heart by God. I would have a great deal more to write if I were to pour out my soul.

signed: M. Mensink.

I just have to stop writing, even though the inclination of my heart is altogether different. We keep on asking that you pray much for us. We hope to do the same. Our sincere greetings to all, greet all friends and those who ask about us. All the folk from Overijssel are well. I know nothing about M. [Gerrit Hermannus] Lankheet; I think that he must have written you by now.

M. Mensink.

[P.S.] If you hear of the ship *Isabella,* advise everyone to take it, because the other people did not fare nearly as well as we did due to lack of space and a poor kitchen and besides that the ship is closed off on the upper level.

Wormser 2

D. A. Budde to J. A. Wormser
Nieuwediep, 27 March 1847

Esteemed Friend and Brother in the Lord,

Every moment we are still with you; the bond of deep friendship and attachment that we feel between us is not broken by being separated from each other. May the Lord reward all your friendship, love, and benevolence bestowed upon us. We are after all children of the same heavenly father, purchased by the blood of his only begotten son to be his eternal possession and bound to the spiritual head, our Lord Jesus Christ. We are of good cheer; until now we are lacking in nothing. The throne of grace is open to us; we are free to approach God in prayer, unitedly entrusting ourselves to his care and faithfulness, asking that he will prosper our faith. As we remember you in our prayers, remember us in yours. All is very well on board; we could not ask for more. The captain, helmsman, cook, and steward are all very friendly and modest. It is only the beginning of the journey, and until now the Lord has been our aid. Thursday (March 25) we boarded ship at Purmerend at six o'clock, having taken a wagon from Buiksloot, so that the *Zeemeeuw* would not fly away without us. I am still not aware that we have overlooked anything of importance; if you should know of anything [send it]; we cannot leave before next Tuesday. If the wind is favorable we will sail that day; they are busy loading even now! We arrived here yesterday, ten and then fourteen horses had to drag us. May the Lord, who has no need of horses, bring us to America with a favorable wind and erelong bring you to us, so that we may once more greet each other face to face and rejoice in him who tied the knot of friendship between us here on earth, to the praise and glory of his name.

We are all in good health. Warmest greetings from us all. Greet the brothers and sisters. Greet my brothers and sisters and please forward the enclosed letter to my brother John for his son Enno.

In love,
D. H. Budde

Wormser 3

C. M. Budde-Stomp to J.A. Wormser and wife
On board the Zeemeeuw, Capt. Kayser in charge, anchored off Nieuwediep, 30 March 1847

Dearly Beloved Friends, Brother and Sister in our Lord Jesus Christ,

Joyfully I take up my pen so I can still write Your Honors a few letters. I hope that this finds all Your Honors well. After we came on board Thursday evening, we tried to make arrangements for our little household. I have had a bad headache for the past two days, and that has bothered me a lot and made me think of you, my dear friends. Our ship had to be loaded on Sunday. We were sitting together and reading in Romans, but we could not continue because of all the noise. On shore we went to a Hervormde Kerk, but it provided no nourishment for poor sinners either. In the evening the loading was finished, and now we were able calmly to finish reading the passage and sing: "Blest is the man whose strength thou art. Thy ways are hidden in his heart" [Psalm 84, stanza 3 in the Dutch versification]. One of the ship's officers, who keeps watch on board ship, was a member of a Seceded congregation, and my husband and I had a pleasant conversation with him, also about Sabbath observance. It is a difficult problem for him; his name is Ros.

Life on board ship is altogether different from life at home, but all of us can adapt to it all right. We are very well taken care of; in the morning we have good porridge and then bread and tea. All of us have a good appetite; it seems that the [ocean] air is good for our digestion. Our children are all doing very well. At first we had very nice weather although it was cold, but Sunday night we had a heavy rainstorm, so that we were glad that we were still in the harbor. My husband and I make very good use of the Boefantes [*Bouffantes*, or woolen scarves] we got from Miss Lothes, and we thank her again for her kindness. We look out on the open but stormy sea. That is not pleasant, but we trust in the help of the Lord who commands the winds and the sea. The captain's wife, the helmsman, and all the crew are very nice to us. They take us to the ship's cabin for coffee and tea. And until now the ship has been free of vermin, which suits us very much. Mrs. Teleman is very happy. For now these letters will be our final farewell. Continue to remember us in your prayers at the throne of grace, in whom we are united together "in the joyous prospect we eagerly anticipate, of perfectly setting forth his praise, and beholding him in righteousness, and sated with the fullness of his divine image" [paraphrase of Psalter 17:8, versification of 1773]. Our sincere greetings to all our good friends: Mrs. Zeelt, Bakker, and Mijntje, and the members of your household.

I remain your friend and sister, ever mindful of you,
C. M. Budde-Stomp.

Wormser 4

J. G. Budde to the young ladies Jansje and Kaatje Wormser
From Nieuwediep, 30 March 1847

Dear Friends,

Having left for Buiksloot at three o'clock, on Wednesday (March 24) after four we left for Purmerend in a wagon and met the ship even before we got to Purmerend, but we boarded her first. During the night the ship lay still, and we arrived at Nieuwediep Friday evening. After that the ship was loaded, which took place on Saturday and Sunday. We expect to head out to the open sea this Tuesday if the wind continues to be favorable. Later on, if the Lord wills and we live, I will continue my account of the journey, having begun already now to fulfill my promise. I am grateful to you for the love and esteem that you bestowed on me, hoping that the Lord may fortify your health and strength. But above all, seek him while he may be found, and pray to him without ceasing, for he will also be found by those who seek him. Once again I greet you warmly and also your parents, and hoping that you will soon follow us.

Your loving friend,
J. G. Budde

Wormser 5

C. M. Budde-Stomp to J. A. Wormser and spouse
On board the *Zeemeeuw*, Capt. Kayser, 1 April 1847

Dearly Beloved Friends, Brother and Sister in Christ Jesus,

I had intended to write another brief note to you who are never out of my mind. We had expected to be at sea by now, but that was not the will of the Lord. Although the Lord's Day (March 28) had to be used to load the cargo, we still have to wait until the Lord gives orders to his wind for us to sail. On Wednesday morning (March 31) all was in readiness, the wind was favorable, the captain took his wife ashore, the pilot was on board, the anchors were lifted, the sails hoisted, and behold the wind died down and turned about completely, so that the captain did not deem it wise to set sail. He fetched his wife back on board, and in the evening we also went ashore and engaged in a conversation with a fisherman who sailed on the little boat of Reverend Scholte. The man complained that he was subject to individuals who were a lot tougher than the Reverend Scholte; they refused to let him have the Sabbath off. He was no longer so opposed to going to America, for he seemed sure that the Lord would pour out his judgments upon the Netherlands.

Now it is Thursday, April 1, and the wind is still contrary. I asked the captain's wife if she would take along a letter for me when she went to Amsterdam. She and all the ship's crew are most friendly. We are all in good health and content, as is Mrs. Teleman and her child and Lubberde[n] and the children; they play together all day long. Dear friends, when you go to our former home, greet our brother and sister, Enno, Ede, Carlien, and Caatje, also Mrs. Flörke and children, and tell Grandfather that we are well. When we are so fortunate to receive some letters from you some time, also let us know how Grandfather and all our friends are doing. On Friday morning (April 2) Reverend Scholte came on board; he had checked out and taken a cabin on the *Pieter Floris*. As soon as it departed from Liverpool, he would occupy the cabin. There will be more wind this evening; we will wait on the Lord.

On Saturday (April 3) my husband experienced stomach pains. We thought we would stay over on Sunday (April 4), but the Lord's Day had to be violated! Today the ship, with sails hoisted, will be dragged out by a steamboat. Now my dear friends, farewell, my dear brothers and sisters, let us join in fellowship before the throne of grace. My husband is not feeling any better, and this gives me some concern, but for the rest we are all still well. Once again, my sincere greetings to you all, also to my father.

Your friend who always thinks of you,
C. M. Budde-Stomp

P.S. Be so kind as to post the enclosed [letter] to Lubberd[en].

Wormser 6

D. A. Budde to J A. Wormser
On board the Zeemeeuw, under Captain H. L. Kayser, 27 April 1847

Esteemed and Dearly Beloved Brother in our Lord Jesus Christ!

I pray that all may be well with you and yours; that is the prayer of my soul. We find ourselves in reasonably good circumstances, although still bobbing up and down on the waves of the great ocean, in the hope that the Lord in his own good time will bring us to the harbor of our destination. The ship is heaving too much for me to be able to continue writing, so we will wait until it quiets down.

May 11. Since we are having very nice weather today and the ship is becalmed, I will again take my pen to write you a bit. You are no doubt aware that we left N[ieuwediep] on Sunday April 4, heading out to sea. The wind was not favorable. It was not long before the dreaded seasickness broke out among all the passengers from first to last. Meanwhile, the ship sailed on across the North Sea to the English Channel, where we could see France on the one side and England with its white cliffs on the other. The wind continued contrary; the weather became most tempestuous, and, since we had always heard that this was a dangerous area, and particularly at night when all is dark, my soul was poured out to God who alone could save us and is a sure refuge in all distress and danger. We exchanged worried glances with each other, asking ourselves if we should have taken this step. Had we given any consideration to the dangers attendant upon a sea voyage? The disciples had their Lord in the ship with them when the danger of perishing threatened them. Should we then not also turn to that Lord, who then revealed himself as the Almighty One in commanding the wind and the sea to be still for their rescue, and seek our refuge in him, our God and Lord? Yes, that was all there was left, and that was enough. In his free grace we had the privilege to go freely to the throne of grace, as poor and helpless sinners in order to obtain mercy. In those moments we also found encouragement and consolation in the word of the Lord on which we, still being together on Sunday, had reflected—Psalm 121, "Our help is in the name of the Lord who created heaven and earth. Behold, the keeper of Israel shall neither slumber nor sleep. The Lord is thy keeper, the Lord is thy shade on thy right hand."

Thursday, the 8th. We were about to go to bed but because of the unusual movements of the ship, sleep was distant, and so we could take all our needs to our faithful Lord and Father. The following night we were already somewhat accustomed to the pounding of the ship and were refreshed by sleep. The wind calmed down some, and on Sunday, the 11th, we had nice weather. [We were grateful] that together we might thank the Lord and call upon him for his care and guidance on our way. We missed being able to worship together as a congregation on the day of rest, but the Lord was good and near to us. We were still united in the Spirit. Gradually, first one then another recovered from seasickness; our Maria and Lubberd[en]'s little Piet scarcely experienced any of it. (It is a real pleasure to see Maria, the way she plays all over the ship, she gets about as easily as the sailors. While we can scarcely remain standing, she walks about as easily as if she were on land.) I was not bothered much by seasickness, except that in the first few days I had no appetite. But all the others had their share of it. Jan was also pretty much over it in a couple of days. The women had their ups and downs. Mrs. Teleman just stayed in her bunk, the best and safest place for her. Diedrich was also sweet and still and fully recovered in about seven days.

On Tuesday the 13th, we had a good wind; after having been at sea nine days, we were one-third of the way across the Channel, which is eighty-three German miles in length. We now sailed the remaining two-thirds in twenty-four hours, and then there was a contrary wind again. On Friday the 16th it became fairly stormy toward evening, and it was no less so during the night. All the common folk had to go up on deck, but we remained quietly below. We were at a standstill but were disconcerted by the tumult up on deck and by the pounding of the waves of the sea, because of which we were being thrown from side to side, and our sleep disturbed.

On Saturday the 17th, the weather remained as stormy as ever. In the morning I went up on deck, but, woe is me, the awful power of the God of heaven and earth was visible to the eye in the waters and the mighty waves of the Sea. His is the Sea; it was brought forth by his might with all the dry land, and everything must obey his laws. And now to this God, who in Christ is my God and Father, my heart poured forth in prayers and petitions to him, who only moments earlier by the Holy Spirit had caused the word of his promise to be quickened in my inward being. When through the deep waters I cause you to go, I shall be with you and the Rivers shall not overwhelm you. It was visible, what the poet of Psalm 93 says: "The floods have lifted up, O Lord, the floods have lifted up their voice." But the Lord is Mightier than the roaring of many waters, yea, than the mighty waves of the sea. Yes, this was also for my consolation.

The captain was also on deck, and I could tell that he was not in a good humor, and that soon was evident. When the first mate came up, and a ship hove into view on the left side, he said: "That is very much like the one that was ahead of us last night." At that very moment the captain burst forth with the most awful curses and cursed him who rules heaven and earth. Even the mate said to me later on, "It's awful the way that man swears; anyone not proficient in it could learn it here." My heart melted within me, and in my mind I called out, Lord, how will we ever get to our place of destination? I remained on deck a moment longer when a huge wave came over the ship, struck me, and threw me against the rear mast so hard that I scarcely knew where I was. The captain and the son of Lubberd[en] also caught it, and we all had to put on dry clothing, for we were soaked through. The captain kept on blurting it out, blaming now this, now that. I was downcast the entire day, sighing before God, the God of my salvation. Oh Lord, do not deal with us according to our sins, do not reward us according to our transgressions; praying for the people that were on board. The Lord Jesus also prayed for his enemies on the cross.

Toward evening, after I had been able to commend everything to the Lord and plead upon his word, things quieted down within me a little. Would you then, Lord, destroy the righteous with the Sinner? No! Lot had to depart from Sodom. The Lord will protect us and keep us. Now the wind calmed a bit, and Sunday the 18th we looked forward with a calm spirit to continuing our journey, looking to God; now the wind was a little stronger, now a little weaker, but for the most part we had contrary winds, seeing nothing but sky and water.

Finally, finally, on Saturday the 24th we discovered land; which came into view suddenly, one of the western isles named Therassom, 314 German miles from the English Channel. Here we also saw an example of the almighty power of God displayed in creation; in the midst of the unfathomable depths of the sea, a mass of land, on which a city with towers; and lovely green farmland, delightful to our eyes. We heaved a sigh of relief. Everyone came on deck except for two of the Lubberd[en] children who had had the measles but had [not] sufficiently recovered. We sailed by the island, which displayed a tall rocky promontory at its edge, another wonder of God's almighty power, and expressed the wish that erelong we would behold the harbor of our destination. The two other Lubberd[en] children now also came down with the measles.

On the 30th we had an easterly wind, but it was so gentle that we made little headway. In the evening the wind became westerly again and on Sunday, May 2, fairly uncomfortable, the weather turbulent, accompanied by rain. It was quieter on Monday, and on Tuesday it was again turbulent. Diedrich now also caught the measles and had to stay in bed. Given how weak my wife was physically, she was generally in good spirits. And we could rejoice together about the great good that is ours in having God as our Father, who will make everything turn out for the best. While we saw the crew members "worshiping the prince of this world," we enjoyed the privilege of receiving strength from our God and Lord in all the unpleasantness of the journey. On the 7th and 8th we again had an easterly wind, then again a contrary wind, and then a calm. The Lord reigns.

New York, May 19, on board.

We have all recovered again. The measles that the children had contracted were a blessing to them; they were off the deck and then back again in eight days! They enjoyed the trip and never were aware of misery or danger; they enjoyed themselves easily and never experienced suffering or danger. Thanks be to God. On the 10th, 11th, and 12th we had so much calm weather that we were driven back a distance of forty-five German miles by the Gulf Stream. Then an east wind came up that became quite violent on Thursday the 13th. Fortunately we were now driven by a favorable wind; the storm abated a bit at times and was raging again on Saturday, so much so that those of us who were unaccustomed to storms could do nothing but cast ourselves into the arms of the everlasting merciful one. This man in trouble called to God, and he delivered him from all his fears.

On Sunday the 16th, the wind let up and we thought about our friends of our Religious Fellowship. The plumb line was cast out and the sea bottom found. The captain, happy, came to us with clay on his finger and said, "That's what we have been looking for so long." On the 17th the weather was nice, and in the distance we saw some land. At 11:30 in the morning a pilot came on board, and in the evening we arrived at the coast of America. On the 18th we sailed along the coast, all healthy and hale; a splendid sight it was.

It is a land where nature is so richly embellished by the Creator that my pen is incapable of describing it adequately. All we can say is: Come and see for yourself. We anchored in the evening and now the doctor has come on board to check whether there are any sick. None. Praise the Lord! On the morning of the 19th, a small steamboat pulled up on one side of our ship, and on the other side a big three-master, and they dragged us to a New York pier, and now we could behold the city. The harbor teems and swarms with more steamboats and other vessels than I could ever have imagined. It was not long before there was a swarm of swindlers on board, Germans and Hollanders. We just let them talk without responding to them. Then H. Hodenpeil [Hodenpyl] of 114 Greenwich Street and an agent for the Holland Society, came on board with a letter from Reverend Scholte, who already was here [urging us] to accompany him. Now I was reassured and stepped ashore with Jan for the first time and went to Reverend Scholte, who had rented rooms for himself in the Holland Hotel. We were overjoyed to meet Hollanders and Christians after a journey of forty-four days from N[ieuwe]diep. Most of those assembled here with us had had a longer voyage.

Now for a walk about town, but was it ever busy! We saw a large steamboat—it was beautiful to see, but the most beautiful thing to see was the Bibles, property of the boat, lying on several tables for the use of the passengers. And Rev. Van Raalte did not exaggerate when he wrote about the city of New York; you just have to see it. Rev. De Witt was not in town. We did not find [John] Neander [Reformed Church missionary to the Jews, 1846-1848] at home either.

May 20. Tonight Rev. Scholte will be preaching in Dutch in a local church. Rev. Van Raalte also had been in the city twelve days ago. Very likely we will be leaving by steamboat for St. Louis tomorrow the 21st. Things were very good aboard ship. I will write again and in greater detail when we have reached our destination in the land on which we have now set foot, and where we will establish ourselves, and which in our eyes is so full of promise.

Remember us and pray to the Lord with us, that his face may shine upon us and go with us. We have very much to be thankful for and [have] great needs in body and soul. May the Lord remain your refuge and ours at all times. Warmest greetings from us all. We thank you for all the love you have shown us. May the Lord reward it richly; his promises are sure. Give greetings to your wife and children; Jan will be writing them later. Greet your brother D, and greet our friends of the Fellowship. Remember us [in prayer]. Greet my brothers and sisters and tell them to communicate the message of our well-being, first of all to those in Ost Friesland. I shall write them later. Farewell, the Lord of Peace be with you and your household. Also the Fellowship at our house. We continue to remember you always.

Your Loving Brother, Bound in Christ,
D. A. Budde.

P.S. Jan spoke to Portenge[n]—greetings—and is thinking of leaving again in a few days.

[*Letter from Scholte enclosed*]

Scholte to J. Hospers at Hoogblokland
Utrecht, 7 June 1847

Esteemed Friend! Knowing of your interest in the experiences of the brethren who have left, I have taken it upon myself to enclose the following copy of a letter by our brother Scholte to be forwarded to Mr. A. A. Schuyt.

New York, 14 May 1847

Dearly Beloved Friend and Brother in our Lord!

Earlier this week, I wrote you in great haste about our safe arrival on the steamboat *Sarah Sand*. Since my family is staying with Mr. Norton in Connecticut and I am here all alone this week, I was able to devote all my time to checking out everything as much as possible. So far I am confirmed in my conviction that Iowa and a part of Illinois will be most suitable for us, and that Van Raalte has made an unfortunate choice. In Albany as well as in New York, the general opinion is that things will turn out badly. In Michigan they are doing everything possible to attract settlers; you can even acquire land from private individuals for less than the government price. In his efforts to get people to go there, Van Raalte has already become thoroughly American. I hope I am never that persistent, and in my opinion a good place for a settlement does not commend itself so much by telling the people what could be done there, but rather by what already has been done and is presently being done. Good locations get populated very rapidly as soon as there is a settlement.

The land in Illinois, about which I had been informed already in Holland, belongs to one of the professors of the "Nieuwwijksche College"; the land is located in La Salle County, a very favorable location, but if no additional land can be obtained, it will not be sufficient for us. In Iowa we can get all the land we need in the neighborhood of Keo[kuk]. Mr. Norton has this land at his disposal. I have already looked into several offerings that I have had to reject because they are not well located or well suited for us. In any event, nothing can be bought until a personal inspection has been made on site. Personally I take notes on everything that looks good in the description.

Not one of our ships has arrived yet. Yesterday I signed a contract for the journey inland: 13 dollars per person above [age] twelve, 6½ dollars for [ages] four to twelve, and below four they go free. Above twelve years you get one hundred pounds of free luggage; between four and twelve, half of that. For everything else, 2 dollars per one hundred pounds. If there is not enough water at Pittsburgh, then the route via Baltimore is the same price. Baltimore would be a good place to land if there were always enough water in Pittsburgh, but that is not always the case. That is why hereafter I will always have to recommend New York as the landing site for the average passenger and, when the season is suitable, New Orleans. From there travel inland is cheapest and also easiest. Our brethren in St. Louis are very satisfied and enjoy much respect and esteem there.

During the annual general assembly of the [Dutch Reformed] churches, I met many ministers, also [Robert] Baird [a noted Presbyterian minister], known among us for his writings. The Dutch Reformed have been after me to join their synod. I told them that I was not so inclined, because I cannot agree with the synodical system. I think Van Raalte will. In that case he will very likely receive an annual stipend of $100. I do not intend, however, to make any hasty decisions, for that has been the misfortune of many in America. I would rather have some extra expenses in the beginning than to have to break off what you have begun. The churches here are all excellent, and the singing is glorious, but I would not like to be permanently settled in one of the big cities. You really do not enjoy life there; it's all too busy and too harried. Quite generally, the war with Mexico is not approved here despite the victories over the Mexican army. The Holland Society for the protection of immigrants from the Netherlands pleases me very much. Mr. [Johan] Wambersie [of the Wambersie & Crooswijk agency] has received the relevant documents. They have already been discussing [the possibility] of shipping cargo on ships going from here to the Netherlands and then to bring back emigrants cheaply, very likely for as little as fl. 30 [$12] per person. It will be more difficult for Dutch ships when the new [U.S.] law, which reduces the number of passengers a ship may carry, goes into effect on May 31.

In Iowa the elections for new state officials have been completed, and from what I hear, very good people have been elected. The people of Iowa by a large majority have voted against permitting places for the sale of strong drinks. The example of the people of that state is being widely praised; in this regard they are an example to the entire nation. This is regarded as proof of the higher morality and virtue of that state, for nowhere else have they achieved such results. As soon as I have had a closer look at things and investigated them, I will write a letter of more general interest, to be published for the Netherlands public. It still is my judgment that no more of our acquaintances should come over this summer, unless it be for urgent reasons. Traveling via New Orleans will be better in the fall, for by then we can be settled and receive more people.

I just now recall that because I was so busy during those last few days in Holland, I forgot to take care of a few minor financial matters; for example, settling an account with Roering in The Hague. If anything should come to your attention regarding this, then please address everything to my nephew in Amsterdam. I am sure that he will write me, at which time I can arrange for payment. I have deposited the money I had with me in a bank in New York and opened an account there. The president and the cashier of the bank are proven Christians. I have not looked into the other financial matters as yet. In all likelihood I will do that today or next week and let you know about that afterwards. There are very good and safe securities here for investment purposes. I have also met Mr. Buys from Amsterdam and got the impression that he did not take any treasures along with him, for he has practically nothing left. But I do not know where his family is.

Tomorrow I hope to go to Connecticut in order to get my family, who are now staying with Mr. Horton, and bring them here, and then go on to the West. I have experienced much friendliness, much cordiality and esteem here, very different than in the Netherlands. There people avoided me; here they ask for me. Till now, nothing has disappointed me; on the contrary, I thank God that he has led me here. I hope that many of my Christian friends in the Netherlands will come and join me in tasting the fruits of genuine freedom. After we get a fairly large settlement in the West, we will soon have considerable influence there, for we are highly regarded in this land. Learning the English language is however a first requisite; make sure that everyone is serious about that. Time does not permit me to write all the brethren in Holland; see to it that this letter is read in Amsterdam, Leiden, and Arnhem and do request that all interested persons be informed about its contents. My sincere greetings in Christ to all brothers and sisters; I always remember them all in my prayers. The Lord grant them grace to remain faithful and clear about the way they should go. Greet especially all the members of your household; on another occasion I shall write them. Remember me in prayer; believe me, I am your loving friend and brother in Christ.

H. P. Scholte

I do not doubt that you will rejoice with me in my safe arrival and all I have experienced; be so kind to share this with all interested persons. I am, after giving you greetings from [Jacob] Maasdam,

Your Friend,
D. Chabot.

Wormser 7

D. A. Budde to J. A. Wormser
Summer 1847, Burlington

Most Esteemed and Dearly Beloved Brother in our Lord and Savior Jesus Christ!

In the expectation that you have received my letter from New York, dated May 19, telling of our safe arrival in this great continent through the faithfulness and goodness of the Lord, you are probably no less interested in knowing how we have fared since then and how we are still getting along. We are with you daily in spirit, and after you have read these letters, we are most eager and interested to have you write us how you are doing in Amsterdam, and how things are with all our friends, and with the Society. O, if only you were all here! There is freedom in all things here, but the distances between us are great, which make it very difficult for us to get together. Thanks be to the Lord who has kept us till now.

I wrote you that Rev. Scholte would be preaching in New York May 20. He did, and we attended the service. A lovely church, though simple; it was nearly filled with an audience of hearers. We were able to speak with several of them; it was a joy to be confirmed in the knowledge that the Lord has his people everywhere. We also engaged in conversation with two other ministers who gave true evidence of their interest in the spread of the kingdom of God and the edification of Christians. The Rev. Scholte was to preach again the next Sunday, and several churches offered their facilities for that purpose. New York is a great turbulent city (principally where most of the ships dock and where most of the trade is carried on); but where the richest people live it is a lovely city.

On the 21st of May we left the city at about six in the evening, leaving by steamboat for Albany, where we arrived at five in the morning. We scarcely had time to get off the boat with our goods before it moved on again. That was not exactly pleasant for us, because we had to cross over to another boat with all our goods while there was a host of people surrounding us, and all wanting to help us, but some in one direction, some in the other. And then relief came in the form of a person, a handy man who had formerly lived with my brother and family on Utrecht Street [in Amsterdam], and who had immigrated here with his family. Every morning before he went to work he stopped by [at the boat landing] to check if there were any Hollanders on the incoming boat. It was he who first took us to a rooming house, and afterward to the Rev. Wyckoff, at 100 Lydius Street. There I met a man full of love for his fellow man, a Christian, who having been liberated by the truth, now lives it. He was exceptional in his friendship toward us and took care of all matters pertaining to our further travels, since it was very difficult for us to do because we could not understand any English. Rev. Wyckoff also gave us a letter of introduction to [the] Buffalo [church]; in it he wrote that he wished to God that he might always be filled with heartfelt love and diligence to assist the Holland Christians. In return Rev. W[yckoff] asked that upon our arrival at St. Louis we would write His Reverence about our journey, which I gladly agreed to do, and also did. After a cordial farewell and a prayer for the blessing of God upon us, we left for Buffalo in the evening by canal boat, a vessel resembling tow barges in Holland but larger and roomier.

On this journey we passed through a number of cities, some larger, some smaller. Frequently we encountered waterways that passed crosswise underneath each other; there was even a railroad that passed underneath us and over which we passed in our boat. On Monday, May 31st, we arrived at Buffalo. It is a large city, 495 miles from New York, and 370 feet higher in elevation; it requires a large number of locks to reach that height. It is a city where you can get anything you need, and that is also why it is a good idea not to take along too much merchandise with you.

We encountered Hollanders here who assisted us, and who also knew and loved the Lord, to whom the Rev. Wyckoff had given us a letter of introduction, and whom we now joined. There was a gracious man who could speak Dutch with us and enjoyed doing so. It was his wish that we should remain here; for, as he said, they also needed good people here. His name is H. van der Poel, (next to the Buffalo Post Office). The friendship he showed us was exceptional; he gave us a walking tour of the town, taking us everywhere, and also introduced us to some other Hollanders. And so it was that we met an old widow lady, H. van Zee, from Coevorden, with four grown children. She had come over with Rev. Van Raalte, but she had not been able to go on any further because she had run out of money. Her contentment [with her lot] was evident in everything; she was an aged Christian who had her feet on solid ground on the road to eternity. It was our privilege to rejoice with her in the faithfulness of the Lord of Lords. From everything it was evident that Mr. Van der Poel was a man who was held in high esteem. We had a two-day layover; all the while this gentleman looked after us and provided us with a letter between stations to guard us against swindling, since in New York we had paid [our fare] all the way to St. Louis. On June 2 we left Buffalo, crossing Lake Erie on a steamboat to Sandusky, where we arrived on the 4th. The Keeper of Israel was our guardian, for though it is often dangerous on this lake, it was calm when we crossed. The name of the Lord be praised.

On the 5th we took a train to Richland, and then, because the railroad was not completed, the next forty-four miles was by wagon to Springfield, where we arrived on the 6th and could rest on the 6th and 7th. This was a tiring journey, wearisome like the one from Albany to Buffalo because of its long duration, even though that boat was being drawn by a team of two horses that were changed at intervals. However, the changing scenery and the fruitfulness of the land through which we were passing provided a pleasant relief in the midst of all our weariness. While we were at the German rooming house in Springfield, a Hollander looked us up and brought with him a German preacher who had been sent by the Bremer Fellowship to establish a German congregation, in other words, to preach the gospel. His name is Joachim Schladermundt, a German Lutheran preacher in Springfield, Ohio. He stopped by repeatedly; our conversations with him were edifying and continued deep into the night [after] everybody else in the rooming house had gone to bed. After taking leave of each other, we gave thanks to God for quickening us in such a variety of ways on our difficult journey and then lay down to sleep.

At 4:30 on the morning of the 8th we left for Cincinnati by train, arriving there the same day. It is a large and bustling city; there are factories of many kinds, all of them powered by steam. We left there on the 10th by steamboat and arrived in St. Louis on the 15th. We found [H.] Barendrecht [Barendregt] and more Hollanders living there. We thought that we would be meeting Rev. Scholte there, because we had been en route for such a long time, but that was not the case. Barendrecht [Barendregt] had also been expecting him for some time already. Since more people who were members of that Society had arrived, and none of them were able to find work, or were able to stand the heat of the sun, it was desirable that it be determined without further delay where all these colonists should be going.

Now there was a parting of ways within our company. W[illem] Lubberde[n] remained [in St. Louis] because his wife wanted to stay; she thought she could have good earnings there as a seamstress. Lubberde[n] would gladly have gone on with us, staying with us, but his wife preferred to stay where there were so many Hollanders. He took a tearful leave of us. Barendrecht [Barendregt] again helped us in getting a letter of recommendation from Dr. Keitz, and we left by steamboat on the 18th for Burlington in Iowa, where we arrived at three in the morning on the 21st of June. We stayed at a rooming house for eight days for 10 dollars, and [then] rented a tolerable dwelling for 4 ½ dollars a month, the one in which we are now living. It has been a difficult journey, but having completed it thus far, and finding ourselves in reasonably good circumstances. Thanks to the goodness of the Lord, all that unpleasantness will soon be forgotten through the pleasant prospect one has of living a quiet, peaceable, and blessed life here.

If a number of Hollanders should want to migrate here together, it is especially important that they learn English, or at least that there be one or two among them who have done so. It was very important for us that we had told Jan to learn some [English]; his ability grew so rapidly through contacts with English and American travelers that often he could be of help to Frenchmen and Germans, clarifying the confusion that resulted from their not understanding the English language.

But let those who contemplate the journey first count the costs, for many people are disappointed in their expectations. They think that once they have crossed the ocean and set foot on land, all their troubles are over, but that is precisely when it starts getting difficult. On the journey everything is expensive, even more expensive than in Holland, although freight costs are not all that high. The above is less true for single persons; for if they still have some money to go on, they can find work, if not in one city, then in another. En route we became very much aware of the demand for workers, and even then it is very important that one can understand German or English.

Generally it is not easy to buy land for little money near the cities through, or past, which one is traveling. Prices range from $25 to $100 per acre, depending on proximity to the city; that is because almost all of it is in the hands of speculators. In several states there is no more Congress land available [at $1.25 per acre]. So it is natural enough that if you are a household, you try to trek further in the hope of getting some land for less money. In the newer states there is still plenty of Congress land, but for someone who has not grown up working the land, everything is strange and difficult since everything is still wild and densely overgrown with trees. It is forest land with large, tall trees everywhere—an enormous number of them in the areas we have traversed, lumber and firewood in abundance, since lumber is expensive because of the labor costs. [Whether] the states that are now the most populated can still hold many more inhabitants, it is impossible to say, because of the great expanse and fertility of the land in N. America. Burlington in the state of Iowa is also a glorious proof of that.

After we had been here in the city for a few days, we met two friends (A. Verkerk and Ch. Beurkens) from Zeeland whose wives were sisters, and each with a child seven years old. We are in hearty agreement with these friends; they did not care to join the colony either and they had also come here as we had, via New Orleans. Now we would like to stay together, close to this city, if that be the Lord's will. They too were amazed at the fertility of the land and how fast things grow: wheat that sprouted here in three days took three weeks in Zeeland. All around the city much wheat is grown—also oats, barley, corn, potatoes, and whatever else the land produces. Garden produce or vegetables are rather expensive here because everything is still so new. Ten years ago there were few houses in the city, and not a single brick house; now they are numerous, and many more are being built. Four new church structures are nearly completed, each with its tower. Old [German] Reformed, Congregationalist, Methodist, and Roman Catholic, but the latter group does not have a priest. Then there are others who do not have a church building as yet but meet in their homes, such as Episcopalians, German Evangelicals, and German Methodists.

During the summer it is fairly warm in the city because it is situated low on the Mississippi River. (Illinois is on the other side of the river.) The land around the city of Burlington lies high and therefore it is not as sultry as in the city. Steamboats go by every day and also stop here. There is a market on Tuesdays, Thursdays, and Saturdays. At that time you can buy everything in the way of food supplies. The rich as well as the poor come to the market with their baskets to buy, the most respected clergy as well as others, there is no distinction. The grandiosity of the gentlemen of the cloth in Amsterdam is unknown here. There is a steam-powered gristmill here, which is operated day and night during the week until Saturday evening, but not on Sunday. There are also saw mills, the one operated by water, another by steam, and still another by horses. Wheat flour can be purchased for four Dutch cents a pound, and an extra fine variety for five Dutch cents a pound; fresh beef is from eight to ten Dutch cents a pound and so is a tasty side of pork, veal, and lamb. In St. Louis the market was bigger and covered a larger area. As the population grows that will be the case here also. The city has about three thousand inhabitants, and this within a space of ten years.

The holiday on which the United States celebrates its independence fell on Sunday, July 4, this year. This Sunday was quiet like any other, the celebration took place on the 3rd and the 5th. On the 3rd there were parades with music in the city, first by an English Society and later by a German one; there were fireworks and bonfires, all very solemn and stately. On Monday, the 5th, there were Sunday school competitions for children from the Methodist, Congregationalist, and other churches. There were a total of 483 children in the churches. The minister spoke to them of the good fortune that was theirs, above others, as free people living in a free land, but above all in having freedom of religion, so that no one would experience any hindrance in practicing his religion. They were free to be instructed in the Bible every Sunday and as often as they wished. And he reminded them of the obligation that now also lay upon them, and then the whole story of how their forefathers had offered their blood in order to gain that freedom.

Then another clergyman spoke of the necessity of attending Sunday school and doing so regularly because they needed to know the truth as it is in Jesus Christ unto eternal salvation. Thereupon they left the church [in a procession]: musicians leading, followed by the clergy and men and women teachers, and then the children two by two, carrying a variety of banners on a parade through the city. The first banner portrayed the Bible; others had sayings such as: In God is my Trust, the Lord is our Keeper, Love, Truth, Patience, and the like. And then they went into the Methodist church where they had a generous meal of refreshments. After getting some assignments from their teachers, they went home.

I cannot tell you how all this affected me. I was overcome with tears at the thought that we and our children, who had scarcely arrived here, were sharing in all these privileges, and so were reminded of all the things that we could not get in Europe. We thanked the Lord our God, who made us of one mind in our determination to leave Holland and who had led us hither under his fatherly guidance.

The festivities in this city were of a wholly different character from those in Amsterdam. There we saw people who debased themselves lower than beasts; here everything was done in good taste—quiet and demure—so that as we reflected on the day's events, our hearts could be active in praise and gratitude to God. In Holland we did not enjoy this kind of freedom, the freedom to do your own thing in matters religious and civil. One is free in everything here, except to do wrong. For there is a jail for evildoers here too, and the prince of darkness has all too many of his servants here as well.

They wanted to keep me here in the city; several friends requested that we do so. Because of my trade I could make a decent living here. I do believe that is true, since earnings, regardless of the work, are greater here than in Europe, and even if you work only three days a week, you have an ample living. But my preference is for the quiet life of the country, rather than again taking on many cares and concerns, and that because the man who works the land can make a good living anywhere here. We have visited just about everywhere in the city and have observed that however much people had to make do with their dwellings (farmers here, except for a few, do not have the nice homes they have in Holland), they had everything else in abundance. We really encountered hospitality among the country folk. Wherever we went, they insisted that we stay for something to eat, even if we were just inquiring about some farmer or other, and that was true even of people who owned nothing at all but rented a log cabin with a small piece of land. To be sure, one city has considerable advantages over another in matters of religion.

Diedrich and Jansje are already attending school here and learning English. But in the country you also find schools at a distance of only three miles, or one hour's walk, from the city. For those of us who are advanced in years it is difficult to hear a sermon in English with profit and edification, simply because we do not understand it, and we do not care for the German preachers. On Sundays Jan attends the English Congregational church; the children go to the same church from 9 till 10:30 in the morning to go to Sunday school where they receive religious instruction. And then we attend the High German services; in the afternoon we have a worship service in our home. The friends we met here also come to our house then. Their names are Adrianus Verkerk and Christoffer Beurkens, from the island of Tholen in Zeeland, but they have since left us and purchased a log cabin and forty acres of land for four hundred dollars in the same area where we hope to settle.

We are still waiting to hear from the gentleman who wants to sell; the property is located three miles or an hour's distance from the city. The fact that we have not written sooner is because we have been waiting for five weeks already, and I would really like to have that property. There is more farmland available, but the acreage is a little much for me. That is why I prefer to wait and see whether this may be the place of my destiny.

Most of the time Jan is out there in the country with the farmers who are ready to instruct us about all kinds of things, and who offer us a helping hand in moving our things from here. Among them is a German, of Reformed persuasion, who is exceptionally interested in having us as neighbors. He also assisted our friends from Zeeland in settling here, the ones who are so exceptionally pleased with their land, and who could not repay him in seven years for all he has done for them. It seems to me that he is a simple, genuine Christian. Other Germans and Americans visited the Verkerks and the Beurkens; they are interested in having good neighbors, for farmers help each other. If your horses have gone off into the woods, you just take one of your neighbor's [horses] and ride off to the city. If someone wants to live only for himself, he is left to his own devices by his neighbors; and when he cannot make it, he finally has to give up his place.

The farmer does not need many helpers, there are machines for everything; the cutting and threshing of grain goes incredibly fast, the one neighbor helps the other, as we have already seen. There are more Hollanders around who also want to move into this area. There are also six unattached persons here from St. Louis, four of whom belong to the Society; they are waiting [for the Society] to purchase land for the establishment of the colony. And two persons want to remain here because of all the discontent in St. Louis, where there are said to be fifteen hundred people. I have also received a letter from Lubberde[n], in which he wrote that Rev. Scholte had arrived in St. Louis on July 5th, that in the church where he preached they took up a collection for the poor (in the Society); that work was too hard for the Hollanders in the city [St. Louis]. There was much sickness, and many were dying. Enclosed there were also greetings from Naatje, Le Cocq, and from Diekinga, both of whose children had died. Lubberde[n] had purchased five acres of land planted with Indian corn and potatoes in Illinois, four miles from St. Louis; the price was two hundred dollars and included a house, two barns, and a well. After everything had been agreed to, the farmer's wife refused to sign and the sale fell through. Now he is thinking of remaining with the colony.

And now here is some information about craftsmen. As I said right from the start, a single person has no problem getting ahead here, but for households it is more difficult. If you have enough money you can take time to look around [before settling in], but if not, my advice is: do not leave Holland if you have a good living. If after completing your journey you can afford to spend five or six hundred dollars to buy some land near a city, and if that is what you really want, you can make a good living at that. I write this on the basis of my experience in Burlington. It may be different in towns farther north; it certainly is true if you go farther inland and do not have to spend as much money for Congress land. But then you do have to put up with many hardships and it is difficult to get one's produce to market. Once Dutch colonies have been established, you will certainly hear about them too. Let me repeat, the land is fertile; you do not find any poor people here. What is very important, even essential, if you wish to settle in a city, is that you understand some English. Though I cannot yet write you that I have purchased a place where we will be living from now on, we are very content here. We may still enjoy the nearness and the mercies of the Lord, and await the one who endures unto all eternity for his children.

Is Santje still living, or is she rejoicing before the throne of the Lamb whose she was during her life upon earth? How are things going for the "Free" schools in Amsterdam? Warmest greetings to your spouse and children from us all, and to all the brothers and sisters of our Society to which I still feel deeply attached; also to Madame Teleman who looks very contented and very happy. Greet Mr. and Mrs. Willink and all who love the Lord in incorruptibility. I continue to remember you in my prayers, your ever loving friend and brother in our Lord and God.

D.A. Budde

Wormser 8

C. M. Budde-Stomp to Mr. and Mrs. Wormser-van der Ven
and their children
Burlington, Summer 1847

Dear Beloved Brother and Sister, and
Beloved Children in our Lord Jesus Christ,

My dearly beloved friend, I live in hope that Your Honors will receive these letters in health and well being. Through the goodness of the Lord we are in reasonably good health and, although some of us were not well at times, we were graciously spared any serious illness. You do not experience the physical distress of seasickness when you are traveling on land. However, travel by steam canal boat and railroad was very difficult because we did not have the best of seats. Fortunately, the Lord directed our way to Burlington, where we are presently living in a fairly good rented dwelling. There are many Germans living here and as a result I do not get to hear a word of English. It is so much a part of us to avoid doing the difficult thing when we can get by with something easier.

This city has really grown in ten years; it already has church towers, a market, etc., and it has possibilities for further expansion in the future. It is situated on the Mississippi River and rises gently toward a wooded hill where there are many brambles, hazelnuts, etc. The land up in the hills is much nicer than that lying at the river's edge. We also have good spring water here, though usually you have to go some distance from your dwelling to get it. Doing the washing, which I had greatly dreaded, turns out to be easier than I had expected. We have a stove with a wash boiler, an oven, for we bake our own bread, and pots to cooks in. We have a yard to dry things; as far as I know they do not have attics here.

Conveniences that are very cheap over there are much more expensive here. The smallest coin is five cents, not a copper coin. Small items, such as matches, chalk, lead pencils, etc., earthenware such as pots, crocks, are crude and expensive; tin ware, such as plates, coffee cans, and mugs, are all more expensive. Dry goods are plain cotton, at ½ dollar per yard. Clothing is very much like in Europe. To protect themselves from the sun the women wear a colored cap—similar to those worn in [the province of] Noord Holland and which is called a bonnet. The land here is beautiful; I was in a log cabin [like the one] that is drawn crudely on a plate in the book by Beijer. There was not a window in it, nor wall bed or cupboard, just a few planks on the beams on which you can set household goods. The Zeelanders had purchased good land here so that they could say: "The lines have fallen to me in pleasant places." It was a lovely sight; in front of the door, some flowers, cabbages, carrots, onions, watermelons, and also cantaloupe, straight from a big beautiful woods where it is a pleasure to walk. Besides, there was a well from which water is drawn, and in the back grew a field of Indian corn and Turkish wheat, as well as butter beans, buckwheat, and cabbage. They already owned a cow and a calf and chickens. And for that reason they praised the Lord their God and acknowledged the benefits received from his hand.

There were Germans on another "farm," the American word for *boerenhofstede*. They had many fruit trees: apple, peach, and cherry, also berries, strawberries, etc., all very lovely. We enjoy a great deal of friendship and assistance from these folk and from others as well. We associated much with the Zeelanders, for in our religion and thought patterns we have much in common. That somewhat softened the loss of our associations with you, for we think and talk of you every day. We are experiencing in a rich measure [the answer] to the prayers that you offered to the Lord [that we might find] hospitality in a foreign land, for the bond of love and friendship which the Lord placed between us has developed deep roots. Our desire to write you was very great, but we wanted very much to let you know our final destination. We would have liked very much to be in the neighborhood of the Zeelanders and the Germans, but the Lord is preventing that so far. We must wait on the Lord and trust his promise to make all things well. It is a new way of life for us, to leave behind all that was dear to us, and the comforts of a life to which we were so accustomed, but we have no regrets about this move. It is amazing how country folk can make do; that makes their housekeeping easier. They are very insistent on good food and drink; they have warm meals three times a day and everything is done with dispatch. In general, people are very friendly and helpful here. They would have liked to keep us in the city, but then my husband would not be able to attain the goal for which he left, but even here a house and land are just too expensive for us.

I write you all with joy, but how great will be my joy when I receive a letter from my dearly beloved friends. Diedrich still often talks about Jansi and Kaatje. Maria is happy and well. Diedrich and Jansi Teleman are attending the English school; the teacher is also interested in us, visits us and talks with Jan. My dear husband looks very healthy, and he has had no chest problems. Mrs. Teleman is healthy and contented, and we go about our housekeeping tasks in the usual relaxed manner. I am very much relieved that there are not many housemaids here; I just would not care to have any foreign help [in my house]. And so the Lord knows how to direct our ways for the best. When you gladden us with a letter, then tell us how all our friends are doing, and whether you hear from my father; whether he is able to adjust to his [new] residence. This time I will not be writing Father, but do give him our greetings.

We are also eager to hear about the Fellowship and whether it is still meeting in our former dwelling. We are reminded of it every Sunday and miss it, for our feelings just are not the same as those of the German preacher. If it should be in the decree of the Lord to lead Your Honors out of the cares and troubles into which you have been placed, and cause us to live together in simplicity and stillness, that would give us great joy. Though we have no certitude about this, [we do] of the joyous prospect of being with the Lord, of being rid of this body of sin, where the loss of this kind of separation is no more. But with all the redeemed of the Lord we shall stand in the purity of love around the throne of the Lamb to bring him our honor, love, and adoration to all eternity.

Be so kind and greet your beloved brother and sister in [the province of] Overijssel for us. It must be said that a man from the country is sooner in his element here than a city dweller who must first learn all about country living. Give our greetings to your brother Dries and his wife, sister Rika, Juff Abrams [Abrahams], Lothes, Luring [Jan Willem Luuring], and all our dear friends. We would like to know what has become of coppersmith Van der Veen. Do kiss your dear Jansi, Kaatje, and Johan for us, if only I could kiss them once. Receive my cordial greetings, dear friends, always remember us in your prayers, and gladden us soon with a letter. As soon as we are established, I shall write you how we like life in the country. It seems very simple to me to live a life of greater stillness and quietude in the Lord. I remain your Sister, remembering you in love.

In the Lord,
C. M. Budde-Stomp.

Wormser 9

D. A. Budde to J. A. Wormser
Burlington, State of Iowa, 15 Aug. 1847

Esteemed and Beloved Brother in our Lord and Savior Jesus Christ!

It grieves me that I did not write you earlier; do not imitate me in this respect. I do not want to make any excuses, because you certainly could be right in being dissatisfied with them. But allow me to make a single observation; I had every intention of writing you where we had made a purchase and what was to be our residence from now on. But since I still cannot do that, I just cannot put off writing any longer. We believe that the Lord will make all things well for us, and therefore we are not in a hurry. We had thought to get something sooner, and we could have, but since this is for the rest of our lives, we were also eager, if possible, to get something to our liking. Our wish for you is that you may be faring well according to Soul and Body. We just cannot sufficiently acknowledge with gratitude all of God's mercies towards us.

There was considerable dissatisfaction among [members] of the Society in St. Louis. Many were running out of money; there was growing poverty. Barendrecht [Barendregt] told us that a ship with 190 passengers, under the leadership of Smink [Smeenk] and Rietveld, had arrived from Baltimore. Rev. Scholte had also been present to sign a contract with an agent to take them to St. Louis for thirteen dollars [each], when they could have gotten there just as well for eight dollars, and so at least two thousand Dutch guilders were lost. We had also utilized the same contract to go from New York to St. Louis for thirteen dollars; we were not all satisfied with the arrangements. The best thing you can do is to buy a ticket from one station to the next. That is what Rev. Wykhoff [Wyckoff] had also wanted to do at Albany. Rev. Van Raalte could have saved a lot of money [by doing this] and so could Rev. Scholte. Rev. Scholte arrived in St. Louis July 5 and rented a dwelling there for a half year; he then appointed a commission, of which he also was a member, in order to buy land. And even now as I am writing, Jan is reading an article in the newspaper, and if it is correct, it reports: "Hollanders, approximately 1,000 souls, are reported to have purchased two townships in Marion County, and they have already selected the site for a city and have laborers of every kind among them. They are nice and desirable people, and the Americans bid them welcome."

And now some news about New York. I talked to the gentlemen at James G. King Sons, 53 William Street, about the money that I still have in Amsterdam, and they said that I could deposit it with the office of Hope & Co., and they would be willing to reimburse me as soon as they received word of this, since they are constantly involved in business transactions with them. And now I would like to ask a favor of you: if you should have gotten all the money, subtract from it all expenses made [on our behalf] and retain one hundred guilders for Grandpa so that he has some spending money, and when that is gone we will provide more. Give him our cordial regards. And do write us soon how things are, for we are very eager to hear from you. And now may I pray that you will not forget us in your prayers before the Lord on our behalf, for we remain the same in our relationship to each other. Neither Sea nor Land can separate us; we are united together for all eternity, when we will find each other again. But as long as we live we shall not forget you all either; often we will find ourselves before the throne of grace together. Warmest greetings, Brother, Sister, Jansie, Kaatje, [from the] American farmer Johan. Give our greetings to Br[other] Lotthes [Lothes] and Mrs. Luuring and the Berkhoud [Berkhout] family, [to] Diekinga, Bousquet, Miss Abrams [Abrahams], Jansen, Schriek, Doornhouwer, your brother Dries and [his] wife and others, from us all. Greeting you again and in cordial love eternally remaining

Your Brother in Christ,
D. A. Budde

Address. Burlington, Iowa, Main Street.
Please be so kind as to wrap a piece of paper around the enclosed [citation] and send it to my brother on the Utrechtse and [Worst] streets. Be sure to read everything, for sometimes something is written in one place and not in another. Jan has developed a fever. May the Lord make all things well.

[Added is a quotation from J. A. Wormser, *Het leven van Albertus Christiaan van Raaalte*, p. 147, part of a letter dated 4 September 1847, from the Rev. P. Zonne from Milwaukee, Wisconsin to J. A. Wormser.]

We may rejoice in continuing good health, which has been almost unbroken for us and the children; however, there are many others who have fevers and the runs, and although few people are dying of it here, the number of deaths in Michigan must be very great. Rev. Van Raalte wrote us that many people were suffering from typhus. It seems to be quite certain that Michigan is very unhealthy, and in particular the site that Van Raalte selected for colonization. I know of no place less suited for the intended plan, and the advantages spelled out in such detail by Van Raalte, if not entirely exaggerated, certainly 90 percent are. The Black River is not navigable, and they are completely isolated from other communities, so that everything is much more costly than here, and sometimes there is almost a lack of the daily food needs. A cow and a calf costs only $25 here; in Michigan it is $50, and still they are not to be had. I fear that they will not be able to make it. And there you have a bit of information on Michigan.

Wormser 10

A. C. Van Raalte to J. A. Wormser
Allegan, Mich. 7 Jan. 1848

By Steamer via Liverpool—*29 Dec. 1847*

For several days we have had severe freezing weather with heavy snows. The snow was half a foot deep; we moved in on sleighs. But now a balmy south wind, not accompanied by rain, removes all the snow again, and it seems to be spring.

Just the other day we heard of a grievous accident. In the northern part of Lake Michigan, the engines of a large steamer [the *Phoenix*] broke down causing a fire to break out. En masse the people tried to save themselves by means of lifeboats, but only 30 were saved, and 150 souls perished, among whom were many Hollanders from Varsseveld and Winterswijk. In all of this we need to hold to our faith that God is just in all his ways and works. Indeed, that he is wise and good.

When I look back on this past year, then I sense a feeling of gratitude in my soul and I must call out: what shall I render to the Lord [for all his benefits]. Yes, I must testify that God has heard my cries. He bore me through it all on his mighty arms of mercy. He has upheld, sheltered, and provided for me, and he has helped and planted an entire people thus far for three years. Given my very lively conviction, I feared that I would go down to the grave having accomplished nothing at all, and now I stand amazed that God has granted me my wish with such a mighty arm. Oh, may he now plant this people to the praise of his name, and in providing for our material needs may he grant us knowledge and godliness. Brother, remember us before the throne of God! God does all according to his good pleasure; the Father of all the life-giving Spirit of the flesh, sends out [his] Spirit and [his] strength. He plants the nations and uproots them, builds up and breaks down. To have such an infinite sovereign as my refuge, who both mercifully forgives and does not chide, this lifts me upon a rock! How blessed is the people whose God is the Lord. And now brother, may God bless you and yours in Christ and keep our generation in the truth.

Our cordial greetings to your spouse and to the beloved in Christ.

Your Brother who Loves You with all His Heart,
A. C. Van Raalte

Wormser 11

D. A. Budde to J. A. Wormser
Burlington, 11 Jan. 1848

My Dear and Highly Esteemed Brother in the Lord!

Grace, Peace, and Mercy be to you and to your beloved wife and children. That is our wish for you, besought of God in accordance with his covenant promise. "Mountains may give way and hills tremble, but not my grace and my mercy." May this God guide and lead you and us, together with all the brothers and sisters in Amsterdam, in his ways to the glory of his name and the salvation of our souls.

Eagerly and painfully longing for some letters from you in response to my letter sent you in the month of August last year, I take up my pen to write you a few letters. All is going well with us here with the exception of John, who has been suffering from fevers off and on since the month of August. But the Lord does not deal with us according to our sins; both he and we may believe that all things, good and ill, must work together for our good...etc. Our departure from Europe was in the name of God, and in a joyful spirit; thus we turn everything over to God in prayer. The condition of our health and that of my wife and children is much better than it was in Amsterdam. That is equally true for Mrs. Teleman and Jansie. We do not have any worries about what shall we eat now and in the future. Our stay in Burlington did seem rather long to me, and that is why I went to work for a boss [shop owner] on August

26 as a wood turner. I work whenever I feel like it, come and go as I please, work three hours or six, or more on a given day, for there is freedom everywhere here, and that makes life pleasant. John also went to work as a wood turner about the middle of October, but he works off and on when he does not have a fever. At first the fever took too much out of him, but gradually you get used to it and you get a little stronger and when the fever is over, you go back to work again. In between we work together, as it suits us, for we work at two [different] shops, and in this way we earn our keep, until we leave Burlington to live in the country in the month of March or April.

Anyone able and willing to work can earn a living by working three days a week. Food supplies are cheap. We bought two pigs, 506 pounds dressed, for two American, five Dutch cents a pound. In small quantities [retail] you can buy the best beef for four American cents a pound, the very finest wheat flour is two American cents a pound. Butter is 12 ½ American cents a pound; milk is expensive if you have to buy it, but most people keep their own cattle. Animals are allowed to roam freely and every animal knows its owner. Already we occasionally meet people in Burlington with whom we feel at home; (for the loss of your company is very grievous to us, and it would be a source of no little joy to us if the Lord were to lead you and your family to come over here. Oh, not a day goes by without your being in our thoughts). The Lord is still good and near to us.

We usually go to church twice on Sundays, in the morning at 10:30 and at 6:30 in the evening. And then we are privileged to hear the Word of the Lord preached in all its fullness by a German Evangelical preacher. In the past it seemed that he avoided having any contact with us. But it has pleased the Lord, through talking and conversation, to get him to embrace the doctrine of the free grace of God in Christ. He was a diligent preacher of the Word, but he was often discouraged because of the hardness [of heart] and the stubbornness of the people. But now he is able prayerfully to leave the working out of the gospel proclamation to the all-powerful work of the grace of the Holy Spirit. We enjoy our associations with him. One Sunday he preaches here twice; the next he goes into the countryside in the morning to preach, and in the evening he is again in Burlington. At nine o'clock in the morning I teach Sunday school at the church. There I speak to the children about the Word of the Lord, while two other persons join me in teaching them to read. If the preacher is in the country in the morning, then I lead the services in our congregation so that we can have [two] regular worship services every Sunday. On Sunday evenings after church I usually have a house full of friends for an enjoyable get together talking about Christendom. We also have a catechism class for men on Wednesday evenings, something very much needed because of the ignorance of the Word of God all around us. At first the minister was very reluctant about it, but now that we have had it in the church for some time, everyone realizes its value, and that it is more beneficial for our spiritual needs than just hearing sermons. There are also [interested] women nowadays, but in accordance with the command of the Apostle [Paul] they do not participate, but they are eager that they be allowed to get together in the same manner. Ah, if only the Lord would strengthen and expand his congregation here, so that many children might be born in Zion.

We live in hope. Generally speaking, also among Americans much of religion tends to be in the externals. John teaches in the [adult] Sunday school of the Congregationalists, and the minister and others have strongly urged him also to teach the children in the Word of the Lord, and this he does do when his health permits. And on Sunday afternoon they also have catechism on the Gospel of John with the minister.

Most of the time Sunday is a blessed day for us. Our bodies are not as exhausted and worn out as they were in Amsterdam, so that it was a hindrance to us in worshiping the Lord. No, the Lord grants us grace and strength to ponder things pertaining to the eternal kingdom and to delight ourselves in a preliminary way in the salvation we have obtained. Magnify the Lord with us, for his great grace granted us unworthy [sinners]. May he grant us grace to devote to him, and in his service, all that we are and receive.

On October 25 the German doctor came by for some letters [of introduction], since he was planning to see Rev. Scholte, because the rumor was making the rounds here that there were so many sick among the Hollanders and the help needed was lacking. I knew him, because we had also had him for Jan, and as a doctor he impressed us very favorably. And it was he who said that our Jan would certainly continue to have attacks of fever this winter, until springtime, and by then he would be able to take the climate as well as any American, and that is exactly what we experienced. As a result we avoided many expenses, and so the other day, instead of sending a letter, I decided to go along to see Pella. Dr. Bruning had a horse of his own and we rented a light wagon, and left together for Pella on the 26th and arrived there in the afternoon of the 29th.

The situation in Pella did not look very attractive to me. There were four houses in the town, one of which was furnished as an inn and boarding house, where two days earlier a Baptist preacher named Post had moved in, having arrived from Feuersfild [Fairfield], located sixty miles from Pella and sixty miles from Burlington. A house was being erected for Rev. Scholte; the cellar had already been built by an [American] mason. There were a few other houses in the area that could be reached only by horse and wagon.

The one night before we returned we stayed with [F.] Le Cocq [Sr.] who had a log cabin, including, he said, 160 acres of land and forest two miles from the city. He had two horses, wagon(s), cows, geese and doves, a hired hand and a maid; he looked contented but weak. His wife also looked well and was learning to adapt to the American way of life, even though they were practically living on top of each other. A large number of people were living in huts covered with straw and hay. You almost had to crawl inside. Some had straw on the ground, others were living on the bare earth. I also looked up Lubberd[en], found him to be in a languishing condition, just as he had been on our journey over here. His youngest child, Piet, had died in St. Louis; another Piet had been born to him in Pella. In the past he had always rejoiced when there was an increase in the family, but not now. The child had not yet been baptized. He had asked Rev. Scholte, but he had told him that there were still no people whose ecclesiastical standpoint he could share, and that he was just another person like everyone else [that is, without

Log cabin interior, Frans Le Cocq, Sr., family

Peter Lubberden (1847-1876), son of Willem Lubberden
(Souvenir History of Pella, Iowa, 1847-1922, Pella: 1922)

ordination]. There were three other children that had not been baptized. Rev. Scholte also said that as long as such things [his deposition by the Synod of Amsterdam] were happening, he could not perform such [liturgical] acts, and Mrs. Lubberd[en] told me that people were really stealing from each other. He had made his cabin from branches stuck in the ground, joined at the top, and covered with tall grass, with a window at one end for light, and at the other a door; a few planks beside the door for her bedstead, a stove in the center, and living just like that on the ground, for to place straw on the ground gives it the appearance of being a pig pen. He had first lived in Pella for five weeks, under some sticks over which sheets hung as a cover.

He still did not know what piece of land he would be getting. The land had been surveyed into sections, but not yet divided into smaller lots for those of modest means, because a prairie fire had prevented the surveyor from proceeding, and they did not know when this would take place. In the month of October, lands with heavy stands of grass are burned off here, because then in the spring [the new grass] is so much better for the cattle. Twice on our journey to Pella, we and our horse and wagon had to pass through territory where the fire [had] burned terribly, for we had almost nothing but prairie the entire eighty miles up to Pella.

Lubberd[en] told me that in Amsterdam things were no different from what we had discussed there earlier. Hengeveld was erecting a hut next to Lubberd[en]'s; in the distance he pointed out some sticks stuck in the ground, overhung with sheets, which had been his dwelling till now. Others were building their dwellings using prairie sod instead of stones. I was told that others had made caves or holes in the ground against the hills in which they were living, but these were too far off for me to go and see for myself. We found a number of sick persons, but there had been many more. [Of the passengers on] the four ships that had left from Holland, 150 persons had died, [some] at sea, [some] in St. Louis, and [some] in the city that still has to be built, Pella. Diekinga and Naatje Schotemeijer were still in St. Louis; rumor has it that Diekinga's wife is dead. The Rev. Scholte had just gone to fetch his wife and family in St. Louis, and while I was in Pella, he had made a side trip and had been to our house in Burlington. He had told so many nice things about Pella, that when I returned, my wife and Jan immediately said that even though I had really enjoyed myself in Pella they still had no intention of moving to Pella. Rev. Scholte had told her that he now did all kinds of things: brick ovens, a lime works (but when I was in Pella I heard that the oven had collapsed), a lumber dealer, a grain dealer, and what not. The land seems to be good; it is 120 miles west of Burlington, but everywhere we traveled it was good [too], so that it seems to me that Scholte could have bought [land] sixty miles nearer, for there is plenty of government land and it is just as good. Pella is located between two rivers: the Des Moines and the Skunk. We rode through one river, the Skunk, with horse and wagon, and the other probably isn't any better. In order to reassure the people, the dream is that soon there will be a railroad, because the capital of Iowa, where the government will meet annually, will be located twelve miles further inland, at the center of the state. But we could all be dead before then. Pella is located eighteen miles farther inland than the last city, Oskaloosa, which is still very tiny, and that is where they will have to go for many necessities or even farther away.

Mr. Scholte told my wife that bad rumors were being spread about Pella in Holland, and therefore he had written a letter about conditions in Pella for placement in the *Rotterdammer Courant*. I would appreciate your sending me some extracts at your convenience if you, dear brother, might happen to read anything about this. I wish that I had found the condition in Pella as described by some emigrants from the County of Lippe, of which the monthly, *De Amerikaansche Boodschapper*, writes as follows:

> In the year 1847 a company of immigrants arrived in Missouri in order to worship God without interference according to their convictions which they in conscience believed to be *the right ones*. They had left their fatherland, because their use of the Heidelberg Catechism and their religious assemblies had been forbidden. Upon arrival in their new dwelling place they gathered together in order to thank God and honor him. In the open field, under a free sky, not disquieted by armed police and threatening bayonets, they held a prayer meeting. One of them made the following statement:

"My Brethren! Let us not forget that we did not come for money, or fertile fields, or even to make a living. We left our beloved fatherland for the bread of life. It is freedom of conscience that we seek here. To be sure, we must expect much toil and trouble; but we had infinitely more grievous scourges to endure in our own country. There we were oppressed, there we dared not instruct our children in the truths of our sacred religion; but in this free air we can pour out our prayers to God without any hindrance. Here we can share with our children the blessed truths of the gospel. So let us not be dissatisfied with our lot. Let us then lay down for ourselves and for our children the basic truths of a simple and pure religion. We will not live for ourselves. We wish to present ourselves a sacrifice to God and to work among our scattered countrymen. Let us therefore pray God, that in the midst of all the trials and sorrows that might befall us, we may become a wholesome leaven among our people, a light to all about us."

These immigrants are strict in their observance of the day of the Lord, and they manifest all kinds of Christian virtues. The periodical ends with the exclamation: "Who would not welcome such pilgrims to our shores?"

We too rejoice and thank the Lord that he has led us here, to be active again in his service for the building up and spread of his kingdom. May he grant us grace to enable and make us faithful, to freely profess his name, for no fear of being called before a secular court of justice and being punished with fines need hold us back.

And now a word about customs here. We had an unexpected thing happen to us: on the 11th of November a farmer and his wife with an eight-week-old child came by and asked us to take them and their sick child to a doctor. While they were at our home the child experienced severe convulsions; the doctor prescribed a warm bath, which we quickly prepared while he was still present, but to no avail. Death prevailed; the child died. We kept the mother and the little corpse at our house overnight. My wife and a neighbor lady made the burial clothes. I went to order a little casket. The father of the child went home, three miles from Burlington, and returned the following morning with a couple of shovels in his wagon. He hired a man, and I went with him to the cemetery to point out where the hole should be dug. Then we went home again, laid the corpse in the little coffin. The father and mother got in the wagon, I handed the little coffin to them, and they took it to the cemetery and buried it. And so it was all over—without anything more. In general corpses are buried quickly here, and it is often customary to have a funeral sermon.

After I had returned from Pella I once again made work of trying to [find a place] so we could continue living in this area. The very next day I was about to buy a farm of 57 ½ acres, but something unexpected came up and the deal fell through. When we were first here I had already looked at an eighty-acre farm, but since it was too big for me to handle alone, I had not given it another thought. But as I wrote above, as we gradually became better informed. The Lord so determined things that a pious man and his wife, with three children, who had been mightily converted by the Lord a good year ago, indicated to me that he was minded to go live on the land with me, since he and his wife knew about farming, and had been practicing it here and in Pennsylvania. They are Germans from the vicinity of Darmstad who already understood English. We can now also speak with them because they kept on speaking German in their home. That prompted us to have another look at that eighty-acre farm together, and everyone told us that it was the best land in the area around the city. It appeared very attractive to us; this summer there were crops of wheat, Indian corn, oats, potatoes, and other garden products, exceptionally beautiful. Watermelons, cantaloupes, just delicious. We bought it on the first of December for twenty-five dollars an acre. It is a half-hour distant from the city.

There is a new stone house in which there are four rooms, a large cellar with a well nearby, and an American type barn for animals; twenty-five acres are uncultivated, and besides there is a woods, or forest, where there are good trees and plenty of firewood; for it is no less cold here than in Holland in the winter, and warmer during the summer. If the people who are living in our new house can again rent a home before the month of April, then we hope to move there in March or otherwise on April 1. I have let out the land, "rented out" they call it here, for a third of the crops, as is the practice here, and then there is nothing I have to take care of. However, I have retained a lovely and wonderful piece of land around the house for myself where we hope to plant an orchard, a garden, and so on. The land is enclosed, or as they say here, fenced in, in order to keep out the animals for whom there is ample forage in the forests in the summer. Thus we are settled in the southern part of Iowa, where we had thought it would not be so cold during the winter; because we had read in Amsterdam that the cattle also remain outdoors in the winter time, but that is due to a lack of barns, since the area is still too newly developed. Thus far the Lord has helped us. His name be praised, and may he remain near to us with his grace, so that we may acknowledge him in all our ways, he who does all things well.

And now let me turn to a matter I mentioned in my last letter, about Mr. King and Sons in New York, concerning the money I still had with you in Amsterdam. If King and Sons only were to receive a message from Amsterdam that the money has been transferred to Hope & Company in my name, then they will send a draft on it to Burlington so that I could receive it, since they always have accounts to settle between them. So will you be kind enough to give an order to Hope & Co.? That will make things very easy for me. Deduct all expenses advanced on my behalf, and also one hundred guilders for grandfather, about which you in your good judgment will doubtless also inform my brothers.

Now, dear brother, may all be well with you. I am much, very much indebted to you. The Lord bless you and your dear wife and the children; may he be and remain with you with his supporting grace, so that you, through the grace and wisdom God has granted, may provide to many weak but upright children of the Lord instruction, renewal and encouragement, and a taste of the blessedness of heaven while the struggle on earth goes on. Yes, your teachings, or the teachings and instructions of the Lord which you, dear brother transmitted, have come even to America. The Lord be your shield and your great reward.

Warmest greetings from me, [my] wife, [my] children, and Mrs. Teleman. Greet your dear wife, Jansie, Kaatje and Johan. Greet brothers Lothes, Luring [Luuring], Berkhoud [Berkhout], Diekinga, Janssen, Schriek, Doornhouwer, Huijding, Gunther and wives. Greet all the brothers and sisters, Miss Abrahams, I still use her little Testament every Sunday. (I don't see, however, how her situation would be any more agreeable in America.) Greet Mr. Willink and Mrs. W. The pen set attests to her cordiality and is very useful to me. Greet my brothers and sisters, and grandfather, and write me how things are going with the Society. With the school system, etc. Oh, if only we might embrace each other once again in this life, but that is known [only] to the Lord. Pray that we may experience fellowship together before the throne of God, that is the desire of,

Your Brother in Christ who Loves You with all His Heart,
D.A. Budde

In my letter of August mailed from Burlington I had included others. When I receive word that one of my letters has arrived, and we are living in our own home, I shall, if the Lord wills, again write to my friends.

Wormser 12

C. M. Budde-Stomp to J. A. Wormser
Burlington, Iowa, January 1848

Dearly Beloved Brother, Sister, and Dearest Children,

Bound as we are to you as children of one family by the bond of love which is in Christ Jesus, the great distance that separates us from you does not result in our forgetting you and all the brothers and sisters in the Lord. Our thoughts and prayers continue to be with you every day, and we yearn for a few letters from you and my dear friend so that we may learn how you all, our Society, and our other friends, are getting along. On the day of the Lord we often said to each other, "Now our friends are again gathered together to praise the Lord."

My husband had had a most friendly, even fraternal meeting with our Evangelical preacher, but his preaching was so general that it did not appeal to us very much, and we sought edification in [the book of] Romans and went to church only once [a Sunday]. But from time to time my husband got into conversation with him about the free grace of God, but he objected with difficult texts. The Lord enabled my husband to refute these until the preacher himself said: "O the depth of wisdom" [Romans 11:33]. That is as far as I had gotten, before I came down with an illness on January 13th that lasted for four weeks and from which I am still very weak. I hope to describe the details of my illness later in some letters to Brother Lothes. Please do read it then as part of a circular letter.

Continuing from where I interrupted my letter: the change in the preacher delighted us; no longer did I neglect any worship service; the men have catechism and the women listen. These folk do not notice a thing about the change in the preaching; they always just say, "It was a lovely sermon." There are very few true children of the Lord, and even they are still very ignorant of the Bible, so that catechizing is most necessary for them. The Methodists are seeking to gain many followers among the Evangelicals. They had a nice opportunity when the preacher was out in the country one Sunday. One of the advocates who belongs to the Masonic Lodge joined the Methodists (there are many Masons here and when there is a funeral they take the body to church in full regalia and have a funeral oration). Now it looked like the entire Evangelical church would be wiped out, but they all returned, even those who do not care to make the Bible their only ground and rule of life but follow their own mind and will, and these people were leaders in the congregation. They wanted to collect funds in a hurry to build a new church, and when they got together to discuss matters they wanted to change the simple name "Evangelical" to "Evangelical Lutheran Reformed." They declared that the Bible was not to be their sole foundation and made other unwise changes. That gave rise to a new conflict and then they all walked out of the meeting together, so that now there is but a small remnant left. Oh, that the Lord might have mercy and cause a Zion to be born here for the proclamation of his name.

During my illness (we must get our mail at the post office), Jan came here on the 29th of January with a letter from Holland in his hand. I was so happy that I had to take hold of myself, so that so great a rejoicing would not harm me in my weakened condition. We rejoice that the Lord has increased your offspring. May he plant it in the garden of his delight and make it to grow with all your children to your great joy. We are hoping that if it be the Lord's will, he will so direct your ways that you may enjoy the good of this land, and find rest for your worn out body as much as can be in this earthly life. If in your opinion it is a good thing, then learn English, the children also, and let my dear friend [your wife] learn how to make butter and especially cheese. There are very few farmers who make good butter; the Americans are fast, but not always all that careful. Cheese is not worth much here; the Germans do wish that good cheese might be coming from Pella in order to market it. Dutch cheese is also known here for its high quality. Farming methods are different here, but we cannot say much about that as yet.

All of us, even including Diedrich, are happy that the Lord has brought us to this good land. Our ties with you, and those with brother and sis, remind us often of the old fatherland, but we have no desire to go back. We hope that the Lord may restore me from my illness and weakness, so that we can move into our new place in the month of March. I look forward with eager anticipation to the future. You recall, my dear friend, how happy I was when Mrs. Zeelt urged me to enjoy the fresh air with my little children. Although our farm is not in a postal district as yet, I do hope we can get one thing and another taken care of to our satisfaction in the near future. It is a beautiful location. Leaving the city you go up a small hill and pass through a woods that is a natural feature in this area. Adjoining this woods is our own woods, and then the first house is ours. My husband wants to plant his vegetable garden in front of the house; he also intends to plant an orchard. As far as we know, the renters will plant wheat, Indian corn, and whatever else they find suitable. We already have a nice brown horse that cost us 137 Dutch guilders, and a wagon, a cow, pigs, and chickens.

Dear friends, hoping also to receive some letters from you now, we wish and pray that the grace of our Lord Jesus Christ may fill your hearts abundantly and that his fellowship may ever gladden you in this troubled life until he releases us to enter into his joy. My warmest greetings to Mrs. Zeelt, Boss Balke, and also from Jan to Jan Hulscher, your brothers and sister, also Riek. Warmest greetings to Mrs. Flörke.

Your Friend and Sister who Thinks of You Always,
C. M. Budde-Stomp

P.S. When you write let me know, if you can, where our niece Heintje and our nephew Johan are living. Also give greetings to our brother, to sister, and Enno. We are gladdened by the birth of a son to brother Ede's son. If the Lord should keep our offspring living on the earth, might they only be consecrated to the Lord.

Wormser 13

D. A. Budde to J. A. Wormser
15 Feb. 1848

Esteemed Brother,

I had already written the foregoing before I received your letter. Because of illness in the family, the letter was delayed. Finally, we received your esteemed letter of January 29, and thanks to the blessing of God we again enjoy good health. Mrs. Teleman is still the weakest of all. In your letter you ask how the land looks to us. It is beautiful, and it is fertile. I have made inquiries about making a livelihood based primarily on interest income without any heavy labor; they calculate that you will need to have four to six thousand dollars. The interest rate is generally 10 percent here. You could then live very comfortably here if, for example, you had a farm as I have, and had a tenant and kept a garden for your own use. The income from the farm would be enough for your everyday needs. [You could have] a horse and wagon to go wherever you please. In time there will be other employment possibilities; there would also be work [for you] in God's kingdom. The prospects for your children are rather better than in Amsterdam: there are schools here in Burlington—in the country; and twenty-eight miles from Burlington, or nine and a half hours distant, is a school where further education is given in all kinds of disciplines.

One can maintain civilized manners here without sighing under the yoke of style or fashion, and that is why I can confidently say with an eye to future generations: **COME OVER.** We expect to move to our farm next month. You could still become my neighbor because there is another farm for sale next to mine. If you were to send me a money draft for $3,000 right now, I could go ahead and buy it for you now. To be sure, it would not yield much interest initially, but as I anticipate that in all likelihood the value of my land will double in ten years, that would be the equivalent of interest. I could make all the arrangements for you. As concerns your brother Dries, I cannot advise him to make a brief trip to investigate matters; it is too costly. The journey from Amsterdam to Burlington cost us about one thousand guilders. The best thing would be for you all to come together.

You write that Reverend Bolks left for New York with about two hundred people. In a newspaper we read that last November 25 a steamboat [the *Phoenix*] on which there were 175 Hollanders burned on Lake Michigan. Of the three hundred persons on board only forty-five were saved. On January 6 I received a letter from Lubberd[en] (whom I expect to see here personally in April), in which he wrote that his land had already been surveyed; he had twenty-nine acres of prairie and six acres of woods. In addition, a church was established, and Mr. Scholte and Mr. Barendregt were elected elders. More will have to be chosen soon, and construction has started on a church and school.

Our address remains the same, except don't include Main Street, because we still have to pick up our mail at the post office. I do not know any other [exchange] house in New York and so the best thing to do is just to send me a bank draft with the necessary information. Give my greetings to your brother Dries, our Hein and Riek and also Pouli [Rev. C.W.H. Pauli]—and Brummelkamp. It gives us joy that the Lord still has kept and increased your family. May he bless you in things temporal as well as spiritual and cause your offspring to grow up in the fear of the Lord.

Hoping to hear soon that all is well, and that the Lord may prepare the way for you, whom we eagerly look for, so that we may welcome you all here in Burlington. Greet Mrs. Flörke and children. May the Lord indwell her heart by his spirit so that if her end should be near, she may depart this life in him.

    Warmest Greetings from your Loving Brother in the Lord,

                                                    D. A. Budde

Budde 1

                J. Wormser-van der Ven to Mrs. C. M. Budde-Stomp
                                            Amsterdam, 24 April 1848

My Esteemed and Beloved Sister in the Lord!

    Since the loss of your presence grieves us daily, just the same it is a pleasure for me to be able to write to you, and when there is a letter from you all then our joy is great. It grieved us very much to learn from your most recent letter that all of you have been ailing quite some, and especially you my dear friend, who are so close to me. But we have also had our troubles this year, although the Lord preserved us from dangerous illnesses, except Johan who was so sick in the month of July that the doctor called five times a day, but the Lord has changed all that and now he is growing up nicely.

    Our Maria is a darling and friendly child, not as rough as Johan was. Every day I think about and discuss with Miss Abrams how much she reminds us of your Maria when she was that small. During the month of February I was not well again: my old problem, but it was so bad that I thought that I might enter eternity at any moment, and had to keep to my room for three weeks. I still have not regained my strength. Fortunately, the Lord has so ordered things that since the death of my mother, my sister Riek is living in with us, and she is very helpful with the children. She sends cordial greetings to all of you. She is happy that by now you must have arrived at your destination. Every day we say [to each other] if only the Lord might direct our ways so that we would end up by them [our Budde friends]. I am sure, my dear friend, that you know how I always objected to making the journey. Although that objection has not been removed, at least with one additional child, I would like so very much still to come this summer. Things are yet so anxious in Europe, as my husband will let you know; we become very anxious when we think of the future of our children.

Mrs. Flörke died of consumption of the lungs on December 1; her children are now with the caretaker. Right until she died she kept on saying how the departure of Budde had shocked her. Luring [Luuring] and his family are living in your house on the Bloemgracht [in Amsterdam], where they are expecting a sixth child this summer.

For the past two weeks my girls have been going to (Crisje) Steenkamp [to learn] sewing. She lives in the [Reestraat]. I visited the family. Aunt de Haas is eighty-nine years old and still [gets about] quite well. Mother Steenkamp is also getting old and Heintje van Vlier died. I thought that I should mention that, since you know that family well. I thought that it might be useful to have my daughters to learn how to sew and to have them taught English and French at home. If ever our pathway should lead your way, then they will be able to get along.

Mrs. Willink had a daughter in February, which they had baptized in their home by Rev. Brummelkamp; they had expected a group [to come], but they had at least a hundred persons from the Bloemgracht [church] and elsewhere. I was prevented from going, I had to keep my bed; but the Lord was good to me; I might be strong in the Lord, my faith was vibrant, and although there still was nothing present of the [religious?] experiences of [bygone] days, it served me well later on in finding rest and consolation, since he has promised that though the earth change its place and the mountains be moved, he would be my all.

Mrs. Abrams asked me to convey her greetings to you all; she would write but does not because the postage runs up so. She said it gave her satisfaction that your husband was using her [New] Testament. She was also still enjoying daily nourishment from the meditations and admonitions [written] by him.

Mrs. Bousquet is not well; it's the nervous ailment that she has had more often. I sympathize with them. Because of the bankruptcy of Roozeboom, he [A. E. Dudok Bousquet] is now out of work. He is full of plans to start all kinds of things, and everything he has tried so far has been a failure. I told Mrs [Bousquet] that if we had such a pointer, then we would go to America. It seems that they are not ready for that.

The Roozeboom family has left the city and has rented a country home in Ede in Gelderland, where they are living peacefully. Miss Jaspers, the governess, has gone with them. Of late they had been attending our group get-together very frequently, and once again we are grieved by their absence. I believe that all the things that have occurred affect

Bousquet deeply and that he could [live with the idea]: sufficient unto the day is the evil thereof. But these days, there is something new every minute, but it is always misery.

The way everything is blossoming in nature, I sometimes think that summer is near. But the Lord also said, when you hear of wars and rumors of war, know that the coming of the Son of man is near. Happy is he who will then found to be waking.

Now my dear friends, sometimes I have hopes that if the Lord will spare our lives a while longer, that we will see each other each again on this side of the grave. Greet Mrs. Teleman and Janse cordially for me. I hope that the Lord may live in your midst, and make your children to grow up and honor him. Every day we talk about Jan. Appreciate your good fortune, my friend; if you were living here you would already be bearing arms; the young people conscripted this year are already encamped at Maastricht. May you be a support and strength to your esteemed parents, and be a constant source of joy to them. My dear friend, do kiss your dear Diedrich and Maria for me. I do hope to embrace them myself some day. At least we are grateful that the Lord has so governed things that we did not get a house of our own, so that we are not so firmly rooted here. Riek sends cordial greetings, and we commend you to the Lord and his grace.

From Your Loving Friend,
J. Wormser-van der Ven

P.S. I hope that when you receive this letter, that you will write back soon, and then do tell how you get along doing your washing, you were looking up against that, and how do you like life in the country, and whether you find you can adjust pretty well to the privations of things so typical of life in the city. Greetings again. Your JW.

Budde 2

Jansje Wormser to Jan Budde
Amsterdam, 24 April 1848

My Very Dear Friend!

We were delighted to hear that there was word from you. It grieved me greatly when I learned from your letter that you had to cope with so much illness upon your arrival. But I hope that by now all of you may

Jansje (Johanna) Wormser (1835-1917), oldest daughter of Johan and Janke Wormser, wife of Carel W. Wüstenhoff
(Courtesy of Jan Peter Verhave)

be in good health again, even as we are. Mrs Flörke died on the 1st of December; but I know nothing of the whereabouts of the children. All of us would so very much like to be with you, but we cannot come as yet. They say that there are again very many people going to America this year.

Doubtless you have heard that we have another little sister; she is getting to be a real darling. Seven weeks later we got a baby nephew, at Uncle Dries's, but it only lived fourteen weeks. I saw it the day it died. The baby was very pale and thin, and it died in the evening. Auntie had also been seriously ill this winter. A few weeks ago we got a baby niece in Overijssel; they now have seven children, four girls and three boys. After Grandma's death, Auntie Riek came to live with us. She is well, but sometimes she has to put up with headaches.

We are taking sewing lessons, and three times a week we have lessons, once in French and twice in English. If we could be there with you, we could talk together in English. Our textbook for English is Merle D'Aubigne and the third volume of the Fairchild Family. We translate from them and also from the New Testament in English. The third volume of Fairchild is very lovely. Mrs. Sherwood put this together with her daughter. Father is now getting lessons in English twice a week. We

"Uprising on the Dam," Amsterdam, 1848

are better at speaking French, but we know the English language better.

There is rioting throughout Europe. On March 24 there was a disturbance in Amsterdam. Windows were smashed on the Herengracht and on the Keizersgracht, but we were spared that. It is said that they wanted to set fire to the city hall, the [French] Comedy [theater], and the Van den Bruijn factory. On the 30th they [seized prisoners] in the Pijlsteeg. The area from the Halssteeg to our house was occupied by the military and also the Warmoesstraat. Dragoons and other military occupied Het Damplein [the Dam Square]. Because of all the rioting, we wanted very much to be with you; everyone is afraid that the French will march into Holland. The conventicle [informal pietistic worship group] is still the same as when you left, except that Santje and one of the younger members of the Gunters have died. Mrs. Bousquet is not well, but I have no information on others,

Every day we think of you; we would so much like to be there with you. Mr. and Mrs. Willink have had a baby daughter. Rev. Brummelkamp baptized it. I was present. It was at the home of Mr. Willink.

My dear friend! Do ask Diedrich, when he is somewhat able to write, to write us too. Dear friend, the Lord be with you all, wherever you may be. Give my greetings to our dear parents and give our greetings to Diedrich. We asked Johan whether we should give you his greetings, and he said, "Yes." Kiss your dear sister Maria for us, and also receive my cordial personal greetings to you.

Your Loving Friend,
J[ansje] Wormser

P.S. Please write me back soon. Give my greetings to Mrs. Teleman and Jansje. Auntie Riek also sends her greetings.

Budde 3

Cato Wormser and J. A. Wormser to Jan Budde
Amsterdam, 24 April 1848

Cordial greetings from your loving friend!

We were very pleased to receive a letter from you; we had not heard from you in a long while you know. My wish is that with the Lord's blessing you may all be healthy and well. I do wish that I could be with you, but that is not possible so I will have to be reconciled to that. We were sad to learn from your letter that you have suffered much from fevers. We are all still hale and well. Johan is getting to be a real dear.

On the 24th of March there was a disturbance here; the riff-raff that smashed the windows was apprehended. Father is convinced that many emigrants will be leaving for North America this year, all the more because there are riots in every city in every locality. People here are getting to be afraid. You are fortunate, friends, that you are over there.

On the first of December, Mrs. Flörke died. Our religious fellowship is doing well, except for Mrs. Bousquet. She has been having a hard time of it. We have gotten a third of the Fairchild family [cf. Budde Letter 2]. We have made good progress in English. Father also started learning English early this month. How are your father, mother, brother, and sister doing? Our little Maria is getting to be very sweet. In Overijssel we have gotten another niece, Maria. Aunt Riek sends cordial greetings. We are already longing to hear from you in America again. Johan says: Give my greetings to Jan. Dear friend! May the blessing of the Lord ever be yours. Do keep thinking of me.

Cordial Greetings from your Loving Girl-friend,
C[ato] Wormser.

Addendum. Duwaër still owes me forty guilders. Things are going better for those people. I have not demanded payment through the courts, because then I will be cutting him off, and you wish to spare him. The war between Denmark and Prussia is getting worse; Denmark has seized the merchant ships of Prussia.

Again with Cordial Greetings,
J. A. Wormser
27 April 1848

Budde 4

Mrs. J. Wormser-van de Ven to Mr. and Mrs. D. A. Budde
Amsterdam, 21 July 1848

Dearly Beloved Friend and Sister in the Lord!

Intimately bound to each other by the bond of love and friendship, it is a very pleasant thing for me to be with you in thought for a few moments, even if it is only on paper. You cannot begin to understand how intensely much I would like to see and embrace you all once again, but I must get on. Every day we long for and anticipate receiving a letter from you all, in order again to learn more about your new way of life. It was grievous for me to learn of your physical ailments in your most recent letter, but it was joy that I also learned of God's good hand upon you in mercifully restoring you again and in sparing all of you for each other. And accordingly, I also hope that the Lord our God will bless you on your farm and that you may have your daily bread in quietness and godliness.

Indeed, I consider you to be fortunate, since Europe is in such a commotion that every evening we consider ourselves fortunate that everything around us is still peaceful. And although I may experience a quiet [acceptance] and peace in God and know that not a hair falls from our head without the will of my heavenly Father, nevertheless, all those events do detach me, perhaps detach me too much, from the country that is our homeland. Although last year I looked up terribly against the journey, now I would very much like to go along with my brother. For a long time I have had the feeling my beloved friend also developed at last: that everything about you is boring, humanity is becoming increasingly godless, and all the misery is more and more wanton. But what shall I say? Every day the will of the Lord is before my eyes and enables me to possess my soul in patience.

The believer will not take rash action. Accordingly, we also wish that the Lord will safely lead to you the friends who are about to undertake the journey. Once again it is a loss for all of us, and given the events of our time, I consider those fortunate who are able to depart. But we remain behind, like a lonely sparrow sitting on the roof, for because of this the number of the devout gets even smaller. We still meet at your house, and it is filled. Many people from the Bloemgracht attend regularly. Raman and his eldest son, Sandbergen, and [Rev. Cornelius] Van Proosdij, who is an exhorter, joined recently. That is all very nice, but slowly on the community is getting to be quite different. Eekhout, Neige, and several others on the past day of rest proclaimed the death of the Lord with us. Old man Janssen is going downhill and cannot work any longer; he regularly gets assistance from our diaconate.

And now, my dear friend, here is some news about us. Our children are growing up nicely. Jansje is becoming quite a fine young lady. Cato is also hale and hearty these days; she is getting tall but not much fatter. After a [troubled] year, Johan is also healthy and is really growing up, but we have the most problems with him. He has a fierce temper and an annoying disposition; for the rest he is a clever boy who is also impressionable. Our little Maria is the dearest, friendly child; at scarcely ten months she already has eight teeth. Till now she has been easier to deal with than any of our other children. Until now she has not had any setbacks such as Johan had. As far as my health is concerned, I still have not fully regained my health and strength after the medical problems that I had in February. Now I am again in my third month [of pregnancy], so that you can well understand that I am weak. As a rule, my husband is really worn out and exhausted [from all his work]. Riek is not getting any stronger either. So, if it be the will of the Lord to grant us a quiet old age, then our choice and wish remains that we may spend it in your midst.

Mrs. J. Wormser-van der Ven

Wormser 14

D. A. Budde to J. A. Wormser
Burlington, Iowa, the ... of June 1848

Dear Beloved Wife and Brother in the Lord,
On the 8th of this month we received your letters [Budde 1-4], some

that were so sad and others that were so joyous and comforting. Every time one of us goes to the city, he stops at the post office to inquire whether there is any news for us, and now Jan came joyfully bearing your letter. With eyes and hearts that wept, we heard the sad reports, the situation that also affected you. Our prayers rise on your behalf and for all the children of the Lord, that you may be strengthened with power from on high. And being confirmed in your trust in the Lord, to keep the eye of faith, which in his unshakable testimony speaks to us: "Call upon me in the day of trouble, and I will deliver thee," etc. [Psalm 50:15]. I too find support in this word of the Lord in the present circumstances, because our Jan is once again sorely beset with fevers. He is the one who is being chastised by the Lord, we share in his grief; our expectation had been that it would wear off in the spring, but that hope has proved to be in vain till now. Thus the Lord has a way of depriving his children of all props and supports. We too feel that all things must work together to the end that we put our trust only in the Lord, but God is faithful. He governs all things and makes them serve the glory of his name, and all things must work for good for those who love the Lord.

Your tiding gladdened us, but in our heart we felt ashamed that we are not sufficiently grateful to the Lord who has lead us so faithfully till now and saved us from so much anxiety and misery. For the general misery in Europe [political rioting] and among you must be very great. We were clearly removed from it all by an omnipotent hand and that is even more evident now as we look back on it. All this misery also had to contribute to the joyous part of your letter, [your decision] to come over here to us, relying on the Lord and his leading. And of those thoughtful reflections—the decision that your brother Dries (our dear friend) desires to undertake the journey with his family in August—is the joyful proof. We will be looking for your brother, and by our words and deeds we will do everything in our power to make his arrival here a pleasant one. In all likelihood your brother will not be able to occupy the farm next to ours as we had intended. Now that we have talked things over with the owner, he is not minded to relinquish eighty to one hundred acres (just as I had gotten eighty acres from his father). I had counted on eighty to one hundred acres plus the house (which is better than ours), and that is why I wrote of $3,000. It is also because land is getting more and more expensive due to the constant influx of settlers. Soon the city will expand; almost sixty brick houses are being built this summer.

The farm I had in mind is No. 1 in the city; it has 318 acres, of which 200 acres are fenced in, 160 acres are cultivated, and the rest is wooded. There is a good well near the house, and there is a spring in the woods that never lacks water, and nearby there is log house for a renter. The owner will only sell everything together for the price of $10,000. The sale price includes 2 horses, 2 wagons with equipment, 250 sheep, 2 cows, 25 pigs big and small, 3 plows, and some miscellaneous items. The supply of wheat, oats, Indian corn, and potatoes is ample for the buyer's needs on the farm for that year. He [the owner] will leave the place two weeks after the contract has been signed. Now this farm probably will be too expensive and too large for you. As far as the price is concerned, generally speaking, people say that it is not too expensive. First of all, because it is the nicest place adjoining the city; a government road runs through, passing the house; and the land is good, and increases in value nearly three to four dollars an acre every year. And now [let me tell you] something about its size. Your entire family could work on the farm and make a living from it, because forty acres is enough for one man. Consider the fact that eighty acres is a ten-minute walk in its length and a five-minute walk in its width.

Next to this farm and also adjoining the city, there is a farm for sale with 450 acres, a large brick house, a barn and a stable, 300 acres are fenced in, and there is a house for renters. The selling price is 30 dollars an acre or 13,500 dollars. On the north side of our farm there is a farm of 240 acres located on a road with a big log house, a big barn, and 2 wells nearby, which can be bought for $30 an acre, for $7,200 dollars. A mile (twenty-minutes' walk) from our house there is another farm of approximately 250 acres, which will probably sell for 14 to 15 dollars an acre. Ten miles further there are 280 acres, of which 50 acres are prairie and 230 acres woodland, none of which is improved, and the price is $1,500. The unclaimed government land still remaining in this area is not worth very much. And that is why I cannot advise you to buy it unless you go farther inland. That is true also for health reasons, for there is much illness where the land is being broken up for the first time. There is a lot of work and effort connected with preparing unimproved land, which may be less of a problem for country folk, but it is very problematic for people like us.

Settling on details or reaching a firm agreement is next to impossible here; the people are very changeable. Today you may reach agreement about a purchase, and then when the contract is about to be written, the seller backs out. I am really sorry that the farm that was just right for you has such a high price tag. Do not let this deter you; every day one hears of changes, that someone or other is again selling his farm; Americans are very fond of moving from one place to another. We can best talk it all over when your brother Dries gets here. Income from land is not great; it seems that because of the disturbances in Europe, fruits of the field have but little value.

If you have anything that still should be taken into consideration, or could have been intended by Mrs. Zeelt, and if upon receipt of this letter your brother might have already left, then do write at once, for then that letter could reach here even sooner than your brother. We were in a hurry to get this information to you, and we will be mailing the letter at the post office this evening. The best route to travel here, we have been told, is from New York to Pittsburgh by train, and from there by steamboat to St. Louis, and then on to Burlington. After getting there ask for Krichbaum, who has a store and lives on the side of the river that is not far from where the steamboat arrives, and he will help your brother on his way. Meanwhile, I hope to gather information where more land might be obtained.

Perhaps you still remember how I bought a fur hat with ear flaps for *f.* 2.25 last winter when I was still with you. It saw good service in the cold weather, and so I would like to ask brother Dries to buy another one for me, since our heads are the same size. Also ask him to get me a pair of communion cups from Rondstad, like the Society has. If you have an opportunity, get seed from Mrs. Zeelt: kale, radishes, red cabbage, big nuts, pear pits, apple pits, cherry pits, peach pits, apricot pits [?], even if it is just a little, so that we get some new kinds, because fruits here are not all that good as yet. We are already eating from our garden, and when Jan is well, he goes down to the market at three o'clock in the morning two or three times a week. For the most part my seeds did not come up; they probably were too old.

I had a message from Lubberd[en], dated April 20, in which he wrote that "they are now all in good health, and the congregation is beginning to settle down, each person is beginning to mind his own business, and doing his own work, and I myself am also beginning to be more at rest within myself. The church building is so far along that that it can be used for worship services. Scholte is preaching about the Acts of the Apostles, and there is a good attendance. Scholte has been down with fever several times. Sunday several children will be baptized."

It is almost unbelievable how many people keep arriving in America. St. Louis is so crowded that people are glad to be able to work for their keep. So many people are coming to Burlington that there is not a house to be had.

    We rejoice and thank the Lord that you still always receive the strength and desire to be active in the work of the Lord, and that your work is not in vain; of that the school in Amsterdam is proof. The Lord strengthen and sustain you and grant that you and yours may enjoy the blessed nearness of the Lord and behold the blessed fruit of your activities, also in the founding and building up of the Society, strengthening in the faith, and leading many unto salvation. Greet the brothers and sisters of the Society. I send greetings to your brothers and sisters. Give my greetings to Grandfather and my brothers. Greet Mrs. Zeelt, Balke, etc.

    I choose to keep silence on the money Duwäer [owes]; you can't expect to get something from nothing. Although I certainly could use it, for the cost of my farm exceeded my capital resources; and still I could not refrain from buying it. I still have to pay two hundred dollars on my farm, and I have had many unforeseen expenses. I would not like to sell the farm for thirty dollars an acre now. And that I owe to your precaution in not sending the money without verifying the manner of its transmission.

    And now most cordial greetings from Mrs. Teleman, from our Jan and Diedrich to Jansie and Kaatje, Johan and little Maria. Accept the cordial greetings from,

Your Loving Brother in Christ,
D.A. Budde

    P.S. When your brother arrives in St. Louis, have him mail a letter to Burlington, so we can be there to meet him.

Wormser 15

C. M. Budde-Stomp to Mrs. J. Wormser-van der Ven
Burlington, Iowa, June 1848

Dearest Friend and Sister in our Lord Jesus Christ,

    We received your precious letters with great joy and rejoice that the Lord has continued to spare you for your family and that he did not take from you your dear Johan. I rejoice with you [in the birth of] your Maria. Ah, if only our offspring might fear the Lord; that is the one thing that can keep us in life and in death. Both of us are reasonably healthy now. Jan had a severe congestive fever in March, so that his life was in peril; to our great joy the Lord heard our sighing and saved him. It was so severe that he took leave of us all, his blood collected around his heart, he could no longer breathe, and he was deathly cold. My husband wanted to go after the doctor himself and left, but I called him back; we did not know whether he had stopped breathing. Another man got on his horse and went to fetch the doctor who returned with him. Then the water bottles (which are very useful to me and I am glad to have them here) were laid at his sides, stones were heated and laid at this feet, [his] hands and body were rubbed with wool, and a big mustard plaster placed on his chest. He [the doctor] immediately gave him spirits and then medicine and said that if he did not perspire, he would not be able to make it. Many people have died quickly from this disease, which is very dangerous. We were very much aware of that. Two young Methodist ministers [died] in quick succession, one of whom had visited me during my illness, and there were others. In our distress the Lord heard our call and gave deliverance. Jan was completely exhausted and because the fevers keep coming back he cannot do any heavy work.

Diedrich got bladder fever again, could not even keep the medicines down, and was throwing up constantly. He certainly is weak, but he is very happy living in the country, and we hope to see him become a good farmer. Maria is healthy and really happy and the others are still enjoying the privilege of good health. Although we are struggling with troubles and hard times, we read your letters with tears in our eyes. Indeed, we are ashamed that we are not thankful enough to the Lord, since his hand has led us so mercifully; for how many cares, how many unimaginable things, would have oppressed us if we had still been in Europe?

We share your anxieties and pray that the Lord will graciously direct your way, because he himself has promised: mine eye shall be upon you. He will not forsake nor leave those who call upon him. Dear friend, our heart is so inclined to forget the blessings of the Lord, and that this earth remains a veil of tears because of sins, and the Lord leads us precisely in the ways his wisdom deems good for us. Your letters were a surprise to us, and the content beyond imagination. The Lord will direct the ways of all his children.

The death of Mrs. Flörke touched me very much. I am deeply concerned about the condition of the children, since they are the little offspring of God-fearing grandparents, for whom my husband had great regard, and that became the occasion for joining up with them. We greatly rejoiced at the birth of a baby to Mr. and Mrs. Willink. My wish is that the Lord may plant it in the garden of his delight, and cause it to grow up to the honor of his great name, to the joy of the parents. He gave them the privilege, like Nicodemus and Joseph, to profess in these troubled times that they present their offspring to the triune God, and only there do they find their salvation and their consolation. I am happy that Rev. Brummelkamp is ministering to you; I believe he also baptized your Maria. How is his health and that of his wife?

The privileges one has in this country are great; we do not experience the aggravating circumstances and oppressive burdens that we had in Europe. It is especially [good] for farm folk who can just go about doing their ordinary work; their station is the best here. There is a lot of work to do on a farm, and if the Lord had not directed our way in making available to us a renter, we would not be able to take care of things. I also help with planting and weeding in the garden as much as I can. I have a cow, and although at first it was difficult for me to learn how to milk, now I can milk her myself. Mrs. Tel[eman] churns the milk, and I prepare the butter. That is a great satisfaction for a household, but it increases the work. I have also made soap; every two weeks we wash everything. They have a board here, with little ribs; you rub the wash over it, and that keeps your hands from going to pieces, although we have heavy sheets and shirts. Then the washing is boiled and if it is summer, laid in the field for an hour or so, treated the same way we used to, and then it is fairly bright. I don't even consider mangling [ironing], but am content with smoothing and folding them [sheets etc.]. They use iron irons here, just like the English washerwomen. As a rule German women are much faster and stronger and so they can do more work. When you have someone working for you, it is usual to provide a warm meal three times a day, and that makes for work. They wear out a lot of clothes here. I do not have any help and I cannot do much myself, so the children wear more clothes that need patching here than they do in Amsterdam, but people do not have scruples about such things here. The lack of city comforts does not bother me much, but the increased load of housework does draw out the perspiration.

The other day I was thinking about Lot's [family] being led out of Sodom and how he had to leave all those lovely things and flee to Zoar, where things surely were not so lovely for him, but he was saved. Thus the Lord leads his children, appointing to them trouble or happiness as is most needful to them. Our change in occupation makes for a very meager income. That is an unpleasant feeling for us, but it does not cause us the anxious concern about the future that you have in the Netherlands because of heavy taxes and dark prospects for the future. That is why the people who come over here must be thoroughly aware of the oppressive situation [in Holland], for else other kinds of troubles might be disappointing to them, for this earth, however beautiful, remains a vale of tears. It is a long, hard struggle getting used to the climate; in winter the cold is severe, and summer is very hot, although the region is a healthy one. Dear friend, the Lord determines the place of each person's dwelling according to his will.

In sending over your brother and his family, the Lord will also make his paths straight. We cannot say much about the future; it all depends on the circumstances. They will be most welcome to us, and we will do everything in our power to assist them. Indeed, we already sense your intimate relation to us, wrought by the bond of love, like David and Jonathan. The dark sky gathered over all of Europe grieves us for your sake, and for all the children of God; we share your fear and anxiety. We would like to see you rescued from all of that and to be in fellowship with us again.

The country is more peaceful here, and it is very good. Our problem is the change of occupation and housekeeping, and that is why a farmer has many advantages. I am ignorant about anything that has to do with country living, and so I must learn everything. The more you know about houses and agricultural matters, the better you can get along. It is a good thing that dear Jansje and Caatje are learning English; my husband and I still don't know it at all, and that is very unpleasant for us. A basic knowledge of sewing also comes in very handy. You can learn it here, but it is more difficult, especially in the country.

If it is the Lord's will that your brother Dries and family come over to us, may he protect them across the great waters and guide them to the place of their destination. I have gotten a good deal of use from some most essential household utensils, such as a dustpan and brush, a tin kettle, a tin hot water bottle, and a light frying pan. I already used it on the steamboat where we had the least room. Traveling is expensive for a family. Upon arrival there are plenty of things you can buy, but because you spend so much money you are thankful to have the most necessary items with you. I had taken bed ticking with me, also a straw mattress for on board ship and several pillows. A lot of packing is a nuisance; often we just lay on the floor to avoid the trouble of packing things again. For a long time I got along without a table or chair, and I bought goose feathers for a bed. But the others are made of straw and leaves of Indian corn, which is cooler in the summer than feathers. An umbrella, a parasol, and a head covering are certainly needed here; also a fan if you still have one. And if it should be your way to come here, may the faithful Shepherd carry you on his shoulder, for that is what he does with his weaker sheep.

Warmest greetings to Miss Abrams, to Mr. and Mrs. Bousquet (we are very much touched by their troubles), to your sister Riek, M[adame] Zeelt, and Balke with Mientje and all our friends. We thank you for all the enclosed letters from our brothers, also Grandfather; it gives us joy that he is well and content. Greet and kiss Jansie and Kaatje, also little Johan and Maria, greet Rev. Brummelkamp. We send our most cordial greetings. May the Lord prepare the way for you.

Your loving friend,
C. M. Budde-Stomp

Budde 5

Jansje Wormser to Jan Budde
Amsterdam, 25 July 1848

Well Beloved Friend!

On the occasion that my uncle goes to you, I will begin and see if I can write you some lines in English and solicit you, if you will be so kind, to answer me in Dutch. That mij [my] uncle goe [goes] to you is well agreable [agreeable] to you, and to Sir Berkhout and Sir Kiesel [Keesel] also, but not for us. Our assemblij [assembly] is very small. Mij [my] father has bought chairs, but it is for the men who comes [come] now and than [then]. We think everij [every] day on you and all friends in America. Upon [at] our sowing [sewing] shop [class], is a girl that goes to Philadelphia. She has there an uncle, whilst his wife and children are here; but those goes with the familij [family] of that girl, at the same time when my uncle shall go. Her mother has still bought shoes of Mr. Kiesel [Keesel], and they have spoke of America.

A Salutation to your parents, brother and sister. Write me when your father write[s] to mine. God be with you and us. I cannot tell you so much, as you to us. We are all in good health, and I hope at you also. Paris have been once more in insurection [insurrection] in time of four days, manij [many] blood is shed. I shall write on this occasion to Miss Sarah Scholte, and I hope that she will answer me like you.

Madam J.J. Zeelt has asked me to do [give] her compliments to you and yours. A Salutation to Mrs. Teleman and her daughter Jennij [Jansje]. Mij [My] brother and sister are very pretty. Be well salued [saluted],

Your Friend,
J. Wormser

The English of this letter is reproduced here exactly as written with occasional bracketed corrections or explanations. The text has many Dutch idioms that are translated literally into English. A persistent spelling error is the failure to distinguish between the Dutch ij and English y.

Wormser 16

H. P. Scholte to J. A. Wormser
Pella, 4 August 1848

Dearly Beloved Friend and Brother in Jesus Christ our Lord!

For some time I have been looking for a letter since I sent my last two, in which I enclosed (the clipping) and the maps. Later I sent another newly published map of Iowa to Bosch in Utrecht requesting that he forward it to you. Since I wrote you in April we have had an election for township officials. I have been elected as justice of the peace and as school inspector. So far I have been fortunate in being able to nip some minor differences in the bud without having to hear them as a judge. On one occasion I had to issue a subpoena, but that was also settled out of court. My principal activity as justice of the peace has been performing marriages; tomorrow I will be again marrying two couples. As school inspector, I have organized the township in districts; two of those districts have been organized according to the legal statutes. The school in the Pella district has been functioning on that basis for two months already. In the Skunk district they are busy building a dwelling and school for Munting[h]. Munting[h] is moving to the Skunk district; Overkamp, with his assistant Hospers, remains in Pella. We still do not have a good schoolmaster for the Amsterdam district, which is not organized as yet, but there are not many children in that district either.

And then there are also two districts under my jurisdiction with mostly American residents.

My correspondence in English is going well these days. I expect to lead a religious gathering for Americans in that language soon. Overkamp was elected to be township clerk, and in that capacity he is also the clerk of the school inspector. Betten and Welle, and an American, are trustees, etc. Thus, as far as our immediate vicinity is concerned, we are already legally organized on an American footing. Building houses, farming and raising cattle, making butter and cheese, all of this makes for a lot of activity. The brickyard is doing well; at the moment two kilns are in operation. I am already running the limekiln entirely with Hollanders. The sawmill, which is also working, stands out for its fast operation. The Hollanders also maintain their fame as cheese makers. We have now shipped three loads [of cheese] to St. Louis. The first two were immediately sold for 1½ American cents more per pound than the American cheese. We still have no word about the third shipment. All of this makes for favorable prospects in things temporal. The agricultural harvest is in full swing these days, and the farm folk are very pleased with the crop. We have also experimented with flax and hemp and the results are beyond our expectation. It is a delight to see the fields. If we could add some factory production to what we now have, that would be nice.

We are located practically in the middle of the state and have water power to run machines, coal for steam engines. The Des Moines River is being made navigable for steamboats, and it is almost certain that within a few years we will have a railroad running through our tract of land to the Mississippi. Areas in which factories could immediately start operating profitably include leather tanning, wool carding, oil pressing, grain grinding, flax spinning, rope making, and beer brewing. The raw materials for all of these are cultivated here, and there is a good market for them in America. Other crafts are again closely linked to these. Scrub makers and brush makers would do well here. As the number of inhabitants and general activity increases, a furniture making shop would also be profitable. We still do not have a pottery and tile works here yet, and there are even raw material for making earthenware for everyday use. By means of such expansion it would also be easy for those who are not farmers and who have some capital [to invest] and live from the interest. The usual interest rate here is 6 percent, but often it is higher. In general American farmers are much more refined than those from Gelderland and Overijssel. Whenever you hear someone talking about another person, they will always refer to "the gentleman" or "Mr.," and they always address each other as Sir. There were times when my wife could not help laughing when she heard an American use the word "gentleman" in referring one of our farm folk. Our farmers have not become gentlemen; they are still peasants. The Americans are free and independent, but they are cultured. I very much enjoy being in their company; they use their good judgment as befits human beings.

In regard to our housekeeping we go our own way; we still do things in a very Dutch way. It is very difficult to keep housemaids, because they marry so soon, for in marriage she finds her livelihood. We have again hired two new maids, but one of them is already engaged. Health conditions are so well here that we do not hear of any special illnesses. The temperature is about as it is in Holland, but drier and fresher, because we are located so much above sea level. The wind can really blow hard, and it really thunders too, but the ground is such that when it has rained hard, the surface is dry again very soon; we never have close, stuffy weather here. During the winter there are constantly cold spells, but it never freezes hard for more than two or three days, so that as a rule we are working outdoors in the open air whether in the woods or elsewhere.

Our colony grows from time to time through the arrival of new settlers from Holland. In New York and in other places, however, there is a type of agent who does everything in his power to direct the newly arrived Hollanders to Michigan. Van Raalte is not wholly innocent of it. I have received requests from New York to send an agent there also, but you realize that I do not wish to recruit in that way. I would rather just wait for those the Lord chooses to send us. Land speculators in the eastern states have no interest in Iowa simply because they do not own any land here. It is entirely different in Michigan, where several companies own land which they have not been able to sell till now. For that reason, they would like, by any means at all, to get people to settle on the land, so that they might have an opportunity to dispose of some of it. In this state much of the land is occupied [by settlers; under the rights of preemption], even though it still belongs to the state. If the settlers are bought out, the government price always remains 1¼ dollars an acre; the government cannot raise the price now that the land is in cultivation. All that is different when the land is in the hands of speculators. I fear that in a few years examples of this [of shady dealing] will indeed be uncovered in Michigan.

My family is well and my wife is expecting a son or daughter. My wife's sister, who is married to Hasebroek [Hazebroek], was delivered of a son recently. A short time ago I had letters from several well-situated Christians living in Zwolle and Kampen, who requested information about our colony. I think that conditions in Europe will induce some of them to come here. Early in October there will be forty [immigrants] coming here from Vuren. If there are any things that need to be sent along for me, that would be a good opportunity. K. v. d. Linden will probably ask you about that. My wife and children send warmest greetings. Greet your wife for me, and all the brothers and sisters. God be with you all; remember in the prayer of faith,

                       Your Dear Friend and Brother,
                                H. P. Scholte.

(On the address side)
If there is no earlier opportunity, then send the copies of *Een Stem uit Pella* [*A Voice from Pella*] that I requested along with K. v. d. Linden, and have two copies hard bound for me. Also request your wife to send along a few chamois. Roelofsz will pay for it all. Ask him why it is that I just do not receive any letters from him any more. After his last [letter], I wrote him twice but have gotten no answer. How is Bousquet doing? If only he were here. Learn English well; that will come in handy when you become a justice of the peace here later on. It does not pay much as yet, but that will also improve as the area develops, because a justice of the peace here can handle many civil services in daily commercial life. In the future send letters via [Le] Havre for the most regular service.

Chapter 3

The Optimism of Jan and Hendrik Hospers
(Hospers Letters 1-65)

The Jan Hospers family letters provide an optimistic picture of the immigration experience. The family thrived in Iowa and modeled the American success story. Their success stands in sharp contrast with the tale of woe recounted in the next chapter by Andries N. Wormser concerning his family's journey to Iowa and their subsequent return to the Netherlands in bitter disappointment. The Hospers letters are very important in relating the story of the founding of Pella.

The Jan Hospers family had its roots in Amsterdam, where Jan was born August 30, 1801. His father (1761-1827) was a tailor who married three times. Only two children of his second marriage, Jan and Anna Cornelia, survived him. Jan, after attending a French school from 1806 to 1813, was boarded out to his uncle, an old-fashioned teacher at Hoogblokland, to teach French to the children. Jan Hospers became secretary of the Christian Seceded Church and also the village of Hoogblokland near Gorcum [Gorinchem], a city on the Waal River in the province of Zuid Holland. In August 1819 Jan Hospers married Hendrika Middelkoop, twenty-one years of age. They had ten children, of whom Hendrik was the oldest.

In April 1847, Hendrik Hospers, then only seventeen years old, immigrated to Pella on the ship *Maasstroom* with his close friend and Pella's first schoolmaster, Isaac Overkamp. Hendrik's decision within two years prompted his parents and siblings to follow in his footsteps (see chapter 5). In Pella, Hospers became Overkamp's teaching assistant.

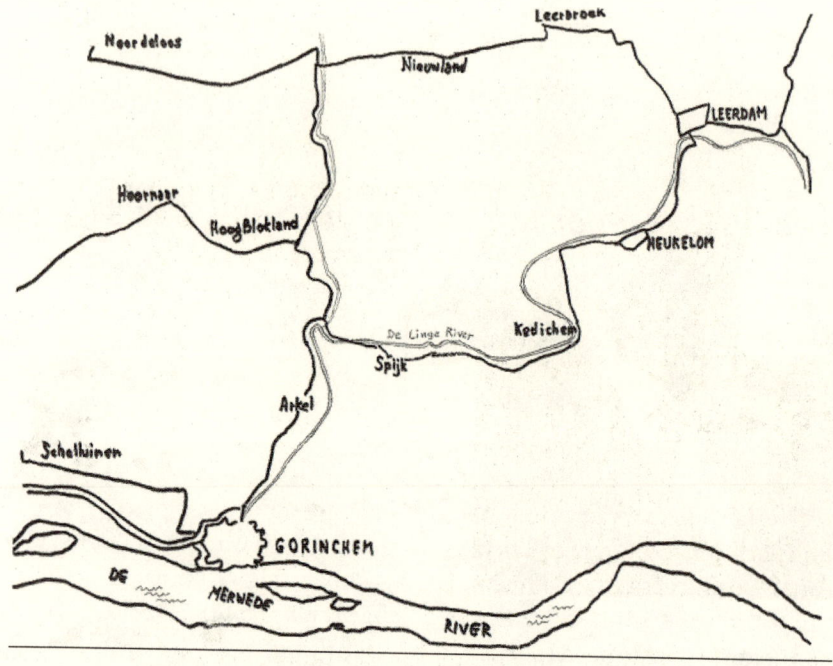

Map of Gorinchem region

In return, Overkamp taught Hospers the English language and his widowed mother cared for both him and Hendrik.

In the years, 1847-1849, Hendrik and his parents exchanged letters regularly, sometimes even weekly, and many are preserved in Pella or at the Northwestern College Library in Orange City, Iowa. Hendrik's early letters tell of his voyage on the *Maasstroom* and of life in Pella in the first months of the new settlement. Later letters describe his surveying work and a land venture on behalf of his parents. Father Jan's letters kept Hendrik abreast of family news in the homeland. Beginning in mid 1848, the letters from Hoogblokland increasingly relate the emotional struggle of the Hospers family about following their beloved Hendrik to the Iowa frontier. To go or not to go was the question. Complicating factors were the many aged relatives, several unmarried, who relied on Jan Hospers for advice and care, and the matter of a substantial inheritance from an uncle without heirs who promised the money to Jan and Hendrika, provided that they remained in the

Hendrik (Henry) Hospers (1830-), Pella businessman and founder of Hospers, Iowa

Netherlands. This put the devout Seceder family between a rock and a hard place—their financial wellbeing in spritually dead Holland or possible penury in spritually alive Pella under the shepherding care of the much revered Rev. Hendrik P. Scholte. In the end, they chose spiritual gain over financial security. But the decision to go cost them three beloved children. At sea, they had to put overboard their eldest girl, Maaike, aged sixteen, and youngest child, Pieter Hendrik, aged two years. Keetje, the second daughter, aged fourteen, died and was buried in Albany, New York. This left Cornelia Geertrui, Nicolaas [Klaas], Teunis de Gelder [called Gelder], Eva Engelina, and Willem Hendrik. (One child died in Hoogblokland.)

    Hendrik Hospers, one of Pella's pioneers and its youngest school teacher, helped develop the colony as land dealer, notary, editor of *Pella's Weekblad*, and mayor (1867-71). Thereafter, he sparked the Orange City colony and founded the town in Sioux County that bears his name. Among the Hollanders of Iowa, Hendrik Hospers was a man of great influence. The letters begin with his leave-taking and end with the departure of his parents, siblings, and mother's parents, Mr. and Mrs. Klaas Middelkoop and their children Sijgje and Gerrit [RPS].

Haven van Rotterdam, 1846 (The Illustrated London News, April 10, 1847)

Rotterdam harbor, 1847

Hospers 1

Rotterdam, April 1847

Dear Parents, Brothers, and Sisters!

Right now (about seven o'clock in the evening) I am in high spirits as I sit here writing letters in the room of a cheap hotel. You probably are puzzled that I am staying at a cheap hotel, but that is because the beds on shipboard are not yet ready, and that is why Mr. I. Overkamp and I are sleeping here at this hotel. Many people come on board ship to have a look, and I have met and spoken to quite a few acquaintances.

Dear Mother! No one on board our ship is crying, nor am I. I could not be in higher spirits. All my trunks are on board. I did not look up [Mr.] Bouw. Rev. Scholte came on board and shook hands with me. The food is fine, and tastes very good! Vanden Berg asked me to come by some time for a drink. It is getting dark because I arrived at our lodgings late, and we will not have any light for a good while.

Well, goodbye Father, goodbye Mother, do not worry about me. I am in good spirits, and I am well taken care of. Goodbye brothers, and sisters, and you too, Uncle. I will write you from Hellevoetsluis (if I can). I remain your loving son and brother,

H. Hospers

P.S. *Je crois qu'Amor tire avec son arc dan mons coeur.* [I believe that Cupid is drawing his bow on my heart.]
Give my regards to all our acquaintances. I. Overkamp

Hospers 2

On board the ship *De Maasstroom*
Saturday, 17 April 1847
On the Hellevoetsluis roadstead

Dear Parents, Brothers, and Sisters!
Here I am sitting most contentedly in a very cramped space without a table, with just a sheet of paper on top of a box that rests on my knees. Friday afternoon we arrived at the Hellevoetsluis roadstead; till now all has gone very well. The *Nagasaki* is also moored here, and so it is very well possible that the first shall be last. The aged Mrs. Overkamp has gotten over her fever, and all the children are well. I just got your package at the post office where I had gone with Bouw to mail my letter.

Mr. Overkamp has answered the following questions. Simply address Mr. Maasdam: To Mr. Maasdam, agent of the English Bible Society in Utrecht. Because Mr. Maasdam is now so well known in Utrecht, that [address] will doubtless suffice for the letter to reach him. I am sure that Father will receive *De Reformatie*, if Father once again only writes Hoogkamer [a Seceder publishing house in Amsterdam]. [Hendrik] Dingemans is on the *Nagasaki* [Dingemans actually sailed on the *Catherina Jackson*].

Please give special greetings to dear Uncle [Hendrik] Van Est for me and also my Uncle De Gelder and all the family. When I am in America and the conditions for writing are better, I will share my observations and critical comments about the journey with you. I have to end now; regular bowel movements, a good appetite, and sleeping well. Well, dear Mother and Father, I must close and wish you every good thing.
Your beloved Son,

H. Hospers.

P.S. Kiss Eva for me.
Amor [Cupid] is firing his arrows, I believe; let him fire away. I have nothing else to do.

Hospers 3*

Hoogblokland, 16 August 1847

Much beloved Son Hendrik!

Since your departure there is one member of your relation less: the wife of Uncle Floor Middelkoop of Vianen died in the beginning of this month. Father [Klaas] Middelkoop attended her funeral. We are well. Except that Keetje has a fever, and Willem Hendrik also. Van Beekum treats them. Your mother is well but does not become stronger. Having no maid she is kept busy, and the baby, Pieter Hendrik, robs her of needed sleep. Three days in the week a woman does the housework and so Maaike and Keetje have time to sew shirts for the coming journey.

Here I am stopped in my writing. Aart de Ruyter came in to pay some interest. That money will go to my debt of ƒ1000 [florins, or guilders] that I borrowed from E. Aanen on Sept. 1, 1846, to buy land in America. I do not doubt but what the land has been bought, and perhaps [Pieter] van Meveren is already working it. The first plowing must be difficult!

All is well at father Middelkoop's. Thus far they did well at farming. The Lord blesses them. In this respect the Lord is blessing all Holland. It is an unusually fruitful year. Potatoes grew well, but we hear that the leaves have turned black in many sections of Holland. Not so bad right here. In this the Lord shows his particular love to us. This shows us that it is in His power to take from us this necessary staple of life and that He is pleased to show us His longsuffering mercy.

Uncle H. van Est [without children or relatives and who planned to make the writer his heir if he would remain in Holland, which legacy of course was lost] lives quietly along. Monday he rode along to Gorinchem in a wagon. He is depressed at present, and is feverish, he says. Yesterday, Sunday, on his usual evening visit, I reminded him that the sorrow of the world works death, but sorrow to God works repentance to salvation.

The uncles and aunts De Gelder [five of them who died unmarried and in age up to ninety-six, leaving their money to their nephew Willem Middelkoop who had remained in Holland] are well again. Very likely they will give up farming. They have discharged their hired men and the maid, and already some have inquired about buying the farm. But Teunis de Gelder was not yet ready for this. "Aai-Oom" [Uncle Arie de Gelder] just now visited us in our sitting room and said, referring to our plans about Pella: "If I were the last one to remain of Teunis and Betje, I would go along with you to America." I have told Uncle Teunis

Immigrant ship *Maastroom*, carried early Pella settlers

all the secrets of your letter. I have told you all about your Blokland relatives; but this of the others. Herman and Koetje [Lubbers (probably), children of Hendrik Hospers's only sister, living in Amsterdam] visited us. Herman cried, surprised by our intention of going away. You have their hearty regards.

Your letter was postmarked, St. Louis, Mo., July 8, with the word PAID, from which I gather that you paid postage up to the ocean. The second postmark is "outré mer, le Havre, 17 Aout 47, and then: Paris, 9 Aout 47" [this letter is lost]. On Wed. Aug 11 at 5 A.M. the Meerkerk mail carrier came to deliver your letter. There was joy! Everybody jumped out of bed! Joy in the household—a veritable feast! As soon as the carrier had left with his fee, the letter was carefully cut open (which had been closed upside down with three wafers), with Mother next to me and Pieter Hendrik at the breast to have quiet, and Maaike, Keetje, Klaas, and [Teunis de] Gelder all around me. Then the letter was carefully read. The mail carrier had ridden fast with his dogcart and had imparted the news to Father, who at once jumped out of bed and came to us, be it noted, sufficiently dressed. We had just finished reading the letter and had not yet recovered from our joy when grandfather stood before us. Your letter was well composed, well written, interesting, and complete.

You have satisfied us very well. Your parents are very well satisfied with your writing.

Sunday morning, Aug. 22, 6 o'clock. There was much anxiety here with regard to your ship, *De Maasstroom. Het Handelsblad* had information that it had sunk. Fortunately, that number came unusually late in our hands. Leerbroek and Nieuwland were full of dismay, as many of their relatives and friends had gone on that ship. In Gorinchem there was much sympathy for all of us. However, the news was kept away from us. When we began to suspect something. P. Vanden Burg wrote us: "God be praised, the *Maasstroom* did not founder." The next day I read that this paper had been severely taken to task for having spread such news without warrant.

My school does well. Klaas and [Teunis de] Gelder are all out of quills. Gerrit Middelkoop, P[ieter] M. vander Ley, and I are studying English since May. Every Saturday afternoon I walk for that purpose to Gorinchem 3 miles. Mr. [H.] Picard is our teacher. We recite from three to five and are home again at seven. It is rather a sacrifice of time and trouble, but I do it with much pleasure and am making progress. It is generally known that we are studying English and so people do not doubt but what Hospers also will leave his Bloklanders. I am very sorry you did not take any English books with you. I hope that Mr. [James] Muntingh, who I do not yet know, has taken care of this.

I visited Utrecht but missed my friends Rev. Scholte, [L.] van Bergeyk, and I. Overkamp. Write much about your circumstances and even the small particulars. How did you come out with your traveling expenses? Anything left? How much land do we have? How much woods? Prairie? How much [cost] per acre? How many Dutch "morgen" does Van Meveren estimate it to be? What is its form? Level or hilly? Does a small stream cross it? What has been done already? What adjoins it? Has a log cabin [blokhuis] been built? If so, give a diagram and indicate it on the map. What are the plans for work? What did P. van Meveren do the day before yesterday? Yesterday? Today? What [did he do] on the day of your writing? What does he plan to do the next day? Do his children also work on our land? Does Van Meveren make decisions alone? Or does he consult with C. den Hartog, Vanden Berg, and with you? This will give me some idea of things. What do you eat in the morning and at what time? Who will be our neighbors? Have they begun with building the "city"? Do you keep school already? Describe it.

Tell Mr. G.H. Overkamp that I have written thirty letters and made trips for him with the result that I have gotten f 115 from the late Jacobus

Kruijt, which matter is now finished. Write me how Overkamp wants this money sent. Greet him, also I. Overkamp. With much pleasure I remember the good time I had with them on my visit. I trust that Mrs. Overkamp will be a mother to you. The most agreeable of all your writing was that you have found such a good friend in Dingemans. God grant that he may prove to you the means to your conversion and bring a friendship as between David and Jonathan. At your request I have written to Dingemans at Rossum and because you mother is so much taken up with that matter I have written at some length. I received a letter for your friend Hendrik D., which is pretty big. Postage to Hoogblokland ran up to 50 cents. How high the postage across the ocean would have been.

J. Hospers

On 22 August 1847 Jan Hospers wrote his son from Hoogblokland:

> Het Handelsblad reported as fact that the *Maasstroom* had perished....It was all kept from us....The next day I read the truth of the matter in the [Nederlandsche] *Staatscourant* with a censure of *Het Handelsblad*: The N[ieuwe] R[otterdamsche] C[ourant] of 31 July 1847, which reports that the *Maasstroom*, under Captain H. Schut, had returned from Baltimore and arrived in Hellevoetsluis on July 30th. The *Zeemeeuw*, on which Budde had emigrated, had returned from New York arriving at Texel on August 5th.

Hospers 4*

[An undated letter of Hendrik's mother and her own handwriting]

Much beloved Hendrik!

The Lord be praised and thanked that at last there has come an end to the silence of my dear Hendrik, and that the Lord has brought you safe across. You have much to talk about with your friend and thank God for. You seem to remain pretty cheerful. That gives me peace. You can think that you are little out of my thoughts. And how glad I am that Jeffrouw [Mrs.] Overkamp cares for you like a mother. Consult her in everything and trust her. How do your clothes fit? Did you lack anything on the journey? You folks must have gotten a very large amount of soiled goods. How inquisitive I am to see you. My heart is always with you. You are a good magnet [*trekplaister or mustard-plaster*] to draw us speedily to you.

Dear Hendrik, if you have a wish for something and you can let Keppel know before he leaves, take advantage of that. Now, dear Hendrik, I entrust you to the Lord and to the care of His people. May the Lord so direct that we may soon see each other in good health. And what shall I write about this place? Everything remains about the same. You have more material to write about than we. Write us everything in detail, but in a separate note what concerns us particularly; and a big cordial letter too. Your letter has been praised and become famous especially by Van Andel and Brand of Gorkum [Gorinchem]. Write whether you are perfectly pleased with all your surroundings; or would you like to have some things different; and whether it is the place for us. I could write my letter full of "dear Hendrik" "dear Hendrik" "dear Hendrik."

Goodbye, *lieve* Hendrik!

Your loving mother

Hospers 5*

Hoogblokland, 28 August 1847

(Side note): Enclosed is a good "Willem" [*a ten guilder gold coin*], a present of Uncle Arie de Gelder. Inform me of receipt.

Dearly Beloved Son Hendrik:

I returned from Gorkum [Gorinchem], whereas on other Saturdays I take lessons in English from H. Prins. All is well, and now I must talk with you. Likely you received my letter of the 23rd. Mr. Kant posted it for me, but he informs me that others also added enough to make it a small package, and so I had to pay $f4.20$ postage, which paid only as far as the western part of England. They were embarrassed about the amount. Your letter cost me $f60$. Write me what you have to pay for letters. A common letter cost $f1.20$ from here to West England. But your letters are worth all the expense.

It is becoming dark. 7:30 pm. I rang the bell for a light and your sister Keetje, who has been sick, brought it. She is very welcome to come in my room, because she has not been here for awhile. You see from this that I am just talking with you. I did write a full letter to you a short time ago, so that now I have nothing special. I hope I can get this to you without expense through Mr. Van Hees, a baker in Rotterdam and an elder in the Seceder church there. He plans to leave for Pella in Sept.

From your letter I at once copied the principal items of interest and sent them to the Seceder Church of Utrecht. I have learned that this letter made the rounds there, was copied, and read with unusual interest, because the land trip was so accurately described, the arrival of the four ships with the passengers, and the result of the meeting to decide on the place of settling.

I learn that Hendrik de Jong has settled in Michigan, where he bought 80 *morgen* of land [one morgen equals about 2 acres] at ƒ 6.25, and 3 cows and 2 calves for ƒ 140. Such pieces of news are devoured here. O, there is so much talk about America here. Without any attempt on our part, your letter has been spread far and wide. From Hellendoorn 150 persons departed, with their luggage loaded on 21 wagons. Another group of 50 persons from that same congregation left; their route was via Arnhem, all of them headed for North America. Rev. [Gerrit] Baai [Baay] wants to leave Apeldoorn with his entire congregation. Rev. Budding is also already leaning towards America.

The year 1847 was unusually productive in Holland. Crops half as large again as usual. O, we would so much like to be in your midst to hear the pure preaching of the Word. Were I a farmer, I would have gone too; but what can a man like myself do, with a large family and no income in my line in America? See to it that Van Meveren takes good care of the land you bought for me. It is the means through which, with God's blessing, I can in time make a living. You know that Maaike and Keetje can make good use of the needle. But what can your father do? From his youth up he has been in educational work. Could I be of any use there? How many scholars in your school? What kind of rooms? What kind of books?

Greet the Overkamps, Scholte, Betten, Van Bergeyk, [Cornelius] Den Hartog, and the family of [Pieter] Van Meveren. Still consider Mrs. Overkamp your mother. This lady must look after you, whether your clothes look well, whether you comb and wash yourself as you should. Do you learn English?

I conclude by reminding you of the Word: "Seek first the kingdom of God, and all other things will be added unto you." This is not merely to obtain things, but from a sense of gratitude because God is so good. The Lord be with you in everything.

Mother will write a little also,
    Your Father,

                                      Jan Hospers

Dear Hendrik:

As concerns your name, you are daily in our thoughts, in our midst. We have pleasant thoughts of you, yes, we are proud of you, our eldest son, who does great things. It comforts me that our son will be cared for surely and protected. My heart often feels strong affection for you, never did I know such love for you as I do now, and this will hasten our journey to you. The Lord may prepare it sooner than we think. It will depend upon the tidings we get from you. Please write us such [tidings] and plainly advise us as you see fit. If we know that you are pleased with your situation, we live in the glad expectation of seeing you in the new land, but then a big struggle awaits us, and may the Lord be near us.

Dear Hendrik:

It is a year ago today that you and Steijnis and his wife were with us and picked all the hazelnuts. There are so many now that you would not do it as quickly. There are also many apples and pears. Tomorrow your dear father will have reached his 46th year. May the Lord spare him long.

Dear Hendrik:

As Mrs. Overkamp mothers you, tell her that you have a weakness not to wash your neck clean—about which your mother complained enough. Give her my regards. Do you have water, as we have here? Is not your way of living altogether different? Do you sleep well? Are you pretty well in your element?

Your dear mother,

Hendrika Hospers (nee Middelkoop)

Hospers 6 [Hospers 3]

Pella, 7 September 1847

Beloved Sisters,

Right now I am sitting in the kind of log cabin [*blokhuis*] that we often saw depicted in that book about America. The log cabin looks exactly like it; the forest about it is also the same, but the trees are of a different kind. Hold the picture in front of you, and then imagine me

Log cabin of O. H. Viersen family

in the woods with a gun on my shoulder to see whether I can shoot a partridge, a prairie turkey or hen, or a rabbit. Or imagine me with an axe on my shoulder cutting up firewood, or walking around in the bushes with one of my friends, for instance, [Hendrik] Dingemans, the son of [Pieter] Welle, looking for bullace (small plums), hazel nuts, or [hawthorn] berries that often grow wild here. I often think of the pleasant hours I spent among the circle of my fellow villagers in the Blokland area. And before I forget, give my greetings especially to Jan Vink, N. Donkerdal, and Roeland. And why don't you have them read this short letter.

How I would like to visit that little village once again, but I would rather see my friends in America and enjoy with them the delight of beholding the splendid location of the Pella region. The prairie is gently rolling. But wait a moment; I am forgetting that I am in America, that I have really seen America's mountains, whose peaks are bathed by the clouds, but my sisters have not; they have not even seen a canal yet. I will have to express myself more clearly: the land, namely the prairie, is hilly. Some sections are level, but then again others have slowly rising hills or small mountains, just about as high as the Blokland church. A woods, which it would take two or three hours to walk around, constitutes the northern and western boundaries of our colony; two rivers, the Skunk and the Des Moines, flow through our land. Now, my dear sisters, you have some idea of my situation. I hope that you will also come soon. You will certainly find some good girlfriends here and probably enjoy more innocent fun than in Holland. In that hope I close, and name myself your loving brother.

H. Hospers

Pella panorama 1851

Hospers 7 [Hospers 4]

Pella, 7 September 1847

Esteemed Uncle Willem and Gerrit [Middelkoop]!

In accordance with your request, I was to write you a few things about American clothing. All the farmers wear wide-rimmed straw hats; white shirts are worn on Sundays as well as weekdays; the farmers' wives are all ladies with veils on their hats and lace on their skirts; whether they look as black as soot makes no difference. All farmers or whatever they may be address each other as Sir, that is, as gentlemen. Everyone rides a horse, and in the saddle; when the women visit each other for coffee, they go on horseback; unmarried women wear no hats at all, only the married women wear bonnets. By all means do not take along a gun, for there are many for sale here among the Hollanders.

I shall close now and name myself your nephew,

H. Hospers

P.S. Mrs. Welle kindly requests that Mother or Grandmother, when they come over, will be so kind as to bring along a small box of Haarlemmer Oil.* I long intensely for some of my favorite food, groat gruel; I certainly do wish that Mother could bring along some groats for me. Buttermilk is expensive here; Mrs. Overkamp needs five American cents' worth in order to cook a porridge. Welle, [A.J.] Betten, G. H. Overkamp, [Cornelius] Den Hartog, etc., send their regards.

On behalf of Rev. Scholte, Grandfather [Klaas Middelkoop] is requested to take along *lubben* [rennet, the fourth stomach from calves] for thirty persons who want to make cheese. There is a great need for them here, and Grandfather can also earn something on them.

*A folk medicine used for internal and external ailments, consisting of three parts turpentine oil, and one part linseed oil in which some sulphur has been dissolved. Haarlemmer Oil had been in use since 1698.

Hospers 8*

Hoogblokland, 30 September 1847

Dear Son!

On my birthday last Aug. 30, Huibert Keppel from Minkeloos had been to Rotterdam with my letter to Van Hees, elder of the Seceded Church there, and the bread baker, Mr. D. Chabot of Utrecht, had written me that he was about to depart for America. I had a letter for you and others to be given along with him, but Keppel came back with word that Van Hees had departed. I now send you these letters in another way. Yours holds a "golden Willem" [a ten guilder gold coin] from Uncle Arie de Gelder who will not have this known to Uncle Teunis and Aunt Betje.

Yesterday I heard that M. R. Chabot, almost a doctor, had died at the age of 28 years from scarlet fever. How this affected me! I liked him. When I was in Utrecht he was my constant companion. And now only Maasdam is left of my particular friends in Utrecht.

Today I went to father [Klaas] Middelkoop to bring him this news and to unburden my heart. O, how delightful is our association with father, I have no other. When I went there I saw all of them threshing hemp. They too saw me and father ran to meet me, saying, "I have news!" When I had brought my sad news, father told me that the Colony had been established. A great thing! Behold, sorrow and joy. Huibert Keppel had been summoned by the old man, B. Pellikaan, of Nieuwland, who had the previous day received a letter of his grandson, Teunis Keppel, containing a full account of Michigan and Marion County. Singing and praising God, I went home where Huibert Keppel already was, and who had given the good news to mother and your brothers and sisters. On this occasion we drank a small glass of brandy and closed the evening with Keppel in considering God's goodness and loving care. The next day father and Willem [Hendrik] came with the original letter. We read all of the eight pages, consulting the map at the same time. Truly, Teunis Keppel is an able young man. When last fall in Utrecht I agreed to include him in the committee to investigate concerning the land to be bought, I did not think there was so much in this Teunis Keppel. But in so many letters we do not hear our Hendrik mentioned.

[part missing] ... and rather read God's Word than occupy my post in church. The words I hear there are not exactly false, but there is no life in them; and when in his written sermons there does occur something fine, then the minister reads it with such fire that I notice that he preaches to himself and it disgusts me. I then cast down my eyes to the floor.

Dinner. Your mother brings in a big plate of fine cauliflower from our garden. Our maid pours off the potatoes. Keetje with Klaas, Willem Hendrik, and Eva are seated at the table. [Teunis de] Gelder took his turn to eat with the uncles; that is still our custom.

We read once more your remark: "After careful consideration, Isaac Overkamp and I advise you to wait with coming till the Lord opens the way without tempting Him in waiting for the death of uncle [Hendrik] Van Est."

On my birthday I received all the congratulations. Eva wished that we might soon see Hendrik; [Teunis de] Gelder produced a nice writing; Klaas had a poem on my name. Willem Hendrik, aged 4, gave me a small piece of paper with 4 or 5 vignettes. Eva had knitted a pair of socks for me. Keetje had made a Greek cap after a pattern found in a ladies journal *Aglaja* for which Maaike had subscribed. Mother and Klaas gave me a silver pocket lead pencil. We had a feast with all around a table, where we drank tea and emptied two bottles and ate currant bread. The children might that evening remain with us till our bedtime. The uncles and aunts, etc., were all supplied with currant bread.

How do you pronounce the word "Iowa?" You will surely make more progress in learning English than I do: I never hear it spoken; my teacher in English, Mr. [H.] Picard, does not like that either: he teaches English but seldom speaks it. Have you ever led the singing in Pella? Is I. Overkamp "voorzinger?"

Friday, Sept. 1. We have eaten, read, and given thanks. No letter yet. We are sorry. I have sent them dated May 29, June 14, July 8, July 19, and Aug. 17. You don't write as busily? Is there anyone in Pella who receives so many letters? We must not be afraid of the high cost of postage. There comes your mother again sweetly caressing (*lief streelem*) and conversing delightfully. The Lord be near you, my son! Keep your eye upon Him. Walk as seeing Him who is invisible. Find your rest and joy not in your works, not even in your best, but in the precious blood of Jesus Christ!!

Your father,

J. Hospers

Saturday, Sept. 3. The mail! No letter from you! I had kept this open but all hope is gone now.
Greetings,

Father

Hospers 9*

Hoogblokland, 3 October 1847

Heartily beloved Brother!
I sit writing here next to Willem Hendrik who is doing all kinds of mischief [*kattekwaad*], as pulling my pen out of my hand, shaking the table, etc. Maaike stands near eating a pear. Willem Hendrik says, "Henne in Noot meca" [Hendrik in North America]. Tonight I have a fever; I get this off and on, more or less. Many sick people around. Now I must rock Pieter to sleep. Hendrik, I send you herewith an English poem and translate it for you:

> Our Bob has got a dog and a gun,
> The dew is on—we may not run.
> At midday it is hot and dry
> Ask Bob and say, why do you cry?
> I do not joy to see him sob.
> Oh! Anna has run a pin into Bob.

From *New English Reader for Beginners* by J. Lagerweij, Gz. Hendrik, every moment I expect the return of the fever. I will close. Hearty greetings from your well-wishing brother,

N[icolaas] Hospers

Hospers 10*

Hoogblokland, 10 October 1847

Dear Hendrik,
Your brother Nicholas has the "double" tertian fever. Since the days are now getting shorter we take our English lessons in the forenoon.

Although it rained hard yesterday at 8 a.m., I went nevertheless with [Pieter] Vander Ley. Gerrit did not go. From Gorkum [Gorinchem] I went via Schelluinen to Nieuwland. That day I walked about fifteen miles. Last Monday J. Gordon of Gorkum [Gorinchem] told Mr. Aanen that [Pieter] Welle intended to return. O, there is so much enmity! Some express themselves openly as wishing that they all would die!

A Rotterdam paper says that Rev. [Pieter] Zonne also arrived in America and has settled at West-Consin [Wisconsin] between Scholte and Van Raalte [Michigan]. In our thoughts we are with you so much. O that we were with our true friends and brethren and today could listen to the true preaching of the Word! O, that blessed proclamation! We are still feasting from the sketches of sermons by Rev. Scholte that I took down. We lack the preaching of the Word in the fullness of faith here. That Word is a treasure compared with which the gold of earth becomes as nothing. That Word, and the experiences of Divine presence, what more can one wish? And yes, daily communion with the brethren would be such a pleasure, as they speak with one another of these things and are led by the Holy Spirit! However deep the reverend gentlemen, Scholte and [A.J.] Betten, may have fathomed that Word, they certainly will acknowledge that there are greater depths still. O, that the Lord may spare them for the church! God grant that I and your mother, brothers and sisters, and grandparents may soon be able to go to the house of the Lord in Pella. May the way soon be open! The Lord knows that I am loose from all my posts and offices, but Uncle Van Est!!!! [Yes, four exclamation marks here: the well-to-do Uncle Hendrik van Est made Jan Hospers, his only nephew, sole heir if he would remain in Holland (Gerrit Hendrik Hospers).]

Dear Hendrik! Greet the reverend gentlemen and brethren Scholte and Betten very heartily from me and tell them in my name of my regard and love for them, not only because of the favors from them but especially because they are such worthy servants of God. The writings of Scholte, the preaching of and conversations with Scholte and Betten were in God's hand the means of enlarging my knowledge and building me up in the faith. The Lord be with them now and evermore.

Your father,

J. Hospers

Hospers 11*

Hoogblokland, 12 October 1847

Dear Eldest Son!

All well. Uncle Van Est had a spell Sunday so that he was not at church. Huibert Keppel was with me in the evening and we were all American. I gave him much information for his journey. Next Sunday he comes again, early, at coffee; father and Vander Ley also come. The Americans will then again be together. I plan to entertain them with a sermon by Scholte, which he last preached in Leerdam. Keppel departs Tuesday. He promises to take with him 400 golden guilders ("Willems"). Do you have money for postage? Do you earn anything? Is it true that a letter of yours came to Utrecht? I[saac] van Gorkum said he saw it from your handwriting.

I write this with a poor steel pen; it is late. Only mother is with me yet. All doors are locked and I hate to get up and get another pen.

October 16

I just came back from Gorkum [Gorinchem] after another lesson in English. At Boderij [a tobacco shop] I bought four German pipes for Keppel to take along—one for you. With each pipe I have bought two smoked-through heads; the extra one, if the other breaks. Boderij selected the best ones. Yours goes now; a special one made for a short or a long stem. I had brought along a box of cigars, but they scare me out, telling me of the high duties imposed, entailing fines and imprisonment. Write what you know about this.

Welle writes that at least a hundred people of our [Emigrant] Society have died, whether en route to or in America. That is an exceptionally high number. There have been, and still are, stranger rumors circulating concerning all aspects of the Society. Thus, it was first said, and then even reported in the *Courant*, that the *Maasstroom* had been lost at sea with all hands on board; furthermore, that there was a plague on board the ships, and that they were not allowed to disembark; that the passengers were dying of hunger; that Scholte had made off with the treasury, and this rumor still persists. That there are many who regret [having emigrated]. That Welle had written "that if he could crawl back on his knees, he would." This report was spread throughout Gorcum.

We are going to see to it that [from now on] all important news reports are gathered together and published, in order in this way to shut the mouth of all those liars and satanic gainsayers. We have already contacted Hoogkamer to see if he is willing to publish anything like that. The writings of Scholte, the sermons and conversations of Scholte and Betten, despite everything, have been the Lord's means to increase my knowledge and to strengthen my faith. May the Lord be with them now and forever!

    Your Father,

J. Hospers

Hospers 12 [Hospers 5]

Pella, 27 [October] 1847

Beloved Parents and Grandparents,
    I am taking this opportunity to send you these letters and to let you know that I am hale and healthy. Since I sent you my second letter, everything remains the same. [Pieter] Van Meveren is still in St. Louis; Rev. Scholte's house will soon be finished; he is now in St. Louis picking up his family. The day before yesterday the family of Rev. Post arrived, and he is now also living in Pella. Tonight will be the first time I sleep in a cupboard bedstead. As I wrote you earlier, [Pieter] Welle will be growing part of his corn on our land. Welle was not exactly happy about that; he talked to Rev. Scholte about it, but since this happens to be the shape of the section [of land], we can do nothing about it. Overkamp advises Father to buy a lot in the city: there is still a very good lot for sale for fifty dollars; Father cannot lose on it, for in time the lots will greatly increase in value. I was very much surprised that Father did not write whether the Dutch were in spirit still yearning for America. Especially greet Uncle [Hendrik] Van Est for me. I think of him often; I even wished to be in Holland once again. Mother, I am eating head cheese tonight made from a [pig] head that was about to be thrown away by the Americans. In hopes of seeing you in good health, I remain your eldest son and grandson.

H. Hospers

Hospers 13 [Hospers 6]

Pella, 27 October 1847

Dearly Beloved Parents!
    I received your letter of October 13 in the best of health and well being. I was surprised, because it came so very unexpectedly. I had come home

about six o'clock in the evening, exhausted from surveying, and so I had developed a healthy appetite. At my first breath the aroma of onions and potatoes filled my nostrils and I was already happy at the prospect of stilling my hunger, when Overkamp said, "Hospers! I have good news for you, there is a letter for you." My hunger was gone, and instead of stilling it, I satisfied my curiosity. I probably should not dwell on this any longer, because paper and space are too precious right now.

After I had written you the letter from St. Louis [lost letter of July 8], the committee to buy land started [on its mission]. The committee consisted of Rev. Scholte, I. Overkamp, [Jan] Rietveld, [H.Y.] Viersen (a Frisian), [G.] Van de Pol, and a son of Keppel. In addition, anyone interested was welcome to join the committee on its travels but at his own expense. The only person who expressed such interest was the aforementioned Viersen. Looking up to God for guidance, the committee left to begin its search. The task that they were undertaking was a difficult one, but God came to their assistance in a very special way. On their journey they stopped at Fairville [Fairfield], where the funeral of a child was taking place. It so happened that Rev. Scholte entered into a conversation with a Baptist missionary, whose name was [Moses J.] Post, and shared their plan with him; the consequence was that this missionary accompanied them on the entire journey. After the committee had been traveling for three weeks, it returned to St. Louis with the glad tiding: "Land has been bought."

It was not long before all the Hollanders in St. Louis knew about the tiding, and because everyone was much interested in this matter, it was decided to hold a meeting, which took place in the Presbyterian church. The meeting was opened with prayer and thanksgiving for the special presence of the Lord in the purchasing of land. Rev. Scholte was president, I. Overkamp was secretary, and the aforementioned Rev. Post was present at all the proceedings. Rev. Scholte then told the following story: After Rev. Post had joined them, the committee purchased land, or rather, staked claims to it. This would have been a very difficult undertaking, had they not had the assistance of the Rev. Post, who is thoroughly familiar with the land and the customs everywhere. The committee took out claims to 2½ townships: part of the land had already been cleared and was under cultivation; there were already forty farms with their own cultivated lands. The owners, or rather the people with claims to the land, were bought out with very much difficulty; this was done with the proviso that claims were also being taken out to the principal points of those 2½ townships, and all in the name of Rev.

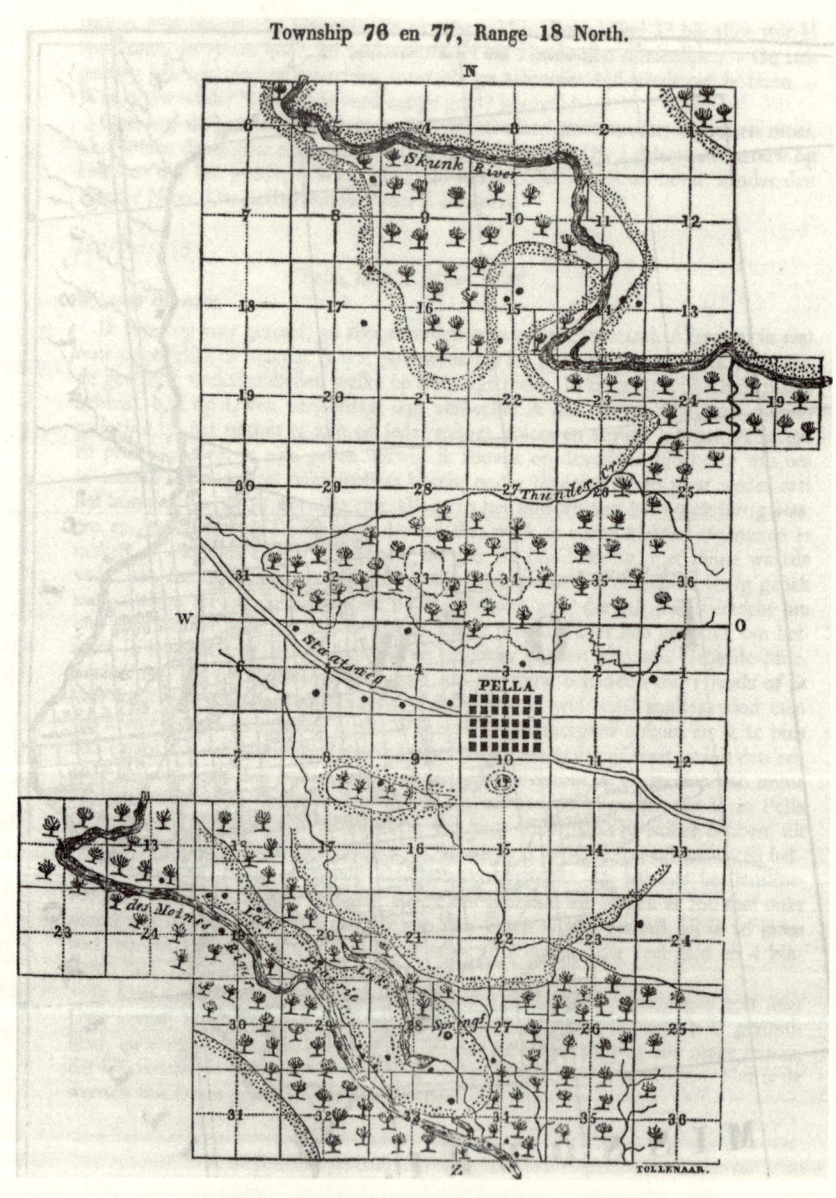

Lake Prairie Township plat, 1848

Scholte. This was done in order to prevent any American from settling in our colony against our wishes.

The nature of the land is in part and mostly excellent black garden soil. There are two coal mines, several quarries, one-third is woods, etc. The surface is gently rolling prairie, slightly more rolling forest, and level along the rivers. Two rivers, the Des Moines and the Skunk, constitute the southern and northern boundaries of the colony. Neither stream is navigable, but the former can be made navigable; both are rich in fish and have good water sources. The principal wooded areas are located not far from the shores of the rivers. The colony is four hours long and five hours wide [walking distance]. The main road from Keokuk to Oxville [Knoxville] etc. traverses the town and the colony. The colony is located in the state of Iowa, Marion County; it is 120 miles northwest of Keokuk. The capital of the state of Iowa, Iowa City, has been moved and now is located eighteen miles northwest of Pella. All this makes the city of Pella very important, and accordingly either a railroad will be passing through the city, or the Des Moines River will be made navigable. The air temperature is very hot in the summer, and in the winter, which is not very long, it is very cold. Rain falls in the spring; in the fall it is very dry; the wind also blows constantly so that it is entirely possible to build windmills.

After Rev. Scholte had given this description, a very realistic one, everyone had to indicate whether he wished to be among the first to leave for the colony, or whether he chose to remain in St. Louis. Most of the landowners left, but most of the workmen remained in St. Louis, as Rev. Scholte had advised that, since more money could be earned there. The carpenters proceeded to set up cabins for the new arrivals.

When that was completed, each person was asked what land he desired to have, whether cultivated or not. In consultation with [Cornelius] Den Hartog and [Pieter] Welle, I applied for as much cultivated land as possible. The meeting closed with thanksgiving. After the meeting it was arranged that [Pieter] Van Meveren would remain in St. Louis until the land was assigned and he could begin his work. A whole steamboat was chartered in order to transport 300 passengers to Keokuk, with a charge of 15 cents for 100 pounds of freight. The trip by land from Keokuk to Pella is very difficult. Everything has to be transported by wagon and this is very expensive. It cost each person [the amount here is torn out], and one dollar for every hundred pounds of freight.

Having arrived in the colony, everyone was put under roof. A grocery store was provided, so that we could obtain what was needed in abundance [*in overvloed*]. Already we are real busy in the dividing of the land.

The city has been surveyed, of which I give you right here the drawing and description, made by the surveyor himself. The English that follows is that transcribed in the letter.

State of Iowa, Marion County

I, Claiborne Hall, Surveyor of Marion County, certify that I have correctly surveyed sixty-four lots in the above named town under my hand this 2nd day of September 1847.

(signed) Clairborne Hall, C.S.M.C.

Description and Plan of Pella

Pella is beautifully situated on an eminence from which may be had a general view of the surrounding country; the streets are one hundred feet wide, the blocks and square are four hundred feet square, and the blocks are laid into eighteen lots, each as seen by the plot is situated about the center of the section line dividing sections 3 and 10 running east and west. The town is laid out at right angles; [t]here is a stone planted at each corner of the square, from which to make future surveyings. The latitude is 90 20" Nine running E."

Hendrik Hospers's drawing of Pella lots, October 1847

On Sept. 12 the clerk of the government of Iowa took an oath in Pella from all male persons twenty-one years of age and above. They have thus been accepted as citizens of the United States of America.

Each of these lots in the first street, i.e., on the Square, costs 100 dollars, and all others sell for 50 dollars. Each lot is 200 feet long and 100 feet wide. If we would sell to Americans, we could easily get 300, 400, and 500 dollars for a lot. The city can be enlarged. All the lots have already been sold. I have colored those that already have houses. Please excuse mistakes in drawing; had no ruler; used the back of a knife. That the Lord may be with you is the wish and prayer of your
   Obedient Son,

Henry Hospers

[The following paragraph was written on the back or address side of the letter]

The principal crops are maize, known to us under the name of Roman wheat, corn, and oats. The farmers have sixty pigs on average; it costs nothing to feed them during the summer because they forage for themselves in the woods. The farmers themselves do not know how many pigs they own; the same is true for chickens and sheep. Every farmer is his own butcher; when he wants to eat bacon, he loads his gun and shoots the pig dead. In the colony bacon costs four American cents a pound, delicious meat two American cents a pound; we eat meat to our hearts' content. Groceries are more expensive here than in Holland, and the flour is without bran and is as nice as flour in Holland; it costs ƒ 6.25 per one hundred pounds. The shoemaker, tailor, etc., is very expensive. There are plenty of potatoes here, but not as good as in Holland. Americans eat three times a day, each with pork and meat. Bread and meat is the principal part of a meal, potatoes is secondary.

This summer the Hollanders have already made cheese for their own use. This will be a success if the houses will only be made fit for it. When I have no work, I generally ride on horseback and can ride at a gallop. The Americans all ride in a saddle and at a gallop. While surveying I have seen two deer and one wolf. Wolves do not hurt anybody. I have seen and killed many snakes.

Across the letter is written the following note from I. Overkamp

Dear Friend and Brother in Christ!

At the request of your son, I hereby inform you what in my judgment is the best way to undertake the journey here. If you leave Holland in the spring or fall, the best route is via New Orleans. I read your son's letter and have nothing to add but my warmest greetings to you and yours, and to our good friends and brothers in the Lord. I am eager to see you and all who are dear to us. Come over here; here is plenty of room to provide everyone a good place to settle. Koen De Jong asks that you give his greeting to his brother Adriaan de Jong at Achthoven when you can, and he is eager to hear how you are doing. And may the Lord be with you and yours, your friend and brother,

I. Overkamp.

Hospers 14 [Hospers 7]

Pella, 17 November 1847

Dear Parents,

I am still very healthy and, according to what they tell me, I really must have grown. I can notice that myself because all my coats and pants have become too small and are bursting at the seams, but I will write about that later, first things first.

It is about ten o'clock on a Wednesday morning, November 17, and it is rainy weather. A fortnight ago Rev. Scholte went to St. Louis to pick up his family and to perform the wedding of Mr. Hazebroek. This gentleman will spend the winter in St. Louis with his new wife and then next spring he will come to the colony in order to open a big grocery store. [Pieter] Van Meveren [Hosper's hired hand] is still in St. Louis. I am doing everything in my power to get that household to move to Pella, since there is plenty of work for them now. It is for that reason that I wrote a little note to Rev. Scholte with the following content (see "Copy" below). What the outcome will be I still do not know.

Since the surveyor had an accident over fourteen days ago, he has not been able to do any surveying during this period. His accident came about as follows. In America there are immense fields of grass that are called prairies. In the fall, when the grass is thoroughly dry, these fields are burned off. It is a grand and moving sight, especially in the evening. We had to start such a fire, and it was because of that fire that the surveyor's face and right hand were burned. However, we expect him on the job soon.

From the drawing I enclosed in my last letter you know the lay of the land. The section of cultivated land happens to be in the northern half, of which Welle has none. It is my judgment, and that of others, that it will come to twenty acres or nine *morgen* in extent, because one acre is 285 (square) rods and one *morgen* is 600 (square) rods. It was decided by lots that the northern half will go to K[laas] Middelkoop and the southern half to J[an] Hospers; thus the cultivated land is in Grandfather's area, and compensatory damages will have to be paid on it. However, the land can also be divided lengthwise, which would be much more desirable for several reasons: for then you will also be located along the road. You can also get half of the cultivated land, and you could build your houses side by side. However, to avoid being partial, I cannot make this division; it is best that you and Grandfather sit down together and make this division. And you should let us know as soon as possible so that cultivation of the land etc. can be arranged accordingly. It would be highly desirable and useful for Uncle Gerrit [Middelkoop, son of Klaas] to come ahead [of the others], for he can be much more useful here than in Holland. He can learn English here just as well.

To break up prairie land, as they say here, costs quite a lot of money. In the spring a number of Americans will be coming through who have special plows suited only for this work, drawn by eight or ten oxen; they will break up the land for prices running between $1.75 and $2.00 per acre. As soon as the land has been broken, you can already sow corn on it, but the next year this broken up land needs to be plowed again, which can be done using two oxen or horses. So, dear Father, to do everything right, and in such a way that the expenses are proportionate to the money I have at my disposal is very difficult.

This afternoon, or in the morning, I plan to visit [Cornelius Den] Hartog to consult with him about several matters. Dear Father, I advise you and I. Overkamp, if possible, to collect all the money, mortgages, etc., and to send it all to Pella. Not only is the money very safe here, but it will draw at least 6 percent, and if you become a shareholder in a mill then there is no limit to the percentages [you can earn] or else just buy lots in the city, for presently everything will increase in price and you can gain as much as 50 percent. Until now no school has been built, and so I am not employed. All this is very costly, although it is very useful that I am here to keep an eye on everything, for if I had not been here, the land would not have been cultivated, and Van Meveren would not have come to the colony.

G. H. Overkamp requests that from the money you have received from him, you take along and pay for the freight on the following goods. [Place the order with] [P.] Polvliet and Sons, located in Rotterdam and widely known there: 6 flat brushes marked E; 6 long-handled scrubbing brushes KB; 6 dozen paint brushes, numbers 1 through 8; 2 fine badger hair brushes; 2 chamois; the finest black fabric for two jackets, 12 steel forks and 12 tin spoons, and ½ box Haarlem Oil. All of these are expensive here, you can count on that. Be sure to have Mother bring plenty of worsteds: these, as well as cloth and duffel, are two to three times as expensive as in Holland. Also bring garden seeds; I bought fifteen newly grafted apple trees because you don't find them here; for ten American cents each. Dictionaries and four-part vocal music books are not available here, and I do want to have them.

In the hope that we will be meeting each other in Pella in good health, I remain your obedient son,

H. Hospers

P.S. Especially greet Uncle [Hendrik] Van Est for me, as well as my grandparents, sisters, and Uncle De Gelder. I often think of dear Eva and Willem Hendrik. I cannot form a mental image of Pieter Hendrik.

Copy

Pella, 5 November 1847
The Rev. H. P. S[cholte] at St. Louis

Reverend Sir!

Having learned from [Hendrik] Barendregt that the family of P[ieter] Van M[everen], which is still living in St. Louis, is very eager to come to the Pella colony, because he will not be able to find enough work to provide for the necessities of daily living during the coming winter, I have looked into ways of providing housing and employment for them after the family will have arrived here. I have already managed to find a place where they can live in with someone else; that is, until such time as they have erected a house or cabin for themselves, and they will have employment right from the start. Thus, it is not only highly desirable but also highly urgent that this family come over here so that during the coming winter they could start making fences to enclose the land of my father and grandfather.

So I have provided for all their needs after the family is here in the colony, but not yet for the financial means to enable them to get to Pella, and for the simple reason that I do not have the money. It is therefore in name of my father and grandfather that I request whether Your Reverence might be willing to advance these monies until such time as I have received the money that is left from the prepaid travel costs for the above-mentioned family and myself. In the event this could be done, my further request to Your Reverence is that you notify P. Van M[everen] to this effect, so that he might be able to start the journey before the most severe winter cold.

Respectfully Yours, and with Reverence, Your Servant,

H. Hospers

Hospers 15*

Pella, Iowa 20 November 1847

Dear Parents!
   I write specially about the expenses of my journey in consultation with I. Overkamp. You know about the sea journey better than I do. The journey from Boston, New York, or Baltimore is tiresome and damaging for freight because of reloading. It is better and cheaper via New Orleans. In New Orleans a steamboat can be engaged which goes up the Mississippi to Keokuk. Rates $4.50 the person and $0.25 per 100 pounds of freight. The riverboat takes the freight right from the ocean liner and unloads at Keokuk. From Baltimore and other places east there are six of these reloadings and we know by experience how much damage was incurred. The river trip lasts 21 days and passengers must see to their own meals. However, quite a bit is left from the sea journey to help out. It is important to take along for the sea journey a large quantity of peas and beans. I hope to meet you in Keokuk with our own wagon, else we must hire one. This will bring both goods and persons to Pella at the rate of $0.75 per 100 pounds (the rate also applies to the passengers). Van Meveren has arrived. No house yet on our land for lack of money. We plan to build a log cabin from trees in the neighborhood on land not belonging to anybody, and we will buy a load of planks at ƒ10.
   Last Sunday the election took place for elders of the church. H.P. Scholte and H. Barendrecht [Barendregt] were elected. Election of deacons later.
   My sisters must not think that they will get ƒ36 for sewing a coat, Naatje Overkamp gets only ƒ2.50. This is the usual charge. Other sewing work commands more. This evening we eat baked fish for the first time.
   Giving this letter to I. Overkamp to be read, he makes the remark that the cost per person from Keokuk to Pella is only $0.75 per 100 pounds, if the persons take their seats on top of the freight. But inside of a carriage it will be easily $2 per person.
   Overkamp asks whether father will be so good as to buy for him a good watch. Your obedient son,

                                                 H. Hospers

Note: That watch was stolen out of the box in New York when it had arrived there some weeks after this.

Hospers 16 [Hospers 8]

Pella, 30 November 1847

My Dear Parents!

Since I sent you my letter of November 20 [written September 17], I have constantly been in good health. It is now Friday evening, about seven-thirty. Everyone that comes in remarks about the cold and crawls close to the stove, which is stoked in such a manner that the Dutch concern about thriftiness in wood [use] need not be observed. Between the words "comes in" and "remarks" I was interrupted by I. Overkamp, who wanted to hear my English recitation and to correct my written themes.

In order to get at the real purpose of this letter, I must give you some information about what Father asked me in all confidence in the Netherlands, namely, whether Father could find a way of making a living in Pella, and if so, when that could begin, and taking into account Father's present circumstances in the Netherlands, for example, a good income, etc. [That is] a very important point, one about which I have thought a great deal; I have also spoken to I. Overkamp about this on occasion. As far as income from the land is concerned, this will not be sufficient to constitute an income in the first two years, if we use no more for cultivating than we are doing presently. But it can bring a good return if we utilize the services of Van Meveren. Both I. Overkamp and I advise Father not to live on the land, nor to engage in farming, but to settle Van Meveren on the land. Father can be very good and very useful in administrative matters.

Because I am not well informed about Father's financial resources, I cannot rightly say what Father is capable of undertaking. There are many kinds of undertakings; for example, the building of a gristmill, or a saw mill run by steam or water power; running a grocery store; or by having a share in one of these and administering it. Above all, I advise Father to buy a lot in the city, for that is good for any kind of enterprise. According to the calculations of Barendregt, a capable carpenter, the cost of constructing a wind-powered gristmill in Pella, with all the necessary appurtenances, would be seven thousand guilders. In the judgment of an able miller, the site and the plentiful winds are most favorable. And because there are few gristmills in the area (the nearest is twenty miles from Pella), such a mill would yield a return of 25 percent. If you could not do this all by yourself, you could take a share in it, as well as in a sawmill and a grocery and still have a good living. In addition to these, there are many more enterprises, so that a person coming to Pella with three, four, or five thousand guilders at his disposal, and who dares to venture something, can become a financier rather than a breadwinner.

As far as teaching is concerned, I cannot write about that as yet, except to say that in the first year there will be no need for a second teacher. But when that should be the case, I have heard I. Overkamp express the wish: "I only wish that Hospers were here then."

Beloved parents! It is difficult for me to tell you straight from the shoulder. Just come over and you will be able to make a living doing something or other for too much depends on that. From the above you can pretty much make your own decision; and if you calculate that you will have only two thousand guilders available to you in Pella, then my judgment still is, do come. But just do not calculate your travel costs too low; they are always more than you anticipate. Also take into consideration that living is very cheap here. And beyond all that, I. Overkamp assures me that there will be plenty of work for Father. As far as I am concerned, in addition to my regular work, I do some surveying; it pays at least two dollars a day, and there is lots of work here. English—and anything else I wish to study—I can learn for nothing with I. Overkamp. In this good man I have found an outstanding leader. Especially greet Great Uncle for me, and Uncle [Hendrik] Van Est, Uncle Teunis and Betje-moeij [a term of endearment for Aunt Betje de Gelder], grandparents, and uncles. The first chance I get I will write you again, and mainly about the land situation.

In wishing you continuing good health, I am,
    Your Obedient Son,

                                        H. Hospers

Hospers 17*

                            Hoogblokland, 23 December 1847

Questions by J. Hospers:
   1. Of what are the present houses in Pella built?
   2. Made by whom? By members of the Association or by others?
   3. How many house were there when the first emigrants came?

4. In how much time were they erected?
5. Is there any gravelling or paving on the streets? If not, they must be muddy in wet weather?
6. How about the main highway between Keokuk and Pella? Of logs?
7. Any more townships near the colony and of the same quality for sale?
8. What is the difference in price of cultivated and prairie land?
9. What difference in value of coal land and the other?
10. How much land still available for new lots in Pella?
11. What expenses are met from the proceeds of 64 lots sold?
12. Where are church, school, and city hall built? On the public plain or square?
13. Did you take up surveying for pleasure, or for gain? How much?
14. Does the government give deeds of ownership? Who has ours?
15. How did you earn the money for the thirty guilders for your gun?
16. Who has enjoyed the produce of our 12 acres of corn?
17. What did this letter cost you? How much for what you send?
18. Cost of transportation at present of an adult from Holland to Pella?
19. How does your account with G.H. Overkamp stand? I had not thought of it that board would have to be paid. If you must pay board, it is surely proper that you should get something for teaching school?
20. Where do you live? In the log cabin that you rented for Van Meveren? Or with Mr. Overkamp? Make clear to us your manner of life.
21. Who are my neighbors north and west of my land? Those west of Father Middelkoop's?
22. In what direction from our land is the city of Pella located?
23. What kind of trees to be found in our woods? How tall? How thick? About how far from each other?
24. How are your clothes? Your mother is interested in this.

Please answer the questions above.

At Noordeloos the church of Vander Aa has called Rev. Koopmans of Heerenveen. Examined in Dordrecht he failed in his examination for languages and was dropped. Heyboer has heard him and says: "He is not Betten." If you write again, don't mention our coming: there is so much enmity. Take good care of your money.

Lovingly,

Your Father

Hospers 18*

Hoogblokland 1 January 1848

Dear Son!
   How much disturbance with all that wishing of a happy New Year! The doorbell rings all the time, to be opened for polite beggars. Maaike is on duty here to do the giving and Keetje does this at Uncle H. Van Est. Whoever of your brothers and sisters goes to wish him a happy new year gets a guilder. Teunis de Gelder went to his uncles and aunt and got an envelope with eight guilders, one for each of his brothers and sisters, therefore one for Hendrik too.

Here follow pages about the absence of a promised letter from Hendrik, which must decide a good deal about the time of going to America. They wait for one mail after the next one with growing anxiety. Grandma says: "I cannot stand it any longer." Grandpa says: "Would we were as intent upon the Word of God as for that letter." Uncle Van Est, wealthy and sick, and from whom Grandpa is to inherit, declares that going to America will put off the inheritance. Grandpa says this will not make any difference. A letter sent from Pella Nov. 17 was received in Jan (Gerrit Hendrik Hospers).

Hospers 19*

<u>Confidential</u>

Hoogblokland, 19 January 1848

Dear Son!
   The stove is burning brightly. It is cold and sharp. Confidential letters are necessary for both of us. We live in the midst of enemies of Pella; your relatives have too much love of Holland. So I write this separate letter so that you may be acquainted with our financial situation, whether we are able or not to come to Pella.
   Last year I have spent altogether $f1500$ for Pella. To that end I made a loan of $f1000$ at E. Aanen; the rest are in notes called in. And now I have again called in for payment two mortgages, each $f300$, and three small obligations ($f230$): a total of $f830$. I still have another lot which totals $f3050$. Subtracting the $f1000$ with Aanen, I am $f2050$ in my favor, if it all comes in. If now I should leave Holland without a legacy, things will not be bright for us, for we will need that $f2000$ for travel, clothes, and

of what must we live then in Pella, we a family of nine persons? Is there any way in which I can earn something in Pella? Will our land produce enough? Remember that expenses are connected with farming and dairying. You would not like to see your parents and your brothers and sisters suffer want, nor may we tempt the Lord. And still my desire is that the Lord will pave the way for us to come next spring. When we come, Baker Heymans wants to come along with us, and he has no money. I have a mortgage on his house for *f*700, but Uncle [Hendrik] Van Est has advanced that money and is to have the interest of it as long as he lives. How will Uncle feel about Heymans going along under these circumstances? I do not feel free to deprive him of these resources, nor of the land which is in my name and of which Uncle must have the interest. I would have to leave all this behind. Uncle gave back to me *f*100 that I had paid him. He had first given me *f*50 because I had respectfully reminded him that I had thus paid over to him *f*2000, and he said he would then give me *f*50. But visiting me the next evening he said he had thought it over and that he would also give me the other *f*50. He thought he would not live much longer. At night he often has spells of oppressed breathing. He speaks of you with respect. Klaas goes there now and then, who has been promised a gold watch on his birthday, May 4.

Now you know our circumstances. I write this because you formerly put us too high. We have a reputation here of being rich. Yes, in a way. The Lord has given us a good income— *f*1300 or *f*1400 and some money on interest. But we also have to pay interest. But now some is in Pella and that brings us nothing. Write what you and your trusted friends would think about our coming without inheritance. I do not see my way very clear: still I want to be in Pella. May the Lord prepare the way!!

With love, Your Father,

J. Hospers

Hospers 20 [Hospers 9]

Pella, 10 February 1848

Dearest Parents,

I had already sealed a short letter [to you] to enclose it in a letter I had written for Overkamp's hired man. And during breakfast today I had already handed it to I. Overkamp, the postmaster, who was to post it with the departing postmail this evening. As we were reading the Bible (in Isaiah 13) after breakfast, D[irk] Den Hartog came in with a letter from Father to G. H. Overkamp (dated November 25, '47, received February 8, '48).

With joy I learned of the good health of my family and was interested to learn of your condition as well. We are longing eagerly for your arrival. On the 1st of February v.d. Linden received a letter from Vuren in which he said that Grandfather was traveling this coming spring! G. H. Overkamp thanks you very much for collecting the small outstanding bills; he asks that you bring the money with you when you come. When you deliver the invoice from Duyzen Van Almkerk to Jan Van Dooijen in Heukeldam (he is co-guardian), he will pay it. I am still happy and content. The school is not yet finished; I work as a surveyor. There is a rumor that a ship with Dutch emigrants has arrived in New Orleans. My guess is that B. Keppel will be among them. The matters pertaining to the cultivation of [the] land are still the same as when I wrote you about them. After that letter of June [18]47, I sent five letters by mail and enclosed four others. I am very eager to get a response to my last letter. Postage costs me very little: twenty cents for a letter from the Netherlands, ten American cents to send one. Shortly I shall write you in greater detail, that is why I am writing so little now; I would be writing more, but it is already enclosed!!! Greetings from I. Ov[erkamp] and family, do the same from me to Uncle Van Est, Grandfather and the family.

Wishing you continued good health and contentment, I am,
Your Loving Son,

H. Hospers

Hospers 21 [Hospers 10]

Pella, 10 Febr. 1848

Dearest Mother,

I am still very healthy, contented, and satisfied with my lot. Everyone who sees me and knew me before says, "That Hospers is sure getting big and fat; how he has grown." People who know Father say how much I look like him. When I was at Jan Rietveld's recently on an errand, and while I was shopping, he said to me: "It's just as though I am seeing your father now, with the same personal features, and my, what a beard you are already getting!!!" I am now already eighteen, and if I were in Holland, I could be registering for the military conscription lottery, taking my physicals. Now I am free of all that. Now I can breathe freely and anticipate a very good future according to the flesh. My dearest Mother! I think of you often and share in your circumstances, namely, living with such oppressive burdens, hostility, and that within a community that has seceded from the people of God. Alas! If only you were here, Mother, I sometimes think. But when I consider your ties with Uncle, and the inheritances you still have coming, then I think that it is better for my parents to defer [coming] a while longer, so that they can then live more comfortably with that money in Pella.

As far as my clothes are concerned, I have outgrown most of them except my underwear. The thick underpants and shirt really stood my old frame in good stead this winter. I can no longer wear my blue rain jacket and the two trousers with pockets; I probably should save those for my brothers. Perhaps you are saying: he does not think they are nice enough, but really, that is not the reason, because it is American fashion "to wear your elbows through your sleeves." My black cloth jacket now looks good on me.

Mrs. Overkamp takes good care of me; she is just like a mother to me. This evening we were treated to waffles because it is Overkamp's birthday. I wish that I could have sent you one of those. Now, dear Mother, I will be writing you soon again, and then I will again include a short note. May God so direct your ways that you come here soon; that is the wish of your obedient son,

H. Hospers

Written through the above:
"Dear Father, this is a homey letter, I sent the same thing to Uncle! The note to Van Deventer is on its way. In a month I will again write a businesslike letter. As a matter of principle, I would very much like to have a remembrance of Uncle [Hendrik] Van Est. And now, dear Father! Believe me that I am and always hope to be your obedient son,

H. Hospers

Accounting of receipts and expenses by H. Hospers.
Receipts:

May 13 Received in loan from G. H. Overkamp	fl.4.00
June 15 Received in loan from G. H. Overkamp	fl.4.00
July 10 Received in loan from G. H. Overkamp (see "a")	fl.4.00
Dec. 12 Received from Rev. Scholte for surveying (a.1)	<u>fl.15.00</u>
	Total fl.27.00

On August 15, 1847, received in loan from C. den Hartog, the sum of two hundred Dutch guilders (fl. 200). The combined receipts therefore are fl. 107.

Expenditures

May 10	Boots resoled	fl. .60
	slippers (b)	fl. .50
May 12	St. Louis, lid for the trunk (c)	fl. 1.00
May 15	black pants patched	fl. .30
May 22	straw hat (d)	fl. .90
May	twelve pens and a bottle of ink	fl. .25
July	postage for letter to Netherlands	fl. .20
	4 weeks school tuition @ 0.25 (e)	fl. 1.00
July 27	B. Verheij 2 hinges [for the trunk]	fl. .20
	10 Sundays for church poor	fl. .30
July 30	Suspenders	fl. .15
	2 haircuts	fl. .15
	crotch of pants	fl. .30
	personal luggage steamboat	fl. 2.00
	chest and trunk	fl. .50
	freight wagon (personal) (Keokuk 1 guilder)	fl. 2.00
	trunk costs	fl. 1.75
	lodging Keokuk	fl. .50
	advance G.H.Overkamp, travel Keokuk to Pella	fl. 1.87½
Sept. 2	1 pair of boots (f)	fl. 2.00
	as per receipt H[ospers]: 1 [passage]	fl. 16.62½
	as per receipt H[ospers]: 2 board and room	fl. 16.00
Sept. 16	gun and powder horn (g)	fl. 12.50
	delivery my chests to home of G.H. Overkamp	fl. .50
Sept. 20	100 cigars	fl. .40
Dec. 2	2 colored shirts	fl. 2.10
	2 axes	fl. 2.50
	2 handles G. Verheij	fl. .30
	small chisel 20 cents, bit 10 cents (h)	fl. .30

Jan. 1	Comb	fl. .15
	writing paper	fl. .15
	Sunday collections	fl. .30
Jan. 12	postage for letter, second mate (i)	fl. .25
	mending working pants	fl. .25
Jan. 20	winter coat (j)	fl. 10.00
	Total	fl. 79.20

Recapitulation

Receipts	fl. 107.00
Expenditures fl. 79.20 church fl. 4.00	fl. 83.20
Favorable balance	fl. 23.80

Based on the true facts, January 31, 1848

signed: H. Hospers

At St. Louis I found that many of my clothes were too small because I had really grown on shipboard. I did not have any money and so Overkamp was so kind to lend me the money; the last four dollars were to defray my travel expenses. While on shipboard in Rotterdam, I had to lodge and eat at an inn the first two nights: that cost me fl. 2.50. I then had fl. 7.50 left: I exchanged a half guinea for fl. 6.00, and with the rest of my Dutch money I bought one pair of wooden shoes, cigars, and spent the remaining fifty cents on food consumption with L. Bouw. I will give an accounting of the remaining fl. 6.00 in my first letter.

I received this fl. 15 on account, and now I still have fl. 25 coming in dollars. I shall apply this as a payment on the lot. (So you see, that when there is work, you can make money.)

a. Because of the sea water all the cloth had come off my slippers.

b. On the last shipment, from the steamer to Overkamp's house, the lid [of my trunk] was broken into several pieces because of rough handling by the Americans, and in order to make the journey from St. Louis to Pella, I had to have it repaired.

c. Everyone had a straw hat but me (I would certainly earn it back).

d. On this item Munting misled me: Overkamp advised me to learn English and thought that he would do it for nothing for me, but at the end of four weeks he asked me for money, because, as he said, he was so short of money. If I had known, I would not have done so.

e. On the trip from St. Louis to Pella a box filled principally with shoes was missing. My boots were in it too. I had the chance to buy a new pair of boots from a Hollander; I did so because a pair of

American boots costs $4.00.
f. I will recover the cost of the gun by the money that I earn with surveying.
g. At the meeting held in St. Louis, about which I wrote you my observations, Rev. Scholte advised us to take along axes and tools, for as he said, "In Pella the word will be: 'help yourselves!'" Because Van Mev[eren] did not have an axe, and it is a necessity, I decided to buy them.
h. I enjoyed great friendship with these helmsmen: they even wrote me a letter from England requesting that I let them know sometime how I was doing; and that I have done.
i. I did not own a winter coat, and because I am earning quite a lot of money I bought one. By all means do not forget to bring duffel [cloth] with you. See behind.

Because the letter would have gotten too heavy, I did not make copies of receipts; when you get here in Pella, you can see them for yourself.

After January 30, 1848, I had the following expenses:

Feb 6	a pants	fl. 2.10
	leather patches for surveying	fl. 1.00
Feb. 9	1 window made for Van M[everen]	fl. 1.25
	2 days, 1 night as per Amst[erdam].	fl. 1.00
	2 chest deliveries	fl. 0.50
	4 deliveries firewood	fl. 1.00
	Total	fl. 6.85
	Recapitulation	
Jan. 30	Positive Balance	fl. 23.80
Feb. 9	Expenditures	fl. 6.85
	Favorable Balance	fl. 16.95

J. Hospers

Hospers 22 [Hospers 12]

Hoogblokland, 21 February 1848

Dear Son!

We are all in good health. Pieter Hendrik, who, as I wrote in my last letter, was ill, has also recovered again. All is well with Grandfather and your great uncles De Gelder. In April, when you receive this letter, the

De Gelders will be having an estate sale. They have between forty and fifty head of horses and cattle that will be sold then. It's amazing how expensive cattle are, especially young heifers. They go for as high as ƒ200, and one was recently sold hereabouts for ƒ240 (horse prices, really). These high prices are the result of exports to England and France. The governor of Zeeland [Province] has already sent a circular to the ruling bodies of the Zeeland cities alerting them to the diminution in the cattle population.

In response to your letter I sent a box with the following items and rennet of the very best quality. The firm advised me to have a box of firewood made, keep the rennet (calves stomachs) dry and in the dark and when received hang it in the chimney to keep it dry. Father [Klaas] Middelkoop packed it. I did this with pleasure because I think it is an important contribution to the cheesemakers of Pella. Surely Americans will be jealous of the delicious cheese which these Pella farmer's wives will make. Pella will become more and more famous for there will be a great demand for the cheese of Pella.

What follows relates to your communication:

A. for Mr. G. H. Overkamp:
1. The requested brushes from Messrs. P. Polvliet & Sons in Rotterdam
2. The silk and woolen goods, from Utrecht
3. A dozen bottles of Haarlem oil
4. A dozen tin spoons
5. A dozen steel forks

B. for Mr. P. Welle (my neighbor)
  A dozen bottles of Haarlem oil

C. for Mr. I. Overkamp
1. A basket of Gouda [white clay] pipes (when my chest is being packed I want to be able to lay them [the pipes] on the rennet).
2. A pocket watch that really pleases me. It costs fl. 16.00, but the watchmaker considers it an especially good one. It took him a lot of time to set it. It has golden hands.

D. for Hendrik Hospers
1. A copy of *Algebraisch Rekenboek (Algebraic Arithmetic)* by Heinkes, vol.2
2. A copy of *Beginselen der Meetkunst (Principles of Geometry)* by J.Prooslij, vol.2
3. An *Engelsche Dictionnaire* by H. Picard, my friend and teacher in the English language
4. Seven ells of cloth for an everyday coat
5. A pair of stockings, knitted by your sister Cornelia Geertrui

6. A pair of black mittens, a gift from your sisters Maaike and Keetje
7. A purse, a gift from Nicolaas and T[eunis] de Gelder Hospers, and made by Keetje
8. The gold coins that go with it, Keppel had already taken along in November 1847

I am worried about this shipment. I could think of nothing better than to enlarge the box for the rennet, which had to be 0.65 ell long [0.65 x 91.4 cm = 59.2 cm.], sufficiently so that a compartment could be added for all the orders. Quite likely an unpleasant odor from the rennet will have penetrated the box by the time it gets to you; but the Pella air will doubtless clear it all up again. Do write me as soon as possible, all of you, whether I have done a good job in carrying out my commissions. It caused me a good deal of anxiety and it took some doing to work it all out here in Hoogblokland. First, I assembled all the items in my house, and then I had a chest made that would hold all the goods. Beforehand, I consulted with Wambersie & Crooswijk [Rotterdam shipping agents] about shipping matters, and now I intend, the Lord willing, to take the chest personally to the shipping agents in Rotterdam on Saturday the 26th.

I made an agreement with [Hendrik] Dingemans: you and H. Dingemans should write a letter every month and enclose another, the one month Dingemans with a letter from Hospers enclosed to Dingemans in Gameren, the next month Hospers, with a letter from Dingemans to me enclosed. Do give my greetings to Van Bergeyk, Betten, and C. Den Hartog. For some time I have been looking for a notice from you [authorizing me] to pay several hundred guilders to Mrs. Van Deventer. Mother has just come back from Uncle Van Est's, and she is bringing me a meal of peas in order to make pea soup tomorrow. But inasmuch as there are so many empty spaces between the brushes [in the chest] and these peas are of such high quality, we are going to distribute or drop the peas in the empty spaces. Will you then ask the Rev. Scholte if he will let you take them [the peas] out in order to plant them in my land; and if it then please the Lord to bless them, I shall find some good peas when I come. My time is up. I have to draw up a marriage certificate for a wedding in Hoornaar tomorrow. My Son! Always keep the Lord before you, whatever happens, and live and act as one beholding the Invisible One.

You will find plenty of letters, perhaps more than you will find time to read in one sitting. What kind of work do you do? What do you do to earn money? How much [do you earn]?

Greetings from Uncle Van Est, Grandfather, Grandmother, uncles and aunts, Great Uncles De Gelder and Great Aunt Betje. The Lord be your guide, trust in him, and do the good. What indeed is the world and all it contains without the Lord? Nothing.

Your loving Father,

J. Hospers

Hospers 23*

Hoogblokland, 24 Feb. 1848

My worthy son!

I wrote this morning to my friend P[ieter] M. vander Ley the following letter:

Dear Friend,

I have had a visit from [Hendrik] Dingemans on Tuesday. I shall take care of your letter to your brother [Jan] Meyer in Pella. I received many such letters nowadays. I am full of business with Pella affairs, and intend to go Saturday in the morning early with the chest to Rotterdam, by steamboat, and my brother also. Pray, give this letter to our master [H.] Picard, if you go to school Saturday. I salute you and your wife and sister. If you have been to school Saturday, give me a declaration of our next lesson.

Your friend,

J. Hospers

Have you much more to learn than I, my worthy son?

Hospers 24*

Hoogblokland, 25 Feb. 1848

To Rev. H.P. Scholte,

From the instant I read your request of November 23, 1847, I have done my best to handle the matter of the rennet, really calf stomachs, with utmost care. The rennet is first-grade quality from thirteen hundred choice calves, each one carefully selected. My preoccupation with this matter gave me much satisfaction, because I consider it a matter of the utmost importance to the cheese farmers of Pella. I am sure that the Americans will be jealous of the delicious cheese the Pella farmers and their wives will be making. That is another reason for Pella to become increasingly renowned, because people will be asking for Pella cheese. (Ship by steamer.)

I have to look after another small company of immigrants. I realize now how busy you were last year with four shiploads. I am busy and I must be careful to do my work well because there are enemies around to report otherwise.

P.S. In the spaces between the [various] brushes you will find some peas; please leave them for my Hendrik, to plant on my land; then I will find a good brand of peas when I arrive.

J. Hospers

Hospers 25 [Hospers 11]

Pella, March 1848

[Hendrik Hospers answers questions of father Jan Hospers in his letter of 23 December 1847.]

1. Of what building materials are houses in Pella presently constructed?

When we arrived in Pella there was an immediate need for homes. So everyone began building a shelter on land relinquished by Rev. Scholte for that purpose in order to be protected against the elements, however minimally. These houses consisted of sods of grass piled on top of each other, and were covered with grass because no reed [for thatching] grows here. About twenty-five houses were built in this manner about ten minutes (one-half mile: they reckon the distance between two or more places in miles here, not in hours) from the site where the city of Pella has now been laid out. Because most of the houses in this arrival area are put together of hay and straw, it is commonly referred to as "Strawtown." Those who could afford to buy a farm moved there and lived in log houses. After the city lots had been platted and sold, most people built on one of those, some of logs, some of wooden planks, and still others of straw and sods.

2. By whom were they built, by members of the [Emigrant] Society or others?

Some, in fact all, the log cabins were built by Americans, because the Hollanders do not know how; all the other houses were built by Hollanders except for Rev. Scholte's frame house on which Americans worked for about ten weeks.

3. How many houses were standing when the first contingent of colonists arrived?

(About) twenty-six farms, or log cabins, and two or three wooden or plank sheds.

4. How long did it take to build them?

The log cabins were already there; eight to ten men can erect a log cabin in one day; the [large] sheds were finished in four days.

5. Are the streets surfaced at all or sanded? If not, then they certainly must be very muddy in wet weather.

They are neither surfaced nor sanded; [they are] clay roads.

6. What is the main road that runs from Keokuk to Pella? Could it be of tree trunks?

They are clay roads, but not built with tree trunks [known as a corduroy road].

7. Are there townships near the colony, with similar soil, that are still for sale?

Yes, if the claims of Americans living in adjoining townships are bought out. However, if this is not done, there are only some sections available, since there are no townships in the vicinity of our colony without Americans residing in them. In the vicinity of the Pella colony, townships usually have similar soil, although there may be a few quarter sections in which there are coal mines that constitute a kind of exception.

8. What is the price differential between developed and undeveloped lands?

The difference in price depends on the cost of buying out improved lands; but when Rev. Scholte will have given an accounting, which is expected soon, I shall be in a better position to answer this question.

9. Is the land on which there are coal mines on them worth more or

less than the rest?

Whenever one buys land [from the government] containing coal mines—or even if they were gold and silver mines—the price, without any exception at all, is still 1¼ dollars. But once an individual has purchased these lands, he can charge any price he chooses. For example, there is a coal mine near our colony for which the owner is asking $2,000. Remember that the land on which you find coal mines is usually rocky, the surface is mountainous, and as a rule these mountains are very steep on one side.

10. How much land is still available around the city of Pella for platting purposes?

The southern half of sec. 3 and the northern half of section 10, together constituting a section of land, has been set aside for the city, and on the map which I enclosed in my previous lettter, you can tell in which direction the level land of the city is located.

11. What expenditures must be defrayed from income from the sale of sixty-four lots?

The 640 acres set aside for the town must still be paid to the state. The 640 acres include two corn fields, which were bought out at a high price by Rev. Scholte, and what other costs will have to be defrayed I do not know. I note that in your question you refer to a fixed number of sixty-four lots, but from my last calculation you can tell how many lots had [actually] been sold as of March 1, 1848.

12. Where will the church, the school, and city hall be built? On the public square or on the opposite side?

From my sketch you can tell that three lots have been set aside for the church and school. Nothing has been side about a city hall so far. The public square is set aside for the market.

13. Was it a hobby of yours that got you involved with surveying? Did you earn any money doing it? If so, by what criteria?

It certainly was not a hobby, for especially in America it is a very exhausting work. At the time I did not have anything to do, and I was bored. I also did it anticipating that in time there might well be need for a surveyor, and for me to learn surveying, the handling of a compass, the different kinds of trees, etc. (and the result is that no one in the colony knows the two townships better than I). I did earn money doing this: I worked about 1½ months, but I do not know how much it will be per day, I guess 75 American cents, which is almost fl.2.00.

14. Has the government supplied any deeds [to the property]? If so, who has ours?

Not as yet, but I hear that it will be happening in the near future.

15. How did you earn the thirty guilders for your gun?

By surveying.

16. Who received the produce of our approximately twelve acres of corn?

It was plowed but not seeded.

17. How much did this letter [from Holland] cost you and how much must you pay when you send a letter?

Your letter cost me ten American cents, and every letter [I send] costs me ten American cents when it is not overweight.

18. What do they now calculate the cost to be for food and transportion for an adult from the Netherlands to Pella?

That depends on the route one takes. It cost G. H. Overkamp and his family fl. 1500.00, but that is too much. You can do it much cheaper by coming via New Orleans.

19. How is your account with G. H. Overkamp? etc.

We have not yet calculated the cost of my weekly board and room; according to my receipts, I have paid off $32.00 [on my indebtedness].

20. How do you find living in a log cabin? etc.

I shall answer this question and have already answered it in part in one of my letters.

21. Who are my neighbors on the north and on the west, and of Father Middelkoop's land on the west side?

There are no next-door neighbors on these sides, because this land has not yet been sold and thus it still belongs to the state (the state is called Uncle Sam).

22. What is the direction of Pella from our land?

See the sketch I sent you of Township 76.

23. What kinds of trees are there in our forest? How tall and how

thick? How near to each other?
(See my enclosed letter).
24. What is the condition of your clothing? Partially answered.
25. How is the morale of the people in Pella?
To put it bluntly: in general there tends to be a feeling of dissatisfaction, which stems for the most part from people having to pay higher prices per acre than they had expected. It is all the more so, because (so far) there has been no accounting, and the result is that people have the impression that Rev. Scholte cannot render an accounting, that he is short [of funds]. But this conception is wrong, and that will be abundantly clear once the accounting is made.

Give my warm greetings to Uncle [Hendrik] Van Est, Grandfather [Middelkoop] , [Uncle] Gerrit [Middelkoop], Willem [Hospers], Aunt Sijgje-moei [Sijgje Middelkoop], Uncle and Aunt De Gelder, Roeland, Rev. Van Dam, Van den Berg, Donkersloot, Keetje [Hospers], and Herman. They should write me once too. Jan Vink should be here, he could really get ahead here, since he probably is [only] a day laborer in Holland now. When you come, my advice is: do not take along a married farm hand, but take a milkmaid and a farm hand [that is, two farm hands]. Greetings to E. Aanen and I. Hoefkens.

Naatje Overkamp and Jan Welle's daughter (Maaike), although unknown [to you], send greetings to my sisters.

Hendrik Hospers

Hospers 26*

Pella, 19 March 1848

Dear Sister!*
Although I am far away from you, I am thinking about your birthday and wish you every conceivable blessing according to body

---

*This sister, Maaike, died en route to Pella on June 6, 1849, and was buried at sea.

and soul. That we may celebrate it together in Pella next year, that is the sincere wish of your loving brother,

H. Hospers

Hospers 27 [Hospers 13]

Pella, 22 March 1848

Dear Mother,
I am still in very good health and very content with my situation. Although at times I do wish that I were with you, when I think of the ordinary activities which take place in my parental home at certain times. For example, the morning of your birthday, I imagined myself being present for breakfast and seeing each of my brothers and sisters making their wishes and giving their presents. About the same time I was busy working alone in rainy, raw weather, in Section 9 of an endless forest, with a $14 compass on my back, marking off several lines a mile long, which we had surveyed the week before. In the evening I imagined to myself the entire family circle, with my dear father at the head of the table, and saw you all enjoying a delicious glass of currant wine and probably some pastry, and all the while I myself was at Rev. Scholte's that evening. He requested that I make a map for him like the one I made for Father in order to include it in a publication that he is preparing.

Dearest Mother! The Overkamps take very good care of me; the Mrs. treats me like one of her own children. I sleep with Mr. I. Overkamp; it is warm and comfortable. Every Sunday evening we have raisin bread with milk. When I am back home (when I am surveying I am gone for weeks at a time) and get up in the morning, I first wash up, have a couple of cups of coffee with sugar, half an hour later have breakfast, and then I go about my ordinary activities.

Dearest Mother, I could only wish that you were already here in Pella (later I will write in greater detail about that). In the first place you can have free sugar from our sugar (maple) trees. Some Hollanders, like the [Cornelius] Vanden Bergs, who were in the know about this, have tapped pails full [of sap] and made very tasty sugar. When we found such a tree while surveying, we made a little hole in it and drank directly from it. The eldest daughter of [Dirk] Den Otter is still healthy and well; she is sixteen years old, and she is already married to a widower from Zeeland [Province] who had much money and four children. They are all enjoying good health.

I visit the [Pieter] Welle family rather frequently; they are very friendly and long for you to come over. He has very nice daughters, dearest Mother! I wish you good health and happiness in soul and body, and may the Lord so direct your ways that without tempting the Lord, you may speedily arrive in Pella. That is the wish of your dear son,

H. Hospers

Hospers 28 [Hospers14]

Pella, 22 March 1848

Dearest Father,

Rev. Scholte has published a book with Hoogkamer & Company, with two maps, one of the State of Iowa and the other of Township 76-77 [these two townships were combined to form Lake Prairie township]. The maps are my work: I copied a large map of Iowa, reproducing it on a smaller scale. It is the most accurate [map] in the entire United States. The map of Township 76-77 was also done by me.

By the time you get this letter, the booklets will very likely have been printed. If you write to Hoogkamer & Co., you should have it soon.

Your obedient son,

H. Hospers

Hospers 29*

Hoogblokland, 1 April 1848

Hendrik!

At the military drawing [lottery], Roeland [son of the Rev. Van Dam of Hoogblokland and Hendrik Hospers's friend] was one of those taken. Jan Vink had the highest number and was free. Roeland got a *"remplasant"* [substitute] for ƒ700—cheap, when we consider the general disorder of Europe these days. The classes of 1845 and 1846 have been called to the colors. Klaas Stam also was called up. We hear of nothing but riot and agitation in all Europe. Although Holland is not free from it, things are reasonably quiet. In Amsterdam a riot occurred in which windows were smashed and stores on its chief business street plundered. A new ministry had to be formed. In this condition of affairs my secretaryship is not pleasant. I had rather be secretary in Pella. See whether you can find something for me there. My work as treasurer is not pleasant either, as the farmers make but little money, 13 or 14 guilders from the hemp....

Today seventeen persons are leaving N[oord] Holland [Province] bound for New York and Pella aboard the *Katharina Jackson*, Captain Stafford commanding. (Van Bergeyk knows the ship.) On June 8, 1848, C. C. Lubbers of Amsterdam writes her nephew H. Hospers: "We have experienced some anxious times, hordes of people came down the canals in our area—smashing windows—my own companion had a fit of nerves, indeed, it frightened many people to death." That is what one housemaid wrote about the revolution of 1848 in Amsterdam.

J. Hospers

Hospers 30*

Hoogblokland, 16 April 1848

Dearly Beloved Son,

It is already a year ago since I saw you pack your things with energy and speed. I am writing this letter in the front room where at that time your boxes stood with goods inside and still outside. In my imagination I now see you walk hither and thither, and I remember what was often told me, "It does not matter so much since in two years we will see each other anyway." But, dear son, I must restrain myself, for my motherly heart felt deeply when you left. Often yet, I cannot express my feelings enough. And now it is my ardent wish and prayer to God that He may grant our wish that we may embrace each other next year in good health. Yes, dear Hendrik, my heart draws to you stronger than to any other of the family and we do not feel free to wait for their property. The Lord might interfere to put off the way to each other. In Europe and here we hear constantly of bankruptcies and great losses; wars and rumors of wars; nations falling out with each other; so that I am in fear and think,

O, that we were in Pella, even with little property.

You refresh me and your father with your letters and cause us to look forward with longing to that time. Our regard for you constantly grows when we notice your progress in everything; and your father lives when he can show your drawings and letters, and everybody says, "Now, Teacher [Meester], your son is smart; and what an interesting style of writing he has!"

I am interrupted now by Van Driel, who comes to talk about his departure. It is Saturday. Father has gone to Rotterdam to investigate everything and direct departing friends. I could not think about writing on Wednesday and Thursday. Those days are the auction of the goods left by Uncle Teunis. No one remembers such a big crowd before. Thursday Maasdam was here. He too likes your letters. Kaatje-moei [Aunt Katie] was here Friday. You will remember she was here last year when you decided to go to America. We talked much about you. She too would like to go but has no means of her own. Her son Willem, then a shoemaker, is now married; Drieka also; if the letters from America are true to fact, they too would like to emigrate.

But, Hendrik, how will things work out when we are there, having only our land and a thousand guilders besides. We have a large family and would not like to be a burden to others. I was so glad that you wrote a letter just to me. Do this again and often. Take good care of our affairs. Next year we hope to speak with you face to face. I am glad you are so well and happy; that you are so fat and look so much like your father, and are getting such a beard. We had to laugh. How anxious I am to see you with your straw hat. I suppose it has a wide rim. Were you so near to Jan Rietveld that you could run an errand there? I can hardly imagine that I have a son who is already 18. To be drafted for military duty is bad, but examinations have their good sides. I gladly believe that you think much of your mother and that she might be with you, and, oh I so much long to care for you again. But, dear Hendrik, I cannot imagine how we shall make our living and whether your father can do anything, and father figures that the traveling expenses will come to 1600 guilders. O that we may only be all together in Pella; I believe that we then will be with the Lord's people.

I am glad that Mrs. Overkamp helps you so much with your wearing apparel. You write about your board money. Does that include mending, sewing, washing? That heavy shirt and pants that did your old body so much good will be going to pieces. I gave along with you a couple of pieces of the same goods for mending. I do hope you will be able to make good money, for in everything you are so dependent upon strangers. Do consult Mrs. Overkamp as a son. I would like to talk with you an hour. I would so gladly have bought you clothes with the money you got as a present from your uncle. But father had so many orders to look after that things got messed up. And he had to advance money for [F.S.] Dikker's traveling expenses. Keppel will have handed over to you the gold ten-guilder piece of Aia-oom [Uncle Arie]. Aunt Betje was sorry that she had not given cheese along for you. Uncle Teunis and Aunt Betje are not becoming more generous. Better enclose a nice little letter for them. You know how to move hearts. No doubt uncle has not understood you about his giving along a remembrance from him, for he right away spoke of giving you, dear Hendrik, two ten-guilder gold pieces. More than four months will elapse before we get an answer on this from you. Write what clothes you need, and what is best to wear there, also for your sisters and for me. We want to take with us all we can.

Yes, dear Hendrik, my writing is very irregular. I have the opportunity to unburden my heart for ten days before this letter will be called for, so I write every day as ideas come into my mind. You left a pair of shoes with the minister; some Blokland dirt still clings to it. Now that you so unhappily lost your boots, these shoes can yet serve you. Willem Hendrik has a daily fever, for two months already. He talks nicely but is not very good. Little Pieter Hendrik sits in a chair next to me. He is the only one of your brothers and sisters you do not know. He is a very nice, dear child. You would be surprised to see how tall your sisters have become. Klaas likes to be a carpenter. Would that be of use to him in America? O, write much and often.

Most affectionately, your loving mother,

       Hendrika Hospers, nee Middelkoop

Hospers 31*

            Hoogblokland, 16 April 1848

Much beloved Brother!
  Eva and I are writing; father in his room is writing to you. Our servant, Miet, is rocking the little Piet to sleep. Since there is no church

here Maaike and Keetje have gone with Gjaje Van Maurik to the Hoornaar church. Just now Van Gelder comes to disturb us by swinging. He came from Uncle Teunis where they all are well but on account of their auction they are much dejected. For, O Hendrik, it is so empty and strange for them, and especially for Aai-oom [Uncle Arie] who was always accustomed to feed. The first evening when they were altogether without animals except two horses and four heifers, I stayed with him in the night; and then they ate rice porridge, and I too. But when Aai-oom [Uncle Arie] got up, he said to Antje van Kekerik, the workwoman, "Now you do not know how strange it is that I cannot feed or water the horses." I can believe that because he was always so accustomed to give the horses such good food. When the auction was held and when Klaas Versluis exercised the horses to see whether they ran right, they were as smooth as a mirror and their hair as nice as I have ever seen it. Aunt Betje and Uncle Teunis are also grieving, and Aai-oom [Uncle Arie] is not free from it. Uncle Teunis could get $f290$ for their youngest horse, but he wants $f400$. O, it is such a nice horse, a gray, that they raised themselves. I do not know of anything more to write. I hope we may soon tell each other the news and desire to remain your loving brother,

N. Hospers

Hospers 32

Hoogblokland, 22 April 1848

Dear Hendrik:

I trust that by now you have received from Rev. Scholte the money for the rennet and other amounts advanced by me to others for travel, a total of $f681.38$. Pay my debt to C. Den Hartog with interest. Take receipts every time, for I might die. You have earned with surveying half a lot in Pella. Earn the other half too so that it can be in your name, for you have quite a number of brothers and sisters.

We still do well in our temporal affairs. I still have my offices and have the full confidence of all. What makes my income less is the money I have sent to Pella. If you think I cannot make my living in Pella or if you have doubts about it, tell me frankly: I do not want to make any false move. We long for Pella, though we may have to live much more simply than here. Very plain, a small house, etc. External things are of this world and do not count for eternity. We desire to ascertain God's will for us from all indications. I have thought: Would the fact of our rather diminished income and our loss of inheritances be Divine indications that we must stay here? On the other hand, this: May I make my going dependent on earthly goods? God is able to give. And Abraham took no thought of earthly means. If you pray in faith, do so for your parents that God my give light. I desire that the Lord may give me strength to submit my sinful will to His Holy will; that I be not worldy, unbelieving, carnal. As things now appear, I will go and have set the time for the spring of 1849. Dear son, save this letter as a proof of and remembrance of us, so that after our death you and your children may know how Pella lay in our hearts. Pray much; walk closely with God who determines all our ways, now and evermore.

Your loving Father,

J. Hospers

Hospers 33 [Hospers 15]

Pella, 26 April 1848

Dear Parents, Brothers and Sisters!

I had already starting writing down the above and was lost in thought on how I might most accurately depict my situation, when suddenly I was disturbed. The place where I was sitting was in the church. It is a building that abundantly attests to the abundance of oak trees. The building is sixty feet long and forty feet wide, and it is entirely of wood. The manner of construction tells the viewer that it is lack of money that prevents its completion. If he enters the church on a Sunday, while the worship service is going on, then, notwithstanding the half finished floor, the rough hewn seats, the crude, clumsy pulpit, the intense attention of the hearers will tell him how much delight they take in the words being addressed to them. And at the same time from all of the above he can learn a lesson, or rather draw a conclusion. It is infinitely better to hear the true exegesis of the Word of God in such a building than to listen to this or that moralizing preacher parading his rhetorical talents in a splendid, beautifully embellished building.

I was just about to write this all down, and was just making a mental sketch of the things to include in my letter when an American walked in. It was George Harrison, a rather tall man, about thirty years of age, and a farmer. [He is] someone who has been and still can be of great assistance to the Hollanders, and accordingly he has won the affection of the Hollanders and is held in high esteem by the Rev. Scholte.

The following dialogue, in English, was also written up in crude English by Henry Hospers:

"Good day, Mr. Hospers! How do you do?"
"I am well, sir, and you. Well come in.
"Mr. Hospers, I have some business for you. I bought about fifty thousand feet lumber and I wish to have measured it; because I cannot make those calculations, you most [must] help me. Do you go with me tomorrow? I will pay you for it."
"Oke, yes sir, I will come tomorrow early in the morning."

A day later we took off with three ox-drawn wagons, six oxen harnessed to each, and while the "haw, gee, giddap" of the drivers echoed through the hills of Marion County, we walked on ahead and beheld the rising sun that appeared on the eastern shores of Thunder Creek and whose beneficent rays you could have first seen a few hours earlier when they appeared from behind Van Maurik's farm. The [saw] mill was located eighteen miles from Pella, in a northerly direction from the town.

Perhaps I had better not take the time to portray for you the beauty of the open prairie, which had been robbed of its cover by the prairie fire during the winter and was now covered with a green crepe, or of the stately oak forests, which from time to time made for a pleasant sight, but I should probably depict for you the condition of Rev. Betten. His farm is located about 1¼ hours from the city in a N.N. Westerly direction. If you can imagine yourself standing in front of his log cabin facing south, you will see a plain, which is bordered by a row of hills that seems to enclose this plain like a dike in the form of a half circle. On one of these hills you will see a farm and also the road to Pella, a road that circles upward like a coiled snake. Turn about and you will see his cornfield, on about thirty-six acres of fenced-in land. Farther out are his woods, located on the shores of the Skunk River, which winds its way from east to west about one-half mile north of his house. It empties into the Mississippi River and, along the way, it powers various grist and sawmills. Entering his log cabin, which is very narrow, one sees several books arranged around a mantle piece clock, which is in strange contrast to the rude logs. If you arrive toward evening, you will ordinarily find Rev. Betten seated on a horse, wearing a cap and jacket, dressed just like any farmer, looking for his grazing cows. His wife and children, all of whom are happy and content, seem to be rather pleased with life in America, but as soon as you engage them in conversation, they always say, "What a difference, your mother will really find that out, etc. etc. etc."

Saturday, April 29, two o'clock in the afternoon. The potatoes and turnips tasted exceptionally good to me, for I was tremendously hungry. Someone might easily have taken me for a man this afternoon. I am really filled now, and I have in mind taking [you on] a walk through town, beginning at the point where the road from Osquiloosa [Oskaloosa] to Monroe enters the town; so it is on the east side that we begin. The road is nice, but you can tell that it rained the day before yesterday. You can also tell by the garden vegetables; just look how nice the lettuce, endive, peas, etc., already look. The first house is built of sod. The architecture certainly is not Corinthian, or Gothic, etc., indeed not, but you can rightly called it the Pella architecture. On the outside the house does not have any walls, and that is because they dug three to four feet in the ground and then managed to secure the rafters or cross beams to the ground surface, in order to form the roof in this manner. On the right side there are four lots on which they have built houses, and they are pretty good frame houses. Several lots further down there are children running about, they are playing, and they probably don't even think that they are all that far removed from their former school mates. There goes the bell! The children stop playing and go to the log cabin. It is the school in Mr. Muntingh's house; he does not conduct school in the church, because it is not yet finished.

What a [large] square space that is over there. It is the public square, and the nice log cabin that stands in the center of it is a house used for [public] meetings, and it is also for the Post Office, as you can tell by the little sign (Post Office) above the door. Now we come to Rev. Scholte's house, as one can tell by the copper nameplate on one of the doorposts, but also by the people who are sitting on the front porch on the street side. And let us not fail to take note of the beautiful, English style garden. In addition there is a small cluster of houses of [Pieter] Kuyper, [G.H.] Overkamp, [Jacob] Van Ham, [A.] Wigny, [Hendrik] Barendregt, [Jan] Meyer, the Store [or Grocery], [Willem] Visser, and a few others, almost all of them on fenced lots. Accordingly, one can very easily see the direction of the streets in this part of the town. Now if you stand on the N.W. corner of the Overkamp lot and walk down this street that runs from north to south, facing south, the first thing on the right side is the lumber yard of Hospers and Harrison, then [Jan] Blanke, Visser, with a sign above the door, "Hollandsch bread and pastry baker"; next Barendrecht [Barendregt], the church, [A.P.] Hasselman, etc. This is the principal part of town. I'll have to quit walking because they are calling for me: "Hospers, are you joining us for coffee?" All I hear about Van Deventer is that he earns lots of money and squanders it all, and in St. Louis he maligns our colonies all he can. Corn. Den Hartog requests that you give his greetings to his family.

H. Hospers

Hospers 34 [Hospers 16]

Pella, undated letter, likely May 1848

I continue to be very healthy and very content, so that I would not care to be back in Holland for all the money in the world, especially after learning in one of the American papers about the happenings in France and the precarious conditions in all of Europe. Consequently, my desire is all the greater that you all, beloved parents, brothers, sisters, and also my grandparents, should come over, before the threatening danger of civil and foreign war breaks loose, which might make it unsafe or impossible to cross the sea. Although here in the new world I can safely hear about the disturbances in a part of the old world, yet in consideration of all this, when compared with the tranquility and freedom we enjoy here, makes it [our situation] all the more precious in our eyes, still my thoughts are frequently in the Netherlands. My wish is, therefore, that the Ruler of the Universe may soon so order all things that all of you can freely come over and witness the further disturbances in Europe with me.

Three weeks ago I quit working as a surveyor after talking it all over with Overkamp, and I did so because I was getting too far behind in my studies. I had to prepare myself for an exam to be legally qualified to be a teacher, an exam I must take with the school inspector, and therefore with Rev. Scholte, who was elected and appointed to this post, and also to that of justice of the peace. Consequently I judged it more urgent to start my studies and especially to practice English. Accordingly, I get free lessons in English from Overkamp, and in other subjects from Muntingh; he and I will settle up later on sometime.

Van Meveren and his family are still healthy and well. They send greetings to all of you. Welle and all of his family are still in good health, but they are very eager to have their neighbors, Father and Grandfather, come over soon. Welle has lost all his hired hands; they left the colony, leaving behind considerable debts. Let this be a lesson to you, dear Father, to be very cautious about taking any people along with you. Welle was deprived of all his workmen in this way, and that is why Van Meveren and one of his sons are now working for him.

I still have not heard a thing from Van Deventer, and I don't believe that anything will ever come of that. Consequently, I have no money at all, and cannot have any work done on our land. But when the chest of rennet arrives, and I get money in my hands for them, it will be to our best advantage to use it to work the land. For it is my impression that there is a greater profit in using the money to work the land, than in using it to pay off on the principal. But taking into consideration the kindness and the friendly disposition of C. Den Hartog, I want to talk this over with him first.

Last week Schijf received a letter from Holland. Schijf is a very able blacksmith, and has more work than he can handle. The letter told of the desire of Bastiaan Vos, who is married to Grietje Kamp, a sister of Schijf's wife, to come to Pella, but it also said that he has money to pay for the sea voyage but not for the journey overland. I have made inquiries about him and, according to [Hendrik] Barendregt and [Aart] Monster who know the man well, he is a good and very able workman, whose conduct is impeccable; and although he is not yet a member of the Secessionist Congregation, he is actively involved. At the time he was living at Hitserd and did not have any children, since he was but newly married. His brother-in-law, Schijf, would very much like to satsify the desire of Bas[tiaan] Vos by advancing him the money, but he did not have an opportunity to send it to the Netherlands. Schijf spoke with me about it last Saturday evening and requested that I ask you to advance to Bas[tiaan] Vos the money for the journey overland, which would come to one hundred guilders. He [Bastiaan Vos] will then come to you with a note from me, which I will enclose in Schijf's letter to Bastiaan Vos. If you then, after having handed him the money, have him write an IOU or receipt [for the money], and send it to me, then I can use that to get the money from Schijf, or rather the amount stated in the IOU. You need have no worries, for I know Schijf, and I have made inquiries about Bas[tiaan] Vos that were very positive, although that really is no concern of mine. You do not have to make it exactly forty dollars; if he needs a little more, that is all right. In any case, he will come to you with a note written by me.

From one of my most recent letters you may have learned that the government of the State of Iowa has granted our request to elect a government from within our midst. On a day designated for this purpose all persons twenty-one and over, who had submitted a declaration of intent to become a citizen of the U.S., appeared and voted. According to the election [results], the following persons were elected: as justice of the peace and school inspector, H. P. Scholte; as trustees, P. Welle, A. J. Betten; as township clerk, I. Overkamp; as treasurer, Roziersz; as overseer of the poor, C. Den Hartog; as constable, C. Vanden Berg; and several fence inspectors and road officials. In respect to church matters the following were chosen: elected as elders, H. P. Scholte, Barendregt, G. H. Overkamp, I. Overkamp, [Jacob] Van Vliet, [K.] De Hoog, and A. J. Betten; as deacons, Meyer, P. Welle, and several others, whose names I have forgotten.

[Dirk] Den Otter and his whole family are well; the man who married his daughter Grietje seems to have money, for he bought a nice farm. Klaas Stam is healthy as ever and lives with an American, about sixteen miles from Pella. Meyer sends you greetings, and so does Vander Ley. Koen De Jong requested that I ask you, when it was convenient for you, to inform his brother A. De Jong, who is married to Mie, [the lady] who lived with us for such a long time, that he and his family are still enjoying good health. Please also give my greetings to Vanden Berg from Gorinchem, and please tell him that now I would like to have a lesson on the geography of the U[nited] States, and then I would like to tell a story about how healthy the air of American freedom is.

Also greet Haefkens for me, and Van Dam, K. Van Dam, especially Jan Vink, Uncle [Hendrik] Van Est, Uncles and Aunt De Gelder. Greetings to Teunis and Uncle Arie from the old Mr. [Adrianus] 't Lam; the man is really contented and healthy. He says, "I would not want to be in Holland for all the world, if only your Uncle Teunis and Uncle Arie were here, just write them that I said so, then we can all live together." Also give greetings to Jan Hansum and J. Steijnes, nephew and niece in Amsterdam, to Donkersloot, and all our other acquaintances. Cordial greetings from the Overkamps, [Pieter] Welle, [L.] Van Bergeyk, [Cornelius] Den Hartog, and [Jan] Meyer.

I hope that all this writing of greetings will end soon, and in hopes of seeing each other face to face, I sign myself as,
Your Loving Son, Brother and Grandson,

H. Hospers

Hospers 35

Pella, 30 May 1848 (received 10 July 1848)

Esteemed Parents, dearest Brothers and Sisters!

Good news from a far country is like cold water to a thirsty soul, says Solomon. The thrust of this proverb I have really experienced, and I do believe [in them accordingly]. Two weeks ago there was a rumor going about that Bart Keppel had arrived in St. Louis. and then had left to come here. The next day I had occasion to inquire about Bart Keppel with someone who was traveling to St. Louis to buy merchandise for [his] store, and at the same time to enquire whether he had dropped off anything for me. Well, you should know that Jan Keppel, a brother of B[art] Keppel lives in Keokuk. As you know Keokuk is located on the Mississippi and is the landing place for colonists going thither. Teunis, son of Jan Keppel, left for [the] Van Raalte [colony], because his bride to be lives there. Teunis Keppel himself would very likely also be heading that way, if he had not already bought land in our colony. (For his reasons see below.)

Last Sunday, May 28, '48, in the afternoon, before the church services were to begin, Walters arrived here from St. Louis thinking that he would really surprise me. Presently, he handed me the little package, and told me that Bart Keppel had left for Van Raalte's. He had attended the church of his brother Jan in Keokuk and had left the little package with him, without a message or even any regards. When everyone had left for church, and I was alone, I imagined myself back in Blokland. The first things I saw were the cigars. I lit one at once, to make the world of my imagining as real as I could.

I will not detain you long by describing what I experienced; every line was most precious to me. But there are other important matters. Only I wish to thank you all most sincerely for your precious letters and gifts. If I ever get a chance I would send Father a pipe, made from an acorn; a nice *vroeter* [possibly an instrument to clean a pipe] for Mother, which is the size of your coconut, the shell of which the Indians use for drinking water. For Mieke [Maaike] I would manage to catch a wolf from whose skin you could make a *boa* (fur necklet), or whatever it is you call it, or underpants. And for Keetje a buffalo skin. Then she would have something to remind her of her brother who last winter, while surveying, slept on a buffalo skin many times.

The Optimism of Jan and Hendrik Hospers

Kaart van den Staat JOWA.

Map of southeastern Iowa

Plat of Pella

An old plat map of Pella, which also reflects the mentality of the founder (from an original in the possession of the author).

Here is a clipping from the Keosauqua *Iowa Democrat* of May 24th, 1847 [likely 1848]:

"Pella has derived more than ordinary interest from the fact of it being the nucleus of the extensive Holland Settlement occupying a beautiful region of country in the northwestern section of Marion County immediately upon the great road from Keokuk to Fort Des Moines. The population is composed entirely of Hollanders who emigrated from the Kingdom of the Netherlands to this country in 1847. In religious faith they are Protestant, having left their native country on account of political and religious intolerance."

Hospers 36*

Pella, Iowa, June 1848

Dear Parents!

The city of Pella has now been laid out in lots. [*Note:* The letter contains a plat of the city carefully drawn by H. Hospers, and in color, on which the streets and avenues are given. The avenues running north and south are named, beginning from the east, Entrance, Inquiring, Reverence, Reformation, Gratitude, Experience, Patience, Confidence, Expectation, Accomplishing Avenues. Taking up the letter again:] The names of the avenues are to express the different stages in which a sinner finds himself when he is converted to God; and at the end of all comes the cemetery.

Dear Father: There is something with which good money can be made here and would be good for you, namely, a tannery—not to work yourself but to let others do it. There is a tanner who is also a shoemaker here with whom I have talked about it because the surveyor recommended it and I too see a good thing in it. The name of this tanner is [Corstianus] Van Stigt, a plain but true Christian. The man has no money for it but advised it. ƒ 600 are necessary to make a start. We can put three vats in the ground, which would cost near ƒ 200 but they are good for thirty years. The hides can easily be bought for $1 a piece. The chance is fine and leather is dear. The leather must remain in the ground for a year, but then the profits begin. If you desire this I will attend to it and watch over it.

A cotton and wool spinning factory, run by horse-power, on not too large a scale, could be built for ƒ1500 and would give a good income. Please let me know at once so that I can make preparations.

Within four weeks I will send you a plat of the City of Amsterdam on the Des Moines River. Would you not like to live in Amsterdam, Father? May we soon see each other. Good day, mother!

Your dutiful son,

H. Hospers

Hospers 37 [Hospers 17]

Pella, 3 June 1848

Dear Parents,

[Hendrik Hospers begins with an unidentified quote about Iowa]
"General description of Iowa. The State of Iowa when viewed in reference to the variety and excellence of its agricultural production—its vast mineral wealth—its great natural commercial facilities—the happy combination of prairie and woodland to the wants and convenience of the husbandman. In a word, viewed in its whole physical aspect and general adaptation to the wants of man, it probably combines as many requisites for human enterprise as is developed in any region or country of the same extent on the face of the globe! This country has alternately been in possession of various Indian tribes, at different periods from the once powerful and warlike Iowas until more recently by the confederated [Indian] tribes of the Vaco and Topes [Sac and Fox], from whom it was purchased by the United States at four successive treaties. The territory ceded to the United States by the last treaty, known as the 'New Purchase,' embraces some fifteen million acres of land. It is probably the most desirable region of territory ever obtained by the nation, either by treaty or conquest. It is well watered and timbered, possessing abundant mill power, and is settling up with a rapidity scarcely paralleled in the annals of history." I found almost the same thing in another newspaper called the *Burlington Hawk-Eye*.

I was really surprised, and no doubt it also surprised you, that B. Keppel left to join Van Raalte; it is assumed around here that it was prompted by false rumors. We hear very little about the colony in Michigan. I am very curious to find out more about it. How can

Heyboer say that all of Iowa has been sold? It must be that he does not have any maps, and he must have a very limited concept of America. Not one-quarter has been sold. On the average more than twenty persons are passing through Pella every day with all their cattle, household effects, and all.

About two months ago more than thirty Indians passed through our city in order to settle farther west. They were oddly dressed, brown in color; the men were tall but the women were small. They were all riding small horses, which are amazingly fast. The men were armed with small-bore rifles; they had adorned themselves by painting their faces with red ocher and blue [pigment]. The chiefs were with them and stood out above the others by their feathers and beads, which hung about their necks and heads. On the whole they looked pretty wild; that was also evident from their very strange language. Two of them spoke broken French and some English. When they arrived in Pella, especially the women were terrified. All of Pella was present, standing in Washington Street to watch the parade, and it was a rare individual who dared to approach them or to speak with them. After arriving at the Dutch store, they all bought Gouda pipes and rode on at a trot with long pipes in their mouths. [Hendrik] Dingemans accompanied them for about two miles, speaking with them in French and English.

I have had your lot in the city fenced in the usual manner, because everyone advised me to do so, and also because it will have to be done some time anyway. Besides it becomes a veritable wilderness when it just lies there uncultivated. The costs are: 70 oak poles $2.50; 800 oak pickets 5 feet long, 3 inches wide, 1 inch thick (oak) $7; 80 slats to which the pickets are nailed $4; nails $1; wages: Overkamp $15; spade work $4.50; 4 bushels of seed potatoes @ 25 cents $1; all told $35 dollars. The quality of the fence is such that it will last at least thirty to forty years; the land will produce at least one hundred bushels of potatoes, which could yield at least $15.

Because of the many problems with stray cattle in the area, which give rise to numerous disputes, there are laws to deal with this matter. Every farmer has to brand his cattle, and if this brand is to be legal, it has to be registered with the township secretary for a fee of twenty-five cents. So if an animal strays and subsequently is located by its brand, the owner has the right to reclaim it. If the brand has not been registered, and thus is not legal, then someone else can adopt the same brand, and that can lead to all kinds of disputes. It is difficult to have different brands for hogs, because they can only be marked on the ears. Although we do not have any cattle as yet, I have registered our brand, which no one else can adopt now, because I was the first to register it. Another reason for doing it now was the fact that if every farmer adopts a brand mark for his hogs, there might not be any left for us. Our brand mark for cows is J. H. on the right horn, for sheep and hogs it is two slits in the left ear. This permit costs twenty-five American cents. Father, do you approve, and do you, Grandfather? If each of you has his own cattle later on, you can certainly design a brand mark to distinguish your cattle. Grandfather should not bring any horse harnesses and above all no Dutch wagons. A Dutch harness is worthless for plowing here, but do have Grandfather bring straps. Welle requested that you bring six to eight guilders worth of twine, as thick as [binder] twine.

Hendrika De Baai married Aart Kool; Pieternella Van Meveren is going to marry Jan Klein. I will be eating pancakes today, Mother. I have a healthy appetite. Next Thursday the school matters will be decided. I will wait with mailing [my letter] till then, so I can let you know about that.

I am your Obedient Son and Loving Brother,

H. Hospers

Hospers 38 [Hospers 18]

[1 June 1848]

Beloved Son,

How far apart our worlds are! There is also a great gulf between us, but one that can be overcome. Hendrik, we have not seen each other in better than a year. We can no longer look in on each other's circumstances. We do not get to know that until six weeks afterwards. At the moment that we read each other's letters, which tell how we are faring, the writer could have long been dead and buried. But it is now—if ever! exactly in circumstances like these, living so far apart, [that we need to keep] our eye fixed on the Omniscient One! He, who sees me, also beholds you. He, whom we worship, you also worship. In him then we have a meeting point. We shall both behold him in the day of his coming. Your parents, brothers, and sisters continue to wish for the day to dawn and oh! if only it might be soon, of our coming to you.

You can already do much in the way of preparation. After all, we shall have to derive our income from the earth. But is there any good opportunity to market these products? Where is the market for Pella products located? Or isn't there one yet? What is the situation with regard to the railroad or making the [Des] Moines River navigable? How [nicely] our woods are located in a bend of the [Des] Moines River. On occasion I have even imagined myself living there. It seems to me that it must be a pleasant place to live, the more so because the surveyor says that it is such good land for a homestead. Is there much traffic on the road to Knoxville that passes through there? How many wagonloads of people per day on the average? Is there a ferry at the end of that road that crosses the [Des] Moines River? If so, is there someone living there, or does he live on the opposite side? How do people make the crossing? Or is the river shallow, so that you can wade across? Those are some of the questions we ask after reading your letters.

People writing letters from America do not sufficiently take into account our unfamiliarity with the land and its people. That is the common observation of all who receive letters, also of a group meeting at my house May 18 and 19, 1848, which included School Inspector Haefkens, Book Dealer Maasdam, and Father [Klaas] Middelkoop. Consequently, when we calmly read your answers (to our December questions), we were constantly asking questions that none of us could answer. I have already mentioned several of those questions. And hard as we all tried to figure it out, none of us, including Maasdam with all his knowledge of letters written to Utrecht, could understand how the prices of cultivated and uncultivated land are determined.

We are still in the dark on that question, but that will probably be removed when we get the [final] accounting. However, since we are as one man in having every confidence in the good order, the accuracy, and the regularity [of the transaction(s)], we do not wish to probe any further into these matters but intend just to wait and see how things turn out. We recognize that these are difficult matters for administrators, and especially for Mr. Scholte. The [overall] calculation [of the breakdown of costs on the large land deal made on behalf of settlers] is important enough, and I have some idea of how complicated and difficult that all must be. In my municipal accounting, which has become very complicated because of Vander Heim, I have on occasion entered monies as paid which in fact had not yet been received. Because of his usual kindheartedness, Mr. Scholte might have done the same, but it is always ill advised; often things turn out wrong! Brother I. Overkamp had better get involved. There is a good deal of talk here about that settlement by Scholte. Why is it so long delayed! People just do not understand the problems that often develop when you are dealing with money matters involving many people. I constantly try to be the defender, and I am happy that, however small, I can be an advocate of the reverend brother Scholte.

With love,

Father J. Hospers

Hospers 39*

Pella, Iowa, 24 June 1848

Dear Parents!

I had wanted to send you a plat of Amsterdam and some sketches of Scholte's sermons. Will do it later. I have enough to write. But do I not write too much? It is expensive in postage.

Now for three weeks I have been teaching school with I. Overkamp for which for the time being I get only my board; soon I will get some more, no doubt. [James] Muntingh will teach in the Skunk district and on these terms: free residence; the farmers will supply him with provisions; use of a horse, and $2 each week; those unable to pay will fence his farm for him. In Pella 40 children are in attendance at school; the number could be 60. It has been ordered that each scholar shall pay a "bit" ($0.125) a piece per week. There are three school districts. You were informed about the Pella district. Yesterday the Skunk district was organized; as directors were chosen [A.J.] Betten, [Jacob] Van Dam, and [Gerrit] Vander Wilt. The Des Moines district is yet to be organized; this will wait a year, and I have the quiet hope to be appointed there. I am studying hard and am making good progress in English.

Your obedient son,

H. Hospers

Hospers 40 [Hospers 19]

Pella, 30 June 1848

Beloved Parents,

  I am busy these days studying, and I really am enjoying it very much. Ordinarily my schedule of activities is as follows: Monday, get up, ordinarily at five-thirty, wash, have a cup of coffee, and then to school at six—my bookcase is located there—then study with Muntingh, for example, theory of arithmetic, geometry, algebra, history of the U.S., geography of the U.S., practical, and English with Overkamp, also French. That goes on till eight o'clock, when I go and have breakfast; then, between eight-thirty and nine, wait for the children in school and plan the activities for my little class, check the school work of the children to determine where some further explanation may be needed, etc.; in a word, I use that half hour or three quarters of an hour in order to be able to teach according to a lesson plan. The beginning of school is announced by a school bell; school begins with prayer. (As long as the school on the Skunk [River] is not finished, Muntingh also conducts classes here, and that is why we alternate on a daily basis in this school.)

  Then come penmanship, spelling books, reading drills, arithmetic drills (ancillary subject), history, etc.—this goes on all week until Friday afternoon. Morning classes last from nine to twelve, afternoon classes from two to four. Saturday, from six to nine [I] study in school, but no longer, because catechism for the children begins then, and in the afternoon there is a meeting of the church council. At home there is no opportunity to study, since there is only one room. So on that day I ordinarily have lessons with Muntingh at his home; he is very friendly. I get there often, almost every day, namely between light and dark, when we have conversations about scientific matters. Science is of little account in the western states; things are much better in the East. I have subscribed to a journal for young people called the *Cabinet*. It is of a scientific nature and consists of compositions written by individuals and submitted locally. (Price $1 per year.) I thought it would be very useful to me to get to know American young people, to learn their style, and not just sit here like a bump on a log in Pella, but also to show them that the Hollanders have something to offer, etc. So I submitted a short piece and promptly received a favorable reply by mail, so that it is likely to be placed. To enable you to see my progress in the English language, I will enclose the composition with this letter.

Mr. D. A. Woodworth
135 Nassau Street
New York

Sir!
There is about a year since I left the Netherlands to emigrate me to the United States en settle me after that in the State of Iowa. It is during this time that I get acquainted with the *Cabinet*. I was very glad to find here the same kind of periodical writings as I was using in the Netherlands. I send you the enclosed you placced, to place. As for the stijle [style], you maiy [may] change whatever you seem more convenient. I beliefe [believe] that it will be not unpleasant to the readers of the youth *Cabinet* when there will receive some communications about Dutch manners and customs. That the enclosed may obtain your approbation is the wish of your servant H. Hospers—Pella, 10 June 1848.

[Copied verbatim]
The enclosed selection is a translation I made from "Van den Berg's belangrijke onderwerpen" [Van den Berg's Important Subjects] etc.

Your son H. Hospers

The following letter is appended:

Pella, 4 July 1848

Dear Parents:
This day, Tuesday, was a holiday for the entire United States. On this day they remember the Declaration of Independence. Throughout the entire United States this day is celebrated enthusiastically, in as many different ways as there are people. We celebrated it too. There was no school. Scholte preached that morning, or finally introduced the people to the condition and the history of the land. The audience was attentive and it was wonderful how he showed the hand of God in everything, and he made an excellent application as well. Church was out at two, after which I ate, and then, at [Pieter] Welle's invitation, I went along with his son and three daughters to their home. We spent the afternoon together pleasantly, and [I] returned home again in the evening.

Hospers 41*

Pella, 6 July 1848

Beloved mother, worthy father and brothers and sisters!

Here is a sketch of your situation, one or two years hence, if all goes well. Imagine yourselves living as in this drawing; to be a farmer, Father, just as [Pieter] Welle, who does not work much any more; who is almost always sitting at [L.] Van Bergeyk, and just looks on.

It is milking time and the following conversation ensues:

FATHER – Go on, Klaas, get the cows; I have seen the folks at Welle already on the way to get theirs.

KLAAS – Have you seen them anywhere?

MAAIKE – Yes, back of the fences over there.

Sketch of Hospers' farm

KEETJE – Why no; these were the oxen.

KLAAS – Say, Gelder, I will go into the woods, and you up the hill.

GELDER – That's all right. While they are getting the cows.

MOTHER – Say, Maaike, get the pails ready; have you turned the cheese?

MAAIKE – No; Kee[tje] was to do that, for have I not been with P. Welle in town; and that is so. Mr. Graves said he would give Father 7 cents for the cheese; that is now the regular price.

MOTHER – Now; you are no longer in Holland to play the lady. What ails you to stay away so long?

MAAIKE – Well, Hendrik was to have brought us on the way, and then we waited till school was dismissed. He said he would come again this afternoon.

KLAAS and GELDER – Hoe ha, hoe ha, dzie, dzie! (Chasing the cows).

FATHER – Where were they?

KLAAS – They were only in the woods.

FATHER – Mother, come right away!

MOTHER – Come here quick, Maaike! They're here already. Where is Kee? She is coming. (Climbs over the fence into the cowshed, for they do not know anything about gates.)

KEE – See, Hendrik is coming there.

HENDRIK – Good day, Father! Here is a paper. It contains quite a bit of news from Holland. I am glad you are out of it. For things are not going well there. You have more freedom here. Just read about it. Meanwhile, I will see Mother. (To mother) Good day, Mother! It is warm today.

MOTHER – Yes, it was too warm to send them with the butter to the city. I think I will devote myself more to making cheese.

HENDRIK – How many cows do you milk now, Mother?

MOTHER – Eighteen.

HENDRIK – Now, isn't it fine here? You just let the cows run and have no further expenses, etc.

Dear Mother! I so much wish that you folks would just come. O, that the Lord would prepare the way for you.

Your dutiful son, H. Hospers.

Note: In this same letter Hendrik Hospers gives his father an idea with a diagram of the way land is surveyed in the midwestern states. He mentions the Fifth Principal Meridian and describes the numbered townships and the ranges, and how a section or part thereof, is described. He then says:

I think you will now better understand how it is possible that our woods located on the Des Moines River can lie in Sections 14 and 23, Township 76, Range 18. *And more of this.* When, then, Father, you compare my two small maps, you will see how beautifully our woods is situated. Thus far the rennet has not yet arrived but is expected daily.

Your son,

H. Hospers

Hospers 42

Hoogblokland, 9 July 1848

Dear Hendrik!

On the 26th of June instant we received your last letter. I have forwarded the letters of [Hendrik] Dingemans and [Pieter] Van Meveren to Gasteren and Franeker. We are still healthy and well and so is your family. Last week, while Uncle [Hendrik] Van Est was back in his garden again, he had a seizure and fell to the ground; he was flat on his back for a while, and finally he got up again. Now he is feeling better; he is still weak, but manages to walk to his neighbor's house just the same. We have asked him several times to go with us to Pella; we make everything as attractive as possible for him and offer him every possible kind of assistance, but he just keeps on saying, "I am too old and too weak for that."

I put off writing until I had heard from Bastiaan Vos. Yesterday Brother Vos, who is single, visited here together with his dearest, Grietje Kamp, a very capable young girl, and still another young man and girl from that area. I believe that the young man is a brother to Grietje Kamp. It just so happened that we were having a general meeting of the teachers in the 4th district at Meerkerk, and as a result I was absent when the young folk from Den Hidsert (or Hitserd) and Klaaswaal visited us. Your mother gave them a friendly reception for they had documents in your handwriting with them. They, the girls, in their unfamiliar [costume] caps and dresses made quite a show as they walked through the village. They climbed the tower and also played on the swings in our school attic. At the meeting I gave your greetings to Steijnen. We walked around Meerkerk together and talked about you. He is without an assistant principal right now, and he certainly does not need one. Alex says that he knows [people for the position of principal]. Many others talked about you.

In their blind infatuation with the Netherlands, many teachers still are not satisfied with what Pella has to offer. Only Haefkens and I are defenders of Pella. At five-thirty I was called from the meeting just as we were eating, and there was Uncle Arie de Gelder with the joyride wagon and a note from your mother telling of the arrival of people from Den Hitserd and expressing the wish that I should return home as soon as possible. I then gave the people 10 guilder gold pieces for which Bastiaan Vos signed a money draft of one hundred guilders which I endorsed to you, and which is enclosed herewith, and on which you can therefore collect the equivalent of one hundred Dutch guilders in American currency.

We are most eager to be in Pella. We have given our word to Father [Klaas] Middelkoop that if he can still sell his homestead and his farmland in time, we also will be ready to leave the Netherlands this coming autumn. We had wanted to just go on ahead, then Geert would also join us; but Father Middelkoop says: "No, by no means! We must go together." As yet, I can not see the homestead and the entire farm being sold *now*; it is now the wrong time: land in the fall and ancestral home [*erfhuis*] in the spring. Heijmans, the baker, [is trying] to persuade Uncle Van Est, so he himself would also be able to come along; because the mortgage of Uncle's money on Heijmans's house is in my name, [money] on which Uncle is drawing interest as long as he lives. I would be conscience stricken if I were to call in the mortgage and thus deprive

Uncle Van Est of the interest, and without inheritances my financial resources are not adequate to take Heijmans along.

  Just spend as much as you can on our land so that it can become a source of income for us. Then all of us better go to work; I anticipate sacrificing pleasures and wealth by the world's standards for the Word of God. I do have the Word here, but it is preached in such a drab way. And besides the situation in Europe is not conducive to wanting to stay here. What temporal peace you people in Pella enjoy. You must already be keeping school by now. Write us all about that, which books you are using, and how they are provided.

  You write that John Harrisson [Harrison] bought 50,000 [linear] feet of lumber and that on your walk through Pella you go by the lumberyard of Hospers and Harrison?? I understand that to refer to a warehouse or a collection site for all the lumber purchased above. I would really appreciate your clarifying that for me. What must I think of that? Is this something that concerns both of us, so that we are acting in partnership with that American Harrisson whom you describe as an able man? Or has our lot in Pella been rented to Harrison for this collection [of lumber]? I certainly hope that our lot is not jointly owned with him. If that unhoped for thing should be the case, then do make work of changing that, so that our lot belongs to us alone. I am very keen about that. After finishing your letter of April 26th you yourself may have realized that by those words, the lumberyard of Hospers and Harrison, you really aroused our curiosity, but did not satisfy it. If upon receipt of this letter this has not yet been done, then write to us at once. Our money is now beginning to arrive in Pella; accordingly, our interest is the greater, especially when a glimmer of light breaks through about income or making a living. I still know nothing about your income from the goods that Keppel took along, the chest with rennet, and the monies for D[irk] Den Hartog. I hope that soon I may be reading pleasant letters with your specific listing of everything that you and others in Pella are receiving; in what condition things are arriving, shipping costs, time of arrival, the condition of the rennet on arrival, etc; whether it is satisfactory [for curdling milk for cheese]; how you are receiving, or have received payment; and what they (the amounts) are, and how they are being spent. Now you will have more to write about than we.

  It is now almost 8 months ago that I sent money along with Huibert Keppel, who spent the winter in Plymouth, but who must have been in Pella for some time by now. But we have not received any word from him. From this we conclude that he had not yet arrived by May 5, the date your last letter was mailed.

The booklet by Scholte, *Eene Stem van Pella* [*A Voice from Pella*], has been published. My friends and I read it with much satisfaction. However, it was just published, so that I still do not know what the reaction of the Dutch will be. I anticipate that they will be pleased with it. A. Scheer in Nieuwkerk asked me only yesterday: "Is Scholte still in Pella. Is it true that he is leaving there, and that he is coming back [to the Netherlands]?" You just cannot believe the strange rumors that are being spread here, all of it figments of the imagination from the States.

I wish you would straighten me out once and for all about the location of our woods. On your drawing it says township 76, [Jan] Hospers section 14, [Klaas] Middelkoop is below that in section 23 on the [Des] Moines River. But those sections are not on your map of Township 76, nor on the back of *Eene Stem van Pella* on the [Des] Moines River. The specific [description] of our timber does not agree with your map. I want to take it along to Pella, so that you can see for yourself. Your drawings have clarified the fences and lot enclosures for us.

Yesterday when I was visiting K[ruijt] in Meerkerk, he promised to send me a letter for Overkamp to enclose in my letter. But I have not heard a thing from him. They are all still healthy and well. His daughters waited on us yesterday when we dined there as members of the Teachers Organization. I hope it will be the last one I attend in the Netherlands. As you requested, I have given greetings to Haefkens, Van Dam, Jan Vink, uncles and aunts De Gelder-Steijen. You had forgotten Uncle Van Est but I managed to write him in the meantime.

I join you in wishing that all this passing on greetings may soon come to an end. Especially give my greetings, and also Father's, to [Klaas] Middelkoop, Rev. Scholte, [A.J.] Betten, [L.] Van Bergeyk, the Overkamps, C. Den Hartog, [Pieter] Welle, Jan Rietveld, B[altus] Van Baaren, P. Van Driel, and H[uibert] Keppel. All the people I gave your greetings send you greetings in return. Andries Van Kleef from Noordeloos sends greetings to P. Van M[everen] and requests that he write him once. Also give our greetings to P. Van M[everen] and family. Herbert Kamsteeg from Giessendam, who has undertaken the [laying down of gravel?] on part of our [road], sends you greetings. A copy of your last letter was sent to Utrecht, to the Van Haaftens. Please give my greetings to Pieter Van Hoorne (a worker for Klein Van Houwelingen, I believe?), who had taken him along. Greetings also from his brother-in-law Gerrit den Besten and his wife; all is well with them. Receive greetings from us all, with the prayer that the Lord may be your Guide in this terrestial life, and that you may ever live with your eye on Him.

Your loving Father,

J. Hospers

Hospers 43*

Hoogblokland, 10 July 1848

Dear Son!

I was busy packing *[these were not yet the separate envelope days]* a letter to you when unexpectedly yours of May 30 arrived. I stopped writing and folding and went with the new letter to your mother who was still sleeping. It was not yet six o'clock. I carefully laid your letter on her face, and waking up she said with joyful tones: "Oh heden, is dat weers en brief van mijnen Hendrik?" [Good grief, is that again a letter from my Hendrik?] At the same time I received a letter from Dingemans, who had enclosed one to be sent by me to his son. It was rather large and postage on it all came to ƒ1.30. Today Uncle Teunis de Gelder comes from Gorkum [Gorinchem] with a letter of H. Kars, which we read with the whole family and are glad to learn that you have a definite job. You know that the conditions made at Leerdam were not fulfilled, because you had to pay board money. Or did you get free of this? The colony cannot earn much yet. It would be fine if you could get your board and clothing out of it. Your proposition to become a tanner, a cotton or wool-spinner, is interesting, but I have no money for that. We plan to come next year and hope we can earn something. If legacies should come (for which I may not long) then I would have funds enough. I am glad to have the new map of Pella; how interesting are the names of the ten cross-streets. I thank you for the territory, population, etc. of the several states from the *Family Christian Almanac* [this is written in English in the letter]. This evening I plan to read it carefully. You know how busy I am by day, especially on Monday. Have the regards of Aai-oom, Uncle Van Est. Your uncles Willem, Gerrit, and Aunt Sijgje [Middelkoop] will see that you get a Viersteeme book [Psalm book with four-part music]. Pieter Hendrik, your youngest brother, can creep on the floor.

Your father,

J. Hospers

Hospers 44*

Hoogblokland, 15 August 1848

Dear Hendrik!

You do not know how glad they all are when a letter arrives from you. When we got your last one everybody had to see your drawings. First Willem Hendrik and Eva, then [Teunis de] Gelder, Klaas, Keetje and Maaike, while Mother and the maid looked over them all to see the pictures of immigrants hitched to and pulling a steamboat and a school. The letters of your friend [Hendrik] Dingemans are spirit and life and please me much. His association with you can benefit you. Without Christ everything is dead for us. I am disturbed in writing this letter. First, Uncle [Hendrik] Van Est comes and inquires after your last letter. Then, in my study, Mother comes with her usual sweetness and inquires after my progress with writing. Then Albert Kars comes to bother me as he pays his taxes. Again the bell rings, and the inquiry: "Is the Meester at home?" Your sister Maaike asks whether there are nice flowers in Pella? "We have seen two nice rose leaves in Dingemans's letter." Your mother says you must not throw away old clothing: we can use it for the smaller ones. We shall likely come with healthy children but not with legacies, unless you advise us not to come, for I cannot work on the land: though I would like to, I am not brought up in this. I notice that money is earned from milk and cheese: therefore cows will have to be bought. It seems to me that in temporalities you are better off than Dingemans, but are you richer than he in things eternal? O Hendrik, seek the Lord while He can be found! We are glad you are teaching school. I take much pleasure in your cards and drawings. Often reading your letters is a delight to me. Hendrik! I feel so much that you are my first born!

Your loving father,

J. Hospers

Hospers 45*

Hoogblokland, 22 August 1848

Much Honored Son!

Zie zoo [That is that]! School is dismissed. My 75 scholars have gone home. Rest! One discovers from experience that this is no easy job. We are looking forward to your next letter with sketches of Scholte's sermons, with a plat of Amsterdam, etc. Have you found a means of subsistence for us? Or is the answer in your remark: "Lumberyard of Hospers & Harrison?" Has any plowing been done on our land? Any cattle there, or a chicken or so? Are the 15 grafted apple trees still living? How about the tannery? We look with great interest to your next letter, but since it arrives in the morning and there is little time to look into it, your mother and I have resolved to lay it aside till evening for reading, and during the day looking at the address and whetting our appetite for what comes. No strangers will bother us in the evening; we shall lock our doors and quietly and slowly read your letter with joy and thanksgiving to God whose good providence rules in our affairs.... Klaas and [Teunis de] Gelder have to re-cut 130 pens (goose-quills) what they like to do.

Aug. 26. This morning I went to Gorinchem to recite a lesson in English. Gone almost two hours. Had a ride part of the way.

Aug. 27, Sunday. Mother is dressing Pieter Hendrik. Keetje dresses Willem Hendrik. Eva Engelina puts on her stockings. Klaas and Gelder are just now getting up. And now Eva brings me a cup of coffee; I'll drink that first. You are sleeping now but soon to hear the fine sermons of Rev. Scholte. What a privilege! I declare that I prefer to stay home here.

Please be particular to greet Rev. Betten and his family. Maaike and Keetje also greet Koosje. As I wrote you in Rotterdam, I was sorry to lose the chance to take leave of him. We hope to see each other in Pella. Tell His Reverence that I am beginning to read in my English Bible. It surprised us that the Overkamps did not let themselves be heard from. My specials regards to Isaac Overkamp. Greet Van Bergeyk from Father and me. Tell him that I have gotten his letter in person from Kentie and without expense. *[Interspersed with this last page there are a large number of greetings to various persons.]*

In these times there are riots in various places. In Leeuwarden the military killed and wounded a large number of rioters. This spirit of riot is spread throughout all this land. In Nymegen also the military had to preserve order.

Please write often; keep on as you have begun. Answer at once. Keetje and Willem Hendrik are improving. Receive the greetings of Grandfather and his family. Uncle Gerrit greets you particularly; also Uncle Van Est, Neeltje, Uncle Floris, and Arie de Gelder and Aunt Betje de Gelder.

Burgomaster Aanen also seems to take much interest in Pella. Greet for me all friends and acquaintances. In the trust that I shall see you in Pella, or else through grace for Christ's sake, eternally in His presence, we call ourselves your loving parents,

H. Middelkoop and J. Hospers

[The first signature in her own hand is that of Hendrik's mother]

Hospers 46

Pella, 25 August 1848

Esteemed Parents!

O, how God's Spirit is at work in Pella! In just three weeks twenty have already been converted, and so convincingly that one need have no doubts about them. And I, beloved parents, may not yet have the privilege of being one [of them]. But the Lord has said: "Pray, and you shall receive; come to me all who labor and are heavy laden and I will give you rest." And when those words come to mind, then I may be still and filled with quiet hope, and once again sing, *"Maar de Heer sal uitkomst geven,"* etc. ["But the Lord will send salvation, and daily grant His favor" (Ps. 42: 5)]. If you were here in Pella in the evening, you would hear psalms resounding to God's praise!

Although I am not yet fully persuaded that I belong to His people, I am part of their fellowship every evening. Oh, beloved sisters! You should really see and hear Naatje Overkamp once now; she is a letter for all to read! Beloved Father, pray for me! I am so convinced that I am a covenant breaker; but it is my hope (ah, if only it were faith) that the Lord may also grant to me the assurance of the covenant He made with Abraham and his seed. As soon as the Lord has assured me of His grace to my soul, I will write you of it, dear parents. Pray for me. How do you do, Mother? Greet Uncle Van Est.

Your son,

H. Hospers.

Copy

G.H. Overkamp to J. Hospers

Pella, 1 August 1848 (received 25 Sept. 1848)

The 1848 Pella Revival

Esteemed Friend and Brother in the Lord!

You write that Europe is in turmoil. We hear that in Pella too. It makes us concerned about our brethren and relatives who are there. Would they were with us in Pella, for it is good to be here. Bro. Hospers, we are not only free from misery and anxiety, but we also have the privilege that on the Lord's Day we get blessed food and instruction for our souls. Seeing this in connection with the events in Europe leads us to an appreciation of the Second Coming of our Lord, as Rev. Scholte pointed out so well in Europe and now here. When he is preaching, the building is sometimes so full that people have to stand outdoors.

I also want to let you know that the Lord is working especially among our young people, so that we have good grounds to believe that they have been translated from darkness into God's wondrous light. Among them, the Lord be praised, is our daughter Aafje [then 14, later married to G.H. Dingemans], who now speaks of the blessed service of God after having experience much sorrow for sin, and declares that what formerly was a burden has now become a pleasure. Altogether they make out a considerable company, girls between twelve and sixteen years who constantly speak of the service of the Lord and urge others to do the same. O blessed privilege and proof of God's love toward us! I thought I had to write to you about this unto your joy, so that I trust that in this way it may also become known in The Netherlands what the Lord is for His people which listens to His voice, and that He may crown it with His blessing.

Yesterday (Monday) evening we had four children at consistory, who made a glorious profession of faith.

I hope the Lord will soon bring you to Pella, so that we may go up together to the house of the Lord and, recalling His mercies, may proclaim His excellence.

Yesterday I received the box with the brushes and the rennet, all in good shape, except the pipes that were all broken and the watch of my brother that was taken out when the box was opened in New York. But

a payment will be made for this. Thanks for your trouble.
Lovingly your brother in the Lord,

G.H. Overkamp

On Sunday, August 27, 1848, Jan Hospers wrote from Hoogblokland:
Today is Sunday! You probably are still sleeping but one of the wonderful sermons of Scholte again awaits you. Oh, what a privilege that is for you in Pella. I assure you that I would rather be alone in my room delighting myself in the Word of God than to take up my post in church. Granted that the words I will hear are not untrue, but there is no life in them—it is all dead!

And then at the beginning of September 1848, we read:

Our levies of 1845, 1846, and 1847 are still in effect, plus substitutions for 48. All the articles of a new constitution have been adopted by the 2nd Chamber and are under discussion in the 1st Chamber. That is to be followed by a chamber doubled in number, and then we shall see what good will come to the Netherlands from that artifice. At least there will be freedom of education. Many teachers are childishly afraid of this.

Hospers 47*

Hoogblokland, Saturday, 2 September 1848
The mail! No letter from you! I had kept this letter open, but all hope is gone now.

Greetings, Father

Hospers 48*

Hoogblokland, 28 September 1848

Dear Hendrik!
I saw an advertisement of a book on surveying. You will be pleased with it and I gladly pay for it and get it to you. Pella costs us a lot of money, Hendrik! For quite a while much of my money brings no

interest. I have to work hard to support my numerous family. The Lord blesses me and gives me strength. Not till in the night could I look at your sketches of Scholte's sermons. Last evening Uncle Van Est and others came to hear your letters and see your drawings. My work for the government had to be done some way also. I had to marry a couple at Hoornaar. Tomorrow I must meet some friends from Utrecht at Arkel, take the canal boat for Gorkum [Gorinchem] and then to Vuren to take leave of Vander Linden.

My schools counts 70 scholars; they are gathering; soon the bell will ring. [Now follows a part of this letter all written in English by J. Hospers himself, indicated by quotations marks]: "I wish to come to Pella. I learn the English language by Mr. [H.] Picard, in the two weeks one lesson of two hours. I must pay for it sixty cents. I learn with pleasure but I have too much business and not time enough to learn my lesson. When I shall be in Pella, I shall always speak English, and at this manner I shall learn very well. The clock strikes nain [nine]. I am going to school. My son, I write these letters without a Dictionary with great haste. I have no more time. *Il n'est bien plus facile d'écrire et de parler français. Salut! Je m'en vais* ["It is not very easy to write and speak French. Goodbye! I am going"].

The same day, afternoon, four o'clock. My school is finished, my dear son! I write now a *nota* [official document] for a marriage this evening in Hoornaar. I believe you will find much faults in this letter. I hope you correct them when I shall be in Pella. Yours."

What do you say of this, Hendrik! If I were only a month among the English, I would be able to speak it.

Lovingly, your father,

J. Hospers

Hospers 49*

Hoogblokland, 10 October 1848

Dear Hendrik!

All well except Uncle Teunis de Gelder who has been sick nigh unto death, but though weak is recovering. He has two persons to stay up with him nights. In the night of Oct. 9 he indicated he had something on his mind. He could not talk. On Monday he got them to understand.

In case of his death he wanted your brother Teunis de Gelder Hospers [named after Teunis de Gelder] to receive ƒ500. Now Aai-oom [Uncle Arie de Gelder] and Aunt Betje de Gelder claim that this ƒ500 is to be paid after the death of all the De Gelders, and so we may easily be in Pella when that has occurred. [As a matter of fact, the last of them died about the year 1880.] I received a letter from you via England, postage ƒ4.00; and one of you via France, postage ƒ1.70. We rejoiced again. Also a fine letter of G.H. Overkamp. When Maasdam, Vander Ley and I took leave of K. vander Linden we read them; also a glorious letter of Scholte.

We just devour all news of Pella, our future earthly fatherland. We rejoice especially to learn of the gracious work of the Holy Spirit in Pella. Of what I sent along with Keppel, I did not get much account, nor of the nice German pipes I sent. Gone? And for the books, not a word. Isaac Overkamp's watch also seems to have been taken out. "Now come over." Your frankness in corresponding with the superintendent of public instruction pleased me. But, beloved son, all with an eye on the Lord, not I (Ps. 15:1).

I thank you for that map of Iowa. No better gift for my birthday. That map has been studied by many here. And the good information on the back of it! How extensive Iowa is. Your explanation of the division of North America now makes me understand better the location of my woodland. The wings of the insect you sent (what is it?) came over in fine shape. They have also been in Vuren. But the sketches of two sermons of Scholte are important. Thus, Scholte is still preaching to many in Holland. But if you again take notes, what you cannot do too much to suit us, take more paper along!?!? The city of Amsterdam is very nice and neatly drawn, perhaps nicer on paper than in reality. You ask whether I would like to live in Amsterdam, but I think you are joking about my birthplace. Would that we were only in our log cabin! Two rooms, to be sure? and 18 cows. But how to get them, Hendrik? And without legacies? But why ask? Before I can get an answer, I will have decided about going. I dare not hesitate because so many are waiting for me. And although I do not know how I can earn [a living], perhaps because of my limited knowledge of everything connected with Pella, I will do and dare and say with Esther: "If I perish, I perish!" I will have spiritual blessing in Pella, and that I seek for my family too.

Today we received your short letter sent through Dingemans. How God's Spirit is at work in Pella! Glorious times! I can hardly remember ever having read with more pleasure a short letter than that one. It contained no references to things worldly or temporal! No, my son, the subject was too gracious for that: it concerned the one thing needful, in comparison with which all things temporal become as nothing. Write us as soon as the Lord has sealed His grace in your heart. May the Lord speedily give us joy. O, how dry it is here spiritually. Yes, the Lord is taking His own away from Holland—a sad sign for our country.

Vander Linden brings with him my Four-parts Psalm book: I could get no other soon enough, so I give mine. But it is really a present to you from Uncles Gerrit and Willem and Aunt Sijgje [Middelkoop], who furnished me with the substitute. K. Vander Linden left Vuren with 30 persons via Rotterdam, Havre, New Orleans to St. Louis. They will winter there and go to Pella in the spring. Greet the friends.

Personal signature follows of your loving mother,

Hendrika Hospers, nee Middelkoop and J. Hospers

Hospers 50*

Hoogblokland, 13 October 1848

Dear Hendrik!

Yesterday I actually sat smoking a pipe with Uncle Teunis de Gelder. He was helped to get up and asked whether I would fill a pipe for him. He lit it, smoked, and asked me whether I would not bear him company. And although I considered the daytime too precious for a healthy man to sit and smoke, I did it. I have sent a letter to Maasdam acquainting him with this delightful spiritual news from Pella, so that the brethren there too may rejoice. Dingemans, Vander Ley, and Father are coming this evening and we shall again feast on a conversation about Pella. Uncle stays at home again.

Monday, October 16. Uncle Teunis is slowly improving. He does not go out doors. My company came the other night. We sat in our best room, one the likes of which probably cannot be found in Pella. We read letters. That one of your friend was a regular sermon. Saturday I attended probably my last Teachers' Meeting in Holland; the next one will be next March, and Mother desires to go. The times are grave. It is reasonably quiet here, but in eastern Europe the tension is great. Your uncles Willem, Gerrit and Aunt Sijgje [Middelkoop] are ready to go with us and leave the other old uncles behind. Tell Corn. Vanden Berg that H. Kars and I think of going to court to compel Gysbert de Groot to settle for his suretyship.

Wednesday, October 18. Cold, and we are using the stoves. Last night I went to smoke a pipe at Uncle Van Est's. I tried to have him go along to Pella, but he said he was too shortwinded as not able to reach the door. Telling him how glad Hendrik would be, he said, "But I am too weak." Hendrik, if the Lord would take away Uncle Van Est this winter, and spare us, we would come next spring, quickly reducing Uncle's possessions to money. Must I leave him behind? What would Pella people say about this, to leave an old man without relatives to look after him?

Friday, October 27. Last Friday Burgomaster B. de Koning came to ask Uncle Van Est whether he would not rent his house. Uncle considers it. His present circumstances do not please him. He wants to live with someone in Gorkum [Gorinchem] this winter already. But he dreads the changes. Uncle seems to get loose of Blokland and so from us. Perhaps he will go with us. He will be 76 next December. We try to note God's leading.

The journey via New Orleans may be the easiest and cheapest, but I will lose a lot of time during which I can still work here and earn. Can you give information regarding the trip via New York, Baltimore, and New Orleans? The less of ballast, the better, is it not?

November 2. I have written the letter to Scholte. Ask to read it. Uncle Teunis de Gelder is improving. He has given me the choice to say who will live on his farm. I suggested the son of Jan Aanen.

Sunday evening your mother and I went to visit Uncle Teunis again. Coincidentally, everybody else was gone, even the maid. Again I mentioned our possible departure to Pella. But I got a shock when I heard these old people complain about our leaving them. I now hardly know when to go. In the spring or in the fall.

Den Hartog has written a letter to Arie de Vlieg that he must have money from Father Middelkoop, and this is read in many places. Father is very sorry about this, for has he not paid the money with all the interest? Hence, coming to Pella, we shall have no debt. Uncle Van Est talks less about going to Gorkum [Gorinchem]. He has rented part of his house. If you were here, you would find everything spiritually dead. The Lord give life to your soul.

Your Father,

J. Hospers

Hospers 51*

Hoogblokland, 24 November 1848

Beloved Hendrik!

We are all well as to the body, but as to the soul it is dry and withered; how can it be otherwise in such dead surroundings. Wednesday we received your letter, which had been two months on the way. Can't you send it via England? That would shorten it two weeks. Your letter cost me *f*1.60.

We learn of your health with pleasure; but we would rejoice much more if you would write: "I have found the pearl of great price." You know that the Lord says that he who seeks, shall find. O that we may yet magnify the Lord when under one roof and at one table we parents with all our eight children may be united! Yes, the children lie nearer to our heart than Uncles and Aunt.

Your next letter, Hendrik, will likely definitely cause us to decide to go. That we live under such arid conditions helps. The matter is weighty; yes, weighty! Yesterday I took your letter to your grandparents who were home alone. I took Nicholas along for company. Your grandparents were much pleased; however, before they decide to go along they will await your next letter to them. I feel pity for the old Uncle De Gelder and Aunt De Gelder and Uncle Van Est. Uncle Arie came yesterday accidentally when I received your letter. I read it to him, and his face blanched. I gave your separate note to Uncle Van Est: you wrote it well; but he said nothing; we will let him sleep on it.

Six pm. Your uncles Gerrit and Willem [Middelkoop] are talking with Mother, and came especially to read your letter. It heartened them and they only hope that you will still be unmarried when they come in order to enjoy with all of you the new surroundings. The Lord give us strength to become loose of our aged relatives. Hendrik, we must live on earth as the pure preaching of the Word; there we live under church disciplines; and there we enjoy the seals of the covenant. It will be a new life. And besides, we have a son who went ahead and prepares the way for us. We can forget the Blokland home. [In 1887 I visited that house in company with Uncle Willem Hospers. It was a neat brick house, schoolroom to the rear, upstairs all one room. The heavy timbers, on a slant to support the heavy tile roof, were pointed out to me as having become smooth because my uncles Klaas and [Teunis de] Gelder (and my father, too, probably) would constantly slide down on them. (Gerrit Hendrik

Hospers.) I plan to take along a drawing of the residence. You write about us taking jobs right with Americans, so that we shall the sooner learn the language. Yes, when the Lord shall have brought us over, we hope to earn our daily bread, and do so as Providence indicates. Yes, I shall be glad to have 80 acres. We come strong in manpower, and I shall be able to pay. Anyway, the land will not spoil and rise in value. My Hendrik's old nature is not strange to me: he prefers having too much rather than too little. In a letter of Sjoerd Aukes Sipma of Friesland it is stated that the state gave a good sum to Pella? Is that so [see p. 217]?

Hendrik, we are pleased with the 17' x 19' log cabin built on our land for us. Is [Pieter] Van Meveren living in it now, or is it designed for us? How much we shall have to see! Greet the Overkamps. Tell G. H. Overkamp that I am still trying to cash in money for him, but I have to deal with tough ones.

Saturday, November 25. Hendrik, do your best to find something for us to do. But remember that I cannot dig ditches. Work on the land does not appear to me unpleasant if I can only do it *slowly* and *sweetly*: but, at that rate perhaps but little will be done, don't you think so? Would you advise me teaching school? But to teach as a sub, or as a second, would not flatter me. I would not be able. But at this distance I cannot judge very well. Greet our neighbor Welle with whom I hope to spend many pleasant days. All the relatives greet you. Aunt Betje de Gelder is still the same stingy one. Klaas and [Teunis de] Gelder are sitting near me, writing.

Lovingly, your father,

J. Hospers

Hospers 52*

Hoogblokland, 28 November 1848

Worthy Hendrik!

Six pm. Am alone in my office, near a warm stove while outside the wind howls and it rains. I hear your brothers and sisters sing Psalm 42 with your mother. Last Saturday I had to count and dispose of two thousand guilders with your uncles Teunis de Gelder and Uncle [Hendrik] Van Est as officers of the township. The two old uncles sit there babbling and smoking their pipes and I must do the work. On going away, Uncle Van Est could not go beyond Heymans, the baker, without being so winded that he could not even speak. He had not visited Uncle Teunis for weeks. And now he cannot leave the house. Hence, we are not quite decided to go. He is getting weaker. If not for this, I would be ready to break up at once. Your mother and your sisters urge me simply to go, the sooner the better. If the Lord wills, you may expect us in 1849.

Hendrik, I hear a noise in the hall. There! It is your little brother Pieter Hendrik. Passing the kitchen, he sees our maid and calls to her, "Da, da!" And now he is at my door and says: "Pa!" Maaike opens the door for him. He enters, looks around, wants to walk on, alongside of the clothes press, but because the stove is burning Maaike will not have him walk alone and she brings him to me. O, now Pieter and father are so busy together!

Nov. 29, evening. Your little brother Willem Hendrik is with me now in my office. He is a healthy four-year old chap. He says that he still knows you and that Hendrik is in "Noot-amerika." O, he is such a dear attractive little man, with fine judgment and memory for his age. Already he can read little words. Today I read that the *Katharina Jackson*, Capt. Stafford [the boat on which the De Gelders, Rietvelds, Welles, etc. had traveled in 1847 to America] had foundered and was destroyed 300 miles from New York. The 196 passengers [none Hollanders] were saved.

Dec. 1. You happily surprised me when this morning I received 8 newspapers from you. Postage, 80cts to Gorinchem. That was nice—worth the postage. My son lets me read the papers! Now I can find out a good deal about Iowa. We can read many hours. We are sorry that your mother is not acquainted with English, else she would gladly read them. Busy today, but first I must go to Uncle Van Est and smoke my first pipe today.

Dec. 10. So busy, I could not write again till now. I get up early and work till late in the evening. The other day your mother and I walked by moonlight to the Baseldyk to visit your grandparents and Gerrit, Willem, and Sijgje [Middelkoop]. Talked with animation about Pella. Yes, they are all ready, if I but give the word to go. But we wait for your next letter. You promise no little thing, saying, "You folks need not be concerned about making a living; if the Lord wills, I will take care of that." Indeed, can you support such a large family? Hendrik, your writing is refreshing, but we want to earn our own living. Would not dairying fit us best? Your letter of Nov. 2 reached us in 5 weeks. That was the fastest ever; it came via England and cost you more.

Your account of how Sunday is spent in Pella and how the Lord crowns it all with His blessing powerfully induces us to come and leave all old relatives and thousands of guilders behind. "Jesus above all the gold of earth!" How gladly I would like to attend all your meetings. Did you think that the service of the Lord would be as gracious as that? And if once you come to taste the love of Jesus, you will testify that earthly pleasures sink away into emptiness compared therewith.

Your father,

J. Hospers

Hospers 53*

Hoornaar, 21 December 1848

Esteemed Friend!

Never did I return home from Hoogblokland as I did last Tuesday. Many, many tears ran down my cheeks. Yes, even when I was all alone. Indeed, no wonder, when one has a friend, a real friend, yes a Surety, to whom one can reveal all kinds of temporal affairs and entrust to. Yea, what is more, one with whom one can freely consult in regard to spiritual things. To learn from such a friend that we must soon part and utter our last farewell, at this thought one's heart breaks. Surely an account of my situation is enough for you. The Lord give you and me strength and teach us to say with the Apostle, "To whom shall we go: thou hast the words of eternal life."

More sincerely yours,

E. Aanen

Note: Mr. E. Aanen was burgomaster of Hoornaar, and a very intimate friend of J. Hospers. On July 4, 1887, when I was in Holland, Mrs. Aanen, widow of the late Burgomaster, was there and I talked with her. Their son, D.K. Aanen, lived in the house. D.K. Aanen was the executer of the estate of Uncle Willem, the latter then still living—Gerrit Hendrik Hospers.

Hospers 54*

Pella, Iowa, December 1848

Dear Parents!

It is pleasant just to talk with you imagining that I am right in your family circle. I am well, only I have made an acquaintance with toothache. There is little sickness; during this year only eleven persons died in this colony. The stork is much in evidence. Rev. Scholte also got a new son. Our Pella farmers make good money. They sell live hogs for 14 cents a pound. Feed costs almost nothing. Carpenters do very well. Welle, Overkamp, and I advise brother Klaas to learn the carpenter trade. Mr. de Gelder better become a farmer: he will love to drive oxen. Just now I receive from Rev. Scholte a list of things he would like to get from Holland, namely: red, white, black "bonte" [currants?] (2-year-old plants); slips of blue and white grapes, early and late; seeds for strawberries; apple and pear seeds; sour and sweet raspberries, cherries; bulbs: 25 hyacinth, 25 tulips, 100 crocus; 25 Duke Van Tol; 25 ranunculus; lilies, keiserskroon; seed of cockscomb, of sweet William, asters, larkspur, cauliflower seed...[*the page is here torn off. In a side-note Hendrik asks for heavy goods for a winter coat because it is so cold in America. A son of Welle asks for the same thing.*]

H. Hospers

Hospers 55*

Hoogblokland, 5am, 30 December 1848

Hendrik!

We have not yet received the letter that you promised your grandfather and Uncle [Hendrik] de Gelder, with an accounting for the first half year of 1848. We need this to settle accounts between your grandfather and me. Your uncle Willem Middelkoop would like to wait another year before going to Pella, but otherwise we all are ready to go.

Well, Hendrik, we shall wait no longer for your letter. We have decided that if the Lord will and we live, and no deaths occur in the family of old people, to continue teaching school until the last of March and leave Holland about May 1. Answer at once if this will be all right

That cheating in America is terrible!

Remember that your next letter is probably the last one you should send us in Holland. Let your schooling go. Get information. Write at once. I will keep on writing till we leave.

The Lord be with you and us. He will be our guide as He was yours. Good morning, Hendrik!

Your loving father,

J. Hospers.

Hospers 56*

[Part of a letter of L. Van Bergeyk]

Pella, Iowa, January 1849

Dear Brother in our Lord Jesus Christ!

Furthermore, since your son Hendrik is a well behaving, splendid son who seeks to serve your best interests whenever he has an opportunity, but on account of his minority cannot proceed as he should, he ought above everything have from you your full power of attorney.

Our Rev. Scholte is very slow in giving his account. What the reason for this is leads to all kinds of surmises. How far there is reason for suspicion is hard to say. It is therefore very desirable that your son Hendrik shall have power to act if necessary on your behalf and in your interest. A young man like Hendrik Hospers can be entrusted with such power. He has good judgment and acts like a man. You would hardly know him anymore; in his appearance he inspires respect. And as God has endowed him with qualities for business, we may believe God will also give him His grace as he himself desire.

Yours in the Lord,

L. Van Bergeyk

Hospers 57*

Hoogblokland, 18 January 1849

Worthy Hendrik!

We are at present in great danger of inundation. The rivers are full of ice. The Waal broke loose. The Merwede [River] is blocked at Hardinxveld. Near Dordrecht and up our way the waters are blocked. No one remembers anything like it. Today at 7am comes Folker Vink, our water guard in such times, with news of what the Dyke Commission ascertained. The water stood at 15 feet above normal and still rising!!!

Today I am going to enter your name for the National Militia. In the Register for the Government I shall enter you as the first one. When the lots are drawn, I hope you will have the highest number [and so fall out of the number called to serve].

Jan. 29 early. A dyke broke in the Land van Altena south of Gorinchem. We are saved! All the ice is gone (Ps. 147:17,18). *De Tweede Stem uit Pella* [*The Second Voice from Pella*] by Rev. Scholte is encouraging enough for people who have money to spare, or who are able to work. [Jacob] Maasdam invites all to a joint effort in the association, in order to travel as a party to Pella in May! I have learned that Mrs. Zeelt has given two thousand guilders, and Mr. Schuijt in Germany one thousand guilders for transportation to Pella for thirty persons from Woerden, etc.

The registration for the National Militia is concluded. In the two communities that are here combined, the full number is 24, from whom the required number to serve will be drawn. In regard to your case, I have written to the governor. His Excellency answered that I had properly entered you.

Uncle Van Est is again improving. Last night we again smoked a pipe together. We have no letter from you. As long as this continues, we dare not come to a full decision. On Sept. 22 you promised to write a big letter with an accounting for the first half year, why not to date? For I get monies whose interest I lose. Many wait for your letter; everything is at a standstill. People want to sell in time, but your delay hinders this. You don't know how we are all looking every morning for a letter, and then such disappointment. People are hopeful when they see the mail carrier; they are despondent when he passes without a word from America.

Jan. 26. Whatever comes from America, we only look for something from Hendrik.

Feb. 3. Yesterday morning we received a letter from Maasdam saying that H. van Dam had disposed of his office. His difficulties are now all gone. Maasdam invites the union of all who would emigrate and leave for Pella on May 1st. Again it is: O, that Hendrik would but write! Last night your mother and I and T[eunis] de Gelder went to your grandparents, to read to them the letter of [Jacob] Maasdam. Indecision! "Why did not Hendrik write?" Said they all, as in concert. They refer to our aged relatives and all feel sorry for them. I read to them Luke 18: 29, 30. Looking to the Lord we decide to go to Pella.

Feb. 10. No letter yet from Hendrik! I have proposed to the aged De Gelder family to take over my mortgages. In April they will receive three or four thousand guilders from their auction and so they could get good interest and can save the expenses connected with succession rights, etc. But their answer was contrary, because they saw clearly that we desired to depart. Uncle Teunis answered that "he had had in mind to place that money in the Gorinchem Savings bank in our names; also to transfer the farm back of the school in our name. But now that we would go, while they, the old people, were in need of us; that Klaas (my father-in-law) and I made each other crazy, etc." O, they were so angry. Aunt Betje cried, and said that we could become rich in Holland, etc. I did not lose my temper but pitied the old souls because they made it so plain that they cared more for earthly things than the spiritual. Next day I went out to arrange for the mortgages. But there was one that needs to go through the courts on account of a child under age. This will take so much time that we cannot get away in the spring. It is a great disappointment. Father, too, has waited too long with the sale of his property. We may have to leave even more behind than we can afford. And the care for the financial affairs of some other people has robbed me of enough sleep. Now I wish soon to know what has been done with the money sent across. Our $f4000$ has not given us a cent of interest. Nor do we know how you do things and whether you earn anything. You should know that your parents surely may be informed so such things.

With love, Your father,

J. Hospers

Hospers 58*

[undated]

Hendrik!

Tell the friends who came from Noordeloos that at present there is much ado about witchcraft in Noordeloos. It is said that there are 86 persons in that community versed in it. There are only two who are bewitched. Arie Brouwer also belonged to this number. He went to a so-called witchdoctor, Lelie, a harness-maker in Gorinchem, who at first seemingly brought much improvement in his condition; but now that patient died suddenly. A certain Hieligje, servant of Andries van Kleef, is accused of unusual ability and energy in that matter. Maria de Jong asks you to give her regards to Reb. Better are those who came from Noordeloos.

J. Hospers

Hospers 59 [Hospers 20]

Pella, 1 February 1849

Confidential

Highly Esteemed Parents!

Although I was advised not to write you about the Pella matters; nevertheless, as your son I feel myself duty bound to do so. An accounting of the costs of the ocean journey and the purchase of lands has still not been completed, and the Pella Christians have proof that it is not good to rely on the arm of flesh and to put your confidence in people.

Several months ago already, a few people went to see Scholte about titles to their land and settlement of the ocean journey costs. But it was in vain; no one could get a settlement. He had no respect at all for the Hollanders; the Americans occupied first place in his mind. Thus, for example, when his house was being built, several American carpenters were working for him. There were also some Hollanders, who were much more competent than the former; still the Americans got 1¼ dollars per day and the Hollanders got ¾ dollars per day. A host of other things happened, all designed to make [him] pope of Pella. At the time, the

Hollanders did not notice it, for if something did occur during the week, then he still won everyone's heart on Sunday by his preaching. The Americans, however, did notice it, and said, "Sch[olte] is a little king, he makes the Hollanders poor, etc." When the mill was being built, the Americans got the job, despite the fact that there were able Dutch millwrights in Pella. The Americans cheated him, and still he was blind to it, although he was told often enough. Gradually he gained various [political] offices, with the result that he devoted his life entirely to the world of politics. He did preach occasionally (in order to throw sand in the eyes of the people), but he acted as if he were ashamed to admit that he belonged to the Holland Christian Church. In proof of this, note:
1. that he did not contribute a penny toward the building of the church;
2. that as a member he did not deign to sign a petition to have the church recognized as an independent corporation;
3. that he did not preach a sermon without admonishing the congregation about its lack of charity;
4. that he always had something negative to say about the congregation; they were always out to get money out of him, etc.

There was no truth in any of this.

He had much building done that was not needed, and he bought anything and everything his eyes fell on and to which he took a fancy. If anyone came to see him about settling accounts, he could never get around to it. And that was true of the rennet as well.

I knew nothing of his having ordered these through you, nor did I know of the [F.S.] Dikker matter. When I first got the news, he began talking about having me sell the rennet. Hence, the agreement between Overkamp and me. As soon as I received word from you about the money advance to [F.S.] Dikker for Scholte, I went to see him seven times about the money, whereupon he finally offered me the said eighty acres. I then wrote you, and you answered that you would take the eighty acres and pay for them when you got here. Yesterday I went to see him again, but he was not well then and asked me to come back in a few days. He took an extortionate profit on the farms. He made five hundred dollars profit on most of them, and then in addition he took the woods that belonged to the farms and divided them among various small landowners. And we have to pay 2¼ dollars on the claim for the woods, 1 dollar more than the government price if he had paid in cash, but now at least 1¼ dollars more than he paid, because he paid with land warrants. Fortunately, there are men like Overkamp and Barendregt in the colony who dare to stand up to him and do so. Fortunately, the association demonstrates that it is worthy of its name by not being afraid to confront him who had won everyone's trust in Holland, but who has made such a scandalous misuse of that trust. Next Monday he will be suspended from his office [as minister]. An accounting of the costs of the journey will be provided to the directors [of the association] within eleven days. We know that there is a balance of seven thousand guilders, but according to his calculation (as told to Overkamp), there still is a deficit...? I will write you of the outcome immediately; I dare repeat [in public] everything I have written at any time, and I have the proof. I would not have written the above if I had thought it would scare you from coming. But I am convinced that you are not coming to Pella for the sake of Scholte, but for the community of saints, which every believer is in need of. And such a community is very special here; we are not lacking in men to proclaim the Word of God on Sundays. O! No! You will be delighted to hear them. And with that I will close.

Father, more and more I am beginning to think about a gristmill. I assure you that it is a profitable venture here. There is a man in the colony, [J.] Smeenk, who has a store, for whom [L.] Van Bergeyk works. This Smeenk is a very fine Christian, one whom you will really enjoy getting to know; Van Bergeyk will attest to his character. This man wants to form a company, which I would also always recommend you join, and that for the following reasons: 1. Initially there are no large capital outlays; if each of you invested one thousand dollars, you would have a steam gristmill, and steam milling is seldom paid in money by Americans, but rather in a share of the crop milled. The result of this is that the grist miller is also the grist seller! and not [only] as a retailer but [also] as a wholesaler. That is why it pays to have him [the miller] here, because he then knows he can sell flour [at wholesale] in St. Louis and also is able to sell flour at retail in the colony. And later on you can adapt it [the mill] to any capacity you choose.

The content of this letter is the principal reason for my writing so soon. I have received twenty guilders from F. Klein, who requests that you kindly pay this sum of money to his poor sister.

How do you like my notes to Uncle! Please do send them on after you have read them; that makes a better impression. Now it is up to you to take over on the [mill] matter. If you are the least bit so inclined, then pay the exchange check drawn on L. v.d. Basaan. He could work on it because he is a good mill builder, but not as though he would be in charge. There are plenty of able mill builders here. Smeenk is a very capable man, has lived in Zutphen, and was the head clerk at the Registry Office. He is a very good mechanic, so he can be very useful in the building [of the mill]. Father, I recommend that you give this your serious consideration. Make your decision as soon as possible, because if there should be more people coming over [to Iowa] then, if we are to go ahead, we must be ahead of them.

Greetings to Grandfather and his household from me; say hello to all the family. Hoping to receive your answer soon, I name myself your obedient son,

Hendrik Hospers.

P.S. Where there is a number, spell it out in letters next to it, and be very sure you do that.

Oh, Father! I had a conversation with some Americans about a gristmill. All of them attest to the fact that there is no better business to get into, if you come here. So do it, soon, before you start anything else. So I expect an answer in....

A testimonial about Mr. [J.] Smeenk by L. Van Bergeyk [enclosed]

The person, Mr. Smeenk, belongs to the Baptist congregation, but we may call him a Brother in our Lord Jesus. He is gifted with various talents externally, and is an able administrator, a dear man. I would say, I have had a second father Hospers in him, and if you were here, you would also choose his company, and in every way praise him that by the grace of God he is a Christian both externally and internally. If you were interested in erecting a gristmill with him, for which there is great need here, then you would have recouped your costs within several years given the blessing of the Lord.

Greetings from me and my wife and children to you and your wife and children, and to father and mother Middelkoop, and so I remain your brother in the Lord Jesus.

L. Van Bergeyk

Hospers 60*

Pella, Iowa, 8:30 p.m., 10 February 1849

Dear Mother!
I think that this letter will arrive quite a while before your birthday

(March 21). On that day my thoughts will be with you, and although I am separated far from you, I can nevertheless wish for you much enjoyment, good health, and the greatest treasure, faith in Christ. O, dear Mother! May the Lord grant that when we meet each other, we may relate to each other what great things the Lord has done to our souls. Indeed that is the most important of all. Then we are prepared for eternity, and can lift up our heads in the midst of all turmoil, knowing that our deliverance is at hand. The Lord is able to perform all things, if only we believe. The Lord grant us that faith, then you would long even more for eternity.

Your loving son,

H. Hospers

P.S. I also wish Maaike the same on her 18th birthday (March 19).

Note. A lost letter dated Feb. 9 and 10 is entirely given to Hendrik urging his father to underwrite the building of a mill. He is most optimistic about its success and gives much detail what to do about it. It would cost no more than $1,600, of which his father is asked to advance $1,000 and Mr. Smeenk $600. He urges that 60 ells of gauze be sent at once, the best, which in America costs nine dollars a yard. "Write at once; with your consent I begin at once. I'll have the tree felled; those will get dry in time, and is no loss anyway, etc."—Gerrit Hendrik Hospers.

Hospers 61*

Hoogblokland, 20 February 1849

Dear Hendrik,

We plan to leave in May. We think we will come 150 strong. Can you get us from Keokuk, Iowa?

J. Hospers

Hospers 62*

Hoornaar, 20 February 1849

Honorable Sir and Highly Esteemed Friend!

Now I have not any longer been able to hide your intention and have informed some friends here as well as in Gorinchem. I can give you the assurance that everybody is shocked to learn of your intention to depart, and thus they share my bitter sorrow.

Once more (I know you will not take it ill of me), while hardly eight more days are set till the execution of your decision, I must once more invite you to continue your valuable activities here. I request that you honor this on the following grounds: If it should be asked of me whether you could be more useful elsewhere than here, I must say, No, as I consider from the youth to the aged. The youth, O, how much they will lose in your departure, not only because they had such an instructive association with you, and I would so dearly have all our own under your care. But what is more so, many seeds unto eternal life have been sown, which, if God be pleased to grant to which I belong and can best understand, we regard as invaluable your gifts used for our good. But I have still greater need: it is known to you, and I have besought God, that regarding this need I might no longer find a helper such as you.

As for the aged, were it only for your relatives, how all their intercourse, all their trust shall have been removed. Those aged ones who were to you almost as parents, and, as I have the idea, regarded you as their son. O, how they shall miss your daily assistance. What is more, who shall now be their guide for the salvation of their immortal souls, when the journey to eternity can so speedily be ended. There, my friend, do consider and weigh this. The Lord grant you light, and grant me support and strength.

I call myself with respect, your Honorable's Servant and Friend,

E. Aanen

Hospers 63*

Hoogblokland, 1 March 1849

Dear Hendrik!

We received a short letter from you through J. Meyer. We have scruples to help Meyer. We notice that money matters between him and Vander Ley are not just right, and others have preference.

Your letter was a corker. Your proposal is grand. I read it to Uncle Van Est and he admired it, and though he would be glad to see you, he considers it must not be required; the sacrifice is too great. You understand it would greatly lessen our chances if you came here. No,

Hendrik, we come to you. We long for your long letter. We may not again write to you because we will be coming so soon.

Hendrik, just a little patience, and we will be there with you. You can no longer reply to us in the Netherlands.... [Jacob] Maasdam was here to see me, and by our calculations, this will be the last group of Scholte followers, but that rear guard will bring money to Pella. Quite a number come with us and that will strengthen Pella a good deal. I have reason to think that Father [Middelkoop] will take along at least f7,000, and though I must leave quite a little, I still expect to have f3,600, from which traveling expenses and everything else will have to be paid. That's enough, isn't it? And then we have seven healthy children and Hendrik. I no longer have any objections, Hendrik! I am happy, and I long for the brethren. I think I hear Van Bergeyk laughing. Greet all our friends, acquaintances, and above all our brothers in Christ. Your eager parents,

J. Hospers

Hospers 64*

Hoogblokland, 20 March 1849

Dear Hendrik:

Your letter of Dec. was received on March 13. The envelope was in bad condition and the edges of the letter frayed. Burgomaster Aanen drew the lot for your military service. It was 19, which made you free.

March 23, 1849

As regards the grain mill I cannot judge. Will the proceeds actually be what you picture to yourself?

March 26, 1849

We intend to go in a full month.

March 27, 1849

Tolling of the bells for His Majesty Willem II who died the 17th. Contain yourself now until the Lord shall have brought us over to you.

Your loving father,

J. Hospers

Hospers 65 [Hospers 21]

Pella, April 1849

Highly Esteemed Parents and Grandparents!

A half-hour ago I received your letter of February 12 in good health and no postage fee, probably because of arrangements made between the postal services of the U.S. and England. I would have written sooner if I had known earlier of your firm decision not to come. To tell you the truth, I shuddered to read the words, "I am coming," for the condition in the colony has not improved. I will write more about that.

As I wrote earlier, [Klaas] v.d. Linden has arrived in America and spent the winter in St. Louis. From there he went to Keokuk and left his family there. He was held back by the bad reports about our colony, and he himself went to Pella with several others to check things out personally. Last week he arrived here, spent several days here, and after a thorough investigation he became only too convinced of the truth and decided not to come here but to buy land elsewhere. In the same way Berkhout from Amsterdam, Bouman from Woerden, and several others from Spijk have also gone back after a similar investigation. Since I am aware that you have been on familiar terms with v.d. Linden for a good while, and I was informed that he is a man of good and solid character, I spoke to him at some length about various matters.

The real reasons for the unfavorable situation in Pella are the following: Scholte is unwilling to give an accounting. This raises suspicions, which, it appears, are not unfounded. Among others there are questions whether the money for the river land, which as you know cannot be purchased as yet, is really on hand. There are many poor people living on that land, and they have spent all their money working the land. Others with farms are getting into a like situation and have no more money, and if Scholte should not have any either to fall back on, then both run the risk that speculators will buy the land. But, you will say, you only surmise all that; you do not know for sure! About four weeks ago Scholte was the subject of discussion at a meeting of the colonists in Pella. The meeting was presided over by [A.J.] Betten, vice president, after two others had been appointed to go to Scholte, president, to request, in the name of the members, that he attend the meeting. But Scholte pretended he could not come, and did not come, because a presidential indisposition prevented him from so doing. The remaining members of the board were I. Ov(erkamp), secretary, and the board members elected in the Netherlands.

At this meeting Overkamp read out loud a letter Scholte had written to the Society. Its principal content was that people were accusing him wrongly, that he had never sought his own interest, but always that of the Society. He proposed that two or more persons be appointed to take the place of the old board, and that they, as members of the society, be entrusted to handle all its business.

We knew what was to be expected, and anyone who did not know the true state of affairs would almost have wept; it was all so religious and so nice. The verdict of the gathering was not to adopt that letter, not to get rid of the old board (because Scholte had something in mind in proposing this), but to appoint several others and strengthen the existing board. The following were appointed: C. Den Hartog, [H.Y.] Viersen, [J.] Smeenk, [G.] Hagens, and [Pieter] Welle. They were to meet weekly, working in the name of the Society, and report on their activities to all the members every other month. Tomorrow, Saturday, March....that will take place. I already know the outcome, but in order to write in good order I will keep notes and pass them on to you in this letter. In a letter that he [Scholte] once wrote to the consistory, he rails at them as stupid blokes [who] did not understand his letter. That's what he thinks of the colony. When some of the elders want to speak to him, it is not unusual for them to be sent away. I. Ov[erkamp] and Smeenk were to help him write [the final settlement] on Saturday[s], but sometimes it does not suit his convenience, and then they will just have to come back.

But now let me tell you about the river land money. To reassure the colonists, and in their name, the board has looked into this with Scholte, who told them that the money was deposited in a bank in New York, but later on he contradicted that again. Do not be surprised. He is a big liar, for what he tells the Society today, he denies the next day. And that is why he was cut off from the congregation last Sunday. Now he is beginning to talk about leaving. And in the face of all this he still says, "If only the people would come asking forgiveness, then I could live with it." Last week when I informed him about the coming of Mr. [Herman] Van Dam, he told me "that he was intending to advise that gentleman to remain in New York until things in the colony were somewhat better."

Hendrik Hospers

What Hospers wrote confidentially, Sjoerd Auke Sipma made public in his *Belangrijke berigten uit Pella [Important Reports from Pella] (Dokkum, 1849)*. He wrote: "Accordingly, religion then is about the only thing that is pretty good; for the rest the actions of Scholte are very naughty. He took up to seven hundred dollars more for claims than they cost him. That is the way the man acted who should have been a father, as it were, acting on behalf of his children, but who goes about filling his own purse."[1]

---

[1] S. A. *Sipma*, Belangrijke Berigten uit Pella in de Vereenigde Staten van Noord Amerika, of tweede Brief...aan de ingezetenen van Bornwerd.... *(Dockum: Wed. B. Schaafsma, 1849), 28-29,* trans. Robert P. Swierenga, ed., *"A Dutch Immigrant's View of Frontier Iowa,"* Annals of Iowa 38 *(Fall 1965): 81-118.*

Chapter 4

The Disappointment of Andries N. Wormser
(Wormser Letters 17-37)

When he boarded a Mississippi steamboat, traveling upstream on his journey to the promised land, the bewildered immigrant had to cope with "vagabonds, swindlers and gamblers, explosions, storms, fires, sandbars, bad food, ramshackle living quarters, illness, suffering, and death." Cabin passengers did enjoy some comforts, but life on the middle and lower decks was often unbearable.

The privations of the immigrants on steamboats were not limited to everyday matters. Epidemics of Asiatic cholera scourged the inland areas during the decades before the Civil War; often steamboats spread the disease from one port to another. There was little sanitation practiced, and many immigrants succumbed to the disease. It frequently happened that when a steamboat lay by, the crew jumped overboard and quickly dug a grave for a new victim. The cold indifference of Americans towards life on these steamboats led Captain Marryat to make the following entry in his journal: "I hate the Mississippi [River] and when I look down on its wild and filthy waters, boiling and roiling, and consider how dangerous it is to travel in this area of high tension, without any social rights, then I can not suppress a feeling of loathing at the thought of perishing in such a filthy sewer, buried in mud, and perhaps to be discovered by a gluttonous alligator."[1]

This quotation from a book about paddle steamers on the Mississippi

---

1. William J. Petersen, *Steamboating on the Upper Mississippi* (Iowa City: State Historical Society of Iowa, 1968), 353-54.

Guillaume Groen van Prinsterer (1801-1876), Seceder leader and founder of the Anti-Revolutionary Party

tells us enough about the journey that was so disappointing to Andries Wormser. In Letters 20 and 22 he tells about the boats and in Letters 18 and 21 about scarlet fever and cholera.

Andries Wormer describes the farm of Budde, the end and turning point of his journey. On 10 April 1848, J. A. Wormser had written to Groen van Prinsterer: "I have received a letter from my friend Budde in America. He is settled on a lovely farm, a half-hour from Burlington, the capital of Iowa; the farm with a brick house, stable etc. cost him 2,000 dollars. They have a pious preacher in Burlington; my friend and his son, a godly young man eighteen years old, are already active in the Sunday school, and he conducts a Bible based catechism class with young men of the congregation, just as we were accustomed to doing in Amsterdam. All of his reports are favorable."

And that is the way Letters 11 and 12 were understood in the Netherlands. Accordingly, Groen would write on 28 January 1849: "The migration to N. America, provided it is under proper management and supervision, might very well serve a great good and useful purpose. It appears, in general, that our fellow believers are doing well, and that there is work and a decent wage for anyone who is willing and able to work diligently. I recently received confirmation of all this in a kind letter from Rev. Van Raalte, which I am enclosing, convinced as I am that you will enjoy reading it."

Groen wrote this at the very same time that A. N. Wormser was writing up his experiences. In Letter 27 Wormser fiercely attacked *Stemmen uit Noord Amerika met een begeleidend woord van A. Brummelkamp* [*Voices from North America, with an accompanying note by A. Brummelkamp*]. The letter of Louise Arnoud, written in Boston September 11, 1846, which had been included in this booklet, is cited and contested by A. N. Wormser. In so doing, he overlooked the fact that it described the situation in Boston and not that in St. Louis or Burlington. He also forgot the following travel account that appeared in the same letter:

> That very night we experienced our worst storm ever; the two of us had two bunks, the one above the other. Well, my husband slept on the top bunk with our little Derkje, and I slept on the lower berth with our two little ones. The ship was in bad shape so that it not only leaked from below but from above as well, and so there was water leaking into our beds and into those of many others, who had to vacate their beds that night. My husband stayed up and lay down on a trunk in front of the bunk bed. At midnight there was such a terrible thunderstorm that the waves crashed over the deck and into the hatches; the foredeck was instantly filled with water; everyone was busy taking down the sails. It was so dark that they could not see a thing; everyone got up, including a man who came from the vicinity of Zutphen, who was deluged with water as he was going up the stairs. When he got to the top of the stairs, he saw nothing but water; he began to weep and called: "Comrades, we are perishing!" I felt sorry for him, for I believe he was worried about his own soul.

The letter contains a warning about the journey and a description of life in Boston that can hardly be called upbeat. But Andries Wormser felt that he had been deceived by it all.

In Letters 23 and 27, J. Berkhout appears on the scene, a misfit who was ridiculed for all his complaints. A letter of his, written to his father, brother, and friends in Amsterdam, was published without permission by G. van Peursem in 1849. Berkhout departed on 28 July 1848. Berkhout, Wormser, and Keesel traveled together as far as New York. From there Berkhout left posthaste with his wife—they had no children—to Troy outside Albany, forgetting his mattress, blankets, and pillows, all left behind at a rooming house. On several occasions he complains about tickets. He got lost in Chicago. "And so after much grief, cheating, vexation, despondency, losses and whatever else can cause pain to one's heart, we finally arrived in St. Louis on the 29th of October."[2]

---

2. *Brief uit Noord Amerika van J. Berkhout aan zijnen vader, broeder en vrienden* (Amsterdam: Van Peursem, 1849), 21.

The Rev. Jan de Liefde, pastor of the Free Evangelical Church, Amsterdam

(© 1999 Foto Henk Visscher)

The scandal-monger Diekinga paints such a bleak picture of Pella that Berkhout stayed on a half-year in St. Louis, ever complaining, but finally he did get to Pella.[3] The published letter of Berkhout appeared with a publisher's announcement on the backside, which says, "Today the press publishes *Klaaglied* [*Song of Lamentation*]), sung in the presence of the king and the nation by H. W. van Rennes." This advertisement spoke to the imagination of the readers (which probably was its intent), so that the rumor reached Berkhout that his letter had gotten the title: "*de klaagliederen van Jeremias*" ("The Lamentations of Jeremiah") (see Wormser Letter 37). The source of the rumor may be the Reverend J. de Liefde of Amsterdam, who on March 7, 1849, wrote of a jeremiad by Berkhout in a letter to J. Smeenk in Pella, "I suspect that it was published without his knowledge." And, "Everyone is having a good laugh at the misfortunes of those two awkward travelers" (Joint Archives of Holland, Holland, Michigan).

Two letters of Scholte belong in this chapter. From them it is evident that Scholte still needed $8,000 and that he borrowed this money from Mrs. J. J. Zeelt at his own risk. According to [Lubbertus] Oostendorp, he purchased 7,600 acres from the land speculator John Armstrong

---

3. Ibid., 24.

Graham for $9,000 and sold 3,186 acres of it to Mrs. Zeelt. He did that to acquire as large an area as possible for the society in the expectation that the Des Moines River would become navigable. At the end of 1848, the *Tweede Stem uit Pella* [*The Second Voice from Pella*] was published in the Netherlands. It includes the plat of Amsterdam, a port on the Des Moines River, surveyed and drawn by Hendrik Hospers.

However, the flood of 1851 put an end to those plans for good. In the light of all these givens, the transaction made by Scholte with the money of a trusting old lady in the Netherlands does seem justifiable. The difference between the purchase price and the selling price of land is understandable, because of the many additional expenses for public facilities and services in every municipality. Many immigrants did not understand that and vehemently accused Scholte of enriching himself. People like Diekenga and Berkhout, who were in no way involved, were the worst gossips.[4]

We read the following about Mrs. Zeelt in a letter of J. A. Wormser to Groen van Prinsterer, dated December 6, 1850:

> On the 14th of this month Mrs. Zeelt will become seventy years old; she has high esteem for your activities. I would be greatly pleased if I could present Her Honor with a copy (of your portrait) in name of Mrs. Groen. She is a woman worthy of our high respect. The lawsuits in which she was involved with her husband in the past speak of [her] "fanaticism" and other such things. Her husband would have liked to have her declared *insane*. The only thing he brought to the marriage was debts. When the marriage was to be contracted, he led her to believe that the marriage deed stipulating the marriage conditions could not be drawn up until after the marriage. When the marriage had been contracted, he said that he had made a mistake. I cannot write any more about that; like everyone else, she has her faults, but they are the faults of a person who from her youth on has been an *exemplary Christian,* who sided more with *poor people* than with *prominent people.*

Mrs. Zeelt, a woman from Baambrugge who was divorced and a Seceder, in July 1850 gave twenty thousand guilders to the *Christelijk Gereformeerde Seminarie* [Christian Reformed Seminary] then being

---

4. Dorothy Schwieder, ed., *Patterns and Perspectives in Iowa History* (Ames: Iowa State Univ. Press, 1973), 68-71.

founded in Amsterdam. Later on she gave even more for the purpose of bringing together the *Hervormde Kerk* (National Reformed Church) and the seceding believers on the basis of the Reformed confessions.[5] However, the Amsterdam plan miscarried. Later, they returned to the plan but within a broader perspective: the history of the *Christelijk Gereformeerde Seminarie* belongs to the prehistory of the *Vrije Universiteit* [Free University] of Amsterdam. The name of Mrs. Zeelt is associated both with one of the first persecutions of the Seceders in Amsterdam and the last persecution in the Netherlands, as well as with the purchases of land in Pella, and with the prehistory of the Free University.

The *Sheboygan Nieuwsbode*, the oldest Dutch language newspaper in America, in Vol. II, number 8 of January, 17, 1851, presents the following summary of the work of Wormser. "Among the Seceders there is a plan for establishing a Theological School, at which the Reverends Brummelkamp and Van Houten and two other scholars will be teaching. With this in mind a number of them recently joined to form a corporate body with the name, *De Christelijk Gereformeerde Seminarie*, established in Amsterdam and have already purchased a building in that city."

This plan seems to be related to an attempt to restore the Secession to its original starting point, not as a separation from the Hervormde Kerk, but rather from the ecclesiastical organization introduced [by King Willem I] in 1816. Thus, it was their desire, as was the case with the Free Scottish Church in Scotland, to give the Secession a more national character and to again free it of the sectarian appearance it had gotten in recent years. Accordingly, they no longer viewed it as being separated from *the church* but from *the ruling ecclesiastical structure* [as instituted in 1816]. As members of the Hervormde Kerk, against whose beliefs and way of life there were no specific objections, they could then also, without seceding, receive the seals of the covenant [the sacraments] for themselves and for their children. This was in accordance with the press announcement that Wormser had prepared.

And then on October 31, 1851, in the 100th number of this paper, we read: "The reverend gentlemen H. A. de Vos and H. de Cock, ministers of the Christian Seceded Congregations at Marrum and at 's Hertogenbosch, have been called as ministers by *De Hollandsche Gereformeerde Gemeente* (The Holland Reformed Congregation) at Grand

---

5. *Tot de prediking van het Woord des geloofs: opstellen ter gelegenheid van de herdenking van de oprichting der Theologische School A.D. 1854 te Kampen* (Kampen: Comité van Uitgave, 1954), 57.

Rapids, in the State of Michigan. The Christian Seceded Congregation at Arnhem has also called the Rev. H. A. de Vos to fill a vacancy caused by the departure of the Rev. A. Brummelkamp to Amsterdam, where His Reverence will take up his duties as docent at the Christelijk Gereformeerde Seminarie in November."

Thus the [Dutch Calvinists] in America read this to mean that after the Revolutions of 1848 [in Holland and Europe], those who had been left behind [in Holland] were still developing new plans. However, the Wormser plan [see above] miscarried because of Brummelkamp.

From Amsterdam, Wormser on October 28, 1851 wrote to the Reverend C. G. de Moen, seceder preacher at Den Ham:

> Esteemed Friend and Brother in the Lord!
>
> I have your letter of the 25th instant. I am not despondent as concerns the work of the Lord, also in our country, but I am despondent as far as the Secession is concerned. A judgment of blindness seems to rest on it. Consequently, it is always losing itself in trifles, and anyone who seeks to build her up lovingly, they cast aside with ingratitude and heap contempt on him. It is not unpleasant for me to write you this; but it is very unpleasant for me, after having worked hard at the seminary for a year, that I now must devote my time in writing letters of explication and in conferences. I have withdrawn myself somewhat from it all, not because Brummelkamp is right, but because he is one of my oldest friends, and I do not wish to take sides against him.
>
> Brummelkamp is the only *overt* cause of all the confusion; Van Houte, who never speaks up at meetings, may well be the *hidden* cause. The confusion all started in such a strange manner, and yet at the same time it was all so very intentional, that it became very

The Rev. Anthony Brummelkamp (1811-1888), leader of the southern wing of the Secession of 1834, brother-in-law of A. C. Van Raalte and Simon van Velzen.

The Rev. Simon van Velzen (1809-1896), leader of the northern wing of the Secession of 1834

obvious that Brummelkamp very much wanted to have the Hervormde docents on his side. Although it is only a surmise on my part, the entire course of events leads me to the supposition that Brummelkamp often suffered from a feeling of his own inadequacy, and that he looked up against being a docent alongside Da Costa and Schwartz, and that Van Houte, seeking to save his own skin, stirred things up. The intent of Brummelkamp to break with the Hervormde docents was most obvious; fidelity to the Afscheiding was merely a pretext. In a gathering of the docents, at which I was present, Brummelkamp developed the thesis (whatever occasioned these remarks I do not recall) that there was not a single *getrouw* [faithful] pastor or member in the Hervormde Kerk. Da Costa replied, "but in *het Programma van Wormser* [the Wormser Program] you did recognize us as *getrouw* [faithful], did you not?" This was the beginning of the *verwijdering* [estrangement]. Brummelkamp rejected that document as not being his. In the discussions he developed principles of fidelity which left everyone dumbfounded. Hasebroek would have to be confirmed in the Hervormde Kerk by Br[ummelkamp], etc. (Wormser Archives).

Brummelkamp again unpacked all the goods he had gotten ready for the move to Amsterdam and remained at Arnhem. He reconciled himself with his brother-in-law Van Velzen. Mrs. Zeelt gave the building to the

The Rev. Carl A. F. Schwartz (1817-1870), German Jewish convert, pastor of Scottish Missionary Church to the Jews, and professor, Scottish Seminary, Amsterdam
(J. C. Rullmann, Onze Voortrekkers, Delft, 1931, 95)

Scottish Missionary Church, which was doing mission work among the Amsterdam Jews under the German Jew, Dr. Carl Schwartz (1817-1870). The Free Church of Scotland and a Scottish seminary were

Scottish Missionary Church, Amsterdam

established in the building. Schwartz and Da Costa were docents there from 1852 till 1860. The building on the Oude Zijds Voorburgwal, in the Stoofsteeg, was becoming too small by 1856, and so in 1886 the *Fransche Comedie* (French Comedy Theater) on the Erwtenmarkt was purchased and deeded to the *Nederlandse Vereniging voor Israel* [Netherlands Society for Israel] under the name Salvatori. The Erwtenmarkt became the *Amstelkade* [Amstel River Wharf] and the building later was utilized by *de Kleine Komedie* [The Little Comedy Theater], [Binnen Amstel at the Halve Maansteeg]. *De Heraut* [the *Herald*], a paper founded by Schwartz in 1850, passed into the hands of Dr. A. Kuyper in 1871. The opening of the Vrije Universiteit was celebrated in the Salvatori Building of the Scottish Missionary Church in 1880, and the first lectures were given there. Thirty years later Kuyper transformed the Wormser Seminary Plan of 1851 into a university with three faculties: Theology, Jurisprudence, and Letters. Thus there is a connection between the Wormser Plan and the Free University, but it is a crooked path, not a straight one. It was like the seed that lies hidden in the field before the new plant sprouts forth.

A son-in-law of Wormser, C. W. Wüstenhoff, was a board member of the Amsterdam branch of *Nederlandsche Vereeniging der Vrienden Israels* (Netherlands Society of the Friends of Israel) in 1860 when Da Costa died. His son supported the Vrije Universiteit with his publishing business. When we seek to appraise Wormser's intentions, we find that the [idea of] the Vrije Universiteit is wholly in line with his insights and plans. He must have been very well acquainted with the views of the dogmatician of the Vrije Universiteit, Dr. Herman Bavinck (1854-1921), and with those of the honorary doctor of the Vrije Universiteit, Dr. C. Rijnsdorp (1894-1982), though each man was unique in his own way. Spiritual annexation is wrong, but if you do not recognize [the importance] of historical perspective, you will be lacking a dimension in your view of reality. Thus, in this chapter we still see new perspectives for Johan Adam Wormser in the Netherlands. But Andries Wormser did not see any future in America.

In the *Tweede Stem uit Pella* [*A Second Voice from Pella*](1848), H. P. Scholte called attention to unbelief and revolution in Europe. "A Christian cannot, in good conscience, choose to side with the liberalism, but no less can he choose the side of the so-called conservative party, for both of them belong to Babel." Scholte's conclusion is Leave Europe = Babel; go to America = Pella.

With regard to the people who remained behind, like A. Brummelkamp and J. A. Wormser, Scholte wrote: "I know that there will be some Christians who judge that it is their calling to remain, to be witnesses for God, and to suffer for his name. Now when this is a person's honest conviction, we do not wish to dispute that conviction but rather pray to God on their behalf, that he may give them wisdom, courage, and strength to render a good testimony and to remain steadfast in suffering. However, at the same time in all brotherly earnestness we call upon all such: search yourself whether you are really genuine about what you allege to be the reason for your remaining in Babel."[6]

By Babel, Scholte understood the last of the world empires mentioned in the book of Daniel, the Roman Empire. He saw that world empire living on in the Roman Catholic Church and in all the European states that wanted to exercise authority over the free church of Christ. In 1843 *De Reformatie* no longer suited Wormser. In that year Scholte published a letter of J. N. Darby with the following postscript: "I thank God with all my heart that he has directed your attention to the coming of Christ and the prophecies." Then follows an article by Scholte about the return of Christ, consisting principally of a listing of [Bible] texts. The third issue contains an article, "The Millennium." In it Scholte posits that there will be an interim period, between the return of Christ and the end of the world, when Christ will rule the world. In this he is a chiliast like Da Costa, but he remains within the confines of the Reformed confessions. The books of Daniel and the Revelation of John greatly fascinated Scholte. To leave Babel was, for him, a prophetic mission. In the revolutionary year of 1848, it is not all that difficult to understand how Scholte misused the text about leaving Babel in order to encourage people to immigrate to Pella. However, for Groen van Prinsterer, Wormser, and Brummelkamp, there remained an important task in the Netherlands.

After the letters of Andries Wormser, the chapter closes with a letter from J. A. Wormser to his wife, who had fled Amsterdam because of a cholera [epidemic] about the time Andries Wormser returned. In reading the letters of Andries Wormser, by all means do not fail to read the following one from his brother, Johan Adam Wormser.

---

6. H. P. Scholte, *Tweede Stem uit Pella* ('s-Hertogenbosch: Palier & Zn., 1848), 27, trans. Robert P. Swierenga, ed., "A Place of Refuge," *Annals of Iowa* 39 (Summer 1968): 322-57.

Wormser 17

S. de Vries [to A. N. Wormser]
Buffalo, the 6th of November 1848

Dear Sir,

I regret to inform you that I still have no word on your trunk. We have been ready for some time to continue our journey, but the [travel] office has postponed our trip repeatedly. Now the gentleman at the office told us bluntly that he is not able to send us on our way because the [travel] money has all been spent. I immediately informed Mr. Van der Poel about this and he went to the office with me. He [the agent] also spoke to Mr. Van der Poel in the same manner and advised us that the New York office had accepted me too cheaply. I told Mr. Van der Poel that I had paid almost fifty guilders too much, and that I had been swindled in New York as well as in Troy. Mr. Van der Poel then told him [the agent] that because of the long journey and other misfortunes I had run out of money. My wife and I and our eight children would be reduced to poverty, since I was a stranger here, did not have a trade, did not know the language, and the like. None of this did any good, and Mr. Van der Poel indicated that he would be writing to New York at once. If I had known all this beforehand, I would have arranged my affairs accordingly, but as it is, here I am waiting and expecting to leave every day. Dear Sir, the prospects here are not good, the prospects of getting work are poor, because the city is jammed full of people. One is deceived by the [travel] office; another is out of money. Some are weary of traveling. A party of four had already decided for Buffalo in Holland or Germany.

My first landlord urged me to move because my family was so large. I now live in a house that costs five shillings a week. This house is a real disaster; the roof is not very good, we do not have a trapdoor to the attic, nor do we have a hearth for heating [and cooking]. For several days we have had to make do by cooking and heating [water] at the neighbor's. Because we were afraid of losing our youngest child, we were forced to buy a stove which cost thirty guilders with [the necessary] implements.

Dear Sir, please write us as soon as possible as per our agreement. We are eager to know how you and your family fared on your journey, and how you are getting along now. Our [son] Piet [works] for a shoemaker and gets board and room and six shillings a week. Hein is working for a whip maker and earns one dollar a week without board and room. Betje still has not found employment as a domestic. We received six shillings from Piet; [so far] that is all the money we have taken in here in America. My own prospects for getting a job are very poor. I wish with all my heart that I could earn enough for my basic needs by working for you. From the above, you will doubtless get some idea of my situation.

Closing with Greetings,
S. de Vries

Wormser 18

A. N. Wormser to Mr. J. A. Wormser
Oude Zijds Voorburgwal Nr. 205
Amsterdam, Kingdom of Holland
Europe, via Liverpool
Burlington, 6 Nov. 1848

Esteemed Brother,

After having experienced much grief on our journey, we arrived here October 29. I had promised to write you promptly upon our arrival here, but we had barely survived one blow when there was another. I am engaged in writing a detailed account of our travel experiences. But since it will doubtless take several days more before it is ready, and [since] Budde asked whether he might enclose a letter of his that will not be ready for several days, my wife and I decided that it would be a good idea to begin by letting you know of our arrival.

Sophia became indisposed two days before our arrival in Burlington, and she developed a red rash. We arrived on Sunday evening, and the next day sent for the doctor who said that she had scarlet fever; her neck swelled up and nothing availed.... She died the following Friday, Nov. 3, after suffering the most awful shortness of breath. Anna now suffers from the same disease, but hers does not appear to be as severe. Very many children who have come here from Europe die here. A few weeks ago, a man left here who had lost three children in eight days. For the rest we are reasonably well. That is also true for the Buddes, all of whom suffered terribly from illnesses earlier; Jan suffered for eleven months.

I hope that all may be well with you and the family. If you wish, you can already write us; for letters from Holland we pay ten American cents.

There is no mail delivery here; from time to time you go to the post office to find out whether there are any letters for you. My address is Mr. N. A. Wormser, Burlington, State of Iowa. Everything around here is rude and crude. My wife and sister send you all warmest greetings. May I ask you to convey our greetings to Mother Portengen and Mrs. Zeelt, Tienes, and all our friends and acquaintances. If you should have occasion to do so, then let Wijnbergen know that I have arrived, and that he must not sell his property to go to America; this is no place for him; it would just ruin him.

Well, Brother, in a few days you will be receiving a more detailed account of our trip.

Your Loving Brother,
A. N. Wormser

N[ota] B[ene]. In Albany I wrote you about our arrival [in America]. Did you get that letter? Wijnbergen lives on the Rustenburgpad outside the Utrecht Gate on the Obdam Square.

Wormser 19

D. A. Budde to J. A. Wormser in Amsterdam
Burlington, 8 Nov. 1848

Dearly Beloved Brother in our Lord, Jesus Christ,

I have received from your esteemed brother the bill of exchange and seven hundred guilders; I herewith return to Your Honor the signed bill; all conforms to the agreement. I thank you for all the trouble you have gone to on my behalf. My heart is filled with love and esteem for you, and I shall honor that whenever I can.

It grieves me that things were rather disappointing for your esteemed brother in Burlington and did not meet his expectations. They had a very uncomfortable journey; the season was not very favorable. They arrived here with one of the children sick, they had to lose a child through death, and their youngest child was sick. With all these things coming together, it seems to me that it was but natural that there was something sad and depressing about everything for him and his family. Had that not been the case, everything would be much more pleasant for them. I have suggested to your brother that they come and live in with us for the winter, so that we can enjoy each other's company, and I can assist them in word and in deed. My renter, for whom I am building a house on my land, will very likely leave us in two weeks, so Dries could move into it already then, which is much cheaper than staying in Burlington.

I must clarify for Your Honor some information I gave in my earlier letter about taking our homegrown products to market during the summer between three and four in the morning. My writing was not sufficiently clear, and accordingly could not be understood by Your Honor. It's like this. We raise many garden products for ourselves—potatoes that were very abundant and very good (because of a long rain spell most of them rotted away in the entire area; no one around here remembers that it ever rained continuously for so long). And there was corn, of which we had more than we needed for our own use. These were then taken to the market and sold for a good price. The market closes at six in the morning, and then everyone goes home again.

I will not write you much about the [general] situation here right now, and initially I will leave that up to Your Honor's brother. I did receive a letter from Lubberd[en] saying that all is now going well in Pella, and that he is very satisfied. Rev. Scholte is preaching on the prophet Daniel.

I thank you for sharing with me the petitions (about education) that were sent to the king of Holland. If only the Lord might look down in mercy once again on this land, once so blessed but now sighing under his judgments for having left the rock of its salvation, and pour out his spirit in rich measure for the revival of his sorrowing Zion, making glad the pious, and shaming the kingdom of darkness. Thanks be to the Lord that you may still see the fruits of your labors and those of the Society. May the Lord ever be present with you with his abundant grace and spirit, so that you may devote the gifts and talents granted Your Honors to his service with gladness and taste much of the heavenly life on this earth. May the Lord ever be with Your Honor's wife and children, bless Your Honor according to soul and body, and to go forth with glad expectation and then to hear his voice: "Blessed art thou, thou good and faithful servant, thou hast been faithful in a few things. I will set you over many things; enter the joy of your Lord."

I hope to respond at greater length to a few things in your letter and also in that of B[rother] Luring [Luuring]. From Brother Lottes [Lothes] I received a letter mailed at Buffalo. We send cordial greetings to all the friends; we are now all in good health again. Jan has not had a fever since June, after suffering from them for eleven months. Madam Teleman sends greetings to you, and we greet all of you together.

Our prayer is that you may all abide in the peace and salvation of our Lord Christ.

D. A. Budde

My wife also hopes to answer her letter on another occasion.

Wormser 20

A. N. Wormser to J. A. Wormser
Burlington, 9 November 1848

Esteemed Brother!

This is the third letter I have sent you since our arrival in North America. Do let me know sometime whether you have received them all. Hereby receive, provisionally, a part of the description of our journey and experiences through this land of wonders. You will be receiving the continuation soon; just now I am prevented by the illness of Anna [daughter] and that is why I cannot go ahead, as I would like. I have gone into some detail in order to give you, to the best of my ability, an idea of how things are and work here, since the reports that we received about America [when we were still] in Holland were of little value. The best thing that we read in order to get some idea about America was the booklet by some *landverhuizers* (emigrants) in North America, a booklet that we considered very exaggerated at the time.

Occasionally I will be writing of things that will very likely disappoint you; that happened to us too. The idea that people in Holland have of America is poles apart from the way things really are. Consequently, ninety-nine out of a hundred emigrants are deceived in their beautiful expectations. Many would like to go back, but the one has no money, the other is ashamed to go back, and a third looks up against making that difficult journey again. It is even disappointing to the Overijssel farmers, who are quite accustomed to wallowing in their own filth, but [there I go] reasoning too much from a Dutch point of view.

Through experience we have gotten to know what travel in North America is like, and surely there is no country in the world where travel is as disagreeable as it is here. I cannot possibly tell you of all the misery, difficulties, poverty, and cares. The letters we read together in Holland made little or no reference to the subject [of travel conditions]. Usually that is because the writers do not want to frighten those left behind from undertaking the journey to North America. People like to see their relatives join them, simply because no one likes to be alone among strangers. So I am sharing with you my impressions of some things that struck me, rather than making much of something new or strange; the good I found, I do not want to disregard, but I want to stick to the truth.

The evening of September 28 we arrived in New York. The next morning the doctor came on board; except for five people who had to go to the hospital, all the others were judged to be well. Then we went to see the city. It is very densely populated; the streets are straight and wide, but when it comes to sanitary conditions, you must not make comparisons with cities in Holland. However, that is often what happens when you read about American cities, because as a rule the writers do not know any other cities, and that accounts for the many disappointments in traveling through the country. The streets are separated: there are foot paths for pedestrians along the houses and a path built of large, rough-hewn stones slightly elevated above the center [roadway], which is an area intended only for carriages. The mud is always a half-foot thick there, and because of that and the large number of carriages, no pedestrians ever walk here, except to cross the street, and for that they have built crossings of large stones at the [street] corners, which carriage drivers may only cross at a walk. It is teeming here with colorfully painted omnibuses in which you can ride several miles for six cents (when I speak of *centen* (cents) they are always American, and of *mijlen* (miles), always English, three miles to an hour, walking). Within a distance the equivalent of that from the St. Jansstraaat to the Pijlsteeg (approximately ninety meters), you can always find at least twenty omnibuses.

New York has a very large number of shops, though there are bigger ones in Amsterdam, especially the cotton [cloth] shops. There are oyster shops everywhere; they say there are more than two thousand, not counting the oyster stalls on the streets. There are many apples, and they are of an exceptional size such as you never see in Holland, but they are not cheap. Sometimes they charge two cents for an apple, but in all likelihood that is because they do not do anything for nothing here, but people must make a living whatever they are doing.

I have been greatly disappointed in how they build houses, make furniture, and hundreds of other things. Mostly it is shoddy workmanship; things are just thrown together. In Holland I had always thought that if the Americans were not ahead of us in house construction, making furniture, and a hundred other things, they were still in a neck-to-neck race with us. But that is not the case at all. The houses are constructed of big crude red bricks of a very ordinary sort, though the texture is finer, and they are much wider than ours, none of which adds to their beauty. The joints are wide and the mortar is gray because of the large amount of sand mixed in with it. That is why the fronts are painted and the joints restored with white paint. The artistically carved gables of Holland you will not find here; that kind of workmanship would take too much time. The inner walls are mostly made of wood [lathes] with plaster thrown in between, as if it were brick; the result is that the floor shakes when you walk on it. I once spoke with one of the Buddes carpenters about the shoddy workmanship in house construction in America. He tried to justify it by saying that if they were to build according to European standards in America, then half the people would be without housing. Some houses have silver doorknobs, and they really brag about that. I for one would rather have a good house with a copper knob than a poor one with silver one. Everything is done quickly but crudely; that is also true of the furniture I have seen; it was not fine workmanship except for a few pieces that reflected good taste, and very likely they were made by Europeans. And mind you, that is the situation in one of the foremost cities. Many people made a big to-do about the big, beautiful houses, the kind we had also read about in letters from America. However, when I pointed out all their shortcomings, they had to agree that this was so. But they said that I should take into account that this was a new country and that everything was still in its infancy. But I for one do not go for new things, if they are not better, or at least as good as the old ones.

Since we had slept on the ship for so long and had suffered so many discomforts, we wanted to take lodgings in the city for a couple of days. We went to an inn run by the brother of our ship's cook. The use of benches for resting on is common all over America. They somewhat resemble a bed but without sideboards or [canopy]. During the summer they sometimes use a kind of net to keep out mosquitoes. Everything possible is done to keep bugs from settling in. To try it out, we also bought one for four dollars. The chairs are usually made entirely of wood, including the seats. That is also done in part to avoid the same discomfort from bugs.

Throughout America they eat three meals a day, in the morning at seven, at midday (noon), and in the evening at six o'clock; drinking tea or coffee outside of those hours is not practiced. All three meals are substantially the same; in the morning people eat bread, meat, cheese, unpeeled potatoes, and coffee or tea; generally they have two large mugs; small cups such we had [in Holland] would be too time consuming. Ordinarily Americans do not ask a blessing or give thanks with their meals, but they eat with head uncovered; Germans do pray for their meals. As a rule Americans do not take longer than five minutes to eat, and when one is finished he leaves the table. The potatoes are large, clayish, and bad, but farther west they are better. The staple foods are beef, pork, bread, and corn pone. The price of meat varies from place to place: in Burlington beef was three and four cents a pound, pork four cents a pound; I bought all the pork chops from half a hog for ten cents. A barrel of the best wheat flour [cost me...]; milk is more expensive; butter costs fourteen cents a pound, cheese eight cents, twelve eggs presently are ten cents, sugar seven pounds for fifty cents, five candles ten cents. When you go shopping [in this state] you should calculate the total so that it ends at five or ten cents, because there are no pennies in Iowa. The chief vegetables are cabbage, turnips, onions, and beets; during the summer there are green peas, wax beans, and radishes. Some immigrants also plant other vegetables, but the Americans do not buy anything they are not familiar with. Everything is done in a hurry here; the milkman at the door shouts, "Hurry! hurry!"

Our goods were removed from the ship September 30, and since we had so much with us, we decided to begin our inland journey at once. The result was a lot of heavy labor. My wife stayed with the children and Leen (Portengen) while the ship was being unloaded. I had to be down in the hold in order to locate the trunks, open a few for the [immigration] officer, and then load them, including some that were fairly heavy. There was such a wild confusion on the wharf that I scarcely know how I managed it all, given the fact that I was alone. The inspection by officials does not amount to much; they just take a quick look at things lying on top, and not all trunks have to be opened. I had to spend a long time in the ship looking for a vat that was hidden under other luggage, but finally I was successful. It was getting late and the boat for Albany was leaving at six in the evening, and so I do not know whether Leen's trunk was left behind on the wharf or whether it was stolen by one of the draymen. I am sure that it did not get lost on the steamboat. I was told that I could not take the route Budde had laid out for me because of all our luggage. I therefore chose a different route, rather than being stranded somewhere.

The steamboat from New York to Albany (one of about a hundred) is 340 feet long and is very fancy; it covers the 150 miles in ten hours.

There was a huge crowd of passengers on board. Like most of the immigrants, we found ourselves below decks. For the accommodation of these two or three hundred passengers, there were six easy chairs to sit on, and all the passengers but those six could lie on the floor and sleep there. But there was a stove; otherwise it would have been pretty cold. Still, this was the best boat we encountered in America and the one with the most conveniences. But you have to keep a wary eye on your belongings, because there are always people who only come along in order to steal. It was still dark when we arrived in Albany, but we waited until daybreak before unloading

The luggage was transferred to a canal boat and then taken farther into the city to be weighed. The canal boats have much in common with our towboats, but they are much bigger and stronger because of the rough handling they undergo on the canal. Every minute they run into each other or the sluice gates so hard that you think the boat might sink. There are about six thousand [tow] boats on the canal. After having our luggage weighed, we remained in Albany the rest of the day. New York did not have many attractions for me, but Albany had even less. Everything is so very somber, the streets are so wretched and dirty, the houses so ugly; all that is even worsened by the barbaric custom of painting monstrous letters on the front facades, all of which makes one eager to leave the city again. There had been an enormous fire in Albany that destroyed at least six hundred houses.

Since we discovered in the morning that Leen's trunk was missing, we were advised to send a telegraphic message to New York. Leen was to stay in Albany overnight, catch the seven o'clock train to Schenectady in the morning, and arrive there at eight o'clock; by that time we also would have arrived there on the boat. But the next morning we were still at the same place, and would not be arriving at Schenectady until night. To put Leen at ease, at noon I also decided to leave for Schenectady at two p.m.

There [I found] Leen with some Americans whose ancestors had left for America two hundred hundred years ago; the entire family still spoke Dutch, especially the father, who spoke it practically as good as we. We waited for the boat there. No news had come from New York, and so we decided to travel on, because I was worried about not keeping (to our schedule). At Albany I made an agreement with someone who had been on the boat with us, to reward him amply for looking after the trunk if it showed up, but I am afraid that he may have left [Albany] already by now.

Traveling by train in America is not something you do for your pleasure. The combined railroad lines cover about five thousand miles. Generally speaking, they are in a dangerous and run-down condition. The locomotives are small, and I do not think that six of them are comparable to one of ours. In the distance they look like moving coffee grinders. They are fired with wood; the cars are longer than ours; they are poorly constructed and sway back and forth like a wallowing ship; the seats are along the sides. The track is so weak and poorly laid that repeatedly they have to go slowly for fear of an accident. While en route you do not see any track maintenance men at work along the track as you do in Holland. Everywhere the trains pass through cities, but there are no crossing gates; they are not needed for the track, and so there are none. The railroad station and the train sheds in Albany are worse than bad. It is said that they make a good profit. I dare say it is true, because their expenditures must be very low; at home [in Holland] we spend millions on buildings etc. so there is but a small return. But here you have the utmost slovenliness. Anything will do, they say, as long as we can get by with it.

The canal from Albany to Buffalo is five hundred miles long, and it is not, as we thought when we were still in Holland, a man-made passage; rather it is a river, that in all likelihood was not navigable in the past. Consequently it has a great many locks; you are lifted at least ten feet in them every time. But just the same the Americans have spent lots of money on it; they have done much excavating, changing the bedding of the river in many places, and they continue to make many improvements every day. When you have entered a lock, the gates are closed, the lock is filled with water, and so the lift occurs. Traveling along this canal was the most enjoyable part of the entire trip for us; the hold was filled with vats and trunks; the passengers had to sleep on these and that was very unpleasant and caused much vexation. At Albany we had first taken the cabin on a provisional basis, and we were eager to stay there, but the captain demanded six dollars extra for that, without meals. I offered four dollars but he refused, but when he saw that we had withdrawn and were already down in the hold, he came down to five dollars; I accepted and had no regrets about it. Here we had adequate space, benches with pillows, a stove to warm ourselves, and we could also sit outside in the front of the boat, where we had a most splendid view of the landscape; we had good sleeping quarters at night. When I got bored of sitting, then I would walk along the road, where we could easily keep up with the boat although it was drawn by two horses. There were also packet boats drawn by three horses; the horses are changed from time to time, there were plenty of them in the stables along the river.

Ordinarily people bring their own provisions, although one can also get food on board from the captain, but that was frightfully expensive on our boat. All along the canal there are stores near the locks where you can buy bread, etc.; that along with milk was our principal food for nine days. Generally speaking, we enjoyed rather nice weather during our trip on the canal, and although it was already autumn, the trees were usually still green; a few were already turning brown. At first we saw nothing but mountains covered with forests; nature was exceptionally beautiful here. All the land here has been sold, but it is far from all being cultivated. Land is expensive here, someone I spoke to along the canal said that an acre costs about a hundred dollars. In the cultivated areas along the canal there are orchards of apples everywhere: they are mostly sour. You seldom see sweet apples; pears are even scarcer, though they are found in America. Hundreds of apples had fallen from the trees and were lying on the ground; everybody was picking them up, so that apples were being eaten on the boat all day long.

The houses on the farmsteads are mostly built of wood; they are painted white, and most of the time they look very nice. You see fewer brick houses, and they are less pleasing to the eye, although in the winter they are warmer. They grow a lot of corn here for feeding hogs. From time to time we passed towns, some larger, some smaller, all depending on how old they were, or how choice the location was. In appearance they differed very much from the cities of New York and Albany, since they consisted mostly of wooden warehouses. Just seeing them as we passed by always gave me an unpleasant feeling, so that I was happy when we had passed them and I could again turn my eyes to the landscape and the mountains. It [those settlements] was like seeing a big cemetery; everything was so stiff and still. To get an idea what such American cities are like, you must go to the Jewish cemetery outside the *Muiderpoort* [in Amsterdam] with each wooden grave marker representing a wooden warehouse painted white, about the size of one of our *poffertjeskramen* (tent-like pancake stands). The scene is somewhat enhanced by the presence of small churches, simple and attractive in appearance, raising their little steeples above the roofs, and although they are not tall, they provide most American churches with a lightning rod.

In general the horses we saw looked good, and even those we saw drawing the [canal] boats were not at all inferior to many of our coach horses. The locks in the canal are built of freestone, which is quarried from the neighboring mountains. And this is not cabinetwork by any means either; the slovenly workmanship is also readily apparent here. In bygone days we had occasion to read in Savary and Volney how the Egyptians laid the big heavy blocks they used in building so closely on top of each other that you could not insert the point of a knife in between. That is not the case here. Here you can put your fingers in the wall joints. They are filled with mortar, but that is quickly washed away by the water.

After completing half of our canal trip, we happened to run into De Vries, who was also going to Buffalo and from there to Chicago, but he had stayed in Buffalo because his wife had a baby (daughter) immediately after his arrival here.

[*The conclusion is missing.*]

Wormser 21

A. N. Wormser to J. A. Wormser
17 November 1848

Esteemed Brother,

Since I consider it of greater importance to share with you my experiences in Burlington and the surrounding area, as well as how I found things at the Buddes, I intend, for the moment, to interrupt the account of our journey. However, I do hope to resume it soon; it may be of some benefit to others intending to make the journey to America, or indeed [to acquaint them with] what awaits them upon arrival there.

On Sunday, October 29, at about six in the evening, we arrived at Burlington, having traveled by steamboat from St. Louis. I immediately went about locating Krichbaum, but that was not as readily done as I had intended or expected. He did have a *winkel* (store) on the river, but he lived in the city. Since I did not know my way about the city, and because it was so dark without any street lamps, I headed back to the boat. There I met a German who pointed out the way to Krichbaum's for me. After that we went to the boat to unload our things and bring them on land. I had already written Budde from Buffalo and did so again at St. Louis. He had received the first letter but not the second, which did not arrive until several days after my arrival.

Budde had made an agreement with Krichbaum to assist us in finding a dwelling, should we arrive in his absence. He did just that, and presently he returned with the message that he had found a house for us. We were overjoyed. The dwelling belonged to his brother-in-law Vonk; it is situated not far from the river. We had our possessions delivered there by a drayman; they were dropped off in front of a low door that was closed with a wooden latch. After opening the door we entered a courtyard similar to Ampie's; our dwelling stood at the far end [of the courtyard]. You can still read the words "Bake House" on the door and from that you may gather what purpose it once served. If an Overijssel farmer were living in it, he would surely write that he was living in a freestone house, and that is correct, but I have never seen uglier houses. It is a kind of loose stone that residents may quarry out of the hills themselves or else have it done. And these, crude as they are, with different sizes and thickness, are all piled on top of each other. The dwelling consists of a single large room, a kind of warehouse; there is nothing to it but four white walls and a hole in the roof for the stovepipe. It has neither cupboards nor shelves. We could get all our possessions in the house except for the big chest; the barrel we had to unpack, the more so because it started raining. Unpacking took up a good part of the night. We spread our bedding on the ground, and so passed the first night in the company of rats and mice. We pay three dollars a month for this dwelling; it is damp and from what we hear it is unhealthy because it is located in the lowest part of the city. But there is nothing else to be had.

The next morning I went with the old Mr. Krichbaum to see Mr. Budde. Everywhere you look you see houses that were built only this year. Although Burlington is not large, still it has the best house construction I have seen in any America town so far. The houses are better, and the fronts are not disfigured with monstrously large lettering. On the outskirts of the city the land is very lovely and hilly; most of it is still wooded, though many trees have already been chopped down. We followed the road and, after half an hour's walk, the Buddes' house came into view. The little Diederik was out in the field; he is a real farm boy. His feet were as bare as the land he walked on; the other children were also barefoot. His jacket looked as if it had been chewed by rats, and there was a pointed fringe on the bottom. As soon as Mrs. Budde caught sight of me she came outdoors, and Budde himself also appeared shortly. They were now all healthy and well again and all appeared to be content, also Mrs. Teleman and her little daughter. They had all been sick last year, but Budde had remained fairly well. Jan suffered from fevers for eleven months, Diederik had pleurisy, and they thought that Mrs. Teleman would die. Budde said that he had had plenty of difficulties building a new small house for his tenant-farmer, about a hundred paces from his own, since he [the tenant] no longer wished to live in one and the same house [with his boss]. It is a small, one-room stone house that will cost him three hundred dollars. He had to borrow the money for the house at 10 percent; the house will be finished in a few days. As we already knew, Budde also lives in a stone house. The entrance is in the middle, with a room on each side, the one being larger than the other. The smaller one they use as a bedroom, and the other is their living room, which is no larger than the front room in *Het Kattegat* [in central Amsterdam] where Riek lived for a time. Part of the family sleeps in the attic which, given the severity of the winters, will not be very pleasant. The walls are just like the masons left them, mortar splashed on them, very rough therefore, and it could also stand a touch of paint. Someone told me that this little house probably cost all of a thousand dollars to build.

Building is expensive here, so that the construction of a good-sized dwelling with large rooms would cost lots of dollars. The money I had brought along for Budde stood him in good stead; he still owes two hundred dollars on his land on which he pays 6 percent interest; he also owes sixty-one dollars to someone who occasionally helps him work the land; and the doctor, I think, must also have quite a sum of money coming, but the doctor reassured him by saying that he would see him about that next year some time. Whether he has other debts I do not know, since he has not mentioned any other debts to me as of now.

As far as his land is concerned, some say that he made a bad buy. The reason they give is that it is such low-lying land. Superficially speaking, one could say that it does not amount to all that much, yet it does appear that all the water from the surrounding lands collects there and stays there. That explains why all his potatoes rotted. He told me that he had counted on a yield of two hundred bushels and got none, although his neighbors still had harvests ranging from two-thirds to one-half. They take them to market to sell them there. Apart from this, it is good, dark, clayish land, and when I visited him I also noticed that his vegetable garden was waterlogged. While his neighbors' land is dry, his remains wet another three days. In addition, his land does not have any woods, though he does have twenty acres of undeveloped land, but that is grown over with hazelwood. It is necessary to have some woods just to exist: it always has a lasting value. He does not even have any timber suitable for fencing purposes but must purchase it from others. A woodlot is essential, for if the crops fail, one can have the wood cut and sell it in the city. Chopping wood is not easy work and we would not be able to do it, but you can have it cut for fifty cents a cart load, you pay fifty cents to have it hauled to town and sold; after all that you have fifty cents left for yourself, because a cartload sells for at least $1.50. You can also just have the wood cut up and haul it to town yourself, if you have a wagon and a team of horses or oxen, and then you have at least a dollar for yourself. If your land includes at least twenty acres of good timber, then, according to what they tell me, you can harvest and sell wood for at least fifty years. Finally, his land is not on the road, and in order to reach it he has to cross over some of his own land as well as that of neighbors. You just cannot always buy a farm that is located on a road; it is no hindrance to him right now, but in time, as the city expands, they usually sell land in smaller lots so that he will have to change his access way to the main road, but his right of access to the main road [an easement] remains.

In my previous letter I wrote you that there might be a farm for sale about a fifteen-minute walk beyond the Buddes' place, very likely for twelve dollars an acre; at least two hundred acres of it, however it still has to be surveyed. It does not have a brick house, but there is a wooden one. The objection to wooden houses is that they are cold in the winter. I asked Budde if there was a woods on this farm, but his answer was no, it was just like his. We were intending to walk part way around it, but the road was so muddy that we gave up the idea for the present. The talk is that you cannot make a living on land in the environs of Burlington, at least if there are no woods.

I seem to recall having written you that I had asked Budde whether he could make a living on his farm and his frank answer was: No. Some people insist that you cannot get more than a 1¼ percent return on the land, but that seems very unlikely to me. Some time later, after I had asked Budde whether he could make a living on his farm, and he had answered in the negative, the subject of making a living on the land came up again; he now began to talk it up, no doubt to make it more attractive to me; he figured that he had a 20 percent return on his land. I asked him how he reached that figure and his answer was that he figured that there was an annual 10 percent increase in the value of the land (that definitely is not true; I do not believe it has risen even 1 percent), and the return from the land was 10 percent. That certainly is not true either, at least not right now. But if I were to assume a return of 9 percent, then his renter gets 6 percent and he gets 3 percent (purchase price $2,000, selling price in 1868 $10,000). But the renters always know the best deal, they know all the ins and outs, they buy and sell wood. And besides they are Germans; they live so penuriously that in three or four years they have been able to lay something aside. Be that as it may, the Budde household really has to plod away, so the name "Plodders' Delight" would not be inappropriate for their place.

Getting rid of the hazelwood with a prick stick was more than Budde could do; he began having pains in his chest, so he had to have it done by others. He sowed winter wheat; I hope that he will succeed in harvesting it. His tenant has no share in this. He did harvest some corn this summer, and that is usually stored in order to feed the hogs and the cattle. Budde has the vegetable garden all to himself. When we were still home [in Holland] I had gotten a mistaken notion of what work was like on the Buddes' farm. If I am not mistaken, we thought that he was living here like a gentleman farmer. His tenant worked the farm and got a two-thirds return, while Budde did nothing but take care of his vegetable garden, his hobby, and got a one-third return. He had purchased a horse and wagon for 150 dollars, so he could take his family for rides from time to time or visit the market. But no, none of this. The tenant works a part of the cultivated land and gets two-thirds; Budde works another part just for himself, just to survive. The vegetable garden takes a lot of work. I thought and so did you, I think, that he worked the vegetable garden for his own use, and as a hobby. But that is not the case; the vegetables are grown in the garden to be taken to market. That explains why we read in his last letter that Jan went to the market with [horse and] wagon at three in the morning, three times a week, on Tuesdays, Thursdays, and Saturdays. And very likely it all begins so early because people start working at seven, and by then the food must be bought, prepared, and eaten. Going to the market is always a man's job; never does a woman go to market to buy anything. The man hangs the basket on his arm and buys whatever is needed, or rather whatever is available; right now there is nothing but meat.

People muddle around making a lot of things themselves here: soap, candles, butter, baking bread, roasting coffee, milking, churning, making butter, chopping wood. Mr. Budde and his family do all this themselves, because they say they must economize wherever they can, even if it is only a penny. But it means endless work, [much of it] never done before. In my judgment it is better to sacrifice a little and buy some articles; for example, you can buy five grease candles for ten cents in the store. If you make them yourself, you have to buy a mold, tallow, and cotton [for wicks], and then five candles probably come to seven or eight cents, but then you don't have a big mess either. You always have to roast your own coffee beans, and in general it makes a pretty bad drink; it is almost nauseating. We still have some [coffee] from Amsterdam.

Budde seems to be fairly content with life here, and from what I hear, does not long to go back to Holland. One evening I was returning from their place, and their tenant who was going into town joined me. He told me that Jan "would not make a good farmer because he had no liking for it, but the old man really plugs away at it." Whatever the facts about farming may be, from everything I see, it is evident that it is a lot of hard plodding without any fruits on your labors, at least in the early years. Even the real farmers, who are way ahead of us, really have to make do in the early years and work very hard; in the beginning you also have a lot of extra expenses (I am only speaking of land that has been cleared). For example, Budde had a well on his farm, but no water; he had to have it dug much deeper and break through a layer of rock, all of which cost him thirty dollars. Then he had to have a house built, and after that he had to have land cleared. From all of this you can gather that the life of a farmer, even with a tenant, is much different from what we had expected when we were still in Holland, although there were times when we secretly feared that it might be a lot of plodding and rough. It seems to me that Americans have little awareness of refined culture or pleasures. Even their houses stand in the midst of stones, clay, or wild growth, although there is plenty of room for a garden. All they think of is work, and that is why most men of forty look as if they were fifty or sixty.

I still do not know why the farm that Budde has in mind for us costs twelve dollars an acre, while he paid twenty-five for his; perhaps it lacks something, or it may be the house. There is a wooden house on the property. B's house, which he had built, cost one thousand dollars, and although it is small, that may have been the going price at the time. This sum is spread over the acreage, and that makes the price per acre so high. It would be very costly to have a large house with many rooms built. Even if one were willing to spend lots of money, no American could ever afford to build a home like "Postwijk" unless he was able to supervise it all himself. Our solid, neatly constructed, and warm [Dutch] houses just cannot be built here. Here all houses have white walls:

House *Postwijk*, country home of
Judith J. Zeelt, Amsterdam
(J. C. van der Does, De Afscheiding, *Delft, 1933)*

wallpaper is almost unknown, although it can be purchased in Burlington. I don't think they use it because of the wall (bed) bugs.

People are as little concerned about furniture as they are about their homes. In the homes I have been in until now, of people not without means, I usually found six wooden chairs, one rocking chair, one table, one chest of drawers (ugly style), one small mirror, one couch, and a couple of small paintings. This may explain why people say that Americans do not steal, but they do when they know that people have money, and they are wild about that. Sometimes there is a carpet on the floor; it is customary to spit [tobacco juice] on it. It is said that some English (Americans) have better taste, but foreigners do not have much contact with them. They regard themselves as much too superior, and anything a Dutchman makes is no good, even if it is ten times better.

And now as far as our life in Burlington is concerned, it is not very commodious or pleasant, even if we do not take into account the illnesses of the children. I have already described our home for you; if you were here, things would be much more pleasant and much easier for us. For example, this morning we were up chopping wood at six o'clock, because the stoves consume an enormous quantity of it. Now, if you were here, then I could saw while you could chop [the wood], and afterward I could go to the market to buy meat while you went to the river to fetch water; and then we would go to the store: one of us could carry a bushel of potatoes, the other a bushel of turnips, etc.

In the state of Iowa there are no pennies in circulation. You cannot get change on a five-cent piece and so you have to round off the cost of your purchases to five or ten cents. If you buy twelve cents worth of something, you have to pay fifteen cents, etc. As in every other American city, the streets of Burlington are dirty, especially in wet weather, because they are not paved. At night there is no street illumination; if you have to cross a street in dark weather, you take a lantern. But these days you do not see anyone on the street at six in the evening. Sometimes you do see a couple of cows or pigs ambling down the street.

Usually there are church services on Wednesday evening. I have no idea how the English and others spend their evenings. On occasion you do see them leaning over a counter talking in some store or other. The Germans do get together in the evening now and then. I have not heard much about newspapers as yet; I just have not inquired into that. At the Buddes I saw two newspapers lying about, one German and one English.

You will understand that I am very curious to hear something about Holland. As far as religion is concerned, every stranger joins the congregation that in his judgment best comports with his convictions. The German and English Methodists gather separately. Budde has joined up with Germans who are mostly Lutherans. They meet in the city in a room that serves as a church. It is a square room, moderate in size. Since the house was built, no whitewash brush has touched the walls, and that is also true of the ceiling, which was also splattered with plaster, nearly half of which has fallen down. Behind the pulpit, constructed of white wood, there are two windows, one of which is almost half again as large as the other. It makes no difference where one worships God, whether that be in a room, in a basement, or in the open air. But if people do set aside a place for this purpose, then why can't they do it without being slovenly or unsanitary? Budde told me that there were plans for building a church, but he thought nothing would come of it. They wanted to call it German-Lutheran which, I believe, did not suit him. Their minister is a German, born in Bremen. Budde told me that the Germans wanted to be rid of him [the minister] again, and he probably would have had to leave of his own volition anyway (just between us, I think that they are planning to starve him to death). He does not have a fixed salary, but once a year everyone pledges what he intends to give him. The Germans usually refuse to pledge.

There is one thing that has been something of a surprise to me. If Budde had had to sing hymns as well as the psalms in Holland, that in itself would have been reason enough for him to go to America. Here it is exactly the other way around; they do not sing any psalms here, only hymns. The first Sunday after my arrival Budde was the speaker; he read a German sermon from a book. The second Sunday the minister preached, and I liked him. Obviously, they do not preach in the Dutch language here, because there are no Hollanders. As a result my family can never go to church, since they would not be able to understand a thing.

In the course of the past year many new stone houses were built in Burlington, and I must say they are more pleasing to the eye than any I have seen in any other American city. They also moved a few wooden houses from one street to another, which would not be such a difficult task, at least not for the Dutch. [The claim] that they can move brick buildings of five stories from one street to another I consider to be a fairy tale, at least when you take into account the poor construction of the houses. Budde does not believe it either.

The most influential people keep a maid and have a midwife when a baby is to be born. The wife of the minister, whose church Budde attends, is one of those people who do not have a midwife, but she helps herself. The men, but especially the women, dress very well, although the value (quality) of the clothes cannot begin to compare with that in Holland. Just as in Holland, many of the women are not moneyed. They are neat in their appearance, own few clothes, and those are washed every week.

And now, having told you some things about America and in particular about Burlington and environs, I come to the most difficult point, whether, after having read all the foregoing, you are still as enthusiastic about going to America as when we were home together. I imagine that it would have as little appeal to you, or perhaps even less, than it does to me. If I now buy land, and you have no desire to come over here, what good is it to you, and to me as well, what good is it for us to be here all alone? Anyone who has enough to eat in Holland should not go to America, and especially not people without children. I do not want to mislead people, as is so commonly done around here; the reports of the Reverends Scholte and Van Raalte are nothing but quackery. Their only object is to attract people to the *Koloniën* [colonies]. Budde and his family themselves commiserate with Berkhout for having taken that step. The Zeelanders, of whom Budde wrote in the past, and who live four miles from here, have assured me that they have also written to

Holland telling how things really are in America. We really have too much, and we have too little to go to America; too much because in all likelihood we could have lived in Holland several more years, if no exceptional circumstances arose and no one should leave before that time; and we have too little to go to America to live without heavy plodding. You could live here without heavy toil if you could bring along another eight thousand guilders to put out at interest, but for me there is no chance of getting ahead. If I were to buy a farm for you, then in three years at best, by dint of hard work I could earn only enough to eat. In any case I have decided not to be in a hurry about buying anything. I think I will first wait for a letter from you stating how you think about it all. Meanwhile, I shall attempt to get to know as much about the country as I can. I have not been here long as yet, and I am greatly impeded by the illnesses of our children. Hein (Wormser) should be in no hurry about leaving, especially if his agency is not discontinued.

And also as far as traveling goes, when the children are young, you just cannot describe all the worries and cares of looking after them, and many young children die. If they are a little older, it is hard to believe what handy helpers they can be and all the things they can do for you. Just tell him to really enjoy his stay in Nijverdal, because he will not find anything like it over here. Of course, the situation will be very different if his earnings stop; that would always change the situation. Life here is good for a certain class of people, and the saying applies to them, that anyone who can work and *wants* to work can make a living here. For example, there is a man here with his wife and child from Hoorn [Netherlands], where he was a painting foreman. He has been living here a year now. He had been led to believe that he could make two to three dollars a day [painting]. He had also read in [immigrant] letters that painters who could not do good lacquer and varnish work might as well stay home. I have already told you what painting is like here, and although many new houses are being built, he could not begin to make a living by painting. But to make a living he now saws and chops wood for the townsmen: that pays him six bits (seventy-five cents) a day. He and his small family can live on that for two days. But that is no work for people like us, because I have all I can do to saw and chop wood for our own household. His wife went crazy here, but now she is reasonably rational again. They say that is why they joined the German Methodists: they had been Baptists before.

Until now I have not heard a thing from Keesel or Berkhout; I really would like to know where they have settled. I am not all that fond of

Berkhout and his wife because they are unabashed spongers. When our ship was anchored in New York, we had a view of the outlying areas of the city. I thought it looked very nice, but Berkhout said, "Well, is that the beautiful America everyone was raving about? It looks like heather to me." But how surprised he must have been as he was traveling through the country itself, probably ending up in the eternal prairies of Scholte.

During our ocean journey Keesel and I talked about our future lot and life in America, for already on the ocean journey you begin to awaken somewhat from your dreams. He recalled his life in Amsterdam, and then how things had been on shipboard, and that now he might have to work as a shoemaker's apprentice, for he had already learned from the farmers on board that farming was no easy job for an inexperienced person. But in America they don't make much work of farming, just so you have some idea when it is time to seed, and after that you just let it grow. Once it is growing, things go very fast, and then you really have your hands full.

There is little wildlife in the environs of Burlington. The hares here are smaller than our rabbits; it is a good thing that I did not buy a gun yet. Budde has not even used his yet. There are many rats and mice here, so many that when we open the door in the evening to let in some fresh air, someone has to stand at the door swinging a broom to prevent any from coming in. During the summer there are many [wall] bugs and mosquitos. In New York I heard that Mr. Roelof's brother left Pella to move to St. Louis. Mr. Roelof himself should not leave for America unless there is an urgent need.

I had written thus far, when I was prevented from continuing. The illness of our Anna had gotten worse. For the last few days it seemed as if her eyes would ulcerate; the stench coming from her mouth was so unbearable that it gave us a headache. In the evening she worsened and again we sent for the doctor who was not very hopeful; her voice became weaker, and at eleven o'clock this evening she was no more. She was conscious to the very last, and just before she died she reached out her hand to me and my wife; it was just fourteen days after our Fietje [had died]. Because of the fear of contagion, we buried her the very next day, in the afternoon, so that was also exactly fourteen days after Fietje. When Fietje was being carried out the door, Anna said to me, "Daddy, isn't Fietje coming back?" little thinking that she herself would be going the same way so soon.

Fietje died in torment with terrible shortness of breath; she was out of her mind for three days, except for the last moments. She pulled the hairs from my wife's head, and until the end she screamed with a hoarse voice: "Oh! Pa, Oh! Pa Oh! Pa." The illness is contagious; the neighbors' children had to take a medicine, and the doctor also gave medicine to his own children. The illness begins with vomiting; as soon as we noticed Anna doing this, we sent for the doctor. The throat swells on the inside and the neck on the outside, phlegm runs from the nose and mouth, the mouth turns black. Sophia was red all over, Anna scarcely at all. The pills they give here are very small and the liquid medicines are usually given in drops from a bottle twice the size of a Haarlem oil bottle.

Little [children's] coffins have a special design here; they are of varnished walnut, after this fashion (drawing of a coffin). They were both taken on the Buddes' wagon for burial at the old cemetery outside the city on a hill. There is also a new cemetery where each grave lot costs twenty-five guilders; at the old cemetery it costs nothing. I sent someone down there to dig the grave. They now rest together, the one above the other; there are two small trees growing at the head end. The earth that is dug out is put on top [of the grave site], and that sinks by itself when it rains, and so that there will not be another burial in the same grave. They place two pieces of wood in the ground, one at the head end, the other at the foot end as follows (drawing).

At the moment Lina is not feeling very well; we hope for the best. During this past week my wife awakened to find her entire left side swollen; the doctor gave her purgative pills, and now she is better again. My neck was also swollen on the outside and my throat felt thick. I went to see my own doctor; I took a strong purgative and drank four or five cups of elderberry with chamomile infusion. That really helped me; the thickness in my neck has disappeared; afterward I still vomited a lot of bile. In eight days we will in all likelihood move in with the Buddes. We are very satisfied with our doctor; he is a German and studied in St. Louis. Some time ago he sent for his father, mother, brother(s) and sister, to have them come to America, but the ship went down (and they) perished in the waves. I must close for now. Shortly I will be sending you the continuing account of our travels through the interior. Please be so kind as to give our cordial greetings to all our friends and acquaintances and especially to your wife, Father Portengen, Mother, and Mrs. Zeelt.

Your Loving Brother,
A. N. Wormser

NB. This is the 4th letter.

Wormser 22

A. N. Wormser to H. Wormser, agent of
the Netherlands Trading Society, Nijverdal
Overijssel, Kingdom of Holland, via Liverpool
Burlington, 27 Nov. 1848

Esteemed Brother,

A few days ago I sent you a letter in which I wrote you in some detail of my reactions to Burlington and to this country; it has hardly lived up to my expectations; now I am sending you the continuation [of the story] of our journey through the interior.

Rochester, a city you pass a few miles before you get to Buffalo, is a rather large and lively city. Recently they had built a large stone bridge to replace another equally long, and although it probably was not even thirty years old, it had already broken down to its very foundations. They do not build for posterity here; ordinarily they say, "If only it lasts our life-time, our children probably could care less."

The ninth day after leaving Albany we arrived in Buffalo; it was a Saturday evening. Here I learned that just then there was no ship leaving for Chicago. The skipper wanted to unload our goods, the alternative being to pay the two dollars he demanded, in which case we and our goods could remain on board until Monday morning, and he would be willing to take them to the steamboat. Since I was not very eager to go to a boarding house, I decided to let it go at that. I looked up lawyer Van der Poel, who is frequently recommended in letters for emigrants who need information. He was out of the city. I wanted very much to consult with him about our [missing] trunk and about the route that I should take. I contacted him on Monday morning; he was not very reassuring about our getting the trunk back, and as far as our route was concerned, he knew less than I did. He said that he knew about as much about that as a cat knows about England. There was a large map of the United States hanging on the wall, the kind that you find in almost every American home. He located Chicago and Burlington on it. You can imagine how much help that was to me. Generally speaking, people here know very little about arrangements and facilities for travel in America. Many carry booklets and maps for looking up places, but what good is that, if you do not know how to get to them? It turned out that we had to travel from Buffalo to Chicago on the [big] lakes, a distance of 1,100 miles. Van der Poel said that I should take a *Repadler*, that is, a screw-driven steamboat, but there would not be one in before Wednesday evening. We went to another agency, where we learned that there would be a very large steamboat, the *Niagara*, leaving for Chicago that very evening, and that we could take it if we paid twelve dollars extra. Since I had no desire to go to a boarding house, and the propeller-driven craft took only three or four days longer, I decided just to put up with that. Van der Poel also advised me to do that, but I do not doubt that he is getting a commission. After all this had been arranged, I went to the boat to transfer our luggage; De Vries was a big help to me in doing all that. In the afternoon my wife and I paid a visit to De Vries's wife, on the other side of the city, while De Vries himself remained on the boat to look after our goods. We had [her] prepare food for us, for which we paid, although at first she refused to take anything for it.

Buffalo is a fairly large city, and like other American cities has somber, badly painted houses, which also displayed their big gaudy numbers. The complaint that there was so little work to be found was quite general. Those who were not craftsmen were working on a new canal lock and earning six shillings a day, but they had to buy their own tools first at a cost of twenty dollars. But people who are seeking employment now are only paid three shillings a day. At the De Vries's home I spoke to a woman who had arrived this spring with her husband; he had gotten a job at a beer brewery for eighteen dollars a month. They had three roomers and so they could get along nicely. De Vries, who seemed to be planning to join up with Rev. Scholte, wanted to try to find work here for the time being. He really wanted to travel with us, and thought that I might be able to employ him. His wife was also very eager to go along, but since she had given birth only a day ago, I advised against that. De Vries had promised to write me and had asked me to let him know whether there was work for him in Burlington. Until now I have not received word from him, and there is nothing for him to do around here but sawing and chopping wood, and often that is not enough to keep one busy either.

Like everywhere else they have more paper dollars here than silver ones. They are usually in denominations of one to five dollars and are drawn on banks in different states. It is difficult for a stranger to determine which are good and which are not. So there are booklets which list all the banks, the good ones as well as those that have failed, because there are *many* banks going bankrupt all the time.* In these

---

* [The reference is to *Thompson's Bank Note Reporter* of New York City.]

booklets you will also find depictions of the over four hundred different kinds of coins from all countries that are circulating in America, each with its value given. I bought such a booklet for only eight cents. You pay six cents for a shave and twelve cents for a haircut here.

The steamboat *Niagara* is among the largest in America; you can get a place on deck as well as upstairs. Price of the latter to Chicago was ten dollars a person, which would have been at least thirty dollars for our family, not counting luggage costs; for that price one gets good cabins to sleep in and a good table, at least on this boat, where everything was available in great abundance. The cabins or rooms run around the deck, and on the inside they form a large hall where you can sit and eat; everything is arranged very nicely there. Things are altogether different for the deck passengers; they get less attention than we would give to animals. On this deck you will find the engine, the passengers, the mercantile goods, the sailors, and the firewood for the engine. There are no benches to sit on, you have to lie on the ground, and if there were only enough space to lie down, you would count yourself fortunate. We had several hundred passengers, so that for our family of seven persons (A. N. Wormser, Miet Wormser-Portengen, Leentje Portengen, Mies, Lena, Anna, and Sophie) we had a space not larger than two Amsterdam yards in length and width. As best we could, we arranged things in such a way that the children could at least sleep at night; we walked around and took turns napping an hour during the day; we constantly had to keep our eye on our goods because they were tossed about at least ten times a day. So this gave us much concern and required a lot of caretaking.

The worst part of this boat was the fact that it was entirely open on the sides; these were closed off with pieces of sailcloth just as we do with our railroad cars. But they were never closed tight, so that there were terrible drafts on all sides. And because our spot was just above the boiler of the engine, we could not be downstairs because of the heat, and not upstairs because of the cold. You have to make provision for your own food beforehand, and so we had taken along a dozen loaves of bread and some ham. However, the steamboat does lay by at times, giving you an opportunity to buy something. But we could have gotten by without buying anything, because the children got everything in great abundance from the cooks. The third day we ran aground, whereupon two steamboats came to our assistance. The men had to get off the boat, but I just stayed on board. It took an entire day before we could continue our journey. The Overijssel contingent left the boat at

Milwaukee, affording us a little more room; we finally arrived at Chicago Sunday morning, and then all the cargo had to be unloaded immediately. The first thing we knew, we again encountered a demand for two shillings, because our goods were standing on the wharf. I refused to pay, whereupon they brought a small cart, seized one of my trunks, and took it to the warehouse. That really made me angry, so that I pushed the trunk so hard that I myself began to worry that he [the man pulling] might stumble and have the trunk and cart land on top of him. But in the end I did have to pay, since it was for that day. But if he did not return the next day, then in all likelihood he had not been satisfied; afterward a Dutchman told me that he had had to pay 3½ dollars.

At Buffalo I had learned that Van den Berg from Zwolle, the same person to whom I brought sixty guilders at the Toll House, was living in Chicago. Upon our arrival there, I immediately made an effort to locate him, but that was not easy since I did not know where he lived. I looked all over town until one o'clock in the afternoon, when someone pointed out an individual to me and my wife who would be able to help us locate our man. He knew that Van den Berg lived in town, but he did not know just where. He directed us to the Presbyterian church, where I would be sure to find him. As soon as we got there, we saw him standing outside. That afternoon I went with him to another Hollander, a Friesian, who had parted ways with Van Raalte only a short time ago. We then began to look for a way to travel together, which turned out to be the canal boat to Peru. It was already evening and we did not see any chance of finding shelter for ourselves and our luggage, so we agreed that my wife and the children would spend the night in a rooming house while Leen [the Frisian] and I would spend the night guarding our luggage. But since there was no room in the rooming houses, my wife and the children had to make do with sleeping in the attic of the Frisian family. We stayed with our luggage on the wharf, the night was cold and long, and so we were happy when day began to break.

Chicago covers a lot of ground; it is sixteen years old and has 24,000 residents living in about 24,000 wooden sheds. The streets are in very poor condition. While we were searching for Van den Berg, a wind gust arose driving up such a terrible dust cloud that we did not know where to take shelter, and we must have looked a lot like people in a sandstorm in a desert as depicted by [the writer] Bruce. In front of the houses there are slightly raised footpaths of diagonally placed wooden planks. There was a certain I. Wormser living in Chicago, but since the house was closed, I did not stop by.

On Monday there were two boats going to Peru, Illinois. The one would transport us for less than the other, the one being willing to transport our persons, luggage, including the trunk, for eighteen dollars, and the other, a competitor, then reduced the price to eleven dollars. But since I knew that this was much too little, I told him that I would take his boat, provided he was willing to give me a receipt. After that had been taken care of, and the luggage loaded, the captain himself came by and again demanded eighteen dollars, since, as he said, he had not made any agreement with me. That I had expected, but I told him that I refused to pay any more, that I had a good and valid receipt from someone whom he had authorized to make such agreements; he was determined to have the luggage removed from the barge, but after much and long bickering and wrangling we agreed that 1 would pay him sixteen dollars. He would give me a new receipt provided I gave the other one back to him. It was still little enough that I paid. Once again we left almost twenty-four hours later than agreed.

The canal between Chicago and Peru is still new, having been completed only recently; the locks had been improved. At least the stones were joined more evenly, but even so, it was not Dutch nautical engineering. When the water had been left out, there were still streams of water spouting forth from between the stones. We arrived at Peru Thursday morning, but on arrival there was no steamboat to take us along the Illinois River to St. Louis. We stopped at the only available rooming house, which turned out to be a discarded steamboat. We had to take our luggage from the canal boat to our lodgings, but that was no easy job for us, given the poor quality and unevenness of the road. Our luggage was stored in the bowels of the steamboat, and we slept upstairs, so that I could not help worrying about things being stolen during the night.

They were building a new wooden house nearby; the carpenters all wore gloves although it was not very cold. It was a terrible workmanship: especially the window frames were "real masterpieces." I can think of no better comparison than that of a box for cat litter without a tree. Lining pieces are nailed on the outside, so that on the outside it only looks like a window frame, with the result there never are, or can be, any leaded windows. Painting and masonry work is just as bad; [but] working tools for farmers as well as for craftsmen are very fine and easy to handle; and they are much more efficient than ours. Everything here is compact and well constructed; for example, a carpenter's square is provided with all the measurements, a hatchet serves both as a hammer and as a nail puller. The axe has the greatest perfection; it will never get stuck in the wood because it always floats on a raised area in the center; at home they are crude and heavy, but they are of no use at all (drawing of an axe).

On the day of our arrival in Peru, we made arrangements for a steamboat to take us to St. Louis for 1½ dollars per person; the total cost for all of us, including luggage, was 11 ½ dollars. A Hollander, who had come from Chicago and was going to St. Louis to look for work, was most helpful to us in every way. Since Peru was a wretched little burg, and it was very early in the morning besides, we could take nothing along but the bread that was left from our previous journey. We counted on being able to pick up something along the way, since the boats stop off at every little place to pick up some freight and also to drop off merchandise. The distance between Peru and St. Louis is calculated to be 250 miles. The captain told us that the trip would take two days, but it took us a full week, so that was a big disappointment for us. First you travel down the Illinois River and then you continue on the Mississippi.

I could have stopped here and waited for a steamboat bound for Burlington, but, since this could have taken some time, I decided in favor of going to St. Louis where there are frequent departures to our place of destination. It is impossible to describe the misery, cold, and deprivation we endured on that boat. All the steamboats that travel on the Illinois and Mississippi rivers are the same make and size, but the deck passengers are located where the animals are in Holland; herewith a small picture of such a boat [not published]. If you are standing on the shore and see such a boat lying in the river, then you might think, especially if you were a farmer, that such a big, beautiful boat must provide its passengers with every convenience, and you might think that the Americans who build such boats can work wonders in comparison to the Hollanders.

The two big iron chimneys at the front end of the boat certainly do make quite a showing. But on closer examination it all breaks down, and you discover once again that everything is only built to make do. For that matter, such a boat can be built very fast, and it is used for hauling freight even before it is finished. Imagine for yourselves a big Amsterdam barge with a ceiling deck built on one side. The engine is located here, and it is also the area that accommodates the deck passengers, the freight, and the sailors. A ceiling, resting on a few miserable posts, has been nailed in place above it, so that you just cannot understand how it can carry the load above. The deck timbers of this ceiling are two-by-fours (at best two inches thick and four to five inches wide), and on this ceiling small rooms have been built with bunks for the passengers. Together these cabins form an inner chamber where you can sit and eat; it is the fanciest part of the boat. Above this, behind the chimneys, there is a small wooden structure for the steersman. At the forward end the boat is entirely open, at the back end there were [supposed to be] two doors, but one was gone, so that there was always a wind blowing from back to front and vice versa, and so we suffered much from the cold. You either sleep on the floor or on the chests. At times there was so much steam that you could not see each other. There is a big stove for boiling water for coffee or tea. We let the children sleep as best they could, and we roamed about during the night, in part because there was no place to sleep, in part to keep an eye on our goods to prevent them from being stolen. For two days we had eaten what was left of our bread supply and still had not been able to buy anything along the way. The third day all we had was a turnip and a little whisky that we had received; that afternoon I had the good fortune of buying a partial loaf of bread and some milk from a farmer.

The banks of the Illinois River are usually still wooded; here and there one sees a few log houses, and from time to time a small town. In most places the banks are low, which makes me think that the river overflows them; frequently there is beautiful scenery. Generally speaking the river is not more than 2½ feet deep; as a result our boat was stuck in the river once for twenty-four hours. We finally arrived at St. Louis, a big mercantile city. There was a host of steamboats anchored there. The city is not attractive, and on the river side it looks as though an earthquake had shaken the ground. We transferred directly from one steamboat to another, one which was to leave for Burlington at four in the afternoon, but in fact that did not happen until the next day. In St. Louis we bought an oven for fifteen dollars. The distance between St. Louis and Burlington is reported to be 250 miles, a distance the captain said we would cover in 2½ days. But it took us nearly eight days, and after putting up with many difficulties, we finally arrived at Burlington on Sunday evening, October 29.

Jan Budde, who had gone to the post office to see if there was any mail for him, just now brought me two letters, the one from an American woman in Hillsdale, State of Michigan, whose acquaintance we had made on the canal boat to Buffalo and whom we had promised to write; the other letter was from De Vries in Buffalo; my wife is making a copy of it [see Wormser 17 above]. From the latter it is evident that things are still not going very well for him. I will immediately write him how things are here, but the trip is very difficult, and especially during the winter. The Hollander who lives here, and who is a very able man, is willing to undertake everything together with him, both in sawing wood, and there is plenty of that and painting, which, given the way it is done here, De Vries can also do.

We are reasonably well now; I gave Mies and Lena, who were not well for several days, an emetic, and that really helped. Warmest greetings to your wife, children, and Riek, to my wife's father, mother, and Mrs. Zeelt and the rest of the family.

> Your Loving Brother,
> A. N. Wormser

Wormser 23

> Excerpt from a letter of J. Berkhout to D. A. Budde
> copied by A. N. Wormser
> St. Louis, 2 December 1848

For the moment, we have moved in with [J.J.] Diekinga, who almost has the dazed look of one who just arrived from Amsterdam. We slept on the floor for fourteen days before and in all kinds of drafts, and so messy that we could no longer remain there. Every day the bed bugs marched across our bedding; my wife even removed them from between her breasts. Not knowing what to do, and since it is neither our intention nor desire to stay in St. Louis, we have again rented a room, one in which we cannot remain. We have now bought a stove for twelve dollars, a cartload of wood, and a pail, but nothing more. We are now living on our own, and we are still sleeping on the floor, but it is clean. I bought wood for a bed, which is now almost completed; our table is still a chest. I am writing this letter on a stool on which a board is lying. We are now the proud owners of two chairs with wooden seats. In addition, we are surrounded by chests, and all the other things we use are standing on the floor and along the wall; it looks a lot like a warehouse.

Our journey through the interior was not at all propitious; on one occasion a lock was broken down in the canal, and on the Great Lakes our steamboat was often grounded. [Jacob] Keesel and his family got off at Sheboygan, in order to go and visit the Rev. [Pieter] Zonne and the several colonies. He was to write me in Pella. I wrote a letter to Janssen in Milwaukee: he also has parted ways with Rev. Zonne. And what more shall I write, brother; we are truly embarrassed to be here. We have wished ourselves back in Holland at least a hundred times. I am not strong enough to work as a carpenter for and among Americans; it will have to be some other trade. I have too little money to start farming. My experience in America has already taught me, now that it is too late, that any decent, well-mannered person perpetrates the greatest folly by going to America. The minute you set foot on shipboard, all delights, pleasures, conveniences, and also the means to nourish your soul, suddenly come to a halt, and for most people it is for the rest of their lives. Religion is not much either, and when it is good, when can you really enjoy it? All you get here is meat and bread; all the rest is bad and often too expensive and too scarce to even get. And in addition to all that, one is plagued by a host of discomforts. At night you have to put up with bed bugs and mosquitoes everywhere. Things are really bad during the day, when it rains [so hard] that you can barely walk down the street without risking your life. And when it is dry, you can scarcely see because of all the dust; one time you are tormented by the cold, another by the heat. The temperate airs, of which we spoke so fondly in Holland, are a fantasy [here].

I just cannot understand how people who have experienced things here can all be so merciless as to cozy up to their friends in Holland, who are well situated, to persuade them to come to America. It is only a good thing for people who suffer hunger in Holland to go to America, but not for any others. But we are now here, and we do not wish to go back. When I think that it was my own folly that led to the decision [to come here], it upsets my mind greatly, etc. etc.

Wormser 24

A. N. Wormser to J. A. Wormser
Burlington, 12 December 1848

Esteemed Brother!
 A couple weeks ago I made a little trip to the forty-acre farm purchased

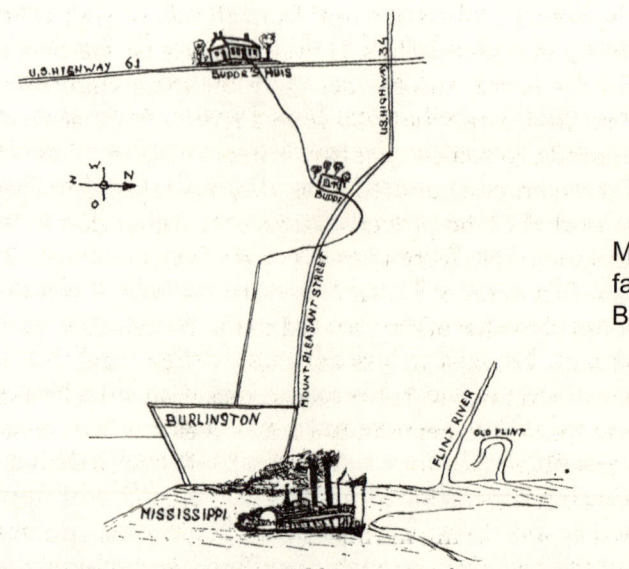

Map to Budde family farm, Burlington

by two Zeelanders (A. Verkerk and Chr. Beurkens). It is located on a different road than Budde is, approximately as shown on the accompanying drawing. From my house, which is located about in the middle of Burlington, I could walk to the Buddes in a little less than an hour; it took me about an hour and a half to get to the Zeelanders. Their land is much higher than the Buddes and looked much better to me. It looks to me that they made the better buy. I think that they will make a better living from their forty acres than Budde from his eighty acres. They paid ten dollars per acre. It must be said that there is only a small log cabin on the land, but they can replace that later on by building a house of their own. If you buy a farm with a brick house on it, then you still have to pay whatever the house cost originally. First they calculate the selling price of the land, then they add the original cost of the house and fencing, and the total amount, recalculated as so much per acre, is what you have to pay. The Zeelanders have a nice stand of woods from which they will be able to fell and sell wood both now and for many years to come. Budde does not have enough timber to build a log cabin for his renter; he had no choice but to have a brick house built, which was very costly.

The land [of the Zeelanders] is also more pleasing to the eye. They figured that they could get seventy bushels of corn per acre, and, at sixteen cents a bushel, that came to eleven dollars and twenty cents [per acre]. Alternatively, twenty bushels of wheat from an acre, at sixty cents a bushel, would bring in twelve dollars. However, nearly all the corn is needed as feed for the cattle, and besides there are many additional expenses at harvest time, even when you have a renter. Forty acres of land is all a renter needs, so you can put two renters on eighty acres. To be sure, if you offer renters one hundred acres, they will take it, but they will not be able to work the land properly; rather they will neglect it. So as a rule you get as much from forty acres as you do from one hundred.

Budde rented out fifty acres of his land, and Jan told me, if you did not take into account the value of the corn fed to the animals, the land, that is the rented land, brought in less than fifty dollars, and that is pretty sad. The combined tax Budde has to pay, including land, house, and cattle, comes to ten dollars per year, and it may even be a little more next year. Budde complains that Jan would rather look at work than do it. But Jan says that his father's mood has changed a good deal from what it was when they were living in Amsterdam. In any case, I do not think that either of them worked as much, or suffered as much cold, in Amsterdam as they have here. But they act as if they do not regret the move they have made. They even act as if it they are pleased at having made the step, although I am convinced that at times they think differently; but they can reconcile themselves to the situation better than we can. For even the Germans, who really know what drudgery is and what it means to make do, have demonstrated that they are especially good at adapting to this kind of life, but then you must not expect too much or be too demanding. And now that the die is cast, I just try to keep them in that good mood. For their sakes I could wish that they had land as good as that of the Zeelanders, for then they would surely do better. Until now they have not even been able to buy a bed, but sleep on corn husks, they are so poor. Jan tried to get work in the pork house [abatoir] but he has not able to get work as yet, since their busy season does not begin until Christmas. There has been talk of his going to the city to saw and chop wood; Budde also talked about [his] going to work for a boss in town as a wood turner.

Stables for cattle scarcely exist here, and what are regarded as stables are so wretched that one feels sorry for the cattle; the snow and ice sometimes is an inch thick on their bodies. But what can you expect of stables when even the houses are so bad that you scarcely know how to protect yourself against drafts. But cattle are cheap here; you can buy a cow and her calf for twelve dollars, a two-hundred-pound pig for four dollars.

Two days ago Budde received a letter from Berkhout, from which we learned that he and his wife are presently in St. Louis. The letter contained some good news for us, namely that Keesel had located Leen's chest, and that it was now in his possession. You will understand that this made us very happy, but the other side of the story is that Keesel is missing a chest that contains a good many valuable things. He now has high hopes that I have a chest of his, but in that he will be disappointed. Berkhout lost his bedding in New York. Berkhout did not know where Keesel was right now; Keesel had left Berkhout at Sheboygan, and was planning to see Rev. Zonne and then to go on to visit the other colonies, for everywhere in America people are getting the worst reports about the Reverends Van Raalte and Scholte. It is reported that most of the people in Van Raalte's colony are sick. While en route, we heard that Van der Veen, the coppersmith, lay at death's door, but then later we heard that he was somewhat better, but that the money he had brought from Holland was nearly gone. Berkhout had not written me, because he did not know whether I had arrived in Burlington. I wrote him at once; his letter, which was about six pages long, contained nothing but lamentations about his folly in having gone to America. I copied a short portion of his letter, which I will enclose. It is just a small sample of the content and what the entire letter is like. He had received the worst reports about Pella and was afraid to go there. First he had moved in with Diekinga, but the mess and the bed bugs chased him away. He had no household furnishings other than an oven, two chairs, and a bed he had built himself, and which was now finished.

I can vividly imagine the regret they must feel at having left Holland, because they have experienced nothing but troubles, worries, and grief since coming here. Their money was nearly gone, melted away as it were. He had also been badly cheated in New York and overcharged on his freight, having to pay again every time he arrived at another destination. I would advise anyone coming here to travel via New Orleans; that is much cheaper, shorter, and easier. Just a few days ago a woman from Bremen arrived at New Orleans in forty-five days, and from there to Burlington in ten days. I wrote Berkhout asking whether he wished to make the journey back [to Holland] with me; he probably would very much like to do that but will not be able to [for lack of funds]. I doubt whether Keesel will feel at home here either. I am really very eager to get a letter from him. Berkhout, who cannot [afford] to go back, is loud in his complaint against the people whose embellished letters containing little truth also lure others to come to America.

Accordingly, I wrote back to Berkhout that the greatest fault lay with advocates like the Reverends Van Raalte, Brummelkamp, and Scholte. The first [Van Raalte] went to America to restore his lost fortune, and, with the cooperation of his brother-in-law, Brummelkamp, they enticed people to come over here. Scholte came mostly because of his wounded ego. But if we may live long enough, then I would not be at all surprised that, when they are rich enough, the Reverends Scholte and Van Raalte will return to Holland, or at least to Europe. What is behind the speedy change in the plans of the Reverend Brummelkamp and Mr. Van der Linde, I do not know, but it is probably related to the same thing. It is generally known in America that they are trying to get rich here. I do not know whether I wrote you this before, but on the steamboat people were saying that Van Raalte was selling land to the farmers that he had gotten from the government, and that he must already have made a tidy sum of money. They went on to say that he should be hanged.

Scholte also insists on having everything in his possession, mills, etc., and everyone ends up by having to go to him. There is a rumor, I do not know whether it is true, that he [Scholte] took out a personal loan for eighty thousand dollars in New York. He has the Americans do his threshing because Hollanders are too slow at it. He says that he is not going to let people here get the best of him as they did in Holland. Let us hope that people will not allow themselves to be misled by pie-in-the-sky letters. In part, it is a good thing for poor people who can get [financial] help from others to make the crossing, but then they will really have to work very hard. The more I realize how things really are here, the clearer it becomes to me that this is not the place for us. People like us, who cannot do heavy work, cannot make a living here.

Budde now also acknowledges that this is not a good place for townspeople from Holland. But he had not thought that we would be gone so soon, he said. He still did not have enough experience to write about everything [at the time], and he had been led to believe that he could live from the land he rented out, which is not true. But what should we wait for? and how long? It is true that his last letter, seen in retrospect, indicated that it was best not to come, because he wrote that there were no farms available for less than twenty to twenty-five thousand guilders and there were no houses for rent, so what would we do there, but all that was not sufficiently clear to us. It would have been better to come right out with it and say there is plenty of land for sale, in pieces as big or as small as you like. It would have been better if we had waited until we had no choice but to leave, that [my] work [in

Holland] had come to an end; then our only alternative would have been to buy land with a good wood lot and have had that cut down and chopped by others and taken to the city to sell—and better too if we had rented out a part of the land. Then, they could have said we had to leave Holland.

Budde must have thought that I knew absolutely nothing [about America], would think that everything was lovely, and that I would immediately go ahead and buy some property. Once he said in jest that it was not a good idea for me to come over first, but I also answered him in jest saying that that was certainly true, because it would have been better for some dumb Overijssel farmer to take the lead in bringing us all to America, even though they do not like it here either. But the De Vries and Berkhout letters have taught him that I am not the only one who thinks unfavorably about America. The winters here are cold and long; below is a table showing the degrees of cold through today. One day it was twelve degrees on the Fahrenheit scale, but it is supposed to get even colder. At the other end, according to Budde, it must be sweltering during the summer; when they were still living in Burlington, Mrs. Teeleman [Teleman] wanted to stay in the basement all day long. Jan said that he had been so sunburned while working that the skin peeled off his arm.

I would very much like to know if everything is still on the old footing in Holland. Then it might be better for us to return to Holland, but the trip is no picnic, and we really look up against it. In the event we do go, it might be best for us to go via New Orleans; we would still have the problem of disposing of our goods. Here almost everyone gets along with next to nothing. I hope that minimally I could dispose of the largest pieces [of furniture]; if there are interested buyers, I would just as soon sell everything except for some clean linens. As yet we have not received a cent for our ribbons and thread. We shall see how things work out. We hope to receive a letter from you soon telling how things are with you and the family. After receipt of this letter, do not send any letters containing anything of importance, for if we should have left here, they would fall into the hands of Budde. If it were not winter, with sailings stalled, we would probably start traveling as soon as we could sell our property; in any case, for the present we do have to wait. But we cannot wait too long, for my wife is expecting a baby about mid-May. We will see how things go, and I suggest that you do not share much of this letter with others, and not the part that concerns Budde either.

Now that the chest is in Keesel's possession, I should be getting it all right, but in no case must we pay him any money until it is in our hands. My wife and children have bad colds; for the rest things are going fairly well, but one must constantly be swallowing rhubarb and phlegm pills; there are no green vegetables here at all: turnips and onions are all there is. Cordial greetings to your wife, to Riek and the children, to Mother and the rest of the family, from my wife as well as from your loving brother A. N. Wormser.

Temperature chart in Fahrenheit

Date		8 A.M.	12 Noon	4 P.M.
November 26		30	32	31
"	27	38	40	36
"	28	43	49	56
"	29	37	36	35
"	30	25	31	30
December 5		25	26	25
"	6	36	38	37
"	7	20	25	23
"	8	20	25	23
"	9	17	24	22
"	10	12	28	20
"	11	18	40	30
"	12	28	40	34

[A. N. Wormser attached the following description to his letter of 12 December 1848.]
Description of a cattle round-up in North America

As is well known, cows are usually not stabled in barns in North America. They wander about in the woods regardless of who owns the land, and they have free access to all lands as long as they are not fenced or closed off. As a result of this practice, it is not easy to stable the animals, and it is even harder to catch them in order to move them from one place to another. Our friend Budde had purchased one of these young cows for eight dollars, a cow which, as I said, roamed about in the woods; he had to catch her to transfer her to his farm. It was two o'clock in the afternoon, and since I am still not sufficiently Americanized to eat at twelve noon, but eat at 4 in the afternoon, I accepted his invitation to help catch the cow. I did so with all the more satisfaction because that cow was said to be on the farm that Budde considered suitable for me to buy. Budde, Jan, and I got under way; we had supplied ourselves with all the things we thought the little cow would enjoy eating, wheat bread, corn, salt, etc. We cut across the fields and several times had to climb over fences as high as a man. I remarked to my friends that the three of us might have quite a job getting the cow over all those fences, but I had sold the hide before catching the bear. Finally, we arrived at the farm. Following local custom, we knocked at the door, and the renter called out, "Come in." Once you are inside, each of you grabs a chair, sets it by the hearth, and sits down. We talked a little while about the farm on which he was a tenant. It was 325 acres in size; of these only fifty acres were cultivated; he said that the woods were poor and that twelve dollars an acre was too high. And then we began our search for the cow. Presently we saw a dozen of them, but we were not sure which one was ours. Budde thought that a red cow with a white head must be the one, and presently we had lured her to us with a piece of wheat bread. Meanwhile Jan, who was holding a rope with a lasso, tried to throw it around her horns but missed. From that moment on the cow mistrusted us and would approach us only very cautiously. Finally, I succeeded in approaching her from the rear and got the lasso around her horns while she was eating, and then the two of us hung on to the rope. The cow, finding herself tied to a rope, began to buck something terrible and ran off with us in tow, so that we had a hard job keeping our feet on the ground. Budde relieved me, but then the little cow took off again and began sauntering off with them. I could see trouble ahead and so remained at a slightly respectable distance.

In order to get her to do her duty [and obey us] a little better, we decided to put another noose around her nose, so that when she pulled hard it would get all the tighter. That was quickly done, but it did not help a thing. She reared and tugged so hard that the rope slipped out of the Buddes' hands, whereupon Jan lost his footing, and long as he was, the cow dragged him through a stand of hazelnut trees. The renter's son and I immediately came to his aid and finally brought the cow to a standstill. Jan got out of it with just some light bruises and torn clothing. I advised him to stop the chase now before we had any more accidents, for a buffalo hunt in Africa could not begin to compare with this. But after standing around the little animal for a few minutes catching our breath, we tried again, but the cow seemed to be tired just like us, at least she refused to budge an inch. We began pulling on the rope and twisting the cow's tail, and every time we did she shot ahead a ways. But since the rope was a little short, she repeatedly walked with her head into Jan Budde's back and he, unable to get out of the way quickly enough, always stepped on his father's heels, which was not a pretty sight. After we had been busy in this way for some time, our cow suddenly took a leap, running as fast as she could go. Budde let go, and, since Jan could not hold on any longer either, the cow took off into the woods trailing the rope behind her. I was happy the game was coming to such a fortunate conclusion; night was beginning to fall, I still had not eaten, and I was chilled through and through from walking through the snow. Since it was Saturday evening, all of us decided to give up the pursuit and to try our luck again Monday, but since the cow still had the rope around her nose, we did have to try to approach her again to get that loose. We followed her for some time in the woods, but, oh my, she always managed to keep a distance of fifty paces between us. So that we gave up the pursuit by just letting her go, which I did not regret, because if we had gotten her to come along, we would have been working late into the night. We left the battle field with silenced drums; on the way home, B[udde] had uncommon praise for the little animal. I thought it was nice too, but the other ones [cows] standing around I found even nicer. It struck me that the hairs were going in the wrong direction, just as in the case of chickens whose feathers stand on end when they have been frightened while they are brooding. [*The letter ends abruptly.*]

Wormser 25

M. Wormser-Portengen, to J. A. Wormser-van der Ven
Burlington, (about the 17th of) December 1848

Esteemed Sister,

As unpleasant as our stay in America may be, I still wish to write and let you know a few things about our situation here. We lived in Burlington for a month and already there we experienced much because of the loss of our two dear children. I cannot dismiss it from my mind for a moment, for we experienced so much together on our journey here, and now all of a sudden they are gone. You will readily understand how difficult it is for me to lose two children to such a contagious disease. Besides our dwelling was one of the most unsanitary ones in Burlington; it was like being in a prison. After our arrival we had a lot of washing to do, because we had soiled so much of our clothing on the journey, and it was so messy and dirty that we just could not get it clean. After many days of washing I could not stand it any longer and became slightly indisposed. One morning I awakened to find my head swollen, as well as my entire left side, and I was completely deaf. I was embarrassed; the doctor who had just come by said that I should not be washing every day as I had been doing, because I could not take it. He gave me some pills, and I was to say in bed until the swelling had gone down. It was a strange feeling. I was completely deaf and without strength, but thanks to the blessing of the Lord I soon was restored. And then, dearest sister, we moved in with the Buddes.

Jan, accompanied by Keizer, the Buddes' renter, came with a wagon to pick up our things. It was bitterly cold and almost too slippery to travel. Besides, it had snowed the day before, so that walking was not easy, for the road is now uphill and then again down. Sometimes we had to walk through water in the low spots, getting our feet wet. The Buddes are almost an hour from the city. Mies and Leena were exhausted, so that we were glad to get there, because our feet were stiff from the wet and cold. Now we have one side of the Budde house, that is, two very small rooms in the dwelling of the renter. The larger one is five Amsterdam ells [91.4 cm.] long and six wide, the other little room is three ells long and four wide, but terribly drafty; we have sealed the windows and plugged the seams of the doors. We hung carpets in front of other doors.

There are plenty of rats and mice here. We have a good view of the land, but it feels like we are the only people alive. It is very cold here; this morning it was twelve degrees. Budde and his wife keep very busy. You would almost say they are not the same people we knew in Amsterdam; all we hear about is work. If they speak on occasion, it is only a few words, they are so very busy. Mrs. Budde said, "My chief complaint is that I just cannot get all my work done; it's more than I can handle, and for me, that is the worst of it." She does not even take the time to sit down for a moment; in the spring it is even worse, and in the summer you just cannot handle all the work. "The worst thing for me," she said, "is that I have so much mending to do and no time to do it; it is a miserable life."

Anyone who likes good eating better not go to America; there is nothing to eat but turnips and onions and dried apples, and they are not cheap. The coffee here is so bad that you cannot drink it; you have to roast your own coffee. It is expensive, fifty nickles [fl 2.50] an American pound. One day we eat potatoes with turnips, the next day potatoes with onions, and the next with apples. And then we start all over again, but we eat very little of it, because the potatoes are so bad that you can hardly eat them. Potatoes are expensive here [forty American cents] a bushel, which comes to one guilder a bushel and a bushel is not much. We have to bake our own bread; I get my butter from Mrs. Budde who makes it herself. [The saying is:] you are on your own, and you just make do; [but] they make far too much of that in Amsterdam; it is not all that easy, as I am now experiencing. People brag about America so much that you would almost think you were late in getting there; but when you do get here you are sorry you came. We have yet to meet anyone who does not regret having come here, even the Germans, but then it is too late. And for children too, life here is just plain rough. This is not Holland, as far as civilization is concerned. In Amsterdam there is such a demand for domestics, but there is no shortage of them here in Burlington. And they do not earn as much as is reported; mostly they are girls between twelve and fourteen who earn fifty cents a week; in a boarding house a domestic earns a dollar a week. I don't think the Budde family cares all that much about being here either, because no one does. Jan says that his father just might move to Ost Friesland some time. We are thinking that it may be best for us to go back. Berkhout would also very much like to go to Holland, but he probably will not be able [to afford it]. I hope, dear Sister, that you and your dear children are enjoying good health. Mies and Leena have colds. For the rest, we are doing quite well.

Your loving Sister,
M. Wormser-Portengen

Wormser 26

H. P. Scholte to J. A. Wormser
Pella, 20 December 1848

Dear Beloved Friend and Brother in Christ,

I have received your letter. Berkhout is still in St. Louis where he will probably remain through the winter. I regret that, since he has Dutch clothing materials with him that people here are eager to have. I think that he is just too cautious and that later on he will be sorry for having done that. Your brother is in Burlington. According to the most recent reports, the Budde family is doing well. I have proposed to Mrs. Zeelt that she consider participating in [the acquisition of] land. She will no doubt consult with you and let you read my letter, and then you will easily understand [what it is all about].

Your acquaintances here are all well. On the first of December the Lord gave me a fine son. We are now completely at home here. The population of this state is increasing rapidly due to the influx of people from the older states. This is now increasing more and more because of the assurance that the Mississippi River will be made navigable. Half of the work has been let and is under way; the other half is now being planned. The chief engineer told us this week that work on it would get started next summer. That is the reason why the [Des Moines] river lands must be paid for sooner than we had thought, and that is why I sent my proposal to Mrs. Zeelt. The spiritual revival is continuing and that is very encouraging for our presence here. How I would like to have you here. Also give greetings to your wife from mine. Saartje also requests me to convey her greetings, but she is too busy to write. The Lord our God be with you, and, if possible, bring you and yours to this blessed land.

I am very curious to learn who was elected president of France. Generally, we get the news from Europe soon. The telegraph comes to this state. Cordial greetings to all the brethren and sisters from me. Do remember me and mine in the prayers of all of you.

Your Loving Brother in Christ,
H. P. Scholte

[*After the February Revolution of 1848 and the flight of King Louis Philip, a government was organized under Alphonse de Lamartine. On December 10, 1848, Ludwig Napoleon was chosen as president. He was Emperor Napoleon III (1852-1870).*]

Wormser 27

A. N. Wormser to H. Wormser
Burlington, 20 January 1849

Esteemed Brother!

Some time ago I sent my sixth letter from America, so this is the seventh. Since I have quite some free time during the long winter evenings, I think I will just use it to write you all. I have already written you about the most important things I have encountered in this land; I may even have repeated things occasionally, but no matter. We are having real winter weather these days and have had for some time. It freezes very hard here, though the temperatures vary a great deal, as you probably noticed from the little chart I included in my last letter. We have already had a temperature of four degrees Fahrenheit, and it is generally coldest in the morning. During the winter the days are about an hour longer here than in Holland. Right now there is so much snow that it is over our knees; not only are the winters severe, but they also last long. On our journey here, we had days of freezing weather already at the beginning of October, and they say that you can still have winter weather as late as April. People are crossing the Mississippi [River] with horses and wagons right now.

In one of my earlier letters I already wrote you how some people can praise the most trivial things to the skies, and thus they mislead others, whether from malice or ignorance I do not know, and lure them away from their peaceful existence to come to America. When I left Holland I also took along a booklet that contains some letters from Dutch emigrants; a booklet that had been published earlier by the Rev. Brummelkamp. Because I had so much luggage I did not care to keep the booklet; instead, from time to time I tore out several pages as I needed them, and so it became more or less customary for me to have a look at the contents before I tore them up. And so I came upon a page, written by a Mrs. Sleyster, if I recall correctly [no, it was Louise Arnoud from Boston], and very likely under the guidance of the Rev. Van Raalte. If you have gotten at all acquainted with the way things are here, you will be scandalized by all the embellishment in this kind of writing. That was the reason I did not tear it up but saved it in my portfolio and later on read it out loud to many Hollanders, all of whom were annoyed by this kind of writing.

Since the booklet is probably no longer in your possession, I would like to copy two pages for you here; they are pages 43 and 44:

> The market is a big brick building, at least a block long; with a large passage way in the center of it. You can buy anything you like here: meat, fish, lambs, whole hogs, sheep, calves, ducks, and chickens; everything is slaughtered and dressed and brought into town in wagons. There is no edible food you can possibly think of, but it will be found here. The area in front of the building and all around it is crowded with wagons filled with meat, vegetables,

potatoes, and all kinds of fruit. Meat costs from 6 to 2 cents a pound; beef is 6 cents, mutton 2 to 3 cents. The sheep are so fat that they are a delight to behold. We eat meat almost every day, there is nothing cheaper to eat; when we cook one-fourth *spint* (1.25 liters) of potatoes at a cost of 3 cents, then we have more than enough, there are still some left. Almost everybody eats meat three times a day; you would almost be inclined to say, "how can things possibly go on this way," but the next morning, says my husband, they are at it again bringing hundreds of sheep and hogs to the market. And when it is very hot outdoors, there is a chunk of ice lying in the center of the slaughtered cattle to prevent anything from spoiling. And everyone is friendly and ready to assist you with all your needs; if there is anything we do not have, they lend it to us. They brought chairs to our room for us to sit on until we were ready to buy, and had purchased six others for 3 dollars, and a bedstead for 2 dollars less ¼ ($1.75). For here they do not have bedsteads and beds like we have [in Holland], but they have open-ended benches to rest on. I think it is for warmth; they sleep with a featherbed underneath and a straw bed on top, but it is all in good taste and neat. Arnhem [with its high-class reputation] does not begin to compare!!!

You do no see any poor people here; there are no beggars, no collection boxes or boxes for the poor, not even in the churches my husband attended. He witnessed the celebration of the Lord's Supper, but no one gave anything for the poor. Schools are free of charge here: when the children are five years old you can send them off to school, boys and girls, each to a separate school. After paying [tuition] for 1¼ years, schooling is free. If a man dies, his wife and children go to a home; they are cared for there, the children are educated until they are of age, and then they are provided for. There are no taxes here and you do not have to pay any license fees.

The trust people have in each other is great, yes, even in strangers. I am convinced that we could get one hundred guilders worth of credit. There are no Lombards (pawn brokers) here; you will not find any taverns for drunks as in Arnhem either. If a drunk is staggering down the street and a policeman sees him, he goes to jail for three months. And if he is lying dead drunk in the street or resists [the police] he gets 6 months, and if they find out which public house he visited, it must pay a heavy fine. There are no public gambling houses here. As soon as the authorities learn of one, they immediately ban it. No one would dare to accost a woman or girl in public. You just do not hear people singing or shouting in the streets, much less swearing.

There is much splendor here, beautiful buildings (!): doors with silver knobs or hand grips, houses five stories high, beautiful churches. They say there are 82 churches here: one Jewish, one Lutheran, one High German Reformed, the others are all English. There are many Roman Catholics here, and only recently a bishop was buried here. You see people going to church by the hundreds, but you are free in all you do; each individual does as he pleases. They are presently busy building three more new churches. If Reverend Budding were here, "wouldn't he pray."

Now what do you think of such an exaggerated and embellished account? Who would not like to live in such land of ease and luxurious living, who would not feel like flying right over there. But it appeals especially to the poor and needy. I don't say that everything said is untrue, but most assuredly it does not reflect the overall situation. For example, to mention only one thing, not a word is said about the fact that there are so many bugs here in the summer that you hardly know what to do; it's almost as though they are falling out of the sky. And there are so many flies that you cannot bring a cup to your lips without having eight to ten flies in it.

But let us have a closer look at the pamphlet: They write: "You can buy anything you want here, meat, fish, etc. There is no edible food you can think of but it will be found here, and in the area in front of and around the building, etc." It is undoubtedly true that you will be able to get more things in one place or city than another. But on my journey through the interior, I did not observe that you could just about buy anything anywhere. One day we eat turnips, the next onions, and the day following, dried apples with potatoes. The potatoes are done for; you can't buy them any longer in Burlington. That is why we use rice instead, though it is expensive and costs ten cents a pound. I had the good fortune of buying a white cabbage for five cents in a store this week. I have seen no fruit here other than apples, and they are three for five cents, but of course it is winter.

"Meat costs from 6 to 2 cents a pound." Here it is not higher than four cents. "Sheep are so fat that they are a delight to behold," but not here. "We eat meat every day, there is nothing cheaper to eat." There are times that we do not have it in two weeks, not because it is not available, but because beef is considered to be unhealthy. However, this is truer during the summer when cows are driven twenty miles and more, are slaughtered immediately, and sometimes are sold when the meat is still warm. As I was told on my journey here, that is the reason men induce vomiting three or four times a year to get rid of bile, but women are purged. There is no such problem with pork, and that is why we always eat it, but never more than once a day, and then only in small amounts. "When we cook one fourth *sprint* (1.25 liters) of potatoes at a cost of 3 cents"; the last time I paid forty cents for a bushel and that is not much. Could it be they had potatoes left from their three cents worth because they were inedible? The farmers still do have potatoes, but they are holding on to them in hopes that the price will go up to a dollar a bushel in the spring. "If there is anything we need, they lend it to us." That surely is convenient. They lend things here too, for example, a blacksmith lends you an iron or a washtub, but you first ask if you can borrow it, and who will then refuse?

"A bedstead for 2 dollars less ¼ ($1.75)." That surely is not very much; I would like to see that masterpiece; the cheapest one costs four dollars here, and I cannot say that that is expensive. "But there are no bedsteads and beds such as we have; instead they have open-ended rest benches. I think it is for warmth." The writer, a lady, knows very well that this is not for warmth but because of the wall-bugs. "And they sleep with a featherbed underneath, and a straw-bed on top." That is strange indeed. Do you suppose that Mrs. Sleyster is the only one who sleeps this way? For bed coverings people generally use the so-called "beggars blankets" (quilts) made from small pieces of colored cloth sewn together. These can be formed into all kinds of designs and some people make much work of it. "But everything is elegant and neat, Arnhem just cannot compare!!!" Her comparison dates back to the time when she lived in Arnhem.

"You do not see any poor people here." What does she mean by that? Very likely, that you do not see any people asking for alms. That is also evident from what follows: "No beggars." True enough, but you do see many individuals whose torn and tattered clothes are such that you would scarcely refuse them a penny in Amsterdam. "Schools are free here." There is said to have been such a school here, but because of insufficient funds it collapsed. "If a man dies...etc." That must also be the case in St. Louis; the city then supports you. "There are no taxes." I already wrote you that B[udde] paid $10 a year in taxes on his land, cattle, and house. "Licenses are not paid here," so it would appear that there are malevolent folk [tax-dodgers] here too. "And you do not find taverns for drunkards here like those in Arnhem either." It may well be that they are not *like* those in Arnhem, but their number is proportionally greater here; along the Albany-Buffalo [Erie] Canal we found one and sometimes three or four at almost every bridge. And they sell alcoholic beverages in almost every store. "When you see a man staggering dead-drunk down the street." The ordinances in respect to this may very well vary from one place to another. In New York we did see a number of them [drunks] staggering down the streets waving their arms, and sufficiently often that we did see one hauled away by the police when it took place there. "No one would accost a woman or a girl on the street." That may be so, but they do just that on the steamboats. "You don't hear any singing or hollering in the streets, let alone swearing." I never heard any singing or shouting, but so much the more swearing. "There is much splendor here, beautiful buildings, doors with silver knobs etc." However this may be, I have commented on it earlier.

By talking things up this way, hundreds of people have been lured away from their cozy situation to come to America, only to exchange all the pleasures they had for toiling and drudging like dockhands and delivery men; that is, if they are lucky enough to get such work. The high day wages also lure many people here; in their letters people say that an apprentice carpenter or mason earns a dollar a day. That is true enough when they are in demand, then that is the price you have to pay. But one should not get the idea that there is lots of work here, because if you come over thinking there is a job waiting for you, you are all wrong. Often you have to wait a long time before anything comes along. In addition you should bear in mind that the winters last very long here, often as much as a half year, and during that time these activities come to a halt; and then you have to live from the income you earned during the summer. People also often leave Holland to improve the lot of their children; but what do they get in this exchange?

Their life is wholly like that of the animals; a horse, for example, eats in the morning and works till midday, eats and goes back to work, in the evening gets his fodder and goes to sleep, and the next day he goes through the same routine. The same applies to human beings. If one is a farmer, he often gets up at three in the morning, sometimes he is going to market while it is still dark, gets home about eight o'clock, eats, and immediately goes to work on his land. At noon he receives his fodder or food, gobbles it down quickly, so he can go right back to work until evening, when it is time to eat and go to sleep, in order to repeat the process the next day, without ever enjoying any satisfactions. Neither do children have anything to make their lives a little more pleasant or give them an opportunity to enjoy themselves. And still there are people who say and try to make us believe, "Really, children have everything here!" But what do they really have when you take a close look at the lives of farmers' children, and that is what we are talking about. As soon as they are able to move their arms about, boys and girls have to do the weeding and other tasks. The boys soon have the opportunity to test their strength by chopping thick branches, fetching water, etc. Like other children in this area, they also have to go to school in town. However, because there is too much work in the field during the summer, as a rule that is put off till winter. Often they have to walk an hour and more; it is bitterly cold or as at present the snow is knee deep, and as a result you are, as it were, cut off from the city. That's about the way children live here; there is no recreation. It is true that if they are brought up this way from childhood on, they do not know any better than this is the way it's supposed to be. But I can only describe their situation as anything but pleasant.

    As far as religion is concerned, that is no reason to leave Holland either, for we are practically deprived of all religion here. Of those leaving [Holland] with a family, the adults usually do not speak any English, scarcely one in twenty-five knows English. As a rule they are too old or don't have the time or opportunity to learn it anymore. They usually try to get along at some German church, comprehending as best they can. If there are an occasional few who understand English, one goes here and another there, one to the Methodists, another to the Presbyterians, like so many wandering sheep. The Hollanders, even if there were enough of them, live too far from each other to form a fellowship. I go with B[udde] to the German Lutherans, or as he called it, the Evangelical Church. I can't say that I am really edified there, and their hymns, which do not have very nice tunes, they belt out as loudly as possible. And that tiny congregation is dwindling; they usually transfer to the Methodists. If you understood English, then it would be best to join the Presbyterians. And it is for that reason that many people would like to be part of a Dutch colony, but the bad rumors about them that have spread all through America keep them from doing that.

    The Hollanders are not highly regarded in America, and Rev. Scholte and his gang have finally dealt them the deathblow. I still do not know the real reasons, but during their stay in St. Louis they were held in such contempt that no one would admit that he was a Hollander, for fear that they would regard him as belonging to the fellowship of the Rev. Scholte. During the past week Le Cocq wrote a letter to Budde, but there was not a word in it about me and Berkhout, although he certainly knows that we have arrived in America, for already fourteen days ago Berkhout wrote that he had sent two letters to Pella. I think that he wrote the letter in the hope that Budde would reply and give him some information about us. There was nothing of any consequence in the letter, only that cheese brought five to six cents a pound after deducting the shipping costs. He had fourteen cows and was building a double log cabin, and he had already been living in a part of it this summer. He writes that while he was in Holland, he had always been hoping to find some leisure in America, but it was the very opposite. Many people had been converted in the colony; among others, they had the good fortune of having a smith in their midst, [but] one whom no one dared get near to because of his wild temperament; this smith is now converted. The daughter of the Rev. Scholte was converted and confirmed; two of his boys were converted, and also another child of eight. I really wanted to visit Pella once, but it is not easy to get there during the winter.

Today I learned that there is a great deal of cholera in New York, New Orleans, and St. Louis. Until now I have not heard a thing from Kessel or Berkhout. Greetings to you and your wife, to Kaa, Margje, and the children, from me and my wife.

Your loving Brother,
A. N. Wormser

N.B. I think that Langheedt [Lankheet], the miller, will not feel at home here either.

On a separate, undated page, A.N. Wormser had transcribed two articles from the Iowa Farmer Advocate, *the first, "Good and Bad Farming," and the second, "Profits of Farming." He makes the following commentary on them:*

From this [first] report it is evident that when the proprietor has others do his farming for him, there is practically nothing left for him to live on, or the capital invested in the land yields no interest. From the other report you can see that the price of corn in Iowa at twenty-five cents a bushel is much higher than it is here, where it is only worth ten to fifteen cents a bushel.

The cost of working 20 acres of land is here reported to be:	$195.91
1,000 bushels of corn @ 15 cents per bushel	$150.00
Thus, the total loss on 20 acres	$45.91

But in addition to this, these 150 dollars are not cash in hand, because this corn cannot be sold, for most of it must be used in feeding the livestock. You have to feed hogs so they can be slaughtered in the fall, beef cattle because you have to have milk cows, [as well as] chickens and a horse; the horse may also be fed oats, but when you sow oats, you cannot grow corn on the land.

The cost of working 20 acres of land sown with wheat is given to be:	$156.25
Less 360 bushels @ 50 cents a bushel (I don't know the current price of wheat locally)	$180.00
	$23.75

If the above mentioned price of 50 cents a bushel were the market price here, then there would be a profit of $23.75. But that does not amount to much either, because there are always so many other costs. For example, when farm hands are working they generally get board and room, and of course they do not pay anything for that, etc. Thus, anyone who is not a farmer, and does not know how to dig in besides, will make a bad showing with his land. And if you take on a tenant, you will do no better. I consider it a misfortune to have to keep a renting tenant, for they eat the meat and leave the bones for the farmer or owner. It has even happened that this year's land did not bring in even a penny except for some vegetables that were taken to market. For what has grown on the rented land is still lying out there in piles, and still has to be threshed, which could not be done until now because of all the snow. And everything is being done under the open sky, because as yet there are no sheds or barns for storage.

Wormser 28

A. N. Wormser to J. A. Wormser
Burlington, 20 January 1849

Beloved Brother,
Budde and his wife seem to be embarrassed about the matter of our returning to Holland one of these days, because they realize that this was not a good place for us or for our children. Ten days ago or so, I had Jan take all the goods I wanted to sell to the city, which Budde had

offered to do for me if I agreed to have his horse shod, which I did. My wife and children accompanied me on the sleigh; the temperature was eight degrees [Fahrenheit]. We took our goods to a Hollander at whose house we slept overnight until they had been sold. I displayed a large share of it in front of the house, and the rest we left inside. I nailed a big sheet of paper against the house with the words "For Sale" printed in large letters. The second day and those following all of Burlington came out, so that in about ten days I sold a great deal. The dresser brought fl 30, the table fl.25, the mirror fl.7.50, but the rest we had to dispose of cheaply. People did not even know what many articles were used for; we could not get our money out of thread, ribbons, and pins. We were offered eighteen dollars for our largest bed, but I did not want to let it go for less than twenty-two dollars, so we still have it. I disposed of a length of linen for what it cost me. Berkhout will do poorly with the cloth he has brought along to sell. When you offer a yard of fine French cottton for ten cents a yard, people tell you that it can be bought for that price here too. But that turns out to be the most coarse and unbleached cotton; here they call it all cotton, ignoring the differences in kinds of cotton. We could not sell our crystal; people thought it was very fine and asked whether the compotes were for syrup. We just said yes, for by then I could have cared less if they wanted to put potatoes in them.

Now we are back at the Buddes; Leen had stayed here while we were away in the city. We are thinking of going to St. Louis in the beginning of February, and from there we go to New Orleans. We hope that the river will be navigable about that time. We are having a very severe winter such as you cannot begin to imagine in Holland. However, in the summer it must be terribly hot. Rev. Eppens told me that the temperature then rises as high as 110 degrees. In the [Dutch] East Indies the temperature is generally 90 degrees.

A few days ago we received your letter of October 27; we were very glad to get it. We had been going to the post office every day to find out if there was anything for us. I hope that I will receive one more letter before we leave. I will arrange for Budde to forward to Amsterdam any letters that may arrive after we leave. It grieved us greatly that you had been so ill; we do hope that all may be well with you now. These days we are all in good health. I believe that Budde could wish that he was still in Amsterdam as he was before, although he still keeps his chin up. Jan says that if he had known how miserable things were here, then (he would) never have gone to America. Budde told me that he had dreamt that he had gone back to Ost Friesland and from there to Amsterdam. I invited him to join us, but then he would not have a business. He said that he could then go in with his brother, but you had better not talk to anyone about this. Jan had told me earlier that his father just might go to Ost Friesland some time, but I don't think he will ever be able to sell his land, at least not for what it cost him. I still have no reply from Berkhout, which I don't understand. Whether he may have gone to Pella on account of the cholera, I don't know. I hope to write you soon again and ask that you give our greetings to your wife, Riek, the children, Portengen, Mother, and Tienes.

> Your loving Brother
> A. N. Wormser

Wormser 29

> Rev. H. P. Scholte to J. A. Wormser
> Pella, 20 January 1849

Esteemed Friend and Brother in Christ!

Enclosed is a letter for Mrs. Zeelt, which Her Honor will surely want to come and discuss with you, and about which I request you to provide her this further clarification. When Iowa was not yet a state, the United

Judith J. Zeelt (1780-1864), wealthy patron of Seceder causes
(J. C. van der Does, De Afscheiding, Delft, *1933)*

States government set aside the uneven sections of public lands for five miles on either side of the Des Moines River to make the river navigable for steamboats up to Fort Des Moines. When Iowa became a state it took over this grant, but while the even sections of the public land were being sold ever farther west, the river lands remained unsold, and the river unimproved. That was the situation when we arrived. However, a commission was then appointed to attend to the river situation. But at the time it was still the general opinion that only a small section would be improved and that there was no thought of doing this farther up [the river]. At the same time, there was a great deal of talk of asking Congress for permission to use [proceeds from] the designated river lands for a railroad. Thus I was not able to pay the claim rights for the purchased river lands. And since it was in the interest of the colony and the Hollanders we anticipated coming to secure as much land as possible, I then purchased more claims on government land and also paid the government fee. I judged that by selling this land, which now could not be taken by the present colonists, to those who would be following, I would surely have again collected sufficient funds so that I, as agent, would be able to pay for the claim rights when the river lands came on the market.

However, now the [river] commission has begun working in earnest on the river, and half of the total project has already been contracted for. They have also called upon the agents who have secured claim rights to pay the government. When I read the report of the commission to the governor, I realized that if our claims were put on the market, we might be in for a big surprise [i.e., prices higher than the original claim right of $1.25 per acre]. And that is why I proposed to Mrs. Zeelt to take over one-half of about ten sections, of which the claims and governmental costs had been paid, for the sum of eight thousand dollars, leaving her the choice of taking half of the whole [five sections] or one-half in the total [in each of ten sections].

The engineers, who recently surveyed the entire river, immediately sent a report of their survey to the legislature, which was in session. And now at the same time that I was mailing my last letter to Mrs. Zeelt, I received a message from Iowa City that the legislature has passed a law on behalf of the River Commission, which recommends the immediate continuation of work on the entire river project. In consequence of this, at any time now all of the claim holders of river land there can be called upon to validate them by paying the government 1¼ dollars per acre. Naturally, the lands that have been pre-purchased in this way cannot be put on the market again, for they have been paid. And so there is no danger that the claim holders will be bid up or outbid. Now I am liable for paying off [the claims]. Our colonists are located on river land as well as on government land, and I have to deliver them free and clear [by paying up]. Given this predicament, I could not first wait for a reply to my previous letter. So the only alternative left open to me was either partially to expose my situation to land speculators and enter into some kind of agreement with them (and that would be undesirable for me as well as for the colony) or to do what I have now done. I have sent Mrs. Zeelt a proof of sale to Her Honor for one-half of specifically designated lands, and against that I have drawn a draft on Her Honor for eight thousand dollars, due fourteen days after presentation. I have sent the draft to Mr. Doremirs (?) in New York, requesting him to present it to Mr. King on my behalf and to send me the money, since I may need it very soon. I have previously handled a number of drafts on Holland for other people in this way. I expect the money from New York by return mail, while the draft goes to Holland, in all likelihood to the banking house of Hope & Co; Mr. King is their New York correspondent.

I hope that Mrs. Zeelt will not leave me in the lurch, for in that event not only would everything be thrown into confusion, but I would be ruined for good. Alternatively, everything remains intact and the value of the money remains present in the land that has been purchased and paid for. I have written Mrs. Zeelt that she can still choose to take either one-half of the whole, that is five sections, or one-half of all the ten sections. I have drawn up the proof of sale in the latter format. If she prefers to put the money out at interest with all the land as security, that is fine with me too; the value is there. Taking into account the higher value of the land when the river is navigable, the river commissioners have proposed to the legislature only to sell the river lands for $1.25 to those who have claims, and not to put the unclaimed lands on the market at the present time, but rather to authorize the borrowing of money [on bonds] to finish the river project and, when that is completed, to put the unsold lands on the market. They estimate that the lands in the Des Moines River Valley will then bring twelve dollars an acre. The state can then enjoy all the gain, which land speculators would run off with if the land were to be sold immediately.

Well, dear friend and brother, I trust that I have enabled you to give some further explanation [of my actions] to Mrs. Zeelt. I hope that she will not be angry that I have put our relationship to such a test. Given the [exigency] of the moment, I knew of no other way to extricate myself honorably from these difficulties, which I was unable to foresee. I knew that Her Honor had the means to help me out, and she may rest assured that I will faithfully look after her interests, which have been so closely linked to mine by this move. I anticipate that looking back she will have no regrets about having invested her money in this way. I did receive your letter of October 31st along with that of Mrs. Zeelt, but my own [letters] were already under way. I was expecting Bosquet; he had not written me about Huijding. I have received word that Bosch, Van Dam, Maasdam from Gorkum near Utrecht, and Kuiper [Kuyper] from Charlois are coming. I have also heard that some are coming from Den Bosch. If the Lord grant us life and health, then by comparison with Europe, we can live here in quiet and in peace. Things really look dark and gloomy in the Old World. The political disturbances everywhere [in Europe] make me shudder, and I could only wish that many of my acquaintances were in America. You have probably noted that many Jews are beginning to think of Jerusalem. In the United States funds are being collected for the erection of a place for the public worship of God for the Jewish people. Permission to do this has already been granted by the Turkish government. This is not all that is to come [in the prophetic return of the Jews to Palestine] but it is a real beginning. What blindness prevails among the peoples, also among the Dutch nation. Superstition and godlessness are gaining the upper hand more and more, and from the Word [of God] we know the frightening Anti-Christ end-time, the falling away, but even then the Lord is also near. If ever, now is the time to watch and pray, and to be in readiness [for the end].

My little Hendrik has had an inflammation of the mucous membrane of the mouth, but he is pretty well over it by now. My wife is still weak, but otherwise she is well. The other children are hale and healthy. Perhaps Saartje will still have time to enclose a short letter for Mrs. Zeelt, [but] a letter to Jansje probably will not be possible this time, because now that my wife must [keep to her room] upstairs, Sara is busy all day long. Warm greetings to your wife and the children and to all the brethren. The Lord be with you. Remember us in your prayers.

Your Loving Friend and Brother,

H. P. Scholte

P.S. Ask Bousquet if I have written him and asked him to bring along some tar brushes. I can't find them anywhere here; also some files for saws; they are cheaper and harder in Holland than they are here.

Wormser 30

A. N. Wormser to J. A. Wormser
Burlington, 20 February 1849

Beloved Brother,

On the 17th instant I received your esteemed letter, dated December 19, which I had been looking for most eagerly (the postage was twelve cents). I had been going to the post office almost daily to inquire whether there was a letter from you, but to no avail. This is the second letter I have received from you here. It gave me much pleasure to learn that you had already received two letters of mine. I had already been fearful that you had not received the letter I sent you from Albany, because the people to whom I had entrusted the letter pocketed the twenty-five cents I had paid for postage. And so you remained without any word about our sea journey. The main thing about it was that we had much stormy weather during our journey; a couple of days before arrival we were on a sandbank before we realized it, because of the misty weather. The captain noticed it by the surf; he shouted for the sails to be taken in, but it was already too late. Fortunately for us, there was enough water on the sandbank so that the stiff wind bowled us over the sandbank in the flash of an eye. The waves of the surf crashed up into each other. Shortly before our arrival we lost the bowsprit to the fierce wind on which only a few moments earlier two sailors had been working. The ship got such a shock that we thought that we had run into something. The sails were cut loose and hauled in, because everything was still tied up in the ropes. Later on I may return to the story of our sea journey.

With deep sympathy we learned of your wife's early delivery of a stillborn baby daughter; however, we were gladdened that she, though weak, was feeling reasonably well given the present circumstances. We hope that she may soon be completely restored. I do hope that my letters were not in any way a contributing cause, because they were not very positive, and all of us had cherished such good thoughts about America when we were in Holland. But I could not write otherwise; I had to report the truth. I did not wish to dish up false reports, as do most of the emigrants. I would have very much preferred to send you different reports, because our goal in emigrating was not to be worse off, but rather to be better off. But I did not want to mislead anyone, as Scholte, Van Raalte, and Bolks are doing, and for whom this is not a matter of conscience. But in order to keep everything in clear focus, I shall answer your letter by starting at the beginning and taking up matters in sequence.

My brother, you write that my letters were dispirited, but on closer reading you will find that that is not the case; otherwise I could never have written them. But they were unfavorable, and that makes it appear that they are downcast. I recall very well reading letters when we were still at home, and if the content was not what we would have liked it to be, we attributed that to despondency; but that was not the case, it was only because it was a little closer to the truth. Later on you realize that it just is not possible to go back, and then you start writing more favorable accounts in order to entice family and friends. You write that some of my reports have the all the marks of being written hastily and superficially, but that is not so. I can quickly discern what is better and what is worse, and then I ask myself, for example: must I do more work here than in Holland? Is the food better or worse, etc? And then my answer must be the truth as I see it.

Now our experience of things here is such that one does not have to deliberate long in order to give a decisive answer to these questions. So it was immediately obvious to me that Wijnbergen should not come over here. I calculated that if he converted all his possessions into cash, and used that to pay his travel expenses, he would not have much left. Perhaps he could buy a few more acres of undeveloped land, but what would he gain by the exchange? Nothing, and he would lose much. And anyone who knows anything at all about the situation here advises against buying undeveloped land. You work yourself to death, and soon you have worn yourself out, and to have the land prepared by others is too costly. You live in a log cabin, you have poor food, a long cold winter, and an exceptionally hot summer. In my judgment, in his present life style he can live on for many more years, and [reach a good old age]. They do not have any children, he lives in a nice little home, and he has a nice little garden from which he can get enough vegetables and potatoes for his family without much effort. That food is good tasting and not like here. He lives in a temperate zone so different from here, and there is no need for him to make such a difficult and expensive journey. If his wife becomes ill, he can get a good doctor; if we get sick and have to call in a doctor, then living as remote as we do now, I surely will have to pay 1½ dollars, and then I still always worry whether they will do more harm than good. The illnesses of Sophie and Anna cost me only thirty guilders [twelve dollars], that is exceptionally little, probably because the treatment failed. [The two daughters died within one week (c.f. Wormser 21, 25).] He charged seventy-five cents a visit; sometimes he came three times in one day, which he counted as a single call. It is true that his office was close to my dwelling, but if the treatment had succeeded, then his tune would have been different. So I can assure you that my letter was written neither in haste nor in despondency. I have already experienced so many things that there is not much that can get me down.

And now we come to the Huijding [Huiding] matter. I knew that in our discussion at home we had concluded that if all went well for us, then Huijding would also be going. In presenting things as I did, I only wanted to indicate that he should not come, and that he would not be able to earn a penny here. I wrote that if he could saw and split nine cart-loads (cords) of wood in a day he would earn three dollars. So if he can do all that sawing and chopping in one day, then he can also earn that in one day. From this you cannot draw the conclusion that wood must be cheap, for inasmuch as Huijding has no wood, he cannot sell it either. But day wages are not low. The thing to bear in mind is that the farmers in the area who have a wood lot chop it down; then they take it to town on a wagon drawn by two horses or oxen and sell it to the residents for seventy-five cents to a dollar per wagonload. But these wagons do not hold very much wood. During the first month I burned three wagonloads of wood. But if I had to buy wood now, I probably would burn four wagonloads because it is so very cold. The wood comes in four-foot lengths, has to be sawed in thirds and then split. Many people do this themselves, even ministers and doctors, indeed even women; but those who do not have the time have others do it for them, like in Holland, where some people have Jews saw the wood in front of their houses. The cost of sawing and splitting a wagonload of wood is 3 bits or 37½ cents, sometimes a little less, because the bottom has fallen out of that too. But Huijding is not suited for this kind of work. Even I, who have always done the sawing and splitting of firewood myself, cannot keep it up for very long. If ever I should return, I will take my big American axe with me, and if perchance Huijding has not left by then, I will let him try it out.

I agree with you that it would be foolish "to buy land hereabouts for twenty-five to thirty dollars an acre." You can get it much cheaper than that and often as much or as little as you wish. Sometimes it is located a little farther from town than the Budde's [land] is, but that makes little difference. Bolks wrote that he could buy the finest land for 1¾ dollars; [but] one can buy the finest land for 1¼ dollars. As is well known, that is undeveloped land. And so at Bolks you are paying half a dollar too much. And where is that land of Bolks located? Assuredly in one of the most unhealthy regions in the United States. It is located in the area of the [Great] Lakes; the condition of the atmosphere is very changeable. I have already written you that there are so very many people sick in the Van Raalte colony all the time. The story here in America is that this is already the third colony established there, but they always died out. You also tell me that Hein wrote Bolks that he was thinking of going to Michigan in August. I need not say much about that; from all that I have written previously, Hein can figure out what awaits him here. And perhaps the day may come when Hein will write you what Berkhout has now written to Budde: "When I consider that it was my own foolishness that brought me to America, then this really preoccupies my mind, and if I then think that this is the Lord's doing, I cannot help crying out, "Oh, God, how hard you have dealt with me!" The only thing I wish to add is that as long as I was not dismissed by [De Nederlandse Handels] *Maatschappij* [The Netherlands Trading Company] I would not go to America. And even if he unexpectedly were to receive a cut in his salary, I still would not go. Hein may very well say, but I cannot live on that, but then he had better learn to live on less, and if he cannot do that, then he will doubtless be taught how in America. He may very well earn a couple of slices of bread and some potatoes in a day. I don't have any more here either, and Budde eats nothing but cornbread, which does remind you a little of sawdust. I cannot even stand the smell of it. If he should be dismissed, then let him start thinking about leaving.

I would like to visit the colony in Michigan, and I have thought about doing so, not that I expect to find something good there, but also to visit and see some other places there. Budde does not have any money for travel, and besides he cannot sell his farm even if he would let it go for twenty-five dollars an acre, and even though he has spent several hundred dollars on it. It's the same here as everywhere else; it is easier to buy than to sell. If he could sell it, he probably would do so, and perhaps move to Ost Friesland. What I have written about Hein also applies to Tienes.

"Bolks," you write me, "constantly sends the most excellent reports." Let us no longer allow ourselves to be misled by clergymen who are looking out for their own interests, but at least let us become wiser through adversity. I have, I think, said enough on the subject of what you should believe of those [exaggerated] reports. For the most part they are false reports, and they keep silent about anything bad, and besides, Bolks is a farmer who can do more with the land than we can. But how does it come about that for the most part people send such glowing reports and seek to mislead others? America is a fish trap, and once you have run into it, it is not easy to get out, and everyone here realizes that, as I think I have written before. One immigrant has just enough money to pay for the trip over, and so once he is here, he cannot return regardless of how eager he may be to do so. Another has sold his things or resigned from his position, and now he would like to return but what will he do upon his return? A third is ashamed to return to Holland after having left there. A fourth dreads the difficult sea voyage. People have left friends and family and now they wish to have them with them. If they send messages telling how it is here, then no one will come, and still they would so very much like to have them near. And some decide, like Bolks, to send the most favorable reports to their friends and family in order to lure them over. I know people in America who have portrayed America to their relatives as a paradise, where you have the most wonderful food, and still those same people have told me that they would hang on to the rudder of the ship if only they could go back.

 The examples of migrants who returned on the same ship on which they came are by no means rare. Recently I heard a nice anecdote about two brothers (Germans) who had conceived the plan to go to America. The one was to go ahead, and if in truth he found everything to be as people had written, then the other one would also come over. The first brother arrives in America and finds everything to be quite the opposite, but he does not have the means to go back, and he also dreads the sea journey, because Germans are not exactly heroes at sea. For a long time he thinks about what to do. If he writes the truth, his brother will not come, and he does not care to be alone either; after long hesitation he decides to have his brother come over and sends the most lovely and enticing report. His brother comes over, but he is disappointed, and as a result they come to blows. Presently they are still living in America. Now that they have more or less forgotten their previous condition, they are more content. It is common for people to say, "We surely can't stay here alone, can we?" They say, "You must have lived here a few years before you get used to it." That is not correct; it is not a matter of getting used to things but of forgetting them, and that takes time, for in time everything wears away. One must forget that once he lived in a fairly decent house; one must forget that he ate pleasant and tasty foods; one must forget that he lived on a well-ordered and well-worked piece of land and that he enjoyed a mild climate, etc. Some people, like the Germans, adapt to such things much faster than others. It is easy enough to get used to anything that is better; it does not take a poor man years to become accustomed to better clothes, food, and shelter. Conversely, it takes a rich man many years to get accustomed to poor housing, food, and clothing, or, I should say, it takes him years before he has forgotten his former circumstances.

I have not heard anything indicating that Van Raalte's government land or that of the settlers may not have been redeemed [paid off]; it may well have been that Scholte wrote this from professional jealousy.

You write, "Hein wants to reduce his entire family to the peasant class [make farmers of them], both in their clothing and in their lifestyle." What is he trying to say? That he wants to apprentice his children to farmers? Or does he want to make them to wear farm clothes? Hein always has to be messing about with something or other. Why doesn't he just keep living on quietly as he has? It would save him a lot of money and headaches. At least if he goes to America he will not have to change his clothing; he might want to have them made according to an Overijssel model and be ridiculed by the Americans. In Holland people always look at things from a Dutch point of view. In Holland, farmers constitute as it were a special class, they have altogether different clothing, food, and housing. This is not true in America. You cannot possibly have an idea of America without having been here; it is either riches or poverty here. For example, people work the land without wearing any stockings or shoes, or stockings with holes in the heels, and people just wear anything they have. When they go to town or to church, then the farmer's or renter's wife or daughter wears white flutes (pleated ruffles) on her legs, a silk bonnet on her head, a veil in front of her face, and a scarf [around her neck]; at home they are bareheaded. But when I mention this finery [of the ladies], please do not think of anything resembling the fine quality of Dutch cloth; of many of them one can say, as they sometimes do in Holland, that lady also has known better days.

And the same is true for men. A German or a Hollander with his broad collar on his dress-coat does not make an agreeable impression on Americans. Here everyone is dressed according to the latest style, in so far as his means allow. The wife of the cop in Burlington wears a very large fur muff. Once a year they celebrate Independence Day in America, and then all the children get together; the daughter of the Buddes' renter then wears a wreath of flowers around her head, but that does not cost all that much. They have exceptionally little cloth here, and to my mind they can just as well import that from Holland.

In Holland there are more class differences; not so here. You cannot tell any difference between a maid and her lady, so that often one is mistaken for the other; the maid walks about the house in a dress and is bareheaded. Generally speaking, cloth is of lesser quality here than in Holland, but it is not cheaper. A black dress coat costs forty guilders [sixteen dollars]. If you cannot afford a silk one, you substitute something else for it. Thus, one sees women wearing big coats, but sometimes instead of being silk they are made of black Orleans or (Lastre´). As a rule, one wears an article of clothing as long as possible, then throws it away and buys another. But when you leave Holland, take along some strong cloth to use on the land, because it is better than the cotton that is mostly used here.

In your letter you speak much of how lacking in manners people are here; you seem to interpret this much more broadly than I do. In general the English are reasonably well mannered. You probably have in mind spitting on the ground, or even on a carpet; or a young lady blowing her nose in her wrap. But that is common practice; we need not dwell on that and besides it need not be imitated. People are well dressed and clean and neat in public. You inquire "whether the lack of mannerliness is attributable to a simple, primitive mentality, or whether it serves the enjoyment of nature, or is it owing to greater health and resiliency, to greater relaxation and less pressing cares." You simply are *compelled* to live in the greatest simplicity here, indeed to such a degree that to a Hollander, however attracted he may be to all that is simple, it is all too simple. For example, people always [use] candles by which you can hardly see. Mrs. Budde and other farmers' wives have a different kind of little lamp; you take a small tea saucer, put some grease on it, lay a tiny discarded rag in it, and light it. They also use still another little lamp made of tin, in which they also burn grease, etc.

And regarding the enjoyment of nature as we understand it, I dare not predict a great deal of pleasure in this respect. You leave a country where everything is well ordered and beautiful and come here to a wasteland (I do not include the cities). I grant that they can make a deep impression on you initially, but presently it wears off and starts boring you. As you are traveling through the land, you often have beautiful vistas of forest-covered mountains, especially along the [Erie]

Canal to Buffalo, but you cannot settle everywhere. In one place it is too expensive or nothing is available, in other places one is completely isolated and there may not be another individual living for miles around. Where people usually settle it is a monotonous woodland. The trees are chopped down; the stumps are not exactly a pretty sight to see, and it will take years to get rid of them. If one has cleared and broken up land, like Budde, there is not a tree in the area. Just imagine a large tract of farm land that is completely bare and flat, and without even a single little tree; more or less in the center of the land stands a house, and in the distance you see trees all around you.

As far as health is concerned in America, I dare not give you a very flattering picture. In my judgment, half a year of severe cold weather followed by a half year of great heat (they scarcely have spring and fall here) can never be conducive to good health. I believe that the severe cold has an adverse effect upon one's chest. No doubt a native is less affected by some illnesses than a stranger, but I have already written you that in general people do not live to an old age here. As concerns us, my wife suffers very much from chest pains; Budde also has a great deal of trouble with his chest, no doubt because of all the piercing cold air. Although I am not any healthier, I am reasonably well, but all of us are lacking in energy. One location or another can make a lot of difference. The region where Van Raalte is located is described as being very unhealthy. Newly cleared areas are also unhealthy. Four years ago twice as many people were dying in Burlington as presently, even though the population was much smaller then than now; now that the land is being cultivated, it is getting healthier here. They also had had to send children to St. Louis for their upbringing because nearly all of them died here. The situation is probably better in the older states, and also more pleasant to enjoy nature there, but the land is too expensive.

You cannot expect to find time for relaxation here, because the land demands the greatest exertion, one that far exceeds our meager strength. As to our cares and concerns, they are of a somewhat different character here, because working conditions are altogether different here. If you have a lot of land, you are always concerned about getting the work done on time. If you have a farm, you do not have to be concerned much about food, but you do have to be content with what you have or can get. So, for example, you eat corn bread dry or smeared with lard, [for] the butter is sold. You can also eat princess [white bean] soup every now and then, etc. Hogs are slaughtered in the fall; there is always lots of work, too much to mention. The result is that sometimes Budde is working in the evening on his bare feet by moonlight. You write that the doctors [there] have advised us to move because our dwelling is so unhealthy, but what would they say if they were here? In a hard wind the candle on the chest is almost blown out. So I cannot see how anyone living on the land the way people do here can have any satisfaction that enlivens one's spirits and makes one cheerful. One works incessantly here; the women as hard as the men. This week my wife said to Mrs. Budde that she could not work in the field all day like she did. Mrs. Budde replied, "Just wait and you will find out otherwise. I cannot do it either, but I have no choice."

While I was living in Amsterdam I occasionally had a headache, and I did not have much appetite. Well, that has not improved here; besides the good food in Holland did entice me to eat occasionally. The way things have been for us here so far, the very opposite is the case. Yesterday my wife boiled some potatoes, and if you had not known, you would have said that they were boiled turnips. Just the look of them is enough to turn my stomach; I cannot eat a thing, and then I generally just eat bread.

I was very glad to hear that the cholera [epidemic] in Amsterdam is over; that gives one greater peace. I believe that I already wrote you that it has been around in New Orleans and St. Louis for some time already. In your letter you tell me to try to get used to American promptness and freedom. That is not where the trouble lies. You seem to give too much significance to that; I for one do not count it for all that much. The greatest drawback for me is that we cannot possibly make a living, at least not those of us who are not used to working [for a living]; you have to work yourself to death. As far as Huijding is concerned, if he is willing to listen to good advice, then let him stay where he is; if he is headstrong, well, let him go, there is no better teacher than experience. As regards Huijding's remark, "You can make money in undeveloped land," that seems to have reference to California. In the spring there will be fortune seekers from everywhere headed that way, Americans as well as Germans. The talk is that one can earn thirty-seven dollars a day. All he would have to do is to cart away the lumps of gold that lie about like stones in the street. In the newspapers they say that people are finding chunks of silver weighing twenty thousand pounds; but if he is going to get a chunk like that on to his wagon, he sure will be sweating. And it is so rugged and uninhabited there that a vat of flour costs one hundred dollars. Would that be rugged enough to suit Huijding?

Before Mr. Bousquet goes to America with his whole family, I would advise him first to make an inspection trip; otherwise I fear that it might be the death of Mrs. Bousquet. And what shall I say about the big speculators in land, Scholte and Van Raalte? Scholte got a loan for $80,000 in New York at 6 percent interest, and for that he has bought a lot of land. Now he has to dispose of that land. What would you say about a shopkeeper who wrote on his wares, "These are no good." Then, of course, he would not be able to sell them. Van Raalte, the story goes, has gotten a lot of government land and he has to dispose of that. They say that he has already made a pretty penny on it; I think that I need say no more. The only thing I still want to ask is why did Brummelkamp, who had made plans to go to America and got the whole thing started, not go to America? Why did Mr. Van der Linde, the brother-in-law of Van Raalte, who already had gotten everything in readiness, not go to America? To say, as he does, that the sight of the ship frightened him off cannot be his [true] reason, because he knew what it was like. He had made several journeys on it as ship's doctor. Dear Brother, I believe that I have answered the main points and objections raised in your letter. Now it is up to you to decide what you think of our present situation; it seems to me that things look pretty miserable for us; we have been misled. This journey has already cost us a lot of grief, sacrifices, and money, but it is only right that the truth has been exposed and that those who seek to plunge others into disaster have been unmasked. This does not do us any good, but someone else may profit from it.

Cordial greetings from both of us to you, your wife, Riek, and the children, as well as Mother and Portengen and the rest of the family.

Your Loving Brother,
A. N. Wormser

8th letter

P.S. Budde said to me that in his note he had forgotten to mention that Mr. Luring [Luuring] should not go to America. I told him that I had already written that. He also said that Huijding, Mr. Bousquet, and Mrs. Abrahams should not come either. Budde was aware that I had been scrutinizing him from every angle. All the while he had been hoping that before our departure a revolution would have broken out in Holland, preventing our departure.

Paris Revolution of 1848

And attached is a kind of diary [of weather temperatures] that I had available when your letter arrived. Perhaps there is something of value to you in it.

Fahrenheit scale

		8 A.M.	12 noon degrees	10 P.M.
January	21	4	18	
"	22	16	40	
"	23	40	46	
"	24	46	56	
"	25	18	24	
"	26	20	31	
"	27	33	46	
"	28	36	32	
"	29	24	28	
"	30	20	30	
	31	19	28	
February	1	14	29	
"	3	8	28	
"	4	25	31	
"	5	4	29	
"	6	23	20	

"	7	7		28	
"	8	30		28	
"	9	8		28	
"	10	24		42	
"	11	26		34	
"	12	20		30	
"	13	22		26	
"	14	3½		11	
"	15	0		13	
"	16	9		19	
"	17	14		14	
"	18	five below zero	-5 extreme cold	11	3½
"	19	16		32	

Wormser 31

A. N. Wormser to J. A. Wormser
Burlington, 20 February 1849

Beloved Brother,

Although to my mind I have already answered your letter and do so also in the accompanying one [see Wormser 20] to the extent I could, I still wish to address some additional concerns in what follows, matters of which no one needs to know. The greater part of the content of the accompanying letter [Wormser 30] likewise deals with matters that are nobody else's business. And that is why I would prefer that not much publicity be given to my letters in Amsterdam. News spreads fast enough, and if we should ever return, then we might look ridiculous. Sometimes it is ok if people happen to know about our affairs, but they do not HAVE to know about them. And on occasion it may be a good idea to give advice to someone who has wanderlust.

Your situation at the present time, I sense it, is far from a pleasant one. The total unemployment and standstill of trade in Holland, indeed in all of Europe, does not show any prospect of improvement in the immediate future. And I realize with you that this, and the large expenses I had to make for the journey, have nearly ruined us and brought us from something to nothing. The pleasant prospects we cherished about America have fled. However, it is not that I do not want to remain here.

After all, we already are in deep trouble here, but I must continue to call out to you: do not come. And what do we do here all by ourselves? As of now I have changed from a solid, well-situated citizen to something less than a dockhand. Some people will attribute that to our own foolishness, and they may not be wrong. We placed more confidence in our friends than they deserved. But I just do not want to accuse everyone of misleading us. I believe that there are also some who did it out of ignorance; for how many people are there not who are lacking in judgment or knowledge, and whose ignorance exceeds that of animals. But most letters are written to mislead family and friends in order to lure them over here. Berkhout wrote Budde in pretty strong language, and Berkhout really stepped on his toes, without directly accusing him. Budde really bears a grudge against Berkhout because of it, because he took it all personally, and he should have. I suspect Budde of having (pocketed) a letter of mine to Berkhout. It's about time that these actions to mislead others be exposed, so that the truth, which they have concealed for so long, can be made public.

But what are we to do in our present circumstances? In the first place, it seems to me that we must not lose courage but keep our heads up as much as possible. And secondly, we must economize in every way possible, to compensate for our diminished income by cutting back. We could wish that many things in Holland were different, but much of what one leaves behind in Holland, he finds back in America. In Holland everything costs lots of money, but you don't get anything for nothing here either. What is cheap in America is expensive in Holland, and what is cheap in Holland is expensive here, so that when it comes to spending money, you can still live cheaper in Holland, and you get better merchandise. If I send my children to school in Burlington, I have to pay more than I paid in Amsterdam. There I paid annually about twenty-five guilders in taxes, license fees, etc. If I bought a farm like that of Budde, I would also have to pay twenty-five guilders, besides 12½ guilders or five dollars for a market stand. And even so I could not begin to earn as much as I did in Amsterdam, and besides I have to work myself to death. Clothing would cost me here more than it did in Holland. I took along coats and trousers, which were four years old and still are very good. And what will it cost me to have a winter coat made here like the one I bought in Holland for fourteen guilders? It would cost me infinitely more here. Fabric is so very cheap in Holland. If you have it made here, it always looks good, even if it is expensive. Regardless of how strong anything is here, it tears apart right away. John told me that in a short while he had already worn out five trousers. A month and a half ago a farmer had a new coat made with silver buttons, and now already half of both sleeves is torn off. I have already worn out more [clothing] here than I did in an entire year in Amsterdam, and I don't throw things out quickly either. My trousers are in such bad shape that you can see more of my drawers than of my trousers.

Furniture is expensive here; that may well be the reason people buy so little of it. But if you so choose, you can buy it in Holland just as well as here. After all, you have acquired them, so you do not have to spend any money on them. If you did not have them, I would still advise you to make few purchases. And if it ever should happen that we come back, then I would buy only the most necessary things; it just takes a lot of work and costs money. Even much that is compulsory in America, you could do voluntarily in Holland; if only people ignored the mistaken notions of others. In America women have to do their own washings, which usually happens on Monday. This alone affords quite some savings. The resulting advantage is that you need not have many linens and other items of clothing, and that means a lot of money saved.

When you wash once a week you need only two tablecloths, you can do without aprons, and there are many other such matters. Furthermore let us not rely too much on other people who are only looking out for themselves, but let us keep our eyes wide open. It is true that it is sad to see our earnings are diminishing so, but let's keep our cool; perhaps when the tide has changed, some beacons can be moved.

As regards Mrs. Huising's business, that gives us much worry and concern. To be sure, when the year is over, the earnings will be in, but the result is that once again you are also less at ease [about the situation]. You will have to consider what can be done about it; you cannot keep on putting in money much longer. They will just have to share in the common misery and take some reduction in salary. That's the way things are here too; if they are not put on hold, they will burst. Meanwhile, we will have to try and see if there is not some other way to resolve the situation.

You cannot begin to understand how much it troubles me that the prospects for us and our children are gone for the time being; our situation has gotten worse because of the money we have lost. Letters written by false friends and jackasses have misled us. We are not the only ones who have experienced misfortune as a result of our American journey. Berkhout, Kiesel [Keesel], and Lankheet will be bemoaning their misfortune their life long. I do not hesitate to include Lankheet among the above, although one individual is more apt to come out with the truth than another. America is indeed equally available to all people, but it is not equally good for all. It is better for a German than a Hollander, and better for a farmer than a city dweller who is not used to heavy physical labor. We [city dwellers] cannot possibly keep plodding away and fixing everything ourselves like a farmer is supposed to do. A good farmer does not have to buy anything but clothing, coffee, and sugar.

How things will work out for us, I do not know. I had written you that I was thinking of leaving in the beginning of February. They are still driving wagons loaded with wood across the river. You cannot take a wagon to St. Louis because it is too cold; we might freeze to death. And the costs are too high. Going to New Orleans by boat is not everything either; cholera is generally worst on the boats. In any case, we are waiting until the river is open in order to take the steamboat to St. Louis, and then I will decide which way I will take. I may travel via Pittsburgh to Buffalo, if it is at all possible. And then I would like to visit the colonies of Zonne and Van Raalte, so I can size up things there. At least then I will know what the situation is there. If my wife's delivery of the baby would be too late for us to leave, then we would have to stay in Buffalo. I have already written a letter to De Vries to inquire whether he is still living there, and, if he is, then I would like to rent a dwelling in his neighborhood if possible. My wife's sister wants to stay in Burlington. There must be some shoddy dealing of Buddes involved in this. She is keeping house for Mr. Krichbaum, a job that Budde got her. It seems that she had nothing to do with this; I believe she earns a half-dollar a week, not more in any case.

I am thinking of writing Portengen in a couple of days. You need tell him nothing about these shoddy dealings; I cannot explicate it all in such great detail. We just hope that they are not misleading her too. My wife will also be sending a letter to your wife in a few days. We greet all Your Honors and wish you all the best.

Your Loving Brother,
A. N. Wormser

There is something about Budde I do not like. When our children died he said to us, "Well, at least you will not have to worry about them any more." I for one can do without such consolation.

Wormser 32

D. A. Budde to J. A. Wormser
Burlington, February 1849

Dear Beloved Brother and Sister in our Lord and Savior Jesus Christ,

As gladdened as we were by the arrival of Your Honor's brother and his family in Burlington, so grievous—unforgettably grievous—is to us their return to Amsterdam. I have asked myself a thousand times over whether I really wrote such *untruths* about America, but could not find any, except for *one* thing; when you are living on a farm like mine, with a tenant-renter, you cannot make an adequate living from a third share of the proceeds. That is what I had written and that is what I had been told. At the time my own experience was not as extensive on these matters as it is now. You can no longer calculate the value of your money or farm at more than 5 percent. But I had also written that you could earn 10 percent on your money, but a farm did not yield that much, that [gain] would have to be realized through the annual increase in the worth of your farm. Outside of that I know of nothing I might have written that would not have told the pure and honest truth, or painted things in brighter colors than they actually were.

I also asked Your Honor's brother Dries whether I had drawn such a rosy picture in my letters that I was to blame for the kind of disappointment that in his opinion he could not help but see now. Not my letters, he said, but all the letters from America taken together had contributed to it. I dare say honestly that until now I have never been disappointed in my expectations—and with the Lord's blessing in another two years we can find ourselves in better circumstances than we did in Amsterdam. All the disappointing, difficult, and sad things that burdened us were not the fault of America; they could have struck us just as well in Amsterdam; it is the hand of the Lord to humble us beneath his powerful hand, so that he might raise us up again in his own good time. It is to test our faith concerning the truth of God, namely, that all things work for the best for those who love him. Indeed, the Lord also had his complaint against us as he did against Israel. My people are guilty of a two-fold evil: they have forsaken me, the fountain of living waters, and they have turned to broken cisterns.

Yes, beloved Brother & Sister, we have had to experience such a great disappointment in our own son, Jan, after the Lord had graciously restored him from his illness in the month of July instant. After that our expectation was to live a quiet, contented, and godly life together—to live unto the Lord for the joys of life—to bear the burdens and the labor of life together; and with hope and anticipation to rejoice already in the future—preserving the good morals of Holland in America and eschewing the evil ones. But alas, to our deep sorrow, it has been our experience that he is abandoning the good morals of Amsterdam, and he is adopting instead morals that are also censured in America; but then again he leaves industry and diligence to the Americans and Germans; instead of now working for his parents, he watches us with indifferent eyes working for him and, when anyone is present, it has the appearance that he is doing everything.

But enough of that, and I hope that you will keep this to yourselves. The Faithful Covenant God is our refuge. He will neither leave nor forsake us, Isaiah 49:15. Considering all the unpleasantness experienced by Your Honor's brother on his journey here, the season, the sickness and death of his two children, the harsh winter, no one here ever experienced anything like it, the high prices and scarcity of foods caused by the protracted rains coming at the time when potatoes and other garden vegetables were to be harvested; all of these, I think, have left Your Honor's brother with the impression that nothing is good here, because now he has had no chance at all to become aware of the fertility of America, so that your brother's way of seeing and judging America differs much, very much, from ours.

There is also a great deal of difference from another aspect, that of glorifying God, and that was after all the immediate cause for thinking about America at all. America is still young, and the fact that not everything in America is as well regulated and well ordered as in Holland is easy to understand, and one could have anticipated that. Everyone tries to work things out to suit himself as best he can. Dear Brother, the delights of country living, above life in the city, sweeten all the toil it requires. But it is not above the circle of our fraternal life together and with each other. Here too the Lord has granted us a faithful friend with whom we can speak from heart to heart, of whom I have made mention earlier, namely, the High German minister.

May the merciful God and Father forgive me if I am guilty of having disappointed your expectations of America. And for the loss of temporal goods caused by your brother's journey in coming here, do forgive me that too. And may the Lord restore the same to you and your children with temporal and spiritual blessings in Christ Jesus. Do not permit the bond of brotherhood to be broken. We sincerely wish that our friendship may continue until we embrace each other before the throne of grace. We continue to live in the hope that we may again be receiving your welcome letters.

D. A. Budde

Wormser 33

C. M. Budde-Stomp to J. Wormser-van der Ven
Burlington, Iowa, [February or March] 1849

My Dearly Beloved Friend and Sister in the Lord,

 I hope that Your Honors may receive these letters in good health and that the Lord may have gladdened you with a successful delivery, and that you may have gotten an offspring for the Lord; that is my heartfelt wish. We were gladdened to hear of the arrival of your brother, news of which was brought to us by the aged gentleman, Mr. Krichbaum. We immediately went to town to see your sister and children. They had immediately taken a dwelling because a child of theirs was ill. The illness soon got worse; the doctor said that it was scarlet fever, characterized by a swelling of the throat, with painful suffering, and usually choking in phlegm. It is very contagious for the other children, so that he gave them medicine too. Sofia was the first sacrificial death the Lord demanded. That was not a pleasant thing for your brother and sister to encounter on arrival.

 Our children Jansje, Telem, and Maria also came down with a light case of the disease, but Diedrich was snatched from the dead for us, as it were. After the death of Anna he became seriously ill; we thought it was a nerve and zinc disease, but the doctor said that the fourth day would tell whether it was the same illness that had affected the W[ormser] children. And so it turned out. His whole body turned red, his throat began to swell; his nose and mouth were so choked with phlegm that he could no longer rinse his throat. Then a little stick with a piece of cloth attached was used to (dab) his throat to prevent him from choking in his phlegm. We had to care for him day and night without ever stopping. When I was exhausted, then my husband again took over the watch. He [the boy] was very patient in his suffering and called upon the Lord many times, Who, to our great joy, also heard the child's prayer. The intensity of the fever diminished, but the swelling of the throat turned outward, requiring constant dabbing, and settled on his Adam's apple. This was no less dangerous and painful. When the doctor came to operate on him, he said that it looked barbarous. My husband was holding Diedrich's little hands on his knees while he lanced the swelling; the doctor himself was glad [when it was over] because he did not like to operate. A very great deal of bad fluid (pus) issued forth and since his suffering persisted, incisions [were] made in other places as well, so that while we were dabbing [the wound], healing was occurring. His earlier hernia ailment also showed up again because of his weakness. That too is better again, but he has to guard against lifting. I also got a callus swelling in my left hand, which gave me a lot of grief.

We are having an unusually early and harsh winter accompanied by much snow. Your brother's arrival and stay in America is not a very attractive experience for him; their departure and return is very grievous for us. It is a costly and difficult journey, and it can even involve risk of life, and they were fortunate making it to us. But the difficulty of imposing on others, against their wishes, a change of status, one that involves much trouble and many difficulties, a choice moreover that he had to make for the entire family, prompted him to go back [to Holland] as agreed.

We have had many difficulties and much unpleasantness this summer. Because of exceptionally heavy rains, an entire field of potatoes, which were exceptionally tasty, rotted away, so that we do not even have any for our own use, let alone any to sell. The renter was in a hurry for a dwelling, because living in with the animals is pretty difficult. After harvesting the fruits, we had to start building. The workers had board and room with us, and that kept me very busy. Building generally costs more than you first thought, but the renter is now living in a reasonably good brick house with a cellar. When your brother arrived, the house was not yet finished, and now your brother was living with us.

[Because of] many unavoidable expenses, little income, and (John) not being able to work in town because of the harsh winter weather, we are for the moment experiencing things that are very unpleasant for us. But who gives us any assurance that our situation in Europe would have been any different? If the Lord does not withhold his blessing, the winter wheat is already growing in the field, a field that was broken only this past fall. When life is all sunshine, a number of difficulties and unpleasant experiences are like so much *moeite en verdriet* (toil and trouble) and cause us to be still before the Lord when he leads us in paths that are not pleasant to the flesh.

Your Honor's brother received your letter in which you asked him to tell us of your miscarriage, for your brother had intended to leave already in February, but the bitter cold prevented him from doing so. I was very sensitive about not receiving a personal letter from you, and it makes me afraid that you are angry with us. It is true, this return is an unpleasant one for Your Honors; indeed it entails a considerable loss [of money] for you. And if we had told lies or deceived you it would grieve my soul, but our conscience does not accuse us in this. We did not leave Europe in order to improve our temporal well-being, for you know, dear friend, that we were content in the life-station in which the Lord had placed us. But it was the suppression of God's people and his laws, on which his wrath will come sooner or later. Add to that my husband's weakness and frailty of body and the prospect of a dim future for our children, these things led us to venture this change in the name of the Lord. And shortly after our departure the troubled times broke out.

Your Honors' letter [about troubles in Holland] caused us to weep before the Lord who had led us out, and to bear patiently the difficulties associated with migration. "In Amsterdam we saw a dark dense cloud spreading over all of Europe" [a reference to the illustration on page 98] and considered the difficulties of farm life easier to get used to than the unanimous report of the dark future for the old fatherland, and even more so for those whose who fear the Lord. We see an evil generation turning its neck [against the Lord], and the result is that the Lord arises to do battle. He will, however, keep his children in safety: indeed, even for five righteous an entire city was to be spared. If it is the Lord's will for you and your dear children and family to remain there, may he graciously keep you all from the evil one. We praise the Lord for having led us here; and if in this life we should not see each other's faces again, then do not let the love and the relationship that developed through our mutual Union in Christ be extinguished, but do write us soon so that I may put this uncertainty behind me.

I hope that Your Honors may be in good health and well being when you receive this letter. Together we both enjoy that great blessing of the Lord. Diedrich is really in good spirits and healthy, and enjoys outdoor life very much; he did not want to return to Holland because his father did not have a garden for him there. Maria is also in good spirits. I have started teaching her to read, and she is doing quite well. [I am] also teaching Diedrich to write, because they will still be too little to send to school in town this winter and I do not wish to deprive them of the basics they should learn in their youth. Jansje Teleman is growing up and Mrs. Tel[e]m[an] is also doing well.

In hopes of being gladdened by some letters from you, and wishing both of Your Honors the choicest blessings of the Lord. May his friendly countenance guide you so that you may know his way with certainty, and with Moses you may be at peace in the way that he will lead you. My cordial greeting to your sister Rieka. Leentje (Portengen), Mietje's sister, is working as a domestic in Burlington and wants to stay in America. Kiss your dear children, Jansje and Kaatje, who no doubt still know us; also Johan and Maria whom we have never seen.

Your Loving Friend and Sister in the Lord,
C. M. Budde-Stomp

Greet all our friends, also my aged father [and tell them] that we are all well and happy.

Wormser 34

D. A. Budde to J. A. Wormser and spouse
[Early March 1849]

In your last letter of October 11, you mention an outpouring of the Holy Spirit at Pella. I learned the same thing, first from Lubberd[en] and then later, on December 13, from Le Cocq. The latter writes me a very nice letter to the effect that sixty persons, young and old, had been converted, also including Rev. Scholte's Saartje and Jan and Dorus of Le Cocq. I also hear good reports about the Hollanders in Pella. Generally speaking, they are very friendly and industrious. May the Lord accompany these letters and your brother and family safely to Amsterdam (since there can be no changing now; for to stay here you have to do it wholeheartedly). Our prayer is that God go with them on their journey. Do remember us in your prayers. And now cordial greetings to you and your dear children and the other friends, and we pray that the grace of the Lord may be with you.

I am Your loving Brother in Christ,
D. A. Budde

On the reverse side:
The 18th of March 1849:
Because your brother's departure was to have taken place earlier, I had also written the foregoing earlier. Now to our joy and with thanksgiving to the Lord, I can tell you that there has been a great change in our son Jan relative to the things I had written about him. It now seems to us that he thoroughly understands that in our [financial] situation we cannot live wholly on the means God has granted us without working. Now, given the circumstances, he is working diligently, so that life has become much more pleasant for us, and our prospects are considerably better.

In the past I also received a letter from Brother Lotthes [Lothes] and one from Luuring, letters that I am leaving unanswered for the time being. That is not due to indifference, indeed not, I trust that even if we remain bodily separated from each other in this life our love will remain. I would not be able to suggest a means of livelihood here for Brother Luuring. Cordial greetings to the two brothers. I do not have much desire to write; because of all the unpleasantness arising from the departure of Your Honor's brother I am not writing for the time being. Just one more thing. No matter how I look at my earlier letters, there is nothing of all I have written that I can take back.

Once again wishing you all the blessing of the Lord, I remain the brother who will never forget you.

D. A. Budde

Wormser 35

A. N. Wormser to J. A. Wormser
St. Louis, 22 March 1849

Beloved Brother!

I have received your letter, dated January 12th instant. This is the third letter I have received from you from Holland. Since I have already written much about America, I can be brief in answering your letter.

In the extract from Keesel's letter I read: "On board the steamboat we already heard about the unfortunate condition of Rev. Van Raaalte's colony. Not only were there many sick people, but entire families had already died out, and that was confirmed here by several other reports.

Someone also read to me from a letter that states that there were households in which four, five, six, and more persons had died. However, I wish to investigate this further, because I have even heard that last year between six hundred and seven hundred persons had died, and that there were not enough healthy carpenters to make coffins, so that corpses had been buried without coffins in the ground behind their houses."

In the fragment of the letter Hein wrote to you I read, "Rev. Van Raalte recently wrote to Rev. De Moen, 'As a relative I would not want *to deceive* you; you can safely come here.'" If Rev. De Moen should decide to go to America, then I would advise him to take his coffin along, since they are much more expensive in America than in Holland. These are the good reports from v. Raalte.

I should really pass over Hein's letter in silence, since it contains nothing but erroneous theses about America. True, it is a batter full, but the letter resembles a dish of pancakes, well buttered and sugared. I could just see them: the grist mills, the peeling mills, and the crushing mills, and my eyes began to dim. That is the misfortune of all migrants; they build themselves air castles. I shall cite only a few points from his letter. Hein writes: "Everything (in America) is governed by just that one thing, which is called *money*. Everyone worships mammon there, and that is the reason for all the hurrying and chasing that drives people over there like a windstorm; they've got to have money! money! Get rich quick, and that is the main idea that governs and corrupts everything. That accounts for all the shoddy business, that explains why they just keep on building and making, not to produce works of art, but to get a good return on their capital, and if at all possible it yields a return, then all is well. From that lust for money!" etc.

It is true that people work for money, but no one has money (I refer to the masses in the working class), so that proposition is faulty. It is so very difficult to penetrate to the inner life of the American; that would take years. Things here are not like they are in Holland. There money tends to remain concentrated, here it flies away, far and wide, and so usually one is without money. That is why I had to sell so much of my property on credit; people will always be in a hurry, although not always to gain money. For example, if a carpenter's helper knows that there will be no work for him the next day, then today he will work as hard as he can to get finished, even though he could work on it a day longer.

And then Hein writes: "However, I cannot say that your reports disappoint me, and that for the simple reason that I *never* imagined

America any different than the way you describe it." When did Hein get these ideas, and how did he get that information? I for one never imagined America to be this way, and neither did you; and if I had only imagined half of it to be like that, I would never have gone. But I ask: If Hein did have such ideas about America, then was it very brotherly of him not to have shared them with me, but just letting me go to ruin. Do I treat him that way? I had always thought that Hein had the same idea I had, to test the move [to America] for our sake and the family's, and not to be worse off, and not either to do the heavy toil of slaves, and on top of that to have no fruits from your labors. Hein seems to have other reasons, and that is why I advise him even now to leave for America himself. If I have just a little time left, I will inform him as best as I can what he should take along and what he needs for the journey.

In all your letters you write that I am not American at all. That is not true, I am completely American in all that is good; naturally not in what is not good. And that is also how I am with regard to things Dutch. If the Dutch is better, then I prefer it; or should I just praise everything, even when it is wrong, only because it is American? I was not aware of that.

Keesel's letter is not very nice really, if one is familiar with matters here, and if one considers that he already had land then. I will save the two hundred guilders for Hein.

In my judgment, Budde might as well have omitted the information he shared to the effect that my unfavorable portrait of America was attributable to fatigue and unfamiliarity. Likewise in my judgment, Hein's remarks about draining water from his [the Buddes] land might also have been omitted, first of all because they are of no use, and secondly because B. positively refuses to accept the fact that his land is no good. At every opportunity he tells me that at any time he can again get $35 per acre, although I know that he might not be able to get even $10 an acre. A couple of weeks ago I talked to an old farmer who told me that in twenty years the Buddes' land would not be worth one cent more than what he had paid for it. Now perhaps I could say to him, "Your land is no good, you are drowning in it," but what good would it do? It would not get any better as a result, and he just might be more upset about it. Now people in Overijssel are writing him what he must do to get rid of the water. If that were possible, people on the spot here would be in a better position to know and to see than those in Overijssel. It is a good thing that you thought of thanking Budde.

If I have any opportunity at all, I want to visit the Holland [Van Raalte] colonies, if I do not have to burden my wife and children too much in doing so. And if I should see that things are better there than in Burlington, and the land is sufficiently productive to provide you a living of sorts, then I will buy land for you. Keesel's land is turning out to be fairly expensive because it is undeveloped land. He writes that there is a ten-acre claim with it, that is to say, cleared land, but that cannot be a claim. No claim can be less than twenty acres, but he still has to pay the claimant, otherwise the claimants would kill him.

The cost of Keesel's land per acre	$4.25
chopping down trees per acre	5.00
clearing stumps per acre	1.00
plowing (breaking up land) per acre	2.00
fencing per acre	1.50
	$13.75

That is thirteen dollars and seventy-five cents an acre. Budde now has sixty acres fenced and still cannot make a living. Perhaps Keesel's land is better, but that makes no difference; then all his trees still have to be cleared and cut up. The journey from Holland to Burlington cost me about one thousand guilders. Keesel is located about midway between New York and Burlington.

Jacob's judgment that things are even worse at Van Raalte's than in Burlington is very accurate, and I fear that it will be no better at Bolks's. On the journey I heard the same complaints about unhealthy conditions. How things are at Rev. Zonne's [Milwaukee, Wisconsin] I do not know, but I shall investigate, and if I can I will go there myself, and also to Rev. Bolks.

I received your letter shortly before our departure, so that I could not answer it before today. We are staying here at an inn and are thinking of traveling to Pittsburgh or Cincinnati if we can. Leen remained behind at Burlington. Budde, but especially his wife, will have it on their consciences that they have plunged Leen into misfortune for the rest of her life.

Our cordial greetings to you all.
Your Loving Brother,
A. N. Wormser

Wormser 36

A. N. Wormser to J. A. Wormser
New York, 2 May 1849

Beloved Brother,

After many difficulties and ups and downs we have again arrived at New York. On our recent trip from New Orleans to New York we enjoyed very much assistance from the bearer of this letter. He was a sailor on the American ship *Clifton*, on which we made the boat trip [to New York]. Besides assisting us in many ways, he was helpful to us in translating, since he was practically the only person on board ship with whom we could speak. And since he happens to be leaving for Amsterdam on another American ship, he was glad to take upon himself the task of taking along a letter for us. We made the [sea] journey via New Orleans because the trip through the interior is too difficult and too costly. I had thought that we would be able to make the crossing to one of the European harbors before the delivery of my wife. There was a ship headed for Antwerp [in the harbor of New Orleans], but since the trip was scheduled to take forty to forty-five days, I was afraid that my wife would deliver at sea. So we decided to travel to New York, and then after her delivery, go on to Holland. However, after we had been at sea for eight days, my wife developed a colic, and after that diarrhea. She was down for twelve days without being able to sleep during all that time because of the pains. As a result of these circumstances, my wife gave birth to a son prematurely, and eight days after the delivery we arrived at New York. My wife's pains abated some after the delivery. The child nursed for a couple of days, but it seems to have taken over the illness in the process. It has been lying there for four or five days without any nourishment; we thought that it would have died already two days ago. It cannot get any food, my wife is weak, and we all have diarrhea. I was told that Jacob (Portengen) is expected to arrive in New York any day. We might be able to travel with him; if not, then we will take another ship, that is, if we are not prevented from doing so by some circumstance or other. We are presently staying in the Pike Slip, corner of Water Street, with Mayer in the Rheinische Hotel. Next Saturday we plan to move into two small rooms that I have rented for seven dollars a month. We hope to be in Holland soon again, where you do not have to be afraid that scoundrels will rob us of life and goods.

Warmest greetings from all of us to your wife, Riek, and the children, and also to Mother, Mrs. Zeelt, Portengen, and the other relatives.

Your Loving Brother,
A. N. Wormser.

Wormser 37

J. Berkhout to J. A. Wormser and spouse
Pella, 11 and 26 May, and St. Louis, 1 June 1849

Esteemed Brother and Sister in the Lord,

Now I wish to pick up the thread of the story of our experiences, or rather of our grief. After the departure of your brother, our hearts were shocked and saddened anew. We felt lonely and abandoned, and although we had no grounds for thinking it, we consoled ourselves with the thought that some day we would be freed from America. God was our refuge before whose countenance we poured out our lament with tears.

After the departure of your brother, we slowly and reluctantly resumed our journey to Pella. Your brother left St. Louis the latter part of March and took the route via New Orleans. We fear that he will not reach Europe before the delivery of his wife. We left St. Louis March 28 and arrived at Keokuk on the 30th. A shortage of money prevents us from taking suitable accomodations, the kind of passage that immigrants almost never take. We spread our bedding up on the upper deck of the steamboat, with just an open roof over our heads, good to keep out rain, open on the sides, and almost in the open air. This was more or less a favor, for otherwise one has to go downstairs where the engine room is located, and where often there is no room either to sit or lie down. This passage costs one dollar without meals; a cabin costs three dollars, and that includes everything

We decided for Pella because, if need be, I could become a colporteur [book peddler] there; but then I would have to own my own horse and wagon, and we already were too short of funds to do that. In addition we had been promised a credit of eighteen hundred dollars if we wanted to open a store, but our funds are not [even] adequate to acquire a log cabin and to pay for the transport of our goods. While we were in St. Louis, I could get a job as a carpenter, but because of my weakened condition, together with the sickly, deadly climate and all the vermin found there, we decided to leave and, if need be, find work in Keokuk, where there was said to be plenty of work.

When we got to Keokuk, the road was in no condition for wagons to travel; accordingly, the wage demanded [for moving luggage] was high, 1½ dollars per one hundred pounds. In addition we heard many bad things about Pella; namely, that the people were poor and you could not earn a penny. A letter arrived from Pella telling us that Rev. Scholte had been deposed. So with three other families, all headed for Pella, we decided to rent a room and then go make an inspection trip. The women and children were packed into one room, the bedding was spread on the wooden floor, which resembled the earth, and we stayed in Keokuk Saturday and Sunday April 1st. On Monday four of us men set out for Pella on foot because it would have cost too much—five dollars a person—to ride. In the meantime my wife had already had a visit from the bed bugs. We paid four dollars a month for rent, with plenty of draft and no way of closing things up. Our chests were standing, partially sheltered under an overhang and left to their fate. Well, if an emergency arises while you are traveling, you can put up with a lot, but to go forty hours each way is almost an impossible undertaking. It began to rain en route, and we had to stay over for 1½ days. We were lodged in a log cabin in which the four of us lay diagonally across the crib with our legs stretched out over a chest and with just a partial cover, and that was our bed. By now we had walked one day, and I already had blisters under my feet and we still had five days to go. By now the road had gotten so bad that we had to make our way through creeks of water, through prairies cut up by wagons and broken up by horses hoofs, everything filled with water, and besides we often sank into the mud above our ankles; it was all uphill, downhill, and then uphill again, up

Pella panorama, 1849

to thirty feet and higher. And so we arrived in Pella on Saturday evening, April 7. I could not contact Le Cocq that evening, but we stayed with a Hollander that night who told us nothing but tales of grief about Pella. On average we had had fairly good beds on our journey; the food was the same everywhere. Bacon with freshly baked bread, eggs fried hard in the bacon grease, bread usually not baked through; sometimes butter and sometimes not. Often we had corn bread and dried apples or pears, a pickle and then as many as you could lay on a saucer. We usually got coffee with sugar. It was the same morning, noon, and night, and it cost us forty to fifty American cents per person per day.

On Sunday morning we went to a church that was very inauspicious. A roughly cut wooden box, slightly elevated, served as the pulpit. [Elder] De Hoog spoke. At the end of the service it was strange to hear the words, "We baptize you" [spoken by a lay elder]. Barendrecht [Barendregt] did the baptism. The Rev. Scholte had been deposed, but he had resigned [earlier] when he saw the dark cloud looming. The reasons for his deposition are deceit and swindling. For example, in the Hagens case he withheld 80 acres of wooded land from the 180-acre claim and made him pay the full price for the entire claim. Thus on [a] $2,200 dollar [claim] he overcharged Welle of Gorkom $500. He overcharged Le Cocq 10 dollars on a claim and, in addition to that, 1¼ dollar on every acre. And rather than citing every instance, I will just sum it up: all those in the original group that went to Pella and acquired land there he overcharged one dollar an acre, and those who came later, like myself, he overcharged 1¼ dollar an acre. He himself did not pay more than 1¼ dollar per acre, whether it was claimed or unclaimed land; in turn he calculated everything at 2½ dollars an acre, so that the people were getting only half as much land as they were entitled to. Moreover, he still has not given proof of ownership [title] to anyone. He cannot do so, because if he gives it to one, he cannot deny it to another, and now it turns out that the land that Scholte claims to own has not yet been paid for. And so one Hollander, who has already put a lot of work into the land, may see it claimed from under him by another Hollander. The result of Scholte's actions has been to impoverish the people; they no longer worked the land as they should have, cultivating it, and so they have suffered want. People are leaving the colony, and others who want to come are being held back. These actions have so offended the Americans that they would kill him if the Hollanders would agree to it. He no longer has dealings with anyone. No one knows how this will all turn out. Apart from that, Pella is a healthy [place to live] and [the land

Frans [Jean Francois] Le Cocq, Sr. (1805-1888), leader of the Pella settlement
(*Souvenir History of Pella, Iowa, 1847-1922*, Pella, 1922)

is] very fertile, and it is practically assured that the Des Moines River Project will be completed in two years, making it available for marketing products. The future is very promising.

Sunday morning I visited Le Cocq, whom I found suffering from a severe case of rheumatism. The others members of his family were well. He had already fenced in... acres. He owns ten cows, five calves, four yearling cattle; five cows still had to calve, and five were being milked; the milk had to be divided between them and the calves. Sometimes they had butter, sometimes not. They had to buy their wheat; they eat it with the bran, very black. They also had to buy their bacon. They generally paid for this with the eggs from seventy chickens. As a farmer, he had some serious setbacks: he lost eight cows, big and small, and they are having a hard time getting over that. If this year turns out well, they will have ample food supplies. Many people suffered great want this winter.

His helper, who had come from Amsterdam with him, was killed by a big block while digging a well. Presently he has a helper and his wife and two children living in with him; they work for their keep. He ran out of money to pay the man, who could not get paid work anywhere in Pella, and so he was very glad to be getting room and board in this way.

So far Le Cocq has not sold anything but a small amount of cheese; others have sold a few hogs, and those who fared best as farmers probably earned between fifty and one hundred dollars [for the year]. At present some are concentrating on raising cattle, and also on making cheese; but in order to raise good cattle, you need to have a good building to feed the cattle during the winter. However, the farmers who are working the land now will be able to stick it out, even though they are not getting all that much money now. But those who have to make a living with their hands, like working men, are having a hard time of it.

Shoemakers seem to be making the best living, but other folk mostly just walk away. Barendrecht did not think he could last as a carpenter. Blanke, a carpenter, has started working as a farm hand for the Americans. The shopkeepers, three in number, did not brag about themselves, but each one of them thought he was doing a good business; that is why they advised me to start a store. One of the three, Wolters and Smenk, was doing almost no business. They had borrowed too much money and lost their credit because they could not pay their bills.

It was terribly cold this winter. One person froze a hand, another a foot, and a still another his ears; chickens suffered frozen feet, cats frozen ears. Almost the entire county is occupied by farmers. At present the Des Moines River is so high that at times steamboats are sailing as far as Pella and beyond.

After spending three days in Pella, I decided that it was not advisable for me to settle in Pella but to look for work in Keokuk and wait things out there, although everyone advised me to come [to Pella]. Le Cocq promised to give me all the help I needed if I wanted to go into farming. I would not need much to get started, etc. If a person starts farming, he cannot count on earning much during the first two years, unless he has broken land. I had neither the money nor the strength for that.

Fenced land, with a log cabin and a well, located between Keokuk and Pella, sells for six to seven dollars an acre. So, for example, there was a plot of 320 acres, half woods, for sale. A farmer told me that a family could live from the rent, that is, a third of the proceeds (but bear in mind that is American style). Undeveloped land, but claimed with only a log cabin on it, costs 2½ to 3 dollars an acre. The information I solicited from farmers comes down to the following: *one* man with *one* boy or *two*, together have all they can do to work 40 acres; and with a good return, they can have from 50 to 100 dollars left to pay for clothes, coffee, etc.

In just fourteen days I was back in Keokuk, thinking to find work there as a carpenter, for it had looked quite promising. It was mid-April, and I was told that carpentry work did not start until June and ended in November. However, I could get work, but then I would have to spend four dollars a week staying in a boarding house with my wife. If I could earn a little more, then I could get shoes for that...get all our provisions at another place and then you have to pay unheard of prices.

I refused to work under those conditions but took the steamboat to Galena, a thriving city, 250 miles up the Mississippi. On the boat I met two Americans, carpenters, one married, and the other single, from Sinsinnati [Cincinnati], also looking for work. Again, my wife remained in Keokuk. I cannot tell you the fears, the anxiety, I endured on that boat. What tears, what cries, what sighs, what prayers I raised to God! God only knows I was not out of my clothes for two days and two nights, lodged down where the boilers were being fired, with nothing to lie on; the little bread and eggs I still had with me were stolen from me. In Galena I looked up a couple of Dutch families and lodged with them; I walked all over the place trying to find work, but to no avail.

One of the two Americans mentioned above was returning to St. Louis two days later; the other offered to sell me all his tools, since he had no money for his return. I went on foot from Galena to Belville, a little town twenty-five miles inland. There should be work there; a Hollander from St. Louis had gone there. Arriving there, I did not find any work, and neither did the Hollander. Everywhere people spoke [well] of the shoemaking business, but everything was uncertain and risky, and I did not care to find out. From there I returned to Keokuk, and my situation was still the same.

May 26, and now I am about to begin a new thread of my tale of misery. I had hoped things would be better, but I cannot tell it other than it is. I found my wife suffering from rheumatism in her chest and back, but she soon recovered.

Just consider, my friend, such circumstances in a foreign land, a land of promise, as it is generally considered to be in Holland, especially as seen from the perspective of our own community: to have to roam about like this when you are older and to have to do that after the enjoyable and peaceable lives we had in recent years. Before our marriage, when I was young, strong, and healthy, I often did this kind of thing in Holland [looking for work], and it never was in vain. But now with our resources nearly depleted, weak and bordering on old age and unfamiliar with American ways and treated as if I am still an apprentice, it is enough to make you desperate, and frequently we are. Sometimes saying prayers, other times not, now gathering courage, then chucking it all away again, now hard [as rocks] but mostly like [melted] wax. What to do next? All doors were closed. To Pella? Once again spend twenty-six dollars traveling on that bad road and cast ourselves into the arms of poverty? We did not know what to do. Suddenly a boat appeared, which was going up the Des Moines River to and beyond Pella. On April 26 we boarded the boat. For the captain the low level of the river was no problem; there were merchants and migrants who had to go forty miles farther than we did. There was also a batch of wooden shoes being returned from St. Louis to a shopkeeper in Pella, because they had not been sold. So we expected to get back to Pella quickly, easily, and cheaply. And, with the help of others, we could then get a small log cabin ready to occupy. We could then return to St Louis to get a little credit, do some shopping, and make some shoes.

But what happened? Twenty-eight miles up the river the boat got stranded, and after working an entire day to free it, they had to give up, and goods and passengers were set ashore and the boat returned to Keokuk. We had to pay five dollars for that little trip and another 2½ dollars if we wished to return. There we were, with still another family headed for Pella, in another quandary. We decided to go back to Keokuk because, *God*, we concluded, did not want us to go to Pella. So everything had been unloaded, except our things. However, when we had decided to go back [to Keokuk], I was seized with such fear, such anxiety, that I could not sleep all night. We reasoned that nothing unusual was happening, for all the passengers were experiencing the same thing, and so we wanted to go on. We were now set ashore, amid the ranting and raving of the ship's crew and the rough handling of our trunks because we were making more work for them than they would have had otherwise. We were now sitting there, like all the others, under the open sky and exposed to weather and wind and without means of transportation, and were at our wit's end. My luggage weighed 1,950 pounds, that of the other family 2,500. There were not half enough wagons for the passengers and their goods, and only one was a covered wagon, the rates high, and the road a bad one.

I could have made it on my own, if I had been willing to abandon the other family to its fate, but then they would have been in deep trouble, because they did not understand any English. Together with an English gentleman, a young lawyer, we decided to rent a wagon for our beds, wives, and children, and to store our other goods in a warehouse. We found a wagon and had to pay twenty dollars for the ninety-five miles to Pella. The lawyer had six hundred pounds, I had three hundred pounds, and the other family eight hundred pounds. The men were to walk, the women and five children stacked atop the bedding. To store the goods we each had to pay one dollar to the warehouse for twelve days; you could see the open sky through the roof, and if it rains it is sure to leak. After getting to Pella we would have opportunity to send down wagons, and have our goods back in our possession before the twelve days had elapsed.

It was now Sunday, the 29th of April. I believe we had left Keokuk on the 26th. The American who was transporting us was to have come with a covered wagon but arrived without a cover. Arguing and protesting did no good; there was nothing else, and we had to be on our way. We had scarcely ridden a half-hour when it began to rain, in just a moment the women and children were soaking wet, and besides it was very cold. In short, the American, unable to put up with the lamentation of the women and children, stopped the wagon, unloaded it, and we could seek shelter in a log cabin. There we stood, wide-eyed like owls, not knowing what to do. It kept raining. But what to do next? The road bad, farmers at work, and no wagons. We stayed until Monday, and then had to take the same wagon for two families for eighteen dollars. The lawyer took the opportunity to go to a nearby little town where he engaged a wagon for himself. I had to pay five dollars of that. We now had a half-baked cover on the wagon to protect the women and children. For the most part the men had to walk, exposed to the rain and all kinds of weather, and it was unseasonably cold, dry, and barren as in winter. On May 3 we arrived safe and sound in Pella, but we could not locate any wagons willing to pick up our luggage. They had just returned from driving their oxen half to death carrying cargo for shopkeepers; their cattle just could not do it, and besides they were needed on the land.

I now instructed the same drayman to get my goods for sixteen dollars; so in all it would have cost me thirty-three dollars from Keokuk to Pella, including food costs. The drayman agreed to take care of it; he had to ride three days before he was home, then he would have to wait three days before he could leave again because of the [bad] road, and then take four days to ride back. So in ten days I would have my goods, around the 13th of May. But immediately after his departure it rained for three days, so that the road was completely impassable. Since then it has rained without stop, and we hear nothing about our goods, and do not know how to get them to Pella. We have nothing to wear but an old suit and my duffel coat; my shoes will be falling from my feet shortly; as to buying new ones, I just do not dare touch the little money that is left. It is almost impossible to go to St. Louis to see merchants and do business with them, especially because of the hot season. I was beginning to feel hopeful, but yesterday, the 25th of May, it rained awfully hard, so that riding is all done for again. There is not a thing we can do here either, because the merchandise for our shop also remained behind, and who knows how spoiled that is by now.

Yesterday an ox-drawn wagon was to leave for Keokuk, and I was at Pella in order to go along, but the wagon was not ready; and now that it had rained so much, the departure was again uncertain. Last Thursday an American told me that a boat was coming up the Des Moines River, and now I had hoped that the man who is storing my goods, and who is located where the boat calls, would send them along, since he knows my address. The boat called at Pella on Saturday, but alas without our goods; the boat was going forty miles farther up the river. Yesterday, Monday, a post rider brought the news that said a boat was coming down and would be at Pella on Tuesday morning; individuals and merchandise should be on location that same evening for loading. He also said that the same boat would be returning to deliver merchandise. Because it is all the same to us, I decided to go there at once, riding on horseback behind the postrider the 1½ hour ride from Pella to the river, splashing our way through the puddles of water.

Last night and also today I am staying with one of Mr. Scholte's farmers named Manster [Monster], who has been living on the ....(?). The weather is good today, and I suspect that the oxen-drawn wagons have been on the move, but whether the boat will still be coming now, you just cannot say, and even less whether it will be coming with merchandise. Getting to Pella is about as hard as it is to get off the island of St. Helena [where Napoleon was held a prisoner]. It is already May 26th and instead of things getting better for us, they are getting worse and worse. It is fast becoming a year since we left Holland, and we still do not know how things will turn out.

I am now on my way to St. Louis to request a credit, and when I think of the Eickman experience, I become worried. Sometimes I think that I have become poor and unfortunate in America. What do I care if I gamble with that American money?

When we arrived in Pella, we stayed with Le Cocq who lives ¾ of a mile from the city. We were welcome, but he complained that it took him a half-hour to pick us up, his cattle had been working all day long, (they) were too weak-kneed, etc. It was not pleasant to hear; if it had not been for you, I would not have done it. It is an amazing boorish mess at his place. He has a man and woman, with two children living in with him, who work for room and board. They live very simply and soberly, because they have to buy everything [food]. It is hard for them to get bacon or meat and good bread; and in the three weeks I have been here, I have learned that many people have a hard time getting a small piece of smoked bacon once a day, and that despite all the loud talk about the abundance of bacon, three times a day—and still it costs [only] three cents a pound—but you have to have the three cents to buy it. Enough of that; I am indignant as I write.

On Sunday, May 27, I arrived at St. Louis; having left Keokuk on the 26th, as a stevedore and stoker on the boat, so that I would earn a dollar instead of spending one; I got one dollar and twenty cents. My limbs really hurt; it felt as if they had been broken. Monday I found out that it was Pentecost Day. You would never have known it in St. Louis, it was one big hustle and bustle; most people have no idea what day it is. And we ourselves, and everyone else, is so overwhelmed by cares that one scarcely ever knows what day of the week or month it is.

While on the boat we heard of a terrible fire in St. Louis; it proved to be true. A steamboat (the *White Cloud*) had burst into flames (on May 17, 1849, at ten in the evening), had cut off the mooring lines, and drifted back along the other side, setting fire to twenty-three steamboats; and these in turn set fire to six hundred houses, mostly warehouses and large shops in the wealthiest section of the city. The damage is estimated to be in the millions ($5,500,000), everything is *one* mass of ruins and nothing was saved. Many people, especially on the boats, were burned or drowned. In addition, an awful cholera epidemic has been raging for six weeks. Sometimes, 130 and more dead on one day, several Hollanders too. What does your friend think of such American blessings? It is dangerous to be here, but I have to be here on account of my work.

I have established credit for five hundred dollars of manufactured goods and three hundred dollars of groceries, the latter to be paid in thirty days, the former in one half year. I did not agree to pay on the due dates, because I do not know what I will be selling and told them that it all depends on that, for I do not have any money. [I spent] another 165 dollars for shoes and boots. The gentleman who was to take care of this for me was ill and could not accompany me, except by means of a note. Another person who had promised to assist me lay on his deathbed, and so another person had to be asked to fill in for me. What a lot of work! What worries! I still do not know how I will get it all to Pella.

Getting a log cabin [store] ready with the help of Hollanders is not possible. It is not difficult when you are dealing with Americans.

Le Cocq assures me of full assistance if I want to go into farming, but I need too much assistance. And besides, I do not dare count on his assistance. On his advice I have rented 1½ acres of land, of which one-third is to be cultivated. He is willing to make the rounds with me to enlist the help of others in getting the land plowed. His cattle were not strong enough, etc. But no one was willing to do it. After an exchange of words, and after reminding him to his face [that he had] lured me to Pella and that I could count on all the promises of [text missing], he [loss of text] a day's work with two horses, all the men had to be called in. Just imagine what would happen if I was [living with him], and that every day I would need something of his, one day a horse, then a plow, then shirts, etc. To be a farmer without a number of children or other help of your own is to be a slave forever, especially in the newly cultivated lands. While I was still in Holland, Le Cocq suggested that I start a thread and ribbon store in Pella and to get my materials from St. Louis. When he was in St. Louis, he repeated the offer, writing, "Even if you had forty-eight chests of fabric, you could sell them all for cash," and now that I am in Pella, he is raising all kinds of objections to my starting a shop. The people do not have any money; there already are three shopkeepers, etc. But enough of all this; it is all deceit just to have a friend or neighbor.

I still do not know what will become of us. I have a credit line of about a thousand dollars with which I will be heading to Pella tomorrow, June 2; but I still do not know how I will get a suitable dwelling. I have rented a small house to have a roof over my head for two dollars a month, but it is not suitable for a shop. If the Lord is pleased to bless us, then we will still be able to make it in this way. Naatje Schotelmeijer and her husband send greetings to you.

My wife and I send cordial greetings to you, your spouse and children, and hope that from all my writing you will have learned to consider yourself fortunate in your work in Amsterdam; and even in the best of circumstances, you would still be moaning and groaning here. That is how I see things; it could be different. I am much weaker in body but for the rest I am healthy, and so is my wife.

We hear that there are many Hollanders coming to Pella; one can only hope that they have plenty of money, otherwise they will be in misery. In the first instance they [those with money] will be a blessing to Pella.

We eagerly wish for a letter from you; do not delay. I have heard that a letter of mine was published. It is not right to do that. It bothers me on account of all those simple, openhearted people. The whole world need not know what one writes to a friend. And I do not believe that if in later letters I present things in a more favorable light, that they will be published. I already can envision the title: "The Jeremiads of Jeremiah." I have plenty of troubles, and it only has an unfavorable effect on my person here. The proponents of America call black white and white black and hate those who tell the truth.

I hear that Maasdam and Van Schelven are also en route. I feel sorry for them. Well, Brother Wormser, God bless you and yours. Give greetings to all the friends who know me, especially those of our [church] fellowship. And, if you can, pray to the Lord for me. Also give our greetings to our aged Father Smit, and tell him that I cannot enclose a letter for anyone else in this one. Ask him to give greetings to my brother and his wife. Believe me that I am your sincere Brother in Christ in the old bond of Friendship, Love, and Obligation.

J. Berkhout

Added from the Wormser Archives

[Beginning of letter]

J. A. Wormser to Mrs J. Wormser-van der Ven
At Leeuwenberg, on the Veldersche Laan, by Nigtevecht
Amsterdam, 27 June 1849

Dear Jans!

I have no news for you! The rumor that the king had died is false, fortunately. The rumor also circulated in Amsterdam. How it got started, no one knows. Sunday an extra paper appeared, which reports that the Dutch in the East Indies gained a victory over the Balinese. Cholera is increasing in Amsterdam, but it is hardly mentioned any more; between June 5 and 25, 466 persons were affected; in the last three days 98.

Thanks to the goodness of the Lord I am well, and I hope that all of you may be faring well too. Our times are filled with strange phenomena; all the judgments and visitations of the Lord have been poured out simultaneously over all the earth, and the people are getting so used to it that they act as if these were ordinary times. That is a sad phenomenon and evidence of hearts that are hardened and refuse to be converted, as in the times that preceded the days of Noah, and which shall also precede the return of the Lord.

Letter of J. A. Wormser to his wife, Mrs. J. Wormser-van der Ven
At Leeuwenburg on the Veldersche Laan by Nigtevednt
Amsterdam, 24 July 1849

Beloved Jans!

Thanks to the goodness of the Lord we are all well. Yesterday afternoon about two-thirty I received a visit from Mr. Elout, which lasted until four o'clock. He was in a very discouraged frame of mind about church and state; apart from that he was very cordial. At four o'clock Dries, Mietje, the two children, and Naatje Portengen arrived at my office in a four-wheeled cab, having come straight from the boat; they are healthy and well. My "love to the saints" has been severely tested, but it has not faltered, although from four o'clock until seven (when I had to leave), and from eight till ten-thirty, the only thing I heard was that our best friends in America, and among them especially Budde and his wife, are among the worst people in the world and the greatest of deceivers. In my heart I prayed the Lord for a calm and quiet spirit, and obviously that was granted to me. I had already heard many times over that they were poor, that they had been robbed of so much, and that the journey had cost them so terribly much. After listening in silence for several hours, I said that it seemed to me that the worst part of this whole matter were the accusations that they were leveling against pious people who had associated with me in all uprightness for many years; that I had to assume that there was a difference in viewpoint between them and our friends, which I could not resolve; but that I could not assume that hundreds of pious and God-fearing people could have suddenly become the biggest rascals and deceivers; that I could not attribute so little power to Christendom and the grace of the Holy Spirit, etc. Later the aged Portengen and the helmsman came by; the latter shouted passionately that the truth and all the deceptions would presently come to light. According to them, there is nothing good about America; everything, including nature, weather, climate, land, cattle, everything was as bad as it possibly could be. And the population of eighteen million souls, including all of our friends, is one solid mass of dissolute deceivers, thieves, and rogues.

Dries will be looking for a dwelling today. I think that it will be at least five-thirty on Saturday before I get outdoors. You should certainly come along to the city on Monday, the Lord willing. I still have much to do, and so I must end now. My heart and mind are at peace and I am strong in the Lord, who will make all things well, but for the rest I am not very cheerful spiritually; that is hardly possible given the circumstances. I am at peace that the Lord is my fortress.

When Dries was leaving New York, a rumor arrived to the effect that Pella had been attacked by the Indians, that it had been plundered and burned, and that a Holland woman had perished in the flames.

Now may the Lord our God be good and near to you and graciously supply all your needs. Give greetings to Riek, the children, and our friends, the Buises, and I commend you all to the Lord.

Your Loving,
J. A. Wormser

The preceding letters from June and July 1849 tell us much about the cholera in Amsterdam; the letter of Wormser to his wife, dated 8 August 1849, contains the following sentences: "Monday I will be sending you, with Orangjeboom [transit], letters from Berkhout and Budde. The letters of Budde have fully confirmed me in the good opinion which we have always had of these friends.... The faith of Berkhout and his wife is wavering; it is because of that, rather than because of their circumstances, that they are having such a hard time, and cannot find rest."

Chapter 5

The Emigrants of 1849
(Hospers Letter 66, Wormser Letters 38-49, Budde Letters 6-7)

In 1849 many individuals again undertook the journey to Pella, this time under the leadership of Jan Hospers, A. C. Kuyper, and Jacob Maasdam. Andries N. Wormser and Johannes Berkhout had gone over on their own in 1849, and we know all about their experiences. [Jan

Jan Hospers, (1801-) leading Pella businessman
(Souvenir History of Pella, Iowa, 1847-1922, Pella, 1922)

Hospers] the father of Hendrik Hospers, kept a record of the journey in a diary, and when he had almost reached the age of eighty-five, he wrote up the story of his life, and did that at Pella, August 18, 1886. [J. S.]

While the 1849 immigrants, 235 strong, faced the typical tragedies of transoceanic travel, they gave the struggling colony a tremendous boost. Among them were educated and highly gifted men of means who became leading citizens and business entrepreneurs, such as A. E. Dudok Bousquet and A. C. Kuyper. This chapter includes many informative letters of Bousquet's wife Henrietta M. Bousquet-Chabot and the biting missives of Jan Berkhout, who called Scholte "A Great Big Scoundrel" [RPS].

From Hospers's Autobiography

I had more income than I needed to live comfortably with my family. But because the education and nurture of children was most important to me in every respect, I could not stand to see the Bible banned from the school and education no longer allowed to be Christian. Even though the Word of God was never absent from my school, as much as was in me it [education] was organized along Christian lines. And although my school inspector, Haefkens, never personally challenged me, I did know what his instructions were, and that is why I preferred to go to a free land, where I would be able to serve my God according to the dictates of my conscience without interference.

This strong urge to emigrate was also encouraged by my association with true Christians, who were scarce in those days. The secession from the *Hervormde Kerkgenootschap* [National Reformed Church] was kindled by the preaching of Rev. H. P. Scholte, preacher at Doeveren and Genderen, and resulted in the founding of several Secessionist congregations. One such group was established in Noordeloos, and they soon built a church and a parsonage, with the Rev. [A. J.] Betten as their leader. My father-in-law, Klaas Middelkoop, who was serving as an elder in the Hervormde Kerk at Hoogblokland, left that congregation to serve as an elder with the Secessionist congregation at Noordeloos. Before long there was talk of escaping the oppression of persecution and seeking a free land.

In order to remain Dutch citizens, we first fixed our sights on the island of Borneo, a large part of which belonged to the Netherlands and was located in Asia. To that end Scholte petitioned His Majesty and the minister of colonies for free passage over for members of the Society [Scholte's Society for Emigration to North America], so they could buy land [and settle] there, but the response was negative. Then our eye was focused on Texas; but there were sound reasons for not going ahead there, including the climate and a populace not friendly to Hollanders. Then the directors of the Society wrote to Rev. De Witt in New York and soon received an extensive and very satisfactory reply (I still have a copy of it in my possession); and so the Society (of which I had been a member since its inception) decided to immigrate to the United States of North America. From that time on, I regularly participated in all the meetings of the Society. When Secretary I. Overkamp was absent, I sometimes had the honor of serving as the acting secretary.

When the emigrants were about to leave, it was decided to appoint from among the members who could not as yet leave and were remaining behind, a provisional committee of eight individuals to assist with word and deed those who would be coming later. The commission consisted of the Messrs. Rev. Brummelkamp, Wormser, Horst, Kant van Andel, etc., and also included me. I then corresponded with the Rotterdam shipbrokers Wambersie & Crooswijk. I was kept busy taking care of our daily correspondence and speaking with the many interested persons who stopped in and doing work that I enjoyed. I could be of assistance to many individuals, and although I was still in the Netherlands, I was very happy that I could be useful to the new Holland colony in America. That lasted for two years, from 1847 to 1849. In the winter of 1848-1849, Messrs. A. C. Kuyper and J. Maasdam joined me to form a committee [to promote] a second expedition to the United States. Kuyper was responsible for Rotterdam and surroundings, Maasdam for Utrecht and Noord Holland, and Hospers for Zuid Holland, Noord Brabant, and Gelderland. On Wednesday, 2 May 1849, we left our homes to go to Rotterdam to embark on the Bremen bark, *Franciska*, under Captain Hagedoorn, with a full load of passengers, and with the Lord's help and flying the Russian flag, to sail to North America. My farewell to the Hoogblokland congregation, the church and school, and the Polder [water control] Board was a very moving one, all the more so because we were leaving behind aged family members who had designated us as their heirs. We were not all that concerned about temporal matters; but it was our wish to obey and follow God rather than men. In this too the Lord has also shown us that he loves us.

Since I supported the emigration with all my heart, I could only be pleased when our group sought my services. Thus, when we were about to set sail, and all our fellow passengers had assembled on deck, at the request of the captain of the *Franciska* and standing on a barrel with the captain supporting me against the rolling of the ship, I read the laws of the sea to the assembly. I could also serve the assembled host when bodies were being committed to the sea. During our sea journey, there were ten deaths on our ship. Included among them was our daughter Maaike on 6 June 1849, seventeen years of age, and on June 11, our infant son Pieter Hendrik, two and one-half years of age. On June 14 our daughter Cornelia Geertrui, almost sixteen years old, became so ill that, being near New York, we took advantage of the opportunity to have a Dutch doctor come on board. She [was able] to come with us to Albany; there she was treated tenderly, especially by dear Miss Jordan;

but the medical assistance was of no avail. In his good pleasure God took her unto himself at eight o'clock in the evening on 5 July 1849. Our daughters Maaike and Keetje gave evidence of being regenerated, so that we have hope of meeting them again with Jesus, together with our covenant child Pieter Hendrik.

On Saturday July 28, we arrived at the home of Mr. P. Welle (in Pella) at 6:30 in the evening. On 3 August 1849 [my father-in-law Klaas] Middelkoop and I, upon profession of faith, were accepted as members of the *Gereformeerde Gemeente* (Reformed [Secessionist] Church). We lived in with Mr. Welle until our new house was ready for occupancy. And so now we had to buy household furnishings and farm equipment, for we had already deposited enough guilders and dollars for the purchase of land and the ocean crossing for ourselves and for the Van Waveren family, as well as some other needy persons with the [Emigrant] Society in the Netherlands. And so we found our land and began to cultivate it, and we are experiencing the blessings of the Lord in a very special way. Indeed, so much so that, if the Lord had asked me how I wanted it, I would not have dared to ask for so many blessings and favors.

Editor J. Stellingwerff continues: And that was the eighty-five-year old Jan Hospers, who had been schoolmaster at Hoogblokland for thirty-six years (1813-1849) and its city clerk for thirty-two years; and following that, he had been a schoolmaster for another thirty years (1849-1879) at Pella, and its city clerk for thirty-eight years (1849-21 February 1888).

Very honestly he noted: "In 1862 the consistory judged that I had enough administrative skills to be their general bookkeeper. From that time on, I had much satisfaction in occupying that position. I have already sought to be relieved of the post, but that is not the wish of the consistory; they say that I must stay on until the Lord relieves me."

This autobiographical account is so much in agreement with other archival documents of Jan Hospers that I am also including the following fragment:

"Early in 1847 Rev. Scholte traveled to New York by steamboat. His Reverence assured me that he was taking one hundred thousand guilders of his own money along with him. All the society members entrusted their subscription monies to Scholte. In an earlier meeting they had expressed the common desire not to insure things with human beings, but to put everything in the hands of the Lord."

In 1847 the emigrants would not have believed that in 1855 H. P. Scholte would become an agent for the United States Insurance Company of New York.

From the travel journal of Jan Hospers [we now include] a fragment about the storm of May 20 and then continue with the entire journey from New York to Pella.

From Hospers's Travel Journal:
Sunday, May 20. N.W. storm. Many waters flood the ship, the rolling and pitching of the ship is tremendous, everything is rumbling, shaking, knocking about, and breaking. Prayers are being offered in two sections. There is consternation everywhere. Cooking is not possible, there is nothing but cold drinking water; we have never experienced a more miserable Sunday in all our lives. The storm increases as the night grows darker, the sailors walk around on deck with knife in hand, ready to cut the ropes in an emergency.

Wednesday, June 13. In the morning we see land; at 10:30 the pilot comes on board; at five o'clock we are in the harbor of New York, where we anchor with land and trees on both sides of us.

Thursday, June 14. Doctor on board to see [daughter] Keetje. Hope for recovery in two days; Keetje is in the cabin; captain and steersman are both most attentive. [She is to take] a pill with a little syrup, followed by half a wine glass of castor oil every five hours, and every two and one-half hours a pill and half a spoon of medicine. The passengers are really delighted by the beautiful sights on both shores. A doctor checks on the health of the passengers. The quarantine doctor that visits Keetje is the same one who comes in the cabin.

Friday, June 15. Thank God, Keetje is calm. A lot of commotion, as everyone is packing, by steamboat from the *Franciska* to New York. Lodgings at 132 Greenwich Street. The population of New York is estimated to be 600,000 inhabitants, indeed some say 1 million. At times there are as many as five hundred horse-drawn wagons riding on a very wide street; the footpaths are wide, constructed of big stone slabs [like you see on graves].

Saturday, June 16, lodging in New York, [pay] Dr. Van Siers $3. At six o'clock in the evening we get on the boat for Albany, four hundred feet long.

Sunday, June 17, we arrive at Albany at six in the morning. On a bridge a dignified young evangelist is kneeling, praying out loud, and surrounded by about fifty American men but no women. After him an elderly gentleman begins to preach. This takes place every Sunday. At an inn near the steamboat they refuse to take in our sick Keetje, who is waiting out in front in a carriage. Then on to a German inn, in the Railroad Street. Unfriendly treatment, only take lodgers for the night, not for the day. In the evening we take a carriage to the inn of William Smit, 41 Liberty Street. A. C. Kuyper is preaching in the Wyckoff School in the evening.

Monday, June 18. Our goods were weighed in Albany, and between nine and ten the two canal boats [left] with our fellow travelers including Father, Mother, Gerrit, Sijgje, Klaas, Gelder, and Van Andel and also Dingemans. Remaining behind in Albany were J. Hospers and his wife, [and the children] Keetje, Eva, W[ille]m Hendrik, and Janna. In the evening Keetje was moved from the William Schmidt [Smit] inn, 41 Liberty St., to Stubenraugh, 213 South Pearl Street. (Our total weight, i.e. for all of us to Buffalo, came to 5,250 pounds.)

Tuesday, June 19. Albany has approximately fifty thousand inhabitants; many houses have silver doorknobs, plaques, number and nameplates on the outside of the front doors. Albany is beautifully located on the broad Hudson River with hills and mountains all around. It is much hotter here than in the Netherlands. Everyone here complains about the heat. At night people sleep with open windows, on mattresses with only a sheet for cover.

Wednesday, June 20. A letter from Albany for Hendrik. In the evening we saw a fire in our neighborhood. At the sound of the alarm, fire engines and men hasten to help. Everything is done with speed and dispatch and still with tact, in the American way; even women who live in the adjoining houses climb on the roofs of their houses in order to sweep away the sparks. The fire got started in a woodpile; that was the only thing burning, and it was soon extinguished.

Thursday, June 21. Went to the vegetable market early to get a bunch of thirteen carrots for Keetje, costing six cents or a sixpence. Kuyper and I have a friendly reception at Rev. Wyckoff's. In the afternoon there was a fire in a house on the hill.

Friday, June 22. Fire twice during the night; temperature 96° Fahrenheit in Albany, New York in the shade 96°, N.Y in the sun 108°.

Saturday, June 23. Zweers, a runner for Doge & Spaan, receives a letter from Kok, who is accompanying our fellow travelers to Cincinnati, with the message that K. Middlekoop had lost his ticket. Zweers provides free duplicate tickets to Buffalo and St. Louis which, with accompanying letters from Zweers and Hospers, are then mailed to Buffalo by Hospers. In the afternoon, Jan, the seven-year-old son of A. C. Kuyper, who died in Albany, is buried there in the cemetery [at the church] of the Rev. Wyckoff. I attended the solemn funeral service in the carriage that bore the corpse.

Sunday, June 24. [Services] at the Reformed Protestant Dutch Church, where Rev. Wyckoff preaches in English on 1 John 2:1; in the afternoon Kuyper preaches on Psalm 115:3 with an introduction from Psalm 97:3. Keetje is sixteen years old.

Monday, June 25. Three new potatoes for two American cents (a Dutch nickel); at three o'clock in the afternoon, an infant of the Nahuis family is buried at Rev. Wyckoff's cemetery from a carriage.

Tuesday, June 26. In the morning to the steamboats and departure of the trains.

Wednesday, June 27. A runaway wagon, two horses in the Hudson River; for the first time I see a horse with its feet tied together. Spent some time looking around in the farm implement shop.

Thursday, June 28. Together with Stubenbaugh and A. C. Kuyper, we looked for and found a place to hold a joint prayer service with the Presbyterian congregation this evening. The Mission Sunday School was relinquished for this purpose. A. C. Kuyper preaches for a group of about forty people about Psalm 36:17 at seven in the evening.

Friday, June 29. If it is the Lord's doing that our children see another spring, then Dr. De Nieve advises that we give them purgatives to purify their blood. [The prescription]: two medicinal ounces of Tamarind to a bottle of water, boiled down to half its former volume, four spoonfuls a day, adding some syrup or sugar. Fire last night at 11:30.

Saturday, June 30. A letter to Hendrik, Pella.

The Budde Letter 6 in this chapter is from the hand of Mrs. A. E. Dudok (Henriette) Bousquet, who with her husband immigrated to Pella with Hospers. It tells the Buddes about the Scholte family and other "women's talk" in Pella. In Budde Letter 7, Johan A. Wormser informs Diedrich A. Budde about activities in the church fellowship in Amsterdam and the origins of the theological school that later relocated from Amsterdam to Kampen. This letter is significant for revealing the growing disaffection in the Amsterdam Seceder congregation between the more broad-minded Brummelkamp faction and the Amsterdam cleric, Simon van Velzen, who championed the staunchly orthodox wing of the movement.

Hospers 66 [Hospers 22]

Albany, 30 June 1849

Beloved Son,

I am writing this letter on the same stained paper I used writing from New York, and more recently on the 20th of June from Albany. Your sister Keetje is recovering some. She is suffering from the results of scarlet fever; she is exceptionally weak and has no defenses. During the past four weeks she has had almost nothing but medicines, but now she is developing a little appetite. Her body is full of sores, also as a result of the heat and lying in bed for so long. The open wounds make her condition a very painful one, and dangerous as well, because of the prevailing temperature of 96° Fahrenheit in the shade. If it please the Lord to restore her, a considerable time will no doubt elapse before we dare to continue our journey with her. That may well be from six to eight weeks. A. C. Kuyper from Charlois, who also remained behind in Albany because of illness in his family, will in all likelihood continue his journey to Pella via Michigan, where he has a son living. He lost a seven-year-old son to death. Then our situation as the only remaining party from the ship *Fransiska* [*Franciska*] will be a rather unpleasant one, but the Lord has enabled us to find lodging with some very fine people, Stubenraugh, a tailor, very well known to G. H. Overkamp. He is a Christian. We get along very well with them. Since these people are also most eager to get to Pella, and if the Lord were to arrange for our departure from here in six to eight weeks, we [might travel together] to St. Louis. Then we could go on to Pella while Stubenraugh and his wife and adult daughter would remain behind in St. Louis with their supplies until there was the prospect of work in his field as a tailor [in Pella]. I would like that very much, because I must say that the thought of traveling through the interior with your mother, Eva and Kaatje, with Wm Hendrik and the maid, does not appeal to me at all, if only because the Americans are experts in the arts of cheating and swindling, and all the more so since I do not know the language well.

If you have not answered my earlier letters yet, please do so upon receipt of this letter. I do not recall whether I gave you my address in the earlier letter. It is J. Hospers, c/o J. K. Stubenraugh, 213 South Pearl Street, Albany. Then do write me what plans have been made for me, what has been done in anticipation of our arrival, whether Father, Mother, Klaas, Gelder, Gerrit, Sijgie, and C. Van Andel arrived in good health, and whether any of our goods were missing en route from Albany to Pella.

(Hospers's chests are 1, 2, 3, 4, 5, 6, 7, 10 and 11; his barrels are 9 and 10; his traveling case is 13. He also has several packages.) I repeat what I wrote in my earlier letter; by all means inform the family of my earnest wish that none of our chests be opened, except chests 1 and 10, in which are located changes of clothes for your brothers Klaas and Gelder.

Should it have been determined in the [Eternal] Counsel of the Lord that our daughter Keetje is to be taken from us, then—barring any other difficulties—our departure from here will take place at once, without any delay. I long for Pella, but the Lord's will be done! My only wish is that Father and his family and luggage have all arrived in good shape; and also that Father may have started a business which produces some profit, so that in Pella we may be gaining what we are consuming here, or that at least things are being set in motion to that end in Pella. Have you come up with any plan better than farming, cattle raising, and dairying? The monies advanced by your grandfather for a wagon, horse or horses, and cows will be repaid upon our arrival; also your advances for hogs, sheep, and chickens.

Do write back soon. If I were to come earlier, that would not be a favorable sign as regards your sister Keetje. Even if it means getting there later, you would no doubt prefer to see us arrive with your sweet and impatient sister Keetje. Stubenraugh sends greetings to Overkamp. Say hello to our relatives and children. Greetings to Scholte, Van Bergeyk, Overkamp, Betten, Welle, Den Hartog, Van Baren, and all my friends who fear the Lord.

It is the wish of your loving Father that we may meet in good health, and that we may soon go up to the house of the Lord, to hear the pure preaching [of the Word]. Your mother, Eva, and Wm Hendrik, as well as myself, are in good health. Tell Dingeman Bot that his mother is still well. She sends greetings to her son.

Hendrik! Teunis Van Klootwijk who, I am told, lives in Pella, is the married brother of Johanna Biesheuvel, the widow Bot, whom we took along as a maid. She is the mother of Dingeman Bot, who also is coming along at our expense and probably has already arrived [in Pella] with our family. The widow requests that you inform her brother, T. van Klootwijk, about the above and to commend to him the oversight and joint care of her son. Greet him on her behalf.

[Jan Hospers]

The travel account of Jan Hospers continues:
Sunday, July 1. Attended Holy Communion with Kuyper in the

Reformed Protestant [Dutch] Church of Rev. Wyckoff.

Monday, July 2. Keetje is very critically ill. A. C. Kuyper is traveling to Buffalo with his family.

Tuesday, July 3. Big preparations, fireworks practice for the Independence Day celebration.

Wednesday, July 4. 1776-1849. Seventy-third birthday of American independence. In the morning a parade by the local militia in uniform, preceded by fife and drum and followed by a fire engine decorated with flowers. The celebration is announced in the early morning by the ringing of [church] bells. All public activities are at a standstill.

Everyone is in holiday attire. On the public squares in the city there are gatherings where speakers standing on raised platforms speak to the people about independence, about freedom, to compare it to that in other parts of the world, and in the process strongly stirring the [patriotic] spirit of the people. Even a highly esteemed preacher appears in public and under the open sky prays that many of the oppressed of the world may be so fortunate to cross the seas, to come and share in the freedom of spacious America. They are playing military music at the principal assembly point, and from there a parade begins, which marches through the city in solemn procession, including the military and their officers, two caissons, then an endless number of wagons and men on horseback, representing every craft and trade, such as teamsters with their drays, loaded with barrels, boxes, and packages; cabinet makers with beautiful furniture, everything displayed most beautifully; carriages drawn by six and eight horses, all of one matching color; organizations with their banners or standards, etc. It is one big celebration, flags [waving], [bells] peeling, [festive] clothes, fireworks, a day of leisure, etc. Everything is calm and orderly, and there is great solidarity.

Thursday, July 5. Cornelia Geertruida Hospers died this evening at eight o'clock; she was born June 24, 1843, and her age at death was sixteen years and eleven days.

Friday, July 6. A hearse takes Keetje and a coach [for the family] to the Wyckoff Cemetery, where she is buried at three o'clock in the afternoon. It is agreed that we will take Jan van de Roovaart and his wife and two children with us, and that in Pella they will reimburse us either in services or in money for expenses made on their behalf, and in this way we will have travel companions.

Saturday, July 7. Our plans to take the train to Buffalo at twelve noon are delayed by the tremendous crowd of immigrant passengers. As a result we are worried about sanitary conditions and overcrowding. At the same time, we see in this delay a gentle, kindly impediment by our Lord to prevent us from desecrating the Sabbath.

Sunday, July 8. The crowd of immigrants arriving with the steamboats from New York this morning include people from Zeeland, Friesland, Gelderland, and also the Preacher Verschuur [K.S. Vander Schuur], who has been called to the ...[South Holland, Michigan, church]. In the afternoon he preaches in Rev. Wyckoff's school church on Galatians 6:14, while [in the Dutch manner] I am the precentor in reading [the scriptures] and in leading the singing [of the psalms].

Monday, July 9. [Albany]. Take the train to Schenectady at two p.m.; Amsterdam (in the State of New York) at three p.m.; in forty minutes from Herkimer to Utica, a fifteen-mile trip. 7½ hours [in all from Albany to Utica].

Tuesday, July 10. Arrive at Buffalo at six in the evening. [Find] lodgings. A bloody mucus discharge prompts me to seek the medical assistance of Dr. Haksteeg in Buffalo. Buffalo did not get started until twenty-two years ago and now already has a population of at least fifty-six thousand souls. Every year more houses are added, all of them brick. It is a lovely city, and it is said to be the healthiest one in all America. It is located on Lake Erie, across from Canada, which belongs to England.

Wednesday, July 11. In the morning we meet Kuyper, who arrived during the night by canal boat. He paid two dollars [for his trip]. He is a friend of Haefkens and corresponds with him.

Thursday, July 12. In the morning we leave the Dutch inn, Washington Koffiehuis, run by Itjen and Haijen, 5 Commercial Street, Buffalo. Together we boarded the steamship *Louisiana*, in the company of A. C. Kuyper, for the trip to Chicago.

Friday, July 13. At ten in the morning we were steaming out of Buffalo, view of Canada. In Buffalo the temperature with overcast sky is 90° F[ahrenheit].

Saturday, July 14. Arrive at Cleveland at 9:45, unusual shouting at the pier by hotel owners and draymen soliciting business.

Sunday, July 15 In the morning Kuyper conducts a worship service speaking on James 1, the first half, while we are steaming on the [St. Clair River] channel between Lake St. Clair and Lake Huron. In the afternoon he continued with the second half of James 1.

Monday, July 16. Making good progress, without any chance for stopovers, since we are sailing on Lake Huron. At three o'clock in the afternoon we are at Fort Mackinaw, the northernmost part of Michigan.

Tuesday, July 17. At ten o'clock in the evening we arrive at Milwaukee.

Wednesday, July 18. At twelve o'clock noon we are at Chicago, a lovely mercantile town, twenty-three thousand inhabitants. There are no streets of stone or rocks because the rain would cause them to sink away. Instead, the streets have a flooring of sawed planks three inches thick and resting on solid stringers; the streets are one hundred feet wide; the side path is four planks in length and 2½ feet below the sidewalk, which runs on both sides of the street along the houses, and is usually covered. At four o'clock we boarded the packet boat for Peru; departure was at seven o'clock. Boys here are especially fond of flying kites. Van Malsum's wife has deserted him for the fifth time; he fears that she will be returning to the Netherlands. He earns $5 a week working in a store in Michigan.

Thursday, July 19. In the packet boat, drawn by three horses which are trotting right along, we travel a straight stretch of ten miles. In that stretch we pass through a wooden trough, set on two stone supports, and cross a river. The canal, its width unchanged, flows through this wooden trough, which has a wooden towpath alongside it. The trough is one hundred yards long, and the river is a hundred miles long. What a marvelous view we have as we pass through it! First a canal and a towpath, then deep down below, a wide flowing river; further on several waterfalls, from, over, and on the rocky cliffs, etc. That night at eleven o'clock we arrived at La Salle, a nice little town.

Friday, July 20. At one o'clock in the morning we boarded the steamboat *Teinolen* bound for St. Louis, to sail as far as Peoria, where we arrived at ten in the evening. A German family in our traveling group tells us of a rooming house, which upon investigation does not suit us. So with permission we stay overnight with our luggage in the storage area of the steamboat.

Saturday, July 21. In the morning we went from Peoria to the Clington House, to the office of the stagecoach company, to make arrangements for taking our family of seven and the Kuyper group of ten to Keokuk in two four-horse coaches for one hundred dollars, including our bedding. The rest of our luggage, approximately five thousand pounds, is consigned via St. Louis to the address of Graham in Keokuk. We left Peoria at nine in the morning, riding in two coaches. We rode on all day and even through the night, stopping only to change drivers and coaches, until on Sunday, July 22, we arrived at Oguawka [Oquawka, Illinois] on the Mississippi [River] at five in the morning. Crossed over to Burlington. Fourteen years ago the inn in which we are lodging was the first house in Burlington, and now it is a city of four thousand souls.

Monday, July 23. My wife is ill.

Tuesday, July 24. Meet Mr. Bousquet. My wife is no better; called in a doctor.

Wednesday, July 25. Accompanied by the Kuypers, we left for Pella at ten this morning in three covered wagons; the price was twenty dollars per wagon, and six shillings a day for each driver for the food of men and horses. We stayed overnight in New London for six dollars.

Thursday, July 26. Stopped [for refreshments] at Mount Pleasant. Mr. Wykoff [Wyckoff] sends word about Hendrik. Arrived in the vicinity of the Skunk River, [staying] at a farm for two dollars. Arrived at Brighton in the evening and stayed there overnight.

Friday, July 27. Saturday, July 28. Arrived at Pella at 6:30 in the evening, lodging with P. Welle.

Friday, August 3. Father K. Middelkoop and J. Hospers were accepted as members [of the church] after making profession of faith before the consistory.

This marks the end of Jan Hosper's journal, as transcribed by his son N. Hospers, one of the nine children who started on the journey, and one of the six who arrived safe and sound in Pella. Both the original copy, part of which was written with a pencil, as well as this copy, were checked by his daughter, Mrs. Hendrika Hospers Cook, who was born in Pella, 3 March 1885.

In 1849 at least 225 persons emigrated from the Netherlands to Pella. In addition to Jan Hospers, his father-in-law, Klaas Middelkoop, A. C. Kuyper, Jacob Maasdam, and J Berkhout, there were two others: Herman van Dam from Utrecht and A. E. Dudok Bousquet from Zaltbommel also went to Pella in 1849.

Abraham Everhard Dudok Bousquet was born in Amsterdam on 6 September 1803, and on 26 November 1854 married Henriette Martha Chabot, who was born in Rotterdam on 13 October 1800. He settled in Zaltbommel as a merchant. He had a factory producing tin-plated ironware and later had an interest in a brick factory. He was an early follower of I. Da Costa, and when he joined the

A. E. Dudok Bousquet, Sr. (1803-c.1856), a follower of Da Costa and businessman who immigrated to Pella in 1849 *(Souvenir History of Pella, Iowa, 1847-1922, Pella, 1922)*

Secession in the summer of 1836, he and his wife faithfully attended the meetings at the Da Costa home in Amsterdam, as well as those of Wormser at the home of Budde.[1]

In Pella he assumed leadership roles in many areas, including building flatboats on the Des Moines River to transport surplus products on them to St. Louis; building a steamboat that was to ply the Des Moines River regularly, and did so a number of times; an attempt, with Scholte, to build a plank road from Keokuk to Pella, of which twenty to twenty-five miles were completed; the pains he took to bring a railway to Pella; his interest in the Elwell Mill; his active role in bringing about the establishment of Central University; and the introduction of the first mowing and threshing machines to Pella."[2] Together with Wolters and Smeenk he established the first business in Pella, The Old Pella Store. Bousquet gave lectures in the natural sciences and also in history at Pella, and he was the leader of the first Sunday school.

Bousquet arrived in Pella with four sons: Piet Hein, born 23 December 1835, who married Sara Maria Scholte 1 December 1864; Jan Josef, who was baptized by Scholte on 23 March 1837; Hendrik Lodewijk, born 14 February 1840; and Herman Frederik, born 16 August 1841. We also find their names with the French spelling, for Bousquet was a French Huguenot family.

Wormser 38

H. M. Bousquet-Chabot to J. Wormser-van der Ven
[Pella], 20 Sept. 1849

Dear Friend and Sister in our Lord Jesus Christ,

Although I put off writing to you much longer than I had thought, and you may possibly accuse me of forgetfulness on that account, I can assure you that that is not the case. And if I should have opportunity sometime to write you in an orderly manner about everything, you will be able to justify my delay. No doubt what I wrote you from Nieuwediep [an anchorage at Rotterdam] has reached you by now and the report of a detailed letter that Bousquet sent to Holland, to provide an account of our journey, must also be in your possession by now, so that I do not have to tell you much about that. Just this, after all that I suffered on the ocean journey, things turned out to be better than I had imagined, and especially because in those moments in which you feel well, your heart is so grateful to be done with all the misery, and of being a good ways closer to your final destination.

1. *Smits*, Gorichen en "Beneder-Gelderland," *1: 279-85.*
2. *Van Stigt*, Gescheidenis van Pella, 2:69.

[*A marginal note in another hand reads*: During which time the wife had a very serious illness, so that we thought that we would lose her, and now she is completely well again.]

Seasickness is a very special and peculiar indisposition, which is wholly related to one's personal frame of mind, and accordingly, the cure must be adapted to that. And thus, even if I wished to tell you or somebody else to use this or that in one circumstance or another, it would do little good. It is my sincere wish, should you ever undertake this journey, that you will not suffer as I did, but necessity teaches one to pray, and praying gives power and strength to the soul, by which the body in turn is sustained. Piet Hein was also sick all the while. Bousquet did not experience the slightest discomfort; the three other children did fine; and Antje, whom we had taken along as a maid, experienced a slight discomfort on only one occasion. So she was quite able to be about and working, which allowed me to take it easy and rest.

I will say nothing about our journey overland; I just want to speak with you a few moments about the day that we spent with our dear friends, the Buddes. When he left church July 22nd, Budde met some travelers on the *Francisco* [*Franciska*]; in talking with them he learned that Zijl had met us in Chicago and so all of a sudden he learned that we were on American soil. That really struck him, and hearing that we would soon be coming to Burlington, in all likelihood on Tuesday, we had the great pleasure of meeting and spending several hours with him after we arrived in Burlington. That was a very delightful moment for both of us. At first we experienced a silent wonder at the Lord's leading of his people. Later we exchanged many expressions of gratitude about the blessing it was that we could meet each other face to face once again after so long a time and overcoming so many dangers. And then we also decided to spend the next day with them on his farm.

At nine in the morning he [Budde] picked us up in his little cart; it was a most delightful day in every way. Mrs. Budde again had several things prepared in the Dutch way that were a real treat. But I do have to say that she also has adopted American ways and that she makes a real effort to master them. They all looked well, and Jan Budde especially had increased greatly in outward prosperity, so that he looks very much like an American. The children had grown a lot. (I don't find any of them, including that good woman, Teleman and her child, to be very neat. *But now after having been here awhile*, my opinion on that has also changed from what it was originally). You can understand how glad they were to hear all the particulars we shared with them about all of you and our wider circle of Amsterdam friends. We were cheered not a little by the favorable temporal prospects of our dear friends, the Buddes. B[ousque]t will doubtless provide you with further details about all that. Leaving them was difficult for me, especially after all we had heard about Pella in a letter from Le Cocq to B[udde].

But the final lap of our journey had to be undertaken just the same. We left Burlington on Friday and arrived at our final destination on Monday; you can imagine with what mixed sensations. I wish that I could just sit down next to you once again in order to be able tell you everything in that regard, since I have such a hard time to communicate everything to you in writing about the real situation here, as it relates to me, without giving you a wrong impression. I will leave it to B[ousque]t to write a letter to your husband concerning the principal matters, ecclesiastical and secular, Rev. Scholte, and rest of the congregation. Shall I now tell you the truth, difficult as it may be, my dear friend? Yes, I must, and then I must discourage you most emphatically from coming here, because of the lack of many amenities of daily living, and because the "help yourself" approach makes it difficult to enjoy helping each other. Life is difficult; but even more than that I miss the pleasant intimacy so peculiar to our Christian fellowship, [a bond] that can strengthen life so much. These matters, without really depressing me, do have a great influence on me and deprive me of feeling a measure of enjoyment in life that I had more or less anticipated. It is possible that my special condition, of which I will give you a brief description, is a contributing factor. But I do have to add here that when I was talking to Mrs. Berkhout about your coming here, she also advised against it. Believe me, there are many reasons why that letter of B[erkhout] grieves me, but it was not so far from the truth. If the Lord should bring you here some day, believe me, the kinds of experiences all immigrants have to go through would be yours also.

And now back to my present circumstances. We were cordially received at the Scholte home, and we were their fraternal houseguests for six weeks. Then we felt constrained to leave; we felt out of place there. Of course, there are no houses available, so then we occupied two rooms that were offered to us for rental. We are living there with our four children and all our goods; the daughter of the farm folk who own the house is serving us more or less as a maid. This young girl, although she is a willing helper, knows nothing at all, so that I also have to keep an eye on the cooking, which is done outdoors. Another person comes to do the laundry, but it will take a good while and some doing before it is ready for the baskets we received from 's-Graveland [Province of Noord-Holland]. It all takes a good deal of time. And drying things out in the open air is not everything either. Well, that is not all that important, but what bothers me more is all this rushing about, which I think results from having so many things that need to be tended to in quick succession. If I want to get started with something else, even if it is only writing a letter, there is no opportunity to do so. Providing for those four boys is a big worry. Until now my health has been reasonably good, but I can assure you that one can also experience nervousness here, and it has plagued me not a little of late. The ray of light that beckons us now is the prospect of getting into our own home. A (small) house is being built on two lots that B[ousque]t bought. The hope is that it will ready in the month of October, and that we will be able to occupy it before the heavy snows come.

October 1: In hopes that this letter can leave in the morning, I shall add something more. Yesterday we again had the privilege of hearing Rev. Scholte. This occasioned a general feeling of joy among the congregation, and it is hoped that it will again put the congregation on the right track, one that was disrupted for some time. He spoke to us about James 5, verses 7 and 8. It was a powerful message, especially for those who were involved in these matters, and for us newcomers there was much that edified us, especially on the return of the Lord, a point on which people think and converse a great deal here. The words of the ninth verse, "Behold, the judge standeth at the door," he interpreted to mean that this could take place at any moment; this becomes the occasion for self-examination in order to be prepared in whatever moment this may take place. I do not believe, dear friend, that this will happen in our lifetime, but I do sense how a powerful impression thereof exerts a good influence on the soul; and how the thought of the end of all things visible makes the present conditions tolerable. As I was leaving the church, I spoke to Mrs. Berkhout. She asks me to give you many greetings; she is not all that cheerful amidst all their troubles. We live very close together, so that when time and roads and weather allow, we do visit each other at times. It only has to rain for a few hours, and it becomes impossible for women to get outside at all, and when you add to that the cold, which everyone here describes as being very bad, then I suppose we will not be getting out much at all. The wife of a doctor assured me that last winter she did not get out of the house for five months.

Piet Hein now works every day in the store in which Bousquet has an interest; so far he likes it. If weather permits, Jan works for a farmer, assisting him with various tasks; he really enjoys farm life; the two youngest attend school. Now you may think that I have lots of time, but that is not the case. After breakfast I have to help prepare the one o'clock meal. I have to get the laundry done every week, and since I am a stranger to ironing, I have to get someone to help me with that. People here really soil a lot of clothes; besides that, you need to be very much concerned about more than one kind of vermin in your clothing and on your bodies. Even when the Lord gives some blessing in the larger undertakings, there are still oh so many little problems that make life difficult, especially for women, to say nothing of the lack of ordinary household and kitchen utensils. Self-denial is a daily lesson.

Saartje Scholte, who was living away from home when we arrived, returned from that farm when her mother became ill; she has developed into such a dear, warm-hearted girl, and she looks fine, a little on the heavy side. And what shall I say about her spiritual state? I did speak with her on occasion, and we may hope for the best, but whether it [a regenerate heart] is presently her primary concern I would doubt very much. In the near future she intends to go to a boarding school near Keokuk to develop her English, and she is very pleased about that. Of course, Maria and Johanna have grown a great deal; they are not all that submissive. They live in a very busy, bustling household, and that is not a good thing for the children; at least it had a bad influence on ours. That little fellow is a sweet child, and he is really growing on cow's milk. The Mrs. is a very competent person, who really does her best to keep everything in good order. I count it a most fortunate thing that she has recovered again.

And now I do have to end and request that you give cordial greetings to all the friends in your neighborhood. How I wish that I would receive an answer from you soon, to hear something about all of you, and also about yourself, and how your stay at Nichteveen turned out, and whether the Lord gave you a blessing on it. And what of the dear Mrs. Willink? Has she returned to the city, or was the Lord's will otherwise? I would like to write her once, if only it would be possible to tell her the good things about us. You have no idea how it bothers me that this letter has been so long in coming, but it also depended on B[ousque]t, who wanted to see how certain matters would turn out before writing. Also give greetings to Mrs. Nol and your children and your husband. Oh, how I long for word from you, but the Lord will also send us that in his own good time. If only it might be for the good, and that we then altogether receive strength to fight the good fight and to keep the faith. Believe me, I am your loving friend in the Lord and Sister,

H. M. Bousquet-Chabot.

Appended from: J. A. Wormser: **The Life of Hendrik P. Scholte,** *pp. 224 and 225*

A. E. Dudok Bousquet to J. A. Wormser
Pella, 29 Sept. 1849

All the laments about not being able to get *deeds* or proofs of ownership are now at an end, for after having waited nine months S[cholte] finally received the necessary documents from the land office, and then immediately set about writing and handing out the deeds. But ignoring for the moment the validity of the grounds for the accusations against Scholte, one can also bring up quite a few accusations against the members of the consistory, and this would be the perfect time and place to thoroughly expose several of them, but what good will it do! Especially since the time of their playing the big boss is pretty much over now. Since the arrival of Kuyper from Charlois, of De Haan from Heerjansdam, of Maasdam from Utrecht, of Hospers and Middelkoop, the congregation has undergone a big change. Kuyper and Maasdam were made elders. There had already been some grumbling about the fact that Rev. S[cholte] was not preaching any more, etc. S[cholte] understood that now was the time to do something about the situation. He wrote a letter to the consistory urging them not to delay his case [S. had been censured and not allowed to preach], because he was awaiting their decision in order to know what he is to do, so that he could again exercise his office as preacher among them. But in the long run things would have to change; and on the other hand, he also asks their pardon, if he might unintentionally have insulted any of them. After a couple of stormy and lengthy sessions, the consistory (some of them protesting) proceeded to lift the censure of the Rev. Scholte; but just how they will work that all out I do not know. Whatever form it takes, it is clear to everyone that S[cholte] has triumphed and they look very foolish.

Postscript

2 October 1849

And so on Sunday afternoon Scholte preached again. He preached on James 5:7, 8. He dealt with everything that had transpired in a straightforward and very wise manner, so that everyone was satisfied. That sermon was well worth my sending you an excerpt of four pages. There were no oblique allusions that would make you smile, but an open, straightforward treatment of matters, without excluding himself.

Wormser 39

J. Berkhout to H. W. Wormser and wife
Pella, 12 March 1850

Esteemed and Beloved Brother and Sister in the Lord!

We were most happy to receive a message from your own hand, and to note that you all were all doing well. About mid-December I sent a letter to my brother-in-law Strikker that included several [letters] to others, and on the eighth of January I mailed one directly to you. I try to distribute the postage costs as much as possible, and sometimes I take the liberty to request that we assist each other in paying the postage costs; but often I pay as far as is practicable. I would have made it my practice to send letters more often to the address you already gave me in Holland. But as a rule when I am sending [a letter] there is no time to lose; and in general it is my impression that it takes a long time for letters sent that way to reach their proper destination. So please excuse me if I should omit doing so again.

I am amazed at how few letters I receive from Holland! A letter from Strikker, one from Hoogeveen, one from father, all enclosed together, that's all; and one from brother Lothes and brother Luuring, and now one from you. Not a single one yet from my brother Gerrit. None yet from Mrs. Abrahams. Perhaps the reason is that not much of my religious life shines through in my letters. While I am writing this, tears come to my eyes, and I do believe that I find in this [loss of faith] a greater source of tears than in my other sorrows.

I hope that by now you will have received my letter of January 8. In it I already came to you with the lament that our amazement [about this country] leaves us speechless; and, mind you, in America we had hoped to find a resting place for Body and Spirit. But indeed we find nothing here but a place of torment for both. Indeed, everyone toils in the earth like a mole to keep his head above water [mixed metaphor!] and still they cannot make it, not counting a few exceptions.

If on the Lord's Day we had found here what we had been missing for so long in Holland, then I think we could have been reconciled to America. But (and I believe that I already wrote this earlier) the calling and commissioning to the office of the ministry is denied here. Scholte is willing to preach now and then, but nothing beyond that. He does not want to be distinguished from others [the laity] in any way as a servant [minister] of Christ. The community of the saints in Christ exists here only in the public worship service. And that is terribly dry and not edifying. They still use the Compendium in teaching Catechism; they know nothing of the [liturgical] formularies. Anyone who is bold enough to speak is the speaker and also baptizes, and does whatever needs to be done without any formularies. No father is seen or even taken into account when a child is being baptized. You only see the mother, as if she were a whore. She stands there with her child, and without addressing a word to the mother either before or after [the baptismal rite], the speaker comes up to the mother and baptizes [the infant] in the name of the Father, of the Son, and of the Holy Spirit, Amen. That's it.

Anyone who wants to, can join [the church], and if he is able to speak [preach] then the crudest errors are tolerated. But if someone, being a member, cannot partake of the Lord's Supper because of conscientious objections to it all, then he is immediately censured. They drive each other so crazy with all their talk about the return of Christ as King upon the earth that one would almost be inclined to get ready to travel to Jerusalem; and by the time you get there, Christ would probably also be there.

They openly deny [the doctrine of] the perseverance of the saints and declare that a fall [from grace] is possible. I even heard Maasdam say that someone whose name is written in the Book of Life of the Lamb can fall [from grace] and in support of that cited the words of Moses: "...Blot me, I pray thee, out of thy book," etc. Moses certainly would not have spoken anything stupid or muddle-headed, nor said anything to God, or asked him anything, that was impossible. This kind of reasoning came from the so-called Pulpit.

Sunday, March 5, I heard Scholte say (in church) that if he wanted to think the least bit rationally, then he would not be able to think of the resurrection as people generally speak of it, and as the ancients always had thought of it: a separation of soul and body [lasting] from one to six thousand years, and that in the last day matter [body] and soul would be united by the power of God, and together transferred to the invisible realm of immortality. No, the Apostle taught differently when he affirmed the resurrection from the parable of the seed of grain. The seed of grain was laid in the earth, and it was not that seed of grain but another that arose, and it was immediately changed to what it was to become. And so the bodies are also sown in the earth as the way of coming to Blessedness or damnation, and thus the Soul was also directly embodied. But that body is immortal, incorruptible, and the embodiment of souls in that invisible realm (that is how he speaks of the realm of the spirits). This is evident from the appearance of angels at the grave, to Moses, Abraham, Lot, and to the three disciples [Peter, James, and John] with Jesus, and that is quite a company. The latter [Peter] even considered them fit to live in tabernacles, others ate, sat down etc.—and God says: I am the God of Abraham, Isaac, and Jacob. God, namely, is a God of the living. Look, they are alive. They all live [in] him, so they are not dead, and so the soul is embodied, and the body is not separated from the soul for thousands of years in the dust; [for] then they would be dead, [but] they are alive [in] him. Surely I need not refute these natural, human ideas for you, and it would be too long for a letter. Alas, that is what happens to a human being when he wants to understand God.

My wife and I have not been able to join such a fellowship and because of that they really look down on us, and we are not esteemed. All the Frisians and many others have no part in their fellowship. In Holland we often complained of the scarcity [of good preaching] and rightly so, but we have never been as up tight as we are here. Getting together is almost impossible because of the distances, and also because of the impassable roads. The Frisians, and several others including me, are involved in calling an orthodox preacher from Holland. Do you happen to know anyone who is mighty in the scriptures, in order to meet head on the host of heresies here? A God fearing man whose desire it is to take his pulpit to America?

It is getting time, dear brother, for me to move on to other subjects, that take you further through our school of disaster and adversity. You know, at least if you have received my letter of January 8, that I stopped at the store of Van Dam from Utrecht and talked about our partnership in affairs of [business]. Shortly after sending my letter, I realized that we could not, and should not go on as we had, and so I began telling him how he had dealt with me, and that I demanded that he make a contract [with me]. A contract was then drawn up, but in such a way that I could not accept it.

He demanded 10 percent on the full capital of five thousand dollars, or of the amount his investment was larger than mine [$4,700]; I had [put in] three hundred dollars. Then he demanded that we share equally in the profits and losses, after subtracting his 10 percent, and assigned all the work to my wife and me. His only task was to do the necessary bookwork and that does not take him even one hour a day, etc.

Another article stipulates that if either one of us wishes to end the partnership, then he must give a three-month notice to the other; the latter may then choose to take over everything at the purchase price, including house and lot, and if he does not care to do so, or is unable, then the one who terminates the partnership will do so.

So all Van Dam had to do was to say in three months, I am quitting, and in three months he would be in charge, taking over everything, and I would be out on the street. He and Scholte, who drew up the contract for him, both knew very well that I had no way of getting hold of five thousand dollars. Now it is clear that this was Van Dam's goal right from the start. If that were not so, why not put the house and lot and merchandise under both of our names? How that all came about I described for you in my previous letter.

I said that I was willing to pay as much interest as the law prescribed without a [written] agreement; that I should have something for my labor, and if the partnership should be terminated in the event he decided to withdraw, then the lot and house should become mine; but nothing doing. Van Dam made no concessions, but said that I had to sign the contract. I asked that it be deferred for a time so that I could investigate the laws and practices in such circumstances.

But what happens? Eight days later Scholte, Van Dam, a clerk, and a process server appear at my door in order to attach my property. The clerk and the process server are English; they read two documents to me, the content of which is that I must appear in court the last Monday in May to give satisfaction to Van Dam for a check and two bills that he had paid for me in St. Louis. Well, we had never had any words or differences about this matter. Scholte said that he had to do this in order to bring our relationship to an end. And so in the afternoon on February 13, 1850, they began writing up my things. They had scarcely begun when they started talking about ways of not proceeding in this way, but I was not ready for that. And when I did suggest some ways out, it all came down to just this: either I take over the business completely, or I get out completely.

The next day the process server [sheriff] served and read to me two more documents, the content of which was that Van Dam declared under oath that he truly believed that in one way or another I was disposing of his goods or removing them in order to deceive or *to do injury* to my creditor, Van Dam. This accusation hurt me terribly and grievously, and just then I could not begin to think of a way out.

I immediately got a lawier [lawyer], who handled the case and advised me not to settle as yet but to send for a justice of the peace immediately and to sell everything that could be sold, to prevent him from levying any attachments beyond the goods and the house. That was done, and I sold, as it was called, two pieces of land and a lot in the city to a Frisian who wanted me to take a draft for three hundred dollars on Holland, and I hope that you have received it in order to purchase woolens and worsteds. They were busy taking inventory for three days, and the third day Scholte came down, preceded by the other four [men] in order to announce that they would now begin [inventorying] our things. My wife said, "Well, I cannot help you with that," and [right then and there] she had such a terrible nervous attack that I thought things would never get straightened out again. I had asked a couple of friends to come over, and just then my lawyer and the justice of the peace were also there in order to prepare the documents of sale. At last they started searching all our chests, etc., but nothing was written down, because everything was homemade and brought from Holland for our own use. Out of fear, we had had a basket of linens taken away, and although it was done when it was dark, it had been seen. Scholte had these fetched and searched, and after the inspection, brought into our house.

This is a story, my brother and friend, unheard of in this county/district of Iowa, and capable of ruining our reputation and [causing us] to lose completely the trust and credit [we had enjoyed]; though friend and foe alike know that Scholte is assisting Van Dam in order to get his dollars and is a **GREAT BIG SCOUNDREL**. But the merchants in St. Louis do not know that.

Then my lawyer and I agreed to investigate the accusation in [K]noxville [the county court house], and there it turned out that their complaint was, "That I am a man dissatisfied with the people and the country, and that I wanted to return to Holland." And that I had signed a note [I.O.U.] with an "X" instead of my regular signature. But the nature of the draft was unknown [not understood] at the court of justice. They have [promissory] notes here, which are used to pay for shop merchandise and everything else. Well, now I realized what it was all about. I recall that when I started a business of my own in St. Louis, I signed a note with an "X," and did that at the request of the bookkeeper of a wholesale trading company. I thought that I had to sign with my signature, but he pointed out to me the place where I was to place the "X," and on a piece of paper showed me how to make it; when I asked, "Nothink (sic) else?" he replied, "No, that's all." And so I made an "X." The note was not yet due when I started with Van Dam; the note was paid and cancelled by Van Dam, and so it is in his possession. That is the extent of my wrong doing, if it is that. My lawyer says if someone signs with an "X" one day and with his signature the next, both are equally valid; he can do as he pleases.

But all winter Scholte and Van Dam have been looking for a way to make me look like a scoundrel, with him in the business and me out. And that, before he, in the ordinary course of decision making, turned out to be a cheat. Be that as it may, we are in a terribly difficult situation with many cares, and it would not be the first time that an innocent man was hanged.

On our road of sorrows we were able to pray to God often and bring our complaint against our adversaries before the High Tribunal. Nevertheless, our anxiety, repentance, and sorrow were often great, and very often we could have murdered them.

My lawyer has become ill, so I have started to stand on my own feet. One advises me to settle, another to pursue my legal case, so we can really expose the rich Van Dam. For legal processes here take long and are costly. Van Dam had to put up fifteen hundred dollars before he could have a process served. When my wife awakened in the morning, she lay shaking in bed as if she had a fever, but I have not dared to let her become the victim, whether we are right or wrong.

After long discussions we had, always with Scholte (I never speak with Van Dam), we agreed to give up everything, including the lot and the house, that I will help straighten out the books, stop living in the house, and that I get a pay-out of 375 dollars, that I am to receive money for the goods I have invested, and that comes to 300 dollars. So I get 675 dollars out of it. We have a notarized contract of all this, drawn up by Scholte, who is a notary public these days, but I fear that I have been deceived, for the whole thing could have been settled in two hours, and now three days have already gone by, and they still are making no progress with the shop record book.

In the twenty weeks that we ran the shop alone, we earned at least 250 dollars on our Dutch goods, and 350 [dollars] while I was with Van Dam, by selling out. That is a gain of 600 dollars, my friend. But it would be sweeter in Holland, even with less. Now we again have no livelihood at all; and we will not be able to get started before May 1. I have purchased a log cabin, 16 x 28, and will build an addition to it, so we have a place to live and a shop for retail business. I did have to build on that lot, the history of which I had already told you, I believe.

But we are not very eager to get started again, and we cannot convince ourselves that we will again be doing good business. Several other Hollanders, who could not make a go in farming, are also opening shops. The talk is that some English people are also building a shop; too many hogs make the hogwash thin. It is almost impossible for us to stay in Pella. Scarcely had the contract of dissolution been signed and Scholte posted an announcement with a warning, as if it involved a thief, that no one should pay me any money, under whatever name, [on purchases past or present].

After making a friendly settlement, it should not be necessary to point out the screaming injustice of it all, the more so because the sales register still has not been checked, and I still have not received my settlement, and I still have debts to collect from my own business. Where can I go with my complaint when the judges themselves are involved in this, and you cannot get enough Hollanders together to enforce the voice of the people. [Pity the] poor soul who is oppressed by the Hollanders here.

Never have I been so much disposed to go to California, and, after collecting enough gold there, to go back to Holland. I have asked my wife to go along with me. She is willing, but she does not dare to do it; it would cost four hundred dollars to go by sea—a little less by land; it takes two months by sea, four months by land. If I were to act according to her wishes, we would return to Holland immediately, but your advice not to return without money makes more sense to me. We could probably take fifteen hundred guilders to Holland, but what could I start with that? I have offered to let her go to Holland alone; I would help her to get underway, and then go to California for a couple of years, and then, if we live, see each other again in Holland. Oh, how I would like that! But she neither wants to nor dares to. I have suggested that she stay here and run a small shop, to wait for the goods [coming] from Holland and sell them, and that I go to California, and then pick her up here to go to Holland, but that will not do either. So we shall have to remain in oppressive Kwella/Pella [*kwellen* means to oppress, kwella Pella thus means oppressive Pella].

Brothers do not find fault with each other. Alas, if only there were no reason to do so, but just consider the following. Le Cocq, an old friend of mine whom I secretly consulted when I first had problems with Van Dam, has not paid me even a single visit in all my straightened circumstances. And Bousquet, who lives right next door, does the same, and just leaves me to my fate; they would be more helpful to me if I were living in Holland than they are here. We have attempted to be on friendly terms with both of them, but they never returned our visits, no doubt because we do not belong to their church. Bousquet could also have joined it [but did not].

I will close for now and kindly request that you send your reply or that of others via Liverpool; then the letters will be here in six weeks. Otherwise it takes three months and longer. I received your letter mid January, just when I was confined to bed with a severe rheumatic attack. At present we are well again, but weak because of all these circumstances. I told Scholte that you had asked me [about coming?]. He said: "Well, that is a good thing."

Enclosed I am sending you a second [money] draft and a list of the merchandise, the address and letter of instruction is gone. I am doing this because I fear the first one may have gotten lost. God bless you and keep you, and comfort you and yours. Greet them all by name.

Your Brother in Christ who Loves You,
Berkhout

Wormser 40

D. A. Budde to J. A. Wormser (fragment)

Burlington, 17 March 1850

Your welcome letter of September 5, which we had been anticipating for a long time, we were privileged to receive in the month of February. We were most happy to learn of your situation, but especially since the Lord made you to experience his promises with power, enabling you by faith to acquiesce in his sovereign good pleasure in the disappointment you have experienced. That was also the problem we wrestled with, but this did reassure us somewhat and enabled us to persevere and to keep going, now that we probably have put the worst of our exodus [out of Holland] behind us. Indeed, the Lord will not forsake his children, whatever trials we may still have to endure in this life. The Lord is faithful, he will not let us be tested beyond our strength, and he knows that of ourselves we do not have the strength to endure. But in the Lord Jesus there is an infinite fullness to fulfill all our needs; and from him we receive consolation, courage, and strength to hold fast to his word even when we think that the Lord is against us, and we are disappointed in our wishes and expectations. The Lord is still good and near to us. Enjoying communion with him already in this life is the most blessed condition of our souls; that also takes the edge off the sense of loss we experience when for a moment we imagine ourselves back in the circle of our old friends. How pleasant and blessed those hours were when we experienced the fellowship of the saints, and that with all our hearts. Even as your conversations then served to encourage and strengthen our mutual faith, so your letters do the same for us now.

You suggest that we stay here if our situation is reasonably good. So far we have no regrets about being here, and we have given no thought to going back. The change is very great, but once you have gotten somewhat used to it all, there are so many wonderful things about an outdoor life, and especially so when you can do without all the sinful turmoil of the world. All of this inspires us to praise and adore the Lord and exclaim, O Lord, how great are thy works!

Our harvest was very profitable last year, the prices were up; the first year we bought our corn (Turkish grain) for ten cents [a pound] and we are now selling it for thirty cents. Grain purchased for fifty cents is now [selling] for ninety-five cents; accordingly, farmers are doing very well. We now work most of our land ourselves, because Jan has changed so very much this past summer and now is enthusiastic about farming. Accordingly, we have bought another horse and wagon. In part this was because we had not needed them earlier; most of the time there had been no work, particularly not for Jan, who preferred to work our own land rather than some one else's. Now we have rented the house and five acres for the period of one year for [only] thirty-five dollars, because it still does not have a well, and water has to be fetched from our well. And now with the Lord's blessing we wish to work together all we can and enjoy all these good things from his hand. For thanks to the goodness of the Lord we are all healthy and well, much better than in times past.

We rejoice about the school in Amsterdam. Praise and thanksgiving be to the Lord who it appears has also been pleased to bless your labors in this regard, and who did not let the *Haagsche Vrienden* [Hague Friends] falter in their labors until they too might see their wishes in this matter fulfilled. May the Lord have mercy on the Netherlands so that public education might again be on a sound basis again.

Last summer we unexpectedly met Mr. Bousquet and his family in Burlington. We were delighted to meet someone from our old circle again. They spent an entire day with us. They just could not cease being amazed at how beautiful things already are in this area, and how much progress has been made, greatly exceeding their expectations. It is their intention to return here if things do not suit them in Pella.

There were two other families, Messrs. Kuiper [Kuyper] and Hospers, from the Rottterdam area who were also going to Pella at the same time. They left with anxious hearts because of the rumors about Pella that have been circulating in America. In April 1849 I received a letter from Barendregt that was not all too favorable; he wanted to come live in Burlington. He [said], "Rev. Scholte could not be persuaded to produce figures and give an accounting, that S. was cut off from the Christian community and was not allowed to preach any longer." Since the aforementioned friends arrived in Pella, the situation there seems to have taken a turn [for the better]. Mr. Bousquet wrote me that "the council had met until twelve [midnight] on September 25 [to consider] the reinstallation of Rev. Scholte and that it was approved unanimously." For as long as the former council was still ruling, this would have been out of the question. In a letter dated Nov. 16, A. C. Kuiper [Kuyper] says, "For some time now Scholte has been going about his work preaching the Word, and that with nearly universal approval of the congregation." From a still later letter by Mr. Hospers, dated February 9, [I cite] the following: "The matter between Scholte and our society has taken a positive turn. In the providence of the Lord the new arrivals in 1849 could assist in bringing this about. Things had gotten so bad that Scholte and the society were completely at odds with each other; each thought that he had the right on his side, and neither party would budge an inch. Satan was really trying hard to bring about an abominable schism. We had meeting upon meeting, with the happy outcome that Scholte was allowed to preach again. The land has been paid for and deeds have been provided. The final accounting has not yet been given, but it will take place soon; there is mutual trust again." It is our hope that the bad rumors about Pella [circulated] by A[ndries

N. Wormser] will gradually wear off, so that Hollanders will not be held in contempt overly much.

Those who live in this area have a good reputation. Janssen and J. Haselhof, who married in Milwaukee, are both still well; a son was born to them December 17, 1849. They only stayed with Zonne for ten months. Berkhout purchased a lot for $150 in Pella; the talk is that he is intending to build a house on it, a sign that things are going well for them; Lubberde[n], Le Cocq, are all well. Van der More [Moor], a house painter in Burlington to whom your brother sold his goods, died recently. He had so much work last summer that he could live comfortably on it this winter, besides having Mrs. Teeleman [Teleman] and Jansje living in with him for four months to do the housekeeping, which his wife was incapable of doing because of her mental illness, and paying her seventy-five cents a week. The local authorities asked me to take care of matters. Jan took his mother to a poor home six miles from here, where she will be cared for. We took into our home the children, survivors of the deceased: Jan, a young man sixteen years old who can earn his board and room in the city, and a five-year-old girl who will stay with us until she is eighteen; then, in accordance with the law, we will outfit her with two sets of clothes, a bed, and a cow. So we again have four children to provide for, and now we wish that Grandfather Stomp also would be with us. Then in his old age he could amply enjoy again the pleasures he had with us in the past, since many of the cares we used to have are now a thing of the past.

Wormser 41

C. M. Budde-Stomp to J. Wormser-van der Ven
Burlington, March 1850

Dearly Beloved Friend and Sister in the Lord,

I read your dear letters with heartfelt joy. We had been looking for them for a good while already, and in the end our hopes were not disappointed. We rejoice in your well-being, and that in the Lord's good pleasure you were gladdened by a good delivery, and may it be an offspring for the Lord. It was a source of comfort and joy to us to see your entire acquiescence in the way of the Lord, also when it involved disappointments. Much as your desire for another country [America] is also ours, and being in your midst in this life, we rest and trust in the

Lord that whatever way he leads you is for the best. Even if we should meet each other again on this earth, it will be trouble and grief. When I behold the great changes and difficulties that accompany a change in one's familiar pattern of living, I could wish to see you spared all that, but if it should be the Lord's will, then follow him even if the path leads to Golgotha. He knows what of trouble or of happiness is most profitable for his own.

We were very much surprised to meet Mr. and Mrs. Bousquet and their family. It happened on a Sunday when I was going to church in the city and saw a man walking behind the stage/mail coach, on which a hamper had been forgotten. He overheard me speaking to Diedrich and asked whether I was a Hollander. He was glad to hear that I was and informed me that his name was Kuyper and that he had lived near Rotterdam. There was another family with them, their name was Hospers, and Bousquet was following them. I was overcome with joy. They remained in town on Monday because his wife was indisposed. These people had also experienced illness and the loss of children en route, but [by grace] they continue to believe and trust in the Lord. Their destination was Pella. It was only a day or so later that my husband met B[ousquet] in the city. They were all well and wanted to stay with us the next day. The Mrs. looked as well as I have ever seen her, and she was very much encouraged [by everything]; the children were all hale and hearty and we really enjoyed each other's company. The Mrs. said that it was your intention to rent a small country seat near Nigtevecht [Province of Hoord-Holland] to enjoy the outdoor air.

Dear Jans, that privilege [fresh air] we enjoy in abundant measure. The children are very happy; they rejoice in the beauty of nature and enjoy taking care of the cattle. My activities are many and varied; the strong air makes for a lot of wear and tear, and [I do it all] now with less help than ever, but I am learning to make the best of it and do the best I can. We have experienced much trouble and many unpleasant things, but there is still hope that with the blessing of the Lord, we will still surmount them all in this life. For the most part, my husband and Jan will be doing the farming themselves. The cattle just keep multiplying and so there is every expectation of increased income to lighten our burdens.

We had anticipated having the pleasure of having a word with the Rev. Eppens about our encounters on life's journey, but that has fallen through. In a sermon about Jesus going up to the temple at the age of twelve and being submissive to his parents, the preacher was rather sharp in the way he addressed the young people about the way they conducted themselves. That displeased some parents so much that when it was put to a vote whether the pastor should remain or another be elected in his place, His Reverence was voted down. This action was in accordance with an article in their constitution: the pastor was to be engaged from year to year. This scandalous article was altered in a new constitution. The Lord did not requite us according to our just deserts, but he still was gracious, and a young, capable, God-fearing minister, the Reverend Mr. Dresel from Basel, who had traveled to America last year with the mother of Mr. Eppens in order to work among the Indians, accepted the call for an indefinite period. He proclaims the way of salvation in all purity and does not hesitate to speak the truth; but he has the gift to say things in a very fitting and modest manner. And again we also have developed a very dear and friendly relationship with him. The congregation is already busily engaged in building an Evangelical church. There is a lot of building going on, and it looks like Burlington is going to be a big city. We are glad that the Lord has placed us in the country.

I was very pleased to hear some things about our family and relations, and for that I thank you sincerely. I cannot fully answer your question about Leentje P[ortengen]. We have never learned why Mietje (M. Wormser-Portengen) was so envious of her sister that she could not stand to have her anywhere near. When Mietje complained to me about the way her sister mistreated her, I was very careful not to take sides; whenever Mietje opened her mouth, not much good came out. Leentje decided to stay here, because in Amsterdam she would also have to be a domestic, and she preferred to be a domestic here. I could not argue with that, because things are much better here for working people. Soon there was talk that she was staying because of Jan. Mietje was eager to confirm that; indeed, she went so far as to make some very indelicate remarks. I inquired of Jan whether this was true [and said] that such a choice would not be pleasing to us. His answer was that he thought about the matter as I did, and so she was not his choice. She became a domestic. At first she did not make very much because she did not understand the language and the nature of the work, but now she is a domestic for upper-class English people, earns 1¼ dollars a week, and the people are very satisfied with her. She is being courted by a German named Sjilp (Schilp), an industrious workman who has a good reputation. Whether it will end in marriage, only time can tell.

Dear friend, we long to be getting letters from Your Honors soon again. Didrigh [Diedrich] and Maria still have not forgotten your Jansje and Cato. They still speak knowledgeably of you. Kiss your dear Johan and Maria for me, and also greet your sister Rika, also our old friend, and my aged father and brothers and sisters; I would love to hear something about them again. May the Lord ever be with You and Yours with his consolation and grace. May he keep your eye always fixed on him through this wilderness on the way to the Heavenly Canaan.

Your Friend and Sister,
intimately united with you in the Lord,
C. M. Budde-Stomp

Wormser 42

J. Berkhout to J. A. Wormser and Spouse
Pella, 25 June 1850

Beloved Brother and Sister in the Lord!

Your esteemed letters of May 13 reached us in good health on June 13. The enclosed letters were too important and too weighty for us to burn them. My wife delivered them personally, and while she was present they had a look at them, but they did not say a thing. The iron-willed Scholte was very resolute in manner and Bousquet was, as usual, very certain of himself. I am a little too busy just now to write you in detail. We are presently busily engaged in setting up our store, both to take care of the necessary carpentry work, which I do myself, and to sort out and price the merchandise, which is being delivered from time to time, etc. In addition there is our garden, where the weeds have taken over, which is crying for help. We have paid for quite some day labor, but the garden cannot make up for those expenses. The rule in everything is do it *yourself*. Really, nothing for which you lay out money can be recouped. Accordingly, anyone who does things on a small scale, and does them himself, is the best businessman. We have now been working in our new store for four weeks, but business is slow. We took in twenty-nine dollars in that period; last year we earned more than we have taken in now. Van Dam sells next to nothing. He has killed off both himself and us. The Hollanders ignore us altogether; the business we do is with the English. We do think that things may improve. One of our supposed friends [mind you], went to Keokuk himself, acquired merchandise of every kind, and now sells it all to his friends, people who are also supposed to be our friends, at wholesale prices, so that we have no profit either from what should be our clientele. How apropos is the word of God that says, "Cursed is the man who trusts in man, and makes flesh his arm, whose heart turns away from the Lord" [Jeremiah 17:5]. It seems to us that God has something to teach and to say to us in a difficult and painful way. We now have a special purpose in all we do, something we have done on several other occasions as well: to seek no help from anyone but God. But how difficult it is to learn to trust only in God, when you experience contempt and scorn from the people [around you].

These days Scholte is championing the slave trade and posits that servitude is preferable to freedom and defends that with an appeal to 1 Corinthians 7:21. He says that the translation in our Bible is wrong here. Yesterday he stopped by with great modesty and with his usual cordiality; we happened to be busy working in the shop. He stayed a while, talking, and said that he intended to send you a letter and did I care to enclose anything? I told him to send it via Nijverdal, that you preferred that. He said that the letter was mainly for Mrs. Zeelt, and so he was sending it to his usual address; and so I am enclosing mine with his. If I were to judge by his appearance and actions, I would have forgotten and forgiven almost everything. However, a little later a person came by who did business with me last year and owed me $160, for which I had sent him a statement, but the money had been collected by Van Dam, and the man had a receipt to prove it. I had spoken to the aforementioned person earlier and told him that he did not [owe] Van Dam the $160, but that he owed it to me. He had then gone to Van Dam to get his money back, but Van Dam had turned him down, saying that he had taken over all the debits [assets] and credits [liabilities], and it was not he, but Scholte himself, who had handled the entire transaction, who had written the invoice.

When I drew up an inventory with Van Dam for taking over the merchandise, he also took over the debts we as partners owed people for services rendered with carpentry, etc. But I had [already] paid all these debts from my own resources even before the inventory existed. But all the debts still owing me he called bad debts, and we never succeeded in resolving that issue. So that I simply went ahead collecting all the obligations due me, and the proof of this is an invoice to Scholte, which he did not pay me until after January. When the business was disbanded I drew up for Scholte a list [of people owing me money], and explained the situation to him, and that these therefore remained obligations owing to me and collectible by me. To which he said that this was none of Van Dam's business. But now he himself [Scholte] is issuing statements for them and demanding payment. And the reason they can do that is because Van Dam is still in possession of my [sales] book, which was also confiscated, but the contract of dissolution specifies that it is to be returned to me when our business is terminated. Scholte does say that the monies have not been collected yet, and so it [the contract] is not yet ended. So if the people never pay, I never get my book back; that was intentional. Van Dam has no right to anything but the merchandise described in the inventory. The list does not show a half sack of wheat, no big traveling chest brought from Holland, no store sign, no account book, none of the debts of which I now speak, and all of these Van Dam refuses to return to me, now that I have signed discharge papers. I think I will have to have him subpoenaed again. Be on your guard for Scholte; I will leave it at that for now. I will be writing soon again. We send our affectionate greetings to you all, and we commend you to the Lord.

J. Berkhout

[*in the margin*]

I thought I would include this half sheet, but too much of it is legible, so I have put in an envelope. The forwarding agents pay the ocean freight and import tariffs and get it back plus their profits from the captain who sails to St. Louis, and the same process is repeated until it is turned over to me. The worries and trouble are too great and are far in excess of the profit they yield. Look over the deed, which is your proof of ownership, if you should get one. At the bottom it must include a separate declaration by a justice of the peace, stating that the wife of the seller, having been separately interrogated, and of her own volition, has agreed to and signed this document. Without that declaration the deed is not official. And it must be recorded with the county register of deeds. Quietly inquire about Hoogeveen's deed; I do not think he wants to admit that he has land here. Scholte sent him a deed this past summer.

Van Dam has written to all merchants [suppliers] in St. Louis that he has had to take legal action [against us], and that he was thinking of taking a bill in Chancery. I believe that stands for a criminal prosecution. But it did not have any effect on those with whom I did business in the past. They all understood that Van Dam wants to get his hands on everything. I paid about six hundred dollars and took a credit of about five hundred dollars.

I do not recall whether I wrote you the following. When I started doing business in St. Louis I signed a promissory note with an "X." That is the only misdeed they were able to allege against me in court, and that I was dissatisfied with this land and its people. The bookkeeper had only asked me to sign my name with an "X," and that is what I did. Mr. Doun [Don] King of St. Louis, whose money draft it was, wrote me to say that the only reason for that [X] was that we could not understand each other well at the time; and he gave me another 150 dollars of credit. I did not want any more.

But it is clear as day that Van Dam began by cheating; while we were still in Pella he tried to gain possession of the lot on which our house was being built. Scholte had written a deed in Van Dam's name, in which I was not even mentioned as a partner. Fortunately, the man who had sold me the property refused to sign the deed, and he was fortunate enough to retain possession of the deed as evidence of their wrongdoing. I was not informed about anything, and so I recounted the history for you even before I knew about any legal actions. Fare well!

Wormser 43

G. Berkhout-Smit to J. Wormser-van der Ven
Pella, August 23, 1850

Dearly Beloved Friend and Sister in the Lord,

It is about time that I am also writing you a letter, my dear friend. The constant turmoil in which we have been involved since coming to this unhappy land of America has pretty much robbed me of all desire to write. Since the first of May we have been living in our own house, on our own lot, which is fully paid. After we had made a down payment on the lot, Scholte tried to take the lot from us by putting it up for sale again. In order to regain ownership, my husband had to draw lots, and drew this one. Now we have fenced it, planted our Dutch garden seeds in it, and now are eating from it: turnips, green peas, snow peas, French beans, wax beans, beets, carrots, kohlrabi, white, red, and Utrecht cabbage, cucumbers, cherries, radishes, kale, endive, purslane, spinach, gray beans, black radish, and potatoes. Garden beans are eaten by some kind of flies! The climate is too hot for cauliflower. You will probably say, dear friend, that must be nice, being able to get everything you want from your own garden. That is true enough, but the work it takes makes it a real burden; the weeds grow over your head. It is hard work, with just the two of us tending the garden and taking care of the store. [Besides] I have to roast the coffee [and] bake bread every other day. We have to get up between 4:30 and 5 in the morning and then with nimble fingers to go to work in the garden; it is too hot during the daytime, and besides we have to run the store. During the summer it gradually gets very hot, thunder storms almost every day, very hard on the nervous system; most of the time we feel so benumbed that we get in our own way. The [hot] air is so oppressive that if I go to the garden for only a few moments, I have to put my hat on; that's how heavy the air is.

We have been *running the store* for eleven weeks now; business is still very slow, but things seem to be slow all over the country. There is very little money in circulation right now, and every day there is a line of Americans wanting to buy merchandise on credit, because they do not have any money. In general they look like poor Jews, plucked and in tatters. This, however, is not a consequence of American freedom. In that regard things here are just as they are in Holland; if one prospers, he dresses the part.

And now I would like to tell you what kind of store we have. [We carry] dry goods, tulle and [bows], trouser materials, hats and caps, shoes and boots, syrup, vinegar, sugar, whisky, coffee, tea, pails, rice, brooms, tinware, stoneware, nails, whole and ground pepper, dry mustards (you have to mix your own), shoe polish, brushes [sweepers], salt, potash, etc., etc., etc.

Beloved friend, I hope that you and yours may truly feel grateful for the privilege of being among your old friends, relatives, and acquaintances. We over here continue to miss the joy of again having good, trustworthy friends. We have no dealings at all with Le Cocq; it is worse than if we had never known each other; the same thing is true for Bousquet. At first I spoke to the Mrs. on several occasions, but when we met the last time [she said], there was no need for us to speak to each other often, as much as saying, just stay away, and that is what I am now doing. The change in her life's circumstances must be very difficult for her. Mr. B[ousquet] is losing weight, getting thin. The children walk around in wooden shoes and go barefoot. You may say that is embarrassing; no, dear friend, that is not it at all. It is because they are needy and suffering want. Everyone becomes poor here. Le Cocq may say that he is well off, but [really] he is poor. It was easier for him to buy expensive meat in Holland than to get meat here at three cents a pound; you should just hear his wife talk. They just do not dare to tell the truth in their letters to Holland, and that accounts for their silence. All women here are slaves rather than queens of the forest. When I was still living in Holland, I often said, if ever I should have to go to America, then I will have left the best part of my life behind me, and it is most emphatically so.

I hope that your dear John may have gotten better, and your headache as well. How are all of our friends in the fellowship doing: Mr. and Mrs. Lottes [Lothes], Luuring, Gunter, Mr. and Mrs. Willink, Mrs. Abrahams, and the other friends, Budde and his wife? How are Diekinga and his wife; is he still a traveling book salesman in Overijssel? Which colporteur is working in Amsterdam?

Sundays here are sad. There is not a single pious person here with whom we get together cordially as friends. While I am writing this, these words [from scripture] come to me, "Trust in the Lord in all things." I believe that the Lord really wants to teach us to find all our sufficiency in him. In most situations I might have the privilege and the grace to ask for self-denial, patience, and submissiveness, and I might rather fall into the hands of God rather than in those of men.

And now dear friend, I must conclude; I have to mail this letter. I have wanted to give you an opportunity to send me a letter written with your own hand. My husband and I greet your husband, your sister Rica, and your children most cordially. Greet all our old friends for us, as well as my aged father and my brother Gerrit, if you should speak to them.

Your sincere Friend and Sister in the Lord,
G. Berkhout-Smit

Budde 6

Mrs. H. M. Bousquet-Chabot to the Budde family
Pella, 4 December 1850

Dearly Beloved Friend and Sister through Faith in our Lord and Savior J[esus] C[hrist],

It would not be very easy for me to tell you in full all the pleasant sensations that the receipt of your most friendly and Christian letter stirred up within me. It was on a Sunday afternoon after church, when Berkhout stopped in to drop it off. Jan Le Cocq happened to be here to pick up his sister Mietje who had eaten with us. I was preoccupied with getting the tea ready, and since it was already becoming dusk, some time elapsed before I got around to reading it. Seeing how pleasant the recollection of the day of our meeting in the month of July was for you, I must tell you that I too could not fail to recall with gratitude the most loving design of the Lord, who arranged all things to concur in such a way that we should have this meeting.

And I must agree with you that in the midst of all the things we enjoy in this world, we still sense the sinful condition in which we live. Nevertheless, amid all this misery there remains joy for the individual, who by grace knows what it means to be a child of God, even though this visible world is still so filled with many things that cause us trouble and grief. Enveloped as we still are by this body of sin, we would be incapable of any higher bliss. But once the last struggle has been fought, we will then be like the Lord and see him as he is.

Since my husband's letter to your husband has reported on many [of our] general activities, I shall limit myself to household matters. All of us are privileged to enjoy good health; for the most part I attribute this to the wonderful climate of this region. For me at least the [fresh] air has been a great influence for the good. I never have been able to take the cold. As I was about to go out this afternoon, I heard others say that it was *very* cold out and that I probably would be the worse for it. But I ventured it just the same, and I am feeling so well that I am firmly convinced that the cold did me more good than harm.

Last Monday our youngest [son] Herman had the misfortune of cutting himself with an axe, right through his shoe and stocking and into his foot. It was pretty bad, but since the wound was not diagonally across his foot and no tendons cut, we need not fear that his toes will be stiff [immobile].

Number 2. Jan also did not feel all that well recently because of a cold he had caught, but he is all well again. Number 3. He and Henry started attending the new school with Mr. Sherman yesterday. Piet Hein, our oldest, is working in the store under the supervision of his father. It is not impossible that he might complete his formal education by going to New Brunswick, a place in the vicinity of New York. That all depends on a communication on the subject, which we are awaiting.

The last time Bousquet went to St. Louis, I had Johanna Scholte staying with me for a short time. Now, during the delivery of her mother, Maria is staying here and Johanna is staying with Mr. De Havre, the future father-in-law of Saartje [Scholte]. These children, having been left on their own a good deal, have various notions that really require some changes, or at least some type of guidance other than that of the father, who is so busy from morning till evening that he can hardly attend to these matters. And the wife, in addition to her children, has a very busy house to run, and she is not one of the strongest. It is a pity that the children, for whom our wish is that they may have a good name, also for their father's sake; sometimes the very opposite is true.

There are a number of people here with whom I can converse very pleasantly in matters relating to our Christian standpoint. But the kind of companionship we had in Amsterdam, among others with the Wormsers and the Willinks, we have not found here so far. I see Mrs. Scholte from time to time, and up to a point I can speak with her about spiritual matters. It works out best after we together have heard a sermon by her husband. She always agrees with it. Right now, after her delivery, she is not all that well. She is very weak, so much so, that today when I was at her house I did not even see her. And I will conclude here, in the hope that you and all your family will receive this letter hale and well. Please be so kind as to give my greetings to your husband, your son, and Mrs. Teleman. It will give me great pleasure to hear from you again sometime. If it would work out for Jan to come here some time, he would be able to tell you much more about us all than we can communicate in a letter. Believe me that I am,

Your loving Friend and Sister in our Lord,
H. M. Bousquet-Chabot

Budde 7

J. A. Wormser to D. A. Budde
Amsterdam, 9 May 1851

Dearly Beloved Friend and Brother in the Lord!

I am in possession of your esteemed letters of Nov. 11 [1850] and Feb. 3 [1851]! We have not written you in a long while, but we have often thought and spoken of you both. On last February first, the Lord visited me with a very serious illness so that they thought that I would be departing this life. I was unconscious because of pleuritis in my chest and an attack of nervous fevers. Thanks to the goodness of the Lord I have been restored again, but I still do not have all my strength back. During my illness we experienced many expressions of interest and concern, more than I dare mention.

It is altogether different than eleven years ago, when [Rev.] Van Velzen had us suspended. Now our work is appreciated more by both Seceders and non-Seceders. The periodical, *De Vereeniging*, is becoming more ecclesiastical. Moreover, we have an excellent daily, *De Nederlanden*, of which Mr. [Guillaume] Groen van Prinsterer is one of the editors, and in which church and school and matters of state are dealt with daily in a Christian manner. I also write in it a good deal.

Our fellowship is still going, but your brother terminated our rental about the first of May, because he could rent it for a higher price. We now meet at Hoogkamer's, but we expect to have a better meeting place about November. The deal is as follows: last December we purchased a big building with a hard stone façade on the Voorburgwal at the Hoofdsteeg for over twelve thousand guilders. We have now taken it over. This summer it is being rebuilt as a church and theological school. Instruction at the theological school will be given by Rev. Brummelkamp, who is moving to Amsterdam; Rev. Van Houten, who studied in Geneva; Mr. Da Costa, whom you know; Rev. Schwartz, missionary to the Jews for the Free Church of Scotland; and by Mr. Teding van Berkhout. The board of directors was constituted by two Seceders and two *Hervormden*; the *Haagsche Heeren* [ruling officials in The Hague] are also participating. Thus, our fellowship will become the heart of a new movement, and we will have more than one preacher of our own. We admit to the sacraments all *Hervormden* who are beyond reproach, even non-Seceders, and we only consider their fidelity to the Confession and their walk of life. That the Rev. Van Velzen will have no part in all of this you will understand. He persists in going his own narrow-minded way.

We are delighted that the Lord is blessing you in the things of this life, although he also causes you to experience the trials of this life. It was with a real inner sympathy that we learned that our good God grants you to experience his spiritual quickening in our Lord Jesus and that he constantly keeps your eye fixed upon the eternal and incorruptible inheritance, which He has set aside for us in heaven. We too may go our way in all quietness and simplicity, in child-like trust in God. Church matters are more demanding of us than we would like, but we dare not pull back, the more so because the good cause is making considerable progress these days, and many who formerly either kept silence or expressed other sentiments now are defending the interests of the Reformed theology.

If the marriage of your son Jan has taken place, then with all our heart we wish him and his young wife and you as well happiness and hope that the Lord may continue to richly bless their union. If the peace of the Lord lives in their hearts and in their home, they are safe under all circumstances, and it will enable them to lighten for each other the sorrows and burdens of this life. We are pleased to hear that Mrs. Teleman and her daughter are doing well; do greet them cordially for us, and also Jan, Diederich, and Maria. Your aged father is still living and is healthy and cheerful; he regularly complains that he is not as alert as he used to be.

I have transferred twenty-eight guilders from Berkhout's account to yours. There are few emigrants from Holland going to America these days. Otherwise things are pretty much the same here. France continues to be one and all confusion and miserable.

Well, dear friends! Cordial greetings to all of you, and we commend you to the Lord and his grace. May he lead and keep you all, and ever fill your hearts with peace and joy through the Holy Spirit.

Your loving Brother in Christ,
J. A. Wormser

Wormser 44

K. de Jong (to family) *Copy*
Pella, 1851(?)

Esteemed Brother,

Since it had long been my intention to write you once, the reason I did not was so that I would be better able to acquaint you with our situation, how we are doing, and what things are like here. Through God's goodness we are still healthy and hale, and we hope the same is true for all of you. We would be sorry if it were otherwise.

We hear that the reports on our situation here vary a great deal. The region where we live is good and fertile; we do not have to chop down any trees for hay fields, pastures, and arable land. There is plenty of that, and it is good. There are plenty of woods for timber and firewood; you could not begin to burn the firewood in the forests in twenty-five years. There are also coal mines, etc., good cattle, and many pigs; there is an abundance of meat and bacon. Good horses are as expensive as in Holland; milk cows sell for 10 to 15 dollars. There are farmers who are already milking twenty cows; cheese and butter are as good as in Holland; cheese sells for 6 to 7 American cents per pound; whey butter 7 ½ cents, good butter 10 cents; a six-pound container of lard is 50 cents. [We have] good garden produce: lettuce, carrots, peas, cucumbers, etc., melons of every kind, good potatoes. And as far as the heat and cold are concerned, it is like Holland, [the climate] is very healthy, we have not heard of any illnesses this summer. The Lord could not have ordered things better for us. We live peaceably and well here, as though we were sitting in the bosom of Abraham, but we hear that things are not so good in Holland. God is great and we do not comprehend him. He does according to his good pleasure with the hosts of heaven and with the inhabitants of the earth. If only we were more grateful for the good things he bestows upon us. We are separated far from you and probably will not see you again on this side of the grave. I wish that my relatives were here; that would increase my joy and happiness. We have not forgotten you, by no means, and we do not think that of you either.

Our congregation is growing; there is regular schooling; my children are learning well. Van Driel could hardly believe that they were my children, they had grown so. We were happy that Van Driel was able and well when we met him; they had been at sea for fifty-four days, [were] a month getting from New York to Pella. Give greetings to his family in Blokland.

Adriaan, I have learned that that there is not much room [left] for you to come over here to us. Yes, brother, if we wait too long, the door may sometimes be closed on us; no wife, no children, no inheritances should hold us back if all is well with us [our soul]. Give my greetings to all our friends and acquaintances. I will add a brief note about our [spiritual] condition. It remains a struggle to enter "by the narrow gate," for there are many bypaths. The words of the Apostle Paul still apply: "Examine yourselves, to see if you are holding to the faith," [2 Corinthians 13:5]; for many shall seek to enter, but they shall not be able. We remember you in our prayers, we hope that you do the same, and in this way we can experience the fellowship of the saints, and the time will then come [in the hereafter] that we will not be separated from each other again.

Here we serve the Lord according to his Word without any hindrances; for church and school this is a good place to be, and that is the greatest blessing for us and our children. We have three teachers here to instruct the young, both in Dutch and in English: Scholte, Barendrecht [Barendregt], and De Hoog are elders; Betten, G. Overkamp, and I.

Overkamp are overseers and deacons. There is preaching twice each Sunday, and catechism is also taught twice, because quite a few people live far from the city. Our church is already much too small, even though it is fifty feet long and twenty-five feet wide. There are also schools being built outside the city. We can let our children go to school to learn, without worrying about being under any moral constraints. That makes us so very happy, and within the year we shall be accepted as lawful citizens of America. We do not have to groan about burdensome taxes here.

The Lord is also working in the upcoming generation; this time there were four girls [who were converted]: one is twelve years old, two others are fourteen, and the other is sixteen. Yes, dear friends, the Lord also desires to expand his Kingdom in this Earthly Pella. And how great it is when the Lord converts young people so that is a great gain for the kingdom of Jesus, and cause for the Lord's people to rejoice. There is already a group of children, ages twelve to seventeen, whose desire it is to serve the Lord. Before, they were the greatest champions in sinning; now they are for Jesus. I cannot tell you how great is the number of those daily being added to the congregation of the redeemed, for they [clearly] are being transferred from darkness into his wondrous light. Often times we melt in tears at the goodness of the Lord, and there are even some seven-year-olds whose desire it is to fear the Lord. Before it was all vanity and frolicsomeness, but now they encourage each other to fear the Lord. They also admonish one another to persevere in prayer; and they are not ridiculed here either, as they are in Holland. Here they come out boldly for his name, and so they glorify God.

Beloved brothers and sisters, I do wish that you were all here, but that is not the case. Now I break off with my pen but not with my heart. And after a prayer on your behalf, I wish you all the choicest blessings of the Lord, and with esteem I remain your loving brother in the Lord.

K. de Jong

Wormser 45

Spouse of K. de Jong to family, *Copy*,
Pella, 1851(?)

Dearly Beloved Brothers and Sisters,

Since we received your letter of [last] June in good health and well being, and from it learned that our father had exchanged the temporal for the eternal. It struck us all the more because he left you sadly, just as we parted from him sadly. Oh, in times like this we see the blessings enjoyed by those who by grace have become desirous to serve the Lord; then death is not the king of terror but a joyous summons, for their [heart's] desire to love and serve the Lord above all is about to be fulfilled. Yes, and many a time that is also our longing too; for oh, my beloved brothers and sisters and all who serve the Lord, we have to let you know, to the honor of the Lord and to the glory of his free grace, that the Lord is working mightily in the hearts of our young people, for converts are being added daily to the congregation of the redeemed. Ah, but we do not hear people talking about anything here but the way to heaven, because the parents are aroused by it, and the children are busy telling of the great things the Lord has done unto them. So again the promises of the Lord are being fulfilled here, "for out of the mouths of babes and sucklings I have brought forth my praise" [Matthew 21:16]. You can well imagine that also means a lot of praying on behalf of our dear children. Ah, but I hope that some day we may be able to write you about all that the Lord has wrought in them; that would make our joy all the greater, as you can well imagine. So we do not know what the Lord has in store for us, but the enemies [of the Lord] have been terribly angry with us, and that has hurt the colony a great deal, and also our dear Rev. Scholte whom we love dearly, not for his own sake, but for the work he has done. Oh beloved family, and all those who fear the Lord, we cannot write you everything, but the precious sermons that we hear from him, and in particular on Sunday morning, when he was so overjoyed about the stirrings among the children, and now affecting even his own household: his eldest daughter, who was also a very worldly girl, but in whom a great change has now taken place. Pella is a place of rejoicing; every mouth is brimming over because of the mercies of the Lord. So you can imagine that we are happy to be here. But I constantly think, oh, if only all my family were here now too. I will not write you much about temporal things [now], but this I can say, it is a land overflowing with milk and honey. But if I were to write about that, you might very well wonder if it were really so, but it is the truth.

(What follows is written in another hand:) Hijn (H. Wormser?) From your letter we learned that your wife, our sister, had a baby.

(Now the first hand continues:) This was written by the wife of K. de Jong.

(The second hand:) At the time he was living at Tienhoven near Ameide.

Wormser 46

D. A. Budde and C. M. Budde-Stomp to J. A. Wormser
Burlington, 26 December 1851

Dearly Beloved Friend and Brother in the Lord!

Your most welcome letter of the 9th of May we have received. It was our privilege to rejoice and be glad. Our hearts were lifted in praise and thanksgiving to the Lord, who, after your very grave illness, restored you again for the well-being of your family and to serve again in the kingdom of our Lord and Savior Jesus Christ and for the building up of the congregation in the Netherlands, which was bought at such a price. May the Lord strengthen you both inwardly and outwardly and grant you to enjoy abundantly the fullness of our Lord Jesus Christ, from grace unto grace.

We thank you for the many important news items that you have shared with us. Indeed, who could ever have thought of our fellowship twelve years ago that the Lord would be pleased to glorify his name through it and cause something to be born of it for the salvation of his church; but it is all in his sovereign good pleasure, to him be the honor! The saying is also true here, "He who was lying bowed in the dust, is raised again by the Lord."

Oh, my heart leaps for joy and I could wish that once again I found myself among my old friends, but the Lord only knows whether it will still happen on this side of the grave. But if not, we shall meet each other in the blessed eternity and join in singing the heavenly hymn of praise,

> To Him who sits on the throne and to the Lamb,
> be praise and honor and glory and power
> for ever and ever, Amen! [Revelation 5:12]

A short time ago, in the month of October, Mr. Bousquet paid us an unexpected visit. He is the very much the same, as talkative as ever. He was en route to St. Louis to procure merchandise for his store and stayed over with us for a day. It was pretty clear to us that his financial situation was not improving, for he said that if he did not have a store, he would not open one now, and he was hoping that he would be getting assistance from Holland. The Mrs. and the children were in very good health. The church situation in Pella was still not a unified one: worship services were being held in three different locations, and Rev. Scholte was a notary public, a lawyer, and some other things. Earlier Mr. Bousquet had written me to come and live in Pella, but now that he saw how things were in Burlington, he could no longer advise us to do so. For there was no money in Pella, and the farmers had a hard time selling their produce; they could only exchange it for other needed items.

Our [son] Jan married Elena van Beek February 28. She is a good wife for him, and to us it does not appear to be hostile to Christendom; she is a quiet person and submissive. If only the fear of the Lord may fill their hearts, then they will be able to bear the burdens of life and have a well-grounded hope for [their] eternal salvation. We are most pleased that they are living on our premises; we get to see and help each other, and erelong we hope to see our family increased. For the coming year I have rented a third of the land to him; then I do not have any cares about it; he now has two horses, and we still have one. The first year was not a profitable one for either of us; it rained a lot in the early summer. We had plenty of food supplies but money was scarce. When our aged father will have exhausted his savings, would you then please advance money on my behalf (if it is convenient for you to do so, and there is a way for me to repay you). Give him our greetings; we are all still well.

And now, beloved friends, the Lord be with you, bless you in all things, and receive heartfelt greetings from all of us. Give greetings to Janssie, Kato, and Johan, and the little one. Greet your friends and ours. Is Mrs. Zeelt happy about the new ecclesiastical situation and its new composition? My wife was not able to write much this time, while I have mailed various letters together. She hopes to do so some other time.

Remember us in your prayers.
Your loving Brother and Sister,
D. A. Budde, C. M. Budde-Stomp

Wormser 47

D. A. Budde to J. A. Wormser
Burlington, 23 December 1852

Dearly Beloved Friends in our Lord Jesus Christ!

We received your long awaited letters of Oct. 4 in good health and well being, thanks to the blessing of the Lord. The tiding that our church fellowship had been dissolved instead of functioning as *De Gereformeerde Kerk* was very grievous to us. If we were still in Amsterdam, I do not think that we would attend the *Bloemgracht* [fellowship] under these circumstances. I can believe and sense how troublesome and grievous it was for all of you, that Brummelkamp had first cooperated in such a brotherly manner and for so long; and then when almost everything seemed to have been settled, he developed scruples, which lead to a complete reversal [of his stance]. The guidance of the Lord is not absent in all of this. Father Jacob, standing before Pharaoh, said, "Few and evil have been the days of the years my life" [Genesis 47:9].

And whatever we undertake, wherever we wend our ways, every believer will doubtless experience this to some degree and bear the same witness. However, by hope we are already blessed, because the love of God has been poured out in our hearts and makes us submissive and still before the omnipotent dispositions of the Lord. Even though our activities on behalf of the church of God are often impure and stained with sin, the Lord attains his end. Then, esteemed Brother! do not let your grievous disappointment in such a great cause, because of Brummelkamp, discourage you from being active in the service of the Lord; even as we rejoice to learn that you are again actively involved in a Christian school—and in writing about infant baptism. May the Lord increase your strength and grant you his Holy Spirit in double measure for the building up of the kingdom of God. We would very much like to have a copy of our own of the ten short articles on baptism, if you should have copies left. They could also be of use to the church of God in America, because the Baptists also have many adherents here. Might there not be a possibility that you could send me three or four copies, along with your brother's brother-in-law (Captain Portengen) to New York in care of Mr. Johannes C. Guldin, 122 Rivington Street, N.Y., with a forwarding address to A. Sprenger at Burlington, Iowa. Then they will reach us here. There is a possibility that my brother's son, [living] in the N. Looyerstraat [Amsterdam] will be traveling to America; then that would [also] be a good opportunity.

We Hollanders, plus a few German families, have affiliated with *De Hollandsche Gereformeerde Kerk* [The Dutch Reformed Church] of New York, and we have a small congregation in Burlington under the name of *De Hollandsche Gereformeerde*. Our Rev. [J. B.] Madoulet is from Nijmegen and preaches each Sunday, once in High German and once in the Dutch language. The financial costs are borne largely by the synod. The church has the same Symbols [creedal and liturgical forms] in their church books as they do in Holland, and that includes the Canons of Dort, but it is all in English. Last October the Rev. Madoulet, A. Sprenger, Jan, and I attended a classis meeting at Ferview [Fairview], Illinois, sixty miles from here. Everything was in English, but most everyone was of Dutch ancestry, and some could still speak some Dutch. We were all like one big family. Three weeks ago the minister of our congregation was installed by the Rev. Wilson of Vervieuw [Fairview] at the Presbyterian church. That church, one in doctrine with us, allows us to meet freely in the lower section [of the edifice]. The good hand of the Lord has so ordained everything that we not only worship in the Dutch language, something we had not even dared to consider, but that we may rejoice in the pure proclamation of God's Word. We now are hoping to build a church next summer, but we do not know whether we will be able to collect sufficient funds. We have already sold at least ten acres of our land for 450 dollars to help the good cause along. The Lord will finish his work, even if we have to wait another year. So now there is a Dutch Reformed congregation (be it small) in Iowa holding fast to the teachings of the fathers. May the Lord continue to crown the work with his approval and blessing; you [I know] unite with us in the prayer: thy kingdom come.

And now, esteemed Brother and Sister, The Lord bless thee from Zion and lift his countenance upon thee, bless thee and thy family, to the rejoicing and gladness of thy soul. Receive our cordial greetings and those of Jan and Diedrich and Mrs. Teleman. Greet Brother Luring [Jan Willem Luuring], and Lothes, and Grandfather, Janssie and Kato, and do not forget,

Your Brother in the Lord,
D. A. Budde

Leentje Schilp-Portengen, gave birth to another son in October; she had sore breasts. They are living on their own land, nine miles from the city, and have built a brick house on it. It is too distant for me to visit her during the winter.

[*This P.S. is in the handwriting of C. M. Budde-Stomp.*]

Wormser 48

>H. M. Bousquet-Chabot to J. Wormser-van der Ven
>Pella, 28 Nov. 1852

Dear Beloved Sister in the Lord,

Even though your letter begun September [18]51 did not reach me until Oct. 52, I must begin by saying that I was most pleased to get it. The passage of time between the beginning and the ending of your letter proved to be the very opposite of what I had presumed; namely, that because of postponing too long, you finally decided to put it off altogether, or that too many cares and difficulties had prevented you from writing. You will agree with me that all too often thoughts arise in an evil heart, thoughts that afterwards put us to shame and, may it be, truly humiliate us.

On this Sunday evening I want to begin answering your letters, which is a distinctly pleasant task for me, but not a very easy one. It is one thing to sit down together to discuss matters, considering them and arguing about them and making immediate judgments and finally ending up by saying, yes, we will just have to admit that it is out of our hands. It is quite different when I am writing and desire to respect the truth without offending anyone, and also without being apologetic. After having received your letter, I happened to meet Berkhout and told him that your husband had referred us back to a letter that he had written to B[ousquet] earlier. And so his wife came over last week with that letter to let us read it. She stayed on a while talking about old things and new, and among others she told me that her husband always wrote very detailed letters to your husband, both about social and ecclesiastical matters, and especially about the latter in very great detail.

From this I gathered that you are acquainted with our very strange situation. Indeed, considering everything, you do have to call it strange. A minister [Rev. H. P. Scholte], of whom I do not have any doubt that he is *a child of God* and which I consider to be the reason why his sermons are always so very powerful and lively, even unbelievers are captivated by them. This same man does not wish to be called a minister. He considers himself to be detached from the congregation; he does not feel qualified to distribute the [elements of the] Lord's Supper. He does not baptize his own children; he does those of others, though sometimes he calls into question the competency of the parents to make the required [baptismal] promises. This is the condition under which we live, and although it is miserable in many ways, we do not see how we can cut ourselves off. We have long accused S[cholte] of being too harsh in his judgment of the people here, especially those who call themselves believers, but having become more familiar with the way things are here, he is not wrong [in his judgment].

You can readily conclude from the matters alluded to here that there is a great deal of division in ecclesiastical matters and the situation is far from what many of us had anticipated. There is a general desire for union, but among only a few is there the desire to do things in the right way, namely, the acknowledgment of wrongdoing and giving up all those rights that make everyone fear having to give in and to be the least. Being passive in all these matters, I would very much like for many things to be different. However, I am not depressed by it all. The Lord gives me boldness and confidence in my faith, and increasingly it is my experience that to be of one mind with the Lord is entirely independent of place and circumstance.

Feb. 17, 1853

Dear Mrs. Wormser,

If I do not at last start writing you again, it would be as if I wanted to imitate you in taking a long time to write you a letter. The long delay was not my fault at all. Often, and that has been true especially of late, I have to write letters on the spur of the moment, and, given the shortage of time for writing, the less pressing letters must wait. I am sorry that it was your letters to which this happened, but you can tell from the beginning that I had every intention of answering you soon.

What a grave and difficult time you lived through during the illness of your husband, your lying in, the death of your mother, and all the related circumstances. In the ecclesiastical sphere, there was also much suffering because of the disappointment regarding the Rev. Brummelkamp, etc., etc. But my dear friend, the Lord, in his own special way, can make things right for every one of his children; indeed, even making a good out of suffering, so that, as it were with one mouth, they must all say: everything was beyond our every prayer and thought. In this connection you speak of the concern and love you might experience in those difficult days to comfort and sustain you. Among others there was Mrs. Groen; I assume that it was a pleasure for you to make her acquaintance. In many respects she is a very blest and gifted Christian, making her most suited for the extensive field of work entrusted to her. When I had the pleasure of meeting Her Honor one time, things pertaining to Christianity were less clear to me; now I would profit from associating with her and enjoy it as well. Because of your present ecclesiastical standpoint, there naturally is much coming together between the dear *Haagsche Vrienden* [Hague Friends], whereas in the past they sensed a distancing [among them] because of that harsh word secession, which now seems to be somewhat softened. Everything we hear from the Netherlands gives us the impression that there is a great deal of Christian unity; and in general things are becoming much more religious; accordingly, some good can be anticipated in the future.

Beginnings are often the hardest. Once the ice is broken on one side or the other, there are soon plenty of followers, and so it all depends on the leaders, as, for example, here in Pella. How many people aren't there who long to see an altogether different ecclesiastical situation brought about! Everyone is talking about it, but no one gets to work on it other than to make suggestions, which are then rejected by others. And so unity remains a distant goal, and that in turn leads many to decide to do nothing at all. The consequences of such a situation are inevitably felt in a variety of circumstances, and these then sometimes lead to unpleasant conflicts, which even with the greatest Christian indulgence cannot always be prevented.

For the past two weeks I have had to be housebound because of the severe cold, and so I did not see anyone of Rev. Scholte's household, since these friends rarely come our way. This morning I sent Herman over there to inquire how the dominie and Marie were doing; they were struggling with colds. Henry, their oldest living child, then came over here and played at our house for a while. He was very sweet and made a pleasant impression on me, which had not been the case before. Having recently recovered from a grave illness, his moral disposition seems to have changed somewhat for the better. He was being treated by Dr. [J.J.M.C. Van] Nus [Nuys], now practicing in Pella, and taking the place of Dr. Roelofs [Joost Roelofsz] who, as you probably know, left for St. Louis. Mr. and Mrs. Van Nus will continue living in the home of Rev. Scholte. They have plenty of room, for not only is the house a large one, it is also being enlarged this summer. Besides, Mr. & Mrs. [Herman] Hasebroek [Hazebroek] have also moved to St. Louis, so their room was open.

I heard that S[cholte] preached again this afternoon. Antje and the children were present; I could not go because I am suffering a good deal from intestinal flu. Bousquet was prevented [from attending] because he left this past Tuesday to go to *Iowaville* [Iowa City] on behalf of matters relating to the steamboat. That is not a cut and dried affair either. There is already competition, and you know B[ousquet], he is easily discouraged, but just as easily he is enthusiastic about the business. Everything here is still so young and so new, and still there has been a remarkable development when you consider that only six years ago the Indians still were living here. The city is really growing and everywhere the farms are starting to be fenced in well. Last Wednesday a meeting was held for the purpose of forming an association in order to provide a safe crossing for people desiring to come this way. Several agents would be appointed, and of course the main office would be in Holland. A certain Van der Linden van Vuuren knows that there are a number of people over there who want to come over; and, as I think I heard, the Rev. Betten would really like to do it all on a larger scale. Since B[ousque]t was not present, I did not hear how it all turned out.

How is everything with you all? Do you still wish to come over some time? Or does the unlikelihood of it happening make you to give up on the idea? According to Mr. Van Nus [Nuys], in every respect things are better here than in Michigan with Van Raalte. V[an] N[uys] seems very much to prefer the prairies over the forests and assumes that because of his reporting many people will be coming here.

Last week Wednesday Mrs. Berkhout spent the afternoon with me. When she arrived I was still in bed, but, feeling well enough to get up, I did so, and she stayed with me in my room for supper. Antje [the maid] presides at the table at which now two more people are seated; we have employed a second girl to assist Antje and myself with some of the work; she is the daughter of a certain Hasselman, you probably know the name. And [we now have] a sweet American boy, fifteen years old, an orphan who wished to have a live-in arrangement so that he could go to school. Mr. Dwight, the present headmaster, now has over thirty young students and gives private lessons in the evening. He is not a run-of-the-mill person; he has studied, has the rank of professor, and, in Mount Pleasant where he came from, he was a preacher. This morning after Sunday school he also exercised that office, since Mr. Curtis who had promised to come was unexpectedly indisposed.

And now to return to Mrs. Berkhout. I promised to send you her compliments, and we agreed that I would inquire of you (also for myself) how the Luuring family is doing? And then that other person, both of us had forgotten his name, he works in the shipyard; and also where Mrs. Abrahams is now, and then also Huijding and his wife, and really about all the friends we know; and we send them our greetings and hope that all will be well with them.

How your girls must have grown. Of course they are of much help and make things easier for you. How everything has changed since the days that we got together at Buddes on Sundays [in the fellowship meeting]; but in the same way *all things* will gradually be changed in form until we all shall share in incorruptibility for *all eternity.*

Bousquet also has to go to Burlington again; and so we will again be hearing something about our friends, the Buddes. I believe that they are again very happy as far as church matters are concerned. Mrs. Berkhout told me that Le Cocq was making but little progress. His sons are beginning to get weary of all the heavy work; he himself suffers a good deal from rheumatism, and his wife still dislikes being in America. One of their younger sons and their youngest daughter make cigars, providing a very good means of support. I think I will just send this [letter] off without [waiting for] responses from B[erkhou]t and Rev. S[cholte] to the letter of your husband. If I have an opportunity to speak to S[cholte], I will ask him whether he has anything to say. Although I have not been all that prompt, you surely must write me once again this year. It is not so much the number of letters as their pleasant content that refreshes one's heart. Knowing that Mrs. Willink and her family are again spending the winter in Nice [France], I sent her a letter at that address. We still have not learned who became burgomaster after the death of Mr. Huidekoper. Well, my dear friend, after extending cordial greetings to you and your husband and children and also Mrs. Kol, I remain,

Your loving Friend and Sister in the Lord,
H. M. Bousquet - Chabot

Wormser 49

H. M. Bousquet-Chabot to J. Wormser-van der Ven
Pella, 1 March 1853

Dear Madam,
This morning Rev. Scholte brought me the enclosed note, which he himself put in with mine, and to be discrete I also had His Honor seal it. As a result, I lost the opportunity for adding a brief P.S as I had

Willem Lubberden (1838-1922), arrived in 1847 and farmed near Pella *(Souvenir History of Pella, Iowa, 1847-1922, Pella, 1922)*

intended. Now this will go separately and both epistles will reach you, thanks to Mrs. Van der Hoeven, my intermediary.

What I had wanted to add were a few things about Lubberde[n] and his family. They are doing well; he is getting on top of things and his son Willem works faithfully along with him. Their daughter Matje is now living in the city with Mrs. Van Citterd. Mrs. L[ubberden] was very seriously ill this fall, but now she is well again. They are also again attending the church of Rev. S[cholte], which was not the case formerly. Last week Wednesday Mrs. Berkhout again had supper with me. But this time it was downstairs with the entire family. She asked whether I had had asked you about Lothes and his wife, and I do that herewith, give them my regards.

How I would have liked to read what Scholte wrote you about the marriage of Saartje. Can you imagine, not once did he speak one word to us or to the other friends about this matter, so that people always had their doubts about it until Thursday, the 11th, when the children came home from school and said to me: "Well, Mama, now Saar is married after all. We saw Dr. Keabels going by in his bridegroom's suit. Mr. Curtis married them and the carriage is waiting [to take them] to Oscaloosa." It was as if someone had dumped a pail of water on my head. Oh well, on Friday I decided to go over there once to tell S[cholte] that after all that had happened we could not possibly attend his church on Sunday, without first having spoken to him. S[cholte] apologized by saying that everything had been as strange to him as it was to me, and since Saartje was of age, his refusal to give permission [for the wedding] had been to no avail. This is her third affair; I have detailed information on how strangely Scholte acted in two of those cases. I do think it is fortunate that Saartje is married. I regret that Bousquet's absence prevents him from adding anything. I received a letter from him that was postmarked Burlington; he was staying with Budde. They

J. A. Wormser's booklet *Infant Baptism* (1838), which so excited D. A. Budde

were all well and had gotten letters from you and a pamphlet on *Infant Baptism*. Bousquet hoped that Scholte would also have an opportunity to read it some time. And now Marie S[cholte] will not be able to complete her schooling, since she seems to have taken over the housekeeping chores from Saartje.

With cordial greetings to both of you, I remain,
Your loving Friend and Sister,
H. M. B[ousquet]

Chapter 6

The In-Between Years, 1853-1861
(Wormser Letters 50-61, Budde Letters 8-25)

The suspensions of Wormser, Budde, and Scholte became the occasion for [H.J.] Koenen to write Groen [van Prinsterer] on April 23, 1840: "I fear that our Seceding congregations have had their finest days (if there ever were such) during the persecutions, and that freedom has been a dangerous gift to them." The freedom of America was not a source of undivided joy for Scholte either. We are all familiar with the insinuations of Diekinga and Berkhout, the confidential letter of Hospers, and the published letter of Sipma. The dispute became so intense that Scholte was suspended in Pella.

Pella was intended as a city of refuge, a haven of rest, and a religious experiment. Scholte was opposed to clerical domination. He wanted a congregational church governed by the elders and deacons, without a preacher. The congregation should come into existence through its own faith initiative; the elders themselves should perform baptisms, administer Holy Communion, and expound the scriptures. Because of a shortage of preachers, the Seceders had already recognized a number of teaching elders, but usually they were soon elevated to the rank of preacher.

It was clear to Scholte that since the days of Constantine the Great, and again since the days of the Synod of Dort, the church had not been free from the state. While retaining the three Forms of Unity as the expression of his faith, he wanted to proceed exclusively on the basis of the Word of God. In so doing he sought to be freed from the Dutch and Calvinistic forms of culture and church organization. Scholte's ideal is comprehended in the name Pella [a place of refuge and freedom], but this freedom could not be realized in Pella. [Even in our time] the church still has to struggle to free itself from all the oppressive bonds of race, culture, and tradition, in order to be become a part of the free, worldwide church of Christ. Free from the state, free from nationalism and imperialism, and especially from the desire to have and exercise power.

On November 13, 1848, the church at Pella was constituted on the basis of these biblical premises by the elders: I. Overkamp, K. De Hoog, H. Barendregt, G. H. Overkamp, A. J. Betten, and the deacons: J. H. Meyer, E. F. Grafe, and P. Welle. Remarkably enough, Scholte himself was not present. Scholte had already been chosen as an elder July 24, 1848, and he often preached on Sunday afternoons.

From the letters of Henry Hospers we know that already in the beginning of 1849 there were complaints about Hendrik Scholte's handling of financial matters. Accusations were going back and forth between Scholte and the Overkamp brothers. Scholte then withdrew from the council, whereupon the elders Betten, Overkamp, and Barendregt reported that this was accepted, because Scholte was disobedient to the Word of God.

In the summer of 1849 new immigrants arrived, including Jan Hospers, who had written his son so astutely about Scholte (cf. Hospers 18). In September 1849 Scholte requested forgiveness for his actions, and after that he again preached as a teaching elder. But the wound did not heal. A nonpublicized matter was the cause for a new break-up on July 24, 1854. Charges were brought against Scholte, and he was visited by a committee consisting of A. J. Betten, A. C. Kuyper, J. Maasdam, I. Overkamp, J. Meyer, J. Van Vliet, and J. F. Le Cocq. According to the charge, Scholte had sold land belonging to the church to a third party. Scholte denied that the church owned this property. He claimed that it was only a matter of making a tentative promise, one that he had every right to withdraw now that he was offering another plot of land in its place. The Christian Church severed relations with Scholte and took the matter to court, which judged in Scholte's favor!

And what was the cause? As president of the Emigration Association, Scholte brought to Pella the chest that contained the money of others as well as his own. With these monies he bought as much land as possible. The members of the association each got a plot of this land.

Compared to all the others, Scholte had a lot of money. He had no use for a farm. He purchased sections 3 and 10 for himself, that is, the entire area within which Pella was being developed. As far as the court was concerned, Scholte was the undisputed owner of the land in Pella.

However, Scholte did not wish to make this public. That was partially the reason why the [final] reckoning was so slow in coming. As the land for the city was being resold, Scholte let the board of the Emigration Association determine the prices. And Scholte gave I. Overkamp and H. Barendregt each a plot of land for all the work they had done, and at the same time he gave a double lot to the church. The quarrel was about this latter plot of land. Scholte won [the case], because there was no deed of transfer nor any written copy of the [unofficial] promise.

But there was more to the matter. Scholte's wife, who was not happy in Pella, had very little interest in Scholte's church. And Scholte [himself] was no longer sufficiently interested in the church, because it no longer made sense to speak of *Volk en Vaderland* [People and Fatherland] in Pella. Scholte's power in Pella was too great because he owned all the land. Scholte wanted equality, but everyone knew that culturally and academically he was head and shoulders above them all. And the fact that Scholte was an Amsterdam urbanite, and continued to be so after his departure from the Netherlands, resulted in his taking a greater interest in American culture and politics than his followers could put up with. He was willing to be a minister of the Word of God in preaching, in publishing, and in political activities, but not as the leader of a church council wrangling about piffling matters. And especially not if they involved him in these matters.

Scholte was against clerical domination, a church in which the clergyman directed everything like an entrepreneur. But Scholte had no problem at all about acting as a capitalistic entrepreneur himself. The congregation at Pella did not have all things in common, as did the first congregation at Jerusalem after Pentecost. Pella was not without its capitalistic social structures.

The Christian Church in Pella, which carried on without Scholte, called A. J. Betten as its shepherd and preacher in July of 1855, even though K. De Hoog, J. Maasdam, and A. C. Kuyper continued as teaching elders. Next to it there was a Holland Reformed church, [but] without a minister. Here an elder had to read from a book of sermons, and the Dort Church Order was observed. Initially they still did this without being affiliated with the older (Holland) Reformed churches of the Reverends De Witt and Wyckoff.

In 1850 the churches of Van Raalte in Michigan were incorporated as an independent classis into the old Reformed Church [now Reformed Church in America]. In Iowa, the Burlington church of Budde was the first to affiliate with this denomination as a needy church requiring assistance, and which existed from 1853 to 1861. The preachers in Burlington were the Reverend J. B. Madoulet, 1835-1855; the Reverend [F.] Delvoa in 1858; and the Reverend Johan Muller, 1855-1861. In 1855 the Reverend John Garretson came from New York to visit Burlington and Budde.

In 1856 the Reverend A. C. Van Raalte, after paying a visit to Budde in Burlington, traveled on to Pella in order to receive the local church, which had been organized March 13, 1856, into the old Reformed denomination. This took place on September 19, 1856. The enclosed letter by Scholte, dated October 22, 1857, shows how closely he followed developments in the Netherlands, and even how he wished to go back. A letter by Van Raalte, written March 5, 1859, during another visit to Pella, shows how ministers, in their own intimate circle, think and write about each other.

The years 1850-1860 were comparatively quiet years. Napoleon III became emperor of France. In England Victoria experienced her happiest years beside Albert, and on March 20, 1852, Harriet Beecher Stowe's book *Uncle Tom's Cabin* appeared in Boston. The American fleet compelled Japan to open its ports in 1854, wars were waged in India and China, the Crimean War of 1855 halted Russian expansion to the Mediterranean Sea, and Italy became more and more unified during these years. And there is not much news to report from Burlington. In the letters we find what struck the Budde family most in the columns of the *Sheboygan Nieuwsbode*, first published in November 1849, and *De Hollander* [published in Holland, Michigan, since the summer of 1850].

The years from 1850 to 1860 saw many publications in the Netherlands. Because of his many articles in *De Nederlander*, J. A. Wormser was an important coworker of Groen van Prinsterer. Especially important was his book published by Höveker in Amsterdam in 1853: *De kinderdoop beschouwd met betrekking tot het bijzondere, kerkelijke en maatschappelijke leven*, [*Infant Baptism, Considered With Respect to Individual, Ecclesiastical, and Social Life*]. Groen republished this book in 1864.

Groen's *De Nederlander* had to cease publication in 1853. In that year Scholte started a new paper, the *Pella Gazette*, in which he voiced his views on American culture, particularly in the area of politics. From Scholte's enclosed letter to the prime minister, J. J. L. van der Brugghen, it is evident that he was also interested in politics in the Netherlands. In 1857 Van der Brugghen introduced the mixed public school, its purpose being to provide instruction in Christian and social virtues. There was no place in it for confessionally based instruction. Groen van Prinsterer left the chamber in protest. This breech constituted the deepest contrast within the anti-revolutionary alignment, and Scholte opted for Van Brugghen, because this involved a consequence of the separation of church and state. In this regard Scholte and Van der Brugghen went much further than Groen. Groen's historical contribution, *Hoe de onderwijswet van 1857 tot stand kwam* [*How the Education Law of 1857 Came About*], clearly showed that a most fundamental matter was at stake here. From the 124 letters in this volume, we cite only the beginning of letter 122:

To [J. J. L.] Van der Brugghen   August 5, 1857

> Most Honorable Sir! I have left your letter unanswered for several days, because the question, "How shall I reply?" repeatedly was a source of embarrassment to me. You are a friend of mine, in the fullest sense of the word, and have been for years on end. Someday you will be my friend again, at least that is my hope and prayer. But to call you that in the present circumstances is scarcely compatible with complete integrity, at least if it is more than just a word, especially given the gravity and great import of the matter which now brings about this separation between us.

Petitions against the Van Brugghen Law were addressed to the king. Wormser also sent a petition to the king. On August 11, 1857, he wrote about this matter to Groen:

> I therefore dictated to my wife the petition which is familiar to you. A young friend wrote it up in perfect form on stamped paper; my hand was then sufficiently healed (from rheumatism) that I was barely able to write my signature. The petition has only six signatures. I have made it a family affair; it was my wish that it be very clear to the Government from whom this petition was coming.
>
> Signers: J.A. Wormser, J. Wormser-van der Ven, their daughters J. and C. Wormser, his brother Andries N. Wormser, and the widow Hall-Pieterse.

Behind the enclosed letter from Scholte follows the beginning and the conclusion of the Wormser petition.

The independent *Pella Gazette*, published by H.P. Scholte and F. H. Grant, carried the following advertisements in its first issue of February 1, 1855

Henry P. Scholte

Attorney and Counsellor at Law and Notary Public.
Pella, Marion County, Iowa.

Is prepared to act as General Land Agent and also to do business for those countries where the Holland, French, German or Latin languages are, or were used in legal and governmental transactions.

Office, Washington Street, North East
Corner of the Garden Square.

B. F. Keables, M.D.,

physisian (sic) and surgeon
Pella, Iowa

Office on Washington Street, North West
Corner of the Garden Square.

Portrait Painting
Henry G. Nollen

Persons desirous of obtaining likenesses of themselves or relatives can be accommodated on reasonable terms by calling at my studio. I can be found for the present at the Book Store on Washington Street, west of the Garden Square. Instruction in this accomplishment can also be given to those desiring to obtain it.

John Nollen

Teacher of Mathematics, Natural Sciences,
French and German and
Vocal and instrumental Music

Pella, Iowa.

The painter Gerrit H. Nollen, born March 6, 1830, at Diedam in Gelderland, came from the Netherlands to Pella with his parents and three sisters, arriving there in 1854. Several of his portraits and some very good paintings of Pella survive. In 1858 Jan Nollen published a small book: *De Hollanders in Iowa, brieven uit Pella van een Geldersman* [*The Hollanders in Iowa, Letters from Pella by a Gelderlander*]. It was published with two plates of paintings by G. H. Nollen: Pella in 1848 and Pella in 1856. The little painting of Pella in 1848 is famous as the first depiction of a town at the edge of civilization. Nevertheless, the depiction is a reconstruction, because Nollen did not arrive in Pella until six years later.

Although John Nollen later published a good overview of *De Afscheiding*, there is nothing in his book about church life. He reports on the first municipal government as follows:

> The following dignitaries have been designated: that of mayor, Mr. Ellis (American). Of the [councilmen] three are Hollanders and three are Americans. The three Hollanders are: J. Berkhout, J. Estreng, and H. Hospers. The treasurer, also a Hollander, is I[saac] Overkamp; the marshall, J. F. Nauhuys, is also from Holland. The recorder or secretary is Hugo Kuyper (Hollander).[1]

From an ecclesiastical standpoint, the visit of Van Raalte to Pella in 1856 was of the greatest importance in connection with the union with the old Dutch Reformed denomination, which he had arranged. Under the leadership of A. C. Kuyper and A. J. Betten, they were once again placing themselves under classical and synodical jurisdiction. A year later Betten returned to Scholte. When no minister wanted to come to Pella, it was decided in 1858 that the preachers Oggel, Van Raalte, and Vander Meulen would work in Pella by turns, for periods of six weeks. Van Raalte came to Pella for the second time in February 1859. His letter to Rev. [J. H.] Donner arrived after Brummelkamp had already written in September 1858 [1859] "that they should give up any idea of getting Rev. Donner from Leiden, because His Reverence could not be spared in the Netherlands."[2] Donner again declined in 1858 [1859]. Finally, the Rev. P. J. Oggel, a son-in-law of Van Raalte, arrived in Pella January

---

1. Jan Nollen, *De Afscheiding* (Orange City, Iowa: De Volksvriend Printing House, 1898), 121.
2. Van Stigt, *Gescheidenis van Pella*, 3:1-7.

The Rev. Pieter J. Oggel, first pastor of the First Reformed Church, Pella (1860-1863) *(Souvenir History of Pella, Iowa, 1847-1922, Pella, 1922)*

15, 1859 [1860]. He stayed there until 1863, when he became an instructor at the Holland Academy in Holland, Michigan, Van Raalte's school. In 1861 he and Hendrik Hospers purchased the printing shop of the *Pella Gazette* and started *Pella's Weekblad* with news; alongside this [weekly], Oggel in 1862 started a monthly for Christian living, entitled *Pella's Maandblad*. He died December 13, 1869, in Holland, Michigan.

Meanwhile, a number of the emigrants thought that the old Reformed Church in America had strayed [from the truth] like the *Hervormde Kerk* in the Netherlands. And even as they had opted for the Van Velzen branch of the Seceders in the Netherlands, so now in America they also thought that they had to secede. In Michigan they turned against Van Raalte, and in April 1857 a number of groups seceded from the Reformed Church in order to establish the Christian Reformed Church. The Seceders in the Netherlands justified this action, and especially after 1872 many new immigrants found it easy to affiliate with this new denomination. While Van Raalte turned against Scholte in Pella, people in Michigan turned against Van Raalte. A Christian Reformed church was also established in Pella, but not until August 2, 1866. The Rev. H. R. Koopmans, a student of H. de Cock, who "had always opposed the free principles of the Rev. Brummelkamp," was the first preacher of the Christian Reformed Church in Pella between 1867 and 1869.

The congregation of Scholte did not have a church council after 1854. Until his death in 1856, A. E. Dudok Bousquet also occupied the pulpit occasionally when Scholte was ill. Scholte was chairman of the weekly congregational meetings and his son-in-law, Piet Hein Bousquet, was secretary. Kommer Van Stigt, who wrote the history of Pella, also belonged to this congregation.

In conclusion, we give an anecdote about interpersonal relationships in Pella. Nikolaas Hospers, born March 4, 1836, the younger brother of Hendrik, did not marry until 1883. His eldest daughter, Hendrieka, born March 3, 1885, went to school under Isaac Overkamp, who died October

21, 1895. On September 30, 1974, she told me that Overkamp was always very serious and began to stutter when he became emotionally involved. She had gotten good, solid instruction from him, also in the Dutch language. She recited [a well-known children's poem] by [Hieronymus] Van Alphen [1746-1803]: *"Jantje zag eens pruimen hangen"* [Little Johnny saw some prunes hanging one day], and she was still enthusiastic about *"De Tocht naar/ De Overwintering op Nova Zembla"* ["The Journey to...: Winter Survival on Nova Zembla"] as related by [Hendrik] Tollens [1780-1856]. In 1851 Hendrik Hospers married Cornelia Welle, and in 1854 he was working as a land agent in Pella. Under his direction, lands belonging to the Overkamp brothers, to J. De Haan, and to A. E. Dudok Bousquet were added to the Pella municipality. The Overkamp brothers wished to have a second cemetery on their land, separate from the Scholte cemetery. Thereupon, Hendrik Hospers, who was dismayed, went to see his friend, the stuttering Overkamp. He realized that his children would never bury him in the much more distant Overkamp cemetery. That is why he was fiercely opposed to the Overkamp cemetery plan, because Hendrik Hospers did not want to be separated from them in the resurrection.

These stories surfaced after I had tried for a long time to get her permission to borrow the family archives in order to copy them. She [Hendrieka Cook-Hospers] would not surrender the documents, because you can have no trust in human beings, only in the Lord God. And because the copy machine could not be moved, she then went along with me herself. And so she related her childhood memories to me during the hours that we were copying her archives under her very eyes: the letters of her uncle, Hendrik Hospers, and the letters and the diary of her grandfather, Jan Hospers.

This chapter also contains eighteen Budde letters, mostly sent from the Johan Wormser family in Amsterdam to the Buddes in Burlington, Iowa. Mrs. Janke Wormser and her teenage children, Jansje, Cato, and Johan Jr., penned most of the letters, but letters from a family friend Johanna Schellinger of Alkmaar and from Mrs. Henriette Bousquet in Pella are interspersed. These missives kept the Buddes well informed about church life and personal news. "Our hearts will not let go of the Netherlands," vowed Diedrich Budde to Wormser (Wormser 53). Pella was another matter altogether. Scholte's doings disgusted Budde and his friends, the Bousquets, and quashed any thoughts of the Buddes to resettle there. In Budde Letters 24 and 25, Diedrich Budde informed the Wormsers concerning the fledgling Burlington Dutch Reformed Church, of which he was the lead elder. His 1858 address to the congregation (copy in Budde 24) reflects the motif of spiritual pilgrimage that pervades Budde's thinking [RPS].

Wormser 50

D. A. Budde to J. A. Wormser and Spouse
Burlington, 29 May 1854

Beloved Friends, Dearly Beloved Brother and Sister in the Lord!

It seems that in America time flies past even faster than in Holland; weeks often go by so fast that they seem more like days, and the months like weeks. When I think to write Your Honor tomorrow, it [actually] takes so long that afterward I blame myself for not having written immediately, and therefore forgive me. It is high time that I reply to your esteemed letter of last February 4. The pamphlets Het Roomsch katolicismus, de Bischoppen, Het Protestantisme, [Roman Catholicism, Bishops, Protestantism] [which had been] placed beside the ballot boxes, we received last summer; and although the author's name [J. A. Wormser] was not given, for us there was no mistake about it, even as I wrote in my letter of last September, but which Your Honor did not receive. When we were reading those pamphlets and the one about infant baptism, it was like old times when we got together on winter evenings to discuss various subjects, and always time was too short, and then we looked forward to another get-together. Having read the above pamphlets, we immediately started walking to and fro in order to share this important good news with others and to spread it about. And since you write that you have been saving another pamphlet for us until you find out whether we have received the above mentioned pamphlets, by now there probably is still another one, and we look forward to them all with great interest. I have often asked myself: from where does *he* get all this wisdom!

From the pamphlets it is evident you are moved with zeal and fire from on high to put the grace and the strength which the Lord grants you to work to expend them in the service and preservation of the church in the Netherlands. The Lord grant that you may still see the wonderful fruits of your work, for the Netherlands has been sunk in a deep morass in recent times, so that it may again serve and honor the God of our fathers. We rejoice in the fact that the Lord is raising up more men in the Netherlands who stand up for the honor of King Jesus, to oppose the total decadence, even though it always constitutes only a small number over against the great host of people who reject the Lord. And yet they cannot be defeated, because their struggle is not in their own strength but in the name of the Lord, even as David overcame Goliath and put the army of the Philistines to flight. Even if you must endure being exposed to contempt and name calling, it is the same thing that our blessed Savior had to endure, because the Enemies of the Lord and of his people cannot withstand the truth.

Blessed are ye, when men revile you...and say all manner of evil against you falsely....Rejoice and be exceeding glad for great is your reward in heaven [Matthew 5:11-12]. The Lord reigneth; that is our consolation, Beloved. Ps. 93. We still believe that we were led hither by the Lord at the right time, since all of Europe is in turmoil and will have to undergo very oppressive and anxious times. And although the Netherlands maintains its neutrality in the war [Crimean War, 1853-1856], nevertheless, we do not believe that it will be able to avoid the general misery but will have to share in much of it. For it is likely that trade and industry will be interrupted to a large extent because of it, and from what we hear, the desire of many to migrate to America confirms this impression.

Our congregation here is not growing much. We have to put up with a lot of grief. It is small, consisting of seventeen families, all by ourselves, over against all the other denominations. We are under very strict scrutiny, and as I wrote you before, the family of our minister does not conduct itself in a Christian manner, and as a result he lost his influence both inside and outside the congregation. So we had no choice but to dismiss him, and accordingly he will be leaving us in the month of July. There is a lot of work involved in getting another minister who can preach in High German and in Dutch. There are six of us who do not understand High German; the others all do—and most of us do not understand English either, so that it is more likely that we will again get a minister who has studied in America and can also preach in High German, rather than one who knows High German and Dutch. The Classis of Illinois is interested in keeping a Holland Reformed Church in Burlington. Although we will not build a church yet this summer, nevertheless we hope and trust that the Lord will make all things well and will not let us become orphans. The Lord is our Shepherd.

I received a letter from Captain Portenge[n], which I immediately answered. Mrs. Schilp, her husband and child, are healthy and well. Burlington is expanding tremendously. The land bordering the city, which I could buy for 20 dollars an acre seven years ago, has been sold for 150 dollars an acre; and that is also part of the reason that not more Hollanders are settling here, since the land in Pella, Michigan, and Wisconsin is not that expensive. Now, loved ones, may you receive this letter in good health and well-being; that is my wish. May the Lord ever be with you and grant you his blessing and multiply his grace by the outpouring of the Holy Spirit upon your children; we send them all cordial greetings. The promise is sure: I am thy God and the God of thy seed after thee in their generations. Most cordial greetings, also from Jan and Mrs. Teleman; we look forward to hearing from you again soon and ask that you remember us in your prayers. I remain

Your loving Brother in Christ,
D. A. Budde

From Ost Friesland we heard that my brother's eldest daughter died in the Looijerstraat [in Amsterdam].

Budde 8

Mrs. J. Wormser-van der Ven to Mrs. C. M. Budde-Stomp
Amsterdam, 26 August 1854

Dearly Beloved Friend and Sister in the Lord!

Yesterday we had a visit from your brother in the Looijerstraat, who told us that his son was planning to set sail early next month with the intention of traveling to you all. I did not want to pass up this opportunity to write you, something I gladly do, but I would even prefer to meet you once! O, how often I think of you, and what would I not give if we could speak to each other once, but that is just the way things are. We will have to make do with letters until the day of reunion dawns when we will never again be separated.

We were deeply moved by your important letter, that the Lord had sent such a visitation upon the family of our friend Jan. But we rejoiced that the chastisement is working such a peaceable fruit of righteousness in him. If only it might behoove the Lord to fully restore his wife again in the body and cause them to walk together before his countenance, then one can bear the adversity more patiently, and the gold becomes so much more glorious in the melting pot. Do give them our most cordial greetings, please.

I am glad that Diederich [Diedrich] can still remember us. Our Johan remembers as little of you as [your] Maria does of us, but Jansje and Cato do much better. When your birthday approaches, they say, if Mrs. Budde were here, we would be sure to get *oliekoeken* [fat balls]. You inquire about our niece Mietje, whether there is any indication of the Lord working in her. The only thing I can say is that we are on a friendly basis, but we do not see much of each other. However, from her early childhood on I always thought that Mietje was much sweeter than her sister Lina, and that is still the case. Recently Mietje expressed to Cato her desire to join a catechism class with Rev. [J.P.] Hasebroek, just like Cato [was doing], but I still do not know whether anything will come of it. I am glad that Jansje Teeleman [Teleman] is out among people, and I hope that things will go well for her. But I cannot recall who Naatje van der Moor is; do let me know sometime.

The people of our fellowship are getting older, like Gunther, and Jansen, a son of Gunther, married a daughter of the midwife Petersen. Kaatje Lijsen is also about to get married, but the daughters of Jaspers are still at home. [J.W.] Luuring still visits us faithfully; his son Willem now works at an office, but every Saturday afternoon he comes over to walk or play together. They do not appear to be getting any more children, and it also seems that our Henriette will remain the smallest [youngest], although I cannot be sure of anything as yet, it seems.

I looked at the picture of Burlington on your last letter, and then I wondered where your home might be located. When you write me again, which I hope will be soon, and on paper like that, put a mark on it, so that we can say more or less, that is where our friends live.

My sister Rica is living in the country [with the lady she works for], but she wrote me that she had coughed up blood again. It was about four times on one day, but it was not as much as it was this winter. In every letter I get from her she complains about weakness and coughing. I only hope that it is the will of the Lord that we may still keep her a while longer. She is my only remaining sister, but as far as we can tell, we need not be concerned about her passing away. I believe her passing will be peaceful. How fortunate that is, because in her condition she could be taken from us unexpectedly. Our sister Leentje in Overijssel also died unexpectedly last March, so that our brother is now a widower with nine children. They were happy together, and then missing each other is not something to be wished for. But for her there was no joy in living, and the children do not miss her much because in the last few years she paid no attention at all to the housekeeping. Fortunately, their oldest daughter, Leentje, is an energetic and nice girl who, with some assistance, is certainly capable of running the household.

Since my husband intends to write your husband, I will leave ecclesiastical matters to him. There is a lot going on at present, as you will see from the booklets we send you from time to time. That is why I have now limited myself to telling you a few things about our old friends. Mrs. Abramsch [Abrahams] is living in Gelderland; she lives in with others, now here then there, and once a year she comes to the city [Amsterdam] and then we get a visit from her, which is still as trying and irksome as it ever was. The Willem, whom Lothes and his wife had taken in, died of consumption six or seven weeks ago. The teacher Scheepmaker also died about the same time, of nervous fevers [*zinckoorts*, literally, "sinking fevers"], leaving behind a widow with six children, three of whom are from his second marriage and are still very young. About the same time Mr. Da Costa lost a daughter to consumption; she left this life in glorious assurance. Your niece in the Loozestraat, about whom your husband inquired in his letter, has passed away. Another [niece] married a son of Krabbendam. Your nephew, we hope, will soon have occasion to tell you about that in person. May the Lord go with him in his travels and bring him safely to you.

Well, dear friend, I certainly have shared much news with you, both good and sad. I dare not say it was bad, because we do not know what is the best. Do make me happy with a letter soon. Jansje and Cato send cordial greetings. Give my greetings to your dear husband, Mrs. Teleman, your dear children, and if you speak to her...from us. I send my cordial greetings to you personally and commend you to the Lord.

Your Loving Friend and Sister in the Lord,
J. Wormser-van der Ven

Budde 9

J(ansje) Wormser to Mrs. C. M. Budde-Stomp
Amsterdam, 1 September 1854

Dear Madam!

Thanks to the goodness of the Lord we may all find ourselves in reasonable well being, and it is my heartfelt wish that you people, too, may enjoy this privilege. We could not pass by the opportunity to send you all a letter without having to pay postage, and that is the reason I am now sitting down to converse with Your Honors for a few moments. I can remember all of you very well, especially His Honor [Mr. Budde] and our friend Jan. How we would also like to see his wife and the baby once. Diederich [Diedrich] and Maria must both be grown up, and they must have changed a lot. I have a hazy recollection of Jansje Teleman, but I have no memory at all of Mrs. Teleman. Every day we think of you and talk about you, especially when one of you is having a birthday.

We now have a Secessionist maid from Utrecht, who will be going to America with her whole family next spring, the Lord willing. A brother and sister of hers left earlier with Rev. Scholte; her brother is living in Pella; her sister lives in St. Louis. The Rev. [De] Moen may also be going with his family. His wife is very eager to go. It is presently being rumored in Amsterdam that Rev. Scholte has died. However, no one knows for sure. The Reverends Van Velzen and Brummelkamp have been appointed as professors at a Secessionist Theological School in Kampen, and they have accepted.

Mrs. Zeelt and her aged gardener, madam Mijntje, are still pretty active. Mrs. [Zeelt] still comes to town now and then. Cato and I spent two weeks with her this summer. A quarter of a year ago Jaspers broke his leg; by now it is sufficiently healed so that the day before he was able to come over and visit us with a crutch and cane.

At father's request, Rev. Hasebroek visited him several times during the time he was not well. The Reverend himself is suffering quite a lot these days; we think that it must be rheumatism. He has not been able to preach for three Sundays in a row, and that is something I really miss; now I am hoping for next Sunday. In the Diaconal Orphanage he catechizes the girls on Tuesday evenings; that is very sweet of him. In the orphanage he is known as Daddy *Haasje* [a sweet, kindly rabbit]. He always has churches filled to the rafters, so that we have to be in church two hours ahead of time; a lot of people take books along, so they can read for a couple of hours.

One of the girls, with whom I made profession of faith, died on my birthday. Her name is Heintje Kropholder; it was wonderful how she passed away. Rev. Hasebroek made a funeral oration at her grave. She died of nervous fever and typhus fever. Things spoken during her illness and the funeral oration are to be published September 2. The Saturday work is now done, and now I take my seat to continue and to finish this letter. We sometimes see the son of Flurke [Flörke] at the children's mission fellowship, but I have not seen Mine in years.

Several weeks ago a terrible murder was perpetrated here. While the husband had gone to the market in the morning, the wife and three children and the maid were wounded terribly. Two children and the mother died the same day; the other six-year-old recovered, and with great effort she was brought to her father. The maid is still in the hospital. You can imagine the father's consternation when he came home. The wretch was a former worker. He was apprehended in England, where he had just bought a ticket to go to New York. The interrogation of the witnesses and trial must still take place. It has caused quite a tumult in the city.

I do not have any more news. It must be unusual for you to receive so many letters from Amsterdam all at the same time. I thank you sincerely for the wishes you expressed on my behalf in your previous letter. I hope that the Lord may confirm them unto me. The profession of faith by the catechumens has taken place. It so happened that the confirmation was by Rev. Spijker [apparently a liberal preacher]; of course we did not go. The rest of the girls had gone to Rev. H[asebroek] to ask what they should do, go or not go. He told them not to go, but one did go anyway. Rev. Hasebroek officiated at the Communion service in the Westerkerk. His text was, "Arise and eat, because the journey is too great for thee" [1 Kings 19:7]. Tomorrow I hope to hear him there again on the third commandment. Now, dear madam, I must conclude. Wishing you and your family the presence of the Lord, and also Jan and his wife, I sign myself with esteem,

Your loving Friend and Servant,
J. Wormser

Budde 10

J. A. Wormser to D. A. Budde
Amsterdam, 2 Sept. 1854

Beloved Friend and Brother in the Lord!

In all likelihood, your nephew will be leaving here on the 5th instant. My many preoccupations, especially in church matters, would almost deprive me of the opportunity to write to you. However, I do wish to send a letter to you, even if it be brief. I am sending along with your nephew the sermons of [Rev.] Beets and three catechisms which together come to four guilders. I am enclosing a petition to the synod and the church council and one to the king. They were written by me. From them and the brochure, *Het klassikaal Bestuur van Amsterdam* [*The Classical*

Directors of Amsterdam], as well as another about Dr. Meyboom, you can get some idea of the nature of our times. The fury and the boldness of the counter party are indescribable. It is clear that our human efforts are of no avail, and if the Lord does not intervene, the Netherlands is going to ruin, religiously and ecclesiastically. The synodical committee will be meeting for several days in order to make a pronouncement in the Meyboom case. Rev. Spijker is president [of the synod], so we can easily guess the outcome. We will still make an attempt to get the matter presented to synod, and to request the king to withhold approbation until after the verdict. However, as always, the synod is very partisan and very hostile. It will be meeting early in July and is meeting even now, for it is very busy. There is a regular shower of petitions from every region of the fatherland. The *Maatschappij tot Nut van 't Algemeen* [Society for General Welfare], of which Spijker is president, by a vote of 794 to 284 has approved the admission of Jews and Mohammedans as members of the society; and, mind you, the society still continues to profess that it maintains Christian principles. The eyes of many people, also those of many preachers, are indeed opening, but there are few people who can work [contribute], and especially most of our preachers are of no use to us. They reason, philosophize, and deal with everything on a *wetenschappelijke* [rational, scientific] basis. There will be no important changes for the good unless the so-called faithful pastors realize that the truth is a matter of life and death, of salvation or perdition.

The rumor is that cholera has broken out here [Amsterdam] and in Breda, but if it is the case in Amsterdam, it is very limited. Thanks to the goodness of the Lord, our health is reasonably good, but my wife and I sense more and more that the strength and vitality of youth are disappearing. It is especially my nerves that are weak, and the injustice in the church does not make things any better.

May these few lines do for now, dear friend! The Lord be with you and yours and cause his blessing to rest on you all. Give our greetings to your wife, to Jan and his wife, to your children, Mrs. Teleman and her daughter, and to other friends.

Your Loving Brother in Christ,
J. A. Wormser

Budde 11

C[ato] Wormser to Mrs. C. M. Budde-Stomp
Amsterdam, 2 Sept. 1854

Esteemed Madam!

The opportunity for me also to send a letter to you across the great wide ocean nicely fits in with my long suppressed desire. And so it is with pleasure that I take up my pen, even though Father and Mother have already written you all the main news from Europe. How much we would all like to see you and speak with you once again. I still have a very good recollection of all of you, only little Maria is beginning to fade a little from my memory. I never pass your home on the Achterburgwal without thinking of Your Honors. I also still have a keepsake that I received from Jan and Diederich [Diedrich], something they no doubt have long since forgotten.

I am taking a profession of faith class with Rev. Hasebroek and if I am spared, God willing, I expect to be confirmed as a full member at Christmas time. Who would ever have thought that, when we were taking catechism classes with Father in the back room with all our friends around us, and Diederich [Diedrich] sitting on the small black velvet chair next to Father. But those enjoyable hours are a thing of the past, and all the things we could talk about together then, now must be compensated for by pen and paper.

The rumor in Amsterdam is that Rev. Scholte has died, but no one has the letter. It's like that time long ago when you left [for America] and were just at sea and there was a rumor that the ship on which you were sailing had perished with all hands on board. Well now, when you answer this letter, do write us whatever information you can about Rev. Scholte; it is news we are very eager to hear. His picture is still in the very same place in the side room. The Seceders have moved their seminary from Arnhem to Kampen, where the Reverends Brummelkamp and Van Velzen will be teaching. But no minister has been called to take the place of Rev. Van Velzen yet. Well, loved ones, the letters have to get to your brother, and so I will have to break off my conversation with you now. If the journey was not so far, how I would like to pay you a visit like we used to do. May the Lord make you experience his nearness in a rich measure, and also our friend Jan and his family, that is the sincere wish of,

Your ever affectionate Friend,
C. Wormser

Budde letterhead, with view of Burlington, Iowa

Wormser 51

C. M. Budde-Stomp to Mrs J. Wormser-van der Ven
Burlington, Iowa (1854?)

Dearly Beloved Friend and Sister in the Lord,
 In my thoughts I often write to you all, my dear friend. I am very glad to hear something about how you are doing, and about our fatherland. You have made me very happy by your letter, and I hope that Your Honors receive this letter in good health. We are quite well these days; my husband has been suffering much from headaches so that working is difficult for him. As I lost my youth, I began putting on weight, so that I have had to let out my clothes. Recently I had considerable dizziness and congestion in my chest. After the death of our grandson, our daughter-in-law Lena had caked breasts, so that she had to undergo surgery; after that she had an infection in her womb, which was not without danger, so that for fourteen weeks she had to be moved from one bed to another. First it was Mrs. Teleman who cared for her and then Jansje; her parents lived close to them, and they provided much assistance. But to our great joy, the question of her salvation began to trouble her; the Lord will continue [his work in her] and bring it to completion. I happened to be with her when I received your most welcome letter, and I said [to her], "My friend sends you greetings and counts you among the people who fear and serve the Lord; that's right, isn't it?" Deeply moved, she said, "When you write also give her my greetings." This affliction was barely over when there was another.
 We got together for a worship service on Sunday [at our home], because our preacher has had a serious illness. In the course of the following week, Johan raised serious objections to being a farmer any longer. His one horse had developed a serious swelling in the chest, and

when it got worse the horse could no longer work, and buying another, borrowing money at 15 percent interest, he did not care to do. But the main thing is that he is not a genius when it comes to farming, and with an ailing wife things were very difficult for him. Since it was the beginning of March, he could give up his rental lease, sell his farm equipment and cattle, and move to the city to look for work there. He ended up in an iron shop running a lathe; he earns one dollar a day, so that his hand skills are still serving him well. This unexpected change shocked me greatly, but since not a hair falls from our head without the will of our heavenly Father, we wish to remain silent before God; we cannot comprehend the [eternal] counsel of the Lord. His wife is so weakened in her vision that she must start wearing glasses at once; she remained so stiff in her legs that she could not climb a stairs and had difficulty walking, and subsequently that developed into swollen water [legs], and now she is again under a doctor's care. In the midst of all of this, Johan has gotten closer to the Lord and manifests a manly clinging to him who directs all his ways. The elder of his young sons is a sweet and clever child of 2 ½ years.

I was very glad that your sister Rica, to your great joy, has been spared and is still in the land of the living; but even more so that she has reached the decision that for her to die is gain. Give her my warmest greetings. Your joy in the privilege of having come nigh to the Table of the Lord with your eldest daughter at the year's beginning, we share. Our Holland congregation also gathered at the Table of the Lord. Because of the severe cold I had not attended; for I cannot take it very well to behold before me the visible elements the crucified Christ has gained for us, and to do so joyfully in faith. My dear little Jansje, before the Lord, just ask yourself his invitation once: My son, my daughter, do you give me your heart? Is your desire an earnest one? Yes, Lord, make my heart your temple and let it be the dwelling of your Spirit in time. My dear Jansje, the future is dark. Your youthful heart will encounter many lovers. Have you chosen the one and only, namely the Bridegroom of souls? He is the mighty one who will crush all his enemies, and he will begin and complete his work in you, to the praise and glory of his great name.

My dear friend, how I would like to join in Catechism with you all; it grieves me to have forgotten so much of our former [Heidelberg] Catechism, and that we need so much to be mindful of the Holy Spirit in order to be led into all truth. It gives me great pleasure by writing about the characteristics of your dear children, because you had the last two after our departure. Diedrich does not forget you people, but

Maria thinks of your brother Dries and his two little daughters. Mietje has drawn my attention on occasion because of her special gentleness and diligent activity, often when her younger sister Leentje mistreated her. Might there be something good for the Lord in that?

Diedrich is a slow learner; he still does not know his [multiplication] tables. He has been learning them for so many years; he does do his best at the English school, and also in Sunday school, so that he has received several commendations and an English Bible from his teachers. He knows Bible [stories] fairly well, and he is eager to hear them. They are also learning catechism, and then my husband talks to them about it in simple language. During the summer it is rather difficult because of the many activities. He is diligent, honest, but very quick-tempered; he is respectful and attentive and he sometimes asks questions that show that the truth is taking hold in his heart. His present stance seems to be more what must I *do* to be saved, than in accepting and embracing Jesus *by faith*. Maria has a quicker mind, but she has a slender frame. It took considerable effort for her to learn to read Dutch with me, and she practices by asking questions. She is very sensitive when she is punished for some misdeed or other. Jansje T[eleman] started working as a maid at the home of our English doctor this spring; the Mrs. is still of Dutch descent. She is very capable and orderly (which is very good for Janjse because her natural tendency is to be rather slow and careless), and she is very religious. Mrs. Teleman is healthy and she is still with us. Naatje van der Moor is heavier than our Maria, but she is a slower learner.

Cordial greetings to you all; remember us in your prayers.

Your Friend and Sister in the Lord
who is always thinking of you,
C. M. Budde-Stomp

Wormser 52

C. M. Budde-Stomp to J. Wormser-van der Ven
Burlington, November 1854

Dearly Beloved Friend and Sister in the Lord,

The arrival of our nephew R. Budde was very unexpected. Mr. Busman, a Methodist minister who also was born in Leer [Ost Friesland], exchanged letters with my husband at the request of the latter's honorable family who also live in Amsterdam, [requesting] that when my nephew arrives in New Orleans, we be helpful in getting him here to us. Thanks to the goodness of God, our nephew arrived healthy and hale at our son Johan's the 17th of November. And in this way your precious letter in the package reached us. Your well being is cause for our rejoicing

This summer an open inflammation developed on my leg, and the leg was so swollen that I could not put on a stocking. And when I tried to stand on it, the pain was so excruciating that I had to crawl on my knees to get from one room to the next. The doctor prescribed medicine for a poultice and salve, and so it slowly healed again. Before I had recovered, my daughter-in-law contracted cholera; the entire family gathered about her bedside. Wearing a slipper and with my leg bandaged, I came along with my dear husband in our little wagon. Her suffering is grievous; the heart appears to be constricted by cramps. The doctor said that if she did not start sweating, she would be a corpse by night. We had our Dutch water bottles with us and laid those on either side of her, warm irons at her feet, warm blankets over her body; every ten minutes we gave her medicine and rubbed her abdomen with medicine. The Lord heard our sighing and gave deliverance. She began to perspire profusely, was extremely exhausted, but the Lord restored her slowly, to the great joy of all of us. My dear husband has quite some chest problems, so that he must guard against doing any hard work.

You have made me very happy by letting me know how our friends are doing. Once a week we have a *Sheboygan Nieuwsbode* from Wisconsin and *De Hollander* from Michigan. They [provide] a good deal of information on what is going on in Europe and in the Netherlands. Recently it included an announcement about the three young Hoedemakers. The son of the Rev. [Cornelis] Vander Meulen and C. Vander Veen—a son by the second wife of the coppersmith Vander Veen (Egbert Vander Veen is married and runs an iron and tin shop)—upon passing their exams, were taken to New Brunswick, New Jersey, by the Rev. Vander M[eulen] to begin their higher education. Another announcement said that a son of the deceased Rev. [G.] Baai had already spent 2½ years at a college for higher education. There was also a story about the sad accident of Rev. [Seine] Bolks of Grand Haven. On the 26th of September, Rev. Bolks and his wife and three youngest children took a carriage to the Holland colony in order to visit sick friends. While crossing the bridge at Port Sheldon, the horse became frightened, reared back, backing off the bridge into the creek where the water is thirty feet deep. Thanks to the assistance of H. Witte and Vijn, the minister and his wife were saved, [but] the children, six years, four years, and six months old, drowned; the horse also drowned.

Whether the Rev. Scholte has died, we still have not heard. My dear friend, you inquire about Naatje van der Moor. Her parents were from Hoorn [Province of Noord-Holland]; he was a painting foreman and had a son now twenty years old, and Naatje ten, just as old as our Maria. They sailed on the same ship with a party of Zeelanders. We were not exactly friends, because he was loud-mouthed and mocked religion. He had abstained from alcohol for six years but then got hooked again, hastening his death. When your brother Dries arrived, the man was eager for more friendship, and they also corresponded. The man had a hard time at first; there was not much call for painting at the time. So he had to make a living by sawing wood and working as a laborer carrying bricks. Then people here and there began to have some painting done; and people were so satisfied that he had plenty of work. His wife had a fit of insanity, whereupon he came to us for advice and assistance. Then Mrs. Teleman took over the housekeeping for four months. She had scarcely gotten home again when the man took ill and died after eight days. He asked if we would take his little daughter and take care of his affairs. After he was buried, Jan took his wife to the poor house, about four miles from here, and that is where she died. She has a sister who lives in Alkmaar, Naatje Schellinger, a domestic. She was quite concerned about the children and she still writes us from time to time.

I would not be able to point out to you our residence on the drawing (see letterhead Wormser 51). In the middle of the street there is a [covered] lean-to like the one on the Fish Market, and that is where the market is. From there a plank road goes as far as Mount Pleasant Road, and our house is a half-hour walk from the city, just a little to the left. The area used to be all woods, but now there are several houses, and so now it is known as Germantown. The city limits have already been extended, so that now we are almost part of the city. Our land is now worth $150 dollars an acre. They are also building a railroad.

The town has grown tremendously. There are four large buildings on four hills for schools, a big church for the Methodists, and a Catholic one. Oh, that the Lord may some day grant us a Reformed one. We have already purchased a lovely lot or plot on this same elevation. We are presently without a shepherd, and so building has been postponed for a time. The foundry or factory where Johan works is located on the river and his house is on the hill overlooking the city and the workshop.

In October Mrs. Schilp, her husband and their little son, paid me a visit. She had given birth to a stillborn baby girl. She had suffered much again, but now she was back on her feet once more. They have experienced quite a number of setbacks. We have had a widespread drought this summer, so that for the most part there has been a meager harvest and that has affected everyone. They also lost a horse and two foals, so that they had to buy another: they cost one hundred dollars these days. Just now we had another visit from Schilp, his wife, and son. They had received a letter, which said that Capt. Portenge[n] was in New York. They answered the letter immediately, so the Capt. would send them money. If the Capt. comes to New York again some time, he would really make his sister [Leentje Schilp-Portengen] happy by coming over for a visit. Just recently, a God-fearing German family, Mr. Biezenbroek, a schoolmaster from Russia, made it from New York to Burlington in fifty-three hours by railroad. If the Capt. were interested, my husband would be willing to take him to his family speedily. She sends greetings to all of you; writing is difficult for her.

Your cordial letters, my dear friends Jansje and Cato, made us deeply happy. It is very clear to us that we may be out of sight but not out of mind to our dear friends and their progeny. Love is wondrous and sweet, stronger than death; it flows from God and returns to him. The mark of the early Christians was: see how they love each other. My joy is great that you dedicate your youthful hearts to the Lord. He is so worthy of it and he is so great for you, who trust in the Lord as Mount Zion. If our flesh and heart should falter, he remains our rock unto all eternity. You see that the Lord can also come to young people, like H. Kropholder. How blessed it is to belong to the Lord. Is it a niece of Mrs. Loheize who was staying with Simons de Smit? May the grace of the Lord and his presence be poured out upon you abundantly; that is the prayer of your friend and sister in the LORD who thinks of you always.

C. M. Budde-Stomp

If your domestic leaves, surprise me again with your letters. Kiss your Johan and Henriette for me.

Budde 12

> Mrs. J. Wormser-van der Ven to Mrs. C. M. Budde-Stomp
> Amsterdam, the 8th of May 1855

Dearly Beloved Friend and Sister in the Lord!

Your esteemed letters of last November 1854 [W 52, 53] we received in reasonable well being, and, as ever, it was a pleasure to hear something from you people. I should have answered long ago, but the days and weeks fly by. I had better not wait with writing until my maid leaves; she had expected to be gone already by May, and that is why I hired another one. But until now they [she] do[es] not have a letter [of appointment], much less any money, but now she is working as a maid elsewhere.

We were sorry to hear that you all have experienced much illness, and especially your daughter-in-law who is ailing so terribly. Early this year my husband again suffered much from rheumatism. From time to time I still suffer from my old ailment: headaches. In all of this the Lord continues to spare our lives, and so we were able to celebrate our twenty-first wedding anniversary yesterday. How numerous are the mercies of the Lord and how great is his faithfulness. It was granted to us to have a good living with our five children; when we celebrated our 12½-year anniversary you were here with us. I do not believe that missing each other is compensated for on this side of the grave. It is rare to find men who are such kindred spirits, and the same is true for women, as was the case between you and us. Even if it is true of men sometimes, then I still do not find a friend in the wife, and vice versa. But such fellow strugglers and fellow travelers, so akin to each other, must be the outgrowth of experience, and that is just the way things are. And our hope remains that in eternity we will not be separated from each other, but that we will praise the Lord together eternally for his leading in our lives.

During the winter we had a gentleman here, a Mr. Hagen[s] from Pella, for whom we made inquiry among all our friends. He came here looking for a Dutch wife, and when his desire was fulfilled, he left again in the spring. He knew you by name. He would not say anything good or bad about Scholte. Berkhout was doing well, and should he live a while longer, he probably will go back to Holland again. Initially Lubberd[en] had a hard time, but now he is doing well. And that was also true for Le C[ocq]: he was poor when he left with Scholte, but now he is prosperous.

Bousquet lost quite some money in his business. We knew of the sad case of Rev. Bolks; he received a call to the congregation of Zonne. Rev. Oggel, from Utrecht, received a call to Grand Haven, and he accepted. He expects to leave soon, much to the regret of his congregation; he is reputed to be a dear evangelical Christian. The Seceders here still do not have a pastor since Van Velzen went to Kampen. They called [Rev. P.M.] Dijksterhuis, but he declined; he did not care to go to the mixed-up congregation of his brother-in-law. Now they have called De Bruin, but it is likely that he also will decline. Almost every week they have had a minister preaching for them, but rarely one who was narrow-minded enough to suit them. From what we hear, no one wants to go to Amsterdam, "for," they say, "that split congregation needs to be worked on to get it united again." To our knowledge, and as far as our friends and we are concerned, there is not the slightest desire to do that. We do not wish to be deprived of our freedom again and to allow ourselves to be subjected to a human yoke; and though things look very sad and even very dark in the Hervormde Kerk; we ourselves cannot affiliate with it. No one [troubles] us, and we are free and can still enjoy the signs of the covenant under the Reverends Hasebroek and Brandt.

Early in January Rev. Kortenhoef Smit passed away. There is not much to memorialize. For three weeks there had been rumors of his impending death, and even when he was dying he did not eat a thing, but survived on his fat. He has the reputation of having been quite an eater and that he was worth six hundred thousand guilders. Two weeks ago his household effects were sold, everybody in town was talking about all the silverware there was, seventeen dinner bells, and everything was commensurate with that. The sale raised eighteen thousand guilders. His books are being sold this week, but there is not much of interest here; there are many novels. He has bequeathed two thousand guilders to the poor, but that is it. Such dead orthodoxy does not do the church much good, and what comes in its place is usually even worse.

We have had a severe winter here and a long one; spring was very sparse. The trees are scarcely beginning to blossom; the north wind is very cold, so that everything is [growing] very slowly and everything is very expensive. There has been much poverty this winter, and presently there are many people who have sinking fever. This spring, there were many big dike breaks and floods in Gelderland and Noord-Brabant; there has been nothing like it in 140 years. Many people and animals drowned, and thousands are homeless, unemployed, and without income. A great deal of money has been contributed, and much has been done to alleviate the situation. But much has also been done that brings the judgments of God upon us; there are comedies, concerts, lotteries. Even in churches where the Lord's death was proclaimed in the morning, there was a benefit organ concert in the evening for [the victims of] the flood. People are blind to those kinds of things these days. Where are we headed? The Netherlands is in danger of being left to its own devices by the Lord if it does not repent to him who is punishing us. We so much wanted to have a day of prayer, but, oh no, people want to have fun and pleasure these days.

Dear friend, your niece Betje Budde, who married the son of Krabbendam, has had a baby boy; I hear that she is doing well. It grieves us that Mrs. Sjilp [Schilp] is ailing so; her elderly father was not well recently, but now he is better again. If you speak to her some time, then tell her that her sister Naatje's husband has died from acute consumption. They were married for only a year and a half. Her brother Karel was to come home on leave from the Far East [Indonesia] this summer, but I hear that has been postponed. Do give her our warmest greetings from all of us, and what more can I say, dearest friend! If I could talk with you, I would have so much more to tell you, but you cannot write down everything.

Only yesterday Mrs. Zeelt came over to see us. She is well, but she is getting old. Mijntje was so ill this winter that they did not think she would pull through, but she has recovered fully. My sister and her children send you most cordial greetings; my dear husband intends to write your husband. We commend you and your husband and your young children to the Lord and send warmest greetings. May the Lord be our strength and support as the years mount. May he lead you safely to and beyond death and into blessed eternity; that is the wish of your friend who loves you dearly.

J. Wormser-van der Ven.

You will do me a real favor by writing me soon. Greetings to Mrs. Teeleman [Teleman] and her daughter. Jaspers, the grit stone mason, is married for the third time with a clear starcher. They paid us a visit; she seemed to be a gentle person. The girls [daughters of Mr. Jaspers] were not enthusiastic about her. Mietje is thirty, Truitje is twenty-six, and she herself is involved in a courtship. They had gotten so used to keeping house for themselves and now to have to say "Mother" for the third time is not much to their liking.

J. Wormser-van der Ven

Budde 13

> Mrs. H. M. Bousquet-Chabot to Mrs. C. M. Budde-Stomp
> Pella, 29 July 1855

Dear Friend and Sister in our Lord,

Your letter, which at the time was [personally] brought to us by J. A. Coffers [Koffers], was most welcome to me. It is a source of joy to hear from old friends and especially when it is for the good. That is the impression I got from your letter. From Coffers, who let me know that he was writing to Burlington, you will no doubt learn how things are going for them here, and how they slept in our shop one night, in the place Bousquet had pointed out for them to place their trunks. It is my sincere wish that religiously they will find here what they are looking and longing for, but I fear that they will be disappointed. Togetherness is altogether lacking here, and everyone agrees that the situation is not a good one, but not everyone agrees that there is nothing we can do in our own strength to change the situation, and that it is the Lord God alone who by faith can make hearts put love into practice. But he is considered not to exist by many people.

Was it not the old believers 100 to 150 years ago who lamented about all kinds of grief and misery, which is something that has not improved to this day? How much more then can we now say, "When the Lord comes, will he still find faith?" Often it seems to me that we are now living in that time. Oh, vanity of vanities is foremost in everything, but then we must not forget the Word of the Lord, that if he had not shortened those days for the sake of the elect, no human being would be saved.

Well, dear friend: Known to God are all his works from all eternity. And since without his will not a hair falls from our head, is not then our only surety that which the Lord does to our soul, giving up on all human wisdom? I could write you about all kinds of things that are going on here, if my head allowed me to write very much, but what good would it do? But one thing is needful, and to possess that with Mary [Luke 10:42] will surely get us to a safe harbor sooner or later.

My health has suffered much since last year; because of extreme changes in the weather here in Iowa, I suffer greatly from rheumatism in my head, arms, and legs. We have two [boys], but often it is more trouble to check on them than to do it yourself. Wednesday I am getting a new maid for the kitchen, a Frisian. Bousquet is suffering much from colic at the moment, but it has not been dangerous so far. Not all our business is going as we would like, and how sad it is that one gets depressed so soon. Cordial greetings to you and your husband.

Our children are growing up; the youngest is fifteen today. Piet Hein has been confirmed as a member of the group of people who constitute Scholte's congregation and are admitted to the Lord's Supper. That is about a half year ago by now. There is not much fruit visible. But I may believe that his profession of faith was sincere, and then the Lord will take care of his end of it. Mrs. Berkhout stops in to see me now and then. So did Le Cocq, to whom I conveyed your greetings. Since I can no longer walk like I used to and visit my old friends, I do not see anyone. You know how everybody in America is always on the run. Now I have to close, and I greet you and all those around you cordially. And I commend you all to the Lord, who after all is the only one that remains when all else is gone. Believe me, I am ever and wholly,

Your Loving Friend,
H. M. Bousquet-Chabot.

Wormser 53

D. A. Budde to J. A. Wormser
Burlington, November 1855

Esteemed Brother in Christ!

Your honored letters of May 11th last have come to hand, and [we] have seen that you, esteemed Brother, are as ever unceasingly active for the well being of country and church. May the Lord of the congregation, bought with a precious price, grant that in this life you may still enjoy the happiness that all things may again go well for Zion, and that the walls of Jerusalem may be rebuilt. The Lord, our faithful God, will not allow your untiring efforts to that end to be fruitless, or to be lost. He will bless you for time and eternity, with blessings on your house and in your generations. For Jehovah says, "I shall honor those who honor me." For after all, the fight you are fighting is about the Honor of God, the honor of our one and only and perfect Savior, who was bereft of his honor by the wily stratagems the enemies of the Cross of Christ seek in the world. The works of yours that we have received are *de nieuwe Bisschoppen, Het Protestantismus geplaatst bij de stembus* [*The New Bishops:*

Protestantism and the Struggle of the Ballot Box]; *het Roomsch Catholicismus* [*Roman Catholicism*]; *Dr. L. J. P. Meyboom en de Regten der Nederduitsche Kerk, het Classikaal Bestuur van Amsterdam* [*Dr. L. J. P. Meyboom and the Rights of the Netherlandic Church, the Classical Church Council of Amsterdam*]; *addressen betrekkelijk de voorgenomen Bijvelvertaling, aan de algemene Synode en aan de Amsterdamsche Kerkeraad, en adres aan den Koning* [*petitions relating to the proposed Bible translation to the General Synod and to the consistory of Amsterdam and a petition to the king*]. We shall be very pleased if we again receive some things from Your Honor for us to read.

When we read the Dutch newspapers here, the first thing we look for is the church news from the Netherlands. Our hearts will not let go of the Netherlands; we are concerned that everything may go well in Zion and that the enemies may be put to shame. If only the time may come that we may still experience, to our great joy and to the praise of God's omnipotent grace, that the Voice of the Lord might be [heard] and beheld saying to the cunning deceivers and the enemies of the congregation of Christ, "Thus far and no farther." Even if Zion may sometimes lament, "The Lord has forsaken me, my Lord has forgotten me," the response to that is, "Can a woman forget her sucking child...; and, "even these may forget, yet I will not forget you. Behold I have graven you on the palms of my hands, your walls are continually before me," thus says the Lord [Isaiah 49:15,16]. "Wait on the Lord, be of good courage, and he shall strengthen thy heart: wait, I say, on the Lord" [Psalm 27:14 King James].

Let that also be our strength—our consolation here in Burlington, since we too still do not have a shepherd and minister in our midst, who leads and feeds our small flock. We too wish to wait on the Lord; he will provide in his own good time. Things are not hopeless yet, for we believe that the Lord still has many people in this city who manifest a hunger for the reasonable and uncorrupted milk of the Word of God. The corrupting leaven has penetrated everywhere in the churches, so that the full Truth, the entire Christ in all the precious wounds [of his suffering] so needed for the poor sinner's heart, are seldom found these days in any but Reformed and Presbyterian congregations. To our great joy we recently had a visit from Rev. [John] Garretson from New York, secretary of the Holland Reformed Church, who could also still speak Dutch, a most dear man. On several occasions we received from him encouraging and comforting letters relating to the congregation of Burlington. Since I also spoke to His Reverence about Your Honor's little work on infant baptism, he very much wished to have a copy of it.

I did not have a copy of it in the house, because Hoedemaker from Utrecht had taken my copy along to Michigan. His Reverence said that on his return journey he was stopping in at Hoedemaker's, and then he would take the work with him and send it back to me again. I promised him that I would write Your Honor whether you might not be so kind as to send His Reverence a copy in a postal wrapper at the following address:

    Rev. John Garretson
    337 Broadway
    New York.

All three booklets I received from you are now making the rounds in America. The Lord will add his blessings to the work; it is a means to open the eyes of many. I will gladly pay for the booklet. Since your brother Dries has sent a money draft to Mr. Schilp and intends to send still another, I can now pay my obligation from this just as well here.

The aforementioned Mr. Hoedemaker had not been in America long when the Lord took his wife from his side through death. He then married another, who also died this summer and left two little children. The man was in a real predicament. [He] traveled about to find a third wife and talked about making a trip to the Netherlands. After he left us to go to Chicago, and after eight days there, and having made the acquaintance of another person, he was confirmed in marriage there for the third time and could now return to his home with a new mother and the children.

We are presently in reasonably good health, but my strength is not such that I can work uninterruptedly. The weaknesses and the infirmities of old age are showing more and more. But in return the Lord gives us [the blessing] that Diedrich is very diligent and steady going in his work, and, in a short time, if it please the Lord, he will be able to give me very much relief. For on a farm there is always work to do, although for the rest it is a quiet and peaceful life and especially good for our children, because the temptations of this turbulent life have such a harmful effect on the youthful hearts of children. And that is also the reason that led our Johan to decide to plan on building a house in the spring next year on our land that is closest to the city, in order to live there, and during the day to continue working in the factory, where his earnings come to nearly twelve dollars a week. Several times he has been asked to become a partner in building a factory, but he prefers to remain in his present situation, free from the many cares and worries that are connected with that.

The city of Burlington is getting bigger and bigger. They cannot build enough houses, and the city limits are about to be moved out again; even our land will now be within the city limits. There are already three exchange banks in town; there is an operating railroad between here and New York, and westward from here [it goes] to Des Moines. Gas pipes are being laid throughout the city for lighting. We hear nothing but good tidings about Pella's growth; many Hollanders are constantly passing through Burlington on their way there.

Mietje, the daughter of Le Cocq, married last March, and Frans and Dorus were next in line. Now, my dear Brother, warmest greetings, say hello to your dear wife, Jansie [Jansje] and Kaatje, and those unknown darlings of mine. Johan, Diedrich, and Maria send greetings to you and also Mrs. Teleman. Give my greetings to Brother Luuring. May the Lord be our expectation and our Peace; world events point us to end times to a joyous expectation for those who fear the Lord, and who will love the appearance of his coming.

D. A. Budde

Wormser 54

C. M. Budde-Stomp to J. Wormser-van der Ven
Burlington, November 1855

Dearly Beloved Friend and Sister in the Lord,

Realizing that this brief letter will be welcome to Your Honors, I also hope that you and your dear ones receive the same in good health. Thanks to the goodness of the Lord we are all reasonably well; our nephew Roelf has been ill for at least eight days on two [different] occasions and suffered high fevers, but he has recovered exclusively with medicines and without the help of a doctor. My dear husband and I are beginning to feel the onset of old age, so that constant work is getting to be difficult for us. My husband has a faithful helper in Diedrich. On July 8th a daughter, Maria Elizabeth, who was very tiny, was born to our son Johan's [wife]. When the baby was about three or four weeks old, she developed an epileptic fever, and so we could only think that we would have to lose her again. I have never seen such a little, old-looking child as it then was, even smaller than your Cato. Beyond our expectations it pleased the Lord to spare it, and although it is small, it is growing and is healthy. While our daughter-in-law was carrying the baby she had quite a hard time of it, but now she is reasonably well again. I have had to do without Mrs. Teleman for about four weeks so that she could assist her [Johan's wife] as a midwife. It was rather difficult for me to do all the work alone.

I had a nice letter from Mrs. Bousquet in the month of July. A Dutch family by the name of Coffers [Koffers] had left for Pella. We had been good friends with these people, which is why we gave them a letter of recommendation to Mrs. Bousquet, and they assisted them immediately. What Mrs. Bousquet wrote about their religious life was not very favorable. She wrote as follows: "Togetherness is altogether lacking; everyone agrees that the situation is not a good one, but they feel that it is not within their power to change things. But the Holy Spirit, who alone through faith can move hearts to the practice of love, does not exist as far as they are concerned."

Their son Piet Hein was accepted as a member by the people who constitute the Scholte congregation and then admitted to the Lord's Supper. When I read the headings like the following in the [*Sheboygan*] *Nieuwsbode:* Scholte & Grand, Bankers, Land Agents, Notaries Public, U. S. Agents for a life insurance company in New Jersey, Editors and Publishers of the *Pella Gazette* and still more, all this contrasts very strangely with being a shepherd and pastor. All the world is a stage, and every day there is something new, and because of sin we have to eat the bitter fruits. But thanks be to God, who has purchased us with his blood, and in his own good time will liberate us from this body of sin to live on an earth where righteousness dwells and the Lord will be glorified perfectly. We are still without a shepherd and experience this as a painful absence. The sermons of Rev. Beets were like ointment on a wound. From time to time my dear husband reads one [a sermon] for the Hollanders, and they like that very much; and so the Lord does not abandon us altogether but keeps us hoping for his lovingkindness.

Geertruida Zonne, married to Arend Lubbers, died at the youthful age of twenty-three from an epileptic fit after giving birth to a healthy son, her second child. Schilp and his wife have rented their farm out for a period of three years, because it is difficult for them to work it without help. They are living in the city, where he works for himself in a quarry and sells stones, and he makes a good living. But they are not as healthy as when they lived in the country; both of them and their little son have some problems with fevers.

We have had a blessed, fertile harvest this year. My husband took two wagon loads of beautiful peaches to market [from] trees that he himself had planted, and often he remarked, if only we could send Wormser a bushel or two, and some cantaloupe. After the market for fruit was over, my husband built a new stable, because the old one was getting so decrepit that we could no longer risk keeping cattle in it. That again involved us in a lot of work, and so we are approaching the end of the year, constantly drudging and toiling. But we may not overlook the faithful help and support of the Lord with all the benefits that encompassed us; with a moderate longing for that new age in which the old shall pass away and [we] shall rise up to eternal life, where the consequences of sin will no longer oppress us, but we shall glorify God to all eternity.

Dear friend, do make me happy soon with one of your esteemed letters and also [may we hear] from your two dear daughters, whose love toward us we have seen poured out in their youthful hearts. May the Lord remain the [first] choice in the hearts of all our children; then they too will love those who are born of God. We commend you and your dear spouse and children to the Lord; Greet your sister Rika, Mrs. Zeelt, master gardener Balke, and Mijntje, and the other old friends, and let us know how they are.

Your Friend and Sister in the Lord
who is always thinking of you,
C. M. Budde-Stomp

Budde 14

Mrs. J. Wormser-van der Ven to Mrs. C. M. Budde-Stomp
Amsterdam, 11 January 1856

Dearly Beloved Friend,

After having looked in vain for a letter from you who were the daily subject of our conversations, we were surprised the day after Christmas to receive your esteemed letter, which is always so gratifying to us. We were glad to hear that all of you were still in the land of the living; that is also our privilege. But that old age is beginning to tell on you, that we can readily believe. We also say the same about ourselves. My dear husband feels that his body is being broken down because of his constant troubles with rheumatism, which were the case rather frequently during the past year. And that is why he formed an association with a young, energetic process writ-server, a Mr. Noordhoek, who had already been making a goodly sum annually off my husband by taking over his work whenever he was not well. And now my husband can turn over the most difficult work to N[oordhoek] without sacrificing all that much, or when he is still weak. When he is indisposed he can take it a little easier, and when he is hale and healthy he can tend to the business energetically himself.

I too feel that I am not getting stronger. Although for the most part I have the privilege of enjoying good health, my chest is getting weak and at times is painful. Fortunately, Jansje and Cato are ready to help me, so that by the goodness of God I do not have to work hard. The old lady who was living upstairs above us, and who was our landlady, died last November. Consequently, our house is being sold in the spring. Fortunately, we have a rental agreement until May 1857, so things here are just like they are in your world, changing every day.

You are aware, my dear friend, that my sister Rika was lady in waiting to Madame Van Cattenburgh; that good lady died of a stroke last December. My sister, and many with her, are deeply saddened, and even though the will is not to be probated before the beginning of February, she has already been assured that Madame has provided for her, so that she will be getting a weekly payment, one on which she, as a middle-class woman, will be able to live. You can imagine that she is very thankful to the Lord for that. It would not be very pleasant for her to be living among others [in a home for the aged], and it would be very difficult for her to live with us, because our house is too small now that the [grand] children are growing up.

As in previous years, we had a good deal of cholera during the months of August and September. In the past it did not carry off so many of our acquaintances, but this time it did, among others: Mietje Jasper, whom you probably still remember. Last Sunday she was sitting next to my daughter in church, mind you; on Tuesday she became ill, and the next day she entered eternity. Those girls [Mietje and Truitje] were not very happy after their father's third marriage; they could not get along well with that stepmother, and besides they were already of marriageable age. So the last time they met the girls, she [Mietje?] complained and said that if you ever heard of an opening somewhere, to think of her. Her sister Truitje is terribly sad, more than the [step-]mother, that you can well imagine. Now it [the cholera] is letting up some. However, measles carried off hundreds of children to their graves this fall; there were times when you saw three [children] from one family being buried at the same time. In both of these contagious diseases, the angel of death passed our house by.

What you write about Scholte, dear friend, is also a puzzle to us. He sent us the *Pella Gazette* several times, but my husband refuses to accept it. He has neither the time nor the desire to read English language newspapers. A few days after getting your letter, we also received one from Berkhout; it was not very cheerful. He complains about the church situation, just as Mrs. Bousquet does to you. If you do not have the pleasure of having your own pastor in Burlington, then you don't have the grief of one either. For years we have noted that wherever S[cholte] went, the congregation was [soon] in a state of confusion. In all likelihood that's the way it will always be. We [suspect] that that is why you do not attend his church. The church situation is not improving here either. Naturally the orthodox and the liberals are separated, even though there is no actual separation. In Amsterdam there is plenty of opportunity for the latter [the liberals] to worship, and of the former [the orthodox] some go here, some go there.

Who could ever have thought that I would hardly ever attend a Dutch church service? But often, and that includes the Lord's Supper, [we worship] in High German. The minister, it is true, leans to the Lutheran side, but it is as clear as day that he has spiritual life [is born again], and that is something you seldom encounter.

It is our heartfelt wish that your son Johan may keep his little baby. Our Henriette was also very small and fragile when she was born; we had a very hard time with her, but now she is a dear, darling child. The Lord willing, she will be four years old in March; she is quick and generally healthy. Jansje and Cato would also like to write Aunt Budde once. To save postage the letters will be mailed with the little books [pamphlets] the first chance we get.

The seminary building in which Rev. Schwartz preaches, and which was newly built four years ago and was very costly, is now too small to suit him. Now he has purchased the *Fransche Comedie* [French Comedy] on the corner of the Erwetemarkt and the Halvemaansteeg. He would like my husband to help him get [financing for] this building too, but he is not at all of a mind to do that. He has not forgotten all the worries and cares about the other [last] building. Four years ago we were thanking the Lord for that church, and now are we just going to put it up for sale again? In that way you can always be starting plants and then be pulling them up again. Now things are turning out this way, we would have preferred to see the Seceders get it [the building], because it is ever so much nicer and at least not smaller. But what can one say? There is unrest everywhere and in everything, and that, I believe, is hastening us to the end of time. May the Lord grant all of you and all of us so much of his grace that we may be found wakeful when he comes.

Give our greetings to all of your dear children; also your daughter-in-law, Mrs. Teeleman [Teleman], and to Jansje, and to all who might still have some recollection of us. My sister also sends you warmest greetings; my dear husband and children also send their greetings. And may you and all your concerns be commended to the Lord by your dearest loving friend and sister in the Lord.

J. Wormser-van der Ven

My husband is writing to Mr. Budde, whom I also greet cordially.

Budde 15

J. A. Wormser Jr. to Mrs. C. M. Budde-Stomp
Amsterdam, 23 February 1856

Esteemed Madam!

I have read your letter that was addressed to me but written in your letter to mother. I thank you very much for the advice and the wishes contained in it. I hope, with the help of God, to act on your advice to fear the Lord. I really wish to serve him with my whole heart, since he also wants to save me, and also died for me.

On November 17, my Aunt Rika also died. Her last words were, "What time is it?" When they said, "Twelve-thirty," she laid her head down and passed on into eternity.

Please give my greetings to Mr. [Budde].

With highest esteem, I have the honor to be,

Your faithful Servant,
J. A. Wormser

Wormser 55

D. A. Budde to J. A. Warner
Burlington, 14 November 1856

Dearly Beloved Friend and Brother in our Lord Jesus Christ!

Grace and peace be granted and multiplied unto you richly from God the Father and the Lord [Jesus] Christ. Your esteemed letters of last January we were pleased and very happy to receive. But you will say, then why did you not reply sooner? I had thought of writing you back sooner than usual, but that intention was thwarted.

Many thanks for the three pamphlets you mailed January 9th, which reached us speedily. On the one hand, we were saddened that wickedness in the Netherlands has gone so far, and on the other hand, we rejoice that the Lord is still working powerfully, and that he girds his own with strength from on high to fight for his honor. No, my dear Brother, your wearisome and exhausting labors on behalf of the fatherland and the church of Christ are not in vain. The Lord is already showing forth its joyous and constructive results. Is it not remarkable that Jews and heathens and Mohammedans are again being excluded from a society that calls itself Christian?

What a cause for joy it is that Mr. Van der Brugge from Nijmegen and Groen van Prinsterer Esq. have been chosen for high office to employ their talents with profit. Even though the number of the God-fearing is small as compared with the liberals, if it is the will of God to save [our] country and church, to cause his honor to reside in the same again—then remember the days of Gideon when the whole host of Israelites was too many to save them from the hand of the Midianites. By God's design it was to be only a few through whom the Lord desired to give deliverance to Israel, so that the Lord alone should be glorified. The Lord is still the same, who can bring about national rebirth by just a few, also in the Netherlands. He poured out the Spirit of faith and of prayers upon his children so that they may follow him as one man, lifting their prayers heavenward, that those men may be equipped with wisdom, strength, and grace so that in their weighty and difficult positions they may experience that the Lord God of Hosts is with them, even though they are but few in number. For he who is with them is greater than those who are against them. The Lord rules!

To my regret I can now inform you that the booklet on infant baptism and the package of pamphlets, which you sent with the *Fosca Helena*, got lost. We waited for it a long time. Meanwhile, I sent two letters to New York and did not receive an answer from the Rev. Garretson, who had been prevented from writing me because of the press of business and illness. It was not until about three weeks ago that I finally received a letter from His Reverence stating that he had not received a thing. And neither have we been able to find out whether that ship arrived safely in New York back then.

Recently the Rev. Van Raalte from Michigan paid us a surprise visit. He has aged considerably; my wife recognized him immediately. He was willing to preach for us, but because it was in the middle of the week and the busy harvesting season, we could hardly try to get the Hollanders together. He was traveling to Pella to see if he could do any good up there. Accordingly, he did manage to bring together a limited group of them who were going to affiliate with the Holland Reformed Church of America. And after Rev. Van Raalte had gotten back home from making his journey, this group did call him, a call which he is considering. It was a distinct pleasure to meet each other in this land in which we are strangers, to unite our hearts in prayer, and to praise and thank the Lord that till now we have been kept in the faith, and the profession of those truths that lead unto salvation, by which our fathers entered heaven. About that time, Scholte was traveling about in Michigan and in Wisconsin making political speeches urging the Hollanders to vote for [James] Buchanan, who was one of the three gentlemen on the nomination. The election took place on the 4th of November. Buchanan received the majority of votes and was elected president of the United States for four years.

Berkhout visited us last winter; he was hoping to get rich overnight. He had bought over 500 hogs in Pella [expecting] to sell them at a big profit in Burlington. The Lord blocked his intention by a severe frost at this time; many of the animals died before they ever got to Burlington. When he got here he found the buyers so overstocked that he had to transport his hogs to New York. The frost continued; it had never been that cold here before. The thermometer registered 10 degrees below zero [Celsius], and on the Fahrenheit thermometer I bought here, it was 28 degrees below zero. Berkhout had become a swine drover; he had to devote his Sunday to the hogs. He was at a complete loss; he was so embarrassed seeing all his losses—in Burlington—and in New York the prices had dropped. Instead of gaining at least 2,000 dollars as he had expected, and then going back to Holland, he lost fully that amount, and his situation is so shaky that he fears he may have to go into bankruptcy. Those who wish to become rich often fall into manifold temptations and into the snares of the devil. That is what the Lord teaches us in his word, and it is recorded as a warning to us.

Mr. Bousquet has fallen asleep in the Lord. He was greatly beloved in Pella, and there are many who mourn his passing. And thus one friend after another precedes us; every day we are one nearer the end of life's journey. May the Lord grant us to be like the wise maidens, with our lamps burning and provided with oil, so that when our hour comes we may also sit down at the marriage feast of the Lamb.

Thanks to the goodness of the Lord I have enjoyed rather good health this year, although my strength is diminishing. Diedrich is a big help to me in all my activities. The Lord does all things well, his name be praised. My dear wife is as healthy as ever she has been. Maria is also doing well. Johan and his wife are also faring well. Mrs. Teleman is failing; she suffers much from a sore leg, but she is content. Janssie [Jansje] is a good, healthy girl.

We still have not gotten another shepherd and minister. Our Dutch friends here do not seem to be much interested. But as for us, we do feel the need of it, although we are again regularly attending the German church, where they have a devout minister, though this cannot fill the absence of a faithful Reformed preacher. For congregational and brotherly contacts stir up more life in one's soul, and make you stand firmer in your faith in the covenantal promises, to the glory of God and the joy and gladness of the soul, to fight the fight of faith in order to receive in Christ the hope of perfect victory over sin and misery; and after completing this earthly life to receive and to enjoy salvation in glorifying the triune covenant God, through all eternity.

Our children greet you; Mrs. Teleman greets you. Please greet for me your dear wife, Janssie [Jansje] and Cato, and your other children. The Lord grant that they may bring much joy into your life, and do instruct them to walk in the way of God's elect. Greet our friend Luuring; we rejoice that all is going well for him. My wife will also be writing your wife about this and that separately. I sincerely expect that you will not wait as long in writing as I have done. And now I commend you and your family to God's grace, and after wishing you temporal and spiritual blessings, I remain with cordial greetings,

Your Loving Friend and Brother in the Lord,
D. A. Budde

Wormser 56

C. M. Budde-Stomp to J. Wormser-van der Ven
Burlington, Dec. 1856

Dearly Beloved Friend!

Your precious letters sent to us in January were a great joy to us. You have shared with me many matters of your life's journey and encounters on this lower (terrestrial) sphere. The bond of love between us is one of deepest joy to me, for I have found nothing like it in this fatherland. But the fact that your dear children are constantly affirming this bond and wish to honor us with their writing is a source of great joy to us.

Day after day we have been waiting for some word from you, but alas we received a letter from Rev. Garretson saying that His Reverence had not received anything [booklet on infant baptism, etc., sent on the *Fosca Helena*; cf.Wormser 55], and so we concluded that in all likelihood the ship had perished.

Thanks to the goodness of the Lord we are in reasonably good health. We hope that in your poor health the strength of the Lord undergirds you to bear all your spiritual and physical labors. Our son Johan bought 1½ acres of our land, had a nice little house built on it, and began living there in July. He goes to his work at the foundry every day and makes a good living. Our joy was but short lived, when the sweet mingled with the bitter. Their little daughter, Maria Elizabeth, who had been so frail, was growing well and was so sweet and cute that everyone loved her. She contracted whooping cough, and, after suffering briefly, the Lord took her to himself, one year and eighteen days old. When she lay in her little casket, her facial features were like those of your Cato when she started walking. Johan was grief stricken by this loss, but, when she was buried, he was given grace to rest in the will of the Lord and to find peace in his inmost being. They still have their elder little son who is five years old and presently has the same illness from which the two children of your brother Dries died.

There was a family, husband and wife and four children, here from Holland and planning to go to Pella where a brother-in law, P. De Jong, lived. The man was a blacksmith, but their money was only enough to take them to Burlington. They went to an inn to inquire about getting transportation to Pella. The drayman refused to take them until he first got half of the agreed price, but they did not have that, and besides the innkeeper demanded twenty-eight dollars for lodging costs and would not let their chests go. These people decided to go on foot with their children, the oldest of which was nine years and the youngest 1½ years; but, after going a short distance, they realized that it was impossible and turned back; the man requested of the innkeeper that his wife and children be allowed to live in the shed. The man resumed the journey and walked to his relatives in Pella in four days. All of a sudden it turned so bitterly cold that the woman and her children sat down in the street, where kindhearted people took them in and gave them food to eat.

When folks learned that they were Hollanders, they got in touch with Jan to help the people. My dear husband and Jan went down there the next day; meanwhile, city folk had already provided them with a room and a stove and with food and drink. The second little child, a girl, became ill; my husband got a doctor who said that it was scarlet fever, and that it was contagious for children. Johan decided to take in these needy people, and, upon father's advice, decided to place (her) little son temporarily with his wife's parents. But (his wife) did not wish to be separated from her child. My husband was surety for the money, got the trunks released, and took them to our house. The little child became critically ill, and for days we thought that it would die. After eight days, the brother-in-law arrived with a wagon to pick up the wife and children. My husband had collected funds in Burlington, so that they were now free to join their family again. I hope that the Lord will direct this testing of Jan to His Name's honor and to our well being.

When I read of the death of your wife (?), I began to wonder whether you might buy the house, and with minor changes use it entirely for yourself, for a dwelling in which the Lord has blessed us, visited us, and saved us has some appeal for our inmost feelings. In my recollection I can see us in the inner room when we were learning our catechism or were talking together. If that should happen, you will doubtless let me know.

Last year we had an exceptionally long and hard winter frost, so that all our peach trees froze. In the spring the blossoms of the apple trees suffered a long drought, so that the harvest was not as abundant as it was last year, but enough to praise the Lord for his blessings. At New Year's Berkhout came to Burlington in bitterly cold weather with a big herd of pigs. Since the prices had dropped considerably because of over supply, and because he had already experienced delay because of unfavorable weather, he decided to ship them to New York, [but] lost so many en route that he suffered considerable losses.

Mrs. Teleman has had a sore leg since November of last year. For a time she could not be about at all, then she could barely get about, but it was so little that this summer she was only able using a cane to see Jan's house on a nice day when it was still just a frame, but she still has not seen it completed. Her miserable condition makes much work for me; the things she used to do, I now have to do, and have to get a washerwoman also for my things. The girls help in the garden and do the milking, because I have six cows; during the winter [the girls] have to go to school. When I push myself to get it all done, then I get dizzy, and I have to take it easy. I am heavier but not stronger, and that is true for my dear husband too. He starts his work with a bang, but soon he has to slow down, and then he experiences discomfort and has to guard against heavy lifting. For the sake of the children and with the help of the Lord, we think it is still best to keep on with our work. Diedrich is a [good] support for his father. Our nephew is stronger and older, and he is healthy these days.

Dear Jansie [Jansje] and Cato, make me happy again with your letters; your love is evident to me; may the fear of the Lord be your [heart's] desire and preference, for then the Lord will keep you in this wicked and seductive world, and, after having fought the [good] fight, he will take you up in glory. Dear friend, the year is again speeding to its end; greet your sister Rika for me as well as the other friends. We extend cordial greetings to you and your children. May the grace and peace of the Lord be with you all, Amen. Your loving Friend and Sister in our Lord.

C. M. Budde-Stomp

Budde 16

Cato Wormser to Mrs. C. M. Budde-Stomp
Amsterdam, 3 July 1857

Esteemed Madam and Dear Friend!

We have not written you for almost a year and a half. I want to thank you most sincerely that you were also willing to send us [girls] a short letter. You probably still think of us living on the Voorburgwal, but last May we moved and now are living on the Achterburgwal #447, between the Hoogstraat and the Stoofsteeg. We like the new house very much. It is much bigger than the previous one, and the office is downstairs. That makes things very quiet for us. However, to all appearances, I will not be living here long because I have been engaged for one and a half years to a porter from Amsterdam, a young man whose name is De Boer and who is twenty-five years old. We are thinking of getting married mid-September, even though I am only twenty. He makes a good living and is an orphan and so now he moves about a good deal. One thing I regret very much is that he is a Lutheran, but he always goes wherever Reverend [L.C.] Lentz is preaching, and he, as you probably will recall, is a good preacher. And by the time you get this letter, I will be living in a different part of the city, close to the Haarlem dike.

The daughter of Lijsen married a few weeks ago; she is the oldest one, named Kaatje. I do not think you know her younger sister. But you misunderstood us in the previous letter about Mietje Jaspers [cf. Budde Letter 15]. You will recall Jaspers, the pumice stone man in our fellowship who had two daughters, Mietje and Trijntje [Truitje], a couple of years older than Jans [Jansje] and I. Now Mientje died of cholera, and Trijntje was here this week and asked me to give you her greetings. Last week old Mr. Gunther died; he was eighty years old.

The Seceders have built a new church on the Keizersgracht, but there has been no preaching there yet. We heard that [Rev. A.G.] De Waal, their present preacher, would be preaching in the new church, and that he would get an assistant to preach in the old church. It appears that the congregation is very difficult to satisfy these days. Rev. Brummelkamp preached here last Sunday, but he did not call on us. We did not know it beforehand or otherwise Jans [Jansje] and I would have gone to hear him. The same thing happened a week earlier with Rev. [De] Moen.

Father and Mother are out for the day visiting Mrs. Zeelt at Postwijk [a country home]. Aunt Rieka is staying there for her health in a rooming house just across the street. Last summer and winter she suffered very much from spewing up blood, so much so that we often thought that she was choking in it. Then she was outdoors and reasonable, although very weak. But now we have gotten a letter saying that the blood spewing had been extremely severe. So now Father and Mother have gone over there to visit her. She has already consulted three different doctors, but they cannot cure her. We do not know what to expect from one minute to the next. One minute she seems so well, given her problem, and the next we expect her to die. It is our firm conviction that she has consumption, but she does not believe it and will not hear of it. The one moment she can await death with calm assurance and contentment, and the next she cannot stand the thought of it.

And now, dear friend, after cordial greetings to all of you, including Jan and his family, and commending you all to the Lord, I remain, as ever,

> Your sincerely loving Friend,
> C. Wormser

Budde 17

> Mrs. J. Wormser-van der Ven to Mrs. C. M. Budde-Stomp
> Amsterdam, 4 July 1857

Dearly Beloved Friend!

I have neglected to write you altogether too long already, but you are in our thoughts every day and often are the subject of our conversations. But life is like a dream; the older one gets, the faster the years fly away, and many of our acquaintances have gone to their eternal home in the year 1856. Early in the spring, Mrs. Burger from the Helsteeg Street died and so did Mrs. [De] Moen. In October, Mrs. Höveker, who had been alive and well, was dead in eight days, and now it is the aged Mr. Gunther. Last March Huiding died; he had been ailing with a chest problem and slipped away quietly. And so our contemporaries are passing away, one after another; but the Lord has spared us together till now. In April '57, my husband again suffered much from rheumatism, so badly that the fevers again affected his head. But, the Lord so arranged things that when it was time to move, he could walk from the Voorburgwal [Street] to the Achterburgwal [Street] and from then till now he has been reasonably well. We have ample reasons for gratitude, since the Lord bestows spiritual and physical blessings upon us.

As you know, our house on the Voorburgwal has been sold because of the death of the aged lady [owner]. My husband would have liked to buy the house for a good price, but one of the heirs bought it for fl.7,000, just fl.150 more than [the bid] my husband had submitted. He wanted to sell it to us, but he demanded a profit of fl.1,000. We were not minded to do that, and after he had been our landlord for two weeks, it reached my husband's ears that we had been living much too cheaply, and so he still had plans to make us pay the expensive purchase price [in a higher rental]. Since this [kind of dealing] was completely out of character for my husband, we decided to move, and lo and behold the Lord had in mind a bigger house for us with a rental of fl.650 with free office space downstairs. Now things can be more restful and better for us. The office is being blessed [with good income], and if it continues this way, we will be able to defray the costs and still have something left. I have written you all this not to boast, but we certainly may mention the lovingkindness of the Lord, the more so since we know that you enjoy it when things are going well for us.

But, my dear friend! In all of this I do not intend to declare that this life does not have its burdens. Oh no, they are many, but they are always intermingled with the loving kindnesses of God. As a result of the death of her lady [employer] in May of '56, my sister became free and independent with a pension of twelve guilders per week. However, in July she had such severe blood spewings, and so many, that in our eyes it is a miracle that she is still in the land of the living. Now, after ailing for a year and being terribly weakened, she has survived another severe attack. On the advice of a doctor, for her health's sake she is now lodging with a devout farmer, who lives across from Mrs. Zeelt, where we visited her yesterday. But she herself thought that more [attacks] would follow, and then we might quite unexpectedly hear that she had entered her eternal rest. Her faith is bright and shining and in all her afflictions she remains calm.

The sister of my husband, Kaatje, whom you probably still know, and who has been living with my husband's brother in Overijssel, is also in a very critical condition. Initially the doctor thought it was an inflammation of the peritoneum, and now she has dropsy; there is no hope for recovery, and her end will probably come soon. If only she may learn at the eleventh hour to cry for grace.

When I wrote you the last time, our daughter Cato had just become engaged. Since it was still so recent, we did not wish to write it to you. He makes a [decent] living, and, since the death of his father, who had given his full approval for the marriage, he has been living with a second mother. Now, if all goes well, they will be marrying in mid-September. He is a fine, well-behaved individual, whose name is Johannes Mattheus de Boer. It will seem strange to us and to her to leave the paternal home, but the Lord will accompany her and the two of them in all their ways.

It is our heartfelt wish that all may be well with you when you receive this letter and that you will not follow my example in waiting so long in writing. But here it is just one thing after another, and if on occasion there is some time, then one is not always immediately ready to write, although I did fix the principal events in my memory to share them with you. By the time you receive this missive, Mrs. Sjilp [Schilp] will probably already have received the death notice of her aged father. If not, you could tell that he died in the latter part of May.

And now, my dear friend, I shall conclude with greetings to your husband, children, and grandchildren from all of us, and commend you to the grace of the Lord. I am your friend who is,

Intimately Yours,
J. Wormser-van der Ven

Budde 18

J[ansje] Wormser to Mrs. C. M. Budde-Stomp
Amsterdam, 6 July 1857

Esteemed Madame, Dearly Beloved Friend!

Since my older sister, and Johan too, have written to you all and Diederich [Diedrich], I can hardly neglect to send you a few lines too. I hope that you will receive them faster than the last time. Since there was no one home in the minister's house in New York to whom Father had addressed the booklets, Captain Visser just took them back to Amsterdam. When he told father at the exchange, father told him that he should take them back again. Upon arriving at New York, he again did not find anyone home but dropped them off at the tobacco shop next door, and that is how they finally arrived at your place.

Your esteemed letter in December of last year [W 56] we received in January, and yours of January reached us in February. How happy we were to see letters from the whole family, from our friend Johan and Diederich [Diedrich], and the little Maria. I still remember very well when I took her into the hallway once to teach her how to walk, and now she fetches cows on horseback. I sure would like to see her once. We talk about you almost every day, and not a birthday passes without our thinking of you. Recently we were going to Haarlem with the family, and we were talking of the time several years ago when you and your whole family went with us to Haarlem, when Diederich [Diedrich] and Cato were sitting in the basket wagon, and how we ate in the dunes. I remember it as if it happened only a year ago, but it must be fifteen or sixteen years ago. I wish that we could still do it all together once again.

You must have read in Mother's letter that we have moved. We now have a much larger house and one that is much easier. We now have gas in our house and waterlines an inch in diameter. You are probably aware that this [water] is a new invention, just like gas; the pipes are in the house, and with [the turn of] a spigot you always have water in abundance. It all comes from the Haarlem dunes. If you were to see the Haarlemmermeer [Haarlem Lake] now, you would not know what you were seeing. It [has been reclaimed] and is now entirely dry. All the land is under cultivation; there are lovely farms, meadows, and farmlands. There is a lovely Hervormde Kerk, and a Roman Catholic one is being built. Rev. Brummelkamp preached there last year, and our Rev. Hasebroek preaches there often; it is not yet an established congregation. It is a great expanse of land.

It will seem very strange to us when Cato is married. It will, no doubt, also be difficult for you to imagine, since you knew her as a baby who could fit into a milk can. Truitje Jaspers has been engaged for some time now; she still does not know when they will get married. She is almost thirty. Last week she asked us to convey her greetings to you. The aged Mr. Gunther is also dead now; his son is thinking of marrying in November. Sientje is now working outside the home. The end of last year Mrs. Abramz [Abrahams] died in Tiel. She must have been ailing for a long time. If you speak to Mrs. Schilp sometime, tell her that three weeks before the death of her father, her sister Naatje Portengen remarried with a retired pensioner from the Far East [Indonesia]. The family of Uncle Dries is prospering. Mr. Luuring's family continues the same. He visits us every Friday evening; he is getting weak, and the Mrs. has aged greatly. Willem still works at the office, and Saartje is our hat maker. She is now also attending a catechism class with Rev. Hasebroek. The aged Janssen is still living, but he is going down hill fast. Today we also heard that the Seceder Simons, the blacksmith, is also going downhill as far as his health is concerned. He has quit his shop and is now retired. The church on the Bloemgracht is closing down; the last preaching service was held there yesterday. Next Sunday the new church will be dedicated. Father has taken seats [rented pews] for Cato and me in the new church. I do hope to make use of it. In spirit Rev. De Waal is like Brummelkamp, not like Van Velzen, and accordingly many people do not like him. Rev. Brummelkamp and Van Velzen do not get along very well at Kampen [Seminary]. That is exactly what was to be expected.

Rev. Meyboom did not fare very well here. In the two and a half years of his stay, he has had to put up with many things. He has been ailing with illnesses much of the time, and now again he has been so critically ill that his children had to leave the house. Several times there have been rumors that he was dead. Now he is improving a little, but he will never be able to mount a pulpit again. Father has already said that if it is true that he can no longer preach, then that would constitute approval of the protest movement. Last year in July, Rev. Bouinier suddenly died from a stroke, leaving us with one less of the good [orthodox] ones. The Saturday preaching schedule looks very meager. Of twenty-eight [ministers], they [the orthodox] have no one but Hasebroek and Brandt to listen to.

The condition of Aunt Riek is not favorable either. You will recall that she was always so pushy and so hot-tempered, but now she is so weak that when I visited her two weeks ago, she needed Mrs. Zeelt's cane to walk with me on the Lindenhof estate. Now she is again suffering from the vomiting of blood. The day after tomorrow, Henriette and I will be going to Mrs. Zeelt and stay over for several days. Then I can visit her [Aunt Riek] again; she just might pass away very unexpectedly, for because of all the vomiting of blood she also has a bad case of consumption.

Well, dear Mrs., I have nothing special to tell you about our old friends. The Doornhouwer family remains the same; we hear nothing from the Schries [Schrieks]. Cato has not spoken to him. We have no word about Lolkes [Lothes] and Mrs. Lottes [Lothes] and assume that they are well. Well, I have gone around the little circle; the other half is in America. Father had a couple of letters last year from Diekinga, the tailor; they are still in Ost Friesland and are doing well. It is our heartfelt hope that you may get this letter in good health. Thanks to God's goodness we all are well. Give our greetings to Jan and his wife, and to Diederich [Diedrich] and Marie. Cordial greetings to you as well as to Mr. [Budde] and may you experience the nearness of the Lord, that is the wish of,

> Your loving Friend,
> J. Wormser

Give our cordial greetings to Mrs. Teleman and Jansje.

Added from *Nieuw Nederland, Christelijk cultureel sociaal weekblad* [*New Netherlands Christian Cultural and Social Weekly*], II-48, of 5 December 1947.

> To J. J. L. van der Brugghen, Esq.
> Pella, 22 October 1857

Esteemed Friend and Brother in our Lord Jesus Christ.

You have not heard anything from me personally for a long time, although you will surely have noticed from the *Pella Gazette*, which has been sent to you regularly, that I have not forgotten my old Netherlands, and that I have also followed with interest the most recent events since your promotion to [the office of cabinet] minister. I have been saddened by the personal opposition that brother Groen [van Prinsterer] and those who agree with him have leveled against you in regards to the law on education. Although I might have approached it all a little differently, I do believe that your direction is more compatible with a good and Christian, or rather biblical, statecraft than that of Groen. On the basis of what I knew about you, I had expected from the outset that you would deviate from Groen's course. Following the governing principles of the brother, the Netherlands can even be thrown into turmoil. And if the circumstances were favorable, a seeming triumph of orthodoxy might even come into existence for a time, but church and state would really have suffered as a result.

The world is still the world, even if it is called Christian, and will not be subject to Christ until the Anti-Christ has come and been brought into subjection in the glorious appearance of our Lord and King. The observation of Luther, "I have certainly seen Christian regents, but no Christian governments," will be borne out to the end of time. The closer my contacts have been, and still are, with worldly governments, the more I am confirmed in my former convictions, that the governments of this world stand under the influence of the ruler of this world. As I have noted from his works, Groen takes offense at my convictions, but I did not become angry because of it; his intentions are good, and he is sincere in his convictions. Seek in him a beloved brother, even though I continue to reject his stance in the area of religious politics. Brothers like Groen just do not understand how a Christian who thinks as I do can get involved in governmental matters. The principal reason for this misunderstanding is that they do not have a clear understanding of the divine governance as it relates to the still ever-pending revelation of the kingdom of heaven of God, for whose coming the Lord has taught us to pray, and the fulfillment of that prayer we await in the Lord's

[good] time with long-suffering and humility.

Because of my position here, I am constantly in direct contact with what constitutes the democratic form of government here, and even so, that has not changed my opinions but rather confirmed them. Here in America I continue to watch with much interest what results the experiment of a pure democracy will yield. Until now, my judgment is that the results will not be favorable to such a form of government. If the majority of people were God-fearing and if that majority chose only God-fearing legislators, judges, and administrative officials, the results could be favorable. However, that is not the case, and the result is that we behold spectacles in America that can only fill the Christian with woe when he considers the divine pronouncement, "Righteousness exalteth a nation, but sin is a reproach to any people" [Proverbs 14:34]. The North American republic must serve some function in the rule of God, but whether the Union will endure is not sure at this point. And when the folly and political fanaticism of the power-driven party leaders drives the masses to break up the Union, then the greatness and prosperity of this democratic republic will be done for. A Christian participating in whatever form of government, when in the providence of God he is called to this task, can by his influence and example do much to avert or to stop the outbreak of evil. But he will never make the world into the kingdom of God.

When I learned that King Willem III had stopped in his course and come to conversion, I rejoiced. It is my heartfelt wish that it may be a Godly conversion. The tiding rekindled my never extinguished affinity for the House of Orange. I saw in this a kind of a fulfillment of a wish once expressed to Willem II in the dedication of a gift of my published sermons presented to His Majesty on his birthday, and which concluded with the following words:

O God verhoor de bee,	Oh God, hear my prayer,
Deel aan den Koning mee	and grant the king
Wat Nederland, wat heel de aard	what all the Netherlands, all the earth
Oranje niet kon geven.	could not give [the House of] Orange.

I was really pleased to see that the king had not accepted your resignation. If the king wishes to rule the Netherlands in the fear of God and truly for the good of the Netherlands, then [J. R.] Thorbecke [Liberal Party leader and prime minister] and his cohorts must be kept out of the cabinet. And if Groen with his ideas could form a cabinet, it would pave the way for the inevitable adoption of the unbelieving philosophical politics of Thorbecke. I therefore wish with all my heart, beloved Brother, that for the good of my old fatherland you will endure the objections of that government with courage, persistence, and patience for the good of my old fatherland.

If the Lord would so order things that I would be able to sell my possessions, which consist mostly of real estate, for a reasonable price, I probably would decide to spend the rest of my earthly life in the Netherlands. As far as the Dutch people are concerned, things are now settled and well ordered here, and however much the Lord has prospered me here, my heart is not in it. America can never become the Netherlands for me. I write you this as a trusted friend so that you might be able to understand me somewhat.

Is it not remarkable that in God's providence the [Far] East is again drawing the attention of the world powers. Russia has been thwarted in its drive to the south but has not changed its political ambitions because of that. What will come of the entanglements in China and India, human perspicacity cannot yet predict, but one thing is certain, that God is at work in the [Far] East. Because of its East Indies possessions, the Netherlands will not be able to stay out of it in the long run. I do believe that something can still be done with respect to these possessions to assure the preponderance of the Netherlands.

I had in mind to visit the Netherlands in the fall, but the illness of our youngest child cancelled that. That intention, which I was very much minded to do after your new [cabinet] appointment, delayed me from writing you earlier. I regularly send His Majesty Willem III the *Pella Gazette*. Is it received and read? As regards the king, there is one desire that I have. I received a gift from Willem II that I have always prized: the first series of the *Archives du Maison d'Orange*. The last volume, which came out after my departure, still was sent to me here. I noticed that the second series has begun. Might not Willem III also be inclined to follow up his father by continuing this gift?

Well, Brother, the page is filled; do let me hear something from you too. My family is doing well these days. I have two sons and four daughters alive on this earth and have as many children with the Lord. My oldest daughter is married to an American doctor, a very able man. Greetings to your family. Greet the brethren. May God strengthen you and cause you to taste his fellowship in the midst of your fellow workers. Remember your friend and brother in love.

Henry P. Scholte

The petition of J. A. Wormser (see below) was directed against the law of J. J. L. van der Brugghen, and thus evidently also against the position of the Rev. H. P. Scholte.

J. A. Wormser, Petition to the King:

That because of the compulsory union of all religious persuasions, a religious education of our youth, in a Christian sense, is rendered impossible; since, because of the Jews, the person of our Lord *Jesus Christ*, including all that the Sacred Scriptures tell of his glory, works and merits, must be excluded; while, because of the Roman Catholics, the entire Bible and the History of the Fatherland must be removed from the School;

that the regulation of Public Education in this manner, in the respectful judgment of the Undersigned, does not meet the requirements of the Constitution, which insists that the regulations shall be carried out with *respect* for—and not by *setting aside* the religious ideas of each individual;

that the argument that one can do without *Christ* in some areas, and that one can do without the Bible, is an argument that does not belong in the mouth of a Christian, who, out of love for his Lord, and for the salvation of people, must be on the lookout for places where he could still bring *Christ* and the Bible;

Because of all of these reasons, the Undersigned respectfully turn to Your Majesty, with the request that you do not give your Royal approval to the presently pending Law for the Regulation of Elementary Education, but by splitting up the Public School into Protestant, Catholic and Israeli Schools, you will want to ensure that the religious ideas of each are respected.

Wormser 57

C. M. Budde-Stomp to J. Wormser-van der Ven
Burlington, January 1858

Dearly Beloved Friend,

Again the year has ended, and I have taken up my pen to answer your letter that I enjoyed so much. Through the goodness of the Lord all of us, and also my husband, enjoy reasonably good health, though we have not been without our troubles and distress. Our neighbor had sold his land to speculators for a high price, but then a money crisis developed, many banks failed, and many places of work, like factories, closed. As a result, the land was neither sold nor rented and remained idle. And so almost all year long we were plagued by stray cattle that repeatedly broke in and destroyed our crops; in addition the Lord sent a drought so that crops were slow in coming up, and because of the shortage of grass, cattle broke in everywhere. The Lord did not deal with us according to our sins but gave a delayed harvest, so that along with the hard times food prices dropped to low levels.

Because of the slowdown in his factory, our son Johan, with the approval of his boss, is now working on a steam-operated saw mill, the machinery of which he had installed; he is staying on there to operate the saws. But he is [working] about six miles inland; he comes home on Saturday evenings and goes back again on Mondays. The family is in reasonably good health; their eldest son is almost six years and goes to the English school with Diedrich and Maria and is learning some Dutch with me. Their little daughter is one year old, walks by herself, is a sweet child, and her name is Elizabeth Maria Sophia.

We rejoice in your blessings, and also in the unexpected increase in your family. May your daughter's entering into holy matrimony be a source of much joy to you, and if it please the Lord to grant them offspring, may you behold the offspring of your offspring, and may the Lord bless them and make them to walk in his ways.

I very much enjoyed your description of your dwelling. I have set many footsteps along that canal. When my parents were still living by the water, we used to go to church through the *Stoofsteeg* and on to the *Hoogstraat* as far as the *Klovenierburgwal*. And I recall a house in the middle of the canal with a lower story and a high stoop rising from the *Stoofsteeg*, not very wide, and a side room with a window, where the old Mr. De Roever lived. If that should be your dwelling, do let me know sometime, and, if it is not, then I can still visualize in my mind the canal where the Lord appointed your dwelling. Having sweet water in houses in Amsterdam assuredly is a great pleasure. The [secular] world makes great inventions; the people of the Lord may also enjoy them. Glorify and praise the Lord for them. Our city also has gaslights in shops and churches, and there are lanterns in the streets.

Since May we have had a preacher in our midst, F. Delvoa. He said that Rev. [A.H.W.] Brandt of Amsterdam was his spiritual father. He does not know much Dutch, and in our judgment he is somewhat flighty. Whether we will keep him, we do not know. We still do not

Scholte Church, Pella

have a church, and the hard times make it more difficult to think about building! Oh, if only we would always call on the Lord for his help, because the silver and gold are his. Our wish and prayer is for a building in which our precious Reformed faith might be proclaimed, for Burlington already has many and large beautiful churches, [but] it still needs a Dutch Reformed one. There are not many of us, and our strength is small; may the Lord graciously grant that we continue to trust in him.

Recently we had a visit from Rev. Vander Meulen; he had attended a classis meeting and was visiting in Pella; he preached in Rev. Scholte's church a couple of times, but then they no longer allowed him to. On his way back he also wanted to pay a visit to the old [Mr.] Budde; we enjoyed it thoroughly. Rev. Klijn, with several members of his congregation, had seceded from the church, but through the efforts of Rev. Vander Meulen they had returned.

You told me of many who are no longer with us. I was especially struck by [the deaths] of Mrs. Höveker and [J.] Barger. If Mrs. Abrahams entered into the rest of the Lord, she is better off, after all; while on earth she was little more than a stranger and wanderer. If your sister Rika is still in the land of the living, my wish is that she may enjoy many of the consolations of the Lord, and if the hour should strike for her to be released from this body, may she then say with the poet:

Zal 't tot sterven gaan,	If death is about to come,
Wilt Gij bij mij staan:	Will Thou then stand by my side:
Door het dal des doods mij leiden,	Lead me through the vale of death,
En tot Uwe wonden leiden,	And lead me to Thy wounds,
Dat ik dan mag gaan,	O may I then stand,
Ter regte hand te staan	On thy right hand.

How are things with Mrs. Zeelt these days, the gardener, and Mijntje? I still often recall that Mijntje had a dislike for Rev. [R.W.] Duin when His Reverence began to wear such a full beard. America is doing likewise: first it was the single men, now it is common for ministers and upper-class folk; some are more coquettish but also include sappers among the military. Is that also the case in Holland? Give my greetings to Mrs. Zeelt, the gardener, and Mijntje. Schilp and his wife returned to their land this fall; they now have two sons and are healthy. I thank you, dear daughter Janjse, for your letter, which I enjoyed so very much; I shall be happy and honored to hear from you again.

And it was you, my dear Johan, who was placed on my lap when your father and mother received the gift of a son. The Lord tested them and let you become deathly ill before you were even a year old, [but] the Lord heard their prayer and gave you back to them again. So then be like the young Samuel and, while you are still young, walk in the fear of the Lord. Yes, my dear Johan, the dear Savior is a friend of children; he called the children to him, blessed them friendly, and kissed them tenderly. What joy it will be for your parents and the people of the Lord [to see] that a young man directs his ways according to the Word of the Lord! David already spoke of being encompassed by vanity, and how much the more in this evil time before [the coming of] Christ. But those who seek their strength in the Lord will not be put to shame. Cordial greetings to your dear spouse and children, most intimately, your friend,

C. M. Budde-Stomp

Greetings from Mrs. Teleman. Her leg is healed again, and Jansje is a domestic in the city.

Budde 19

J. A. Wormser, Jr., to Diedrich Budde, Jr.
Amsterdam, 20 February 1858

Dearly Beloved Friend Diedrich!

With joy and pleasure I received your dear letter yesterday. Your dear letters, the letters for Father, Mother, my sisters and me, arrived very quickly, it seems to me. In January, Father again experienced an attack of rheumatism, so that he could not leave the house for three weeks. Fortunately, he is well again now. My mother often has severe headaches

Johan A. Wormser, Jr. (1845-1916), Amsterdam law clerk

in this time [of year]. Yesterday she had to go to bed already at eight o'clock; she could not stay up because of her headache. I shall be very happy if we can become as good friends as our parents were, even though great seas separate us from each other. We should just write each other every time that our parents send each other letters, for it will give me great pleasure to receive a letter from you.

My aunt Rika also died in the night of November 17. I am very saddened by it, but it is lovely that we can believe that she is in heaven. My sister Cato married Johannes Matheus de Boer September 24. What a long time ago it seems that she got married. It is almost a half year ago already. All is well at our house, and so are Cato and her husband. I hope that that is also the case for you and your family. My Aunt Kaatje, father's sister, who lives in Overijssel, is very ill, and we expect a death notice at any time. Perhaps your parents know her. For the rest, our entire family is well as far as we know. Please do write me soon again.

A few months ago a new pastor arrived here in Amsterdam; he preaches a very nice sermon, and we do believe that he fears the Lord. His name is Hugenholz, and we have heard him many times already. He is very young; we think he is about thirty years old.

February 22

Last night my father and mother went to hear Hugenholz; he preached a very fine sermon. Last night Jansje and I went to hear Hasebroek. He also preached a nice sermon. It was on the eighth Sunday [of the Heidelberg Catechism] on the Trinity. Among other things, he said that some people do not believe in it because they cannot comprehend it, but he said, "Then do not believe either that you are saved by grace, that his blood cleanses us of all our sins, etc., for you cannot understand that either." "Oh," he said, "then what is left of the Bible?"

We are having a very mild winter here, almost no snow. It has been freezing a good deal of late, so that the ice skaters are out. I do not know how to ice-skate, but last summer I did take lessons in swimming; I enjoy it very much. Here in the Achterburgwal the ice is not very nice, and no one is skating. In the Voorburgwal there was quite a lot of it [skating], but not here. We find it very pleasant living here. The office is in a spacious, well-lighted basement, so that it is completely separated from the house. The stoop [entrance] to the house is on the Hoogstraat, and we have two windows in the side room. When you walk into the hallway a little way, you come to a wide step that leads to the chamber, a nice, spacious room. If you go up three more steps, you come to the mezzanine, the playroom of my two younger sisters, and then, having left the mezzanine, you go up another stairs, you come to a spacious nice front room. Up still another stairs you enter the lower attic. In the rear part off that attic there is a nice small room, where my sister Jansje sleeps. Up another stairs you come to the upper attic, where there is a [miscellany of things]. And above that there is a large open attic, in which there is a window that opens on to a flat roof, from which you have a view of half the city.

In thought, I go back down to the hallway, which you can walk through a little farther, and then you enter an inner room in which there are a couple of large cabinets. From the inner room you look out on a small court. Proceeding further through the hallway, and passing the court, you enter a sizable kitchen in which there is a ladder. Going up on it you come to a room, which is half the size of the chamber-room, which is very high, with two windows that look out on the court. That is my room, where I sleep and have a desk with books. Above it there is another room of the same size, which is the maid's room; our maid sleeps there. Going downstairs and entering the hallway again, there is a stairway opposite the court that goes downstairs and takes you into a cellar for wines, potatoes, and other things. Passing through that cellar a little way, you come to the peat storage room, and passing through that you come to the office, a very spacious and [rather] bright cellar room. We have three cabinets there. Finally, going up the steps of the office, you come to the outdoors again. At the moment, our office personnel consists of ten persons. We have eight reading and writing desks, and two people are running errands all day long. Things are rather slow at work these days, so I am now writing at my desk in the office.

In Amsterdam, a certain R. C. Meijer, a book dealer belonging to the Walloon congregation, has written a letter, in which he says that he no longer believes in the fairy tales and fables of the Bible, that he no longer is a Christian, and that he no longer wishes to belong to any of those sects. He requested the Walloon congregation to take note of his renunciation of the faith. What do you say to that? Mind you, that is how far things have gone in Amsterdam.

Feb. 23

For a half-year and more I have been attending a profession of faith class with Rev. Hasebroek on Tuesdays from eleven to twelve, and I like it very much. We have to answer about twenty questions on paper every week, and we have to learn five or six from memory. I attended the class again today.

It is still freezing here all the time. But the ice is very poor just the same, because when it freezes at night, the sun, which is already pretty strong, shines on it again. There are some people falling through the ice here, but in Amsterdam they are very numerous. My niece, the daughter of Uncle Dries, who lives near Amsterdam, assures me that on Sunday and Monday thirty fell into the ditch behind their house. And according to what I hear, eight fell in on Sunday in the city; whether it is true or not, I do not know. And yesterday two fell into the Kloveniersburgwal [canal]. Fortunately, no one drowned as far as I know.

Eight days ago there was a very big fire three-and-a-half canals from our house. Two houses were burned out completely, and the third was badly damaged. It began at seven o'clock, and by eight-thirty they had the fire "under control," according to the newspaper, but I heard that it was still burning at one-thirty. I went over to see at seven-thirty, and then it was burning at its worst. I had never seen a burning house before. A fire is something I find pitiable and terrible, but the fire, as such, I find nice [to see].

Now, esteemed friend, I must conclude. Give my greetings and those of my parents and sisters to your dear parents, to your sister Maria, and also to your brother Johan. With highest esteem, I am,

> Your loving Friend,
> J. Wormser, Jr.

Budde 20

> Johanna Schellinger to D. A. Budde
> Alkmaar, 5 April 1858

[Dear] Sir and Friend,

Thanks to the friendly offer of Mr. and Mrs. Coster (formerly Mrs. Bleekser), I have this opportunity to send Your Honors a small package, and I hope that you and your wife will not mind that I have a little favor for your daughter. Since I learned from your letter that the young lady is Naatje's age, I wondered if it might not be nice to honor both of them with a small silver pocket book, and my nephew Mathijs with a silver cigar holder, as a kind of remembrance, and hoping that it will be to their liking.

Your Honors' reports concerning my beloved sister continue to be sad and move us deeply. And since she has been in this deplorable condition for so many months, and even while Mr. Van der Mooren [Van der Moor] was still living, there is little hope for recovery. The thought of her sad lot often reminds me how dark the ways of Providence are. And then our only hope is in the Lord, that he may grant us strength to bear what his wisdom and love decrees for us. I [wish to] express my sincere thanks to Your Honors for the reports.

Concerning the inheritance of Van der Mooren, [the important thing] for us is that with the blessing of the Lord he had acquired sufficient capital, so that everyone got the money he had coming, and that there is also something left for the children, though not much. It was very comforting to me to note from your letter how involved Your Honors are with my Naatje, nurturing her in the fear of the Lord. And that in Your Honors she has found people who hold religion in such high esteem; that is very important to her and to us. I can well imagine how much effort it has cost you and your wife to bend her will to yours. There doubtless was much lacking in her education, because it must have been neglected not a little because of sad circumstances. I will always be gratified to receive some word from you, since I prize highly the friendship with which Your Honors have been willing to honor me. And so I commend myself graciously to Your Honors, with the sincere wish that it may please the Lord that you and all your relations may receive this [letter] in well being. And so I extend my best wishes to Your Honors and all yours, even though they are unknown to me, and to Naatje. I call myself, with highest esteem,

The humble Servant and Friend of Your Honors,
Johanna Schellinger

Budde 21

Mrs. J. Wormser-van der Ven to Mrs. C. M. Budde-Stomp
Amsterdam 26 April 1858

Dearly Beloved Friend!

As ever, we were just delighted when we received your esteemed letter of January [W.57]. To our joy we might learn from it that you were in good health. Still, it did grieve us to see that you too get your share of troubles and sorrow. But what else can we expect, as long as we carry about this body of sin on this sinful earth? We too are enjoying many blessings and prosperity, but we are not without our trials as well. My dear husband continues to suffer rather frequently from rheumatism. He has already had two attacks this year, and over time that does undermine your system and your joints get stiff.

Our daughter Cato entered into matrimony on September 24, and presently she has [my] former condition [health problem?] for the second time already. Both times it was caused by a scare: the first time it was the death announcement of my sister Rica, who died in the Lord on November 16. My husband and I had spent the entire evening with her [Rica]. She was fully conscious and spoke [to us]; from time to time my husband spoke and read to her and prayed with her. At twelve-thirty, she said it was all right for us to go home for a while. Although she lives just diagonally across from us, on Hetruslandstreet, we had scarcely gotten home when [Mr. J.] Sielof came over to tell us that she was no more. She was a firm believer, trusting in the promises of God, and thus she has entered into her rest. I miss in her the last of my sisters. My husband's sister, Kaatje, in Overijssel, is also in a very critical condition, and so we expect her death tiding at any time, but she cannot await her end with such assurance [of faith]. Mrs. Siemons passed away on the 3rd of February, and [just] a week later her husband [died]. It was quite moving; he had been ailing for a long time, and his wife was hale and well. A few days before her death she began to cough, and then she passed away before her husband. About six or seven weeks ago, the aged Sielof, coppersmith on Het Ruslandstraat, passed away.

As far as the church situation goes, it remains very sad. To be sure, we have Rev. Hasebroek who is good; for [Rev.] Kortenhoef Smit [we now have] [Rev.] Hugenholz, who is passable to listen to.

The German [Rev.] Brandt, like your German [preacher], is also something of an enthusiast. He is not getting any better of late, and he is always admonishing in his preaching, as if he never has any believers in his audience. That is all right for a time, but after a while one feels the need to be edified. And that pretty well sums up all that we have to listen to in the *Hervormde Kerk*.

Things are also sad among the Seceders. After Van Velzen left for Kampen, they called Rev. De Waal. The man declined two times, but the third time he accepted. We met him and his wife for several hours at the home of Mrs. Zeelt last summer. To us it seemed that he was not a very learned Christian, but sincere and adhering to Evangelical principles. However, the well-known group of old believers made life so miserable for him that the man left joyfully for Assen, where, I am told, his salary is fl.500 less. Yesterday he preached his farewell sermon, and rumor has it that the congregation is now dividing into two groups. So we do not for one moment regret that we are no longer members there; at least we can go wherever we wish, and no one bothers us. We surely can view the disputes with sadness, but still it is not as grievous as when we ourselves were involved.

My dear friend, you ask whether we are living in the house of the aged Mr. De Roever. I also distinctly remember having read that name often. But it is exactly next to that, in the direction of the Hoogstraat, so that our doorstep adjoins theirs. Our house has two side room windows, and we like it very much. Every day we speak of it, how the Lord has provided us with such a good dwelling. Now that Cato and Jansje are not at home, there is quite a lot of work for one maid. Now I will be getting Fientje van Gunther as a second girl in May. The old gentleman is dead, and the widow [Fientje's mother?] is most happy about the work arrangement. Fientje is nineteen years old, has learned how to sew, and if I teach her how to do the washing, she can be of much help to me. It is all getting to be too much for me; the housekeeping and the children demand too much work.

It grieves us that our friend Jan is having such a hard time finding work. The money crisis has also been a hardship for many people here, and many a business went bottom up. But it did not have any ill effects for us. They were very busy at the office protesting checks for nonacceptance. We sincerely hope that business conditions may soon change for the better for you, and that your son may be able to earn his daily bread for his family in your midst. Johan is enclosing a note for you and Diederich [Diedrich], but because of postage costs Jansje will not do it this time.

Mrs. Zeelt, the gardener, and Mijntje [his wife] are all still in good health. This very day we had a farmer who lives opposite her visiting at our house; he said that she is getting to be an old dotard. She does not come to town often, and when she comes she always has someone with her, and she has a cane. She is seventy-eight years old now, but she is as restless and active as ever, so that we do not care to spend even one day there every summer.

And now my dear friend, let us not always keep each other waiting for word any more. We always long to hear from you, and we are very interested in how you and your children are doing. Give them our greetings, and your friend who loves you deeply commends you and your husband to the Lord and his Grace.

J. Wormser-van der Ven

Budde 22

J(ansje) Wormser to Mrs. C. M. Budde-Stomp
Amsterdam, 27 April 1858

My Dear Ma'am, Esteemed Friend!

I had first intended to pass up this opportunity to enclose a letter, but since there were still some matters about which mother did not write, I changed my mind. I wanted to write you in somewhat greater detail what the wedding day of my sister was like. Our quay was under repair, which was a big nuisance, since it meant that they could not marry from our house, because the carriages could not ride up the quay along the canal. Then Father asked Mr. Noordbeek if the bride and bridegroom and all the family might come to his house, just as if that were the home of the bride. Mr. Noordbeek lives on the Voorburgwal across from *De Oude Kerk*. Mr. and Mrs. Noordbeek approved of this; they spent the whole day with us. Early in the morning the bride, dressed in her workaday clothes, went with mother to Mr. Noordbeek's home. She got dressed there, and then waited for the family to come. She was dressed in a black silk gown, dark [interwoven] cloth, and a white hat made by Saartje Luuring. At ten o'clock we had to be at the city hall, and at twelve in the Oude Kerk, where Rev. Hasebroek was to marry them; the church was filled. The text of the minister was, "Our citizenship is in heaven"; the three points: (1) Our citizenship from heaven, (2) for heaven, and (3) to heaven. It was very sweet the way he married them, and everyone was moved by it. After they were married, the wedding moved to the home of Uncle Dries. After church the minister immediately went along in the carriage. We then had a very delightful afternoon. We sat down to eat at two-thirty, and by five-thirty the wedding was already over. The minister began with prayer, talked about various subjects with Father: first about marriage, then about baptism, church, and school. Afterward Father said that it seemed more like a synod than a wedding. In between, the minister had us sing Psalm 116, verses 7 and 8. After Dominie had closed with prayer, everyone went home, and they took us, our family, and the newlyweds to their dwelling. That evening they left from there to go by train to The Hague. Then they made a nice little trip through Germany. Now it is already more than a half year ago; my sister was not even twenty-one when she got married.

April 28. That is as far as I got copying last night, when Truitje Jaspers stopped in for a visit. She came to tell me that she was to become a bride the next day; she is marrying a certain [Mr.] Scholz, a carpenter's helper. He is twenty-four and Truitje is turning twenty-nine. They are going to live in the Eerste Weteringdwarsstraat, across from the Walloon orphanage. Things were not very nice for her living with her third mother. Truitje asked me to send you her cordial greetings. Kaatje Lijsen married Van Lente in June. They have a potato and [door]mats business in the Weesperstraat. I visited them once; they have very nice living accommodations and the house belongs to them. We hear that they are very happy. Eight days ago Kaatje gave birth to a son. Everything is going according to plan for them.

The eldest daughter of Höveker, Betje, whom you probably still remember, was first keeping company with a student, but she could not love him, and because of his consumption it came to an end. Now she is going with an office man; recently he coughed up blood, so that is also a sad prospect.

Well, dear Ma'am, now I still have written a good deal. Willem Luuring has been working in Father's office since November. The Luuring family is well, but the Mrs. is aging fast. The Mr. [Luuring] still visits with us every Friday evening. Mrs. Jansen [Janssen] has had her tenth stroke attack; she is completely paralyzed on one side. Mrs. Gunther is caring for her. Old [Mr.] Jansen [Janssen] is still the same; nowadays he belongs to the church of Rev. [Jan] De Liefde. At the Doornhouwer home everything is still the same; his daughter Truitje suffers much from nervous attacks, so that from time to time she is hospitalized for weeks. The eldest daughter of Uncle Dries made profession of faith with Rev. Hasebroek shortly before Easter.

And now, dear Ma'am, I hope you and the whole family may receive this letter in good health and well-being. Thanks to the goodness of the Lord we may also be well. After giving my greetings to all the family, I name myself,

Your Friend who loves you sincerely,
J[ansje] Wormser

P.S. I hope that next time you will include a few lines to me.

Budde 23

Johanna Schellinger to D. A. Budde
Alkmaar, 9 June 1858

[Dear] Sir and Friend!

I have postponed writing to Your Honor too long. Because these matters were of too little interest to you, I did not want to bother you with trivia. And if it might please the Lord that my letter should reach you, and if I have not spoiled things too much by my neglect in writing, it would make me very happy, and it would even increase my joy, if I might receive any message at all from you. And although I did not write you, still in my thoughts I have been at your dwelling so very often, with the sincere wish that the Lord may teach you, and that he may have spared all those who are dear to you.

My niece, if she is still living, must almost be a full-grown girl. And if she could enclose a short letter within yours, be it ever so brief, she would really surprise me so, and I would enjoy it so much. It has often given me a sense of peace that she is so well placed with you. How much the education in the fear of the Lord she gets at your house will soon teach her to realize that there is a loving Father who directs all that befalls us, and that among the many good things that we receive from him, he also grants us the great privilege that we can share our thoughts with each other, despite the great distance that separates us. I appreciate this all the more, because my dear sister was not favored with such good fortune, and there are many like her.

Since I last wrote you, Sir, I have again experienced many things. I believe that I wrote you about the passing of my good, aged mother. And now I have also lost my highly esteemed *Mevrouw* [mistress]; an illness of long duration terminated her life. I served Her Honor [as a household maid] for thirty-three years. Her husband passed away already when I had been there a good year. Most of her life my mistress was suffering from this ailment or that. She had a *Jufvrouw* [lady] for forty years. But the rest of the (workers?) alternated more. Accordingly, the mistress made [financial] arrangements so that we are freed from servitude [i.e. no longer having to work as household servants]. Now the lady and I agreed to live together in much smaller quarters. And I was deeply grateful that I was so very fortunate, because I have also always thought highly of the *Jufrouw*, because she was such a noble and sweet person. But my good fortune was of short duration; it was given to us to live together for only six months, when a brief illness also took her from me. Losing her struck me very hard, since I am losing an upright friend in her, one I will not find again in anyone else. We had so much wished to taste some of the joys of life; just having our freedom [from work] provided us much pleasure. The family of *Mevrouw* would have wished a longer life for her, also because she had spent so much time with our [ailing] Mistress and had always dealt most patiently with everything. They had high esteem for her, but what is man and what are his prospects in this life? They are gone in a moment. It teaches us ever to look up to a higher life, where there is no more separation. It is the Lord who directs our destiny, and I should be reconciled to that. Indeed, all he does is in wisdom and love.

The good *Jufrouw* has also remembered me [with a bequest], so that I have rented a small house and live all by myself. And since I have always enjoyed being alone, this quiet life does agree with me. Being able to think about the beloved dead unhindered, and thus to focus on the things above, gives one so much consolation. And since I am fond of reading and, since to my joy I own *Het Bijbels Magesijn* [the *Biblical Magazine*] and still other things, I am never bored, which puzzles my friends at times. My highly esteemed mistress bequeathed me some money on a weekly basis, which stops when I pass away. She also gave me a thousand guilders, which I may dispose of as I wish, and which I have put out at interest. She also gave me some bedding, tableware, and furniture. And now it was my desire, since we do not know the day or hour death, to have these things officially recorded, the things that I can now legally call my own. It probably will not amount to much, if it is to be divided. But if I do not have it recorded, much of it will just disappear, and strangers will run off with the things for which I have worked so long and gotten with the Lord's blessing.

And that is why, Sir, I kindly request whether Your Honor would be so kind to inform me whether my niece, Johanna van der Moor, is still living. I would also very much like to find out something about Mathijs van der Moor, where he is living and how he is faring. Here in the Netherlands I only have two nephews, both sons of my oldest brother. I had nine brothers and sisters, and all of them are dead and buried with the greater part of my family.

I hope, dear Sir, that I have not demanded too much of your [time and] attention, but I know your interest in the fortunes of our family. And for that I hope that you may experience the blessing of the Lord in rich measure, and also that I may receive good reports from you. Herewith, I request that you give my sincere regards to you and your family and also to my dear niece. I sign with highest esteem,

The faithful Servant of your Honor,
Johanna Schellinger

My address: Joh. Schellinger, Doelestraat, Alkmaar

Wormser 58

C. M. Budde-Stomp to J. Wormser-van der Ven
Burlington, 10 December 1858

Dearly Beloved Friend!

Thanks to the goodness of the Lord we have received all your honored letters in good health. Our wish is that all may also be well with you when you receive this letter. We rejoice in the hope of the blessed death of your beloved sister Rika. When I saw her for the first time, who would have said that she too was one of the chosen of the Lord; I loved her dearly.

This spring our parental heart was saddened. Our son Johan's working arrangements came to an end. Because of the hard times, no work was to be had, and Jan just does not care much for farming. He decided to travel to St. Louis to see if he could find work there. The separation was very hard on us; my dear husband wept like a child, [but] we had to acquiesce in the ways of the Lord. And he was back soon again and [decided] to help his father work the farm until there would be work at the foundry again. On the 4th of November the Lord granted them a daughter, and they called her Elena Louisa. My daughter-in-law is doing passably well, but once again she had a caked breast that required surgery. They now have three lovely children. The oldest is a son, and they have two daughters.

Six weeks before Easter our Rev. Delvoa announced—like a farmhand—that he was leaving. It came as a surprise; no one knew anything of it. My dear husband asked him where he was going, and he answered that the Lord would provide. Looking back, it was clear that he had done more to break down the congregation than to build it up, and that he had set the members against each other. Now it looked like everything was done for; the congregation was scarcely willing to get together once a month on the day of the Lord for worship. My husband immediately wrote a letter to New York. In our great distress the Lord had mercy on us; the board of the Dutch Reformed Church immediately sent a minister, Rev. J. Muller, born in Saxony. He was converted under the preaching of Rev. [Johannes C.] Guldin in New York. He is now thirty-two years old, studied English for seven years, and his ministry in an English congregation for seven years was blessed. He had a desire to preach the gospel to his countrymen in Burlington. His wife is an English lady of Dutch descent, whose mother still speaks Dutch; she was glad to be going to the Hollanders, but she died while they were still packing [for the trip]. They have a little son of three years, and a second child was due soon. He was installed July 25 and his text was Proverbs 4:1, "Hear, ye children, the instruction of a father, and attend to know understanding." I wish that you could have heard the sermon, but the Word of God remains unto all eternity and therefore the people of the Lord will understand it more perfectly in the blessed eternity, and may the Lord in his grace bring us thither. His Reverence is now preaching three times, [once for us] and twice in English for the Presbyterians; their minister had left and now they have asked him to preach for them until they again have a minister of their own. Our children follow him in English. Diedrich can practically also understand him in German, so that we are able to discuss the sermon together.

And now we really had to get to work; it was a matter of necessity that we have a church of our own. And so it was decided to build a chapel on the lot in the back section that could hold at least 160 listeners. Later, if it is the Lord's will for the congregation to grow, it can be used as a parsonage. Plans are to dedicate it on Sunday, December 19. We are sure that you will rejoice at this with us, and praise the Lord for his mercies and that our [Reformed] witness may also be located in the Far West under the protection of the Lord.

In the course of the summer we had a visit from Rev. Oggel. His Reverence was on his way to Pella to preach there for six weeks; you see, the Reformed people have built a church there. They had asked the Holland minister to preach there until they would have called a minister. His Reverence lives in Grand Haven, Michigan. We really enjoyed His Reverence, and on his return trip he paid us another visit. In the course of our conversation, we looked up something in the Bible [and explained] that Mrs. Zeelt had been instrumental in its [the Bible's] publication. Then His Reverence [suggested] that Mrs. Zeelt be requested to furnish a number of [Dutch] Bibles for their academy. I had remembered this request, and when our cause was making so much progress, it occurred to me that we request that Her Honor give a Dutch Reformed Bible in her remembrance to the Dutch Reformed Church in Burlington. If Your Honor approves, then please be so kind as to ask her for me; that seemed better to me than writing. Our minister uses the Dutch Bible on occasion; it is closer to the English text, because the German text often diverges. Although most of the time he consults the original languages, and that was also the case when a Dutch minister preached for us once.

Walking is difficult for me, especially when it is slippery. Our old, trusty horse is aging, the younger ones have not been sufficiently broken in as yet. And you always have to be on your guard with them. We had lots of rain this year, so that we could hardly get anything in the ground. Later on, the Lord gave us favorable weather so that we were still granted a forfeited harvest. The city has again been enriched with a new market building, much like the covered one in Amsterdam. There are fancy covered [stone] counters on both sides, in which each butcher has his own area. In the center there are big columns where the farmers have their section. In the winter there are four stoves where you can warm up. There is market every day. During the winter Diedrich goes; my husband cannot take it any longer.

Gladden us soon with a reply. Be so kind to give our warmest greetings to Mrs. Zeelt, the gardener, and to Mijntje. Greet your esteemed spouse and children, the manly Johan, Mr. and Mrs. De Boer. Also give greetings from Mrs. Teleman and daughter. The Lord bless you and keep you all as the year comes to an end. May his countenance go with you into the new [year] and enable you to go on until the struggle is done and we enter into eternal joy.

> Your Friend who thinks of you always,
> C. M. Budde-Stomp

Budde 24

> D. A. Budde to Church at Burlington
> 19 Dec.1858
> (Opening address for church in Burlington)

This memorable day is important, as well as a time for rejoicing. I am also deeply moved that I may address a few words to my Dutch fellow believers. But let us give expression to this emotion by singing the rhymed version of Psalm 118, verse 12:

> *Dit is de dag, de roem der dagen*
> *Dien Isrels God geheiligd heeft.*
> *Laat ons verheugd, van zorg ontslagen,*
> *Hem roemen, die ons blijdschap geeft.*

[A free rendition of this verse follows:]

This is the day, the day of days,
Which Israel's God has sanctified.
Let us rejoice, free from cares,
Praise him, who gives us joy.

This is from the Lord. It is a day of glad rejoicing that we, My Brothers and Sisters, are experiencing today. Do you not recall with me, when we arrived in this good land, how we also found the Dutch [Reformed] Church, with all its institutions, and how it served to strengthen us in our faith, and to rejoice in God? The confirmation of our faith was confirmed no less when we met Brethren from other regions of this world, who joined with us to be a part of the Congregation of Christ in the land of our Sojourn. And though we experienced various trials and adversities, our experience was like that of the Dove that Noah let out from window of the Ark, which did not find a resting place for the hollow of its foot.

What adversity did we not encounter after we were barely two months into the year that has flown past? Did it not seem that it was all over for us here in Burlington? And still in the midst of all these all ups and downs, never once did we conclude that the Lord might not be favorable to us. No, the Lord remembered us as he did Noah, who roved about on the waters, in grace and mercy. The Lord upheld us, however often we lost heart and gave up the idea of getting a house of prayer for him. And what did the Lord now do? He sent one of his servants to us. We were encouraged to build a house unto the Lord. We were made willing to contribute. Indeed, the Lord, whose are the silver and the gold, softened the hearts of so many to contribute, to all of whom we today express our thanksgiving, even as today we may, for the first time, solemnly consecrate this House to the worship of God, and to the glorifying of his name. Now our joy rises, now we clap our hands, now we may rejoice, this is from...[the Lord].

When we call to mind the love and affection of our American Brethren, how very clear it is that their Dutch blood has not yet been extinguished in them. Let us highly esteem that Confession for which our Fathers sacrificed their all, their lives and goods. We have no less reason to rejoice in the Lord our God, since it was for that confession that in the old Fatherland we suffered defamation and contempt, money fines, and some of our Brethren even had to undergo punishment in prison. Rejoice and be glad in God. We are no longer limited to the number twenty, but now we may sing of the glory and praise of God with all those who love the Lord.

Yes, indeed, we can and may rejoice now that for the first time we have assembled to proclaim the faithfulness and truth of our covenant God, who is mindful of us in the land of our Sojourn. And he will also prepare the table on which the manna of heaven will be handed to us. The Lord Jehovah himself is our fountain-head, whereby our hearts are abundantly lavished, quickened, and strengthened, as long as we remain here below in the church militant in order to overcome all the difficulties of this life.

Rejoice and be glad, Beloved. The Lord does not do unto us according to our sins. He has established with us an eternal Covenant of Grace, which is well ordained in all things. Just consider our small Congregation. In ourselves we have nothing lovable for which Jehovah might look upon us in grace. No! Nothing but sin! Leprous from head to foot, so that we ought to cry out: Unclean—unclean. Rejoice and be glad, Beloved. Let the praise of the Lord be proclaimed by us in our profession and walk of life, so that it may be evident that we are no longer our own, but that we belong to Jesus Christ, purchased with the precious blood of God, so that we may live unto him.

But may the voice of rejoicing and gladness be mingled with the voice of lament today by some Dutch friends, as was the case in time past at the laying of the foundations of the second temple, because we do not now hear the word of life being proclaimed in our Dutch language. Is this not just a minor loss for some among us, since our children understand it in the English language, which is becoming their mother tongue? Yes indeed! If they walk in the fear of the Lord, they can also propagate the truth, and the Kingdom of God will be enlarged. But I must be brief, so that I do not bore the friends who do not understand Dutch.

And now a word to our young people, in connection with the blessings that have been ours. Let your choice be that of the psalmist in Psalm 104, verses 23 and 34. I shall [praise?] the Lord, that is the sincere prayer of David (Psalm 119, verse 5). Oh, that my ways [were directed to keep thy statutes!] You will then become an ornament of God's church and be a blessing to others, just as we experience this today in the land of our sojourn.

Beloved! I repeat it once more, with regard to the day that we are experiencing today. This is the [Holy One[?]. O Lord, do good unto Zion and build the walls of Zion for thy name's sake. And now let us take our harps from the willow trees once more as we sing Psalm 100 [stanza 1:]

[All people that on earth do dwell, sing to the Lord with cheerful voice; him serve with mirth, his praise forth tell, Come ye before him and rejoice.]

And Psalm 134 stanza 3:

[Jehovah bless thee from above, From Zion in his boundless love,
Our God, who heaven and earth did frame; Blest be his great and holy name.]

[From *Psalter Hymnal, Centennial Edition.* 1959.]

Wormser 59

D. A. Budde to J. A. Wormser and Spouse
Burlington, 21 December 1858

Esteemed and Dearly Beloved Brother and Sister in the Lord!

  I should have replied long ago to your esteemed letter of May 6th instant, but a number of things have contributed to its being postponed so long. We rejoice greatly in your well being both in body and soul. Thanks to God's free grace and favor, that is true for us also. All of us find ourselves in reasonably good health right now, with the exception of Maria who coughs a great deal. We surely have a rich God and Father who provides for all our needs according to body and soul for the sake of his Son Jesus Christ. In the past we were well off in Amsterdam, and by the grace of God we were privileged to acknowledge that at the time. Our good God lives and cares for us so well and so kindly in America that we often say to each other in all simplicity, "How well the Lord has provided for us in a foreign land." We are lacking in nothing and have everything in abundance; and we may quicken each other and feel happy together when we leave church to recall and discuss the Word and promises of God. Then we realize that we have learned only the first principles of the inexhaustible Word of God that leads unto salvation. How wonderful it will be when we shall have laid aside the body of sin and death, and the veil of our blindness, which is now rent, shall be wholly removed, so that we may enter the holy of holies to praise God unto all eternity!

  As far as church matters are concerned, we have made one step forward. After wandering about in a foreign land for several years and having had to struggle with many ups and downs, we had made no progress. To be sure we did have a minister on two occasions, but we just stayed where we were. They were men who were not suited for the church in Germany either [Rev. Madoulet and Rev. Delvoa], like so many others who come here. And because of the scarcity of ministers, you have to make do with them, just as we had to at the beginning of the Secession. To counter this, the synod passed a resolution not to accept as ministers in the Dutch [Reformed] Church any men coming from abroad until they had spent a year at their academy and satisfactorily passed an examination. Last April we were again without a minister; the situation of our little group was sad indeed. It appeared that the Reformed community in Burlington was about to die out completely. I wrote to New York, telling them how things were here, and behold the Lord did not deal with us according to our sins. Jehovah prepared the heart of one of his servants so that he was ready and willing to preach the gospel in Burlington.

We received word that Rev. [John] Muller would be coming to us. His Reverence was generally known and respected; he had studied at the Holland Academy and was qualified to work in our church. Rev. Muller arrived here last July, and his first sermon among us was on Isaiah 49, versus 15 and 16. ["Can a woman forget her sucking child, that she should not have compassion on the son of her womb? Yea, they may forget, yet I will not forget thee. Behold I have graven thee upon the palms of my hands; thy walls are continually before me."] It made us ashamed, but at the same time it was comforting, so that it seemed as if everything among us was again coming to life from the dead; there was movement among those dead bones. And so far he has remained constant in his preaching; esteem for him is growing. And since he has been preaching for us in High German, and in English for the Presbyterians, he has become so well known that among the religious element he stands out above all other ministers in Burlington. We may say that his preaching is a manifestation of the Spirit with power, wholly free, and without regard for persons, for that is a great evil in the English churches, so that the world has such a large presence there, rather than Christ alone.

Last September we began discussions about building a small church or chapel. We were all agreed that there was a need for it, but what about the costs in such a bad time as this? I said that if we do not build a house unto the Lord now, then we will never do it. A fortnight later we drew up a [subscription] list in order to determine how much money we could raise in order to get started. The house was contracted out for 1,150 dollars, to which 100 dollars can be added for unforeseen expenditures. The dimensions of the building were to be 27 x 38 feet and 20 feet high on the inside. And then the builders got to work—the consistory members canvassed the town for funds. The Lord, whose are both the silver and the gold, inclined so many hearts to be generous that friends and foes alike contributed, and so we can already meet half the costs, and when the other half must be paid three months from now, the Lord will also make provision for us.

Last Sunday, on the 19th of December, the building was consecrated as a house of prayer to the Lord for the first time. Rev. Muller began the service with prayer, followed by [Scripture] reading: 2 Chronicles 6. [Then] a hymn, prayer, hymn; the text was II Chronicles 7, 15-16: ["Now mine eye shall be open, and mine ears attend unto the prayer that is made in this place. For now I have chosen and sanctified this house, that my name may be there forever: and mine eyes and mine heart shall be there perpetually."] The Lord was well pleased with Solomon's temple. The Lord heard Solomon's prayer. The Lord gave Solomon more than he asked for. After the sermon our Dutch friends sang stanza 12 of Psalm 118:

Dit is de dag, de roem der dagen	This is the day, day of glory and renown
dien Israels God geheiligd heeft	Which Israel's God has sanctified;
Laat ons verheugd, van zorg ontslagen	Come, let us rejoice, free from cares
Hem roemen, die ons blijdschap geeft.	And praise him who gives us joy.
Och Heer, geef thans uw zegeningen	Oh Lord, now give your blessings,
Och Heer, geef heil op dezen dag	Oh Lord, grant salvation on this day.
Och, dat men op deez' eerstelingen	Oh, that on these firstlings we may see
Een rijken oogst van voorspoed zag!	A rich harvest of prosperity!

[free translation by W.L]

And after I had spoken a few words to them, we sang Psalm 100 and stanza 3 of Psalm 134; then the minister did the closing prayer, we sang, and he gave the closing benediction. It was a memorable day for us and for Burlington. To the existing thirteen church structures, a fourteenth has now been added, in which the Reformed confessions with the same institutions for which our fathers sacrificed life and limb might be carried on, to the praise of God's free grace. In the afternoon His Reverence preached in English, a service attended by many Americans. We then went homeward, contented and happy. Our feelings are expressed in stanzas 2 and 3 of Psalm 126:

God heeft bij ons wat groots verricht:	God has done great things for us
Hij zelf heeft onzen druk verlicht	He himself has lifted our burden.
Hij heeft door wond'ren ons bevrijd, *Dies juichen wij en zijn verblijd.* *Breng, Heer, al uw gevang'nen weder,*	He liberated us by miracles, And so we sing and rejoice. Oh Lord, bring all your pris'ners back,
Zie verder op uw erfvolk neder,	do look down on your inheritance,
Verkwik het als de watervloed, *die 't zuiderland herleven doet.*	refresh it as the flood of waters which the south land doth revive
Die hier bedrukt met tranen zaait,	Who downcast with tears here sows,
zal juichen als hij vruchten maait.	Shall rejoice when fruits he mows.
Die 't zaad draagt, dat men zaaien zal,	He who carries the seed to be sown,
gaat wenend voort en zaait het al,	Goes forth weeping and sows it all,
maar hij zal zonder ramp te schromen *eerlang met blijdschap wederkomen*	but with no fear of calamity, erelong he shall return gladsome
en met gejuich te goeder uur	and come rejoicing when the time is ripe
zijn schoven dragen in de schuur.	Bearing his sheaves into the barn.

[Free translation by W.L.]

I cannot write you much about the revival that began in this land last year. It got started in the Reformed Church in New York. An hour of prayer was begun, at midday, between twelve and one, which was so well attended that within a short time fourteen churches were opened to follow this example. And so it has been taking place mostly in the big cities, and it still moves on slowly. In Burlington we have seen no traces of it.

Receive Cordial Greetings From Your,
D. A. Budde

[*on the backside*]
Since I hear nothing from my relatives in Leer, please be so kind and mail the enclosed letter for me. Cordial greetings, give my greetings to your dear children. D. A. B.

Wormser 60

C. M. Budde-Stomp to Miss Jansje Wormser
Burlington, 21 December 1858

My Dearly Beloved Friend,
Your warm affection towards us gives me joy. The detailed account of the wedding day of your beloved sister, Mrs C. de Boer, reminded me of the enjoyable meals with friends at the home of your very dearly beloved parents. We have not had such communal get-togethers since then. We do enjoy esteem, but there is not the communal bond of love that was intensified by shared oppression and troubles. We live in the hope that after having fought the good fight, we shall be present at the wedding feast of the Lamb and meet each other there to adore and praise the Lord for his mercies, in greater holiness and more glorious than we can possibly imagine here. Your Honor wrote of the clothing of the bride, and I was happy about that. In the old fatherland, and also here in America, among fashionable people, it has become customary for the bride to appear at the altar with her hair dressed, that is, with her head uncovered. As I see it, that is contrary to the Word of God, and so they cannot expect the Lord's approval. People follow the fashion [of the day], and how many will even give it a second thought? I rejoiced that your young niece has been experiencing the means of grace [Word and sacrament]; may the Lord grant her a love for the truth. I was attracted to her already when she was a child. I also rejoiced about Truitje Jaspers, and I wish her the blessing of the Lord in her marriage.

Before the year's end, the Lord let us experience a remarkable and joyous day: the solemn dedication of a Dutch Reformed chapel in Burlington by our esteemed minister, the Reverend Muller. With all our hearts we sang, "This thing is from the Lord Almighty, it is a marvel in our eyes" [Psalm 118, stanza 11, *Psalter Hymnal* #233]. The text was 2 Chronicles 7, verses 15 and 16. It is a neat, nice little church, an American pulpit, bright gleaming white, a flat lectern covered with a blue flannel cover and fringe on which the Bible rests. Behind it there is a cushioned bench with arm rests, one foot above the floor; three ministers can sit on it. From now on the morning sermon will be in High German, and the afternoon one in English.

Well, dear Jansje, I hope that I have fulfilled your wish and now I look forward to being honored with a couple of letters from Your Honor. I hope that you receive this letter in good health. After friendly greetings to your dear parents, sisters, and brothers, I wish Your Honor the blessing of the Lord, and I remain with highest esteem,

Your Friend,
C. M. Budde-Stomp

Our son Johan, Diedrich, and Maria send warmest greetings to you and your dear parents and relatives.

Addendum from Documentatiecentrum Nederlands Protestantisme, Vrije Universiteit te Amsterdam [JS].

The Right Reverend Mr. [Johannes H.] Donner, Preacher at Leiden

Pella, Iowa, 5 March 1859

Beloved Brother,

A letter from Van Raalte, really! Yes, my dear friend. We live in an age of miracles. So just do not be overly surprised. You have received a call from Pella, and now I would like to put in my two cents worth. I, too, would so very much like to have you here, and that is why the cat licks the candle stick [is buttering you up]. There, that is the whole story in a nutshell. But long ago, when I was young, they used to say, "Quit your kidding." Well, let's talk seriously. I am eager to see you here if it would please the Lord, and I have my reasons for that. A very large number of Dutchmen live here, and it will continue to be a drawing point for [people in] the Old Netherlands. For years I have been deeply concerned about Pella. I was aware that God's people were being shamefully destroyed here, and that the worship of God, and the godly orientation of the congregation, was being completely banished from the consciences of the people; that the poor ignorant mass [of people] was not being ministered to; indeed that the seed [young people] of the congregation was becoming a prey to the world. For years we had to let them muddle along, and Pella was a slander on the name of God and a disgrace to the people of the Netherlands. The people became weary of it all and in their distress called upon God. That also provided an

The Rev. Albertus C. Van Raalte (1811-1876), Secession leader and founder of Holland (Michigan) colony, leader of the Midwestern wing of the Reformed Church and constituted First Reformed Church of Pella in 1856

opening for preachers from Michigan for at least two years. I found a Babel [of voices] here, which I probably better not describe for you, but the state of affairs was almost too great an ordeal for my courage and patience.

Through the goodness of God the two principal factions were united; the preaching of the Michigan preachers drew many people. God cleared the path of some knuckle timber [stumbling blocks], gave the people a big church (I believe it holds eight hundred people), and converted many people here during the past year. Thus, a well-ordered congregation, inspired by fixed principles, is calling you; it is encompassed by a host of dispersed and scattered people that fill up the church, but really another church is needed to hold them all. A year ago they called me; and I was ready to go. But when I was about to act on it, in the providence of God I was held back, because I saw an influence at work bent on moving the Holland Academy to one of the larger cities just to accommodate the principal. I realized that I had to seize the bull by the horns and to withstand my enemy by erecting an academy building. It was very hard for me to give up on Pella, for my soul was tortured by the heartless wasting away of God's sighing people, and I was constantly troubled by the much feared destruction of the weak young people's society. But the name of God be praised who turned away the evil we feared. Moreover, Pella as a field of labor was dear to me because I saw that this field was especially, and in every way, ripe for cultivating. I saw them thirsting for spiritual pastoral care after years of nothing but seed wasted by those who are called shepherds and who could not have looked less [like shepherds]; and so all [real pastoral] work was gratefully received. Moreover I envisioned a body here that was pre-eminently suited to establish a second Holland Academy and at the same time to lead the people to an efficacious Christendom, especially on the mission field. And so I was pressed on all sides by deep compassion for these poor people of God, whom I desired to save, and for that host of untended sheep wandering about without a shepherd whom I desired to care for. And so I was drawn by the prospect of a hopeful future and most pleasant prospects to hasten to Pella.

Although I have not been able to take on this field of work, my interest in it is undiminished, but to me it is of the greatest importance that you should come to labor here, if that be the Lord's will. And be assured that, if God entrusts this field to you, then in my judgment, you may thank God for it on your knees. Pella weighs heavily on my heart, and that is why I wish and I pray that God may send you for Jesus' sake. We also need a brother here who can unite Pella with the other congregations. For in unity there is strength, and that is what we need, for the Dutch have a great and noble dwelling here. God is blessing them, and on all sides they are invited to be an ennobling influence, as long as they do not neglect the task of education and higher learning and are willing to work for the kingdom of God. That is the way they must go, for otherwise they will decline and fall into worldliness with all its consequences. We need someone who can see and appreciate this broad calling with us. Your coming here will also enable us to better serve the interests of our good people along the Mississippi. So you can sense how important your coming is to us.

We are not inviting you to a cave to languish there, nor to a post that is hazard filled. No, my dear little brother! Do not allow such spooks of the night to crisscross or torture your soul, for the very opposite is true: it is a beautiful country. And I will not even respond to all the idle chatter about America being a land of uncivilized natives where you cannot enjoy leisure and pleasure, for you are old and wise enough not to pay any attention to such old wives' tales. This is a land where the minister rides in his own cushioned carriage, where they play pianos and reed organs. It is a land in which people, with a simple, warm-hearted mind of Christ, still have rejected a dead and deadening formalism and every binding shackle. I assure you that it is *natural* to breathe freely here, and one need not be on his guard about stupid trifles in order to read in the people's eyes what they think about a given matter. All that counts here is whether you are willing to throw yourself heart and soul into the things of the kingdom of God and give your all to it; that is all they ask.

If I were with you, you would surely want to ask me this and that about the congregation. Well, I can tell you this: I can well imagine that because Pella has played *such* a role here, you may well think of the Pella people as difficult folk, with all kinds of crazy notions in their heads and puffed up with a professorial quasi-knowledge. A large number of these people was constantly under the leadership of Scholte. As you know, he always had new ideas and was prominent by his speculative theology. They had admired him for years, even though they were not able to put up with his insipid niceties for some time already, and like tame sheep they followed him. However, an accumulation of matters, because it did take quite a lot of them, drove them away from him in disgust. They were cured (most of them at least) of all those speculative, quaint new ideas, and people began to thirst for a spiritual, godly ministry [of the Word]. The banning of Scholte [from the pulpit] was acceptable to them all. The leaders are solid, God-fearing men, the kind I would very much like to have in my consistory. There are still some strange elements [among them], unusable knuckle timber, but they are on the outside, outside the congregation. And since it is publicly manifest that the congregation is larger and more stable, it has and is constantly gaining more influence on the consciences of people. As a result, the aforementioned people [the knuckle timber] are receding altogether into the background, and that befalls them most justly because of their former conduct. There certainly continue to be very many children of God dispersed among the several little groups and bunches. But their souls are almost all sick and tired of all the wrangling and squabbles, and clearly it is their hope that the congregation may get a capable minister. All groupings that oppose the congregation are scattering like chaff; not one of them has a fixed principle or goal toward which they wish to steer things. This is the fourth time that one of our ministers is visiting them within a space of two years, but the influence of this scant effort is not all that large. In a word, I must say it again, it is a noble field, ready for harvesting.

Moreover, the congregation itself is sensitive and alert to [the need] to work in higher callings. I proposed that they lay the groundwork for higher education: immediately they pledged the sum of nine hundred dollars in cash and building materials, and seven hundred dollars' worth of real estate, and mind you not nearly the entire congregation was assembled for this meeting. They decided to ask the Board of Domestic Missions to provide preaching in English for the Americans, so that this clergyman might at the same time be designated by the Board of Education for doing the groundwork for setting up a Latin school. They promised the board a school and church building and an annual financial contribution. I have great hopes that if you come here you will find faithful support and assistance at your side to support this cause in the American language, and that would make things much more pleasant for you. I share all this with you so that you can see that this is a people that is willing to work and also has the capacity to do so, and to provide you the pleasant prospect of having a Christian brother and a welcome helper at your side.

But perhaps you may on occasion wonder whether Scholte is someone to look up against; that lion in the street is dead, as dead as a worm [nail]. Yesterday he got home from neighboring Knocksville [Knoxville], where the court of justice was in session. He presented a flood of lawsuits against the citizens of Pella for money [he claimed] they owed him. He lost all of them except for the defendants who did not appear. And now he says that they are the most uncivilized people, and that he intends to move to another big city in another state where he can find civilized people. And even before he himself said this, I had said that Scholte would be leaving Pella sooner or later, if only he could succeed in disposing of some of his properties. This may continue to be a stumbling block for him, but if he can, he will be going. From the above instance you can gather how things are going for him. He has lost all esteem among Americans and Hollanders. It is true that he does have a church of his own, and he preaches there on [Sunday] afternoons; but although he does have supporters and followers, no one really dares to defend him. The only reason they give for hearing him [preach] is, "He preaches the truth." And if you ask them whether he builds up and encourages faith and godliness in his preaching, they dare not say that he does. But they do say that as soon as he leaves the pulpit, everything goes wrong. I assume that in considering this call you would like to know something about Scholte, and that is why I bring it up, although I hate to do so. But I am sure that you will keep what I have written in confidence, for there is no point in disclosing this scandal to all the world. Without going into any further details, I just want to add this, that the congregation and Scholte have nothing to do with each other, and that, now they are freed of him, there are no more problems. They leave him alone, with a kind of aversion, sorrow, and compassion, knowing that he is beyond the reach of any warning or loving admonition, since he has vilified all and continues to do so to all who will not acknowledge his rule. The congregation no longer believes that he is a minister. Indeed, it seems that he does not insist on it all that much either, although he preaches and administers the sacraments without an organized congregation since, as he says, he is unable to find any elders and deacons. However, it does seem that since they [the elders and deacons] censured him in the past, he does not care to be kept under constant surveillance by such people around him. Scholte is finished. May God still grant him a resurrection from the dead.

And so I have communicated to you, it seemed to me, the kinds of things you would be asking about. May the Lord graciously incline your heart to this field of work. You know that Leiden can be filled more readily than this place. I am well aware that in the fatherland there will be a hue and a cry about such monstrous behavior: that you should leave the fatherland. I have long wondered that there is no ecclesiastical ban against such a preacher. But just consider the following. They [the Mission Board in the Netherlands] at their own expense solemnly sent a missionary to the colony of rich Dutch farmers at the Cape [of South Africa], and they can let thousands of Dutchmen in Pella and along the Mississippi [River] fritter away and remain the victims of dispersion. Not only has their blood turned cold against them, but, what is more, when they stretch out their hands to the Netherlands for spiritual food, then what comes is a rejection full of indignation, for they say: they have committed the sin of migration. Let them perish. And if perchance they still had some ballast to throw from the ship, they could get it here. But God has determined better things for us: First, an [Rev.] Oggel, now a Donner; that is how they are being picked out for us. And many a patriotic Dutchman, who has a hard time breathing in the Netherlands, will come here for a breath of fresh air and enliven the work of God, causing the rays of truth to spread, especially to Japan and Java where the name of the Netherlands is a disgrace to all the world because for a hundred years we could trample the cross, that is, let millions of people die in ignorance without having worked among them.

The Lord has also performed many miracles in Pella in converting many people. During the past fourteen days three families, husbands and wives, were brought to a [saving] knowledge of Christ. I have seen much of the religious revival. It is a blessed work, a great work! But now my hand is weary from of all my scribbling, and so I shall end wishing that God by his Holy Spirit may attune your heart to his will. Meanwhile, we will beseech the Lord on your behalf. Greet your spouse; though unknown to me, the Lord make her willing to follow her husband and to plant her children in the great expanses of America. Greet Mr. Teleman and family for me; also Mr. De Moen, should you speak to him; my family is doing very well, thanks to goodness of God.

Your friend and brother in the ministry [of the Word],
A. C. Van Raalte

P.S. I must stay here three more weeks. The isolated location of Pella is coming to an end. They are building a railroad, and it is hoped that it will soon reach Pella.

Budde 25

J. Wormser-van der Ven to Mrs. C. M. Budde-Stomp
Amsterdam, 1 August 1859

Dearly Beloved Friend!

Last January we received your esteemed letter. We were really happy to hear something from our old friends again, although it grieves us that your son Johan is having such a hard time with his work. With an increase in the family, that is not very pleasant for him, nor for you; it is our wish that the Lord will also provide in this situation. In the midst of many trials, we have received countless blessings from the Lord, also most recently. My dear husband suffers much from rheumatism, and he has had another attack, which kept him bed-ridden and confined to his room for seven weeks. All this has left him weak, so that he can spend only an hour or two a day at the office. However, the Lord has again helped him till now, for which his name be praised.

In the fall of 1858, Johan, Jansje, and Henriette had scarlet fever, and at the same time my husband had an attack of rheumatism. After that our little one got whooping cough, but the Lord has rescued us from all of these [illnesses]. On the 7th of May instant, we had the privilege of celebrating our twenty-fifth wedding anniversary, and on the same day the Lord made us grandparents. Since our daughter Cato gave birth to a son at seven in the morning, it was a double celebration for us. The night before, I was tired, since we had had people over for coffee and had asked some others for a mid-day meal. I was about to go to bed when our son-in-law appeared to pick me up, so I will not readily forget that night. She became a mother, and she sure knows it [she had a hard time of it]. I immediately sent a note by porter to my husband, telling him that Cato had delivered her baby and that I would come home as soon as possible. You can imagine how surprised our three youngest children were. They had gotten up early and were walking about in the house singing, waiting for father and mother with their present. Then father came down alone. "Where is mother?" they asked with a single voice. To Cato? That is not nice of mother, but they were overjoyed when they heard that they had become uncle and aunt. Cato remained weak for a long time, and, as soon as she was up and around again, she lost her milk and the baby became ill. But now she has a wet nurse, and the baby is growing well. But then she developed breast fever, but by now she has also recovered from that. A good many women die in childbirth these days. Six or seven weeks before Cato delivered her baby, Truitje Jaspers delivered her first child, and on the seventeenth day after [the birth] the Lord took her [home]. That hit us rather hard.

Our Jans [Jansje] has been going steady with the eldest son of our friend Wüstenhoff, who works with my husband at Mr. Van Hall's office. It gives us great pleasure, for he is a handsome young man and a clerk at the shipping office Messrs. Blaauw and Co. But he does not make enough to get married on. Neither of them is in a hurry, and they live happily. When Rev. Hasebroek heard of it, he said, "My two best catechumens are going together; I like that." He immediately came over to congratulate us. He also participated in our domestic festivity [wedding anniversary] on May 7.

Last Friday my husband and I visited Mrs. Zeelt; she is getting old and is going downhill fast. On the 2nd of December last year, Mijntje, her gardener, passed away. Madame [Zeelt] misses her much; but the old man [Mijntje's husband?] [misses her] no less. He wanders about, very much a lonely man. He too is already seventy, and the older you get, the less you can miss each other. That is what we would say, humanly speaking, but the Lord carries out his plan, and silence becomes us. Dear friend, we dare not ask Mrs. Zeelt about Bibles, because she denied our request to publish them at a reduced price. Your Honors still know how she is; you just do not dare come with any such request. The book publisher Höveker has married again with a Miss Van der Linden, a lady about thirty years of age.

I must still tell you something. As a reminder of our silver wedding anniversary [on May 7, 1859], we had a painting made of our family sitting together around the table in the front room, and father with the open Bible [before him] fixes our attention on the privileges of this day. Johan is leaning against father's chair, and everyone is looking at father except the youngest, who is standing with a doll in her arm against my lap and is laughing at me.

In the frame below me, it says, "As for me and my house, we will serve the Lord" (Joshua 24:15). In the frame below my husband, it says, "Except the Lord build the house, they labor in vain that build it" (Psalm 127:1). It turned out to be excellent and arrived here the day before yesterday. Come and see if it is not an exact likeness.

The oldest son of my husband's brother in Overijssel, named Hendrik, has been working as a clerk at the brokerage firm of Esquires Ooyens and gives complete satisfaction. He is living in a boarding house. His oldest sister, Leentje, who broke your doll, is going to marry this fall, in Deventer, with the Seceder preacher [J.] Schuurman, a widower with two children.

Now that I reread my letter, it looks much like a news report, but I understand that my friend is eager to find out something about her old birthplace. As far as church and state are concerned, I hope that my dear husband will write a short letter to your husband, and that is why I limit myself more to things about which he does not write.

I hope that you and yours receive this letter in well being and that you together may continue to go on your life's way with good cheer. Give greetings to your husband and your dear children, even as our children also send their greetings. As ever I am, intimately associated with you as,

Your Friend,
J. Wormser-van der Ven

P.S. The eldest son of our friend Luuring is working at our office, and my husband has a good clerk in him. His sister Saartje is our hat maker. Cordial greetings, and greetings to Mrs. Teleman and Jansje!

Wormser 61

D. A. Budde to J. A. Wormser
Burlington, 18 December 1860

Dearly Beloved Friend and Brother in the Lord!
    It is my sincere wish that you and yours may receive this letter in good health. I should have answered your letter long ago. Since it had been en route so long before our deep desire to hear something from our dear friends might be fulfilled, it was all the more necessary that I take up the pen at once. Accordingly, that is exactly what we intended to do, but time has passed so swiftly that we have nearly reached the end of the year without having heard anything from each other. Yes, and again we are already longing [to hear from you], and we do not doubt but the same is true for you also.
    I have also been ailing a great deal in '59 and have endured many troubles, cramps in my stomach, and then in my chest. None of the doctor's medicine might avail, and finally I took twenty drops of Haarlem oil every evening. The Lord gave his blessing, and so this past year might be a good deal healthier one for me. At times I even thought that I would regain some of my strength so I could do a little more work, something I still really enjoy doing, but that [strength] does not seem to return as you get older. Well, in this situation the Lord has also supplied our present needs. Our dear Diedrich, who is now about twenty years old, is well behaved and industrious. Religion is his delight, and his life is not without evidences of the fear of God. What a blessing, what a great privilege we presently enjoy in things spiritual; it is with joy that we go up to the house of the Lord with our three children every Sunday to hear the pure preaching of the Word. Earlier on our Johan had affiliated with the Congregationalists; and after we had gotten a good minister here, he remained ecclesiastically separated from us for two years. That grieved us, because, by his own testimony liberalism, not the full truth, had the upper hand in that church. But the Lord heard our pleadings and caused the truth to triumph. Now he is active in our Sunday school.
    During the past summer, our thoughts were often in our room on the Achterburgwal [in Amsterdam] when you were interpreting the Letter to the Hebrews for our fellowship, because Rev. Muller was also exegeting this book consecutively on Sunday evenings. We had forgotten much since those days; much was new to us again, and what we did remember was the same truth in America as in Amsterdam: food

and nourishment for the soul. The same Lord Jesus, our great High Priest, who with his own blood entered the holy of holies and brought about our eternal salvation, and who now still perfects the salvation of all who go unto God through him. The Lord Jesus is our perfect Savior! What a comfort for us poor sinners who have nothing to point to but our sin. He alone is our *all*, the *hope* that never is found wanting. What a pity that so few people acknowledge him for that and believe in him. There are constantly new people coming to our church, but the language is too overpowering, it is too demeaning for the haughty individual. The Lord alone can remove a heart of stone and give a heart of flesh.

We also have an hour prayer meeting on Tuesdays at two o'clock, specifically [to pray] for the outpouring of the Holy Spirit, that it may please the Lord to make our small flock wax and increase, that the preaching of the Word may be a savor of life unto eternal life for many. Might you, dear Brother, depending on circumstances, be willing to unite with us in spirit during that hour to pray, "Thy kingdom come." I know that you will also be mindful of us, even as in the past we together participated in the prayer revival for American Christians. Indeed, you will surely rejoice and praise the Lord when you learn that also in Burlington many have been taken from darkness and brought to the marvelous light of God. To be sure, there are still some who have not bowed the knee to Baal (the False God of the Free Will), but as says our Rev. Muller, who is better acquainted with the American churches than we are, there is little spiritual life evident in them. Everything seems to be dead in Burlington; there are no stirrings, no movement in the right direction, for there is one [a movement] that combats the truth as it is in Christ Jesus. The Lord is present in many places in America and also in many other lands, with the outpouring of the Holy Spirit for the conversion of sinners, the gathering in of those purchased with the blood of Jesus Christ. However, the outside judgments about it all [the revivals] vary greatly. Judging by what we have heard and also read in periodicals, our petition goes up to God that he may have mercy on Zion, and that the Lord Jesus may make his entry into the hearts of people, and that also in Burlington there will be inhabitants with his Spirit and grace, and that many may be found who with hand and heart subscribe [to the testimony], "We are the Lord's."

May the Lord be near you all with his Spirit and grace. Cordial greetings to your wife and dear children. Greet our friend Luring [Luuring] for us, and [I] ever remain our beloved friend and brother in the Lord.

D. A. Budde

Chapter 7

The Later Years, 1861-1873
(Wormser Letters 62-88, Budde Letters 26-61)

In Letter 62 there is reference to the family portrait that J. A. Wormser had painted on the occasion of his twenty-fifth wedding anniversary. We see the entire family on it:

Johan Adam Wormser (born June 17, 1807).
Janke van der Veen (born March 9, 1810).
Jansje Wormser (born August 10, 1835), married C. W. Wüstenhoff.
Catharina (Kaatje) Wormser (born October 20, 1836), married De Boer, died 1870.
Johan Adam Wormser Jr. (born October 9, 1845), married Catharina Johanna Höveker (September 16, 1869, died March 7, 1916).
Maria Louise Wormser (born June 10, 1847).
Maria Hendrika Wormser (born March 25, 1852).

On the list we read, "1834–7 May 1859" and two texts: Joshua 24:15, "As for me and my house, we will serve the Lord," and Psalm 127:1, "Except the Lord build the house, they labor in vain that build it." This painting is the property of H. A. Höveker, the oldest son of the oldest daughter of J. A. Wormser. Jr.

J. A. Wormser died only a few years later, on November 1, 1862. In May of that year, he and his wife had stayed a month at the home of Mrs. J. J. Zeelt to recuperate; she was then eighty-one years old and would survive Wormser by two years. On May 19, 1862, Wormser wrote to his children in Amsterdam: "When we were about to go to bed, and I was

Floris Adriaan van Hall (1791-1866), Amsterdam Seceder leader and jurist

about to wish Mrs. Zeelt good night, I stooped down a little, and the result was a shock to my loins which caused me to cry out and threw me to the floor, greatly frightening mother and the numerous bystanders. Fortunately there was nothing in the way, and I did not hurt myself."

When Wormser passed away, there was a letter of condolence from The Hague, dated November 5, 1862, from the [cabinet] minister, Baron F. A. van Hall, L.L.M.:

Much as I was grieved by the sad announcement of the passing of Your Honor's spouse, still I am grateful to you that, on this sad occasion, you by this announcement have proven that you are convinced that I sincerely and deeply share in your loss. Your Honor was not mistaken about that. I very much share in the grief that has befallen you and very much lament the passing of my former servant [cabinet minister], whom I loved as a friend. May the infinitely good God grant Your Honor his choicest consolation!

Believe me that I am ever with esteem,

Your Honor's faithful servant,
Van Hall

The only son of Johan Adam Wormser took over the publishing company of his father-in-law, H. Höveker (1831-1886), and for years he was the important publisher of Dr. Abraham Kuyper, of many Free

University publications, and of *De Heraut* and Kuyper's newspaper *De Standaard*.

In this last series of letters, we read about the American Civil War of 1861-1865; about the assassination of Lincoln; trips that a few immigrants made to Europe; and the deaths of H. P. Scholte August 25, 1868, Janke Wormser-van der Ven February 26, 1872, C. M. Budde-Stomp July 25, 1872, and D. A. Budde April 18, 1873; and also about marriages of the younger [second] generation.

Three daughters of H. P Scholte, from his [first] marriage with Sara Maria Brandt, married in Pella are:

Sara Johanna Scholte, born November 9, 1833, married Dr. B. F. Keables, and died October 18, 1914; she was survived by three sons and two daughters.

Sara Maria Scholte, born June 6, 1839, married P. H. Bousquet; she died January 14, 1876, leaving behind two daughters.

Sarah Johanna Suzanna Scholte, born June 3, 1842, probably named after Helena Susanna van Hall-van Schermbeek, married Jan Nollen in 1864 and died in 1937.

Sara Maria Brandt died January 23, 1844, and Scholte remarried June 13, 1845, with Maria Hendrika Elisabeth Krantz (born March 26, 1820). Of her nine children, six died at a very early age.

Theodora M. J. Scholte, born November 23, 1858, died May 22, 1870, at twelve years of age. Two sons reached adulthood. Henry Peter Scholte, born November 30, 1848, was the father of one daughter and two sons; he died October 26, 1918. David Scholte, born in 1862, was still living in 1914; he was married but childless.

During the American Civil War, twenty-five years after the Secession [of 1834], S. van Velzen Jr. published: "*Compleete uitgave van de Officiëele stukken betreffende den Uitgang uit het Nederl. Herv. Kerkgenootschap van de Leeraren H. P. Scholte, A. Brummelkamp, S. van Velzen, G. F. Gezelle Meerburg en Dr. A. C. Van Raalte.*" Scholte used this opportunity to address once again *De Geloovigen in Nederland*. In this publication, Scholte gave a further explanation of his secession and the position he later took.

Before the Civil War, Scholte wrote: "In the present dispensation all national distinctions are eliminated. He [God] calls all men everywhere, unto the farthest ends of the earth, to turn to him, with the unconditional promise that it is his desire to make them happy for all eternity." He then declares that Babel is also present in America. "We are fully justified in calling Rome the heart and center as well as the oldest part of Babylon, but at the same time we must recognize that in

The Rev. Hendrik Pieter (Henry Peter) Scholte (1805-1868) in his latter years, leader of the Secession of 1834, founder of Pella colony and its chief promoter

the course of the centuries various Protestant districts have been added, and that this [outward] expansion still has not come to a halt. The United States of America do not stand outside this development. Although, to all appearances, the European model of the union of church and state has been censured and rejected, every impartial observer must admit that the Spirit of Babylon also reigns there [in America] and is evident in the intermingling of religious denominations with political parties, so that through mutual support they can get the upper hand over each other."[1]

And again Scholte referred to the imminent return of Christ. He wanted to remain Reformed but would never put doctrine before the individual. He continued to see a contrast between church and state, between belief in the scriptures and philosophy, and he did not see a place for Christian politics and Christian philosophy. Above all, he wanted to live simply, close to the Bible, including the prophecies.

Scholte wrote as follows about the Secession:

> For any attentive observer of the events that followed upon the Secession from the Reformed churches, it is clear that there were

---

1. Scholte, Aan de geloovigen in Nederland (1863), 227.

several groups among the Secessionists. As far as the ministers are concerned, one grouping, represented by the Right Reverend Mr. De Cock, had focused its attention principally upon the doctrines of the Reformed Church and the Church Order as it was drawn up by the Synod of Dort between 1618 and 1619. This group undoubtedly constituted the majority of the Secessionists.

Although I believed and professed the doctrinal teachings of the Reformed Church with all my heart, still it was not so much church doctrine, and even less church order, that was in the forefront of my attention. Having come to the knowledge of the truth exclusively through the reading of the sacred Scriptures apart from any church organization, my attention was principally focused on the person of Christ. Having found in him the way, the truth, and the life, and having come during my years of study into friendly contact with lively believers from several church communities and countries, my attention was and is constantly on the community of which Christ is the head. Consequently, the sacred Scriptures were my model, and never, not in any period in history, have I been able to see any church community as the example of perfection, either in doctrine or in form. And that is why I was never much concerned about *quia* (because) and *quatenus* (in so far) in the subscription form of the Hervormde preachers.*

This I knew with certainty, that the orthodox Gereformeerde Kerk, represented by the Synod of Dort in 1618 and 1619, had upheld the confession that the Word of God was above all else and that no human writings, however good, could be compared with the sacred Scriptures [Art.VII].

During my tenure of service in the Nederlandsch Hervormde Kerkgenootschap, no preacher or church council can accuse me of ever having quarreled with the formularies or church ordinances; the Word of God was my only weapon. That is the reason my personal secession took place immediately, as soon as the church council forbade me from preaching, without any accusation at all that I had violated [the authority of] the Word of God. My misdeeds were that I had preached and baptized without the approval of an [appointed] clerical counselor. As a minister in the Hervormde Kerkgenootschap, I was qualified to perform both activities, and

---

* In 1816 the national synod of the Hervormde Kerk altered the Form of Subscription ever so slightly (by replacing *quatenus* with *quia*) and thus made its meaning ambiguous.

besides I had been invited to do so by a legally constituted consistory.

That secession, in which I was followed by my congregation and consistory, with the exception of a very small number of persons, immediately put me into contact with other secessionists. Since I was acting in good faith, it certainly could not be expected of me that after that secession I would subject the Word of God to any ecclesiastical system of doctrines, or that I should want to bind the newly liberated congregation to the letter of a church order more than two hundred years old. I was fully convinced that this had never been the intention of the Dort fathers, and I knew for a certainty that in their church rule those fathers themselves were not independent of the secular government. At the first synodical gathering, the differences in thought and direction were clearly evident, although the Word of God kept the upper hand there. However, among the secessionist congregations there immediately were complaints about deviation from the old ways, and from that time on the differences among the secessionists increased, [but] these need not be recounted here.

Most of my former Christian friends remained opposed to the Secession, not because they were less opposed than I to the godless heresies in the Hervormde Kerkgenootschap, but mostly because they considered the step to be a premature one, and also because they thought that they could still find the historical Gereformeerde Kerk in the Hervormde Kerkgenootschap, notwithstanding the fact that some of them acknowledged with the noble Groen van Prinsterer "dat wij van het kerkgenootschap gescheiden waren om in de Kerk te blijven [that we had seceded from the Hervormde Kerk in order to remain in the church]."

In regard to the publication, *Aan de Geloovigen in Nederland* [*To the Believers in the Netherlands*], Scholte wrote as follows to Rev. H. J. Buddingh on May 16, 1866:

As far as my stance and position to the things of the kingdom of God are concerned, I have spelled that out as clearly as possible in the postscript to the new edition of *The Articles pertaining to the Secession*. I noted that this postscript was not exactly to the liking of the seceding preachers in the Netherlands, and I do not doubt that they would deny me their pulpits if I should ever return to the

Netherlands....There are all kinds of Christians here too. I still am the minister in the Christian church in Pella. The truth of the personal and visible return of Christ has become more and more precious to me and encourages me in all my trials and disappointments. I am, outwardly, thanks to the goodness of God, independent of human beings; the church [building] in which I preach belongs to me, and everyone can hear me free of charge. The three daughters from my first marriage are all married and live in the same street with me. I also have two boys and one girl from my second marriage. During my stay here I have had to wrestle with many problems, and I have developed some understanding of human beings. The Lord has put me to the test, but he has not abandoned me.[2]

During the last years of his life, from September 1866 to August 1868, Hendrik Hospers continued to publish *De Toekomst* [*The Future*] for Scholte, with the masthead, "The Lord is coming!" In line with Da Costa, Scholte was still looking for a millenium, a reign of peace for one thousand years, after the return of the Jews to Israel. The church that proclaimed itself to be the true church, or in one way or another sought to gain a position of power in this world, he called the Whore of Babylon of the Apocalypse. A dissertation at the Free University sums it up as follows: "His Reveil individualism, biblicism, and romantic idealism unfit him for bondage to crowd, creed, or custom....He who had disappointed the hope of the Reveil, led and quarreled with the Afscheiding, co-captained the migration, founded and failed the colony, the greatest and most disillusioned politician among the immigrants [died virtually alone, a stranger in a strange land]."[3]

When Scholte was felled by a heart attack, the mayor of Pella, Henry Hospers, had the following resolution adopted at a special meeting of the city council:

> Inasmuch as in the death of Henry P. Scholte, the city of Pella, and its environs have suffered an irreparable loss, therefore be it
> Resolved, that, while with humble submission we bow before the inscrutable providence of God, we greatly lament the loss of our

---

2. H. J. Gunning, *H. J. Budding, een leven en arbeid*, 2nd ed. (Rhenen: Van Nas, 1909), 598-99.

3. L. Oostendorp, *H. P. Scholte: Leader of the Secession of 1834 and Founder of Pella* (Franeker: T. Wever, 1964), 191.

beloved friend Henry P. Scholte, the founder of our colony, who by his honest character, his upright walk and brotherly affection had become dear to us all.

Resolved, that in Henry P. Scholte we recognize an able theologian, a deep thinker, and a sound interpreter of the sacred Scriptures, an example of a good-hearted, wise, and moderate-minded human being whose memory will live in the hearts of all true and right-minded citizens, not only in our beloved dwelling place, but also in Holland, the land of his birth.

Resolved, that with all our heart we share in the loss which has befallen the relatives of the deceased Henry P. Scholte, and that we hereby give evidence of our genuine grief, praying that our loving Lord, whose ways are unfathomable, will pour out on them the heavenly balm of his consolation.

Resolved, that the above-mentioned resolutions be published in the Pella newspapers, and that a copy thereof be presented to the relatives of the deceased.

H. Neyenesch, City Recorder.
Henry Hospers, Mayor

At the time of Scholte's death, Maria Kranz was forty-eight years old. She remarried July 2, 1870, when she was fifty—although she said she was forty-nine—with Robert Beard, an American who was twenty-four years old. This was two months after her daughter Dora died at the age of twelve. She continued to live as Mrs. Beard for a good twenty-two years and died September 18, 1892. On her deathbed she said of herself, "I am dying as a stranger in a strange land."

Budde 26

Johanna Schellinger to D. A. Budde
Alkmaar, 16 September 1860

Sir and Esteemed Friend,

With grateful feelings I received your letter, and I must confess that tears of emotion flowed freely when I learned its contents—that the loving Father has still spared you [for all that are dear to you]. How much good the Lord grants on our life's pathway. Happy is the person who observes it and quietly acquiesces in his loving rule. However much we trace the rule of the Lord in all that befalls human beings, and though often it appears dark to us, we cannot be grateful enough for all the good that flows forth from it, and all too often is not observed by us. I had many different feelings as I read your letter. How I would love to stay with your family once, but since the great distance prevents that, I am more than content with the friendship by which you honor me.

I am very sensitive to the kind attention that your dear wife has for me [by her willingness] to send me the picture of my dear niece. Would you approve of enclosing it with a letter, if that is possible? I could then put a frame on here. I am so free as to make this suggestion, but I hope that you will do whatever suits you best. I will gladly pay whatever it costs. It is worth very much to me to see her picture. I have been deeply moved that you think so nobly of my niece, having her learn her catechism and making her profession of faith, and so have promoted her eternal welfare. If only she may some day realize and by thankful conduct show and prove the gratitude she owes you. But may the Lord who beholds all things reward you for all the loving attention you have shown her.

The two girls have surprised me not a little, although I did not expect any thanks from the dear Maria. If the distance were not so great, I would love to send them something or other. I do not doubt but Johanna will do her best in learning to write, because Maria is way ahead of her. Then I look forward to the prospect that she too will correspond with me, under your tutelage, although I am satisfied that she has already progressed so far. The few letters that I may be receiving from the two dear girls will be most welcome to me.

Mathijs van der Moore [Moor] seems to keep the indifferent character I noticed in him even before he left from here. If he had learned a trade, once he was well placed, that would have provided him with a better prospect for the future than just being a menial help in a coffee house. Well, at least it is something that he can make it on his own. If only the fear of the Lord does not leave him entirely, and he does not realize too late the consequences of his frivolous behavior. That is my heartfelt wish for him. It gives me joy that you continue to keep Johanna under your tutelage. The vanities of the world so readily create the wrong impressions on youthful girls. It is most fortunate when one is preserved from that and learns to realize it early on.

After receiving our letter, I had a lawyer draw up the necessary papers to fulfill my wish in deciding the disposition of the things I may call my own, in order in this way to meet the obligation that was mine. And now, my dear friend, if you and yours may receive this letter in the well being in which I find myself through the blessing of the Lord, that will be most agreeable to me. Receive my cordial greetings to Your Honors and your family, and also my dear niece. Herewith I remain with highest esteem,

Your Honor's Servant and Friend,
Johanna Schellinger

Wormser 62

C. M. Budde-Stomp to J. Wormser-van der Ven
Burlington (late 1860 or early 1861)

My Dearly Beloved Friend!

On May 26, 1860, we received Your Honor's dearly longed for letter of August 1, 1859. Thanks to the goodness of the Lord, we are doing well these days. Our son Johan again had a daughter, Flora, but she soon died in the arms of her mother, and so they have only two children left. It was their sixth child. The oldest boy is nearly nine; he comes to my house to read Dutch and to learn the [Dutch] psalms. The little girl is three years old. We were privileged to witness the [public] profession of faith of our children Diedrich and Maria in the Dutch Reformed Church of Burlington on June 19, 1959. Rev. Muller addressed them personally with texts [from the Bible]. That of David was Psalm 119, verse 9: "Wherewithall shall a young man cleanse his way? By taking heed thereto according to thy word." And for Maria [the text] was Isaiah 43 verse 1: "I have redeemed thee, I have called thee by thy name, thou art mine." Shortly thereafter, both girls got the measles. Naatje got over it quickly, but Maria developed diarrhea, and her case became critical. My husband talked to her about dying, and whether she could give herself up into the hands of the Lord Jesus. She gave a sound reply, that it would be difficult for us, and she did wish to be reassured [on that point], but after that she was willing to die. Then she said to me, "I would just like to throw my arms around *Him*." In the fall she had had an attack of cholera; in three hours' time she had wilted away like snow before the sun. To our great joy the Lord did spare her then. But now Naatje van der Moor developed a bilious [?] and nervous fever, which was not without danger, [but] the Lord restored her again so that no one in our midst has yet been taken away by death. We just go quietly on our way; every now and then one of our old friends is called away, like Mijntje Da Costa, Truitje Jaspers.

It seems only such a short time that we celebrated Your Honor's copper wedding anniversary [twelve and one-half years] in your [living] room, and see now it is already your silver [twenty-fifth anniversary]. You invite me to see the lovely painting of Your Honor's family circle [cf. p. 4]. If I could do that, then I would also be with you and could embrace you, but the gift that the Lord gave you could not be adequately expressed in art. The motto, "As for me and my house, we will serve the Lord," was expanded so that all of you may taste the blessing of beholding the offspring of your daughter. Father Abraham gave instructions to his household to fear and serve the Lord, and that is the desire of all of you. May the God of Abraham fulfill his promise to you and to your seed after you in succeeding generations, so that many more of you who praise the Lord may still be born in Zion; that is the heartfelt wish of your loving friend.

And you, my dear Cato, Mrs. and Mr. De Boer, rejoice in the treasure that the Lord has entrusted you; again entrust it to *Him*; instruct her in the fear of the Lord so that all of you, after having fought the good fight, may enter into the inheritance of eternal salvation and may say, "Lord, [here we are], and the children thou hast given us."

And you, dear Jansje, you have pledged your hand to a young man. If Your Honors have not yet entered wedlock, it is my wish that both of you may choose to live together in the fear of the Lord, for in marriage one ordinarily encounters more trials and tribulations, cross[es], and adversities than in the sweet spring of youth; therefore it is such a great privilege to take your refuge in the Lord together.

My dear Johan, how are things with you? Is it your greatest desire to keep your path pure and untainted according to the Word of the Lord? Vanities and sin will surely encompass you, but by enlisting in the service of King Jesus you will learn how to do battle and in *His* power to overcome.

We have the great privilege, [and] we wish that you might also share it, of hearing the preaching of the gospel. Our minister is outstanding as a man of faith; his preaching is sound and powerful, but the Lord is putting us to the test. It [his preaching] is not without blessing among our young people and that includes my son Johan; in the past he joined the Congregational church, and now he has returned to the confessions [faith] of the fathers. The church is not growing. The board of the Dutch Reformed in New York has been giving $300 a year toward salary, but that will not go on forever. Besides, we are burdened with a big unpaid debt incurred when we were building the church, so that our minister became apprehensive about what to do. In this crisis situation we know of no other way but to call on the Lord, who creates light out of darkness and governs all things according to the council of his will. To that end the consistory felt compelled to set aside an hour of prayer every week in order to present the general and particular concerns of the kingdom of God before the Lord; in addition there is a weekly hour of prayer for all. The minister leads in prayer, takes a text, for example, "Moreover, it is my wish that the House of Jacob call upon me in prayer about [their need]." [He then] briefly explains the contents, calls for something appropriate to be sung, calls on another to pray, and then he closes. And if even here below it is blessed to join in prayer to the Lord, then what will it be like in the hereafter, singing and praising the Lord perfectly?

Recently Jan Le Cocq stopped by to visit us and stayed for several days. He had been in Chicago for eight months in order to gain some information for their business affairs. The three sons of Le Cocq and his daughter Maria are all married and have children. Jan and Frans have a store together, but because of the money [financial] crisis, their income was greatly reduced, and that is why Jan tried to increase their business by making cigars. We really enjoyed talking about old times and new, and also that Your Honor's catechism class for children had not been without its fruits. His father had written him a happy tiding: his youngest sister Christina, who is still unmarried and who, after being troubled and concerned about her salvation for three years, might now believe in the Lord Jesus [as her Savior].

Rev. Oggel and an elder are faithful in doing house visiting, and they might see the fruits of their labors. His Reverence is married to a daughter of Rev. Van Raalte. The congregation in Pella is very satisfied with Rev. Oggel; it is fairly large and they have built a church and parsonage. Rev. Scholte is still preaching in his church; he is very much involved in politics, and his reputation is really tarnished in the newspapers.

Rev. Vander Meulen is serving a new Dutch Reformed congregation in Chicago; it has a very nice church. At the dedication they had the rare privilege of hearing the father and his two sons preach: the father in the morning, one son in the afternoon, the other in the evening. The student, C. Van Veen, has also preached already, and he did very well. The son of Rev. Baai serves in a Dutch Reformed congregation in

Keokuk; he is married to an English lady. The Dutch Reformed church is expanding considerably in the West.

Jansje Teleman married an American, Jannawa, in September. He has no specific trade or craft but does what his hand finds to do. She had earlier become a Methodist; she was then keeping company with a widower who had a child; he was a carpenter. Last Saturday he and she stopped in to see us; they were here to visit her mother. The next week he had to marry the woman with whom he had been boarding; later on he drowned. Mrs. Teleman is still living in with us; she is healthy but has an open wound in a swollen leg so that she cannot wear a shoe.

I hope that all is well with you when Your Honors receive this letter. Greet your esteemed husband and your beloved children; cordial greetings from me, and all of us. Your Friend who loves you dearly. Surprise me with a letter soon.

C. M. Budde-Stomp

Cordial greetings to Mrs. Zeelt, the gardener, and friends.

Budde 27

Johanna Schellinger to Maria Budde and to her niece Naatje
Alkmaar, 30 May 1861

Dear Maria,

How surprised I was to get your letter. I thank you very much for your attention, and I rejoice that, thanks to the goodness of God [both of] you are again fully recovered, and that both of your young lives were spared. May you, and all who are dear and precious to you, long continue to experience that privilege. May the good Father in heaven, who governs all things in love, grant that.

Dear Maria, in my imagination both you and Naatje must be the same age because you can enjoy so many things together; and how much both of you can learn from your dear mother. It gives me so much joy that Naatje has such a good friend in you, and that she receives so many indications of your interest, and that of your dear family, in her. And now, dear Maria, I hope that you and your family may constantly experience the blessing of the Lord. With esteem I am,

Your Loving Friend,
Johanna Schellinger

[Letter to Johanna Schellinger's niece Naatje]

Dear Niece,

I received your picture in good health, and I look at it frequently with amazement. It seems to me that you look very little like your mother. When you left us as a child just a year old, I certainly could see her in you, but at your age a human being changes so much. Still, your mother's features were also a little dark, just like yours. I write you this, dear Niece, because no doubt you will want to know what I think of your likeness. I am very happy that I now possess what I have wanted to have for so very long.

But, my dear Niece, I notice from your writing that you have made little progress since I received your last letter. If you would just make more work of your writing and were able to write me a letter from time to time, wouldn't that make you feel good? It seems to me that already you are able to tell so much, like the things that occupy your time. Just do your best, as much as you can, dear Naatje, and do be more obliging in trying to please all those about you. Then everybody will love you, and you will rejoice that the Spirit of God who is love itself is directing you. Then you may hope that your prayer is being answered, that the image of Jesus our good Savior is being planted in your youthful heart. At your age, it is so good to consider well how well the heavenly Father has cared for you and will continue to do so, if only you pray much for that good Spirit, which makes us so thankful for all the good things we receive and makes our life so pleasant.

And now, dear Niece, I greatly rejoice that you have again been so completely restored from the illness that struck you so hard last year, and it is my sincere wish that you and your dear friends may receive this letter in good health. Cordial greetings from,

Your Loving Aunt,
Johanna Schellinger

Budde 28

J(ansje) Wüstenhoff-Wormser to Mrs. C. M. Budde-Stomp
Amsterdam, 19 October 1861

Esteemed Madame, Dearly Beloved Friend,

It is high time that we get around to answering your dear letters. It is a task my mother hopes to fulfill, but I also wished to write you a few lines. We hope that you all may continue to enjoy good health, a privilege that we also continue to enjoy. As regards the war, things look very sad in America, so we learn from the newspapers. We were talking about you just recently, and we hope that it is no hindrance to you. We hope that our wedding announcement arrived there in a timely manner. Our marriage took place August 15th, and the ecclesiastical consecration was performed by Rev. Brandt. Many interested friends were in attendance. Rev. Brandt was a guest at our wedding. His text was, "Whatsoever he telleth you, do it" [John 2:6]. You are probably wondering why it wasn't Rev. Hasebroek. The reason is that His Reverence had gone to Germany for health reasons, and because we also wished to make a little trip to Germany, we could not wait until His Reverence returned, because of the time of year. Our little trip was delightful.

I distinctly recall that when you were still living in Amsterdam, and I was still very young, that you showed me a tinder box with grains of wheat it and said [to me], "I have brought those a distance of two hundred hours from Germany." During those two hundred hours of travel, you probably were in some of the places we visited. I will only mention the main places, without the excursions we made, for that would take too much time. We left from Arnhem, taking the train to Düsseldorf, from there to Bonn, and from Bonn by steamboat to Coblenz, where we stayed from Saturday till Monday. And then on again from Coblenz to Bingen, and then to Wiesbaden, nowadays the high point of splendor and wealth. Then we took the train to Mainz and then back to Arnhem. And to delight ourselves in the mountains with Father and Mother, we went back to Bonn and environs and to Elberfeld. We saw very much. Our little trip lasted fourteen days, and then we traveled back to Amsterdam together.

We live on the Bloemgracht, [which is] well known to you, a few houses past our friends, the Luurings, next to the house of [Mr.] Vis, the mason. I think that you may still remember him. Our life is very happy, and that is a blessing that exceeds thousands of others. I wish that you could see us sitting here in our house. Our house is small, like that of my parents on the Voorburgwal: an inside room and suite and hall and kitchen, a small room above the kitchen, and a small inner court.

I cannot tell you much about old friends. A week ago Monday the aged Mr. Jansen [Janssen] passed away. His son is married and has a baby. He lives at the Botermarkt and runs a basement eatery. The

Luuring family is prospering. I saw Jaspers and his wife as late as last Sunday. The situation of the Doornhouwer family remains the same. We never hear anything from [Mr.] Schriek, and the same thing is true for Mrs. Otten. Mrs. Zeelt is getting old and weak. Father visited her as recently as eight days ago. The caretaker is well. Betje Höveker got married in May. During our bridal days, Uncle Dries celebrated his silver wedding anniversary. His wife is ailing and recently she vomited blood. My sister, her husband, and child are well. Father has not had a severe rheumatic attack this year. Mother was generally well this year, except for headaches. Johan, Marie, and Henriette are growing up. Well, my dear friend, my letter is a lot like a newspaper. My husband and I greet you cordially, including our friend Jan and his family, Diderich [Diedrich] and Maria. Give greetings to Mrs. Teeleman [Teleman] and Jansje. Do make us happy with a letter again soon, won't you? Once again, warmest greetings, and be commended to the Lord by,

Your Loving Friend
J. Wüstenhoff-Wormser

Budde 29

C(ato) de Boer-Wormser to Mrs. C. M. Budde-Stomp
Amsterdam, November 1861

Dearly Beloved Friend!
The very thought of writing you, the oldest friend I have, if memory serves me right, gladdens my whole heart. Often you all are the subject of my conversation, even with my husband who has never seen you. Today we may be glad to be in reasonably good health, although I am frequently ailing. We still have only one child; I just cannot tell you how sweet he is. He is two and a half years old, and his name is Johan. He speaks distinctly and walks nicely. He is cheerful and a fast learner. Thanks to the blessing of the Lord, we have not had any setbacks with him so far. We spend Tuesdays with Father and Mother, and now I cannot punish the little fellow any worse than to say, "Johan may not go along." You can see how fond he is of his grandfather and grandmother.

Your niece, Grietje Krabbendam-Budde, visited me once this summer. She is doing well. She was expecting her fourth child. She sends you her greetings. The oldest daughter of Uncle Hein, our cousin Leentje, married a minister, a Seceder whose name is [J.] Schuurman. Life in Amsterdam is very expensive. There is hardly anything that is reasonably priced except bread, so it is used for the midday (warm) meal by the poorer classes. We, and also Wüstenhoff, who is married to my sister Jans, have been highly privileged by the Lord in that our husbands earn enough so that we can live like respectable, middle-class people.

Mr. and Mrs. Luuring are well, but he always gives the appearance of working too hard, although Saartje is always busy making [women's] hats and Willem works at the Singel office. Betje, the eldest daughter of Höveker, married a short time before our Jans, to a certain Van der Land, a Christian young man. I do not think you know him. Aunt Mietje, the wife of Uncle Dries, has been ailing quite a lot. She has vomited blood several times, but presently she is convalescing. The cousins are still at home with their parents.

Well, my dear! I just took out a few moments to chat with you, and while I did so, I had all of you clearly in my mind's eye. I still have a drawing of Jan, with his signature, also a breakfast dish given to me on my birthday by you, my dear friend. I also have an egg holder of which I am very fond and still always use, I dare say with thoughts of you. We only hope that we may get some word from you soon. You cannot imagine how happy and grateful that will make us. Our relationship with you all is more than an ordinary one. May the Lord be near and good to you, and console us with his presence. That is the wish and prayer of,

Your loving Friend,
C. de Boer-Wormser

Cordial greetings to you all, also from my husband, and also to Jan and his family, Diederich [Diedrich] and Maria.

Wormser 63

C. M. Budde-Stomp to J. Wormser-van der Ven
Burlington, December 5, 1861

My Dearly Beloved Friends,

For a long time we had been longing to get some mail from you, and then we received the wedding announcement of Your Honor's beloved daughter Johanna and Mr. [C. W.] Wüstenhoff. It would have been appropriate for me to respond at once, but I was hoping that a letter from you might follow. It is our wish that you may experience much joy for some years to come, and that they may walk hand in hand in the fear of the Lord, which as you have found, is the most blessed life on earth and will be made perfect in heaven.

In the period since our last letter to you, a great deal has happened here. In the month of June, I was seriously ill with summer complaint and dysentery. My dear husband and children were very worried, but the Lord was with me with his grace and mercy. At the same time our beloved minister, the Rev. J. Muller, accepted a call to Silver Creek, where he was attending a classis meeting. It is a Dutch Reformed congregation, mostly Ost Frisians, much larger than we are, and they also already have a lovely church and parsonage. The Rev. Wagner, who was also known to us, was returning to Germany for health reasons. They are capable of providing for their own minister. We could not object, because he served us as a missionary preacher and received $300 of his salary from the board, the balance being supplied by our congregation. Because of the pressing [financial] conditions at the time, the board could not assist us; it already had big debts of its own. All this really affected my nerves so that I could not get any sleep, day or night. I could only thank the Lord for his mercy in having granted us three years of sound gospel preaching. The Lord now demands that we put our trust in *Him*; he will not forsake the work of his hands. Our Sunday gathering [for worship] goes on; every other week an evangelical minister from the area serves as our guest preacher in order to keep our congregation together as much as possible, until the Lord have mercy on us.

Our fatherland is at war with the South, as you are doubtless more aware than I can [possibly] write you. We also experienced much unrest this summer due to the fact that our land borders on the fairgrounds [or exhibition grounds]. They built [temporary] huts there in which three thousand soldiers were encamped. From five in the morning till evening, they were exercising with drums and music. Soon there was a shortage of water at the fairgrounds; during the exercises, two to three hundred men at a time would then come to our house to drink water from our well, and every morning and evening they came with big iron pails to get water for cooking purposes. The well has never run dry, and it has very good water. We had it dug right after our arrival [here]. It [the well] often became the subject of praise to the Lord, also in conversations with soldiers, for example, [the story of] the Samaritan woman [at the well] (etc.). Worship services were also conducted [in the encampment] on Sundays and as well as evenings. Although the greatest number of them is frivolous, some of the English, German, and Dutch [soldiers] were religious [i.e. serious about their religion]. A Dutch Lieutenant De Heus, whose uncle owned the big button factory at the Leiden Gate [in Amsterdam], heard us talking about Pella and told us that a son of Mrs. Bousquet was also in the [military] services, and that she had followed him to the encampment at Keokuk and stayed on there until they left.

A daughter, Christina Maria, was born to our son Johan on the 21st of March. The child was very healthy, but she came down with the same illness I had. It lingered on for seven months; then the Lord took her to himself. The middle child, a girl of 4 1/2 years, was spared; she had a throat illness, one that affected very many children here and from which many died. The throat gets swollen, the tongue turns black; she coughed up blood and pus; she could neither eat nor drink, nor could she speak. The rattle in her chest was so vehement that we were afraid that she might choke at any moment. These days all of us are in reasonably good health.

While I was writing this, Johan brought over your letter of October 28th instant, one we were eagerly expecting. We were all glad as it was being read aloud. When we came to the sentence in your letter which said, "D[iedrich] and M[aria] will no longer know us," Diedrich expressed the wish, "I'd really like to see the portrait of Mr. Wormser once." That really struck me; his character is so open and genuine. I saw how frank and open he was in his relationship and love toward you people. When he was younger he could still recall many things about Amsterdam, but now he scarcely remembers. As far as Your Honors and the family are concerned, his recollection is very much alive because of our correspondence. M[aria] still has a good recollection of the time your brother Dries [A.N. Wormser] and family visited us, because their youngest daughter Leentje was always teasing her. She does not remember anything about Amsterdam. Dare I ask Mr. Wormser about D[iedrich]'s wish, even if it were without a frame?

We share in the pains your dear husband has to suffer, but we know that the Lord uses these for his own purposes. My dear husband also suffers much pain from stomach cramps and gases, so much so that the usual home remedies no longer avail. He weakened so much that we called in the doctor. At present he is somewhat better physically, but he is still not completely healed; it is very painful for him to want to work and not be able to do so. I am sure that you remember from way back that it was never his desire to gather many [earthly] treasures, but the needs of the family demand constant labor. D[iedrich] is a faithful helper but he cannot do everything alone; he goes to the market three times a week for three-quarters of the year, and once in the winter. In addition to milking [the cows], both of our girls have to work in the field and in the garden. Our nephew is healthy and strong, but he is very slow. When he is alone, he does almost nothing, and so everyone has his troubles. The Lord governs the course of all things. This enables us to acquiesce and to sing, *"met mijn kruis al zachtjes naar huis, enz"* ("with my cross gently to my home I go," etc).

Household provisions are not expensive, except things coming from southern regions: items like coffee, tea, cotton, wool, etc. We are [now] getting half price for vegetables. For example, butter, which used to be twenty-five to thirty-five cents a pound, is now twelve cents. This makes for lots of work but less income. And now, dear friend, in hopes that you will receive this in good health, our heartfelt prayer is that the Lord may continue to be with you and yours and grant that they may walk in humble fear of the Lord. Greet and kiss Johan, Maria, Henriette. Mrs. Teleman sends you greetings; she is completely recovered.

Your loving Friend,
C. M. Budde.

P.S. Mrs. Schilp recently gave birth to a daughter.

Wormser 64

C. M. Budde-Stomp to C. W. Wüstenhoff, et al (letter with much of the text lost)
Burlington, December 1861

Highly Esteemed Friend and Lady-Friend,

The announcement of your intent and desire to enter wedlock reached us speedily. On the 4th of August it was thirty-seven years ago that we entered into matrimony; we then also felt the need of the Lord and his blessing. The Lord was pleased to grant our petition and increasingly detached us from earthly things and awakened in us a greater desire for the things above. In days of sickness and adversity, and other vicissitudes of life, the Lord was ever near us, encircling us with his fatherly help and care. He moved us to cleave unto him more closely, so that we may say, "The trials of the righteous are many, but the Lord saves them from them all." As we increase in years and in the weakness of the body, his promise is that he will not abandon nor forsake us; even in our old age we will still be bearing fruits that were planted in the house of the Lord. We rejoice that it is also Your Honor's desire to enter the important [marriage] state with the Lord. Go forth in this way and the Lord will continue to crown you with his blessing. And if it be his will to grant you offspring that is consecrated to the Lord, may he grant you length (of years) and may he cause you to taste the sweetness of love, peace, unity, and the fear of the Lord. And when the fight of faith has been fought and finished, you will appear at the wedding [feast] of the Lamb that will never end; praise (honor) and worship and adoration shall be rendered to the triune Lord unto all eternity. That is the sincere wish of your loving friend.

Do surprise me with your letter and [tell] how you are doing. In my thoughts, dear Jansje, (I still see you) sitting on your father's lap playing with his watch, while (your dear mother) has your dear sister Cato on her lap. It was a pleasure for me to watch you growing up...(text missing)...it is from God, and that is why we love the brethren...(text missing)..."to the joyous prospect that delights me" [Dutch Psalter, Psalm 17, stanza 8, the first line alone was enough to recall the entire stanza of this familiar and beloved psalm. Translated by WL].

Maar - blij voooruitzicht dat mij streelt	But pleasant prospect that delights me
Ik zal, ontwaakt, uw lof ontvouwen,	I shall, awakened, thy praise unfold
U in gerechtigheid aanschouwen	in righteousness thee behold
Verzadigd met uw godd'lijk beeld.	Sated, thy godly face I see.

[The next 5 lines cannot be translated because they are so incomplete. They appear to describe a trip made to Germany by Mrs. C. M. Budde for health reasons. It was a trip from the Netherlands to Ulm on the Danube in Germany; the return trip included stops in Cologne, Elberfeld, and Düsseldorf, all in Germany. She concludes by saying that she had had two infections, and that the trip had been very good for her.]

In our family we keep on using the Dutch language; Diedrich and Maria can understand and read German fairly well. English is their mother tongue outside the home. Last winter all three of them attended a singing school. The Germans have some very beautiful songs. We also have a Reformed translation of the psalms. In my youth I was rather familiar with German tunes. We still frequently enjoy singing a nice hymn. Then Jan rehearses with us until we can sing it, for example:

Ich will streben/ Nach dem Leben,/ Wo ich selig bin;/
Ich will ringen ein zu dringen/ Bis das ich's gewinn./
Hält man mich, so lauf ich fort./
Bin ich mat, so ruft das Wort:/
Fort gerungen, Durch gedrungen/ bis zum Kleinod hin./

I want to strive/ for the life,/ Where I am blessed;/
I want to struggle/ to enter in,/ until it I win/
If they stop me,/ I'll run away/
If I am weary,/ the word tells me stay/
Fight on/ keep on, until the gem you've won.

Well, my beloved, may the Lord place us together in this struggle, for without a struggle there can be no victory. "To him that overcometh, I will grant to sit with me on my throne" [Revelation 3:21].

Your loving friend, C. M. Budde-Stomp.

And now a note to you, my dear Cato, Mrs. De Boer.

I rejoice greatly in your well-being and your joy because of the blessed growing up of your dear little Johan, which is also a joy for your esteemed parents. Your get-togethers on Tuesdays remind me how I, along with several friends, used to be catechized by your father, whom I highly esteemed. It was a delight to me. Even now, when I have a look at the catechism materials, they are like a bottle of that which has been poured out. When you put a cork on it, its potency stays inside, so that you can still recognize it. But thanks be to God, his Word endures forever. If it was bliss just to gather around the Word of God here, just imagine what it will be in a state of perfection. I am much obliged to you for keeping us informed about our old loved ones. From it we have noted that all our family is still well and there are no...[text missing]. [We] have not written them in a long time, and neither have we received a letter [from them]. If Your Honor should ever have occasion to speak to them, then please give them our greetings, and [tell] them that we are reasonably well. [What follows is a very garbled text with numerous missing passages] would like...something from our old friends. And then one is removed by death...[text missing]...and who is with her to take the place of faithful Mijntje? ...greetings ...[text missing]. Do you ever hear anything from the Lothes? Greetings to Mr. Luuring and ...[text missing] no longer know us, and also all [our] friends. My son sends you greetings...[text missing] also your dear parents and sister; greetings also to Your Honor's husband...[text missing]...dear little daughter nine months old I had...[text missing]...wishes to blow out the candle of her life with us...[text missing].

Budde 30

J. A. Wormser [fragment] to D. A. Budde
[no date]

[The text begins with several incomplete phrases]

......has fooled us and....
...[the] battle of religious [points of view]....
....the strength of extreme liberals....

[A possible reconstruction on the basis of what follows might be:]

[Our goal in the struggle of religious points of view is that the strength of the extreme liberals and that of the extreme orthodox party will really be broken....]

When the soul realizes its guilt before the Lord and feels the need for reconciliation and forgiveness, the teachings of a lifeless liberalism are not enough to satisfy her, and neither are the arid concepts of an extreme orthodoxy, which put their trust in *election* and not in the *atoning blood* of Christ. The so-called little alternative churches are multiplying very rapidly here, but they have little to recommend them. The truth is distorted in them, and it is always presented in a cold, abstract, unfeeling manner, so that souls are only confronted with the *decrees* of God and not sufficiently with the *revealed* will of the Lord. That does much harm and leads to a careless, offensive walk among not a few. However, it is also true that this crust of orthodoxy is being opposed more and more on all sides.

Recently we got to know a work by the American pastor Spencer, *Schetsen uit het dagboek eens leeraars* [*Sketches from the Diary of a Pastor*], which pleases me exceedingly. For the rest, our life moves on in stillness and simplicity.

The Lord grants us many blessings and has acquitted himself well towards us. We may rest in his grace, grounded in the reconciliation brought about through our Lord Jesus. May his grace also be with you all. Give cordial greetings to your wife and children, to Mrs. Teleman and her daughter from us, and believe me, that I always am,

Your loving Friend and Brother in Christ,
J. A. Wormser

Wormser 65

D. A. Budde to J. A. Wormser
Burlington, 16 December 1861

Beloved Brother in the Lord!

Since my dear wife has already written yours, I very much wanted to add a few lines of my own. Really, you cannot believe how happy we were to hear something from you after having waited so long. It gave us genuine pleasure to learn how well you all were doing and how happy and contented life was within your family circles. The mercies of the Lord are great toward us. What can be more pleasant than to be able to praise and thank the Lord together with one's children for the free manifestations of his favor, in which we may share with you? How many Christian parents are deprived of that? Now that I am getting older, weaker, and ailing more, I have much support from our Diedrich. And so the Lord is able to lighten the burdens of old age. Often I have to accuse myself of ingratitude toward the Lord, instead of constantly admonishing my soul [to] "forget not all the benefits which the Lord has shown and is showing you" [Psalm 103:2], the very opposite occurs. And then I have to flee with this and all my other sins to the atoning blood that cleanses us from all our sins.

As you know, one part of the American nation is at war with the other. The situation is just awful in those areas where they have taken up arms against each other. If war between nations is always a fearful matter, how much the more a civil war such as we are having here in America. It is one of those terrible judgments that the Lord visits upon the land and its people because of their sins. [To judge] by the reports we receive from various parts of this great land, it seems as if the Lord has given America over to the mutual consuming and destroying of each other. Nearly a million soldiers from the South and North stand opposite each other. In the month of October, Washington spent ninety million dollars, in the entire preceding year it was just nine million dollars.

Entire cities are put to the flame; entire lands are laid waste. Those who live in the South, that is, in the slave states, and side with the Union, must flee for their lives, leaving everything behind. Destruction, plunder, and killing are the order of the day. Raids are constantly being carried out, which manifest a hellish hatred. And who knows how far the judgments of the Lord may still have to go? The American nation was getting too haughty with all the blessings it enjoyed above all other nations. It forsook the Lord of heaven and earth. And then the wrath of God was spread over the earth in his judgments. And was there then a turning to the Lord who is striking us? Oh No! We will put down those firebrands in short order was the general boast and now look. Losses and disappointments, that was the answer of the Lord. The Lord lays low, and he raises up. So far the prospect continues to be very wretched. Here in Iowa we still have been spared, and we may still enjoy the goodness of the Lord in tranquility and peace, but for how long, only the Lord knows. God the Lord rules. Psalm 93.

Well, I must conclude, and I hope that soon we will be hearing from you. May the Lord continue to be with you all and grant that you may enjoy the consolations of the Holy Spirit.

Give my greetings to your dear wife, and children, and to old friends.

Your Loving,
D. A. Budde

Budde 31

Mrs. H. M. Bousquet-Chabot to Mrs. C. M. Budde-Stomp
Pella, 18 February 1862

Esteemed Friends, the Buddes,

Last night we were gladdened by a visit from our friend and brother Le Cocq. In the course of the conversation, we learned that he intended to write you within the next few days, and that really aroused my desire to enclose a few lines to you. As I was about to start writing today, the thought occurred to me how one delight flows forth from another, if only we have a listening ear and an attentive heart. The pleasure of meeting Le Cocq now brings me into contact with you without the least effort on my part. But such are the dealings of the Lord with his people who let themselves be led by him, only by free grace, and who have no other desire than that of the Father who is in heaven. Sometimes it can take a long time before a poor sinner, who through the love of the Lord Jesus has received the right to call himself a king and a priest. This is just as he is and before he can make the right use of those great privileges, which for the most part are still completely hidden from him. Still, through the blessing of the Spirit in the study of the Scriptures, so much has been made known to him, in beams of light as it were, that he may be ready to make the great transfer [to the hereafter], which will be the beginning of his everlasting bliss.

When I have met individuals from time to time and noticed that they had been in Burlington, I always inquired about our friends the Buddes. The general reports were always good; of course, you never get any detailed information. But, among other things, and I take it as a sign of wellbeing, I heard that Mrs. Budde, whom I always knew to be very thin, now has become a heavy set lady. It may not all be health, but it is a big change just the same. By the same route, this time from people who have acquaintances or relatives in Pella, you may have heard that two of my sons are now in the army. This matter, although very grievous in itself, had blessings for me and mine that could only be attributed to God's fatherly governance over us. Herman, our youngest son (he will turn twenty-one in August), had been involved in a spiritual struggle for two years. Now before he left his parental home to go into military service, [the Spirit of God] empowered him freely to confess that he belonged to the Lord Jesus. You can imagine what a relief this was for us at such a sad departure. I cannot write you all the details, but his letters confirm for us that the Lord has upheld him in his struggle and difficulties. Herm had just finished his studies at the seminary.

When some of Herman's friends, who were also the friends of Jan, our second son, were in Pella on furlough, they talked him [Jan] into going along. At the time he was a clerk in the Berkhout store, where he had to work hard, [put up with a lot], and learned little. As far as human contacts and experience go, he now has greater opportunity to become a man. When he left he said to me, "Mama, do not worry about me; I am going with the Lord and the Lord is going with me." And there is complete confirmation for this: he is a dear Christian, loved by all, and helpful to all.

Now about the two remaining [children]. They are both doing very well, each in his own work. So when I look at my children, I have many reasons for gratitude. My health is good, as long as I can only stay inside in all this cold weather.

And now my dear friend, I hope that when you receive these lines you will have as much pleasure as I had in writing them. It is not likely that we will see each other face to face in this world, but then let us slowly on get ready for the great encounter up above. Believe me, I am,

> Your loving Sister in the Lord,
> H. M. Bousquet

Budde 31a

> Mrs. H. M. Bousquet-Chabot to Mrs. C. M. Budde-Stomp
> 18 February 1862

[This is a fragment of a *kladbrief* [first draft] Budde-Stomp, Wormser 63]

That was the kind of situation I was in, dear friend. I still recall when I was eight, ten, twelve years old and was, as it were, persecuted by many Christians [urging] me to love the Lord Jesus. The way to get me to that point took many different forms. This condition, with rising and falling, lasted until my fifty-fourth year. Then I occasionally felt what it means to stand in the freedom of Christ, until I now, at the age of sixty-two, can say with full assurance of faith that through free grace the Lord has become my portion unto all eternity.

Le Cocq did not pick up the letter yesterday, and after rereading it I realized that I had to add the above in order to clarify what I had written. The war tidings seem to be very favorable for our cause. What a sense of peace the Christian has in being able to give everything into the hands of the Lord.

> Once again receive my cordial greetings. H. M. B.

Budde 32

> Pastor Johan Müller to brother D. A. Budde
> Silver Brook Parsonage, 21 April 1862

Dear Brother Budde,

Aren't you thinking that I have forgotten you? No wonder. I should never have kept you waiting so long for a sign of life from me. My only apology is that I am always so busy. Last winter it was cold in nature here, and it also seems to have been cold in the hearts of people. Only two people from among the large number of people have come to walk beneath the Banner of the Cross, one aged gray-beard and a woman who was still young. Today I visited two families—in one a sick man; he laments that his heart is hard as steel—in the other, a woman who had been ill. She has found the Lord but has an inner struggle about baptism; her father is a Baptist. Oh, it not only takes a lot of work in this congregation, it also requires much wisdom. I do not have an abundance of that, but, "If any of you lack wisdom, let him ask of God, that giveth to all men liberally" [James 1:5]. The Lord, who is ever gracious, will not fail to give his help.

Last fall I spent several pleasant days at classis [meetings] in Milwaukee. I stayed with your friends from Amsterdam, the Janssens, dear people. I am to send you cordial greetings [from them], and if you and your dear wife come to visit me here, he promised that he and his wife would also come. This spring we could not go to classis because of the bad roads. Let me know whether you are coming this summer, so that I can let your friend Janssen know. Also write me what his first name is; I have forgotten it. My wife asks me to tell your wife that if she were to come, she [my wife] would be able to speak a few words in German.

In February I again had my neck problem; I could not preach for three Sundays. A short time ago my wife had cold fever, but now we are all healthy again. Last fall I sent you my picture; did you get it all right? If not, then we will have to try sending another. Will you be so kind to have the enclosed release for my wife from the church at Burlington signed and send it to me in your next letter? I think of Burlington and the church there often. If only the Lord might grant that his work there might prosper just the same.

Give warmest greetings from me and my wife to your entire dear family and to all the brethren and sisters.

Your loving Brother in Christ,
Johan Müller

Budde 33

        Mrs. H. M. Bousquet-Chabot to Mrs. C. M. Budde-Stomp
                                       Pella, 14 Sept. 1862

Dear Budde Friends,
    A worldly courtesy would require that I begin with an apology for having kept you waiting so long for an answer to a letter of no ordinary everyday content. But, it is exactly the more than ordinary expression of Christian love, and the heavenly-minded sentiments expressed therein, which no random moment, even if there is no special task waiting, can set the soul in the required direction for the cultivation and development of that which is still to be experienced when we, released from this body of sin, shall see the Lord as he is.
    The refreshing emotions that the Lord causes us to experience now and then, whether it be through a personal encounter or a written communication (as is the case between us now), are often needful to us for the strengthening, encouragement, and building up of our faith and putting our trust in the promises of our Lord. As I see it, such times are entirely in the hand of the Lord, and it seems to me that if we view them in this way, there is blessing in them for us. And so, my dear friend, even though it may be a while before I, the Lord willing, may again get an answering letter from the two of you, I will not complain about having waited too long, nor that the content is too brief, if only my soul may again be refreshed as it was in your letter of April 1 [1862]. We must use the talents we have received to build each other up, but especially to glorify the name of the Lord.
    Recently I had a sweet visit from Burkens [Beurkens]. While I was speaking to him about you and said that I hoped to write you soon, he requested that I mention that his wife is recuperating these days from a sickness that really was very debilitating. No doubt you know that Burkens is now living on a farm. He was in town here with a young man who had lived at his house for four years, and whom he had brought here to enlist as a volunteer in the army. The brother of his son-in-law was a very well behaved young man. It really seemed to hit B. hard; as you know he is a very sensitive man.
    And now, my dear friend, even as I reported to you in my previous [letter] that Jan's second son volunteered [for military duty], so I must now inform you that the third [son], Henry, has also joined the same company of [Matthes]. They have a believing captain; that is not everything, but it is much. At the moment they are still in Oskaloosa,

only eighteen miles from here, so that there still can be constant travel back and forth, but that too will end soon. And who knows how far they will be from us then, but never too far to be out of the eye of the Lord. What an encouraging consolation it is that if only we commend and bear up our children [to the Lord] on the basis of his own promises and the covenant made with us in baptism, by faith we can assume that there is a better and safer Guardian watching over them than any earthly father or mother can be for their children. The Lord is especially [near] to me at the departure of this third child, so that I may hope that this matter too may redound to the renown and glorification of his great name.

[It takes time], but we are getting the most satisfactory reports from the two others. They were in a camp near Memphis, Tennessee, for a long time, but they have left from there for an unknown destination. The health of the children remains very good despite heat and fatigue; and, except for their daily activities, they have very much enjoyed the beautiful countryside and bemoaned the fact that through the wantonness of people it is being destroyed so. The many changes that have occurred in the war situation since you last wrote me may also have required that some of your friends and perhaps relatives have been called up for duty. If that should be the case, then the Lord certainly did not test you beyond your capability, without comforting you in the usual fatherly manner, but let me not expand on this with assumptions.

Are you acquainted with Rev. Oggel, the present Dutch Reformed preacher here? (I certainly may call him the Reformer of Pella.) He is a very dear and pleasant person, and although my children and I do not belong to his congregation, there is still a pleasant association between us, and that is true also for the Rev. Fimpton, the English preacher in that church. Rev. Oggel is leaving for Michigan tomorrow to pick up his wife, who had been at the home of her parents to have her baby; at the same time he is taking leave of his brother Oggel and his brother-in-law Van Raalte, both of whom are going into the army. And so every one gets his share in this time of worldly confusion, so it would appear, but our strength is in the carrying out of the divine promises and their fulfillment.

You probably have heard, with some sympathy, of the increase in Rev. Scholte's family; his wife gave birth to a son last night. It is his fourteenth child, of which seven are now living. Saartje, who is married to Dr. Keables, has three children: two boys and one girl; they are very well-to-do, [lazy], wild children. About three months ago the doctor joined the army; he is working in the Third Regiment, in which my children also are.

The Berkhout children, whom you probably still recall, visit me fairly often. They now have their store across from us on the square in the busiest neighborhood, and they share with everyone else the pressure of these hard times, and that is not always all that easy to bear. Berkhout is a big supporter of [Rev.] Oggel and his congregation; he also teaches in the Sunday school.

It is about time for me to transfer my thoughts to Burlington, that is, at least to you on your farm. I can readily understand how changed everything must look from the time that we spent a day there in the summer of '49. Oh, how I remembered the way my dear husband acted when I read the story about the apple trees [Johnny Appleseed?]. It was the joy and delight of his life to advocate such a thing [planting apple seeds?]. On the 10th of this month it was six years ago that his corpse was committed to the earth. As much as I still miss him every day, I must say his cup of troubles of this life was filled, and so the Lord's time had come to take him unto himself, where he now lives freed from all misery. By faith I can glory in my invisible husband and father of my children and experience blessings beyond my prayers and thoughts.

It gives me joy that as your years mount toward old age, the Lord also provides assistance through your children. That is far to be desired over getting assistance from strangers. The greatest joy in life is to experience rest and trust in your daily associations with others. I was also very glad that through you I got to know something about our dear friends, the Wormsers. Although they experience blessings in their family, still [Mr.] W[ormser] seems to experience much physical suffering. At the moment there is no occasion for me to write them from here, but if you should happen to write them again, then be so kind to send them my sincere greetings. Although it seems that all who once were alive are cut off from all Christian ties in death [text not clear here], still one day the never-ending time of quickening life will commence, and the longing for that, does, after all, constitute the consolation and strength of every true child of God.

Because of a minor indisposition I was prevented from going to church today, but in my reading and reflecting I might rejoice in the presence of the Lord, and having spent the evening writing to you, there is again an abundance of new material for gratitude before the rest of this night begins.

Sept. 16. I did not have an opportunity to finish this before now. I hope that it will find you and yours in good health and greet everyone for me. How much farther we are presently separated from each other than when we lived in Noorderbosch in Amsterdam?

And now, dear friend, may the Lord strengthen our faith in these trouble-filled days, and may he constantly make us to wish and to strive for the good that remains when all else perishes. My son Piet Hein, who is in the room just now, sends his greetings to you all. In this child I really experience the blessing of the Lord, especially in that he makes use of this world but not as one possessing it.

Now may you both be assured of my Christian remembrance of you. Believe me that I am,

Your loving Sister in the Lord,
H. M. Bousquet

Budde 34

J. Wüstenhoff-Wormser to Mrs. C. M. Budde-Stomp
Amsterdam, October 3, 1862

Esteemed Madam, Dearly Beloved Friend,

Your letters, which we are always so glad to receive, should have been answered sooner. We were so very happy to receive your letters toward the end of December, and that we might learn from them that the Lord still has spared all of you for each other. It was the extended serious sickness of my dear father that is the cause of the delay. And since probably an even longer delay will follow, at the request of my parents I have taken my pen to let you know about our experiences and the manifold trials that have been ours during the past year.

Early in November, Father [Mr. J. A. Wormser] had a severe attack of rheumatism, so that for days he could not use any of his limbs. That lasted until the end of December. After doing a little work at the office for three weeks, toward the end of January he got another attack, as severe as the previous one, so that he was completely exhausted. The doctor advised that as soon as the weather turned warm, Father should be outdoors. Father was too weak to make a trip, and the weather was too variable, so that it was decided that Father and Mother should enjoy the outdoor air for a little while at Mrs. Zeelt's [country home] in the hope that the Lord would restore his strength there. Father and Mother left on the 5th of May, but that might not avail either. Repeatedly he got attacks of rheumatism in his back and loins, so severe that one time Father fell down on the floor, and we had to send medicines almost every day.

The latter part of May our parents came home again. Father had made no progress at all, and the next week Father suffered much from rheumatic toothache, and his face was so swollen that even we could scarcely recognize him. But on the 6th of June Father had another attack in his back; on the 8th of June, the second day of Pentecost, it reached a highpoint such as you cannot begin to imagine. It was twitches of gout, coupled with very severe nerve pains. Father would be sitting on a settee and repeatedly get a convulsion [so severe] that at times we would not hold him down with the five of us. Then he would become terribly sleepy, and at the point of falling asleep, he would get another convulsion. That day we thought that Father would succumb because of it, and it was Father's wish that we should stay with him. The doctor said he had never seen anything like it, and the only thing he could prescribe was to make a sop and rub with chloroform. This situation lasted from eight-thirty Monday morning till Wednesday evening at nine o'clock, without any interruptions, when we finally were able to get Father to bed. All that time Father, supported by at least two people, had to sit straight as a candle on the settee.

Those attacks were repeated again and again with severe palpitations, and so there were many fly blisters on his back, and when they [the blisters] were open, morphine powder was strewn into them. Later on, Father had ten *koppen* [blood suckers?] on his back, and these finally served to quell the pain. But this was followed by an unbelievable weakness, so that by human calculations this sickbed may well become Father's deathbed. Since the 6th of June, Father has not left his room, and at night there has always been someone keeping watch with him, and of late it has been two persons. Recently, Father was so miserable that Mother did not get to bed for fourteen nights, but only slept for a few hours in the morning. And now my husband and I are keeping watch together every third or fourth night. Then it is Mother's turn to sleep. My brother-in law De Boer, Johan, and Uncle Dries take turns watching. So far we have been able to get along without any outside help.

Every day my sister Cato and I spend the whole day at the home of Father and Mother, but my sister is constantly weak and ailing, so that she just cannot do without her nightly rest, and she cannot be away from her child all the time either. Five or six weeks ago, Father said to us that if things continued in this way [with him] getting slowly weaker, he thought that it must be the will of the Lord to take him away, and for that he is prepared, and so if we had anything to say or ask, we should do so. And that is what we have done, and now there is a great calm and peace in the house, accompanied by the grief of having to lose him.

When we think of our enjoyable Sunday evenings and the ordinary Wednesday evening of catechism lessons [with Father], and the loss for Mother and the youngest children, sometimes we are very nervous and sad. On the other hand, considering his suffering and weakness and his desire to be *ontbonden* [to be released by death], then at times we say to each other, would it be love on our part if we wanted to keep him here like this? Last Monday, Father said that when he considered the pending glory, then it was as if he were going to a feast, but if he were healthy then he would want to stay with us for a time.

Thus far, you have an account of Father's condition. You certainly will understand that Mother is in no mood for writing now. At times all of us are equally tired, because it always takes two people to move Father, or to raise him a little, and sometimes he is just a dead weight. Yesterday, Thursday, we were able to change his bed for the first time since Saturday, which for some weeks now has taken four people to handle. First we carry Father to a cot, and then back to the bed. I am writing this [letter] in the sick room; Father knows that I am writing, and he has asked that I send cordial greetings to all the family, and also to friends who know him.

Your and our friend Luuring passed away August 14th. As you know, he had been ailing for years, but in the last eighteen weeks he was home; and he finally succumbed to consumption and vomiting of blood at the age of fifty years. It was grievous for him as well as for Father that they were not able to meet each other one more time. Because of the emotional impact on his wife and children, he was insistent that there should be no talk about death, not even remotely. The Lord is making special provision for the family since his death. Willem is working at another office where he earns much more, and, also, the work is sent to him, as it were. The girls make hats and do sewing for people, so that this and that will be adequate for them to keep on living on the same footing that they have been used till now.

You probably will say that you are not getting a very pleasant letter. Apart from Father's condition, we have more serious illnesses in the family. My mother-in-law is suffering from a liver disease and was in a very critical condition this week. My husband's only brother is suffering from vomiting blood, and thus he is always in a dangerous condition, and so we always have to be going from one sick person to another. Fortunately, the Lord constantly blesses us with health and strength.

Mrs. Zeelt is still living, but when Father and Mother were staying in the country [last June], she was so miserable that we expected to receive a death notice at any time. However, she has recovered somewhat and spent eight days in Utrecht once again. But she could go any day; she is eighty-two years old now.

And now I must still inform you that Father and Mother, with the assistance of Rev. Hasebroek, have transferred their membership to the Hervormde Kerk. Without our ever being aware of it, our Luuring friends had the same desire, so that Rev. Hasebroek arranged it for them also. They did not have to make a profession of faith, nor make a confession of having wandered away in the past, but they only had to express the desire to be received as members into the church again. But the children might not be transferred, and now Maria is the only Seceder in our house. Last March, Johan was received as a member of the congregation.

Well, dear friend, I have written you about all the news I know. We hope you will not wait as long [with writing] as we did. Father himself, when he had a rheumatic attack in his right hand, said that he would write again when the hand was healed, and so nothing came of that. We hope that the war does not hinder you in any way, and that you can get our letters regularly and we can get yours. And do write us something about it [the war] once.

The German hymn, *"Ich will sterben"* ["I Want to Die"], is the favorite hymn of my husband; he plays it on the piano often. He has several books on German hymns; many of them [hymns] are very beautiful. The verse you quoted in our house has gotten the name, "Mrs. Budde's verse."

Well, dear friends, I had better conclude. We hope to receive a more cheerful letter from you than you are receiving from us. We extend cordial greetings to your entire family, to friend Jan and his family, to Mrs. Teeleman [Teleman] and her daughter, as well as to all the friends who know us. My parents, spouse, mother, and brother, all of them greet you cordially. I do not know whether it is already known to you that the aged Jansen [Janssen] died some time ago. Once again, with warmest greetings from your friend, who loves you cordially, and commends you to the Lord.

J. Wüstenhoff-Wormser

Budde 35

Mrs. H. M. Bousquet-Chabot to D. A. Budde
Pella, 21 Oct. 1862

Esteemed Brother,
 I do not know what there is to say about what happened to the accompanying letter. A few days ago I happened to see some papers of my son P[iet Hein]. I discover with them my letter to you that I had asked him to mail on Sept. 16. I considered that rather careless, and so I was disappointed with the thought that you should not have received a message from me. But, when I consider that this neglect now provides me the opportunity to add a few additional lines to it [the unmailed letter], then I must again say that this is the way it had to be.
 And so with a few words I still wanted to notify you of the great privilege that we have experienced through the love and nearness of the Lord when our dear son Jan was wounded by a bullet in his right leg above the knee. It happened on the 7th of this month [October] in the battle of Corinth. His regiment was not in the most intense fire, just in the reserves, but just the same a bullet entered his leg, and on the outside of the leg it was held back by the skin. Dr. Keables then cut it out. Miracle of miracles, no bone was hit, and so if there are no complicating circumstances Jan will be able to keep his life. He himself wrote a few lines, and he too is struck by the goodness of the Lord. Herman had a gall [bladder] disease and had not recovered sufficiently to go along when it was time to march. But he is improving slowly. Henry is still in Oskaloosa and has the great privilege of having been chosen as clerk by the colonel, a post in which he appears to be doing very well, and one in which the responsibilities are doubly compensated for by the advantages.
 So you see, dear friends, that these few lines are not the least important ones of my letter, since there are so many evidences of God's faithfulness and love contained therein. He does not reward us according to our unrighteousness. Believe me, I am,

Your Friend who loves you in the Lord,
H. M. Bousquet

Wormser 66

H. M. Bousquet-Chabot, to J. Wormser-van der Ven
Pella, 8 December 1862

Dear Friend,
 In our daily lives there are some circumstances more than others that remind us of the Lord's directing hand, which extends to every little detail. Thus, about two weeks ago my mind was preoccupied with the course of events (too lengthy to relate to you) by which Mrs. Berkhout, who was visiting at our house that evening, had gotten your letter. When she opened the letter, we learned of the great loss that the Lord has brought upon you [death of J. A. Wormser, Nov. 1, 1862]. When Mr. B[erkhout] came to pick up his wife, I said to him that I would very much like to enclose a few lines when His Honor answered your letter.
 Since that letter will be leaving today, it is my pleasure to carry out my intention. The teaching of the Lord [to] "rejoice with them that rejoice, and weep with them that weep" [Romans 12:15] remains ours, and the fulfillment thereof is our heart's desire, so that, dear Friend, carrying out this obligation is at the same time an acknowledgment of our desire to fulfill that lesson (however imperfectly). What shall we puny people say to each other that is of any comfort at all, unless it be rooted in that all-embracing word? "You are my people." "I have known you from before the foundation of the world." This declaration says it all for the believing Christian. If we do not always experience the strengthening power of such words of consolation, then the reason for it can only be found in us. One day when we, like our friend, will have laid aside the body of our sins, the time of eternal blessedness will also dawn for us. I know, my dear Friend, that the Lord will comfort you, but in his own good time, for God who knows that we are dust and ashes also knows what it means for a wife and mother to lose her dearly beloved husband and spouse. Such a deep wound must heal somewhat through the passage of time before there can be any of the true comfort promised by the Lord to widows who are widows indeed. By grace it was given unto you and also to me to take hold of these promises by faith, and from experience I can assure you that they will never fail.
 December 9. Through a small coincidence I have the opportunity to add a few lines about our present situation. Because of the increasing ease and speed of communications, you are no doubt somewhat informed about the sorrowful condition now prevailing throughout

the United States, and I shall say nothing about that.

A letter is just too limited to explain the situation to you, but I shall tell you how, because of these internal disturbances, three of my children have taken up arms in order to be of assistance in putting down the rebellion of the South. Herman, the youngest, left on May 29, 1861. John, our second son, left November 19, 1861, and Henry, the third son, left September 2, 1862. The circumstances were different for each one, but they were such that I did not feel at liberty to restrain them; indeed, I was able to acquiesce in the way the Lord wants to lead me in these matters. In the given situation, which is far from an ordinary one, I must say that the Lord strengthens me greatly, also by so ordering all things, that it is not difficult to discern that His guiding hand is very much outstretched over our children.

In April of 1862 a bullet passed through Herman's cap without a hair being singed. Before he left he professed his faith in the Lord Jesus, and in his letters he has been sharing with me the ups and downs in the development of his faith in a truly childlike manner. Jan had already become a [professing] member of Scholte's church, and for him too, though in a different way, a training school has been opened to test his faith. In a battle fought last October 4 and 5, he was wounded in his right leg, but in such a way that, humanly speaking, he will be getting back the full use of his leg; but as he wrote me yesterday, the wound is healing very slowly. He is presently in a hospital at Keokuk, only 120 miles from here. We are doing all we can to get him a furlough to come to Pella, but so far we have not succeeded. But we are not giving up yet. Since the person to whom I had written at Keokuk was out of town, I might still be getting a positive reply from him later. He is able to walk with the aid of a crutch, and, having several friends there, even in that situation he does have some small satisfactions. [These include] Rev. Baai, at whose home he is a frequent guest.

Henry has been especially fortunate; he left with a company consisting entirely of people from Pella: Hollanders and Americans. He knew the captain and the latter utilized him as a clerk. He appears to have done very well in that capacity, so that he is now being used by a colonel in the same capacity. But because of this promotion he is completely relieved of military duties and is being used as a writer; the situation is a good one for him since his health is not all that good. So you see, under the present circumstances I have many reasons to be thankful; there is nothing I wish for more fervently than to surrender myself and all my family entirely to the leading of the Lord. Letters may be a pleasant means of communication between friends who are separated, but still there is a certain limitation, and so I must now conclude.

We have had some glorious days for this season [of the year], so that until now I have been going out every day; that was quite different in other years. This afternoon I hope to visit Mrs. Scholte once again. She had her eighth child in October; it is a fine boy, Scholte's fourteenth child. Saartje, who, as you may know, married a Dr. Keables, has three of the most darling children, but she deplores the absence of her husband, who is serving as a doctor in the army. And now I hope these lines may reach you in reasonably good health. From our friends, the Berkhouts, I learned that both of your daughters have married; by my reckoning, I think your son must be about eighteen years old. You will do me a real favor by conveying my greetings to friends whom you happen to meet, and who, you think, still remember me. Some names of people I can still visualize include Mr. Luuring and his wife and Mrs. Kaspar. Our old friends, the Le Cocqs, are living on their farm; two of their married sons [live] in the city, while Jan, who is still single, lives in with them. I recently started corresponding with our friends, the Buddes, in Burlington, so that very likely I will be getting some Netherlands news now and then via that channel.

Although we are now very distant from each other, we are all still very closely linked together, so imagine what it will be like when all of us are united together, without sin, and in the presence of the Lord Jesus.

If you should run into Mrs. Da Costa, then give her my greetings; and what of Mrs. Willing, is she still here on earth or is she with her Lord!

Believe me, I am still your loving Friend,
H. M. Bousquet

I do have to add a word about Piet Hein, who is such a faithful business manager for me. His health is perfect, notwithstanding the fact that his activities are many and very exhausting. He has been blessed in his many undertakings, and as a notary public and lawyer, he is a counselor to, and manager for, many people.

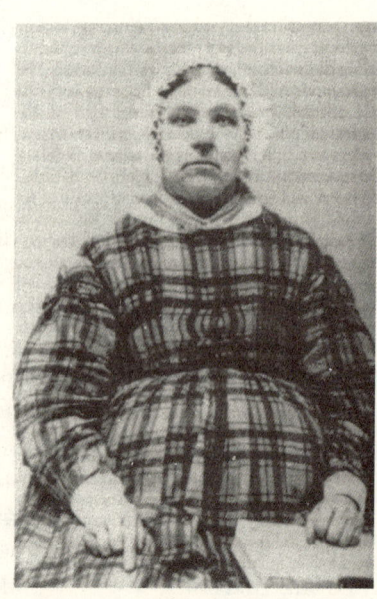

Christina Maria Budde-Stomp (1802-1872), wife of Diedrich A. Budde, friend of Janke Wormser-van der Ven and faithful Iowa correspondent with the Netherlands
(Courtesy of Jan Peter Verhave)

Wormser 67

C. M. Budde-Stomp to the widow Mrs. Wormser
and her children and children-in-law
Burlington, December 1862

Dearly Beloved Friend and Sister in the Lord,
 On November 30 we received the sad tiding we had been expecting of the death of Your Honor's beloved Husband and Father, our highly esteemed and beloved Friend and brother, Johan Adam Wormser. We also share with interest in your grief and loss, hoping that in your rightful grief Your Honor may gaze after him in his eternal bliss. Granted that his suffering here was very heavy, his Savior bore it with him; his great High Priest had to be sanctified by his suffering, thus becoming the source of salvation for all those who are saved. And "so, he had to taste [drink] the dregs of [the cup of] his suffering, following his great master, to where God shall wipe away all tears. And so rejoice with fear and be glad with trembling, that God will be your strength, for he has promised to be a husband to widows and a Father to orphans." That is the heartfelt wish of your loving friend.
 And you, my beloved Johan, cannot begin to realize the moving emotions I experienced when I saw your signature seal instead of that of your dear father. Your God-fearing parents have dedicated you to a

triune God and in your baptism you received the seal thereof; you have also been accepted as a member of the Christian congregation, but that is not all. In his Word the Lord says: "Behold I stand at the door and knock. If any man hear my voice, and open the door, I will come in to him, and will sup with him, and he with me" [Revelation 3:20]. King Jesus wants our heart, that is, all our mind and affection, and he [desires] to give us his Holy Spirit, and to govern us according to his good pleasure. Many a young person has tasted the sweet voice of the Good Shepherd in his youth, but suffered shipwreck in the enticing adolescent years. King David sings: "Wherewith shall a young man, surrounded by vanities, cleanse his way? Surely, by taking heed thereto according to thy holy word; with my whole heart have I sought thee; mine eye is fixed on thee" [adapted from Psalm 119:9-10]. If that is also your choice, my dear Johan, you will also follow in your beloved father's footsteps, and you will be your dear mother's consolation and support, and an ornament in the house of God.

The song that you love so, "Ich will streben" ["I want to strive for..."; cf. Wormser 64], gives me the glad hope that you and the lovely couple, Mr. & Mrs. Wüstenhoff, are striving with manly vigor to enter by the narrow gate. The firm resolution of your dear father-in-law was, "As for me and my house, we will serve the Lord." May the Lord graciously grant that unto his servant even unto generations to come!

It was a great joy to us that we might receive [your] father's cordial greetings from his sickbed. When things quiet down for [your] mother or one of you, would you be so kind to write where his [father's] final resting place is and how old he was? It is such a precious thing ("Behold the place where they laid him") [Mark 16:6]. Your nice letter should have gotten an earlier response, but a whole series of events were taking place here just then. A daughter, Johanna, was born to our son Johan September 24, the eighth child, of whom two are still living. It was a healthy and lovely [baby], which the Lord took to himself when it was three weeks old. At the same time, his father-in-law, Van Beek, who lives next to them on our land, became ill and died two days before the baby, so that they had two corpses in one week.

In addition to chest pains, my dear husband suffers much from stomach cramps; of late it worsened so much that I became dejected as I observed his decline. One evening, we were eating when it seemed that something was stuck in his throat; he could not breathe. He struggled hard until water was running from his mouth. This had exhausted him so much that he had to stay in bed and he became even sicker, so that in his mind it was as if he was being translated [to Heaven], and he was greatly concerned. The doctor said it was a billiard fever [an evil humor with high fevers] and stomach cramps. It pleased the Lord to bless the [medical] means, so that he did recover, but very slowly. The Lord be thanked who continues to spare us from losing him. I also experience great lassitude; when I do anything out of the ordinary, my head gets very dizzy, and [I have] sleepless nights that leave me feeling very worn out. I have also had rheumatism in my right thumb for over a year now, and that bothers me a great deal when I am sewing or writing.

From time to time we have a very nice exchange of letters with the widow, Mrs. Bousquet; it is already six years ago that Her Honor's husband passed away. And she is over sixty-two. In her fifth year [as a widow], she came to the full assurance of faith and can say, "By free grace the Lord is my portion unto all eternity." In another letter she requested that I send Your Honor her sincere greetings. She is very upbeat and active, given her circumstances. Three of her sons enlisted and are in military service; her second son, Jan, was wounded in the battle of Corinth on October 7, a bullet penetrated his right leg above the knee and was lodged against the skin on the opposite side. Dr. Keables, Rev. Scholte's son-in-law, who is also in the army, cut it out. Quite amazingly, it had not struck any bone, so if there are no other complications he will survive. Piet Hein, the oldest son, is still with her and is a notary public. Saartje Scholte has three children; a son was recently born to Rev. Scholte, his fourteenth child, of whom seven are living.

Your Honor asked whether the war hindered us in any way; until now our state has been spared any battlefields, but we are constantly worried about a draft of men between the ages of eighteen and forty-five. While I am writing, we read in a weekly that if the number [quota] is not filled by New Year, the government will be compelled to conscript men by a lottery, and that can also affect our children. The situation in America is a very sad one, the fighting has gone on for one and a half years. Thousands of casualties have fallen on the battlefields, and there has been no progress at all. To be sure, the South is rebelling, but the Lord is chastising the North as well. [Like] Israel against the Benjaminites, the nation has turned from the Lord. What a lot of war expenditures both on land and sea, which will have to be paid by every one of us! You hardly see silver money any more; it is all paper money, right down to the small change. The Lord did give some intervals of mercy by granting us a fairly bountiful harvest; if only the Lord might humble the people and sheath the sword of war.

And now I cannot help thinking that I have satisfied your desires. My son Johan [as well as] Diedrich and Maria share in your grief and wish Your Honor the consolation of the Lord; he who alone can assuage your grief. Diedrich is very much attached to Wormser. The death of our friend, Luring [Luuring], distressed me greatly. My heartfelt greetings to all of you, Mr. and Mrs. De Boer. Kiss Maria and Henriette for me. I commend you to the Lord and his grace.

Your most loving sister and friend in the Lord,
C. M. Budde-Stomp

P.S. Mrs. Teleman is with her daughter; I have not spoken to her since your [last] letter.

Wormser 68

D. A. Budde to Mrs. J. Wormser-van der Ven
Burlington, 9 December 1862

Esteemed Friend and Sister in the Lord!

I never could have thought that my dear friend and brother would have ended his pilgrim journey even before me. And that he would be

Diedrich A. Budde (1800-1873), Burlington farmer and friend of J. A. Wormser
(Courtesy of Jan Peter Verhave)

taken from your side into the Paradise of our God. We all share in your grief. I cannot find the words to express myself adequately, and since my dear wife has already written, I will only add a few lines as a token of my sympathy, with the prayer that our dear Lord Jesus, who sympathizes with those who mourn, may make up to you what you have lost in your beloved deceased one, with his blessed consolation and with the consolation of the Holy Spirit. What consolation do we not find in the precious word of the Lord to his children when we read, "For thy Maker is thy *husband*, the Lord of Hosts is his name" [Isaiah 54:4]. You may mourn freely, but not as those who have no hope. If your future pathway does not look all that smooth to you, never fear! The precious truth was granted as consolation for the downcast and stricken of heart. Therefore, "Commit thy way unto the Lord; trust also in him; and he shall bring it to pass" [Psalm 37:5]. And since it is very likely that you will not be getting this letter until the year 1863, I will conclude with a wish and a prayer for you, esteemed Sister, and all your dear relatives. As we find it in Psalm 32:8: "I will instruct thee and teach thee in the way which thou shalt go. I will guide thee with mine eye."

With heartfelt greetings [to you] and all yours, I remain,

Your Friend and Brother,
D. A. Budde

Budde 36

C(ato) de Boer-Wormser to Mrs. C. M. Budde-Stomp
Amsterdam, 23 Jan. 1863
Mrs. C. M. Budde nee Stomp

Dearly Beloved Friend!

We were very happy to again receive a tiding from you on Dec. 31st of last year. The tiding of Father's passing away surely reached you fast. We are still in mourning, dear friend, how could it be otherwise, you know *what kind* of father *ours* might be. Now we wish to be thankful for the privilege of having been allowed to keep him for so long. With all my heart I hope that, with God's help, I may follow Father's example in bringing up our only son. That nurturing falls mostly on my shoulders, since my husband is out of the house almost the entire day. It is no easy task, since I want very much to see him walk in the fear of the Lord when he grows up. But my parents have taught me to know him who said, "Open your mouth, and I will fill it."

All of us, married and unmarried and in-laws, gathered around Father's bed when he was dying. That was very much Father's wish and desire, and I do not know of any wish that remained unfulfilled either before or after his death. Father was very patient during his suffering, and he admonished us all to abide in the Lord. He still was praising the goodness and greatness of God just hours before his death; then he took leave of everyone by name. But I must not forget to tell you that we experienced very much love, heartiness, and help from Uncle Dries; he was with us day and night. The last night we were together with the nine of us. We have learned to love him, and he certainly is worth it; he has now become guardian. And after having taken leave of *all of us*, Father seemed peaceful and lay down to await death. So Father passed away, slowly and gently, and now he is with the Lord whom he loved and served for so long. I have to be so very brief on paper. How I would like to tell you everything personally, things that I must now pass over in silence. That night Father commended his soul to God with the words of Stephen. Granted that it is true that we always confess the omnipresence of God, but after those words it was as if we could distinctly feel that the Lord himself was present in the room with his angels. In a word, it was a solemn night, and right after that the sure knowledge that Father was already joining in the hymn in honor of the Lamb.

How soon Father's death followed that of Mr. Luuring; there were only seven weeks between them. The [Luuring] family is well, and everything remains on the same old footing there. Our mother is going to move to the Noorderstraat and so is my sister Jansje. I think of you often in connection with the war. It gives us great joy that you have been spared so far. Mother has letters from Berkhout and Mrs. Bouquet. And now you must by all means not write us any less. If possible, my sister and I would prefer to receive our letters on separate sheets of paper so we can save them. And now I must greet all of you, Mr. [Budde] and Jan, Maria [and] Diederick [Diedrich], of whose greeting and devotion Father still took cognizance. I can still recall all of you, but you best, my dear friend. And now I give my common greeting to you all, and commend you all to the Lord.

Your loving Friend,
C. de Boer-Wormser

Budde 37

Mrs. J. Wormser-van der Ven to Mrs. C. M. Budde-Stomp
Amsterdam, 23 January 1863

Dearly Beloved Friend and Sister in the Lord!

Your cordial and sympathetic letter has reached me in reasonably good health and well-being. I thank you for it. Indeed, dear friends, there are times when I say, "The Almighty hath dealt bitterly with me" [Ruth 1:20] by taking such a worthy man from me, for the greater your treasure, the greater your loss. But in calmer moments, I can acquiesce more in the way the Lord is taking me. Then I can thank him that such a man was mine for 28 1/2 years. If the Lord had taken him sooner, I would also have had to keep silence. It is, after all, the way of all flesh; man is born to die. He is with his Lord whom he loved and served, for whom he longed so. His suffering was long and heavy, but he bore it calmly and patiently, so much so that Mr. Groen van Prinsterer, who visited him twice, said to me: "It is a privilege when people in The Hague tell the story that a Roman Catholic, Dr. Rive, felt impelled to testify that Wormser was a model of suffering, but also a model of patience."

He never had any fear of death. I did hear him say, "When I think of you and the children, I would like to stay a while longer, but when I think of the eternal glory, it is as if I am going to a feast." When I asked him from time to time, "Is everything still clear within?" then his answer was, "Christ is my rock, he will never fail me, whether I live or die, I am the Lord's." And one night at four A.M., after he had called us all together, he said with a loud voice, "Lord Jesus receive my soul," and at seven in the morning of November 1, he passed away. And so you see, my dear friend, as his life was, so was his dying, unfaltering in the faith. And grieve I must every day, and grieve I may, but my lonely pilgrim journey cannot last all that much longer either. Then I shall go to him and the Lord, whom we served here with many shortcomings, and together we shall praise and glorify [him] perfectly.

Thanks to the goodness of the Lord and the care and concern of my dear husband, I can have a good living with my three children. Mr. Noordhoek will be moving the office to his home on the Heerengracht in May. I am going to move to the Noorderstraat near the Vijzelgracht in a lovely house with a garden for fl.290 [per month]. Jansje and her husband will be moving right next door to me, so that via the side door we can reach each other as well as get into the garden. Every month they bring me one-third of the net profit of the office for as long as I live, and after my decease, until our youngest child reaches maturity. That is how the contract reads, so that if the office does not totally collapse, I can live well. If the Lord now accompanies me, all will be well, and he certainly will. And he is not an arid desert to me either. My loss cannot be compensated for on this side of the grave, but in the midst of all the strain I have much consolation and love from the children that the Lord granted us; they walk in the right way. The mother-in-law of Jans [Jansje], Mrs. Wüstenhoff, also went to her [eternal] rest on the 19th of this month. Her husband's brother is in the last phase of consumption, and our friend Luuring passed away eleven weeks before my husband. From all this, we can gather that our time will also be short.

How gladly we would have granted your wishes, and how often we talked about sending you the portrait of my dear husband. But his condition was getting steadily worse, and in that condition we could not go ahead with it [making a copy]. Fortunately, I do have the painting, but I dare not promise you anything, because making a copy costs a lot of money here. I will keep it in mind and I would be glad to send one to you, convinced as I am of your intimate affection that you cherish for the deceased. On the 4th of June he turned fifty-five, and his mortal remains rest in the St. Anthonis [Anthony] Cemetery, on his orders. Our child is also buried there, and he always said, "Absolutely not in a church, because God's house is not a charnel house." He asked Rev. Hasebroek not to make a eulogy at his grave but rather to be with me and my daughters while his corpse was being buried. For to pay tribute to the individual at the moment he receives the wages of sin [death] is a contradiction in terms. I am a poor sinner saved by grace. The dominie said, "Brother your will is my law," and he kept his word, although, contrary to my wish, when he received the death tiding he went to Höveker and said, "A hero has fallen in Israel." Mr. Groen [van Prinsterer] unburdened his soul in the weekly *De Heraut* and once again seriously praised all the writings that had issued from his pen. May his ashes rest in peace until the resurrection morn.

And there you have it, everything written as well as I could, in brief. A letter allows for only so much, otherwise I could go on. I most heartily rejoice in the fact that our children, yours as well as ours, feel something of the bond that unites us; mine are constantly talking about you all. It grieves us that our friend Jan experiences so many afflictions. If only the heart grows nearer to the Lord through them, then our burden is light and soon comes to an end, even as it works an excellent weight of eternal glory. I had also sent a letter, like mine to you, to the Berkhouts in Pella. And now I have received one from him, and enclosed in it was a lovely Christian letter from Mrs. Bousquet. I hope to answer them both.

On February 12th, I had written the letter this far when I became indisposed and had to take to my bed that afternoon. I sent for the doctor, who said that it was a nervous collapse and that I was thoroughly exhausted. I do not take many medicines, but I did have to take many restoratives [strengthening food], and I still do. I was so very weak that I could hardly be up to sit around; the first few days I thought to myself, might I be seeing my dear husband so soon again? and I must say that did appeal to me. But the Lord blessed the means [of recovery], and although it is slow, I am slowly regaining my strength. And now I wish to serve out my time according to the [eternal] council of the Lord, since I also do care to stay a time longer with my children, and the younger ones still do need my care so very much.

Well, my dear friend, it will probably be at least May before I get a letter from you again. But standing at the end of our life's journey, let us keep each informed as long as possible whether the Lord is calling home any more of us. My address is:

    The Widow J. A. Wormser-van der Ven
    Noorderstraat at the Vijzelgracht
    Neighborhood A.A. 427
    Amsterdam

And now beloved friend, in the hope that you are well when you receive this letter, may I ask you to greet your esteemed husband and children cordially from me and my children? May you be commended to the Lord and his grace by your deeply grieving but dearly loving friend,

    Widow J. A. Wormser-van der Ven

P.S. Our Jans [Jansje] hopes to write you again the next time [I write], since she is very busy these days with the sick and dying. She and her husband are most happy. They make a good living and are now also inheriting quite a sum, but they are not expecting any children as yet and that gives them much freedom in the present circumstances.

    Widow J. A. Wormser

Wormser 69

C. M. Budde to Widow Mrs. J. A. Wormser
Burlington 27 January 1863

Dearly Beloved Friend,
   We had no idea when we received Your Honor's last [death] announcement to us, that we would be making a like report so soon. It pleased the Lord, who has power over life and death, to take unto himself on January 15 at five o'clock in the evening our youngest son, Diedrich Christiaan, at the age of twenty-two years and nine months.
   For some years he had indicated by his quiet and humble walk that he was not of this world but detached from it. He lived in communion with his God and Savior, and although he acknowledged that he was a great sinner, he also knew that all his sins and guilt had been washed away by the blood of Jesus. He could give everything over into the hand of the Lord (also the desperate circumstances of our country, in which we were never certain for even a moment, whether he might be called to the field of battle). He was being prepared for Heaven, even while he was able to perform his daily labors with tireless enthusiasm and diligence, and in his contacts with all kinds of people (although some of them mocked him) he was sweet and charming, and he was much liked. As his illness was coming on he was full of the love of God in Christ Jesus, such as the Lord sometimes lets his loved ones enjoy [already] in this mortal life. Already on the first day that he had to keep to his bed, he said that he was only going ahead of us, that we would be separated for only a short time. The fevers became so severe that already on the second day there was no hope of recovery. Meanwhile, at intervals he even preached to the bystanders—and prayed earnestly that they might all fear and serve the Lord. A short illness (nerves and sinking fever?) of only five days brought an end to his earthly life. We live in the full assurance that he has entered eternal salvation; that is the text from Revelation 14:13 ["Blessed are the dead which die in the Lord from henceforth: Yea, saith the Spirit, that they may rest from their labours; and their works do follow them"], which was chosen for the interment of the mortal remains on the 17th of this month.
   As grievous as this ordeal was for us, we were privileged in that we could entrust him unto our faithful God and Father, and the Lord stood by us and gave us the strength to bear this heavy cross; he belonged to the Lord, and we might have the great privilege, indeed a taste of the

bliss, of having nurtured a child of God, a citizen of heaven.

We may mourn and weep over this loss, but not as those who are without hope; the sufferings of this age cannot be compared with the glory that shall be revealed unto us. We are assured that you share in our grievous loss and commend ourselves in your intercessory prayers before the throne of grace; and after cordial greetings [to you] and all your beloved relatives, we remain united in the Lord.

Your Friends,
D. A. Budde
C. M. Budde-Stomp

(We are very eager to get a letter from Your Honors)

Budde 38

Pastor Johan Müller to D. A. Budde
Silver Brook Parsonage, 30 March 1863

My Dear Brother Budde,

I have received your letter with the mournful tiding of the death of your dear son. I can readily imagine the intense pain the passing of your good child has caused you and your wife. A dear child has, after all, grown up in mysterious bonds with the heart of the parents. The breaking of such bonds can only be painful. But for the Christian it is not a visitation that crushes but one that elicits the blessing of the God of grace. This is another of the afflictions that work the peaceable fruit of righteousness to those who are exercised thereby. And it is the oil of peace of true consolation that must lighten your mourning, when you consider that your loss is a greater, unspeakable gain for your child. Out of longing, of struggling, of waiting, of renewed wrestling, of stumbling, of redoubled fighting for the faith, to be deemed worthy, so early, to enter into Rest, into Beholding, into Light, to be deemed worthy, yea, deemed worthy to enter.

Why is it that we, although already at a riper age, still are not there? It would be audacious to want to look into God's [eternal] Counsel, and still the answer is near. We are not completely ready, as he was, for the inheritance of the saints in light. Well, parents like to look out for what is best for their children. Here, the self-interest that permeates all things has reached its limits; the child only beholds the parental eyes with joy as they as they gain every advantage [for the child]. In your son you have been offered the greatest joy. He now shares in the greatest Advantage. Looking back on the beautiful features of his character, and beholding his blessed lot in heaven, you can only join with me in saying with me, only more intimately than I:

Stilles Herz, sanftes Wesen.	Heart of still acceptance, tender being
Treuer, liebervoller Sinn.	Faithful, ever loving mind.
Jesus Christus war dein Leben,	Jesus Christ your all,
Sterben ist nun dein Gewinn.	Death is now your gain.

As a gap has arisen in your family, so in ours there has been an increase. On the 8th of February a baby boy was born to us.

The Word of God is not lacking in power in our congregation. I believe that I observe growth in grace in the Christians, and many a soul unconcerned before is now wrestling for the greater part [salvation]. Pastor [John M.] Wagner, of West Leyden, N.Y., was critically ill, but now he is better again. Pastor [John] Guldin in New York died about five weeks ago.

Give greetings to your dear ones from me, my wife, and all the brethren and sisters. I should be writing a few more letters to Burlington. In particular, I received a letter from Brother Biesenbek [Biezenbroek] a long time ago and still have not answered it, but I do not have the time now.

Your Loving Brother,
Johan Müller

Budde 39

Johanna Schellinger to D. A. Budde
Alkmaar, 30 May 1863

[The special tone and style of the letters of Mrs. Schellinger reflect her social status in the lower class of Dutch society in many ways.]

Sir and Esteemed Friend,

Your Esteemed Letter, including the picture, I have through the Blessing of the Lord received in well being and with great Pleasure. I thank Your Honor and your Highly esteemed Wife for the trouble this has Cost you. I look at it often with thankful joy that I possess it, and what joy it gave me that I might learn from your letter that our Loving

Heavenly Father has Spared All Your Lives. It gives me Great Satisfaction that I may receive so many evidences of Friendship from you and your dear housemate. But Esteemed Friend, I read and reread your letter often, and I feel my inability so strongly that I am embarrassed to answer it as is behooving; and still I want to hope that you will forgive my faulty writing style if it should not please you in many respects. I thank Your Honors for so much interest as you show in me for this life and for the next life, and also for the comfort and encouragement that I might receive from your honored letters. How much good does not the Lord grant us on our life's journey. It is so surprising and uplifting when one meets genuine friends who mean so well for us, and I am also so Happy that the few friends with whom I associate here also show my genuine Friendship and which I always appreciate.

Still it is always true, as you write, how much of greater worth is the consolation that the Word of God grants us, especially when one is so lonely. How fortunate then is the individual who has the desire and the good cheer to do that, and who can ward off boredom and then may taste that consolation and peace which Excels all understanding. He has certainly chosen the better part. Since we all one day must descend into the somber stillness of the realm of the death, one is all the more obligated to pass the time in the service of God and the Son of his Good Pleasure. How infinitely much does not the individual fall short every day. The Goodness of the Supreme Being that we should observe in Everything is so seldom considered as it ought to be. And still, the individual is under obligation to occupy his thoughts, as much as in him is, with the leadings that the Heavenly Father has with us, all of which work together for the Good, and yet are so seldom observed. How often I think, but what is man, O Lord, that thou art Mindful of him, and doth show him so much Love, and the Love that Thou has made so great in the sending of thy son, in whom we have an intercessor, by whom we have been bought at such a price. If only I might reflect on that more and thus diminish that worldly mindedness which never satisfies and which cannot measure up to the peace of the word of God.

And now, Esteemed Friend, I must still inform you that last Year I was surprised by a visit from your brother in Amsterdam. He had business in Alkmaar and hoped to get some word about you from me, since he had not heard from you in such a long time. But since I could not fulfill his wish, he resolved to write you soon, and I do not doubt that he must have received word from you long ago. I hope and wish that you and your Esteemed wife may have much pleasure from my

Niece, and that she herself may Well realize the thanks that she owes you. Now that she is getting to be of age, she can do this and that in keeping the house. I do wish that she shall be obliging and willing. Without the approval of both of you, [her courtship] with Mathijs van der Mooren [Moor] will never turn out well in the end. He had had such a Good Position, and there is little Good to be expected from someone who is ungrateful and indifferent. If only he would consider once what serves his peace. Esteemed friend, I do commend myself to your thoughts as well as those of your beloved wife. I will be most pleased if you and your beloved spouse receive this letter in good health. And after making my Cordial Greetings, I remain with highest Esteem,

The Servant and Friend of Your Honors,
Joh[anna] Schellinger

Budde 40

Jansje Wüstenhoff-Wormser to Mrs. C. M. Budde-Stomp
Amsterdam, 24 Aug. 1863

Esteemed Madam, Dearly Beloved Friend,
 You probably are thinking that we have forgotten you, but that is not true. From the date on the enclosed note, you will see that I wrote you shortly after we had received the death notice of Diederich [Diedrich]. Since Mother was not finished [with her letter], the mailing was delayed until today. On the 8th of April we were saddened anew by the death of my brother-in-law. As we were coming out of church on the first Pentecost Day, my husband and I thought he looked greatly diminished, and we could tell that he was dying. He was very short of breath, but his spirit [mind] was clear and his faith firm. Mother and Johan visited him that evening, and then he said to Mother, "I am about to die, how well off I soon will be," and he also spoke to Johan most endearingly. On the second Pentecost Day he was short of breath briefly, and when the doctor came he asked whether it would be much longer. His answer was no. "Oh," he said, "then I will be up above [in heaven] before the fourteenth after all."
 He had a rather quiet night; Tuesday morning his father and my husband had to go to their offices, so the maid and I were the only ones staying with him. A few more people came by to take leave of him; but at one o'clock in the afternoon, he said that my husband and I should

stay with him that night, for it would soon be all over, and that I should send for my husband. He did a great deal of talking all that day; because of his shortness of breath he was lying on a canapé. I was sitting next to him and could understand many of his prayers, though they were spoken very softly. Among others, he prayed that the Lord might spare him great shortness of breath and let him gently sleep away. That evening at eight-thirty he had a raw egg and requested that the gaslight be turned up a little. He then took two morphine pills together and slept for a little while. About ten o'clock he again took a cordial leave of us all, and then he began singing: Psalm 89, verse 1

[*I'k Zal eeuwig zingen van Gods goedertierenheên,*
uw waarheid t'allen tijd vermelden door mijn reên.
Ik weet hoe 't vast gebouw van uwe gunstbewijzen
naar uw gemaakt bestek, in eeuwigheid zal rijzen:
zo min de hemel ooit uit zijnen stand zal wijken,
zo min zal uwe trouw ooit wank'len of bezwijken.]

[My song forever shall record/ The tender mercies of the Lord;/ Thy faithfulness will I proclaim/ And every age shall know thy name./ I sing of mercies that endure/ Forever builded firm and sure./ Of faithfulness that never dies/ Established changeless in the skies./

Psalter Hymnal: Centennial Edition, Publication Committee of the Christian Reformed Church, Grand Rapids, Michigan, 1959.]

After that he sang some more, but we could not understand any of it. Later on, he cried out while singing, "Now I am home, now I am home. Oh, how beautiful it is here. Oh, how lovely heaven is." That continued for some time; finally he fell asleep again, and at twelve o'clock he had already entered his eternal rest, having received his request that he might pass away in his sleep.

For us, life is very empty now; three of our dearest relations were taken from us within a half year. Mother and we moved on the 1st of May, and now we are living next to each other in the Noorderstraat. Towards the end of his life, Father expressed the wish that we should live as close to each other as possible. We were not looking for housing next to each other, but the Lord led us in finding it. Mother has a lovely garden behind her house.

On the 6th of August, a big mission fest was celebrated at Wolfheze near Arnhem, on an estate made available for that purpose by a lady. My husband and I also attended, and we enjoyed it very much. There were over six thousand people in attendance: Hervormden (National Reformed Church members), Seceders, and Lutherans, they were all there. Speakers included the Rev. Brummelkamp. He was very generous and broad in his perspective; the German Rev. Brandt also spoke. The intention is to have such a [mission] fest every year for the edification and cooperation between Christians of all denominations.

Miss Chrisje Steenkamp, whom you no doubt still remember, died a fortnight ago. Beyond that I am not aware of any news about any of our acquaintances. Mrs. Zeelt is still living but she is very obtuse. We hope that you have not suffered as a result of the war. If you write us, then do give us some information on the sons of Mrs. Bousquet. Cordial greetings from my husband and me to you and all your family. Wishing you and your house the blessing and presence of the Lord.

Your loving Friend,
J. Wüstenhoff-Wormser

Budde 41

C. M. van der Veen to D. A. Budde
Pella, 23 Sept. 1863

Beloved Brother,

In answer to your little note, the following. If the Lord prospers my way, I hope to arrive in Burlington by cars [train] Tuesday evening. Also, the arrangements for the worship services are at your disposition, since you are more knowledgeable about what is easiest and most pleasant for the little flock. Whatever you decide is fine with me. I am at your disposal for that day.

If only the God of the covenant deigns to make this a day of salvation and blessing through my labors, my soul could not ask for more. Let us pray for that.

Wishing you the benediction [of the Lord] and warmest greetings.

Your Brother in Christ,
C. M. vander Veen

Wormser 70

C. M. Budde-Stomp to Widow Mrs. J. A. Wormser
Burlington, October '63

Dear Beloved Friend and Sister in the Lord,

We received your precious letter of January 23 in reasonably good health on March 4. We realized that our letters had crossed each other. [We lived] in hopes that we would again be receiving a letter of sympathy from Your Honors regarding our grievous loss, but it took so long that I thought that Your Honors had not received our letter; besides Johan mentioned to us that about that time several steamboats had perished. Finally your long-awaited letter of August 24 arrived. I do not think you will mind if I tell you a few things about the life and death of our beloved Diedrich, whom you held on your lap on Palm Sunday of 1840. His childhood years were just simply sweet, faithful, diligent; in the year '58 we noted that the Lord was at work in his soul. One day he came up to us to ask forgiveness for having insulted us, because the Lord had also forgiven him. Anyone who comes to the fountain [of life] on his own does not need to be shown the way. At the time, Rev. Muller had been our minister for three years. He [Diedrich] was very eager to attend the worship services, and after the sermon we had great pleasure in discussing it together. In his lifestyle he was a quiet, unobtrusive person, upright, and manifestly withdrawn from the world. On Sundays after church he read in his big [Dutch folio] Bible [authorized version dating back to 1637], and together we sang beautiful hymns; [we also read] Bunyan's *A Christian's Journey* in English and really enjoyed discussing it. His spiritual life manifested itself clearly in his life style, but we had no idea that this plant would be ripe so fast.

Our minister had been called to Silver Creek some time ago, and so we were without a shepherd. About that time, a Rev. Rijnhout van Brederode wrote us from Zeeland that he had preached in Brazil and that he had labored among the Germans (he had been recommended to us by Rev. Guldin, who had always served us so faithfully). He was a minister in the Dutch Reformed Church in New York, an American by birth; his ancestors were Swiss and his grandfather was a minister. He preached in the German language; he is now already at rest in the Lord. Brederode had come to us from New York. There happened to be a convocation going on for eight days, one in which Christians were called to prayer and thanksgiving, the kind we also used to have together in

Amsterdam. The minister was to preach in German in our church, but it was more Dutch [than German]. He stopped in the middle of his sermon, saying that he did not feel well. That evening he was to lead in prayer in the Dutch language, but it was so pitiable that we immediately realized that we had been deceived and advised him to return to New York. Friday afternoon Diedrich took him to the city in the wagon; that was the last work he did. This was a most unpleasant matter for us to endure.

On Friday morning it happened that Jan, Diedrich, and I were in my room, still talking about this matter. Then Diedrich spoke up, with a heavy heart it seemed, "How wonderful things are for the righteous," [and] then I noticed that there was again something stirring in his soul. He left quietly again until evening, when I had his bed brought to our room, and on Saturday Jan was to go to the city and take his place; that was all right with him. In the morning we were standing at his bedside. "Father and Mother," he said, "I am going ahead of you, and it will not be long before we shall be together for all eternity. Oh, Father, I really would like to tell you something [about the vision I had], but, after all, Paul [the Apostle] was not able to do it either." This touched our hearts so deeply, that though we cannot help missing him, we cannot but thank the Lord with gladness that he saved him. It was now apparent to us that he was getting sick and we told Jan to fetch the doctor at once. "Fine," said Diedrich, "if it is the Lord's wish, then the doctor can do something [for me], and if not, then he cannot do anything either." He [the doctor] came quickly and said that it was nerves and...fever. That evening Father was about to lead us in prayer, but then he wished that it be done in his own room, and he joined us in sweetly singing Psalm 146, verse 6:

| *De Heer betoont zijn welbehagen* | The Lord shows his good pleasure |
| *aan hen, die need'rig naar hem vragen.* | to those who humbly seek him. |

On Sunday the doctor said that he was afraid that he would not make it and gave him some (moschatel herb) pills. Saturday afternoon he [Diedrich] told Maria that he was going to die, whereupon she wept bitterly. Sunday afternoon Maria and her beloved were standing at his bedside, and then he said: "The two of you are pledged to each other; it is my earnest wish that the two of you might also fear and serve the Lord. Will you also do that too, Barend and Maria? How I would like to see that." It was so solemn to hear our dying darling speaking [like this]. And then he prayed, "We praise and thank thee, Oh Lord, that thou dost accept us out of grace, and none of us here have any right to believe this; Lord, help our unbelief for the sake of thy dear Son, Amen."

On Monday Mrs. Teleman and Mrs. Verkerk came over and visited with him and sat up with Jan that night. About noon he broke out in tremors, shaking like someone having a fit of epilepsy, so that we had to call everyone to help hold him down; it looked like someone who is involved in a struggle. He called with a loud voice so that the wall echoed [the sound], "Ready, born again, inside, the bell is tolling," and meanwhile it really seemed like the clock was striking. Then things quieted down, and [he] asked for something to eat. The doctor had prescribed chamomile to drink, and after that he perspired some; accordingly, I still had a faint hope, but before he had eaten anything we could tell that there was no improvement. The high fevers got worse, but from time to time he was in full command of his faculties. Whenever a German, Englishman, or Hollander stopped by, he spoke to each in his own language; twice he sang an English hymn so sweetly that it sounded angelic. During the seizures he was very strong [and violent], dangerously so, so that we finally decided to bind him with sheets [to restrain him], and his hands with sacks and cloths. He was still constantly calling for Jan; Jan, I really love you, even though he knew that he had bound him; Jan was seldom gone from his bed; the Lord strengthened and supported us. They also put Spanish flies on his back and chest, and they were still (drawing blood). Wednesday evening his face was already (broken) and Thursday morning his hands and feet were already getting cold. The doctor said that it would be over in less than an hour. Only three minutes before he passed away he still called for Jan, and then he passed away quietly. He was buried Saturday morning, and four young men carried him to the funeral coach and to the [final] resting place where Jan's children are buried. Sympathy and participation was widespread; even worldly people respected him for his uprightness.

In the spring we had a visit from Mr. Le Cocq and his son, Frans, who is also already married and has children. They wanted to meet us in our [present] situation and were pleased that Jan was taking the place of Diedrich. About the same time, my husband was suffering from severe stomach pains so that we were worried that Father might soon be following Diedrich, but it pleased the Lord to spare him for us and to bless the ministrations of the doctor. He was without pain for five months and recovered completely. In September the ailment returned, and he still is having a hard time of it. Le Cocq did not even know that Luring had passed away. Mrs. Bousquet is presently in the Netherlands; the week before Pentecost, she had written us that we should come to Burlington on Monday after Pentecost to meet each other there. Unfortunately, Jan left the letter in his pocket, and we did not get it until Tuesday at the very time that Mrs. B[ousquet] was leaving Burlington. Miss Boekenoogen, a girl of twenty, accompanies her. We were terribly sorry, but knowing that no hair falls [from our head] without the will of the Lord, we have to be resigned to this. Now we have no idea of what her plans are, [but] if you should meet her, please let her know what happened, and if the Lord brings her back here, will she be so kind as to honor us with a visit.

Our church situation is grim; we have not had a Reformed minister for three years. It was the Lord's good pleasure to refresh us on one occasion. Rev. Oggel of Pella went to the baths because he was not feeling well, but since he did not improve, he is presently staying with his father-in-law, Rev. Van Raalte. The doctor recommends that he give up his ministry for the time being. Presently the classis periodically sends a minister for six weeks. Quite unexpectedly, the oldest son of the coppersmith Van der Veen, who is a minister and studied in [New Brunswick], New Jersey, stopped in to see us on his way to Pella. My husband requested that he preach for us some time; on his return trip he did just that on October 30 and administered both seals of the covenant [baptism and Communion]. In the morning his text was 1 Corinthians 5, verse 5 (we also have a Passover, etc.) [probably should be verse 7: "For Christ our passover is sacrificed for us"]; and in the afternoon Ps. 42, verse 12 ["Why art thou cast down, O my soul? And why art thou disquieted within me? Hope thou in God: for I shall yet praise him, who is the health of my countenance, and my God."]. It was a day of [spiritual] uplift and strengthening of our faith. The Lord has equipped him for the office of preacher and has fulfilled the wish of his father, made at his birth, that he might be a pillar in God's church. His father died joyfully; and this also left an impression on his youthful heart. The Lord really made his good pleasure known to this household; his mother had remarried with a widower, Mr. Tolsma, who had no children. He enjoyed the three [step]sons so much that he sacrificed everything possible for these children; her sister Rika is still living with her. When the need of the fatherland became great, he, along with one of the sons and some other young people, enlisted for military service, but he succumbed in a hospital; his end was a peaceful one. Now the minister [Rev. Van der Veen] is able to support the family. And so we witness the faithful care and leading of the Lord [in the lives of] of friends, both men and women.

I had written this letter up to here when we joyfully received your esteemed letter of October 26, '63. We thank you most sincerely for the portraits and we were eager to send you our two guilders, but winter was upon us, and then it becomes pretty hard for us to get to the city. The old folks slow down; this winter I suffered a great deal from rheumatism in my hips, so that I could hardly even find a place to lie down. This often made me think of our unforgettable friend Wormser and his suffering. Today I am again suffering from r[heumatism]. [The next three paragraphs are not legible.] We are most happy with your portraits, [and] especially that now we know the face of Mr. Wüstenhoff; the other [pictures] are of Johan and his spouse. For this time, my dear friend Cato will have to be content with only general information. May the Lord grant her a glimpse of his friendly countenance in her soul; until such time her friends will just have to stand on the side lines.

Our church situation here seemed to be done for. In this situation the Lord provided a Presbyterian minister, the Rev. Brücher, who preaches for us every two weeks. A God-fearing man, he is a powerful preacher, so that our weary souls are refreshed again and we can only praise the Lord. We are ready to leave the future to God. If Mrs. Bousquet is still in Amsterdam, will you be so kind as to acquaint Her Honor with the contents of this letter and give her our cordial greetings? Do gladden us with an answer soon. Do you happen to know whether our family is still well? Our greetings to you all and to Johan, your dear son; we commend you all to the Lord and his grace. Kiss your dear Maria and Henriette. Greetings to your brother, Dries. Tell him that Krichbaum passed away.

Your most loving friend and sister in the Lord,
C. M. Budde-Stomp

Esteemed Friend,

I feel obligated to add a few lines to the letter of my spouse and to thank Your Honor's friends for your cordial friendship in sending Your Honor's portraits, and also that of my now blessed friend and brother who died in the Lord. Although the living person is missing in the portrait when we look at it, it does remind us of our intimate association, which was so salutary and strengthening for us on our pilgrim's journey;

he already enjoys peace there, with the battle won and suffering done. While I am writing, I am again constantly suffering from attacks of stomach cramps. Oh, it is a good thing that we do not have an abiding place here; our Lord, sanctified by suffering, has gone before us, having become the source of eternal salvation to all who will love his appearance. [The rest is not legible.]

Wormser 71

J. G. Budde to J. Wormser-van der Ven
Burlington, Iowa, 5 June 1864

Beloved Friend,
  In Your Honor's last letter, you requested that I write much more about the war, and immediately after reading your esteemed letter, it was Mother's wish that I answer that part of your letter. I then intended to provide you, to the best of my ability, with an extensive account of the cause, the principle, and the present status of this most terrible civil war. But since I later learned that Mrs. Bousquet was visiting Your Honor, who could relate all this to you in much greater detail, I decided to limit myself to the present situation. On this side the war is most intense in the state of Virginia, with both armies between Washington, our capital, and Richmond, that of the rebels. The goal of our generals seems to be to capture the latter city; the several battles waged there in the past month have not achieved that result so far. On our side there were fifty thousand casualties, dead, wounded, or taken prisoner, but nearly the same number on the rebel side. Our army has now advanced to within thirty English miles of Richmond, but even bloodier and more violent battles will have to be fought before our army can reach Richmond; because the enemy utilizes every means and every tactic to prevent that, but God alone can say: so far and no farther.
  Because our people had been privileged to enjoy so much abundance here for many years, they became backsliders, forgot their Lord and Maker, and became wanton. The Lord is chastising our country severely, and until now, the people are not willing to humble themselves. Only last week I read: Never before has sin, affluence, sin and deceit reached such a high point as it has presently in Washington, the seat of our government. Pride and arrogance are becoming dominant. Only [let us] never expect the victory through our own strength and the power

and speed of the horse. To be sure, there is also a segment here that has not bowed the knee to Baal, and if it were not for the people of God, this country and people would waste away and perish. It is a great consolation to us, is it not, to know and to believe, that our God reigns, and however things may turn out, it will be to the honor and glory of his great name. Seen from a political point of view the question remains unanswered. Can people, under a Republican form of government, be capable of governing themselves in the long run? Past histories prove the contrary and mighty nations under such a form of government have fallen and been destroyed by internal, civil disturbances.

The number of human lives this civil war has cost is almost incalculable; already a million lives have been lost on each side, and the prospects continue to be very dark, despite all the talk in our newspapers. Charleston, South Carolina, continues to be bombarded without success; the western armies are constantly engaged in skirmishes. Right now all eyes are anxiously fixed on the eastern army. One of the greatest hindrances is the divisiveness and the party spirit that prevails among us in the North; one faction seeks to oppose the government in whatever it undertakes, so that their faction will gain the upper hand. The land is full of spies. And there are those in the army and in the government who side with the enemy, so that the enemy knows everything as swiftly and as accurately as our own generals. You can imagine our cares and concerns, since the history of our own fatherland provides the same kind of examples. If our hope and trust were not in the Lord, things would be miserable for us. May the Lord grant that this nation humble itself under his mighty hand, bow beneath his rod, and acknowledge that he alone is God, that is our prayer. May this letter reach you in good health in A[msterdam]. With cordial greetings to the rest of the family, I am and remain,

Your Friend,
J. G. Budde

Budde 42

Johanna Schellinger to D. A. Budde
Alkmaar, 26 August 1864

Highly Esteemed Esquire and Lady Friend,
    It was a delight to receive your letter. But at the same time I was saddened to read that the Lord of life and death had taken away one of

your loved ones. Time passes quickly with sadness and lamentation, but the remembrance of our loved one does not disappear so swiftly. And I hasten to add my condolences, my esteemed friends, with such a grievous loss, and it is my wish that you may meet each other again in a better place, where there will be no more death or mourning. May it be a continuing consolation for all of you that your loved one had such a joyful outlook on Eternity. How great is not the Peace in God for all those who know it. It provides such a peaceful acquiescence in his wise and loving rule in life and in death. May our good God grant you that blessed peace and long continue to spare your lives with all those who are dear and precious to you.

I cannot thank you enough, esteemed Friends, for the care and concern that the two of you have devoted to my Niece. Now that she is already capable of making a living on her own, may she always continue to realize what a privilege she has enjoyed. May she by her grateful and good conduct demonstrate how much she appreciates your interested friendship, which I find to be so noble and so great, taking her into your home with that terrible illness of which everyone is so afraid. May God's visible blessing rest upon you, also for the labor of love that you have shown her.

Before I received your letter, I often wondered about how my esteemed friends in America were getting along. For how grievous are the tidings that reach us about that war, which gives rise to so much trouble. If only the Almighty might direct it all to a Good End. For to the Lord the peoples are but as a particle of dust in the balance scale, and he does with them according to his good pleasure. After all, it is the Lord who sends suffering and distress, but also rescue and deliverance to those who hope in his help. There is much distress in the world now and always has been. Happy is the man who holds fast to our great Redeemer who has overcome the world.

Esteemed friends, most gladly I shall fill your request to send you a picture of me. I just have not seen any need to do so until now, since my good friends here can see me every day. I am also sending one for your dear wife. She may well want to put a sixty-year-old girlfriend in her album; I do not doubt that at all. I was quite surprised to read, dear friend, that Mathijs v.d. Moor was living so close to you again, and that he is married. My only wish is that he just lets Naatje be, and that she not do anything without your permission. I also hope to see to it that the money [inheritance] that I have set aside for her does not get into his hands. You just cannot expect anything good from him.

Here, everything is just the same, I am still living in my own little home, since there is no vacancy as yet in the *Hofje* [a courtyard of small homes for elderly indigent women provided by rich benefactors], a home that the family of the deceased Lady I worked for set aside for me, and which also provides many other advantages. But our lot is determined by our loving Father, who knows what is best, what is useful for us, and in whom we can always trust. Thanks to the blessing of the Lord I am very healthy, although I am never without rheumatism, but this kind of thing is often associated with old age. And now, esteemed friends, I commend myself to Your Honors to keep me in remembrance. I would be gratified if I might hear from you that you had received this letter in health and well-being. And after sending you my sincere greetings, and also to your dear spouse, I remain with highest esteem,

Your Faithful Servant and Friend,
Johanna Schellinger

Budde 43

C(ato) de Boer-Wormser to Mrs. C. M. Budde-Stomp
Amsterdam, 24 Oct. 1864

Dearly Beloved Friend!

I have not written you in a long time, and that makes the present occasion all the more pleasant. How many things have transpired during that time! How soon your son Diederich met our beloved Father. We still are affected by your loss, because we can so well imagine what a support he was to you in your old age, but that does not begin to compare with the blessed reunion. It is a privilege that we may see him go before us with joy.

On the 18th of April instant, we were privileged to rejoice in the birth of our second son, whom we named Johan Adam after Father. I was very happy that after waiting for five years I might suckle such a dear tender child myself, a privilege that was denied me in the case of our oldest child. But after the child had suffered much, it pleased the Lord to take the dear child to himself on the 7th of October; that hit me hard and does so still. However, the Lord was kind to him, and in this way he did not suffer so very much of earthly sorrow, and he was spared many things. He is much better off now than I ever could have provided for him, even with the best of intentions. We had him buried with Father. In life and in death he did look like Father. Now we only have our oldest little son, who was born on the 25th [wedding] anniversary; he is now five and a half years old, and he has been growing nicely till now.

Your pictures really surprised us. Jans [Jansje] brought them to me and told me one by one who everyone was. But I did not recognize you people, and I could hardly believe her when she said who everyone was. On close scrutiny I began to recognize some features, but [bear in mind] how young I was when you all left, though I still remember it distinctly. I also remember getting a scolding from Mr. [Budde] once because I kept my eyes open during prayer in the catechism class. I also still have a little plate and an egg holder that I received from you. If I have my picture taken some time, I will also send you a copy. I would like to know whether you all recognized the pictures; they all look excellent. My husband asked if you would be willing to write something about the war sometime and whether you have still been spared [its effects]. We all recognized Mrs. Bousquet immediately [when she came back]; she is still exactly the same, though she seems stronger than she used to be. Everything is still the same at the Luurings; no one has gotten married as yet. No doubt Mother has written you that Uncle Dries died so suddenly on February 1st. Auntie and the nieces are still living [together] just as they always did in the past.

Well dear friend! I want to give my greetings to you, as well as to Mr. [Budde] and Jan and Maria, whom I can still recall as a little child with rosy cheeks, who was being carried wearing a small brown coat. How nice it is to maintain friendships, as we have done. My husband just cannot understand what it means to me, people whom I can scarcely recall any more, but he is not aware of the narrow bond that unites us, that is, the bond of faith. Now it is my pleasure to anticipate having a letter from your hand in my possession. [I send] cordial greetings from my husband and child, though they are unknown. And I commend you both to the Lord and with warm greetings.

Your loving Friend,
C. de Boer-Wormser

Wormser 72

D. A. Budde to J. Wormser-van der Ven
Burlington, Iowa, 10 January 1865

Dearly Beloved Friend,

Since Mrs. Schilp is sending [back] a proxy from her brother in Loenen [province of Utrecht], and we were helpful to her in this matter, I cannot pass by the opportunity to include a few lines of my own, in hopes that you and your loved one may receive this in good health. May the Lord our God be your and our stay and support, our one and all in Christ Jesus, as the new year begins. Then we can continue our pilgrimage through the wilderness with joy in the midst of all the changes, of all the disappointments we encounter, and which at the same time must be for our best. That is to be blessed in the midst of it all. We have a God who helps us and a Lord who saves us from death. We were deeply struck by the tiding that Dries had already passed away quite some time ago, as we learned from the letter of Mr. K. F. C. Portengen. We had been eagerly waiting for some word from you, esteemed friend, how you and your dear family were doing and now we hear of deaths; and that makes us all the more eager to hear from you, since it was last summer that we wrote you last and also sent you our pictures.

We are doing very well. I still suffer from stomach cramps, and, in addition to that, I have such rheumatic pains that there are times that I cannot lie on either side. But the Lord will not suffer us to be tempted beyond what we are able. The interventions of his mercy shown to me, an unworthy sinner, are many. For the most part Johan's wife is in very poor health; toward the end of last year they again lost a darling little girl of about eleven months through death. But his strength is in the Lord his God, and in all of this he may gladly be submissive to the will of his God. My dear wife and Maria of whom we now have clear signs [that she is born again] has changed so much during the past year that her brother's wish, [expressed] when he was dying, may be fulfilled [namely, I will see you again in Heaven, cf. Wormser Letter 70]. Both of them are fairly healthy and so, in this world of our banishment, they live their lives, falling and rising, guided by the shepherd and leader of our souls, until the earthen house of the body is also destroyed and they may enter into the Dwelling of Peace, to be with the Lord evermore.

May this brief note not be a trifling one. Schilp and his wife are sitting here, waiting as I write. I send my heartfelt greetings to you, and also to your dear family, from my spouse, Johan, and Maria. The Lord be with you all; how much we would like to get together with you once again. But we are sure that that it will happen one day, with all our dear acquaintances, who have loved the Lord Jesus in incorruptibility.

Your Friend and Brother in the Lord,
D. A. Budde

Wormser 73

C. M. Budde-Stomp to J. Wormser-van der Ven
Burlington, 10 October 1865

My Dearly Beloved Friend,

Finally, I will sit down to write you, my highly esteemed friend and children. When we received your dear letter of December 1964 we were reasonably well; our sincere wish is that you also will receive this letter in good health. Again I have to begin by recounting to you the troubles of this life. It behooved the Lord to have Johan's youngest daughter to grow and flourish until she was almost a year old. She was a darling child, raised on cow's milk to their great joy, but then the Lord demanded this sacrifice. She developed a swelling and soreness in her throat, and within a few days the Lord called her [home]. Her mother had been ailing, and now it affected her nerves so that she was unconscious for long periods of time and had to be watched night and day. She was pregnant at the time, and because of her exhaustion the fetus became detached and so she had a [premature] delivery; and oh, the wonder of it all! I had an infant of six months alive on my lap; it died two days later. It was a girl, the tenth child; the mother remained in a critical condition for a long time. It was a big burden for Johan and for us, but the Lord supported us to the praise of his great name.

My dear husband continues to suffer so much trouble from stomach pains, with the result that his body is greatly weakened and it is difficult for him to work. Old age has its infirmities. How good it is that when the house of this earthly tabernacle is dissolved, we have a building from God, etc. We are slowly being weaned from earthly things and long for the rest that is reserved for the people of God. I was also visited so badly with rheumatism this winter that it made me weep; my right hand was so paralyzed that I could not hold a thing. I thought of you all and feared that I might no longer have the use of my hands to write you all. The Lord has graciously healed me, his name be praised.

I cannot comply with your request for a picture of Di[edrich]; his simple, sincere desire for the picture of our never-to-be-forgotten friend J. A. Wormser prompted our decision to send you our picture. None of us had had our picture taken. There was one thing in my letter that you misunderstood. I was busy writing it when your pictures arrived, and then we decided to send you ours. The letter, which I had already partially written, mentioned what the dying D[iedrich] had said to Maria and her sweetheart. [Cf. Wormser Letter 70] I did not feel like writing it all over again, because so often I have rheumatic pain in my right thumb, and that makes writing and sewing difficult for me. So then I made a little mark at that place, and at another place I wrote: the knot is broken.

So far Maria is not working; she is a big help to us. Farming is getting to be difficult for us. The promise of the Lord, that he will not leave us nor forsake us when we are old, enables us to put our trust in him.

You are also involved in our Civil War. Although we were graciously spared from being near the fighting zone, it still drips down, affecting us all. Constantly we live in fear that Johan will be drafted, that is, his [lottery] number drawn, although as a citizen of the city he has already been called up for [military] service. At the beginning of the year things still looked somber. Every four years, the people choose a new president. Pr[esident] A. Lincoln was reelected by a majority. He was a man of sterling character, who had the welfare of the country at heart. Four years long the North had fought in vain, [but] now the Lord gave the victory. One fortress after another was captured. Fortunately, General Sherman broke through the southern lines, with the result that the South was being attacked on two sides, front and back. Richmond was the capital of the South, and President Davis was there; the fighting was stubborn, the lines were broken, and Richmond taken. The Negroes were the first to march in[to the city]; the slaves are free, the president fled and was captured in women's clothing. The South has been ravaged something awful. Entire cities have been laid waste; there is nothing left in them but women, old men, and children, [and they are] terribly impoverished. That was the end of the revolt; that is how quickly the Lord caused the situation to change. The first battle was at Fort Sumter, where we lost; after four years, it was retaken and the Union flag raised.

The government declared a day of thanksgiving and prayer, and in the evening a play was presented at a theater, and, oh my, the assassin's shot rang, our President Lincoln was the victim and succumbed the next morning. A wounded general, who was lying on his bed in his room, was the victim of a surprise attack and his caretakers were beaten to death. This all happened on Friday in April, and by Saturday the news was already known in our city via telegraph. There was a grievous sadness; all houses, churches, etc., were draped in black and white; the saloons were closed. Men and women were weeping in the streets; people everywhere were grief stricken. The feelings of elation caused by such a happy victory were now plunged into such deep sorrow. We were also deeply touched by it all, and especially because the murderer's bullet struck him in a theater. I do not want to pass judgment, but let us walk circumspectly so that we are not conformed to the world. At his inauguration into office, he felt the need to urge Christians to pray for him. In the papers I read many things about him that gave me hope that he was truthfully seeking the Lord. It is my wish that he may have entered by the narrow gate outside of which no one will be saved. The murderer was shot dead as he was being captured; he came to his end rather soon, but eternity will be long enough anyway for his dastardly deed. Now you can just imagine how the people felt, after such a joyous victory, such grievous mourning. May we and the people of this country acknowledge that this is of the Lord. To him be the honor, the adoration, and the thanksgiving. The revolt has been overcome; many of our soldiers have come home.

In the month of March we received a letter from our relatives in Leer [Ost Friesland]; they were making plans to travel to America, Mr. Hulsebosch with two sons. His wife is the daughter of my husband's oldest brother. They made it here safely, and although we were very happy, it was quite a busy time for us. Presently their youngest son, Enno, is with us and is critically ill, but there is hope for his recovery. Johan immediately made work of trying to locate land. They did succeed in that and have purchased 120 acres for six dollars plus per acre. They are located twelve miles, or a three-hour [walk] from us, and they visit us frequently. The father is going back again in October to get his wife and eight children. One son is a steersman and wishes to continue sailing. The Lord willing, they are thinking of coming in the spring.

Our church situation has also changed; our entire congregation has joined the Old School Presbyterians, because we could not get a minister or support from the Holland Reformed Board. We must attest to the fact that preaching among us has not been unfruitful, and sinners have been converted to the Lord. May the Lord be and remain with us, Amen.

I have not yet had a visit from Mrs. Bousquet. I have not heard a thing about Mr. and Mrs. Wüstenhoff in your letters. I hope that they may be well in body and soul, also your beloved son, Johan, Maria, and Henrietta. Dear friend, do surprise me soon with a letter; I commend you to the Lord and his grace. Warmest greetings from my dear husband, [and from] Johan and his spouse and Maria.

Your dear Friend and Sister in the Lord
who thinks of you always,
C. M. Budde-Stomp

Budde 44

Mrs. J. Wormser-van der Ven to Mrs. C. M. Budde-Stomp
Amsterdam, 20 January 1866

Dearly Beloved Sister in C[hrist],

When I received your esteemed letter of October 10 [Wormser Letter 72] towards the end of the year [1865], I was so very happy that I immediately had the desire to write you very soon. But the weeks and years fly past so swiftly that one scarcely knows where all the busyness and cares of life come from. It grieves me that our friend Jan has to lose so many children. He and his wife are already getting a good share of the trials of this life. May the Lord sanctify them to their hearts and enable them to acquiesce in his rule.

All of us may rejoice in reasonably good health, but, dear friend, I have a tribulation that I have kept from you for a long time already, but now I must unburden myself to you. The husband of my dear Cato has become an alcoholic. It caused us a great deal of grief already when my husband was still living, but since then it has become very much worse, so much so that there is the threat that he may be dismissed from the Veem (a prominent storage company) at any time. They are keeping him on out of compassion for his wife; he borrows money everywhere and then tells them that he has [is married to] a daughter of the Wormsers. He just keeps on buying and has everything sent home, and Cato gets the bills. He is head over heels in debt, stays out until the wee hours of the morning, and then is incapable of working. Under those circumstances, she prematurely gave birth to a baby boy on July 21, 1865, [a baby] that to everyone's amazement is still living. Although Cato had told him in the morning that she was not well, he came home terribly drunk [that night]. One sin leads to another, so that Cato is thinking seriously about separating, and she then will come to live with me with her two children. Imagine what grief that will be for us.

I often have headaches from all the thinking and all the grief. Fortunately, my other son-in-law and my own children are a real delight to me. Jansje is happy, and, if it should please the Lord, I would really wish for them to have a baby. They make a good living. My Johan is well behaved, and he is beginning to look more and more like his father. And now my daughter, Maria, who is just a little over eighteen years of age, already started keeping company this summer with my nephew, Johannes Wormser, from Nijverdal, the second son of my husband's brother, whom you no doubt know. He has the same name as my husband, is twenty-one years old, and is a devout dear boy, with the sobriety of a man. In Nijverdal he is the director of the Solomonson Esquires Factory. He has free housing, a gentleman's mansion with a large garden, and a good income. His sister, Kaatje, is his housekeeper, and she has a maid of her own. And although Maria is still young, I did not feel free to refuse this [keeping company], provided that they did not marry too soon.

And Henriette, my youngest, is almost fourteen years old and learning how to sew with Mrs. Steenkamp. And even if I did not feel that I was getting old, if I only take a good look at my children, they certainly do tell me that my task here is just about done. But that is something I consider calmly, and sometimes even with gladness. How fortunate we are that whatever befalls us we can take refuge in the rock of our safety, Christ, to whom we can go with our every lament, with all our cares, and who will also grant us succor for every trial.

Mrs. Bousquet has long since returned to Pella. I got a letter from Berkhout, who reported that to me, and also that he and his wife were thinking of again coming to Holland. His intent was to dispose of his store this winter; and if the Lord spared our lives, then we would be seeing each other again. I shall not flatter myself into thinking that that will be the case with you. Now that age and gray hair have come upon you, you will probably be staying in America, and we shall be meeting each other again where there is no more separation, and where all sorrow will be forgotten. It grieves me that you are still ailing so because of rheumatism; it is a terrible visitation. Still, your last letter is written so beautifully that I could notice nothing of it. Now you will do me a great favor when your hand is free of pain, if you will just write me a letter soon, the kind that I am always longing for so.

As far as the war in America is concerned, we keep informed about it through the newspapers. I am sorry that I did not understand what you wrote about the engagement of your Maria. What is the cause of the break-up? Give our most cordial greetings to your esteemed husband and children, and I commend you with all your cares to the Lord, and receive most intimate greetings from,

> Your loving Friend,
> Widow J. A. Wormser-van der Ven

Wormser 74

> C. M. Budde-Stomp to Widow Mrs. J. A. Wormser-van der Ven
> Burlington, 14 March 1866

Dearly Beloved Friend and Sister in the Lord,

We read your letter of January 20 with genuine interest, and we rejoice that you are all doing well. I wanted to write you back immediately, but I was about to leave by railroad for Mount Pleasant, twenty-eight miles from Burlington, getting there in [only] two hours. "Many are the afflictions of the righteous: but the Lord delivereth them out of them all" [Psalm 18:34]. Truly, [it is] a great tribulation for you and the family, a blow that strikes you in your very heart. I noted in Cato's letters that her spiritual life was growing, and now the Lord has seen fit to draw her to himself by such a heavy trial and cross. God knows what is most expedient for his own, whether it be misfortune or fortune; when we experience tribulation, it does not seem joyous to us, but thereafter it will bring forth in us a peaceable fruit of righteousness characteristic of those who are exercised thereby. With all our troubles we may and must go to the Lord, who will direct their outcome in such a way that we can bear them. May the Lord graciously bless his chastising hand to all your hearts, to the honor of his great name, and to your well being, that is my heartfelt wish.

You asked me about the reasons for M[aria's] breakup. The engagement did not go through on the conditions stipulated, namely that Maria who had made profession of faith, had to keep company with a man who walked in the ways of the Lord. It was because Maria had promised this before God and the congregation that we allowed her to have an honorable courtship. Later on he refused to be the least bit complaisant with us; he seemed to have decided to call on M[aria] on Sunday evenings and stay till after midnight. That distressed us, and although we asked him in a friendly manner to go home on time, he chose not to do so. We had much unpleasantness about this matter, and finally he told M[aria] that he was quitting [the engagement]. That suited her because she could not stand the idea of being estranged from her parents in this way. She remained firm even when he sought to ask her hand again.

The Lord had better things in store for us. In the summer of '64 our Rev. Brücher asked us to his house; he was having a song service of members at his house, and there we met [members of] the congregation. Also present was an Andreas Singer, who had been called powerfully from popery to the worship of the Lord under the pastor's preaching, and we then made his acquaintance. As we got together from time to time we found all this to be true. In October '65 he came to ask for Maria's hand. In her heart she preferred to have a man who feared and served the Lord. He is sixteen years older than she, but he is a young man, a German, born near Mainz on the Rhine. He is a bread and pastry baker by trade and has a shop where he sells small Nüremburg wares, and thanks to the Lord's blessing, he makes a good living. On December 11, '65 they were united in matrimony. Though the Lord had taken a precious treasure from us through death, he now gladdened us again by giving us another who honors and loves us with all his heart. We had a very pleasant wedding so that the older people could tell how good it is to serve the Lord in one's youth, to begin your marriage with him, who blessed it with his first miracle. We, [as well as] Johan and his wife, are also very content [about the marriage]. It also involved a big change for us; the loss of Maria meant I could no longer attend to farm activities like churning butter, etc., but we exchanged dwellings with Johan, whose house is located at the entrance to the land. He is now in charge of the cattle and everything connected with that. Father is considerably weaker, and he is eager to take it easy.

The young folk do not lack trials either. M[aria] is having stomach troubles. Starting January 2nd she vomited for three days so that she had to keep her bed and became so weak that she could not stand on her feet. The doctor gave her medicine and put a mustard plaster on her chest; then she calmed down and got better. They had promised to visit us at New Year's, and that is what they did. They had scarcely gotten here when the same thing happened all over again, and she could not go back with her husband, because he could not neglect the farm, and she was in good hands. The Lord soon restored her to health, so that after she had been with us a fortnight, we could take her back to Mount Pleasant. We stayed with them for eight days in order to (make sure everything was all right). We have decided, the Lord willing, to sell our land, because Johan cannot work the [entire] farm without father's help. Despite the best intentions, his wife remains a weak and ailing person. On January 2, '66 she was again delivered of a stillborn son, the eleventh child, and again she had been ailing all the while. Singer had proposed that they go into business together, because he has four workers and would like to have his own overseer. If it be the Lord's way, the family would very much like to be together. Mount Pl[easant] is a quiet country town, famous for its asylum for the insane; I have not found an institution as well appointed as this one anywhere. There are many churches and schools and also two churches for freed blacks who are very numerous here.

I really wanted to see one [of these churches]; one reads so much about the conversion of the heathen, and they even have some of their own ministers already. It was on a Sunday evening [that I attended], not a beautiful building, but a simple schoolhouse. After all, during the Secession our eyes were turned from fancy things, but we were thoroughly content if only we heard the pure proclamation of the Word of God, even if it was only in a workshop. There was a black preacher, and although we still do not understand English, we could see the respect and earnestness and also the attention of the listeners. His prayer was one unbroken flow. Singer was with us and told us that the text was from Luke, chapter 2, the story about Joseph and Mary and the little child. The singing was simple and enthusiastic. We stayed until the sermon was finished; it was a Baptist congregation.

So your Maria is already engaged too; I thought that the family tie was a little close, but I am not sure of it. Then I wish them the blessing of the Lord so that they may walk uprightly before his countenance, and that they may be your joy and give you happiness; that is my sincere wish.

The father of our family went to Ost Friesland this fall; he sold his farm, and on March 21 he and his wife, who is a daughter of my husband's oldest brother, are going to America with their eight children. Both of their sons are already on land they bought and are farming nine miles inland, a three-hour's ride from here. The family will first be arriving at our place; may the Lord grant them a safe journey.

Again we will be confronting an unpleasant prospect, our esteemed preacher, the Rev. Brücher, will be leaving us about May, and so we will again be without a shepherd; may the Lord have mercy on us.

I shall close for now. Mrs. Teleman and her daughter send greetings; she already has three daughters and they were all at the wedding. Heartfelt greetings from all of us to your esteemed children and your married children and also to your Johan; very likely he will not become an American farmer. The Lord strengthen you and support you all on your difficult life's way, and grant that you acquiesce in his ways; indeed all things must work together for good. Make us happy with an early reply. Your Friend and Sister in the Lord who thinks of you always,

C. M. Budde-Stomp

Added from the Risseeuw Archives of the Documentatiecentrum Nederlands Protestantisme V[rije] U[niversiteit], a fragment of a letter from Van Raalte to his son, Ben, Kampen [Netherlands], June 11, 1866, about the Netherlands as seen through the eyes of an emigrant [JS].

Mother and I are both doing very well—Mother had a slight stomach upset, but it was just mild. Mother, it seems to me, has already put on weight and her cough is very mild, so that this gives us much reason for gratitude. Since our ocean voyage I have been eating better than I have for some years, and this makes me stronger.

The synod in Amsterdam has come to a close, and I was pleased the way it ended. It was a most pleasant experience for me, and I was received with so much love and cordiality that I was ashamed and embarrassed by it. I am glad that the meeting is over, because of all those stinking canals, and, besides, working late into the night (making days of the nights) does not agree with me. But here too they have their evening meal between ten and eleven.

You certainly will be able to understand that I have my eyes wide open here, but although the countryside in the prosperous areas is beautiful, still there is nothing here that would attract me. And besides I do not find a thing here that we do not also have in America. The cattle are numerous and beautiful, but I saw cattle no less beautiful in America. I do not see any horses as fast as that of Dirk; the horses move like the people—at a very leisurely pace. Accordingly, I shrink from hiring a [farm] laborer. They are too slow to suit me, and even at that they are not used to tackling anything new. There is plague among cattle in Noord and Zuid Holland and Utrecht, but it has spread across the whole country—in some places it is very severe. Altogether eleven farmers had lost...ever so many head of cattle. Cholera is slowly spreading throughout the land; however, it is not as severe as in times past. And still it is (very bad) for commerce and country. God grant that it may also be for its hallowing. The threatening postures of the armed forces that oppose each other in Austria, Italy, and Prussia also results in stagnation of trade here. The bankruptcy of banks and prominent mercantile firms adds to the general malaise. But the building of railroads and various public works do provide a good deal of work for the laboring man.

Addition from Ponsteen: Van Noetzele at Nijverdal [Province of Overijssel]. In the periodical, De Vereeniging Christelijke Stemmen, of March 15, 1867, Hein Wormser gives a report of the first year of the school he founded in 1866 and in it expands as follows about the condition of factory workers [JS].

We read about native tribes in North America and elsewhere which, after coming into contact with Europeans, begin to languish and gradually die out. This phenomenon of wasting away we are also beginning to observe in our midst: and if the government waits much longer with regulating hours of work in factories, the class of factory workers, if not augmented [with workers] from other classes, will gradually cease to exist. In America it may well be brandy that is the chief reason for the dying out of native tribes, but here it is [the problem of] of labor, begun too early in life, and for too many hours a day, that destroys the factory worker physically and intellectually. Do we not observe among the draftees for military service, that a host of these lads do not meet minimal physical requirements? Was it not reported to me only yesterday that a child of one of the factory workers had died, the tenth child in the married life of these parents to be carried to the graveyard. Scarcely does the child begin to grow up and the parents begin to realize that it can be a source of benefit to them. The farmer not only utilizes it [child labor] in his activities during the summer time, but also in the spring and fall; the factory worker also pursues his own gain with the child at an early age. It is an evil against which all Christian admonition and persuasion falls on deaf ears, and that will not be prevented as long as the government remains totally indifferent to the needs of the children of the Netherlands who are sacrificed in the arms of the factory Molochs. It is almost incomprehensible how the legislative powers in our fatherland can be so laggardly about passing a law controlling working hours in factories; and that notwithstanding the fact that those who are familiar with and even involved in factory

The Later Years, 1861-1873   547

production have publicly expressed the need for such a law for years in order to put an end to the intolerable situation in both physical and moral respects.

In the original Wormser struck out the following, in all likelihood so that the report would not become too long.

....Or should there not be some kind of arrangement for the young woman who works in the factory until the last minute before asking permission to go home to bring a child into the world; and in a couple of days is again standing at her loom, only nursing the baby at meal times, and for the rest entrusting it to the care of an aged grandmother or neighbor lady? Is this practice in the Netherlands very different from what used to take place on the plantations of Suriname?

When will the time come (will it ever happen?) that the Netherlands government will put an end to the exploitation of children and give them the opportunity to be able to enjoy their youth in education and play? Presently, when a child is ten years old, sooner or later, he will be joining, somber faced and lack-luster, older people headed for the big factory and waste his youth there like someone confined to prison.

To enable the reader to judge the age of the children in our school, we provide the following extract from the quarterly report submitted to the municipal government on April 15, 1866:

	male	female
Under 6 years	11	9
6, 7, or 8 years	23	22
9, 10, and 11	7	8
12 years and older	0	1
Total	81 children	

What a sad relationship! Sixty-five children under the age of eight and only fifteen between the ages nine and eleven, and one twelve-year-old.

What can we begin to do with children below or at eight years of age, who constitute our entire student population but for sixteen? When they get to be two years older, they are probably taken from school. Quickly teach them reading and writing, and a little arithmetic; any language, history, and geography, any further educational development is out of the question.

In response to the above, J. Esser wrote an article in the weekly "De Heraut" [The Herald] entitled: "Kindermoord in Nederland" ["The Murder of Children in the Netherlands"] [JS].

[*From the Wormser archives.*]

J. Wüstenhoff-Wormser to Mother J. A. Wormser-van der Ven
Paris, 21 July 1867

Dear Mom,

Since I think it has been rather a long time since you have heard anything from us, I decided to write you once again. We have been enjoying ourselves very much and think it is a real pity that our time is nearly over. We are now always eating and drinking at our hotel, since it is not all that expensive and much better than it is in the cafés. We unexpectedly found out that the porter and his wife are Hollanders, and very nice people, who are happy when they can talk Dutch with us; the food here is outstandingly good and is fixed in the Dutch way.

We bought a couple of stereoscope views so that you can have some idea of how busy it is here. On Wednesday we climbed the Arch of Triumph, from where you can see all of Paris. Among others, we saw a street so wide that I could count eight rows of lanterns. The next day, we went to St. Cloud, saw the palace, walked in the park, and took the steamboat back. The next day it was the Louvre, where there were innumerable paintings to be seen. Yesterday we took the train to visit Versailles. Carl and Johan took turns sitting on top; we also saw the palace there and walked in the woods. Last night we visited the shops and bought a few things. Everything here is done early in the evening and late in the morning, and the people here are never in a hurry, that is sure.

The climate here is just splendid, though we have had some rain, but yesterday and today it was very nice again. It is so warm here that my barrège gown [of buttons] sometimes is too warm, and we always sleep with open windows.

This morning we walked until twelve o'clock and attended the Reformed church where Rev. Grand Pierre is the preacher, so it was very good. From there we went to visit the Père La Chaise Cemetery, which is a city all by itself with broad streets and sidewalks. And now Carl and Johan are not allowing me any more time to write because it is seven-thirty, and they still want to take a walk. I do not think that you have ever heard and seen as much traffic as we did today; Sundays just are not pleasant here.

If we do not get home Wednesday evening, it will be because Carl has gotten a letter with business matters which may delay him a day, so do not get worried. Johan will probably stay then too. With cordial greetings from us all to you all, I remain your loving daughter,

J. Wüstenhoff-Wormser

Wormser 75

C. M. Budde-Stomp to Widow Mrs. J. A. Wormser-van der Ven
Burlington, August 1867

To my Dearly Beloved Friend and Sister in the Lord and her Children,

After waiting in vain a long time to hear from Your Honor, I finally must take up my pen. We received your letter of January 10, '66 with sympathy, and in '66 we sent Your Honor a letter in which we described many and important matters regarding our children and ourselves at great length. May I kindly request that you write me whether you have received that, and if not, I will have to write that again.

This winter my dear husband suffered greatly from a stomach ailment from time to time. When the pains are severe he is incapable of doing anything. In the month of May he developed such terrible pains in his head that he could not stand it. We sent for the doctor, and the Lord blessed the means and soon he experienced relief. He had gone downhill so badly that we feared for his recovery. The children quickly came from Mount Pleasant to see Father once more; the Lord heard our prayers, and to our great joy restored Father. However, he remains too weak to do much work. That had always been his chief delight, but in this respect he will now have to practice renunciation and suffering and do what the Lord wills.

I have been plagued with rheumatism a great deal this winter, and if I exercise myself the least bit, my heart pounds so that I must sit down quickly. Last June we had a farewell visit from Berkhout and his wife. They planned to travel by steamer to Bremen and from there to the Piedmont to take the baths. He was hoping that he would get over the pain in his back; it might be fall before they would get to Holland. They have not changed at all; B[erkhout] looks a little older. They promised they would write when they got to the Piedmont. They told me that Mr. Lothes had died and that Mrs. Lothes was [living] in Utrecht. Mrs. Teleman has also been called home. She was still well on Sunday, but during the night she became indisposed and restless. Jansje gave her some camphor; that calmed it down and she sent for the doctor. On Wednesday afternoon when J[ansje's] husband was coming, Johan's wife came along at once. She was no longer conscious. Her eyes had broken, and she lay in quiet slumber. In the evening we came down by wagon; she was still in the same condition. Jansje related that a pious old woman asked her whether she still clung to her Savior. She smiled, even nodded yes. During the night she had her husband on her mind and she called, "Father, are you there?" We had to leave and Lena stayed with her. Not long after we left, she passed away peacefully. She was buried August 1 '67, aged sixty-five years. She lay in her coffin with a happy look on her face. (Jansje is expecting her fourth child; her husband is well behaved, an American, and he makes a fairly good living.) For twenty-four years the Lord was to her a husband of widows, and she lacked nothing, and he makes her to lie down and rest in the earth until the last day. Our children were greatly attached to her, so that she was not regarded as a stranger but as a sister in the Lord. My dear husband has gone to Mount Pleasant to be with the children. Maria is now in good health, and, the Lord willing, I expect to go there about mid November, because she is in a state of blessed expectancy, and then they like to have their mother around. Johan's wife had a son, stillborn, last winter, their twelfth child; they have one son and a daughter living and are reasonably well these days.

There is quite a revival among the Germans in Mount Pleasant. They are building a German Presbyterian church; there are already English-speaking ones, and in all likelihood it will be completed before winter. Our [friend] Singer is also an elder; he is very diligent in the work of the Lord. Burlington and Mount Pleasant share a minister by the name of Smit. We have partial support for the minister from the Presbyterian Board. The Holland Reformed no longer have students who can preach in Dutch. The church in Burlington is not growing. To make sure that we would not be entirely without preaching, and with the approval of the entire congregation, we joined the Presbyterian denomination. They have the same doctrines as we; they use the Westminster Catechism and have their origins in Scotland. In our childhood years, we had a reader that told the story about Countess Jacoba van Beyeren, who was very unhappy that in her fourth marriage she had to give up the title of

"Countess" in order to get Frank van Borstelen as her husband. In like manner we have to give up the name "Reformed" in order to keep our preaching. We were most happy about the Evangelical Alliance in Amsterdam, and we expect that you will enjoy blessings because of it. After all, it is an association of God's children who really are nothing but the Christian church, the congregation that the Lamb has purchased with his blood. He knows them all by name and keeps them so that together they may talk about the things of the Kingdom, and give each other the hand of fellowship, whether they are from distant lands or near, and unitedly work for the Lord and in his service. Ah, may the Lord's blessing descend on them, his favor from Zion be their stay, that is my prayer [Dutch Psalter 134:3].

The Lord works in mysterious ways. In Paris man's art, science, and technology are on display [remarks occasioned by the visit of Wormser children to the World's Fair at Paris in 1867]. And there too the Lord shows how far and how manifold his divine Word, the Bible, has spread even to lands once closed to it, in order that all the called may be gathered in. We are fast coming to the end of time; blessed is the servant whom the Lord will find alert and waiting. And in the midst of so much commotion—a chapel in which one can hear the Word of God preached: how marvelous! The Lord reigns, Psalm 93; the favorite psalm of your beloved husband.

Since I am writing a joint letter about our situation, your dear children will pardon me for not writing each one individually. This is difficult enough for us to do; but love does press us to talk somewhat on paper, so that we may get to know something of each other's experiences. Now, dear friends, write us back soon, after all we have been waiting such a long time, and let us know whether you have received our letter, which was an answer to your letter of January 10, 1866. Warmest greetings from our Johan and his wife, also from our Maria Singer. I hope that my dear husband will also write a short note. May the Lord be gracious and near to you all.

Your loving Friend and Sister in the Lord,
C. M. Budde-Stomp

Wormser 76

                                                 D. A. Budde to J. A. Wormser-van der Ven
                                                                    Burlington, Sept. 16, 1867

Dearly Beloved Friend and Sister in the Lord,
    My dear wife was so very eager that I should include a few lines with her letter. As long as the Lord spares us for each other, I may not refrain from doing so. It is eight days ago that I, after limping along for a long time, was felled by a new kind of illness that consists of severe pain and misery in the lower parts of my body, which in a very short space of time has reduced me to such a condition that I can scarcely walk any more. But thanks be to God that today, with nice weather and being out in the fresh air for the first time, I may feel myself somewhat more cheerful. My wife and I are glad to see that we have left behind the final milepost in our preparation as pilgrims and strangers here, including the manifold troubles on our life's way; and through the faithful assistance of our faithful God and Savior, we live in the faith and trust that his promises will not fail us to the very end, that of serving and glorifying the triune God unto all eternity. The Lord grant that you and your dear children, dear Sister, may be able to cast all your cares and concerns in the bosom of our heavenly Father; only there will it be safe, blessed and holy. Amen. By the same mail I am sending you three selections, taken from the publication about the day of rest, written by your husband of blessed memory, and which I have had translated into German—and printed. I hope to distribute them to sundry persons, and with the Lord's blessing, may it increase the fervor of many (to abandon the seeming and ever disappointing rest of this world) for the eternal rest that is laid aside for the people of God in heaven. Wormser still is not forgotten. Heartfelt greetings to you and your children; the peace of the Lord Jesus Christ be with you all.

                                                                          Your Friend in the Lord,
                                                                              D. A. Budde

Budde 45

>Jansje Wüstenhoff-Wormser to Mrs. C. M. Budde-Stomp
>Amsterdam, 3 Oct. 1867

Esteemed Madame, Dearly Beloved Friend,
   Last night mother received your and Mr. Budde's letter in reasonably good health, and this morning it was forwarded to me to read. You have good reason to be angry with us, since we kept you waiting so long to hear from us. But by constantly postponing, time moves by so fast, that it takes another letter to come, with grumbling reminders, before one gets started. And that is why we have immediately taken our pen in hand to thank you for all you all that you have shared with us. It grieves us that Mr. Budde, your husband, is again ailing so. May the Lord long spare him for you. [Here] we may all rejoice in continuing good health; mother is ailing somewhat at times and still continues to have days of severe headaches.
   We have had a very busy summer and have enjoyed ourselves very much. You ask whether we had rain during the Evangelical Alliance. I will be telling you this and that about it. You also make a passing reference to the world exhibition in Paris, and I will also tell you some things about that, since we did visit it. What do you say about that? Our next journey abroad will, I hope, be to New York, where the next meeting of the Alliance will take place. The American gentlemen were so excited about the reception in Holland that they promised that they would then send a big steamboat to fetch all the Hollanders and take them over free of charge. If the Lord spares our lives, I hope that we may then have the desire and the opportunity to see a small bit of the New World. For like Paul, who wanted to see Rome, so I would also like to see New York once.
   I had better begin by telling you in good order the things that kept us so busy. In April my sister Cato left for Baambrugge; no doubt, mother wrote you in detail about her sad story. In June, my husband came home from the office one day and said to me, "Now you are free to go to Paris, if you wish, my employer offered to let me go there for a few days." Well, you can imagine, they did not have to ask us a second time. We left at six in the morning on July 16th, and at nine o'clock in the evening we were in Paris. It is enchantingly beautiful. The city itself is splendid, and the exhibition is dizzying. We visited it only three times, and mind you it takes four months to see it all. We visited the [Centennial] Park

extensively; there are no less than three hundred large buildings, most of them of cut stone. There [you will see] the diamond cutting shop of Coster in operation, a Dutch farm house, Japanese dwellings [and] Chinese, a very big Roman [Catholic] church. And from pagan lands there are temples of false gods. And let us not forget America: we went all through a farmer's house [and] an American school, in which only the children were absent, maps hanging on the walls, paper and ink in the desks. There was also a Dutch elementary school and a Prussian one. We also visited the American bakery just when they were baking bread. Also a portable house made of cypress wood, very beautiful. In that house, my husband bought a map of America.

In your letter, your refer to Bible distribution. Indeed, it is great; there are two houses where they hand out a portion of the Holy Scriptures free of charge to every person going by, and in whatever language they wish. We each got one Dutch and two French New Testaments. There is also a small Protestant church that can hold five hundred persons and where they serve the Holy Communion every Sunday. There is also a large room for conferences, where every evening there is opportunity to have discussions concerning the kingdom of God. There is also another large room where you can see all the triumphs of Christendom over paganism, among others, the club with which missionary Williams was killed. You may be familiar with the story. After the murderer of Williams was converted several years ago, he turned over that club to an English society that saves things like that.

There was also a building of Jewish antiquities, very old books [scrolls] from the beginning of our era; on tables [there were replicas] of the entire temple and temple worship of the Old Testament; all of Jerusalem, Gethsemane, the Mount of Olives, etc. On Sunday we were in the Protestant church where we heard the Rev. Grand Pierre preach a very vigorous sermon. We also visited palaces in St. Cloud, Versailles, and the Louvre, known for the [St.] Bartholomew night [massacre]. In the Louvre we also saw everything that had belonged to Napoleon, also all the things he had used on [the island of] St. Helena. After having enjoyed all of this, we arrived safely home on July 24th. There we found Mother and my cousin Jansje with her husband, Kollen, who had come by that day to take leave before their departure to America. Kollen has a store in the colony of Rev. Van Raalte. After we had been home a few days, my sister and her children came over to stay with us for a few days so that they could join [with us] in celebrating my birthday. After they left on August 12, Rev. Brummelkamp and his wife arrived on the 17th and stayed with us during the [Evangelical] Alliance. This was [in accordance with] an agreement made the year before, when the Reverends Brummelkamp, De Moen, and Van Raalte ate at Mother's one afternoon.

The [Evangelical] Alliance was opened by Rev. [J.J.] Van Oosterzee on Sunday evening in the Nieuwe Kerk [in Amsterdam]. The meetings in the Park Assembly Hall began on Monday with a time of prayer at eight o'clock. I attended all the meetings but two, but I assure you that it is tiring. There were many speakers from New York. The prayer times were striking. Every morning there were devotions in separate rooms for the French, the Germans, the English, and the Dutch. We liked those of the English best. The first night there was a reunion in the garden, and you could just talk to anyone whose acquaintance you wished to make. Mother spoke to Mr. Groen van Prinsterer; my husband spoke with the sixty-three-year-old Prof. Tholuck from Halle, whose name probably is known to you. I can do no more than make the briefest reference to matters, but I do want to say a word about the blessing and edification we enjoyed at the communal celebration of the Lord's Supper. It was held in the Remonstrant Church at two o'clock in the afternoon. Rev. Hasebroek began by speaking briefly on the words: "With desire I have desired to eat this Passover with you" [Luke 22:15]. A German preacher spoke, then a French one, and then an Englishman, the Rev. Birks. We had a hymnal in four languages; after the joint...[blank] the Rev. [M.] Cohen Stuart read the Institution of the Lord's Supper in Dutch, and then the three other [clergymen] did so in their languages; the English was by Dr. Mullens of New York. Then they all sat down: men and women of many languages and nations, a mix of many religions, but one in Christ, and united through faith in him. After the sacrament had been administered, the four ministers, in the four languages, [individually] concluded with the Lord's Prayer; and, after jointly singing a hymn, everyone left for home. To me the most striking aspect of it all was the fact that no message was given; the ceremony spoke for itself and did everything that was needed. I do not believe that I will ever celebrate a more satisfying Lord's Supper, or it should have to be at such an occasion as this.

The next evening Mr. Baxter from London was present at a meeting in one of the upper rooms to discuss the work of the Lord in England and Holland. We also attended. Before it started, one of the Baxter ladies spoke to me and asked whether I had been present at the Communion service yesterday. She had enjoyed it so very much.

There is another Englishman in our country who just keeps on conducting prayer meetings in the English and American way and to admonish people to repent, without delay, today. After his address, he allows several minutes for prayer, and then he is ready to talk to any one who so desires about his spiritual condition. A goodly number of people took advantage of the opportunity; usually he spoke twice a day. As far as we know, he is still in Zeist [province of Utrecht], where there has been a considerable revival as a result of his speaking. It was a blessing to many people. The week before, he was in The Hague. He had bread, tea, and [honey] cake distributed to one thousand mothers and children, with an address. On the designated day it rained, and the baker inquired what he should do with the bread. His answer was to take it to the school for the down and outers, and so his expenses were doubled.

Rev. Brummelkamp was in a rapture of delight during the Alliance [gatherings]. For once he could get away from the narrow-minded mess. Recently his son preached in the Hervormde Kerk. Synod has allowed that since a year ago.

Well, my dear lady, you certainly did have to wait long to get this, but at least now you are getting a double letter. I just cannot believe that your daughter Maria is married and is about to become a mother. In my mind's eye I still see her staggering in our hallway, wearing her blue dress, one and a half years old. Please give her my greetings sometime. Your little house on the Achterburgwal still is in the same old condition, but the canal has been filled in. Now it is a street. The day after the Brummelkamp friends left, the Berkhout friends suddenly showed up. They have not changed at all; they have only gotten a little older. If you and Mr. [Budde] were still strong enough, I would hope that we might still see you here too sometime.

Well, dear lady, cordial greetings to you and Mr. [Budde] and your son and his spouse from the two of us, and we commit you to the Lord.

Your loving Friend,
J. Wüstendorff-Wormser.

P.S. Mother will send you reports of the Alliance. Shorthand writers took notes, and every day there was a paper. There are many errors in it, and it is very incomplete, but then you can at least follow events more or less. The addresses by Lord Radstock, about which I wrote, have all been translated; our preachers have been very busy translating. Once again, cordial greetings. We regularly enjoy hearing Rev. Huet [preach];

last Sunday he preached in English, about three weeks ago he preached in the French church and baptized the first grandson of [Isaac] Da Costa. So that now there is again an Isaac Da Costa.

Budde 46

> Mrs. J. Wormser-van der Ven to Mrs. C. M. Budde-Stomp
> Amsterdam, 3 October 1867

Dearly Beloved Friends in our Lord!

Procrastination is the thief of time. To my shame I have proven the truth of this saying by my long delay in writing. Yes, dear friend, I do have in my possession your esteemed letter sent to me last year, which kept me informed about your situation. Last night I was surprised by yours of this past August, and I now want to start answering it at once.

When I received your previous letter, my daughter Cato was staying at my house with her two little children. Her husband was misbehaving so badly with his drinking and making debts and going out with wanton women that she could stand it no longer. In February 1866 she arrived at my house at eleven P.M. with her little ones. [She] began divorce proceedings and, as the daughter of Wormser, was treated with utmost consideration by all the members of the court. In March of this year, the Divorce Decree was proclaimed. She received all the household furnishings in compensation for the debts he had left behind. But he continued his reveling and was dismissed by the storage company [his employer], and for the longest time now he has been living in the greatest misery in both soul and body. As you can well imagine, he was admonished frequently, but nothing availed. The whole affair did not do my health any good, and I could not stand all the activity in my little home either.

We concluded that it would be better for Cato to live in the country, and the Lord led us in finding a good location. She is living in Baambrugge in a small, free-standing house in a neighborhood of dear pious people, whom we have acquainted with her circumstances and who are very fond of her. Jansje and her husband pay the rent, but for the rest she depends entirely on me. The Lord rules and cares for us as a Father, that I have amply experienced, since my income is adequate to support their household as well as my own. Old bossman Balke, [Mrs. Zeelt's gardener until she died in 1864], who is living all alone in

Postwijk, feels sorry for her [Cato] and constantly supplies her with vegetables and fruit [cf. Budde Letter 26]. And since it [Baambrugge] is so close by, we visit her with some frequency. She has quieted down by now, and, given her situation, she is as happy as possible. When she first came to my house, no one thought that she would survive. Accordingly, she was under doctor's care for a quarter of a year. Finally he said, "I do not have any medicines for you, what you need is a quiet life." The whole thing of becoming separated from her husband really took a lot out of her. But after the divorce she heard of so many other scandals [involving him], that by now she feels free of him. She enjoys the consolation of the Lord and lives in communion with him. Now that it is all over, it is easier for me to talk and write about it. I suffered many headaches and experienced much nervousness because of it.

It grieves me that you are having so many physical ailments, but our life's journey is shortening, and it cannot be much longer before we see each other again and are reunited with my dear husband, [with] Mrs. Teeleman [Teleman], and all with those who have gone before us into the eternal rest to praise the Lord perfectly with never any interruption.

I thought that you had been living in with your daughter Maria at Mount Pleasant for a long time already. But last month Berkhout and his wife stopped by and gave us your greetings written in Burlington. I was very happy to receive them. I said to my children, if only our friends, the Buddes, would drop in on us like that once. It looks like B[erkhout] earned a good deal of money: they bought a small house with a garden on the Zaagpad just outside the Utrecht gate. They were scheduled to move in this week, and that may well be the reason I have not seen or heard from them during the past eight days. They arrived too late to witness the wonderful [Evangelical] Alliance days. Jansje will also be writing you, but more specifically about the Alliance, and that is why I will just talk about myself.

Each of us, including me, bought a pass that cost fl 2.50 per person and gave admittance to all the sessions. On Sunday evening, Professor Oosterzee gave the opening address for the Alliance at the Nieuwe Kerk, but I could not attend because of a headache. On Monday I was able to go along to the Park [Congress site], and, although they were speaking in many languages so that much was lost to me, still the sight of so many believers from all over the world was moving just the same, and it made a deep impression on my soul. That evening, when there were friendly encounters in the park gardens, I was so moved that it upset me. A veritable host of old acquaintances: Mr. [Guillaume] Groen van

Prinsterer, Rev. [N. H.] De Graaf, [Otto G.] Heldring, Nonnebel [?] van Rijn, Mr. and Mrs. Ooyens. Mrs. Voute from the Asylum [Shelter?] came up to me to shake my hand and to tell me of the blessings they had enjoyed because of him [Mr. Wormser] and inquired at length how I and my children were faring. [He commented that though] Wormser was not present here, he was celebrating the Alliance above [in heaven]. I also went down on Tuesday, but then the joy of it all was more than my body could take, and I sometimes had to skip sessions. I was constantly thinking, "How things have changed, when we were first getting acquainted [as Seceders] we were dispersed whenever we assembled to hear the Word of God, and to pray together, and now there are hundreds of us together for days, doing nothing different from then, and now we are treated with greatest courtesy on all sides."

You have had to give up the name of *Gereformeerd* [Reformed] in order preserve the preaching of the Word; that was somewhat the case here too. Everyone was represented: the Remonstrant Rev. M. Cohen Stuart from Rotterdam was also a member of the governing board, and what that man said and did was more significant than what many Reformed preachers dish out to us from their pulpits these days. I believe that the time is drawing nigh that it will be one flock and one Shepherd, and whether we are in this group or that will not then matter. If we only belong to the one flock and are under the loving guidance of the Shepherd, then we will know him and not follow any other. Our present church situation is one that is not tenable in the long run; there are certainly good preachers, but there are also many who are very modern [liberal], who have said to the Alliance that they too wanted to see what was going on at that spiritual kermis [carnival].

I have not received the [German translation of the] Sabbath pamphlets yet, but your high esteem for Wormser's work makes me very happy. His memory abides as a blessing for you even as it does for Mr. Groen [van Prinsterer].

My favorite preacher is still the High German Rev. Brandt, who always emphasizes faith and especially its fruits. A ruling has recently been adopted in the churches that all preachers of existing fellowships [independent church groups] may preach [in the Netherlands Reformed Church]. And just a few weeks ago Rev. Hasebroek invited the Seceder, Rev. Van Dijk, to preach in his pulpit, and he enthusiastically had us sing several hymns. And shortly after the Alliance had ended, Johannes Brummelkamp, the second son of our Brummelkamp, and a Seceder preacher in Thiel [Tiel], preached for Rev. Vinke in the Nieuwe Kerk and gave much satisfaction. I had a long visit from him and told him that he was a strange Seceder, [but] now I hear that [the Seceders] take it ill of him [for preaching there], and that they are thinking of suspending him.

October 4.

Everything is astir in church and state, and the Lord is carrying out his [eternal] counsel. In the midst of all those stirrings, it is safe to take refuge near the Lord and to entrust our lot and way into his hand. I hope that your receive this missive before you go and visit your Maria, and that she in the Lord's good time may become a happy mother. Our friend Jan certainly has been most unfortunate in [the loss of] his children. I hope that they may acquiesce in the will of the Lord. They still have two left. When Job was bereft of all his [children], he still said, "The Lord gave, the Lord hath taken, Blessed be the name of the Lord" [Job 1:21].

At the moment my Maria and her beloved [Johannes] are out having a look at the School for the Poor and Neglected. Johannes is in town in order to celebrate their birthday, which is on the 6th instant. Their birthdays are on the same day; he is turning twenty-three and she twenty, a little young to get married, though he does talk about it. Saartje Luuring married a bookbinder's helper this summer. She has to do a lot of sewing in order to help them make a living. Willem, the eldest son, got a position with the Handelsmaatschappij [Netherlands Trading Company]; he is going steady. The youngest son, Johan, is suffering from consumption and will not live much longer. Mrs. [Luuring] is aging very much.

Well, my dear friend, I am getting tired; writing always is a big effort for me. You have given a fine example in writing to me, although it was my turn. Now please be so kind and write me soon again. Who knows how few letters we shall still exchange, and it is always so comforting to get a letter from you. Cato does not know that I am writing you, and so I cannot give you her greetings. All my other children do send you and yours their cordial greetings. May the peace of God in Christ Jesus fill your hearts and may all of you and your concerns be commended to the Lord.

Your Intimately Loving Friend and Sister in the Lord,
Widow J. Wormser-van der Ven

[In the handwriting of J. Wüstendorff Wormser]

Mother asks that I mention to you that Johan, my brother, went to Paris with us. Mother trusted him to go to that worldly city in our company. He is as satisfied as we are. We brought back some stereoscopic plates, all views of Paris. Recently someone loaned us 100 plates about America.

Wormser 77

C. M. Budde-Stomp to the Widow Mrs. J. A. Wormser-van der Ven
Burlington, Jan. 1868

Beloved Friend and Sister in the Lord with her Children,

We received your esteemed letter in good health on October 26, '67. We were all very happy about it; after such a long wait it was even surprising. Through the revival and the newspapers, we had already heard about and rejoiced at the coming (Evangelical) Alliance in Amsterdam. We rejoiced at the great blessing that you all had enjoyed and now again have shared with us. The Lord is the faithful covenant God who does not let his people be tried beyond what they are able, but causes the trial to end in such a way that we can bear it. Doubtless you have observed that instead of being persecuted, Christians are now being treated with respect; and in all countries they may [freely] assemble to speak with each other about the kingdom of God, to praise and glorify the Lord. You caused us great rejoicing with your reports on the Alliance. My son-in-law Singer read them with me and he was delighted in them, as were Holland friends at Mount Pleasant. Our Rev. Schmidt did not have much use for the Alliance, and so I did not show them to him; he has a rather narrow outlook on things.

On Sunday, November 3, '67 the church at Mount Pleasant was to be dedicated. It is a small church with a little tower and the preacher's house is behind it. We all wanted to go down to participate in the festivities, and I would then stay with Maria until after her delivery, at the end of the month, she thought. I put my household in order and got the washing done on Monday so I could go to Mount Pleasant on Friday. Monday morning there was a telegram with the message, "*Merie heeft een bebe (kindje) al wel kom over*" ("Maria has a baby (little child), all is well, come over"). We were all scared. Now I had to hurry to get there as soon as possible, by the first train that did not leave till evening. The unexpected tiding led me to fear the worst, but lo and behold, the Lord had made all things well. She had still been running errands on Saturday afternoon, and as a result felt somewhat fatigued; during the night she did not feel very well, and then things calmed down again. Finally Singer said, "I am going to get the doctor"; it was three o'clock. He [the doctor] said, "The baby will be coming soon." Now she became embarrassed, no mother there, and no telegram could be sent because it was Sunday. Now she had to place herself completely at the mercy of the Lord. They got two lady friends to be with her, and they attended her faithfully. On Sunday morning, the 27th, before church began, she was delivered of a healthy baby daughter. You see, there is a church service at their house, just as there is at ours. Father came on Friday with niece Etje, the oldest daughter of his brother Johan, who has been living with her family about twelve miles from us for two years already.

The building was solemnly dedicated to the Lord. In the morning, Rev. Kliebenstein preached on Isaiah 57:15; in the afternoon, Rev. Schmidt [preached] on Zachariah 6:12, and in the evening he preached in English on Isaiah 54:17. It was a day of rejoicing in the Lord, also for us, for we have seen this congregation grow and we share a preacher. Our children share this too. May it be a Bethel, where the Lord is adored and sinners are converted to him. Father and the family went home to Burlington; I stayed with Maria for six weeks. Father returned again on the 25th of November, and we, with Maria and Singer, presented our granddaughter, Anna Maria, to the Lord in holy baptism, Rev. Schmidt officiating.

My dear husband's health is up and down; he has quite a few intervals when his stomach pains are rather bearable. But we both are growing weaker. Presently we are again in Burlington; there still is no buyer for our farm; we must bide the Lord's time.

Your dear Cato's lot grieves us, but we are glad that a caring mother and supportive family mitigate her grief. May the Lord comfort her and cause her to flee to him all the more, and may he spare her long for her offspring.

Reading about the Rev. Cohen Stuart was wondrous to me, but then it occurred to me that perhaps it is a case like that of Rev. Ter Borg and the Mennonite Church, whom the Lord converted. But when I read in the reports of the [Evangelical] Alliance, and recognized his voice there, I was completely satisfied. I was also surprised that the Remonstrants allow their church to be used for the celebration of the Lord's Supper; it probably was the best available.

The Lord has the hearts of men in his hands and guides them like springs of water. Everything must serve him, so the Egyptians bestow gifts of gold and silver to the Israelites and let them leave. It [the story] elicited a good deal of comment in America; it appeared in the English language in religious papers, and then it was again translated into Dutch, just as Your Honor wrote us. What a foretaste of heavenly joy you have all enjoyed, and we too share in it all, even though we are not present. The joyous prospect of gathering together with all the people of the Lord, in whom and through whom we shall all be one, and bring praise, adoration, worship, and thanksgiving unto him who sits upon the throne and to the Lamb through all eternity, Amen.

We are glad that you still enjoy your Maria and the other children, and that in this way your grief is assuaged, and when she enters matrimony with Johannes may the blessing of the Lord accompany them. It is already a great privilege to walk together in the fear of the Lord, the most wonderful thing one can enjoy on earth. I thank you for sharing with me some things about our old friends. If you have not yet received the pamphlets about the day of rest, my dear husband will send them to you again. It was published in a periodical called *Der Wächter*. It is not complete, but includes only what would be useful in America. Without my husband's knowledge, the printer omitted the name [of the author] and "translated from the Dutch." Well, the work speaks for itself. My dear friend, I must conclude. Warmest greetings to you all from us, from Johan and his spouse, also from Maria and Singer, to whom I have read your letter. We commend you all to the Lord and his grace.

Your loving Friend and Sister in the Lord,
C. M. Budde-Stomp

P.S. Do surprise us soon with your reply. Greetings to Berkhout and his wife. He did not keep his word; he was to write us as soon as he arrived at the baths.

"*Gott ist getreu! Sein Herz sein Vaterherz Verläs[s]t die Seinen nie.*"	God is faithful! His heart, his Father heart Never forsakes his own.

[Six stanzas follow that have not been printed.]

Wormser 78

C. M. Budde-Stomp to Mrs. J. Wüstenhof-Wormser
Burlington, January 1868

Dearly Beloved Friend and her Spouse,

The detailed account of your visit to Paris, as well as the glad [news] about the [Evangelical] Alliance, were a happy surprise for us and I thank Your Honors for it. I saw such grandeur in it all, those arts, sciences, antiquities, etc., which also often confirm the truth of the Bible; and whose only source is, after all, the Lord. For he gave human beings the knowledge needed to produce these arts and sciences, but they deny the Lord and rob him of his honor and make themselves Gods, as if they had made these things by their own hands. Indeed they go so far as to deny the Lord God, and put nature in his place. Despite them, the Lord shows by the spread of his Word, that

God, de Heer, regeert	God, the Lord rules
Beeft, gij volken, eert	Tremble, all ye nations, reverence,
eert zijn hoog bestel.	reverence his high decree
	[Dutch Psalter 99:1] etc. but
Hoe zalig is het volk,	How blest is the people,
dat naar uw klanken hoort ...	That hearkens to your voice
	[Dutch Psalter 89:7]

All the earth, with all that it holds and enfolds, cannot be compared with what God has laid away for those who love him.

If it be the Lord's will, and we are living, and Your Honor might be visiting New York sometime, I flatter myself that Your Honor will also continue your journey and visit us in Burlington and Mount Pleasant. During that time you can stay with us. How happy we would be to embrace Your Honors; you will be lodging here free of charge.

On October 27 Maria became a happy mother with the birth of a healthy, well-formed daughter; her name is Anna Maria. They are very happy and they walk together serving the Lord. I stayed with them for six weeks and read to them the letter from Your Honors. They send most cordial greetings. Your Honors will find enclosed pictures of us; the faces are all right, but for the rest they did not turn out very well. I had a hymnal and glasses on my lap, but the glasses did not get on the picture. I still enjoy singing very much, and I have translated a couple of stanzas into Dutch for your sister, some that I thought would be good for her. Well, my dear friend, I must close now; my head feels weary.

If my dear husband does any work at all, he does it slowly, or he is just there to direct things. Johan continues to farm as long as it is the Lord's good pleasure. He has a hired hand and the son of our nephew, who is now sixteen years old, also gives a hand; during the winter he attends school; he is a good student. We would very much like to be [living] together in Mount Pleasant, but the Lord knows what is best for us. Do surprise us soon with a reply. May the Lord be your guide in this newly begun year so that your footsteps may be in his paths, and that your feet may not slip, as Psalm 17 says. That is the sincere wish of your fellow traveler to the Heavenly Jerusalem.

Your loving Friend and Sister,
C. M. Budde-Stomp

P.S. I cannot recall the maiden name of your niece Jansje Collen [Kollen], who went to America. Does your Uncle Marinus have any children yet? I recall that you are rather fond of German hymns and that is why I wrote one at the end of your mother's letter, because there was still some room there.

Budde 47

C(ato) de Boer-Wormser to Mrs. C. M. Budde-Stomp
Baambrugge, 30 Jan. 1868

Dearly Beloved Friend!

Yesterday I was happily surprised to receive your most welcome letter and the two photos. I was happy to note from this how you also are mindful of the children of your old friends. Sincere thanks for all your kindness. I can now visualize your spouse; I had forgotten his facial features, not his figure. But you, my dear friend, I can still recall, at least in your actions. I also possess a copy of *Der Christliche Ruhetag* [*The Christian Day of Rest*]. The translation of the booklet shows me how my dead father is still held in honor and esteem in distant lands. May that work, in that language, and so concise, still be a blessing to many so that both the writer and the translator have been instrumental in promoting the more precise keeping of the fourth commandment.

Mother has written you all about my present circumstances; I thank you for your interest and concern. With the help of God I have gotten through so far, and as you so rightly write, God has not abandoned me nor forsaken me. But the cross is still there; it has been greatly relieved and changed, but it is still there. If only I may be taught thereby so that it may be evident that the Lord did not chastise me in vain. Oh! I have experienced so much good amid it all, and the Lord has helped me so often, and preserved and strengthened me. As you know, I always was a weak and tender child, but the Lord has often granted me the strength I so much needed at a given moment. And so now that it [the divorce] is over, I can do nothing but exalt and praise his name.

When the way was difficult the Lord proved to be strong, and whoever puts his trust in him will not be put to shame. And it is that experience that prompts me to persevere [in wondering] whether it may still please the Lord to convert De Boer [her ex-husband], for with the Lord nothing is impossible, and I shall continue to hope for that.

I really enjoy being here in Baambrugge. I live in a very lovely location. I look out on the Postwijk [estate], although that will soon be torn down. My nearest neighbors are devout people, and through them I have again gotten to know others, so that my friends are their friends. I enjoy very much friendship and cordiality. My neighbor says that he remembers seeing Mr. [Budde] at Postwijk; he immediately recognized his portrait. His name is Welsink. He was already living here when he was a child and went to church on the Postwijk [estate]. I shall pass on your greetings to Baas Balke [old man Balke], but he is not well just now and I cannot get there during the winter.

My oldest son is growing up. He is almost nine years old already and enjoys living in the country very much. My second little son died when he was a half-year-old, and the youngest, also a boy, is now two and a half years old, but he is retarded and a weak child. He has already suffered much, and we never thought that he would reach this age. He is a very dear child to me. It is my wish and prayer that both of them may walk in the fear of the Lord and serve him all the days of their lives.

If I had a portrait of myself I would include it, but I do not have a single one. But I have given my word [promises] for very many of them that still have to be made, and [when they are ready] I will also be glad to send you one. I also met Mr. and Mrs. Berkhout and would have recognized the latter at once but not the former. Our cousin Jansje Wormser, daughter of H. Wormser, married [Mr.] Kollen and together they went to America where he had already established himself [in business] earlier. Their reports are favorable.

Well, my dear friend, cordial greetings in the Lord to your husband and children, whom I can still recall as they were at your departure and I commend you all to the Lord.

Your Friend who loves you dearly,

C. de Boer-Wormser

Budde 48

Jansje Wüstenhoff-Wormser to Mrs. C. M. Budde-Stomp
Baambrugge, 14 February 1868

Dear Beloved Friend!

I was most delighted to receive your friendly letter of this past January, and I sincerely thank you for the pictures. The old friends of my parents have a big place in my heart!

I was pleased to see from your letter that the reports of the [Evangelical] Alliance had reached their destination in good order. After the Alliance was over, we still greatly enjoyed the addresses of Lord Radstock. It [the Alliance] has left us with many blessings, especially in Zeist, but also here. After Lord Radstock left mid-September, a Negro from North America, Captain Chester, who fought for the freedom of his people under General [Ulysses S.] Grant in the most recent [Civil] War, spoke in one of the churches. We heard him, and my husband made his acquaintance. He spent a Sunday evening with us in the company of our friends, the Berkhouts, and another evening with mother. We continue to receive friendly letters from him, and this summer he hopes to visit us again. He is studying law in London in order to become a lawyer. Following Mr. Chester, Bishop Goba(t) from Jerusalem spoke here about his forty years as a missionary, first in Abyssinia and later in Palestine. He had known King Theodorus [?] already as a child; older, he inclined very much toward the Christian [religion], but now he is said to have gone far astray. Much that has been written and said on this subject is greatly exaggerated.

Presently there are again two English evangelists preaching in the streets of Amsterdam; they speak especially and frequently in slum quarters. Last Wednesday they were in the cooperage of the beer brewery *De Gekroonde Valk* [The Crowned Falcon]. I was also present, and it was very much to my liking.

The ease of manners, so characteristic of the Americans and English, does seem a little strange to us Hollanders, and equally so their candor in acknowledging the name of the Lord in public. In May, Lord Radstock and Francis Tucker will be coming back, and perhaps Richard Weaver as well, but he is presently ill. By attending all those English "meetings" I am getting good lessons in English, if ever in my life I should be going to America. Monday evening my brother Johan was translating for the English gentlemen, and he was doing it on what formerly was called the French path, now the Willemstraat, a street where they do a great deal of evangelizing. Last night my brother [who lives] in the Elandstraat was translating for them. Wüstenhoff would also have done it, but he comes home too late from the office in the evening. I have copied a couple of stanzas from the Alliance hymnbook for you. We sang #30 with our black friend. The other one you probably know. I want to thank you for taking the trouble to copy [a number] from the German hymnal for me. We have the hymnal that Rev. Brandt uses. At the Alliance [meetings] on Sundays we often sing from that hymnal, which is printed in four languages, and then we usually sing in [three] or four languages, which makes for a jolly time.

The fact that I am writing from Baambrugge is because I am staying with my sister De Boer for a few days, and [also] a few days at the home of the preacher who is married to a cousin of Wüstenhoff. This provides an endearing conversation for my sister; the preacher and his wife are devout people. Baambrugge is a great improvement over what it used to be. The "Postwijk" [estate] has been completely demolished; I should say that they are presently tearing it down: the painted copula is gone, and so is the rear copula. All the big trees alongside the house are gone; the house is the only thing that will remain standing. The little hill will also stay; the canary [hide away] is also gone.

In the paper I read that Mr. Budde's brother remarried three or four weeks ago. Your house [in Amsterdam] is still the same as ever; you could still be living there, but it is settling a little. The canal has also been filled in and now it is a wide street, which would be nice if there were new houses. Now the old ones look ugly, but that will all improve in time. I also want to thank you for sending the pamphlets on the Sabbath as a day of rest. It is really pleasing for us to know that Father's work is still appreciated in far away America.

A great change has taken place in the Hervormde Kerk. The synod has decided that the congregations may now choose whether they wish to continue having the appointment of elders, deacons, and the calling of preachers done by the council, as was the case heretofore, or whether it will be done by the male members themselves. In those congregations that have more than 100 voting members, the election must be performed by an electoral college. In Amsterdam the electoral college consists of 270 persons, plus the [members of] council, altogether at least 400 persons. And now the orthodox party has gotten the upper hand, and only right-minded people have been appointed. Not a single Modernist [Liberal] was chosen, so that all those gentlemen are siding together, and this past Sunday a modernist preacher even refused to announce the newly appointed slate. Mr. Höveker was appointed as an elder, also Mr. Feringa, teacher at the [...] School. I do not think that there are any of your acquaintances among the others. Messrs. Pierson and Ooyens, probably known to you by name, were also appointed as elders. Wüstenhoff is a member of the Electoral College but does not have time to be a deacon, so that he was not appointed. On an earlier occasion he had also been asked to fill that office. If Father had still been living, he would doubtless also have become an elder, just as his friends who were now appointed.

And now, madame, it is about time for me to conclude again. Give cordial greetings to your children, congratulate your daughter on the birth of her child; it is my sincere wish that she may grow up [in the fear of] the Lord. I hope that the health of both of you may be adequate and that Mr. [Budde] may have less trouble with his stomach. That is also Mr. Berkhout's problem. We are both healthy. My dear husband sends his greetings, as does my sister, although she [herself] already wrote you several days ago. I also extend to all of you my sincere greetings and commend you all to the Lord.

Your friend who loves you dearly,
J. Wüstenhoff-Wormser

[a postscript from Mr. C. Wüstenhoff, Jr.]

Dear Madame, Mother wrote you about our new house. I [wish to] reciprocate and request that you and Mr. [Budde] come and stay with us when we have moved in. We have a free room for that purpose.

28 February 1868

I just want to add a few lines. Mr. Frigo, fellow sufferer with Matamoros in prison in Spain and exile in France, was here early in December and requested some contributions for the evangelization and education work among the young Spaniards in France. There was much interest in that here, especially now since we had a past martyr in our midst, who rejoices greatly that he participated in the suffering and fighting for the cause of the Lord.

And now, dear friends, greetings again.

Your affectionate Friend,
C. W. Wüstenhoff, Jr.

Budde 49

Mrs. J. Wormser-van der Ven to Mrs. C. M. Budde-Stomp
Amsterdam, 28 February 1868

Dear Beloved Friend!

Your very precious letter of last month reached us in good order. My children and I were all happy, also because of your pictures. I still vividly remember that shortly after your departure I wrote you: No ocean, no death, can break the bond that unites us together, and I still say that. We probably have exchanged most of the letters we will ever write. All of us are getting older and weaker, but we are also getting all the closer to the union where there is no more separation.

I sincerely thank you for sending the pamphlets on the Day of Rest. I received them a few days after I had mailed you my previous letter. They have been translated very well. And so we need not make use of your offer to send me another copy in case I had not received it. But my children said, "I wish that Mr. and Mrs. Budde would do so anyway, then we each would have a copy," but I may not demand that of you. Separately, I have the pleasure of sending you the pictures of Johannes Wormser and my Maria, who, the Lord willing, will be entering matrimony in July or August, and then she will be moving to Nijverdal, and that is still eight hours of traveling by train; and, mind you, my second daughter also leaving the city [for Baambrugge]. But our lot and that of our children is in the hand of the Lord; you do not even have your only daughter with you. But the Lord is present everywhere and helps where human help is lacking. Your daughter Maria certainly experienced the faithfulness of God when she had her baby. May the Lord bless the parents and offspring and make it to grow up to his honor, that is my heartfelt wish. May he also direct your way so that you may still live to enjoy some quiet and peace with your children, and that he will soon send you a buyer for your farm. I also want to thank you for writing out the hymn: "*Gott ist getreu!*" ["God is faithful!"], which is not unknown to us. We have it in our German hymnal and also sing it in Rev. Brandt's church, which I almost always attend. We also often sing German hymns at home; I find them so heart warming.

On the 3rd of this month I celebrated my 58th birthday, and for that occasion I invited Berkhout and his wife to my house and reminded them of their promises to write you. They said that they were lazy writers and [asked me] to extend their greetings and tell how they were faring when I wrote to you. I am willing to do that, but I am doing it *sub rosa* [in secret]. They bought a little house on *het Noordelijk Zaagpad* outside the Utrecht city gate, a long way down the path along which you can also take to [Stadlander?]. There are two small rooms for fl.1600. I advised them against it; it would be better for them first to rent and then to take their time in buying something. But oh, no, and now we hear nothing but complaints: it is too small, too poorly built, too far from the city, too cold, and now they want to get out of it again, the seller has deceived them, etc. But I know them; they will never be satisfied. Apart from that, Amsterdam suited them very much, and they would not want to go back to America. They received a letter from Mrs. Bousquet, which must be a very somber one. Another son of hers had gotten married, and she seems to have fallen back into a life of toiling and slaving [for a living]. What a privilege it is to entrust ourselves wholly and with all our concerns to the Lord. I also have times when I am inclined to brood and worry, but if only I can get to the point of saying, "Oh, my soul, foster that old trust and confidence again, and remember God's faithfulness, then my soul is again at rest, and I enjoy the blessed assurance that his Father's eye looks upon me in love, and that he will make all things right." [This is a paraphrase of stanza 7 of Psalm 42 in the Dutch psalter.]

Enclosed you will find brief letters from Jansje and Cato. May I request that we receive a return letter from you soon? Last Wednesday, Wüstenhoff and Jansje bought a house for fl.10,000 on the Prinsengracht between the Utrecht Road and the Amstel [River]. I have seen it; it is very nice, sturdily built, and has plenty of room so that if the Lord will continue to spare my life till my son would also finally decide to get married, then I and Henriette could go and live in with them. But as long as I have a son at home, that would be less desirable. I must say that I am beginning to feel strongly inclined to rest and leisure!

My niece and namesake, who married Kollen and went to Overijssel [Overisel] in America where he already had a store, likes it very much there; her letters are always cheerful.

Well, dear friend! May the Lord continue to spare you and your husband together for a long time. To me his face appears less wasted on this last picture than on the one I got three years ago. If there still is one of Maria and her husband, then I would very much like to request one. After all, I do have some right to it, being the one who was the first to hold her on my lap when she came into this world and still recall the little dribble well. Give my greetings to your children. My children also send greetings. Be commended to the Lord in all things.

Your Friend and Sister in the Lord who loves you Dearly,
Widow J.A. Wormser-van der Ven

P.S. Do write back soon.

Budde 50

Mr. and Mrs. J. Berkhout to D. A. Budde
Amsterdam, 14 Feb. 1868

Esteemed Brother in our Lord!

From Mrs. Wormser I learned of your reminder of not yet having received a letter from me since our departure for Europe. When we arrived at Piedmont on July 27 in reasonable well being, but exhausted (we left New York on July 4), we still had to find lodgings, which was not all that easy because everything was so very crowded. We thought it was really quite expensive.

We waited about eight days before we wrote at all, and I really was not allowed to write or exert myself in any way that involved thinking. And still I had obligations to write much to many people. To make it easier for myself and not have to write the same thing many times over, which is tedious as you know, I decided on a common answer to many people at the same time, and that via *Pella's Weekblad*, and to do so in considerable detail, and so to be done with it all at once, and then to see to it that Your Honor received a copy of the newspaper. Henry Hospers, the publisher, had asked me if I would be willing to prepare something like this for his press. However, when he received the letter, he had rearranged the content so much, that in the meantime its value for my friends was lost. If Your Honor cares to know the details, then it would be best for you to write to Mr. John Nollen, Esquire, at Pella and ask him if he will give you the letter I sent him from Piedmont. And next [ask] Mrs. Bousquet for the letter I wrote her from here, which tells of special dangers and rescues by the Lord on our journey, and which occurred in New York. My friends in Pella have to be satisfied by retelling the story, or by sharing the letter with each other. And then you would have to send a third [request] to Mr. P.[C.] Lankelma at Pella for the letter written from here, in which our experiences here [in Holland] are continued. Writing letters is not my preference, especially not when you have to say the same thing over many times, and besides paying postage for many letters is expensive.

We arrived here early in September, took lodgings for a few days, and after renting an interior furnished room for four weeks, we bought a small house outside the Utrecht city limits on the Voorpad for nineteen hundred guilders from an elder of the Seceder congregation in Amsterdam, a [Mr.] De Winter, miller of a sawmill, on the above mentioned path. The man appeared very trustworthy and pious to us, and since we had no knowledge of the value of houses, we thought we should ask him for his best price and take it. But now, when experts have a look at it, it turns out that he charged us at least seven hundred guilders too much. In addition, he sold our rainwater barrel. No one could see it, because there was a big stone opening cemented on it, and so if it does not rain for eight days, we are out of water. To fetch water from the city costs fifteen cents each time; and mind you, these were all things that we had specifically inquired about. There are many things about which he misled us, too many and too shameful to even list. We were very pleased with our purchase because we counted on having a pleasant association with the family, but that is all over with now. We were of the opinion that you need not worry about such deceit among Hollanders, much less so with a pious man and an elder like De Winter.

But we have more to tell. In an old reputable bedding shop, where no one would doubt their honesty, we bought bedding and paid fl.1.90 per pound for half down and half prime lively goose feathers. Instead, they stuffed the ticking with heavy dead stuff, and instead of new springs in the mattresses they put in old rusty ones, and there is more.

And now we think that we must say that we never encountered anything of the kind in America in business matters, in which you can only rely on the trustworthiness of the other. All this and more has aroused in me a dislike for the Netherlands.

    We are not settled in as yet. We cannot stay where we are now living; it is just too far from everything. In the city, dwellings are terribly expensive. Still, we rather liked Amsterdam. Whether we shall be living somewhere in [rural] Gelderland we still do not know. Our lot in life and the place of our dwelling is in the hands of the Lord who knows whether trouble or prosperity will serve our salvation best. If only this might always possess our heart and will; our life cannot last all that much longer, our years are mounting, my body is weak. The baths of Piedmont did me good in many respects, but slowly on, all the old (eruptions) are returning. My stomach has become so bad that as of now I can hardly eat anything without being plagued night and day by every kind of stomach ailment. I am always taking something or other [medicine], and it gets worse and worse. We like the climate very much, and many other things. You can get all kinds of help here....Comforts. Religious life has many advantages over America, at least over Pella. Here believers sing and pray together at their [meetings] and in Pella only.....[?] And so there are terribly many meetings where one can be edified, but you have to be fast enough [able to get around] to profit from that. We are too old to go from one [meeting] to another, and everything takes place at night; that is what we hate and avoid. There is little left for us in this life than to say that it is all vanity of vanities and to wait patiently for the time of our being released from this body, for after all, that will be far the best. Our best days are little more than trouble and grief, indeed they are few and evil. Oh, [my] friend, how wonderful it will be to be released from the body of sin and death, the body that always bears the marks thereof within, and to be made like unto the glorious body of Christ our Lord, and to enjoy all lovely things with him, things that no eye has seen and no ear has heard and which never has occurred to the mind of man. I did not think that you would have survived this summer, but that you would already be sharing in the joys of Heaven.

    And now, my friend, God bless you and yours with his best blessing and cause you to share in the joyous expectation of his never ending and perfect communion. We greet you and yours lovingly. Greet those who know us and believe me that we always will be,

Your affectionate Friends,
J. Berkhout and Spouse

Budde 51

M. M. and C. H. Budde to the Budde Family
Amsterdam, 21 April 1868

Esteemed Uncle and Aunt and Brother,

We were most pleasantly surprised to receive your letter and the portrait pictures, and some weeks later that of my brother. We thank you most sincerely for them and we are happy that you are all feeling well. We rejoice to say that the same is true for us. And accordingly we do not want to delay long in writing, and in mailing you a letter and portrait picture as soon as possible. On several occasions, Father and Mother bemoaned the fact that Mrs. Worms[er] did have your portraits [and they did not], but quite unexpectedly, they have now been satisfied. Although we are not seeing each other in person again, just the same, it does seem to satisfy our longing for our relatives more. That is especially true when we may observe the way in which God's help has led you and our dear brother, and will lead us all. If we give heed to the Voice that comes to us so often, there can be no doubt that we shall see each other again [in the hereafter]. Then our hope, that we shall be reunited never to separate again, will not be put to shame.

Dear Rolf, you write that you were happy that I had not forgotten you. How could we forget those who are so dear and precious to us: our Brother, and our Uncle and Aunt, to whom you and we owe so much. Oh no! Even though you are so far from us, and we might not be with you in order to express our feelings on occasion, we frequently pray for you to God, who is near to us everywhere, and who directs the lot and the ways of men. How fortunate we deem ourselves to be, that we may hear from you, that though you are alone, the Lord is with you. Continue to put your trust herein and all will be well with you. We wish to follow your advice to read the Word of God much, so that we may become partakers of the glory which is prepared for those who are steadfast in believing that we can be saved only by grace through the suffering and death of Jesus. And though our life's pathway may sometimes be difficult and precarious, the end will be sure some day, and we shall be freed from all earthly cares. Therefore, also remain contented as much as you can, and remember that though you are separated from us, it is for your own well being. For what good would it do you if you and I had jobs in the same town, and you seldom saw your parents? I have been working here for thirteen years now, but I still have never been home for even one day. That is how busy we always are there, and we have a very strict employer besides.

And now, dear Rolf, I would like to share with you some things about the family. Father's leg still has an open sore, and he has not been outside for the past half year. For the rest, he is healthy and content. Mother also manages quite well. After reading your letter, the immediate desire of both of them was to fulfill your wishes and to send their likenesses off to you. I do not doubt but that you will really be pleased with them. [A picture] of Lena will follow later, otherwise the letter gets too bulky.

Lena and her husband and children are doing fairly well, and they are all in good health. We tell them from time to time that they have an uncle in Burlington, and then they say, "I want to go there, too." The children of your sister Grietje and brother-in-law [Willem] Schaarwächter have had many, many ailments in recent years. Grietje's husband has had an open sore in his leg for the past six years. He suffers terribly because of it—working hard during the day and not sleeping at night because of the pain. As a result, they did not get ahead at all, sacrificing everything for it. The only thing that might help, according to the doctor, would be to move to Germany, but that is easier said than done. But behold, after suffering comes rejoicing. God's help once again was plain to see. Quite unexpectedly there was a letter from Germany in January asking Willem whether he might be inclined to come to Barmen to get a job as master and supervisor in a copper and iron works factory. To make a long story short, he took the job and has been there since last February to see whether it suited him, and now he is coming in May to pick up his wife and children. Amazingly, the sore in his leg is practically closed [healed], and he has almost no pain. You can imagine how happy we were about all this, and that their situation now looks somewhat better. However, moving away is still going to be strange for Grietje, now also having to take leave of everyone. But that's the way things are; the one's gain is the other's bane. We are convinced that both of them were happy and content, also when their suffering again..., and that is why we may be thankful to God for all the blessings bestowed upon them.

Well, dear Uncle, Aunt, and Brother, I have shared a few things with you. Hoping that you all may be healthy and well, I remain with many greetings to my parents, brother, and sisters,

Your ever loving Sister and Niece,
M. M. Budde

P.S. I have left a little space for Mother and Father; to fulfill your desire both of them will write a few lines. It is very difficult for them.
—

Beloved Son, Brother, and Sister,
Since Lena has told you this and that about us and the rest of the family, I do not know what else to add, since it covers everything and is in accord with our hopes and wishes; but this is only proof of our desire to write and to fulfill the desire of our Rolf.

Accept the pictures of Father and Mother, and may this also fulfill your desire just as it is our satisfaction to have yours today. [text unclear] I cannot write you with a pen all the time.

Your loving Mother

P.S. Rolf, do write us soon whether you have received this and that.

It was with the greatest effort that I succeeded in having my picture taken. May it be to you as if I am presently speaking to you personally and call out to you, "Be of good courage, my Son, your faith shall keep you, remain firm to the end, and we shall see each other again." Ever continue to put your trust in this and all will be well with you. Also receive greetings from all of us. I ever remain,

Your loving Father and Brother and Sister,
C. H. Budde

Wormser 79

C. M. Budde-Stomp to the Widow Mrs. J. A. Wormser-van der Ven
Burlington, May 1868

Beloved Friend and her Children,
We were gladdened to receive in good health a letter, dated Febr. 14th instant, from you and your children. My dear husband has been relatively free of stomach pains, though he is coughing more in the morning; then he slowly gets on the job again, to make sure that things are getting done. The Lord be praised for this relief. Our intention had been to visit the children in Mount Pleasant at Easter time. I could not write back immediately, but I took the letters along, and they were a source of real pleasure to the children. Thanks to the goodness of the

Lord they are all well; little Anna is a sweet gentle child, not all that big, but she is growing nicely and is quite chubby. After getting home I did not get around to writing right away either; we are getting to be very slow, but we must thank the Lord for all the good things we enjoy together.

We thank you sincerely for the pictures of your Maria and Johannes Wormser; how nice it is to get to know someone's face from a picture. We wish them the blessing of the Lord in their intention to enter the wedded state. May their beginning be in the fear of the Lord, and may both have the intention to walk together before the Lord. It is a great treasure on earth, under the cross and the ups and downs of life that come to every child of God, that we may walk together hand in hand. May the Lord gladden you with children, so that they may grow to become a large family that fears the Lord. Maria and Singer have not had their pictures taken yet; as soon as they do so, I will send you their pictures. Mari[a] hopes to come to Burlington with her baby this summer. Singer cannot leave his business affairs for long. She has not visited in Burlington for a year. My loved ones, it is difficult for me to write each of Your Honors separately, and that is why I shall just go on with this one; after all, it's all in the family. My head is starting to feel weaker, and so I will have to take it easy as I continue.

Your dear Cato really made me happy with her letter. May the Lord be to her a faithful covenant God in whose presence she may find shelter. He always has his eye on the needy and will be their helper, counselor, and refuge, until one day the battle is done, the course run, the faith kept. Then the Lord will wipe away all tears from our eyes. May the Lord grant this to us all my dear Jansje.

Mrs. Wüstenhoff, to what trouble you have gone to write me so much, your old friend. How wonderful love is; it passes from generation to generation, this love that has its roots in the Lord. And your dear husband, Mr. Wüstenhoff, has attested to his delight that you have in your midst one who suffers and struggles for the name and the cause of the Lord. I have read much by Matamoros, who has given us great joy that the Lord works in this way, and that the new day is dawning (Thy Kingdom come). Spain, where Paul once set foot, is being opened to the gospel. I rejoice in the thought of being together with all who fear the Lord in incorruptibility, eternally to praise and glorify the Lord. He has purchased for himself a congregation from among all tongues, peoples, and nations to glorify him forever. The [Evangelical] Alliance has had much fruit in our old fatherland; our ecclesiastical situation does seem to be in a winter [of deep sleep]. May the Lord graciously grant us a spring [of new life].

And you, my dear Johan, whom I received on my lap upon your entrance into this world, have you set your foot on the way of life? You yourself answer before the Lord and say with the poet of Psalm 17 verse 5, "Hold up my goings in thy paths, that my footsteps slip not"; that is my heartfelt wish for you. For the present, our son Johan and his family are doing reasonably well; in March his wife again had a stillborn son, their thirteenth child, and again she was not well the entire time. He does have his cross, but in all of this he is a very moderate man, believing that the Lord imposes the cross and gives strength to bear it, for his own good, so that he may be tried and tested by it.

Via Pella we received a letter from the Berkhouts. From the letter it is evident that they did not find Amsterdam to be a Paradise either; what can we say but

| *Hoog, omhoog mijn ziel naar boven* | Look up, up on high, my soul, |
| *Hier beneden is het niet.* | It [paradise] is not down here below. |

[Source unknown].

Be so kind as to give them our greetings. Your Honors wrote us something new: the remarriage of our brother Ede Budde. We had expected to get a letter from him but have been waiting in vain so far. And now, my dear friends, it is your turn; do surprise us by a letter. All my children join in sending you all cordial greetings, and so do I; my dear husband will write a letter of his own. May the grace of the Lord be and remain with us all.

Your dearly loving Sister and Friend in the Lord,
C. M. Budde-Stomp

P.S. In Mount Pleasant I heard someone from Pella say that [Jan] Hengeveld from Aalsmeer had hanged himself in Chicago; what a frightful ending. Because of delay this letter was held up.

Wormser 80

D. A. Budde to the Widow Mrs. J. A. Wormser-van der Ven
Burlington, 20 June 1868

Esteemed Friend and Sister in our Savior Jesus Christ!

I gladly comply with the wish of your esteemed children to again send you six copies of *De Christelijke Rustdag* [*The Christian Day of Rest*]. I would have liked for Berkhout to take them along last year, but I did not dare burden him with them. At the time B[erkhout] asked me whether I made any profit on them. "O no," I replied, "I am not doing this for temporal gain, indeed not! I only had them printed in the hope that they might be useful to strengthen in wavering souls the conviction that this commandment has the same force as all the others." Nor was that the purpose of your husband of blessed memory, my esteemed friend and brother, in putting together and publishing this article. And it was not to gather treasures for this world, to be a restless slave to them. Indeed not! Love of God and his Truth was compensation enough to rejoice freely in the thought that it may still serve the kingdom of God. And since here in America the Prince of Darkness does everything in his power to gratify his followers, even going so far that great mass meetings are held, in order, if God were to allow it, to finally destroy the commandment of God by a majority vote.

God, the Lord, reigns. In many congregations that love the truth, they are now also insisting on preaching on the Sabbath. Thus it was, and is, my goal to distribute these pamphlets about the Christian Day of Rest far and wide, wherever there is opportunity, and in this way the works of Brother Wormser will also continue to speak in America. I have already received a personal letter from the editor of a Christian weekly in Cleveland, in the state of Ohio, saying that the article on the Sabbath was a very good one. It was also printed in a *duitsch* (*sic deutsch*) [German] theological work named *Der Wächter*, which appears every three months. In this way scholars also get to know about it, and it is even being sent to Germany. Although Wormser has died, he lives on. He lives in my memory, and I often see him in my dreams at night, as I knew him in Amsterdam twenty years ago. Not what I see now when I look at a picture of him, for, as far as I am concerned, he had changed a great deal already. "It is not all that long ago that I was engaged in a conversation with my friend Wormser, and told him that on several occasions I was in his presence in my dreams, and W[ormser] asked me whether there was really anything to this? I said that this very moment attested to that; when I was going up the street to the church, outside, looking through the windows, I saw you sitting there. After the minister had pronounced the benediction and left, we stayed behind together for a little while in the front part of the church (the assembly also was still in the church), and W[ormser] invited me to spend the evening with you all; to which I said, that is fine, I have not even seen your new house yet. After a bit Wormser goes by, a little to the side, and in a loud voice calls out to the assembly in German: '*Lasset uns dem Herrn ein Loblied singen zur Ehre Seiner Gnade.*' ('Let us sing a hymn of praise to the Lord in honor of his grace'). It seemed as if the entire assembly wanted to kneel, and I awakened, and behold, it was a dream."

And now my esteemed friend, our pilgrim journey is coming to an end. We have enjoyed genuine friendship with each other. I am already sixty-eight years old. There is nothing new in telling you that we are getting weaker. It is proof that our earthly home too can be broken up soon, and what then? Then we will be going to the mansions of the Father that Christ has prepared for us, that we may live in them together forever praising God in undisturbed bliss. Just read the promises in Jeremiah 32:38-41. A respected writer says of them: "O, what promises these are! What more can our weak faith desire to put an end to all its doubts. How great is God's goodness to his children, that he, knowing their frame and that they are dust [Psalm 103:14], for their good and that of their children, has laid a foundation for their faith on which they can build without fear, and having been established on it, they can fight the good fight of faith, being assured of the victory." [Source not given.] And should we not, my esteemed friend, then profess the Lord's grace and faithfulness, for ourselves as well as for our children?

I have deep sympathy with Cato in the changing fortunes of her life. She too is embraced in the promises [of God]. I also rejoice in the well-being of your children. Give our greetings to all your children. The Lord bless you and your children. And I conclude with the prayer that you and yours, and we and ours, may be strengthened, whether it be in beginning, or in continuing, to walk the way to the heavenly Zion, where eternal joy abides, and where sorrowing and sighing will forever flee away.

With prayers for your soul's well-being,
D. A. Budde

Budde 52

> Mrs. J. Wormser-van der Ven and J. Wüstenhoff-Wormser
> to Mrs. C. M. Budde-Stomp
> Amsterdam, September 1868

Beloved Friend and Lady Friend,

When I returned home in July, to my great joy I found one of your letters, always so precious to me. I was most happy to learn that both of you were in reasonably good health. Mine...[text missing] not over. Last April [I suffered] much from constriction in my chest, which weakened me very much; I thought that my end was near. However, the [eternal] counsel of the Lord [for my life] had not run its course. I recovered a little, but very slowly, until in June, on the advice of Doctor Rive, I had to go to Bloemendaal north of Haarlem, because he said that I needed fresh air for further healing, and I needed some ocean air. I spent five weeks there, but that did not do much good, because I probably will keep that constricted chest and always have to look for relief from my ailment by suppuration. Sometimes I am terribly constricted and cannot stand anything that tires me in the least. The doctor would have preferred that I stay in the open air longer, but since the marriage of my Maria had been set for August 13, I could not be away from home any longer, since the necessary preparations had to be made. Maria has been taking care of housekeeping matters in Nijverdal for three weeks already.

My house seems very quiet now; three of my children have already left home. And while I was out in the country for a week, I received a letter from my son, Johan, saying that he was [getting engaged] to Kaatje, the youngest daughter of Höveker, a darling girl, who fears the Lord. He had been going ahead with this with my approval when I left, and I had to thank the Lord that He had prospered his way so. Höveker is also very pleased and said to me, "Höveker and Wormser: your husband and my wife [both deceased] would certainly be pleased with that." At least he is also in a good religious circle, which is very important for a young man, and he spends many of his free evening hours there. They probably will have to wait with getting married because his income is not adequate as yet.

I have also lost my son and daughter Wüstenhoff as my neighbors; in March they bought a house on the Prinsengracht between the Utrecht Road and the Amstel River. They could take possession in mid-August; now they have moved in for a fortnight. It is very nice, has six rooms, a kitchen, basement, and a garden and cost him fl.10,000. It is much too big for them right now, but if the Lord should spare my life and Johan would just get married, then Henriette and I would move in with them. (The older I get, the more assistance I need). And then I could break up my housekeeping. After my death, my underaged [daughter] would move in with them anyway. Now what do you have to say? Haven't we spent an important summer? Until now Jansje is still without children, but I do not know what is a worse trial, not to have them or, like your Johan, to have to lose them again immediately. I am glad to see that he bears his cross with resignation.

Esteemed Friend! I want to thank you most sincerely for myself and for my children for sending the pamphlets on the Day of Rest. They were very happy to get them; it is very important to them that the friend of their Father has that much interest in it. I need not tell you that my husband of blessed memory is always in my thoughts. Just the same it is a precious thought to me that you and Mr. Groen van Prinsterer still keep him in mind. There is some truth to your dream. Not one of us has seen the new [heavenly] dwelling of Wormser, but our life's journey is getting shorter and our Savior said, "In my Father's house there are many mansions," and so there is also a place for all of us. May the Lord grant that no one from your generation and mine will be missing there, and may this not turn out to be a dream but the real thing.

Berkhout and his wife are now living across from me, but presently they are again off to the baths of Piedmont. He still persists in wanting to restore his old weak body to health, wastes a lot of money on it, and is getting to be peevish and grumpy. I have advised him that he should give up that hope once and for all and rather bear his trial submissively, and to look for the land of [rest and peace]. But they have earned a lot of money and their hearts seem attached to that. They hardly dare to live a good bourgeois life on it. And then they still lose it [their money] in other ways. They have a much smaller home than I have; they sold all their books in Pella and have been here for a year now, and always I hear the lament that they do not have any books. Well, I do have a library with many good works in it, which my husband acquired for the poor who cannot afford to buy books. But I cannot lend those books to them, then I would just encourage them in their stinginess, and what good does all that reading do if it does not produce any fruits?

And there, dear friends, I have shared some things with you again. My children know that I am writing you. I will ask them if they have an opportunity to add anything, and in case they do, I will wait with mailing this for a few days. My dear Cato and her little children are reasonably well, but this week I heard that the situation of her husband is most grievous; he is poor and in such a condition that they are making work of getting him into a hospital. How unhappy sin makes people already here [in this life]!

There is a rumor making the rounds that you have sold your farm for a good price, but I have said that I do not believe it, because then I would also have heard about it from you.

And now, dear friends! Give my greetings to your children and to your married children, and you are commended to the Lord by,

Your dearly loving Friend,
Widow J. A. Wormser-van der Ven

Sept. 15

Dear Friends!

I did not have an opportunity to write you separately, but being at Mother's today, she asked me to close the letter for her, and could I add a few lines. I have no news at all. I have been very busy moving, and now I have a big washing. And so I am still very tired every day. I have asked Mr. Berkhout if I might read the *Christian Intelligencer* [a Reformed Church in America magazine], which I enjoy very much. You probably know it too. [There are] lovely short selections that appeal to me very much; I began translating some from English to the best of my limited ability in the language, just for my own sake, and read them out loud at our Dorcas Society. Then a gentleman came by who had been converted during the [Evangelical] Alliance, and I let him read them too. He asked me if he could have them and asked me to continue [translating them]. He is a deacon in our congregation and could make good use of them in visits to the poor. He had some of the articles published in a Christian periodical, and Rev. Huet used them in the pulpit. So dear friends, you see how fond I still am of America. How I would like to attend a prayer meeting in Fulton Street.

The deacon I referred to is the son of Rev. Van Velzen in Weesp, whom you must have met at Mrs. Zeelt's. But it is not the Seceder Van Velzen; this minister is Hervormd (Reformed).

The Dorcas Society of which I wrote is led by Mrs. Höveker during the winter, and then the thirteen of us are busy sewing for poor children, who cannot attend Sunday school because they lack clothes. We visit the parents, etc. Mr. Höveker generally comes by to explain a chapter from the Bible, and that is interspersed with singing.

Well, dear friends, I do not have any more time; my brother is waiting for the letter. Warmest greetings.

Your Loving Friend,
J. Wüstenhoff-Wormser

Wormser 81

C. M. Budde-Stomp to the Widow Mrs. J. A. Wormser-van der Ven
Mount Pleasant, November 1868

My Beloved Friend and her Children,

Early in October, while we were still in Burlington, we received your esteemed letter; we also received the announcement of the wedding between Mr. J. Wormser and your dear Maria. Your vacillating health reminds us of the breaking down of our earthly tabernacle with its warning: O man, put your house in order, for you shall die.

We have had a hard time of it, but the Lord sustained us mightily. The rumor about the sale of our farm spread early and quickly; the right buyer came along and everything moved along rapidly. On Wednesday, September 30, we sold the place including everything on it such as horses, cows, wagons, etc., for $10,000. Already on Thursday the people, a family of nine, started moving in with Jan, for they had just come up from the South. They had made a journey to Germany, but things did not suit them there, and they came back to Burlington, where they had a single room and boarded with a relative. They are people of means, and they really liked our place. Jan sent his family to friends in the city, and he remained with the people to assist them in taking over the market stand. Our cousin Roelf also stayed with them, because he knew how to care for the animals and besides he could do the farm work with which they were not yet acquainted. They had had a store in the South, but the man had been a gardener in Germany and now they were more interested in living on the land. We immediately started packing as best we could, and on Monday we were happy to arrive at our children's place in Mount Pleasant. Johan first took care of all the business matters and arrived eight days later with his family. It was the wish of both Johan and Singer that they should go into business together. May the Lord grant them his blessing for their mutual well-being and satisfaction. Johan bought a house and garden not far from Singer's place, very pleasant with a lovely view, for $2,225, and he is already living there. Our intention was to stay with Maria for the winter. I resisted going on our own; the winter is hard for us to take, and having strange help [in the house] is not always very pleasant either. We will leave the future to the Lord. From our earliest years he has been our hiding place in dangers, etc. [Psalm 90]. Things may be ever so good for us here below, but there always remains a void until we enter the rest that is laid away for the people of God.

You must have heard of the passing away of Rev. Scholte. Johan's mother-in-law just happened to be in Pella enjoying herself. She related that his illness was but of short duration; he became indisposed, and for several hours the doctor did not think that he was out of danger. After that he felt better, so that he was walking about in his room. On Tuesday afternoon he said to his wife that he had developed pain in his side; she was to prepare a mustard plaster for him. He lay down in his bed, and mind you, it was to die there. The family scarcely had time to get there [before he died]. He was laid on a bier, so that all who still wished to see him could do so, and he was buried on Thursday. It did shock me. You are aware how our relations with him have been; I would greatly prefer to remain silent on that subject.

In our reading we noted that Rev. Budding had deviated from the orthodox truth [of Reformed theology]. Did you hear anything about that? How often people change over time, and therefore, it is he who perseveres to the end who will be saved. In the papers I saw a reference to the Rev. W. Raman; is that a son of our Raman? The ecclesiastical situation among the Reformed people here is not so very favorable either. Again there are secessions in many places, and they call themselves the true Reformed [church]. [What would we do] if the Lord had not promised in his Word that he himself would sanctify and purify his church? The mountains may give way and the hills shake, but my mercy will never leave you, and the covenant of my peace will not waver; thus says the Lord who has mercy on you. Let us then hold fast, as seeing him who is invisible [Hebrews 11:27]. After all, he shall guide his church into the eternal rest; here it remains the struggling church, and blest are we if may be members thereof.

We are all reasonably well. Father's stomach and chest are also doing fairly well; if I exert myself a little, I have heart palpitations. Living in with Maria gives me much relief.....Also Johan and his family and Singer and Maria....[are well?]. The little Anna is now a year old, she almost walks by herself. She is very sweet although at times it is also evident that she was begotten of sinful seed, and so she needs to be transplanted into the olive tree [Christ] in order to bear good fruit. And so slowly on we get older.

And now about your Johan. In his early youth, his father called him the American farmer, and now he is already about to take his father's place. I find his decision to take a daughter of Mr. Höveker [as a bride] very sweet. It is my wish that they may have the desire to receive the Lord into their hearts and homes. He is our best friend, indispensable in life and death, and the only one with whom we can stand before God. We thank your dear Jansje, Mrs. Wüstenhoff Wormser, that she still continues to think of us regularly. May the Lord grant her the desire and the buoyancy of spirit to labor for the kingdom of God.

Greetings also to your dear Cato. The Lord will make all things well; may she ever cleave unto and follow him. And greetings to all your children and their spouses. Greetings also to Johan and his wife; he is very busy preparing for his new profession and getting his house in order. Maria and Singer send greetings. Gladden us soon again with a letter, that is, as long as we are privileged to share our circumstances with each other. It still gives me joy to see how we have communicated what was in our hearts and what we have experienced with each other, and how we were helpful to each other in everything. Dear friend, I commend you and yours to the Lord.

Your Friend, who thinks of you always,
C. M. Budde-Stomp

P.S. Caroline Schilp came to us with the friendly request that, when we send you a letter, we inquire whether you could report something about her oldest brother Portengen, to whom I had written several letters on behalf of Mrs. Schilp, and to which there has been no reply as yet. In hopes of an answer, I continue to pray for the Lord's choice blessing on you and yours. Your friend and Brother in Christ Jesus,

D. A. Budde

Our address is the same, Mount Pleasant instead of Burlington.

Budde 53

Johanna Schellinger to Mrs. C. M. Budde-Stomp
Alkmaar, 5 June 1869

Highly Esteemed Friend,

Your messages received in February [Wormser 81] were a true source of rejoicing for me, since I might learn from them that the good God had still spared the lives of you all, and that you all may experience reasonably good health. How much has happened since I received your last messages, and what changes in our way of life have befallen us. The Lord be thanked; it was all to the good.

How we are reminded each day that putting our trust in the Lord is not in vain. My heart rejoices that you realized your wishes in the sale of your farm, and that now your wish to live with your children has also been fulfilled. May that satisfaction be yours for a long time, so that you may rejoice in each other's presence for many years to come. It is really a true joy to be with one's own at an advanced age. That relieves many burdens.

It made me happy that Naatje married someone whom was known to your family. For, if you would had had any objections to it and had called that to her attention, she surely would have listened to your advice. After all, she owes you so infinitely much, and I am sure that she values your friendship very highly. It seems to me that it will be a real pleasure for her when she can pay you and your family a visit. I just hope that they will be happy together; all the more so since she was again a household help for strangers, and her life was not all that pleasant. She will certainly experience the difference now that she has someone who bears life's burdens with her, and so they can make life more agreeable for each other.

My esteemed friend, don't you find it attentive of the Ruler of our Destinies that it was exactly we, who love each other so much, that had to enter upon a new way of living [having to move] at the same time. For I too received a notice from *Het Hofje* that a death had occurred in September and that I would have to make arrangements to fill the vacancy by November. It really was a sacrifice for me that I had to say farewell to my quiet days and freedom. I had occupied the little house that suited me so well for about ten years, and with so much satisfaction, that I was scared when I received that message so unexpectedly. To be sure, it is more economical, and now I can give a little more to others, and that is a true delight for me, and I would be sinning if I did not gratefully acknowledge that. This *Hofje* is a small [enclosed] area, and three single women live there. Two of them have reached the age of eighty and have been here for thirty years already; they are not exactly pleasant people to associate with. My best lady-friend, who was loved by everybody, was just taken from me [by death], and I have to take her place, but that is how things are in this world. Everything has its bright side and its dark side, and all of us are under the Rule of the Lord, and therefore my only hope is that I may go my quiet, cheerful way, wherever the Lord leads me. How often man proposes, but the Lord disposes the way we are to go.

I have observed that again in plans made by my cousin. His wife was often indisposed and very much disliked the busy life of their bakery, especially in the fall. So, my cousin bought a house suitable for them to live a quiet life, and into which they expected to move in May. But the Lord took her to his eternal home. She died in November '68. And now my cousin is staying in the bakery with his two children. His son works with him, and his daughter runs the housekeeping. Both of them are doing all they can for their father.

And now, my esteemed friend, my sincere wish is that Your Honors may receive this letter in well-being. I would have liked to write you much earlier, but my indisposition prevented me from doing so. I have much rheumatism in my head, so that reading tires me quickly, but thank God I am healthy again. I herewith send you and your family my cordial greetings, and remain,

Your loving Friend,
Johanna Schellinger

Budde 54

Johanna Schellinger to Naatje
Alkmaar 5 June [1869]

Much Esteemed and Beloved Niece,

How surprised I was to receive the notice that you were married. It was most pleasing to me that I might learn that your marriage partner was not a total stranger to you, since he had been working for some of your best friends. Heartfelt congratulations to you, dear friends, on your union. May it increase the joy of life for both of you; and may you also remain constant for each other in joy and sorrow. To that end may the good God grant you his indispensable blessing and, even if things are not always clear in the future, then keep in mind that a loving Father governs your lot in life, and that no one is ever put to shame who puts his trust in him. And shall not he, who granted us so infinitely much in the Son of His Love, will he not also cause all things to work together for good; if only it might always be gratefully remembered.

Dear Nephew and Niece, it seems to me that the two of you are busy enough. [Just so] the job you have started working at does not demand so much of your youthful strength that it might not be good for you. Your dear mother, for whom heavy lifting and hard work was the joy of her life in her youth, suffered much from a discomfort [disablement?], which she took with her to her grave. I hope that that there will be some relief for both of you soon, and that your work may be somewhat more [productive] so that you do not have to think to yourself every night, "I just do not have time to come to myself," and so you might forget the one thing needful, which our good Savior regarded so highly in the noble Maria.

What a great pleasure you would do me, if you could send me pictures of both of you. O, be so kind, and make work of it. That would really make me happy, being able to see you, since we will not behold each other from nearby in this life. I hope that both of you may receive this letter in good health.

I have not been well all winter, but I think that much of it is the result of fatigue, since I have now been placed in a small courtyard [of houses for elderly widows and single women]. Because of the moving, I probably was cold a good deal, and that is not the best for rheumatism. I suffered much from headaches, so that I constantly had to postpone writing to you. But now, thanks to the goodness of God, I am somewhat better again. The last Sunday in May, I went to church again. I was confined to quarters for a long time, but when God's Word illumines your soul, you can march on the pathway of life with joy. And now, dear Nephew and Niece, receive cordial greetings from,

Your loving Aunt
Johanna Schellinger

My address is now: At the Hofje of Oosthoorn
    On the Koningsweg

Budde 55

Mrs. J. Wormser-van der Ven to Mrs. C. M. Budde-Stomp
Amsterdam, 16 August 1869

Dearly Beloved Friend,
Days and years fly by like thoughts and to my shame I must acknowledge that I have been much too negligent in responding to your dear letter. I was pleased to learn that you were now living in with Marie and that you enjoy more rest there. I will be following your example soon, the Lord willing, for my Johan is getting married in mid-September and is already in Höveker's business; and beginning at New Year, the business will become Höveker and Son. Since Höveker does not have a son, the marriage must first be solemnized and become a matter of public record. Höveker found in my son a man of real ability and solid quality; although he had many persons seeking to become business partners and soliciting the hand of his daughter, he has always turned them down. But Johan was seeking the daughter's hand and never thought of getting into the business, and now Höveker himself has offered it to him. They have rented an upstairs in the Reguliersdwarsstraat near the Koningsplein, because Höveker will continue living on the Heerengracht. Johan also has to get to know the [publishing] business first. As soon as Johan gets married, we, Henriette and I, will move in with Wüstenhoff and Jansje as soon as possible. Then I will have fewer cares, and we will enjoy each other's company.

My house has been rented, with an October occupancy date, to a son of Lieutenant Smit; he is a preacher in the Churches Under the Cross. However, a month ago a Synod of Middelburg decided to unite the Seceders and the Churches under the Cross, and so now there are three preachers and three churches in Amsterdam. But I hear that the members are not as much in agreement on this as are the preachers.

The tiding of the death of Ds. [Rev.] Scholte I received very quickly through Berkhout; in addition, his widow sent me a printed letter. His death also struck me; and so our contemporaries pass on. If only we might learn from this to keep our lanterns burning like the wise maidens, so that we may be prepared when the Bridegroom comes.

The rumor that Rev. [H. J] Budding[h] is a Modernist is generally known; he is said to deny the most precious truths. Oh, what is man? Let him who stands see to it that he does not fall. Rev. Raman is the son of an old acquaintance of ours. He stopped by at my house about three years ago in order to drop off a message from Rev. Brummelkamp. He is a spoiled little man who probably is not proud of the fact that his aged mother still works as a dry nurse. I did not like him at all.

I brought the Portengen family the message of Mrs. Schilp, but her brother Carel told me that he had written her. She had another brother, Willem, in the [Netherlands] East Indies, who has been away for twenty-five years; he is now here on leave and intends to apply for his pension. He is to become a bridegroom next Thursday, and his bride does not want to go to the East.

Like the rest of us, my sister Mietje is getting old. Her daughters still have not gotten married. They wear such dressy clothes that it is nauseating to see. By comparison, my daughters and Kaatje Höveker look like their maids, and still it does not do them any good.

In the month of April, Johannes and Maria stopped in to see me. I still had not seen any of their home furnishings, so Henriette and I went along with them and stayed a full three weeks. It was a delight to see how happy and contented they are together; the fear of the Lord lives in their home and in their hearts. They have been married a year now, but occasionally she feels the need to go see me and the family. She will be coming here again in September for the wedding of Johan. There still is no prospect of an increase in the family.

My health and that of my children is satisfactory; only the constriction in my chest is not getting any better. That makes every movement and speaking as well difficult for me. We are hastening to our end. This very day the mortal remains of Mr. Horst are being buried in Utrecht; he suffered a great deal from (dropsy?). Rev. Hoedemaker from America, who is a nephew of Höveker, is married to a daughter of Horst and is the preacher of the Hervormde Kerk in Veenendaal in [the province of] Gelderland.

Are you also intending, the Lord willing, to go to New York in September 1870, to attend the Evangelical Alliance? You probably are aware that the English brethren, after having enjoyed themselves so much here, do not wish to wait any longer. They will seek to work out an agreement for getting the passage price reduced, and there is an open invitation to one and all. They will also do all they can to arrange for lodgings for the foreign guests. All my children and their spouses, from the oldest to the youngest, would like to go, but it will take more time and money than they have at their disposal. I personally would also still enjoy it, but I think I will count on the Alliance in the hereafter. It will not be a perfect delight until we are united with our dear loved ones who have entered [eternal] rest before us.

My dear friend, I too constantly think of our intimate contacts with each other; granted that human beings are happy creatures. I also still have friends, but that intimacy, that sharing of joy and sorrow with each other, I think, a person can enjoy only once in a lifetime. You and I shared that and so did our husbands. I always sense that very deeply, and that is why your departure to America struck me so hard. But I console myself with the thought that Christians never see each other for the last time here [in this life].

I have to tell you one more thing. The first day that Johan worked at Höveker's, he sold the first copy of "Infant Baptism" by his father. That really touched me. Well, my dear friend, as a result of waiting so long, you are now getting much news and a long letter, and now it is your turn. Do make me happy in my new home soon with reports about yourself, your husband, and your children. My address is Widow J.A. Wormser/ Prinsengracht between the Utrecht Road and the Amstel River/ at the home of Mr. C. W. Wüstenhoff. Receive greetings from all my children. Jansje is a member of the Dorcas Society that visits and cares for poor children. Cato and Maria and Henriette each lead a Sunday school class. May they be a blessing to all in their work. Give my cordial greetings to your husband and dear children, and may you yourself receive the most cordial greetings, be embraced in thought, and commended to the Lord by

> Your loving Friend and Sister in our Lord,
> Widow J.A. Wormser-van der Ven

P.S. I still have to inform you that Lijsen's second wife died a half year ago, and now at the age of sixty-nine he is going to marry the seamstress. His twenty-seven-year-old daughter could do a very good job of keeping house. The family is angry about it, but he pays no attention. If the children don't like it, they can lump it.

Wormser 82

> C. M. Budde-Stomp to the Widow Mrs. J. Wormser-van der Ven
> Mount Pleasant, 20 Dec. 1869

My Dear Friend and her children,

We received your welcome letter on Sept. 2, and it found us reasonably well. We also received the wedding announcement of your son Johan with Miss C. J. Höveker. It gives us great joy, and we wish them the blessing of the Lord for their temporal but also their eternal well-being. May the Lord grant them the privilege of his presence, which the Lord himself linked to marriage in his first miracle.

In the month of August I read in a German weekly, *De[r] Evangelist*, that the death of that godly man Gerhardt Terste[e]gen [1697-1769] had been commemorated in Mühlheim [Germany], and that a great host of people had participated in the festive occasion; there were even two from neighboring Holland. The oldest one was a [Mr.] Höveker, a book dealer from Amsterdam, a man with a *wunderbaren Lebensführung* [amazing life story], etc. By means of his publishing business he has contributed much for the spread of Terste[e]gen's writings in the Dutch language. You can imagine how pleased I was to read the above in an American publication, especially since I had been blessed by the reading of Terste[e]gen's writings in my youth. When we were still courting, my [future] husband gave to me as gifts: *Das Blumengärtlein* [*The Flower Garden*] with its hymns and *Das fromme Glückspiel* [*The Pious Lottery*]; we still prize them. Many [of his] hymns have been taken over in High German hymnals. Another, *Die Brosame die von des Herrn Tische fielen* [*The Crumbs that fell from the Lord's Table*], had refreshed us greatly. Dear friend, if you can get it in Holland, by all means do so; I have no doubt but that you will like it.

We really enjoy living in with Singer and Maria and thank the Lord for this arrangement, which enables us to take it easy; but it is a great change, [instead of increasing] to decrease and to become the lesser ones. It is so contrary to our nature; we feel as Paul [sic Peter] did: "When thou wast young, thou girdest thyself....but when thou shalt be old, ...another shall gird thee" [John 21:18] and thus to be dependent. Let us hold fast to the promise, "Those that are planted in the house of the Lord shall flourish in the courts of our God. They shall bring forth fruit in old age; they shall be fat and flourishing; to show that the Lord is upright" [Psalm 92:13-14].

I felt like answering immediately, but I wanted to wait just a little longer. On Nov. 4, our daughter, Maria, was safely delivered of a well-formed daughter, named Elisabeth Christina. The Lord made all things well. A little one like that makes for a lot of work, and a grandmother can also do her share. Last summer we made a little trip to Burlington with Maria and her little daughter and visited the farm. The people were very friendly, but we do not feel at home there any longer.

A bridge has been constructed over the Mississippi on which trains cross. A section of the bridge can be opened mechanically to allow steamboats to pass. We had only seen this construction from a distance before, but now we saw it from close up, on the bridge. How great are the works man makes; like the Suez Canal and others, in his own good time the Lord will make use of them for his purposes. And so we gradually approach our end. We visited a brother-in-law of Johan in New London, a couple of miles from Mount Pleasant. They had been married eight years and had just gotten a daughter. They had been very quiet about it up to the time she was born.

I gave a young Dutch girl, who was going to visit her parents who lived in Pella, a letter for Mrs. Bousquet to let her know about our change [of residence]. She wrote a sweet letter in return; mentally, she is somewhat retarded. The trip to the Netherlands did not have a good effect on her life in Pella. Her oldest son, P[iet] H[ein], married Maria Scholte. Twice she brought a child into the world under very difficult circumstances; the first lived a few hours, the second not at all. Now people are saying that they fear for her life, should it happen again; her health is not all that good. She was greatly affected by the death of her father, and she still has not recovered from that. Mrs. B[ousquet] is living in with P[iet] H[ein]. Saartje married a doctor; her father made her go to church. Johanna has two children who still are not baptized. The church of Rev. Scholte was dissolved; the congregation has rented the church from Mrs. Scholte and they have called a Rev. Vos, I do not know from where. Henri B[ousquet] is still unmarried; the others have married and are doing well.

On Dec. 13 the Rev. Oggel also was called from this life after a lengthy, and at the end, a very painful suffering. He was a faithful servant of the Lord and was a blessing to many. His work was very different from that of H. P. S[cholte]. The Rev. Vander Meulen preached the funeral sermon on Thursday. I am not aware if you know that he lost his dear spouse very suddenly and that he went to the Netherlands after that. Did you happen to meet him?

Our church is making slow progress. Our minister has a narrow outlook, and that is not very pleasant for us, but we must abide the Lord's time; he will work out everything according to the counsel of his will. Even if we live, I do not think that any of us will be visiting the [Evangelical] Alliance, not from disdain, but their situation [Johan and Maria] will not allow it. Our Johan and his family are in reasonably good health; his son is reading Wagenmaker and really enjoys it.

The girl goes to school and helps her mother. Lena's mother also lives in with them, and so they live together pleasantly. Separately, I am sending you a picture of A. Singer, Maria, and their oldest daughter. The little one would not sit still, and that is why it turned out as it did. Did I rightly conclude from your letter that Cato is again [living] near you? That would make me very happy. Maria wants to string a necklace for the little baby to wear around her neck from the small blue beads of the little purse Cato made for her when she went to America, because she is very plump, and as a reminder of C[ato].

Cordial greetings from us all to your dear Jansje, Mrs. Wüstenhoff, and her husband. If they should ever cross over to America, we should be happy to have them visit us. We also wish your son Johan and his spouse and all your children and in-laws the blessings and the peace of the Lord. Cordial greetings also from me, and I commend you to the injunction of the Lord: Let your Widows trust in me.

Your Friend and Sister in the Lord,
affectionately thinking of you,
C. M. Budde-Stomp

Budde 56

Johanna Schellinger and Johanna Akkerman
to Mrs. C. M. Budde-Stomp
Alkmaar, 20 October 1870

Most Esteemed Friend,

Your honor's letter was most welcome, and I must attest to you my thanks for the trouble you have taken to tell me various things, which always afford me so much pleasure. My hearty congratulations, dearest friend, with the increase in your lovely family and that it has pleased the Lord to again bring rejoicing to your beloved daughter with this pledge of the marriage bond. I hope that this joy may later be increased by the birth of a son. I hope that the darling little one may grow well, and that you may long enjoy the blessing of being grandparents. What a pleasure it is that you can see each other so often. How many people are separated from their parents, like happened [here] recently?

A young Woman [upper class], an acquaintance whom I often used to visit at her home, has now had the good fortune that the life of her third son might be spared. And thanks to the blessing of the Lord, it became a darling, prosperous child, to the great joy of the entire family circle. Mr. [unnamed] was a paymaster here and received notice from The Hague to leave and move to [the province of] Noord-Brabant. That was indeed advantageous for him, but a great disappointment to the grandparents and other family members, and, since they were such nice people to associate with, it was a great loss to me too. The Mrs. was also very sweet to me. She had the same name as my best Lady, the one whom I was privileged to serve for so long. I received a picture of the dear child. Initially things did not go well for it, since he was so restless and they could not quiet him down. But the Lord suddenly had music played, and then he suddenly quieted down so that everything turned out well. He is now eight months old.

I hope, esteemed friend, that my writing will not be tedious to you, for after all, out of the abundance of the heart, the mouth speaks, and you do want to air things on occasion. But I know of your interest, which was always so sweet toward us, so much so that I need not be worried about that. I am glad to hear that Akkerman has again gotten a job. It is probably better to be a shop hand than the boss, since all that machinery brings on so many changes. I am most happy that my niece was so fortunate in her first delivery and that the Lord blessed her with a speedy recovery. She certainly has many reasons for gratitude, considering how beneficently her life's pathway has been directed until now by a most loving Father, who wishes to be a loving Father to all of us in our life's walk if only we honor the Father in the Son of his love, our savior, in a holy walk of life.

And now, my esteemed friend, I hope that you and your family may receive this [letter] in the best of health and well being, in which I also find myself to be through the blessing of the Lord. After loving greetings I remain,

Your Loving Friend,
Johanna Schellinger

25 March 1871

Dear Aunt,

We send you herewith our pictures, hoping that you may receive them in good health. We are all well. The little Willie is really growing and already has teeth, crawls all over the floor, and already wants to stand by the foot-warmer. After loving greetings from me and my husband,

Your loving Niece,
Johanna Akkerman

Budde 57

Mrs. J. Wormser-van der Ven to Mrs. C. M. Budde-Stomp
Amsterdam, 12 Nov. 1870

Dearly Beloved Friend,

"Put it off, and you'll never do it." Nothing could be truer, now that I have gotten out your letter of last year [Wormser 82], I am ashamed that I did not respond sooner to your letter that I enjoyed so much, but the weeks and months go by so fast that it amazes you. And even as time flies, so great [world] events follow each other in quick succession. It is hard to believe all the things that have happened in 1870! And what things can still happen before the year is over. Happy the man, who in the midst of all that transpires, bows before the King of Kings and feels safe and secure under His Rule.

This year has also been rather important for me. My dear Cato was still living in Baambrugge with her little children, but she was always ailing so, that she needed someone to care for her, and was going downhill all the while. At the end of June she felt like staying in Amsterdam for a time, and at the same time be under treatment by a professor. At the beginning of July I went to Nijverdal once again with Henriette to visit Maria, since Cato had now been entrusted to the care of Jansje. While I was there, that bloody war [Franco-Prussian War], which makes every human heart tremble, suddenly broke out.

On August 3, I returned and found that Cato's condition had declined greatly. On the 5th of August, my son Johan picked me up in the morning, and at eleven-thirty we rejoiced at the birth of a Johan Adam Wormser; at one o'clock, another son arrived, who is named Hendericus after Höveker. They are not heavy chunky boys, but they are healthy. The mother developed caked breasts, which are only now beginning to heal. The children are bottle-fed and are becoming very sweet. When they were four weeks old, Ka came and showed them to Cato, and that was the only time [she saw them]. She still wanted to make a quick day trip home, but we could tell that she would come to her end at our house. And that is how it turned out, as you learned from Johan's letter. On the 6th of September, she entered the eternal rest in the full assurance of faith in her Savior, after a troubled life. She lay dying fully conscious for three days and nights, so that she had great shortness of breath when she said to me, "Nothing matters within, Mom, all is peace there; it is only something in the body. I shall continue to entrust myself to my faithful Savior regardless of what happens." You know from experience how grievous such a loss is, but I can acquiesce in the will of the Lord. For her, the joy of life was so totally destroyed [in the divorce from her alcoholic husband] that she could only succumb to it.

Her oldest son is now attending a boarding school near Nijmegen under Mr. Gerritsen. We were given to understand that he needed to be under the leading of a firm Christian. Her youngest son is five years old and is now with Maria. Our cares and concerns with the children have been many, since Cato was only separated by bed and board. She did not want a complete separation at the time, and so, by law the father was the guardian. Cato did have a legal document drawn up by a lawyer whereby her brother Johan was appointed guardian, but this must be confirmed by the court. Now our first concern after her death was to keep the children out of the reach of the father. We sent De Boer a notice of her passing. He came to see the body; she was already in the coffin. He was deeply moved. He had known nothing of her illness and felt that she had changed so. Jansje said: "[Don't forget,] she also suffered a great deal. No one thinks she looks thirty-three years old; she looks more like sixty or seventy. I am sorry that you have come to see the body of your wife, and that you have been drinking." He beat his hands against his forehead. We were glad to see him go. Since then he came to see me to ask my forgiveness. I said that as a human being and as a Christian that was my duty, and that if he showed improvement in his life, our home and heart would be open to him, but if he continued in the old way, we would also be as before. He has the court decree at home whereby the care of the children is entrusted to Johan. The father still does not know where they [the children] are.

The Lord, to whom they have been committed in baptism, and to whom the mother offered so many prayers, will, I trust, be a Father to them in Christ. In the midst of all those circumstances, I frequently thought of writing you, but I did not have the mind or desire to do it. Now I have been waiting the last few weeks, because I thought that I would have to provide you the death notice about Berkhout, but he is still living, though any moment could be his last. Everything he eats tastes good to him but everything turns sour, and he throws it up; all efforts to induce bowel movements are futile.

Who would ever have thought that the wonderful [Evangelical] Alliance would have to be cancelled because of war and blood letting? Although none of us could go, still we do know people who were planning on it. While I was in Nijverdal in July, two children of my husband's brother left for America, a son Andries, who is going to study, and his daughter Maria, who is living with her sister in Overisel, in Michigan. They had a good and safe journey.

What pleasure you have given me by sending me the pictures of Mrs. Singer! I would not be able to recognize in them the little Maria as she used to sit on my lap. And for you to experience having children again at this time in your life really makes me glad. How I would like to see and embrace you all, but I doubt there will be much chance of that; if only we may all meet each other before the throne of the Lamb. For me it is a pleasant thought that my old friends are living in with their children, just as I am, and that the evening of our life may be a restful one, to the extent that is possible in this world so full of unrest.

And now I want to add a word about [the German poet] Tersteegen. When I still attended church, I almost always went to the German church of Rev. Brandt. There, as at home, it was a great pleasure to sing his [Tersteegen's] hymns. It is a real sacrifice for me that because of my chest I cannot walk down the street, but always have to ride, and I do not do that on Sunday. I always spend the day of rest at home, but I have no demands to make, and enjoy so many undeserved blessings that I have every reason to be grateful. My daughter Jansje has a troublesome throat ailment, which is always inflamed, and as a result she can only get out in the fresh air when the weather is mild. My other children are all healthy and well. They send greetings to you and your husband. May you and all yours be commended to the Lord, with my most cordial greetings from your deeply loving friend and sister in the Lord.

Widow J. A. Wormser-van der Ven

P.S. I certainly may request that you do not follow my example, but make me happy soon with some news about you people. If I recall correctly, it is your birthday this very day, dear friend. May the Lord grant you many more years and cause you and yours to experience his lovingkindness.

Wormser 83

C. M. Budde-Stomp to the Widow Mrs. J. A. Wormser-van der Ven
Mount Pleasant, 20 Dec. 1870

[To] My Beloved Friend and her Children!
On Dec. 11 we received Your Honor's long anticipated letter in reasonable well being;
On November 12, my 68th birthday, we received the printed announcement of the birth of your two grandsons; we were joyful that even after his death, the lineage of our dear friend W[ormser] lives on. We trust that the parents of the children have surrendered themselves to the Lord and his service, and thus have also consecrated their children to the Lord and educate them in the fear of the Lord. May the motto and the choice of the grandparents, "As for me and my house, we will serve the Lord," [Joshua 24:15] continue into future generations. The Lord grant it.

I noticed there was another letter, sent by your son Johan, which we did not receive. I regret that very much, because I would so very much have liked to hear from him. Well, I hope that when it is convenient, I will also be getting some mail from him. The sad tiding about your dear Cato was most unexpected. We loved her dearly, but no, we must rejoice that the Lord has called her to him, and thus took her to her heavenly home prematurely. May the Lord comfort you all on this loss, and also stretch forth his fatherly hand, so that when the battle is done, they may, with all the children of God, sing praise to the Lord through all eternity and praise him for his great love in Christ Jesus. If possible, I would very much like to have a picture of her, for when she was still living she promised me one in a letter. If that is not possible, then we shall have to wait patiently until we have been translated [into glory] and live together through all eternity.

This summer we met a grandson of [Minister] Van Hall, one of more than thirty-two [in the group]. He was a tall young man, nineteen years old, here with Greve from Leiden, the son of a surgeon. I thought that his parents also lived in Leiden. They had old acquaintances living in Mount Pleasant and wanted to take up farming there, but that was not quite as easy as they had imagined. He said he was still young and that he wanted to have some fun in life first. We told him that we had known an uncle and aunt of his, who had given themselves to the Lord and his service, and both of them had died an early but blessed death. We advised him that if he truly wanted to be happy, to seek the Lord with all his heart and to serve him, to say farewell to the world and all its vanities, and to choose to serve the Lord. He was very friendly; Greve went to Kansas with another person, and Van Hall went back [to the Netherlands].

How much things can change in a short time. Who would ever have thought that the pope would have his temporal power taken from him without even a struggle; the help on which he relied was just a reed and dropped him. What terrible bloodshed, and how will it all end? We are approaching the last days. The Lord is coming; let us keep our lamps filled and trimmed.

Things have been very busy for our children this year. Before we knew it, the year was over. We were living above their store, and the children did not have any fresh air. Singer bought a lot, five houses from Johan's dwelling, and built a house that has a hallway and a stairway in the center, with two rooms on either side; the upstairs is the same. It has a good-sized kitchen and cellar in which we eat together. On one side we have a room for our use, and next to it is their bedroom. If anything goes wrong, we are all together in no time. There is a lean to, and a garden where the children can play and we can also enjoy the fresh air. We really enjoy the children a lot. The youngest is a year old and walks all by himself. Anna is three years old, and I am teaching her the Dutch A,B,Cs. In all this the Lord has been very merciful to us. My dear husband's health is fairly good. In the fall his chest and stomach pains worsened; as a result he became weaker. He sees the doctor, but he still manages to be up and around. My heart rate is fairly moderate, but I do have to avoid activity. How fortunate that we are not pressed by work and may take it easy. Singer and Johan get along well and faithfully help each other.

Our Johan is not very strong either; he suffers from high blood pressure. The doctors in Burlington do not agree; the one says he has a heart condition, the other says it is his lungs. We must wait on the Lord. If it is consonant with God's plan, then he may be spared for us, for he is a faithful son, and his wife and children are understanding as well. His wife's mother lives in with him. In America we had heard that Berkhout was dead, and then again that he was still living, because someone in Pella had received a letter from him. They [the Berkhouts] were not liked all that much in Pella. Rev. Scholte's wife remarried with a young man (Robert Beard, twenty-four years old; she is forty-nine).

And now, dear friend, I hope that you may receive this letter in good health. While this letter is still en route, we will again be entering upon a new era. The Lord knows what we shall encounter in it; if only we find ourselves in his hand, he will also guide us through this vale of tears. Cordial greetings from Johan and his family. He was deeply moved by [the passing of] your dear Cato. Greetings also from Maria and Singer, and from us too. We commend you to the Lord and his grace,

Your loving Friend,
C. M. Budde-Stomp

P.S. Many greetings to Mr. Höveker. Do write us soon again. We might not be able to do so much longer.

Budde 58

Mrs. J. Wormser-van der Ven to the Budde family
Amsterdam, 2 Feb. 1871

Dearly Beloved Friend and Spouse and Children,

Your most welcome letter of this past December [Wormser 83] reached me in good order. I must begin by correcting an error. In my previous letter, I wrote you that my son Johan had written you; that is not so. We had talked about it at the time of my dear Cato's death, since I was about to write you anyway, but nothing came of it and so no letter was lost. When I learned of your desire to have a picture of her, and [because] she had left behind so many lady-friends who also desired one, I resolved to have several copies made. I now have the pleasure to enclose a copy; it is not from the last part of her life, but for that reason it is all the better, because at the end she looked to be sixty to seventy years old.

Shortly after [I sent] my last letter, Berkhout died. When they arrived in Holland, they had a nice middle-class sum of money. He visited me, and since my son is a dealer in stocks, I asked him as a favor to [assist Berkhout in investing]. One day he [Berkhout] came with a proposal to speculate with a large sum of money, to which my son replied that he would not do that unless he knew how much money Berkhout possessed. Berkhout took his money to another dealer. One time he gained fl.2,000; by another he lost fl.10,000; until in the past year, at the beginning of the [Franco-Prussian] War, they came over one evening after ten, completely crushed. The trading company had gone broke, and they were poor as church mice. We think that it did a great deal of harm to Berkhout's health, but now that it is all over, and the people in Pella [are again] paying [on] time, the Mrs. will be able live on that for a little while. She could not continue living in their dwelling because of the high rent, and she now has one room with the book dealer Van Peursum in the St. Jansstraat [in Utrecht]. How unfortunate it is when a human being is not satisfied even when he has plenty. When he wants to become rich, he falls into a snare and into many temptations. My request to you is to keep this history to yourselves, because I do not know whether those [family?] in Pella would even want to know this. I have [asked] my son to enclose...[text missing]. He has promised [to do so, but he] is very busy. He has the principal responsibility for running the store of the book company. He is the father of two children, is the guardian of Cato's children, and now he has been appointed deacon in the church. Besides, he also has to become a [a member of] the citizen soldiery this year, and all that, mind you, at the age of twenty-five. At the moment he is a little feverish and that is why I just started writing. My health also parallels my situation. Because of the shortness of breath in my chest I can do almost nothing, and so the Lord arranges things so I do not have to. I no longer attend church, and I seldom go out except occasionally by carriage to my children. I cannot be thankful enough for such a happy old age; living in with Carel and Jansje, and my Henriette with me, I can be calm as I see my life span growing shorter. What a privilege it is that we do not seek our happiness or satisfaction here below, but have our eyes fixed on a better fatherland.

I sincerely hope that your son Johan may regain his health. I can well imagine that the death notice of Cato [struck] him. [No doubt he still] remembers Cato. At least they, [the Wormser children] can still recall him [Johan]; they even still know your Maria as a child just beginning to walk. [Translator's reconstruction of a passage with missing text.]

I sincerely hope that none of our children or grandchildren will be missing in Heaven, where we all as a family in immortality may eternally serve the Lord, exalting and praising him. I have asked my sons and daughter-in-law for pictures for you, but they do not have any. Cordial greetings to your husband and children from me and my children, and in everything you are commended to the Lord by,

                        Your Friend who loves you dearly,
                        Widow J. A. Wormser-van der Ven

Budde 59

> J. A. Wormser, Jr. to Mr. and Mrs. Budde
> Amsterdam, 22 Feb. 1871

Esteemed Sir and Madam!

I am pleased to respond to your honored request, addressed to me in your last letter to my mother, [namely] that I send you, by my own hand, some sign of life and friendship. I have little time to spare on correspondence, that is true. My responsibilities: the father of twins (and the two little boys like to play and roughhouse with their father), the guardian of the children of my sister Cato, a book dealer, and, since the first of this year, a deacon in the Hervormde (Reformed) congregation [of Amsterdam]. All these things do give me other things to do.

My dear wife also has her hands full taking care of her two sons, who are over a half-year old now. Caked breasts that were ulcerated have given her lots of trouble. Happily she is now well again and can devote herself completely to the boys. They are growing and getting to be as sweet as can be. You may know their names. Johan Adam, the oldest, is named for me, and consequently also after father Wormser. Henricus, the youngest, is the namesake of father Höveker. Because of this double blessing our home soon became too small, so that we consider it a boon that the landlord, by canceling our rent, has compelled us to move into a new and also more spacious dwelling next May. We are staying in the neighborhood of the store on the Heerengracht, but we will be living a rather considerable distance from Mother.

In 1870 Europe lived through a year such as has rarely occurred in the history of the world. We now do have hope that peace will be signed, may the Lord grant it. Thousands of human lives have been wasted or shortened through death and crippling by the rulers of both warring parties. And all this for one Imperial crown! Happy is he who has a higher perspective and knows that through all the human passions and sin God is able to prepare and to achieve his glorious purposes. Without that firm faith one would despair.

And that is true in every other respect, also in ecclesiastical matters. Hardly have we been delivered from the tyranny of modernism in Amsterdam but the threatening spook of an orthodox inquisition is at the door. One orthodox party is intemperate in the way it clings to the [creedal] formularies, raising them as shibboleths between brethren.

To be sure, it is more or less a natural reaction, but it is painful just the same, even though we know that this kind of zealotry cannot last more than a few years. Still the gates of hell will not overwhelm the congregation of the Lord (under whatever name). That promise is sure and puts to shame all such reprehensible attempts.

My wife and I will be pleased to hear good reports about you and yours soon. We ask you to convey our greetings to your children, who remember me better than I remember them. May you all to the Lord be commended to the Lord.

Your loving Friend,
J. A. Wormser

Wormser 84

C. M. Budde-Stomp to the Widow Mrs. J. A. Wormser-van der Ven
Mount Pleasant, May 1871

My Beloved Friend and her Children,

It was a pleasant surprise to me to receive your letter of February '71, including the picture of your dear Cato. We would not have recognized her, she looked so very sweet and lovely. I thank you most sincerely for having fulfilled my wishes. If it should work out some time, I would appreciate getting a picture of your son and daughter-in-law for my album. Our tie with the Wormser family on this earth has been so cordial and so close knit, like David and Jonathan, and also with their children. Your failing memory reminds me that I should repeat my request from time to time.

Our health is not all that bad; my dear husband's chest continues to give him trouble, and consequently he is quite weak. My rapid heartbeat and rheumatism kept me down this winter. We had much stormy weather this winter. I wanted to write you back at once, but I could not because I felt faint. Thanks to the Lord's goodness, the rest of the family is enjoying good health and prosperity. Given the outward prosperity and blessings, it is not very pleasant that there are so many disagreeable maids here; they are very headstrong and do as they please. If you say anything, and we leave, they are unwilling to do much work and take off when it suits them. Maria does not even have one [a maid] these days; that makes things rather difficult for her and the children. May the Lord provide a helper in her need, one like the servant of whom the centurion spoke, "I say to this man, Go, and he goeth; and to another, Come, and he cometh; and to my servant, Do this, and he doeth it" [Matthew 8: 9]. Our surety, J[esus] C[hrist], also had to do without and lamented, "He that eateth bread with me, hath lifted up his heel against me" [John 13:18]. May the Lord grant us patience and meekness to bear what he lays upon us. The world is a vale of tears, nothing but sorrow and trouble. We have no abiding place here, and when the battle is done, the course is run, God will wipe away all tears from our eyes, and there will be no more trouble and grief, but we shall praise and glorify him through all eternity, Amen.

I was pleased to receive a friendly letter from your dear son, Johan; how much work has been laid upon him in his youth! Oh well, it is good for a man that he bear his yoke in his youth [Lamentations 3:27]. The burdens that the Lord lays upon us, he will also enable us to bear. "But seek ye first the kingdom of God and his righteousness; and all these things shall be added unto you" [Matthew 6:33]. "Those who fear the Lord shall lack no good thing;...they shall still bring forth fruit in old age" [Psalm 92:14].

May the blessing of the Lord rest upon you and your loved ones to length of days, your dearly beloved friend.

Cordial greetings from us all to our dear Jansje, Mrs. and Mr. Wüstenhoff. May the Lord bless you all, so that you may still be there to make life pleasant for your dear mother, and to be a support to her as her years increase, so that the blessing of the Lord may attend you; greetings to our family at Nijverdal, and to your Henriette. Greetings from Johan, and Singer and Maria, to you all. We commend you to the Lord and his grace. Do surprise us again with a letter.

Your Friends who think of you always,
The Buddes

P.S. Greetings also to the aged Mr. Höveker and family. Is your daughter-in-law from his first wife or from the second marriage?

P.S. The grandson of Minister Van Hall has returned here again; he is living in with a farmer. After he has been there a year, his parents want to buy a small farm for him; his parents live in Leiden.

Jansje Wüstenhoff-Wormser, later correspondent with Budde family, and her husband, Carel W. Wüstenhoff
(Courtesy of Jan Peter Verhave)

Budde 60

Jansje Wüstenhoff-Wormser to Mrs. C. M. Budde-Stomp
Amsterdam, 15 Jan. 1872

Esteemed Mrs.! Dear friends!

Your esteemed letter of May 1871 [Wormser 84] should have been answered earlier. Mother received your letter in June, a couple of days before she left for Nijverdal, where she and Henriette were going to spend a few weeks with my sister Maria. After being there a few days, mother began to throw up blood, which weakened her considerably. Having recovered some, they traveled home again. The cause [of the indisposition] was very likely the thin air.

About the same time I was staying at Velp, north of Haarlem, for reasons of health, mainly the recovery of my throat. Since the stay had been planned for at least six weeks, this was a nasty confluence. Since Mom had recovered enough so she could return home a little earlier, I could stay out my time at Velp. After I had been home a few days, the same indisposition recurred in Mom, and since the bedrooms are two floors up, Mom had no choice but to stay upstairs to avoid climbing stairs. And that is how it is all the time now; Mom has been upstairs since August already. In November, Mom was getting worse by the day so that we were worried [for her life], but fortunately she has recovered from that set-back and she has regained much of her strength. However, last Friday Mom again vomited a little blood, but now Mom is quite well again. Nevertheless, Mom feels too weak to write letters. And so that you would not have to wait any longer, Mom instructed me to share a few things about life here.

My throat has improved somewhat as a result of being in the outside air, although that was not noticeable until later; but in rough, stormy weather it is very sensitive just the same. Rest and quiet are the most important medicine. Fortunately, that agrees with me pretty well. The other members of the family have been fairly healthy during the past year. My brother Johan's twins are now one and one-half years old; they are as cute as can be. Cato's children are also healthy. Marie and her husband were here for Christmas, and they are also well, although Marie is not strong either. We sincerely hope that everything may still be the same with all of you, and that you and Mr. [Budde] may enjoy reasonably good health at your advanced age.

No doubt you have heard about the sudden death of Mrs. Berkhout. We still miss her all the time, for she visited us rather often, usually on Monday evenings. That was also the case on Monday, October 23. She was first downstairs [with me] for tea, then she went [upstairs] to keep Mom company for an hour, and then came down again to have a sandwich with us, and so she left for home, happy and cheerful, at ten-thirty. Little did I think, when I let her out, that I was seeing her for the last time. We got the death notice Wednesday afternoon. My husband immediately went to the Van Peursems, where she had had a room of her own since May. He wanted to learn a little more about what had happened and to see her once more, but even that was not to be. She had gone out on Tuesday afternoon, and gone out again in the evening, and had returned home safe and well at ten-thirty. When she did not answer after the milkman rang her door-bell repeatedly, one of the Van Peursem girls went to her room and found her [in a coma] from a stroke. She died the next morning at eleven-thirty, but they never heard another word from her. She certainly followed her husband fast, and what a sad life those people had. The saying, "Those who want to become rich fall into a snare," certainly was confirmed in them, for I do not know whether you are aware that in the war of 1870 they lost all their money. It was kept rather quiet at the time, but now that they are both dead, and you were such old friends of theirs, I may write you this. After the death of Berkhout, she could manage to live by being very thrifty, but she saved every penny she could. On top of that, since Berkhout died, she did not receive any interest from America, so that it is a puzzle to us what she lived on. That just shows that it is better to enjoy whatever God gives with a free and happy heart; [for] now, to tell the truth, they had nothing, and the best they had was only trouble and sorrow.

Four weeks after the death of Mrs. Berkhout, the Lord suddenly took another friend of ours to himself. He visited us on Saturday evening as usual. On Monday Henriette visited his wife and the baby, which was only four weeks old. He was in bed, with what they thought was a bad cold. On Wednesday, Wüstenhoff went to visit him and again he was in bed, but no one thought it was anything but a cold. And already on Friday we received word of his death. You can imagine how shocked we were. On Thursday he had developed smallpox, and he died that same night. They had been married less than a year, and they had absolutely no family in the city, just a few friends. When his wife told him that she was afraid that he was getting smallpox, he said, "Well my dear, whatever happens, we are in the hand of the Lord." He even said what to tell the family, and even before the family in Nieuwediep got the message, he was already [in heaven] above. When we went to the house of the dead that evening, we found the young mother and child with neighbors. The family had just arrived, and they were also at the neighbor's. It was a sad scene. The grandfathers were seeing their grandchild for the first time, but they were not even allowed to see the body [for fear of contagion].

We suggested that the widow and baby spend a few days with us, since she was not allowed into her home. On Saturday her husband was buried, exactly one week after he had discussed the baptism of the baby with us; and now the widow was coming to our house. After she had been at our house for a few days and had arranged her affairs, she went to Nieuwediep with her relatives, and, mind you, after being home a few days, the baby came down with smallpox, and it was fairly serious, too. However, it survived the illness, and so far the Lord has spared its life for her. That is no small thing to experience at the age of twenty-four, don't you agree? However, she is calm and comforted. Her father [husband?] said he had his luggage packed and was ready for the journey [to eternity]. That is a great consolation for the relatives and friends. My husband is losing his best friend in him, and we still feel very hollow and empty. He and Mrs. Berkhout were our most frequent visitors.

What terrible fires have afflicted Chicago and Michigan. Several children of my uncle in Nijverdal live in Holland, [Michigan], but fortunately they have been spared any losses. One of them had some damage, but they are being reimbursed. How sad the years 1870 and 1871 have been, first by the sad, destructive war, and then the consequences thereof, to wit the Commune of Paris. And illnesses everywhere. Our hearts bled at the reports that came from Paris every day. Having seen Paris at its best, in our mind's eye we were able to follow the reports of destruction street by street. The splendor and opulence [of Paris] had reached its peak, and now so much has been destroyed that it is a miracle at all that so much is left. In America, too, opulence seems to be increasing at an alarming pace from what we hear, and that has now been shattered to such an extent that the labors and efforts of so many years have been destroyed in a flash by the flames. How fortunate we are to know that in all of this the Lord rules, and that nothing shall separate us from his love.

Our church situation is not all that pleasant, at least as far as Amsterdam is concerned. In the past the appointment of elders and deacons and the calling of ministers was the work of the council. As you know, in recent years that was done by an electoral college consisting of the council and members of the congregation. In the past the council was for the most part liberal, but at present the electoral college and consequently the council has become as rigidly orthodox as it could possibly be. Already it is about as far out as it used to be among the Seceders of the most rigid sort. People who never went to church now are seated in the elders' pews, and when an orthodox preacher has a hymn sung, they very piously close their psalter-hymnals. We have gotten a Rev. Kuyper, just thirty years old, who used to be an out and out modernist. He is now the other extreme, as rigid as possible. He draws many people and gives a certain tone to the council because he now has many kindred spirits in it.

Fortunately, the milder wing has still gained a victory this year by calling Rev. De Graaf as a counterpart to Kuyper. You may have a faint recollection of him. As a student, he and the Rev. Gildemeester, then also a student, were once part of the audience that heard Father in your home on the Achterburgwal. I recall it very distinctly. Rev. De Graaf is the son-in-law of Mr. Pierson. He is very orthodox, but not so rigidly narrow, [but rather] *vrij en blij* [unfettered and joyful] as becomes the Christian. In addition, he is very popular, so that the most simple-minded can understand him. He would be eminently suited to be a street-corner preacher [evangelist], if that were the practice in our country. As the widow of his old friend, he visited Mother twice during her most recent illness. He has been here [in Amsterdam] since October, so that his work schedule is not completely settled as yet. I have asked him to start a catechism class for women members; he will keep it in mind. Orthodox preachers are doing this more often now than in the past. Rev. Kuyper has over one hundred [in a class]. But with so many, it [the class] unwittingly turns out to be a lecture on the Bible, and that is not exactly the intention.

Well, my dear friend, it seems to me that this long letter has compensated you for your long wait. I still have to answer a question of yours: my sister-in-law is the youngest daughter of Mr. Höveker from his first marriage. In February they are expecting another baby. I hope that your daughter Maria now has a good maid again; getting one is a big headache here, too. I have reason to complain, because next May it will be twelve years ago that she [her maid] came to Mom as a little girl, and she was has been with us almost eleven years now. Given all her shortcomings, she is still very loyal. Well, dear friend, all of us send our most sincere greetings to you and all your relatives, and you are commended to the Lord.

Your loving Friend,
J. Wüstenhoff

Wormser 85

C. M. Budde-Stomp to the children of the Widow J. A. Wormser, deceased
Mount Pleasant, 28 March 1872

Beloved Friends and Mrs. J. Wüstenhoff,
Quite unexpectedly, we received the death announcement of your dear mother, our dearly beloved friend. It struck us, because we were always happy when we received a letter from you. Her affection for us was also evident when she instructed you to write us, and we sincerely thank you for doing that. We received your letter on February 5th. I wanted to reply at once, but I suffer from heart trouble and I cannot be about, but have to keep very quiet. I dare not even occupy my mind. All winter long I had a bad cold and pain in my throat. Then it improved some, but with cold weather it comes right back again. The doctor gave me

some medicine, and now I am somewhat better.

My dear husband has been suffering from severe pains in his chest and stomach for over six months; he became so weak and so thin that we were worried whether father might be taken from us. The doctor thought that father had a blockage in his lower abdomen. [They] worked on that and there is some improvement, but he still suffers pain and must remain in the house. We have had a long, cold winter with many storms. Fresh air and a little exercise would do my husband good. The Lord alone rules; he directs the course of clouds, air, and winds. But all things must work for the best of those who fear him. Who can discern God's wise and wondrous and ways? He does all things well.

Our son Johan is also being visited by the hand of God. His dear wife has been sick for over a half-year and cannot go beyond her room and bed. She has been visited with numerous ills. Recently they discovered that she had a tapeworm; with medical assistance she got rid of that. It filled a beer glass and looked like a white ribbon the width of a cushion ribbon; the head pointed like a needle. She is still suffering, has a great deal of pain in her left side; the doctors say that she has a liver ailment; no one has succeeded in curing her of it. Their son has learned wagon making and his apprenticeship will soon be over. Their daughter is fifteen years old; she is big and healthy. Her mother is living in with them, but because of an unfortunate fall, she has to walk with two crutches. She is quite healthy and a big support with all the housekeeping. The rest of the family is well, and so we slowly move on to our final destination. Simon and Johan are in business together and get along well with each other. Our Maria is expecting an offspring again about June. I hope the Lord will bring her safely through.

Dear Jansje, Mrs. Wüstenhoff, do make up for me the absence and loss of your dear mother by writing us, at your convenience, how you are all doing. I can still remember you very well from when you were young. Your parents have already been released [from this life] and are with Jesus whom they served here. We still have to cross the river of death; the promise of the Lord is that he will give eternal life to his servants and lead them into Canaan. May the Lord comfort you all and enable you to hope in a blessed reunion. Sincere greetings from all of us to your husband, Mr. Wüstenhoff, your brother Johan, and the rest of the family. Also give our greetings to the old Mr. Höveker and family. Please pardon my poor handwriting; putting down my thoughts is getting hard for me. We commend you to the Lord and his grace. Your loving friends,

C. M. Budde-Stomp

[P.S.] Surprise me with a reply.

Budde 61

                    Johanna Schellinger to Mrs. C. M. Budde-Stomp
                                      Alkmaar, 10 May 1872

Highly Esteemed Friend,

  I have received your honored letter with great pleasure, and how cheering that from it I might learn that by the grace of God all your lives have been spared till now. May those illnesses in your family also be removed. How much more pleasant that would make life for all of you in this beautiful and glorious season, but we are people who are here today and gone tomorrow. We know nothing. We certainly may desire to bear about a healthy body, but if it is decided otherwise in the Lord's wise council, then our consolation is to acquiesce in his loving governance. However dark our way may be, for everyone who believes, it is a glorious prospect that whatever befalls us is sent us by a loving Father. How many are the undeserved blessings we receive beyond our prayers and imaginings. If only we take note of it.

  I do hope with all my heart that your beloved daughter may erelong also be blessed with a successful delivery, and that all of you may rejoice in the blessing, which is also so indispensable to her at that time. I also rejoice that Naatje is so happy with her offspring. I can readily imagine that she was overjoyed to have a daughter. What a pleasure it must be for you to live so close together; how easy, then, it is to help each other. I thank you, dear friend, for encouraging Naatje to send a letter. It is also so gratifying to me.

  And since I am so convinced of your well-meaning interest in me, I must share something with you that happened to me. In the past I have on occasion written you about a friend who was a sister to me, and who worked with me as a household maid for an unforgettable Lady. She [my friend] was much younger than I, and rather a quiet sort, and so thoughtful in her trade that everyone liked having her work for them. She lived a very healthy life but always complained about headaches. The result was that she could not always think as clearly as she had in the past, and so completely unexpectedly, she took her own life. That tiding hit me hard. One day before she turned forty-five, on March 16th instant, she made that ill-fated decision. Her mistress missed her in the early morning, and she herself came to me. Did I know anything about her whereabouts? But I had not seen her in a week. Later on she was found in the peat attic. It is something that is unforgettably with me. I cannot imagine what the reason is, but I have given it over to the Ruler of our Destiny, to whom no thoughts are hidden. If she did it in complete confusion of mind, I hope that the Lord will be gracious to her and save her soul from eternal damnation. How dark things can get on our life's pathway. How wise and good our heavenly Father is that we do not know the day of tomorrow. We may just entrust ourselves to his leading and governance; that gives us so much rest on life's way. I have also received much sympathy from my good friends. Many of them held my friend in high esteem, and many of them would like to provide me some distraction. I cannot ignore that either, but I feel most at home in the quiet of my room.

And now, my dear friend, it is my dearest wish that you and your family receive this letter in reasonable well being, even as I experience that myself, thanks to the blessing of the Lord. And hereby receive my heartfelt greetings and remain with [high] esteem,

Your loving Friend,
Johanna Schellinger

Wormser 86

D. A. Budde to the children of J. Wormser-van der Ven, deceased
Mount Pleasant, 13 February 1873

[Copied and concluded by J. G. Budde]

Esteemed Friends,

Since I lived in such intimate fellowship with your father and associated with him when we were both still in the church militant upon earth, I wish to comply with your wish that we write in greater detail about her [Mrs. Budde's] passing to the abode of the blest, like the one we received from you about your mother of blessed memory. O, Mother's longing to hear about that was so great that I had to console her repeatedly, [telling her that] I had already sent my letter to Amsterdam. She also longed to leave this life, but only very moderately, although there was no external matter involved in that. For the Lord had done everything so well for us, that in our later years everything was so good and enjoyable between and among us, that in all our years we could not have been able or even dared to imagine it. As concerns her health in recent times, it was fairly good, and her heart palpitation was not all that bad either. Let me give you just one example. When Maria was happily delivered of her third daughter on the 25th of May, she was so happy and well that Mother insisted on doing all the midwife's work; no one else was allowed to do it until Maria herself had recovered sufficiently to do it herself. And until her death she was privileged to see that the Lord had blessed mother and child more than usual.

Shortly before her death, Mother was still so well that one summer day all of us together, including the children, could go for a carriage ride to see the farms around Mount Pleasant. About that time I too was again sufficiently recovered that now and then, when the heat of the day had abated, I could go for walks to visit various people. And so it happened that toward evening on the 25th of July, I said to mother: "Why don't we go to Aunt Lena's with the children." She was ready shortly and then we went into the garden; mother and the children went to the cherry tree and ate to their heart's content. Then she also walked around in the garden, which is quite large, looking for (black)berries, but it was too late for them And so we were all able to enjoy ourselves in the fresh air and cool off until it was getting to be bedtime for the children. Then we went home, and when we got to the gate, I went in the house with the little ones. Mother said, "I just want to get a glass of lemonade at the store," which was once again as far as we had already walked, but then she could walk better than I. Singer fixed it for her, and after she had rested, she [got up] and passed Johan who was working on some job or other, and said to him, "Good night, Jan." After getting back, we sat down on the balcony. Mother sat down beside us and said, "I just had a nice glass of lemonade," and then joined the conversation with a Hollander named Van Hall, who was opinionated enough to think that he could prove that man originated in the plant kingdom. After we argued against him, basing ourselves on the divine witness [of the Bible], the conversation ended.

We had already withdrawn from it several times, since he is a free spirit, and we know from our own experience that the Lord only can put to shame the wisdom of the wise by the power of the sacred gospel. I said it is getting time for us to turn in. "That is fine," she said. "Good night, Mr. Van Hall, I hold fast to the simple word of the Bible." And then we got ready [for bed], had our usual evening devotions, and then, as we were going to our bedroom, she herself blew out the candle, and went to bed.

As usual, I awakened an hour later and heard M[other] moaning. I called, "Mother where are you?" "On the chair and I cannot breathe." Singer and Maria were there immediately, since their room was next to ours. She was promptly washed with something that would refresh her. Maria asked whether she should give her the drops she always used for her heart palpitation. She said, "That may be all right, but it is not the heart palpitation; it [the pain] is from under my arm." After it had diminished some, she again went to bed, and so did the others. I said that I would stay up and keep the light burning. "That is fine." After having been quiet for a while, she said, "Too bad that I am so restless," very likely so that I might also enjoy some rest. Now she was on the chamber pot, then back in bed, and when she was again sitting on the chair, she cried out, "O Lord, help." Again the children were there immediately. Singer asked, "Shall I get the doctor?" "No, then I'd rather that you get Jan, he knows a lot." Singer immediately left for Jan's [house], only five houses away; she was again sitting on the chair and said, "I have to get into the night chest." I opened it, and Maria and the maid helped her to it; she embraced Maria in whose arms her head was resting, and said, "There is a cloth in the second drawer; get it for me, I am getting a little cold." No sooner said than done. As the cloth was hung about her, her head drooped in Maria's arms. She had departed into the dwelling of peace. Singer and Jan, although they came immediately, did not find her alive any more. Then they had to lay her on the bed, and since she was so very heavy, it took the five of us to do it. Now you can picture our situation to yourselves. We all kept our wits about us, and willing friends assisted in laying out the body.

Then we had to decide when to bury her. It was so very warm, and it could not be delayed. In the morning she was laid between layers of ice, and in the afternoon laid in the coffin. Nevertheless, the body was already beginning to decompose, and the corpse was getting bloated. Rev. Schmidt gave a funeral sermon at the house before a large crowd of people, as is the custom here, and spoke on the words, "Blessed are the dead which die in the Lord [henceforth]" [Revelation 14:13], and then we might bring the soulless body to the quiet resting place of the dead in God. A day earlier soul and body were still walking on the earth, and now the soul is rejoicing in the midst of the great hosts of the redeemed and the friends that have gone before, and with whom they were so closely united in the Lord. And accordingly, this was our quiet peace and joy, and who would begrudge her that she had gone before, especially after being seized with fear on more than one occasion that I might precede her. It was my desire that this boon might befall my beloved before me, and accordingly I acquiesced in the Lord's will. And so we went our way together, with falling and rising, until the Lord fulfilled her wish. For fourteen days I might rejoice with a holy stillness and gladness that it was Mother's privilege already now to participate in the wedding of the Lamb; but then it all revived again, my preference to have kept her [here]. And now I began to understand somewhat the words of the Savior, "The Spirit is willing but the flesh is weak," and what it means to "acquiesce with body and soul in the divine good pleasure." But since her whole heart was focused on Jesus, what must it be like now to behold the glory of the Lord, rejoicing with the great host before the throne of the Lamb. And that again comforts me to wait patiently for my faithful life's companion with whom I had walked our Pilgrim way for more than fifty years. He is also the faithful Savior who manifested his love and concern for us and will also guide me into the Father's house to praise and thank the Lord with her forever.

I have already mentioned that Maria now has three children; the oldest is Anna Maria, five years old; Elizabeth Christina is three years; I will send you a picture of her as a remembrance; the third, Flora Lydia, is still too active to sit still [for a picture]. The three children are a real delight. May the workings of the Holy Spirit ever preserve them as they grow up in this apostate world. We have the promise, and it is sure. Maria and Singer are both well, and so is Jan, and they work together well, although Jan is not as strong and healthy as Singer. Jan's two children are already grown up and healthy. He has many cares because of his wife, who has been ill for over a year. [Her] two doctors were also often at a loss what to do, and none of us saw any prospect for her recovery. Then it turned out that she had a tapeworm. The doctor managed to get rid of it in almost exactly the time he had predicted. We now thought that that she would speedily recover, but she was physically so weakened that her mind went blank and she had to be treated like a little child. The doctor said that could last for a year; in late summer it did improve some, and now she is up and about, as best she can, but she is not capable of doing her regular work. Her mother, who gets about on two crutches because of a fall, is in the house with them and she is pleasant as ever. And so the Lord has his way of keeping Jan humble and an example of submissiveness and to gain from this a peaceable fruit of righteousness so that he too may finally be delivered from this terrestrial ball and enter upon eternal salvation.

In all likelihood you will not be getting a letter about ordinary matters, because that would require too much time. Many times I was busy [writing] and then once again I had to exclaim, "I just cannot go on," even though I really wanted to put my thoughts on paper. Then everything got jumbled, my feelings got the best of me, and I am still under a doctor's care and do not want to write anything about my grief and suffering to excuse myself that I kept you waiting so long (if you should care to hear about my children).

[J. G. Budde, a son, continues]

Dear friends, up to this point, I was transcribing my father's notes, since he is no longer capable of doing it himself; hope of recovery led to postponement. Since Christmas a disease has settled in his legs, accompanied by so much pain that he is not able to rest day or night. He can not even lie down any longer but constantly has to remain seated on a sofa or hospital chair. His legs are swollen up to his knees. First his left leg began to swell, beginning at the ankle. It was opened up with poultices, but very little matter came out. In moments like this it seems harder to bear, and he has such pain that he constantly takes his refuge to the God of his salvation for grace to be able to bear with meekness and patience the bad things he sends us in this vale of tears, and to kiss the hand that refines. Six weeks later the other leg also began swelling like the first, but it did not break open because the doctors first wanted to avoid lancing it, but the pain in this leg also became so severe that they felt constrained to do so. The doctors themselves had little hope of recovery because it looked as if there might be (gangrene) in his legs. Also, because his body is so weak and worn out and his life's blood can only flow slowly through his arteries and veins. Father himself is also prepared, if it be the Lord's way, to exchange this mortal life for the immortal, to join her who preceded him in singing and praising their Lord and Savior forever. So Your Honors can well understand the circumstances in which we find ourselves.

But then our expectation is only from the Lord who does not try his children beyond what they are able to bear. But he also constantly puts his balm on their wounds and the admixtures of his mercies are ever so great, for he does not chastise us in his wrath but for our profit, so that we might become partakers of his holiness. And our prayer is: Lord grant us faith and trust that what you do is well done. And now I wish to pick up again the thread where Father left off.

If Your Honors may wish to honor us with a letter, we would appreciate it very much. It is true that I did not write often, because my beloved parents kept up the correspondence. But it was with real joy and desire that I read and reread Your Honor's letters, recalling the days of my youth and the very pleasant hours we already then spent together in the service of the Lord. I need not write you how pleasant it would be for Father if he were to get a reply from Your Honors, if the Lord should spare him that long.

And now humble greetings from us all, and wishing you the blessing of the Lord. I remain most respectfully,

Your Friend,
J. G. Budde

Wormser 87

J. G. Budde to the children of J. Wormser-van der Ven, deceased
Mount Pleasant, Iowa, 16 July 1873

Esteemed Friends in the Lord,

We received your last letter with great joy, because in his last days Father was very eager to get word from you all once more. We got it two days before he passed away, and when I read it to him he said, "All is well," and as regards the church situation [he said]: "Jan, things over there seem to be pretty much as they are here, did you notice. Rigid sectarianism must disappear, and we must again return to being a simple community living together as the children of God, moved to reciprocal love by the love of Christ." Father was getting weaker all the while. The sensation of pain diminished, and since he had developed bedsores from sitting so long, his prayers to be released [from this life] became more urgent, but at the same time he prayed for strength to bear patiently what his heavenly Father laid upon him. Just a few hours before his death, he affirmed the family prayer with a triple Amen, and that is how our beloved Father passed away in the Lord after four months of very painful suffering.

Yes, my dears, the ways of the Lord are wondrous. Mother, so to speak, passed away into blessed eternity without any pain, Father was quite different. He did say to me, I always thought how good it was of the Lord to take Mother to himself without any pain at all. I thought that I was more capable of enduring pain, but the Lord makes me so aware of my own impotence that I must constantly cry out, "Lord, help me." I need not tell you how much we feel the loss of our parents, but would we wish them back in this vale of tears, now that together they are praising our Lord and Savior in the full joy of blessedness with those who preceded them, indeed not. But we shall soon follow in the Lord's good time, for this earthly life hastens away. When I think that twenty-six years have passed since we saw each other last, I wonder, where has the time gone? How many [we knew] have exchanged this temporal life for eternal life in those intervening years? And ere long the call will also come to us, prepare thy house, for thou shalt die.

My dear wife is doing fairly well at the moment, except that she continues to have chronic diarrhea. The Singers also experience blessings. May the Lord especially comfort my sister in the daily loss of Father; may she accept it without complaint and acquiesce in the good pleasure of the Lord.

A month ago we had a convention here of Presbyterian preachers, who were quartered with members of the congregation; we were privileged to spend blessed hours together.

If your brother, sir, has not yet had an opportunity to send me a [pulpit] Bible, then have him send me two, since I promised one to our preacher. And now, my dear friends, I hope that you will continue to maintain the bond of love that existed between our parents and us, by letting us know about your experiences from time to time, and we hope to do the same.

We greet all of you and commend you to God.

Your loving Friend,
J. G. Budde

Wormser 88

Sara Keables-Scholte to Jansje Wüstenhoff-Wormser
Pella, 29 Dec. 1873

Esteemed Friend,

You are probably surprised to receive from me an answer to a letter you sent to Mrs. Bousquet, but since it is getting difficult for her to write, I have taken it upon myself to answer you. She is in reasonably good health and looks very good for her age. I was sorry to hear about the passing of your mother; it is always grievous to lose our friends, even though we know that they have entered their [eternal] rest, but if we love our Lord, we shall soon be joined with them again. Life speeds by so fast, does it not? I noted from your letter that Mr. Budde and his wife had both passed away, and also Berkhout and his wife. They had such a good living here. If only they had not been so difficult, they could have made themselves beloved by all, and they could have done much good. I still often think of the kindness of your parents in taking us in and providing for us, and now that I have children, I appreciate it all the more. No doubt you know that my husband is an American. We have been married for nearly twenty-two years: my oldest son is seventeen, my only daughter is fifteen, and the two youngest are thirteen and eight years, respectively. All of them are still in school. My daughter joined the church last year, and with all my heart I believe that she is a child of God. Since my father's death we have joined the English Reformed Church. My sister Maria is living in with me; she married the oldest son of Mrs. Bousquet. They have a daughter who is two years old. Mother remarried and got a very good man. Of her nine children, two are still living; the oldest son lives at home, and the youngest was transferred to our capital. She lost her youngest daughter a year after Father's death. It was a hard blow, because after Father's [death], they [the children] were always together. She was a dear child, the same age as my Katie. Most of the time people took them for twins; they were dressed alike most of the time. Our oldest brother looks just like Father and is a fine young man. He is now twenty-five years old. They live all on the same street and see each other every day. The daughter's parents and sister also live in the city. You see we are well provided with relations.

 No doubt, you will find some spelling errors, for I never write in the mother tongue, and I read it very seldom; the children speak both languages. My sister married Mr. Nollen. She has two sons; last summer she lost her only daughter. Nollen and Bousquet are in business together as bankers and lawyers. Two of Mrs. Bousquet's sons have American wives and live in the city here. Her second son married a Dutch girl and lives a day's journey from here. Well, I may have written much that you already knew but not what you really wanted to know. But it is difficult to write to a person whom you have not met in so long. But since I hope that you will answer me, things will be better in the future. I also hope to hear from your sister, Cato; I do not know the younger children, though I would like to hear about them, as well as yourself and your family. My sisters send their greetings, and give greetings to your husband from me.

Mrs. B[ousquet] will probably also add a few lines, but if she is not able to do so, she sends many compliments. Wishing you a happy New Year, I sign myself

Your sincere Friend,
Sara Keables Scholte

My address is
Mrs. B. F. Keables
Pella, Marion County, Iowa

...8th of June, the second day of Pentecost, it reached a highpoint such as you cannot begin to imagine. It was...[text illegible]...er's wish that we should stay with him. The doctor said he had never seen anything like it, and the only thing he could prescribe (*in hard copy, text picks up again here*) Spirit, and rule us...

Chapter 8

In Memoriam:
D. A. Budde, J. A. Wormser, and H. P. Scholte

In 1874 Groen van Prinsterer characterized Budde as follows: "A Christian of the hard working middle class who for a long time made his house available for the [worship] meetings and catechism classes of [the Secession Fellowship]. He left [for America] in 1847. Their friendship was kept alive by a fairly regular correspondence. His wife died in 1872, and he followed in 1873. Their children are doing very well just as they [their parents] were also prospering soon after their arrival. Wormser and his wife always spoke of them as being among their best and most noble friends in America, and he [Budde] was almost the only person with whom the fellowship ties were maintained through regular correspondence."[1]

In their "fairly regular correspondence," Budde and his wife set forth their thoughts in considerable detail. Their letters and the other things we learned about them confirm the judgment of Groen. Budde is diligent, loyal, and hospitable. Their letters provide us a direct glimpse of the way ordinary people lived in the nineteenth century with its impotence over against the burdens of old age, contagious diseases, and infant mortality. Budde founded the first Reformed church in Iowa, but when the congregation in Burlington became too small, he affiliated with the Presbyterians. His great grandchildren are still members there.

---

1. G. Groen Van Prinsterer, *Brieven aan J. A. Wormser*, 6 vols. (Amsterdam: Höveker & Zn., 1874-1876), 1: 91.

Grave of the Budde family,
Mount Pleasant, Iowa
(Courtesy of Jan Peter Verhave)

His name is still borne in Mount Pleasant by a number of his descendents, but his descendents will die out with the present generation. A small street in Burlington, a stone [monument] in Mount Pleasant, and several books will long keep alive the memory of his name.

In the present book, especially in the later letters of Budde and his wife, we find a very clear expression of the manner in which the faith of an individual can penetrate his entire being and constantly find expression in his insights and observations. Naturally, this is true not only for the Reformed faith, but also for Roman Catholicism, liberal capitalism, Neo-Marxism, and crass materialism. Often that remains hidden, but in letters like these, it can find free and full expression.

Budde and his wife were of German descent, from Leer in Ost Friesland [Germany]. Ecclesiastically, the Reformed churches in Ost Friesland and in Graafschap Bentheim are affiliated with the Netherlands [churches], and after moving to Amsterdam Budde and his wife became true Dutch citizens. Wormser and Scholte were of Dutch descent, but they themselves were born in Amsterdam.

After J. A. Wormser's death, Groen van Prinsterer characterized him in the following words: "A Christian, whose friendship and advice I remember as one of the outstanding privileges that have come my way. A man, whose influence in his writings and actions on behalf of the

Johan Adam Wormser, Sr., in his later years

Protestant Christian way of life has been both incalculable and unnoticed (at least by many of the great, the noble, and the wise of this world). Wormser was a believing Christian of outstanding gifts. Not only did he have an open eye, but also a keen one that took in our entire ecclesiastical and social situation at a glance. Perhaps no one has equaled him in making intelligible to the public the Christian historical principle as it applies to church, state, and school."[2] In 1874, Groen added: "Exemplary in modesty and simplicity. Gifted with a seldom matched perception, one that is ever thoughtful, and which, informed by the Word of God, at times reached the heights of prophetic insight."[3]

In the days when Wormser was devoting all his energies to the establishment of the Christian Reformed Seminary in Amsterdam and had to mediate between Heldring and Beets, Da Costa and Schwartz, Groen and Brummelkamp and Van Houten, he wrote to Groen on December 11, 1850, "And so in the *Afscheiding* [Secession] I have always had to plod along with the rashness of Scholte, the closed-mindedness of Van Velzen, and the vacillating of Brummelkamp."[4] In all of this, he

---

2. Ibid., 1:4
3. Ibid., 1:6
4. Ibid., 3: 69. The letter written in the morning of December 11, 1850, in the Wormser Letters, is also that of the morning of December 11, 1850, in the Groen Letters.

did not say a word too much; he was always trying to bring people together by committing them to their biblical Reformed origins.

Until the emigration of 1847, Wormser worked together much with Scholte, but after that very much with Groen van Prinsterer. If he [Wormser] had gone to Pella, the Reformed community in the Netherlands would have suffered considerably, and Pella would only have gained one more pioneer. At best he would have been able to correct Scholte and act as an intermediary between Scholte and Van Raalte. In all likelihood, it was the letters from his brother [in America] that kept Wormser in and for the Netherlands.

The Secession wanted to regain its roots in the Reformation, but its knowledge thereof was scanty. Seceders read *de oude schrijvers* [the old writers] of the eighteenth century. On more than one occasion Wormser relates that the Seceders, who appealed to the Three Forms of Unity and the Church Order of Dort, as it turned out, did not know these documents. Wormser himself was extremely diligent in his educational efforts to teach the congregation, old and young, the content of the Reformed faith in Bible classes and in publications.

When Scholte formed the Seceded Congregation of Amsterdam, he warned the people to "be on the watch for itinerant strangers who seek to infiltrate the congregations....Where there is not a qualified and regular leader, the congregation can be edified in the common assemblies by the writings of those preachers who died in the Lord and who still speak after they have died; for example, the sermons of Lodensteyn, Van der Kemp, and Vermeer on the Catechism; the several works of Comrie, Smytegeld *Christenheil en sieraad* [The Christian's Salvation and Adornment]; the sermons of R. and E. Erskine and still others."[5]

Wormser, however, was not one who endorsed the reading of sermons or of the "old writers." He went back to the Reformation of the sixteenth century and the Bible itself. He explained the Heidelberg Catechism and the Bible to children and adults. That was his strength, and, in so doing, he augmented the work of the historian and politician Groen van Prinsterer. As early as 1837, he was also augmenting Scholte with his insights.

In 1837, D. D. Drukker of Veendam published *Eene korte verklaring van den Kinderdoop* [*A Brief Exposition of Infant Baptism*], with an

---

5. H. P. Scholte, foreword to *Adressen aan Zijne Majesteit den Koning...* (The Hague: Van Golverdinge, 1835), 7.

introduction by Rev. H. de Cock. In it the practice of baptizing the children of members by baptism was also sanctioned. Illness and a busy schedule prevented Scholte from responding.

Instead, Scholte published an article by Wormser, "since in all respects it reflects my own feelings, it can be viewed as if I myself had written it." For anyone who is familiar with the problems and the terminology, the following observation by Scholte is curious indeed: "From it one can learn that he can be rigorous in administering [the sacrament] without being a *Labadist* [a Darbyist], that one can be free of all human systematics, without becoming an *Independent*. From this one can also learn that one can advocate a biblical practice of Holy Baptism that is most closely linked to the Forms of Unity, and therefore also to refuse to baptize infants, other than those of Christians, of believers, of the beloved in Christ the Lord, without introducing a semi-Mennonite theology."[6] Scholte himself was accused of Labadism and Independentism, just as he was later of Darbyism.

Wormser taught that baptism was a sign and seal of the covenant between God and the believers and their children. Baptism is not limited to the believing individual, nor is it general for all nominal members of a national [establishment] church. The covenant is made with believing, Christian families. And H. de Cock's problem with the believer who has not made profession of faith and still wants to have his child baptized does not exist for Wormser. He takes the baptismal questions seriously, and the parents, in answering those, are after all making a profession of faith. They are then no longer members by baptism, but professing Christians. Wormser developed his thought further along these lines, whereas Scholte held to a less orthodox course.

The second important point for Wormser was the petition to request [official] recognition of the seceded congregations. Scholte was the first to request recognition in Utrecht in December 1838. Without consultation, the independent Scholte requested recognition while relinquishing the Reformed name and rights of the original Reformed churches. Scholte wanted to maintain the Reformed confession, but he regarded the rights and name as dubious [inconsequential] matters. Wormser, however, was of the opinion that on this point the Secession was falling into a trap. It was not so much that he was concerned about property, but because new churches were being formed. He did not want

---

6. H. P. Scholte and J. A. Wormser, *Bijdragen ter Bevordering der Regte Kennis aangaande de Leer en Praktijk des Heiligen Doops* (Amsterdam: H. Höveker, 1837), vii-viii.

separation from the original church, only from the new church government that had been introduced from the top down [by the Ministry of Internal Affairs.] The object was not a new independent institution, but the maintenance of the historical tie with the Reformed church, with the church of the Reformation and before. History was far more important to Wormser than it was to Scholte. It is for that reason that Wormser always sought cooperation with the Reformed believers in the Hervormde Kerk. Scholte did address the *vorst en volk* [sovereign and people] again and again, but he was less precise about seeking cooperation where and when that was still possible.

In the third place, Wormser sought a connection between church and state. Scholte was already anticipating the end of the Constantinian legacy [of the state church]. He had felt the threat of the state, and he had opposed the seizure of power in the church. He wanted the church to be entirely free of the state. That is why Scholte opposed the Church Order of Dort.

Groen van Prinsterer and Wormser felt their responsibility as citizens of the state. They engaged in the struggle for a Christian school, and they were personally involved in both church and state. In his book *De Kinderdoop beschouwd met betrekking tot het bijzondere, kerkelijke en maatschappelijke leven* [Infant Baptism Viewed in Relation to Private, Ecclesiastical and Social Life], Wormser writes: "So State and Church, even though they may be called separate, in *my* person they do not seem to be *separated*, but in some measure at least, they seem to be *united*. It is expected of me, indivisible person, and I believe rightly so, that I have as much interest in the State as I do in the Church."[7]

In saying this, Wormser proceeds from the actual situation in 1853 that a high percentage of the people of the Netherlands was baptized. On that basis he lays the foundation for Christian politics, something for which Scholte no longer saw a place. Wormser wrote, "Although I am neither a politician nor a theologian by profession, I simply wish in my capacity as a *member* of the entire *body* of the nation to raise my objections to the removal *of all Christian principles from our national institutions*; and my basis for doing so is the fact THAT OUR ENTIRE NATION IS BAPTIZED."[8]

Wormser concludes his book with the following summary: "In the midst of all the turmoil and activity, it may not be deemed superfluous

---

7. J. A. Wormser, *De kinderdoop, beschouwd met betrekking tot het bijzondere, kerkelijke en maatschappelijke leven* (Amsterdam: Höveker, 1864), 2.

8. Ibid., 4.

to remind ourselves that, like every Christian truth, so also every Christian institution *needs to be revived* in the heart and mind with regard to the Christian profession."[9]

In this way, Wormser laid the groundwork for the development of the Reformed Christian social and political mind in the Netherlands. He maintained contact between the Seceders and the later *Doleantie* movement [of the 1880s]. He was in the front ranks of the struggle for the Christian school and Christian politics. With the seminary in Amsterdam, he laid the foundations for the later *Vrije Universiteit*. His son became the publisher for [Abraham] Kuyper of *De Heraut* [the *Herald*] and *De Standaard* and many Free University publications. His work, along with that of Groen van Prinsterer and Kuyper and very many others, bore so much fruit in the Netherlands that not until 1975 was there again talk of the end of the Constantinian period, and likewise the completion of the emancipation of the Reformed community.

According to Wormser, it was Scholte who let the Secession run into the governmental fish trap. From a letter to Groen (23 March 1843), it is evident that Scholte did not apply the criticism of his friend Wormser to himself: "Our brother Wormser wrote you: 'The Secession has run into a fish trap.' In some respects I agree, it is especially true in Amsterdam, but in a fish trap the fish is still in its natural element. The fish does not have to leave the trap in order to get in the water. Even the Amsterdam Seceders still lack something that promotes the real essence of the Christian church." The fish trap here refers to the internal situation in Amsterdam, where Wormser and Budde had been suspended and were still in their pulpits. Scholte was blind to the criticism of him for relinquishing the Reformed name and rights; he did not think of history concretely.

Groen van Prinsterer had already gotten to know Scholte personally immediately after the Secession in November 1834. "I had a rather extended visit with Scholte here recently. In many respects he made a very good impression on me, and it does not surprise me at all that he is well received and has considerable influence on his congregation. I regard him as a person who combines many skills and judgment with much faith and zeal, a faith and zeal that well may put many to shame, and that includes me. But because of that zeal, or rather by being overzealous, he has been carried away to do things of which he will later very likely disapprove." Just contrast that with Groen's judgment

---

9. Ibid., 134.

of H. de Cock, as expressed in one sharp attack: "I will have nothing to do with the impertinencies of Cock and others; it seems to me I have said all that was needed on that subject on p. 37 of *Maatregelen tegen de Afgescheidenen aan het staatsregt getoetst* [*Measures Against the Seceders Examined by Constitutional Law*]."[10]

And so already on their first acquaintance, Groen was favorably impressed by Scholte. He was filled with religious zeal and widely educated, but because of his rashness and independence, it was not easy to work with him. On March 20, 1837, the burgomaster of Amsterdam spoke of Budde as being timorous, but Budde was steadfast, unwavering. Scholte certainly was not the least bit timorous, but he certainly was not reliable on more than one occasion. On the contrary, Wormser went about his work fearlessly and deliberately, always moving steadfastly towards cooperation on a clearly Reformed course.

> Contemporaries described Scholte as a man of the people, familiar and friendly in his dealings with all, and at the same time ready to assist people in distress as he was able. Notwithstanding the opposition he encountered from a small group of people, he was dearly loved by the masses. People, who censured him unmercifully in his absence, were so charmed by his personality that in his presence they acted as if there was not a cloud in the sky. He was not vengeful and was able to rise above opposition, attributing it to ignorance or a faulty narrowmindedness.[11]

Scholte was very susceptible to [momentary] impressions. He was at Ulrum when things got tense there; from the start he was involved with the emigration movement. He was also knowledgeable about what was going on in Europe and elsewhere in the world. In addition, Scholte had a prophetic vision. He foresaw the return of the Jews to Palestine, he clearly realized the problematic aspects of the Church Order of Dort, and in his own mind he had already experienced the end of the Constantinian period [in church history].

As regards his faith, Scholte was Reformed, but he had a very independent character. He encouraged separation between church and state, because the freedom of the church was dear to him. There was no

---

10. Letter to C. J. Van Assen, September 20, 1837.
11. H. Beets, "H. P. Scholte's leven en streven in Noord-Amerika," *Nederlandsch Archief voor Kerkgeschiedenis* 23 (1930): 274.

room in his thought for the adherence to Christian principles in politics and the struggle for a Christian school. The free school in Pella was a public school that did not charge tuition, and Scholte was a trustee. Wormser emphasized that the whole [indivisible] person played a role in the church as well as in the state, the school, the family, and the society. How can one be a Christian in the church and not in the school, the state, the family, in society? That question was only partially answered by Van Raalte in America. And Scholte completely ignored the question. Instead, he was very much preoccupied with the return of Christ. Additionally, the unity of the person was less perfectly realized in Scholte, because of a counter force in his marriage. There were many factors, including his marriage, the separation of church and state, his independence and sometimes rash actions; these and the hostility to him that developed in the Netherlands and in his own circle [in America] prevented the unity of his person, which he as a Christian should have been, from coming into its own. He escaped the calling to be a Christian in all of life by withdrawing from the situation in the Netherlands, by emigrating to Pella, by withdrawing himself from the ecclesiastical developments in Pella, by giving his attention to the immediate here and now, and by transferring Christian politics, Christian school, and Christian social action to the future coming of Christ.

If we judge by his educational level, gifts of mind, imagination, powers of expression, and his heart, then Scholte far excelled Wormser and Budde. But Budde was more steadfast and faithful, and we must esteem Wormser more highly for his Christian-historical perspective [on life]. The question of Wormser still remains pertinent, also in America: how can a baptized Christian be so divided a person that in the area of school and politics he does not struggle for Christian principles and Christian institutions? That struggle will have to teach us whether there is still room for Christian political parties and other Christian organizations, or whether the only thing we are left with is a Christian church community. If there is no possibility for a Christian party in America, then the need for a radical Christian political movement remains.

Chapter 9

Pella and Amsterdam

According to Eusebius's account about the siege of Jerusalem in the year 70 A.D. in the third volume of his *Church History*, the Christians took timely refuge in Pella. The congregation at Jerusalem had received a revelation to go to Pella, and when those who believed in Christ had left Jerusalem and Judea, judgment fell upon the Jews at the hand of the Roman Titus. This story is known to us only through Eusebius. Pella was located close to the Jordan [River], opposite Beth-San, thirty kilometers south of Lake Gennesaret. The city belonged to the Decapolis, a ten-city federation. These cities were not Jewish and had self-rule under the Roman governor of Syria. They were cities with a strong Hellenistic influence. If the Jerusalem congregation indeed went to Pella, the move was significant in that it was a flight from a great disaster, a break with Israel, and that it began the Hellenizing and Romanizing of the church.

When Scholte went to Pella, it signified a flight from Europe in time to escape the Revolution of 1848, a break with the Netherlands, and the beginning of the Americanization of the immigrants. The name Pella is heavily laden with a vision of Europe as Babel, the city in which the church is persecuted, like the Jerusalem on which judgment bursts forth. And that is then the Roman church of the Constantinian period, which is organized as a system in which the power of the church unites with the power of the state in order to regulate and organize the freedom of the children of God, and thus to enslave them.

Van Raalte did not share this vision of Europe as Babel, and Scholte discovered that American freedom is not the same as Christian freedom. Pella is also located on this earth and is no more than a temporary hiding place from a limited judgment. Scholte writes in *De tweede stem uit Pella* [*The Second Voice from Pella*] that the Roman Empire never repented from the sin of Pontius Pilate, who said to Christ, "Do you not know that I have power to crucify you or to let you go?" All the governments of Europe, the Netherlands included, acknowledge this Roman principle.

> The sin of Pontius Pilate cleaves to you as a nation. And that is not just now, it was true in the most flourishing times of the commonweal. Note it in the title of your national Bible translation: *Op last der Edel Mogende Heeren Staten Generaal* [By Order of the Noble High and Mighty Lords of the States General]. And note it in the Acts of the Synod of Dordrecht, in which those Noble High and Mighty Lords give orders about what may or may not be dealt with, entirely in the spirit of the Roman Empire under Constantine the Great.... And are we then safe in America? My answer is: the people of the United States of North America have a great host of sinners in their midst, but as a nation it has not been guilty of the sin of the Roman empire....
>
> The liberal principle in Europe and in the Netherlands is: religion is an indifferent matter to the State and therefore everyone may think and believe as he pleases. The North American principle is: the State has not received power over conscience, and it is not qualified to judge in matters of religion. God alone is judge of that, and that is why the State does not have anything to do with it....

In good conscience a Christian cannot join the side of liberalism, but no less can he be on the side of the so-called conservative party; for both of them belong to Babel.

Thus, a Christian cannot become a member of a conservative party or of a progressive liberal party. That is why Wormser and Groen van Prinsterer chose for a Christian party. Scholte considered it to be the Christian's calling to immigrate to America. He has a very favorable impression of America:

> The Declaration of Independence did not flow from a theoretical principle of freedom, but from the practical recognition of justice

and righteousness. The vast areas where millions of people can still make an adequate living were not taken from their former owners by force, with bloodthirsty weapons; they were bought and paid for. The Babel [Constantinian] principle of the world empires in the North-American Colonies, transplanted from Europe from the start, was totally rejected when the Union was formed....The worship of God is held in honor without financial support from the State; but also without being fettered by the State.

Not until the Civil War does Scholte acknowledge that Babel is also present in America. Babel is the country where Israel sojourned in exile. Babel-Rome is the world power that arrogates to itself the right to tell congregations of Christ what their place [in society] is. "America is not entirely free of that; the spirit of Babel also rules there," Scholte wrote in 1863. Pella was a place of refuge and a place of rest, but not for long. The grain fields of Iowa are of greatest importance to the entire world. With the resources of Iowa and the Midwest, "Washington" decides the quality of life for a number of nations at international food conferences. It is no longer possible to escape culture. The earth is round, and there is no rim to civilization. World problems cannot be escaped anywhere.

Amsterdam, a city of burger homes, so human in their dimension and encircled by canals, is a city at the forefront of the culture struggle. In Amsterdam, German, French, and English cultures interact in a center of progressive, democratic tolerance. Whatever one finds in the metropolises of Berlin, Frankfurt, Paris, London, Jerusalem, Rome, New York, Montreal, Toronto, and San Francisco is also present in Amsterdam. In Amsterdam, the descendents of Wormser, Brummelkamp, and Donner, under the leadership of Abraham Kuyper, worked together in establishing and developing the *Vrije Universiteit*. It is now a progressive Christian university that gives much attention to the third world. Those countries prefer to maintain contact with a small country, rather than with the great centers of power.

The Free University has shown little interest in Pella. There is much interest in, but less sympathy for, Washington as a center of world power. The Christian interest of the Free University is directed above all to the suppressed and the poor. The center of interest is directed less to seventeenth-century immigrants of Netherlands descent and the migrants of the nineteenth century. The United States of North America themselves constitute a pattern of cultures between two oceans, which as a whole makes a unified impression. Especially the Midwest, with

Pella located between Chicago and Omaha, gives the impression of keeping to itself and being conservative. And imperceptibly, Christendom there has Americanized, as in Europe it has Hellenized and Romanized.

The emigrants of 1847 wanted a free, Christian school. But Scholte became a school inspector of the public school. In Pella, Scholte became a banker and life insurance agent. In 1859, on one day he was a delegate to the Democratic state convention and suddenly on the next a delegate of the Republican Party. Of course, a man may act that way in a free country. Still, those are signs of the Americanization of Christian life.

When one views all the above and compares it with the reform efforts of Groen van Prinsterer, Wormser, and Kuyper, then, seen from a distance, this development [Americanization] is most striking. The end of the Constantinian period signifies the end of the secular power of the church. That is the end of cooperation between the church and the state, the [church] and social and cultural structures, the [church] and political and other secular powers. Many churches discover that the gospel has been so hindered through that cooperation that gradually they have become sterile, cultural organizations. And often the ruling authorities have no further need to cooperate with the churches on behalf of peaceful governance. In the modern world it is precisely the power of the church that is an obstacle to the church in giving shape to, and witnessing to what inspires the church of Christ. The Hellenization, Romanization, and Americanization of the church is coming to an end. A Christian will no longer automatically be a good citizen and soldier. And the churches that continue to derive their power from a scholastic doctrine, an Episcopal hierarchy, the Roman Curia, the Apostolic Succession, the Declaration of Independence, or the Rights of Man, can no longer make an appeal to the Holy Spirit. They are losing their spirit.

These observations are concerned with understanding the time in which we live. We are speeding toward a world culture, one in which Pella and all cities and villages on earth are moving to the cultural front lines. Again the sign of Israel has been raised in Jerusalem, and all nations and all the peoples of the world are involved. The God-is-dead theology turned out to be a slogan. And the words, "He scares me so. I want him so. I love him so," resonate in the hearts of many the world over.

In Amsterdam and in Pella, in Europe and in America, we shall have to liberate ourselves from many cultural, political, and national obstacles in order to follow Christ as the Savior of the whole world in a new era.

Biography of Johan Stellingwerff

Johan Stellingwerff was born in Groningen on December 5, 1924, son of Jan Stellingwerff, teacher, and Wissiena Bügel. He was the oldest of nine children, of whom four immigrated to Canada. He attended a Christian high school in Groningen, and, after the Second World War, he studied civil engineering at the *Technische Hoogeschool* [Delft Polytechnic University]. He received his doctorate there June 24, 1959, with a dissertation entitled *Werkelijkheid en grondmotief bij Vincent Willem van Gogh*. Employed first by N.V. Philips and then by the municipal government in Eindhoven, he was named acting librarian for the newly formed Technical University in Eindhoven. He became the librarian of the Free University of Amsterdam in 1960, a post he held for twenty-seven years, until the end of 1987. He reorganized the library, supervised the removal to a new campus of its holdings scattered in various locations in downtown Amsterdam, and began the automation of the library.

His publications are in the areas of philosophy and history. In 1959, he and a number of students initiated the publication of the commemorative volume, *Perspectief*, for the twenty-fifth anniversary of the *Vereniging voor Calvinistische Wijsbegeerte* [Society for Calvinist Philosophy]. This was followed by the series, *Christelijk Perspectief*, of which he edited twenty-six volumes. In 1999 he published *Inzicht in Virtual Reality: een media-filosofie als reisgids voor het landschap van de geest*. His latest book, *Doeff van Deshima, kenner van Japan, koopman en diplomaat*, is in press.

List of Letters

List of Letters
Number   Sender   Addressee
                                   Place and Date

Chapter 1
Extra   H.S. van Schermbeek   Children
                                   Utrecht 20 Dec. 1843

Chapter 2
Extra   H. Hospers   Parents
                                   Pella 20 Nov. 1847
W. 1   M. Mensink   H. Wormser
                                   Albany 30 Dec. 1846
W. 2   D. A. Budde   J. A. Wormser
                                   Nieuwediep 27 March 1847
W. 3   C. M. Budde-Stomp   J. Wormser-van der Ven
                                   Nieuwediep 30 March 1847
W. 4   J. G. Budde   J. and K. Wormser
                                   Nieuwediep 30 March 1847
W. 5   C. M. Budde-Stomp   J. Wormser-van der Ven
                                   Texelstroom 1 April 1847

W. 6	D. A. Budde	J. A. Wormser New York 11, 19 May 1847
Extra	H. P. Scholte	A. A. W. Schuyt New York 14 May 1847
W. 7	D. A. Budde	J. A. Wormser Burlington Summer 1847
W. 8	C. M. Budde-Stomp	J. Wormser-van der Ven Burlington Summer 1847
W. 9	D. A. Budde	J. A. Wormser Burlington 15 Aug. 1847
Extra	P. Zonne	J. A. Wormser Milwaukee 4 Sept. 1847
W.10	A. C. Van Raalte	J. A. Wormser Allegan 7 Jan. 1848
W.11	D. A. Budde	J. A. Wormser Burlington 11 Jan. 1848
W.12	C. M. Budde-Stomp	J. A. Wormser Burlington January 1848
W.13	D. A. Budde	J. A. Wormser Burlington 15 Feb. 1848
B. 1	J. Wormser-van der Ven	C. M. Budde-Stomp Amsterdam 24 April 1848
B 2	Jansje Wormser	Jan Budde Amsterdam 24 April 1848
B. 3	Cato and J. A. Wormser, Jr.	Jan Budde Amsterdam 24 April 1848
B. 4	J. Wormser-van der Ven	D. A. Budde Amsterdam 21 July 1848
W.14	D. A. Budde	J. A. Wormser Burlington June 1848
W.15	C. M. Budde-Stomp	J. Wormser-van der Ven Burlington June 1848
B. 5	Jansje Wormser	Jan Budde Amsterdam 25 July 1848
W.16	H. P. Scholte	J. A. Wormser Pella 4 August 1848

Chapter 3

H. 1 [1]	H. Hospers	Parents, Brothers and Sisters Rotterdam April 1847
H. 2 [2]	H. Hospers	Parents, Brothers and Sisters Hellevoetsluis 17 April 1847
H. 3*	J. Hospers	H. Hospers Hoogblokland 16 Aug. 1847

List of Letters 643

H. 4*	Hendrika Hospers		H. Hospers Hoogblokland, undated
H. 5*	J. Hospers		H. Hospers Hoogblokland 28 Aug. 1847
H. 6 [3]	H. Hospers		Sisters Pella 7 Sept. 1847
H. 7 [4]	H. Hospers		Willem & Gerrit Middelkoop Pella 7 Sept. 1847
H. 8*	J. Hospers		H. Hospers Hoogblokland 30 Sept. 1847
H. 9*	N. Hospers		H. Hospers Hoogblokland 3 Oct. 1847
H. 10*	J. Hospers		H. Hospers Hoogblokland 10 Oct. 1847
H. 11*	J. Hospers		H. Hospers Hoogblokland 12 Oct. 1847
H. 12 [5]	H. Hospers		Parents and Grandparents Pella 27 Sept. 1847
H. 13 [6]	H. Hospers		Parents Pella 27 Oct. 1847
Extra	I. Overkamp		J. Hospers Pella 27 Oct. 1847
H. 14 [7]	H. Hospers		Parents Pella 17 Nov. 1847
Extra	H. Hospers		H. P. Scholte Pella 5 Nov. 1847
H. 15*	H. Hospers		Parents Pella 20 Nov. 1847
H. 16 [8]	H. Hospers		Parents Pella 30 Nov. 1847
H. 17*	J. Hospers		H. Hospers Hoogblokland 23 Dec. 1847
H. 18*	J. Hospers		H. Hospers Hoogblokland 1 Jan. 1848
H. 19*	J. Hospers(Confidential)		H. Hospers Hoogblokland 1 Jan. 1848
H. 20 [9]	H. Hospers		Parents Pella 10 Feb. 1848
H. 21[10]	H. Hospers		Mother Pella 10 Feb. 1848
H. 22[12]	J. Hospers		H. Hospers Hoogblokland 21 Feb. 1848
H. 23*	J. Hospers		H. Hospers Hoogblokland 24 Feb. 1848

H. 24*	J. Hospers	H. P. Scholte
		Hoogblokland 25 Feb. 1848
H. 25[11]	H. Hospers	J. Hospers
		Pella March 1848
H. 26	Hendrik Hospers	Maaike Hospers
		Pella 19 March 1848
H. 27[13]	H. Hospers	Mother
		Pella 22 March 1848
H. 28[14]	H. Hospers	Father
		Pella 22 March 1848
H. 29	J. Hospers	H. Hospers
		Hoogblokland 1 April 1848
H. 30	Hendrika Hospers	H. Hospers
		Hoogblokland 16 April 1848
H. 31	N. Hospers	H. Hospers
		Hoogblokland 16 April 1848
H. 32	J. Hospers	H. Hospers
		Hoogblokland 22 April 1848
H. 33[15]	H. Hospers	Parents, Brothers, and Sisters
		Pella 26 April 1848
H. 34[16]	H. Hospers	Parents
		Pella [undated, May 1848]
H. 35	H. Hospers	Parents
		Pella 30 May 1848
H. 36	H. Hospers	Parents
		Pella June 1848
H. 37[17]	H. Hospers	Parents
		Pella 3 June 1848
H. 38[18]	J. Hospers	H. Hospers
		Hoogblokland 1 June 1848
H. 39*	H. Hospers	Parents
		Pella 24 June 1848
H. 40[19]	H. Hospers	Parents
		Pella 30 June 1848
H. 41	H. Hospers	Parents, Brothers, and Sisters
		Pella, 6 July 1848
H. 42	J. Hospers	H. Hospers
		Hoogblokland 9 July 1848
H. 43*	J. Hospers	H. Hospers
		Hoogblokland 10 July 1848
H. 44*	J. Hospers	H. Hospers
		Hoogblokland 15 Aug. 1848

List of Letters 645

H. 45*	J. Hospers	H. Hospers	
		Hoogblokland 22 Aug.1848	
H. 46	H. Hospers	Parents	
		Pella 25 Aug. 1848	
Extra	G. H. Overkamp	J. Hospers	
		Pella 1 Aug. 1848	
H. 47*	J. Hospers	H. Hospers	
		Hoogblokland 2 Sept. 1848	
H. 48*	J. Hospers	H. Hospers	
		Hoogblokland 28 Sept. 1848	
H. 49*	J. Hospers	H. Hospers	
		Hoogblokland 10 Oct. 1848	
H. 50*	J. Hospers	H. Hospers	
		Hoogblokland 13 Oct. 1848	
H. 51*	J. Hospers	H. Hospers	
		Hoogblokland 24 Nov.1848	
H. 52*	J. Hospers	H. Hospers	
		Hoogblokland 28 Nov.1848	
H. 53*	E. Aanen	J. Hospers	
		Hoornaar 21 Dec. 1848	
H. 54*	H. Hospers	Parents	
		Pella Dec. 1848	
H. 55*	J. Hospers	H. Hospers	
		Hoogblokland 30 Dec. 1848	
H. 56*	L. Van Bergyk	J. Hospers	
		Pella Jan. 1849	
H. 57*	J. Hospers	H. Hospers	
		Hoogblokland 18 Jan. 1849	
H. 58*	J. Hospers	H. Hospers	
		Hoogblokland, undated	
H. 59[20]	H. Hospers (Confidential)	Parents	
		Pella 1 Feb. 1849	
Extra	L. Van Bergyk	J. Hospers	
		Pella 1 Feb. 1849	
H. 60*	H. Hospers	Mother	
		Pella 10 Feb. 1849	
H. 61*	J. Hospers	H. Hospers	
		Hoogblokland 20 Feb.1849	
H. 62*	E. Aanen	J. Hospers	
		Hoornaar 20 Feb. 1849	
H. 63	J. Hospers	H. Hospers	
		Hoogblokland 20 Feb.1849	

646   IOWA LETTERS

H. 64*	J. Hospers	H. Hospers Hoogblokland 20 Mar. 1849
H. 65[21	H. Hospers	Parents and Grandparents Pella April 1849

Chapter 4

Extra	J. A. Wormser	C. G. de Moen Amsterdam 28 Oct 1851
W. 17	S. de Vries	A. N. Wormser Buffalo 6 Nov. 1848
W. 18	A. N. Wormser	J. A. Wormser Burlington 6 Nov. 1848
W. 19	D. A. Budde	J. A. Wormser Burlington 8 Nov. 1848
W. 20	A. N. Wormser	J. A. Wormser Burlington 9 Nov. 1848
W. 21	A. N. Wormser	J. A. Wormser Burlington 17 Nov. 1848
W. 22	A. N. Wormser	H. Wormser Burlington 27 Nov. 1848
W. 23	J. Berkhout	D. A. Budde St. Louis 2 Dec. 1848
W. 24	A. N. Wormser	J. A. Wormser Burlington 12 Dec. 1848
W. 25	M. Wormser-Portengen	J. Wormser-van der Ven Burlington [17] Dec. 1848
W. 26	H. P. Scholte	J. A. Wormser Pella 20 Dec. 1848
W. 27	A. N. Wormser	H. Wormser Burlington 20 Jan. 1849
W. 28	A. N. Wormser	J. A. Wormser Burlington 20 Jan. 1849
W. 29	H. P. Scholte	J. A. Wormser Pella 20 Jan. 1849
W. 30	A. N. Wormser	J. A. Wormser Burlington 20 Feb. 1849
W. 31	A. N. Wormser	J. A. Wormser Burlington 20 Feb. 1849
W. 32	D. A. Budde	J. A. Wormser Burlington Feb. 1849
W. 33	C. M. Budde-Stomp	J. Wormser-van der Ven Burlington [Feb.] 1849

W. 34	D. A. Budde	J. A. Wormser
		Burlington March 1849
W. 35	A. N. Wormser	J. A. Wormser
		St. Louis 22 March 1849
W. 36	A. N. Womser	J. A. Wormser
		New York 2 May 1849
W. 37	J. Berkhout	J. A. Wormser
		Pella 11, 26 May 1849
Extra	J. A. Wormser	J. Wormser-van der Ven
		Amsterdam 27 June 1849
Extra	J. A. Wormser	J. Wormser-van der Ven
		Amsterdam 24 July 1849

Chapter 5

Extra	J. Hospers	Autobiography
		Pella 18 Aug. 1886
Extra	J. Hospers	Travel journal
		20 May-3 Aug. 1849
H. 66[22]	J. Hospers	H. Hospers
		Albany 30 June 1849
W. 38	H. M. Bousquet-Chabot	J. Wormser-van der Ven
		Pella 20 Sept. 1949
Extra	A. E. Dudok Bousquet	J. A. Wormser
		Pella 29 Sept. 1849
W. 39	J. Berkhout	H. W. Wormser
		Pella 12 March 1850
W. 40	D. A. Budde	J. A. Wormser
		Burlington 17 March 1850
W. 41	C. M. Budde-Stomp	J. Wormser-van der Ven
		Burlington March 1850
W. 42	J. Berkhout	J. A. Wormser
		Pella 25 June 1850
W. 43	G. Berkhout-Smit	J. Wormser-van der Ven
		Pella 23 Aug. 1850
B. 6	H. M. Bousquet-Chabot	Budde family
		Pella 4 Dec. 1850
B. 7	J. A. Wormser	D. A. Budde
		Amsterdam 9 May 1851
W. 44	K. de Jong	Family
		Pella 1851?
W. 45	Mrs. K. de Jong	Family
		Pella 1851?

W. 46	D. A. and C. M. Budde	J. A. Wormser Burlington 26 Dec. 1851
W. 47	D. A. Budde	J. A. Wormser Burlington 23 Dec. 1852
W. 48	H. M. Bousquet-Chabot	J. Wormser-van der Ven Pella 28 Nov. 1852
W. 49	H. M. Bousquet-Chabot	J. Wormser-van der Ven Pella 1 March 1853

Chapter 6

Extra	H. P. Scholte	J. J. L. van der Brugghen Pella 5 Aug. 1857
W. 50	D. A. Budde	J. A. Wormser Burlington 29 May 1854
B. 8	J. Wormser-van der Ven	C. M. Budde-Stomp Amsterdam 26 Aug. 1854
B. 9	Jansje Wormser	C. M. Budde-Stomp Amsterdam 1 Sept. 1854
B. 10	J. A. Wormser	D. A. Budde Amsterdam 2 Sept. 1854
B. 11	Cato Wormser	C. M. Budde-Stomp Amsterdam 2 Sept. 1854
W. 51	C. M. Budde-Stomp	J. Wormser-van der Ven Burlington 1854?
W. 52	C. M. Budde-Stomp	J. Wormser-van der Ven Burlington Nov. 1854
B. 12	J. Wormser-van der Ven	C. M. Budde-Stomp Amsterdam 8 May 1855
B. 13	H. M. Bousquet-Chabot	C. M. Budde-Stomp Pella 25 July 1855
W. 53	D. A. Budde	J. A. Wormser Burlington November 1855
W. 54	C. M. Budde-Stomp	J. Wormser-van der Ven Burlington November 1855
B. 14	J. Wormser-van der Ven	C. M. Budde-Stomp Amsterdam 11 Jan. 1856
B. 15	J. A. Wormser, Jr.	C. M. Budde-Stomp Amsterdam 23 Feb. 1856
W. 55	D. A. Budde	J. A. Wormser Burlington 14 Nov. 1856
W. 56	C. M. Budde-Stomp	J. Wormser-van der Ven Burlington Dec. 1856

B. 16	Cato Wormser	C. M. Budde-Stomp Amsterdam 3 July 1857
B. 17	J. Wormser-van der Ven	C. M. Budde-Stomp Amsterdam 4 July 1857
B. 18	Jansje Wormser	C. M. Budde-Stomp Amsterdam 6 July 1857
Extra	H. P. Scholte	J.J.L. van der Brugghen Pella 22 Oct. 1847
W. 57	C. M. Budde-Stomp	J. Wormser-van der Ven Burlington Jan. 1858
B. 19	J. A. Wormser, Jr.	Diedrich Budde, Jr. Amsterdam 20 Feb. 1858
B. 20	Johanna Schellinger	D. A. Budde Alkmaar 5 April 1858
B. 21	J. Wormser-van der Ven	C. M. Budde-Stomp Amsterdam 26 April 1858
B. 22	Jansje Wormser	C. M. Budde-Stomp Amsterdam 27 April 1858
B. 23	Johanna Schellinger	D. A. Budde Alkmaar 9 June 1858
W. 58	C. M. Budde-Stomp	J. Wormser-van der Ven Burlington 10 Dec. 1858
B. 24	D. A. Budde	Church Speech Burlington 19 Dec. 1858
W. 59	D. A. Budde	J. A. Wormser Burlington 21 Dec. 1858
W. 60	C. M. Budde-Stomp	Jansje Wormser Burlington 21 Dec. 1858
Extra	A. C. Van Raalte	J. H. Donner Pella 5 March 1859
B. 25	J. Wormser-van der Ven	C. M. Budde-Stomp Amsterdam 1 Aug. 1859
W. 61	D. A. Budde	J. A. Wormser Burlington 18 Dec. 1860

Chapter 7

Extra	F. A. van Hall	J. Wormser-van der Ven The Hague 5 Nov. 1852
Extra	H. P. Scholte	H. J. Buddingh Pella 16 May 1866
B. 26	Johanna Schellinger	D. A. Budde Alkmaar 16 Sept. 1860

W. 62	C. M. Budde-Stomp	J. Wormser-van der Ven Burlington [late 1860]
B. 27	Johanna Schellinger	Maria Budde & Niece Naatje Alkmaar 30 May 1861
B. 28	Jansje Wüstenhoff-Wormser	C. M. Budde-Stomp Amsterdam 19 Oct. 1861
B. 29	Cato de Boer-Wormser	C. M. Budde-Stomp Amsterdam Nov. 1861
W. 63	C. M. Budde-Stomp	J. Wormser-van der Ven Burlington 5 Dec. 1861
W. 64	C. M. Budde-Stomp	C. W. Wüstenhoff Burlington Dec. 1861
B. 30	J. A. Wormser	D. A. Budde Amsterdam [no date]
W. 65	D. A. Budde	J. A. Wormser Burlington 16 Oct. 1861
B. 31	H. M. Bousquet-Chabot	C. M. Budde-Stomp Pella 18 Feb. 1862
B. 31a	H. M. Bousquet-Chabot	C. M. Budde-Stomp Pella 18 Feb. 1862
B. 32	Johan Müller	D. A. Budde Silver Brook 21 April 1862
B. 33	H. M. Bousquet-Chabot	C. M. Budde-Stomp Pella 14 Sept. 1862
B. 34	Jansje Wüstenhoff-Wormser	C. M. Budde-Stomp Amsterdam 3 Oct. 1862
B. 35	H. M. Bousquet-Chabot	D. A. Budde Pella 21 Oct. 1862
W. 66	H. M. Bousquet-Chabot	J. Wormser-van der Ven Pella 8 Dec. 1862
W. 67	C. M. Budde-Stomp	J. Wormser-van der Ven Burlington Dec. 1862
W. 68	D. A. Budde	J. Wormser-van der Ven Burlington 9 Dec 1862
B. 36	Cato de Boer-Wormser	C. M. Budde-Stomp Amsterdam 23 Jan. 1863
B. 37	J. Wormser-van der Ven	C. M. Budde-Stomp Amsterdam 23 Feb. 1863
W. 69	C. M. Budde-Stomp	J. Wormser-van der Ven Burlington 27 Jan. 1863
B. 38	Johan Müller	D. A. Budde Silver Brook 30 March 1863

B. 39	Johanna Schellinger	D. A. Budde Alkmaar 30 May 1863
B. 40	Jansje Wüstenhoff-Wormser	C. M. Budde-Stomp Amsterdam 26 Aug. 1863
B. 41	C. M. van der Veen	D. A. Budde Pella 23 Sept. 1863
W. 70	C. M. Budde-Stomp	J. Wormser-van der Ven Burlington Oct. 1863
W. 71	J. G. Budde	J. Wormser-van der Ven Burlington 5 June 1864
B. 42	Johanna Schellinger	D. A. Budde Alkmaar 26 Aug. 1864
B. 43	Cato de Boer-Wormser	C. M. Budde-Stomp Amsterdam 24 Oct. 1864
W. 72	D. A. Budde	J. Wormser-van der Ven Burlington 10 Jan. 1865
W. 73	C. M. Budde-Stomp	J. Wormser-van der Ven Burlington 10 Oct. 1865
B. 44	J. Wormser-van der Ven	C. M. Budde-Stomp Amsterdam 20 Jan. 1866
W. 74	C. M. Budde-Stomp	J. Wormser-van der Ven Burlington 14 March 1866
Extra	A. C. Van Raalte	Ben Van Raalte Kampen 11 June 1866
Extra	H. Wormser	about factory work Nijverdal 15 March 1867
Extra	Jansje Wüstenhoff-Wormser	J. Wormser-van der Ven Paris 21 July 1867
W. 75	C. M. Budde-Stomp	J. Wormser-van der Ven Burlington August 1867
W. 76	D. A. Budde	J. Wormser-van der Ven Burlington 16 Sept. 1867
B. 45	Jansje Wüstenhoff-Wormser	C. M. Budde-Stomp Amsterdam 3 Oct. 1867
B. 46	J. Wormser-van der Ven	C. M. Budde-Stomp Amsterdam 3 Oct. 1867
W. 77	C. M. Budde-Stomp	J. Wormser-van der Ven Burlington Jan. 1868
W. 78	C. M. Budde-Stomp	Jansje Wüstenhoff-Wormser Burlington Jan. 1868
B. 47	Cato de Boer-Wormser	C. M. Budde-Stomp Baambrugge 30 Jan. 1968

B. 48	Jansje Wüstenhoff-Wormser	C. M. Budde-Stomp Baambrugge 14 Feb. 1868
B. 49	J. Wormser-van der Ven	C. M. Budde-Stomp Amsterdam 28 Feb. 1868
B. 50	J. Berkhout	D. A. Budde Amsterdam 14 Feb. 1868
B. 51	M. M. and C. H. Budde	Budde family Amsterdam 21 April 1868
W. 79	C. M. Budde-Stomp	J. Wormser-van der Ven Burlington May 1868
W. 80	D. A. Budde	J. Wormser-van der Ven Burlington 20 June 1868
B. 52	J. Wormser-van der Ven	C. M. Budde-Stomp Amsterdam Sept. 1868
W. 81	C. M. Budde-Stomp	J. Wormser-van der Ven Mt. Pleasant Nov. 1868
B. 53	Johanna Schellinger	C. M. Budde-Stomp Alkmaar 5 June 1869
B. 54	Johanna Schellinger	Naatje Schellinger Alkmaar 5 June [1869]
B. 55	J. Wormser-van der Ven	C. M. Budde-Stomp Amsterdam 16 Aug. 1869
W. 82	C. M. Budde-Stomp	J. Wormser-van der Ven Mt. Pleasant 20 Dec. 1869
B. 56	Johanna Schellinger	C. M. Budde-Stomp Alkmaar 20 Oct. 1870
B. 57	J. Wormser-van der Ven	C. M. Budde-Stomp Amsterdam 12 Nov. 1870
W. 83	C. M. Budde-Stomp	J. Wormser-van der Ven Mt. Pleasant 20 Dec. 1870
B. 58	J. Wormser-van der Ven	Budde family Amsterdam 2 Feb. 1871
B. 59	J. A. Wormser, Jr.	D. A. & C. M. Budde Amsterdam 22 Feb. 1871
W. 84	C. M. Budde-Stomp	J. Wormser-van der Ven Mt. Pleasant May 1871
B. 60	Jansje Wüstenhoff-Wormser	C. M. Budde-Stomp Amsterdam 15 Jan. 1872
W. 85	C. M. Budde-Stomp	Children Wid. J.A. Wormser Mt. Pleasant 28 March 1872
B. 61	Johanna Schellinger	C. M. Budde-Stomp Alkmaar 10 May 1872

W. 86	D. A. Budde	Children Wid. J.A. Wormser Mt. Pleasant 13 Feb. 1873
W. 87	J. G. Budde	Children Wid. J.A. Wormser Mt. Pleasant 16 July 1873
W. 88	Sara Keebles-Scholte	Jansje Wüstenhoff-Wormser Pella 29 Dec. 1873

Bibliography
Edited by Cornelia Kennedy

Acte van Afscheiding van het Nederlandsch Hervormd Kerkgenootschap: den 14en October 1834 te Ulrum geteekend benevens de notulen van de eerste kerkeraadsvergadering der Afgescheidenen. Nijverdal: Bosch, 1915.

Adres, ingediend aan Z.M. den Koning, ter begeleiding der Provinciale kerkeördening door inwoners van de Provinciën Zuid-Holland, Utrecht, Noord-Brabant en Gelderland. Amsterdam: Höveker, 1837.

Algemeen Reglement voor het Bestuur der Hervormde Kerk in het Koninkrijk der Nederlanden. The Hague: Algemeene 'sLands Drukkerij, 1816.

Algra, H. *Het wonder van de 19e eeuw: van vrije kerken en kleine luyden.* 3rd ed., rev. Franeker: T. Wever, 1970.

Bartlett, Richard A. *The New Country: A Social History of the American Frontier, 1776-1890.* New York: Oxford Univ. Press, 1974.

Beets, H. "H. P. Scholte's leven en streven in Noord-Amerika." *Nederlandsch archief voor Kerkgeschiedenis* 23 (1930): 260-76.

Boeck, G. A. "Transportation Fever in Burlington, 1845-1855." *Iowa Journal of History* 56, no. 2 (April 1958).

Bos, F. L. *Kruisdominees: figuren uit de Gereformeerde Kerk onder 't kruis.* Kampen: J. H. Kok, 1953.

Bos, F. L. and A. Goslinga, eds. *Archiefstukken betreffende de Afscheiding van 1834.* 4 vols. Kampen: J. H. Kok, 1939-1946.

Bosch, J. *Figuren en Aspecten uit de eeuw der Afscheiding.* Goes: Oosterbaan & Le Cointre, 1952.

Bouma, H. *Een vergeten hoofdstuk: een bladzijde uit de worsteling van de sedert 1834 wedergekeerde Kerken voor gereformeerd schoolonderwijs.* Enschede: J. Boersma, 1954.

Bouwman, H. *De Crisis der Jeugd: eenige bladzijden uit de geschiedenis van de kerken der Afscheiding.* Kampen: J. H. Kok, 1914.

Brief uit Noord Amerika van J. Berkhout aan zijnen vader, broeder en vrienden. Amsterdam: Van Peursem, 1849.

Brugmans, H. *Stilstaand getij, 1795-1848.* Rev. ed. by I. J. Brugmans. Vol 2, Geschiedenis van Amsterdam. Utrecht: Het Spectrum, 1973.

Bruins, Elton J. *The Americanization of a Congregation.* 2nd ed. Grand Rapids, Mich.: Eerdmans, 1970.

Brummelkamp, A. *Evangelische Alliantie: Rede uitgesproken bij het overdragen van het rektoraat aan de Theologische School der Christelijk Gereformeerde Kerk, op 6 dec. 1873.* The Hague: S. van Velzen, 1874.

——. Foreword to *Adres, ingediend door de Gereformeerden, in Overijssel en Gelderland.* The Hague: Van Golverdinge, 1836.

——. *Levensbeschrijving van wijlen Prof. A. Brummelkamp, hoogleeraar aan de Theologische School in Kampen, door zijn jongsten zoon.* Kampen: J. H. Kok, 1910.

——. *Uitgang uit de Gemeenschap met het Nederlandsch Hervormd kerkbestuur noodzakelijk Gemaakt door Afzetting.* The Hague: Van Golverdinge, 1835.

——, ed. *Stemmen uit Noord-Amerika.* Amsterdam: Hoogkamer, 1847.

Brummelkamp. A and A. C. Van Raalte. *Landverhuizing, of waarom bevorderen wij de Volksverhuizing en wel naar Noord-Amerika en niet naar Java?* Amsterdam: Hoogkamer, 1846.

Capadose, A. *Ter Gedachtenis aan Dr. Carl Schwartz.* Amsterdam: H. De Hoogh & Co., 1871.

Cohen Stuart, M. *Evangelische Alliantie: Verslag van de Vijfde Algemeene Vergadering gehouden te Amsterdam, 18-27 augustus 1867.* Rotterdam: Wijt & Zn., 1868.

——. *Gedenkboek van de zesde Algemeene Vergadering der Evangelische Alliantie: in Amerika gehouden te New York in october 1873.* Amsterdam: H. De Hoogh & Co., 1874.

——. *Zes maanden in Amerika.* Vols. I and II. Haarlem: Kruseman en Tjeenk Willink, 1875.

Coleman, Terry. *Passage to America.* London: Hutchinson and Co., 1972.

Corwin, Edward T. *A Manual of the Reformed Church in America, 1628-1902.* New York: Board of Publication of the Reformed Church in America, 1902.

Couprie, J. C. *Welmeenende Waarschuwing, aan degenen die zich aan de Afgescheidene Gemeente onttrekken naar aanleiding van een onlangs uitgekomen geschrift van D. van der Werp en W. W. Smit, overgezien door S. van Velzen.* The Hague: Van Golverdinge, 1840.

Da Costa, Isaac. *Vijf en twintig jaren, een lied in 1840.* Amsterdam: D. Groebe, 1840.

De Bey, B. and A. Zwemer. *Stemmen uit de Hollandsch-Gereformeerde Kerk in de*

Vereenigde Staten van Amerika. Groningen: G. J. Reits, 1871.
De Jong, J. A. *As the Waters Cover the Sea: Millennial Expectations in the Rise of Anglo-American Missions, 1640-1810.* Kampen: J. H. Kok, 1970.
De Liefde, J. *Gevaak! En geen vrede!: een woord tot de slapenden en in slaap gewiegden.* Zutphen: A. E. C. Van Someren, 1844.
De Moen, C. G. *De Toestand der Hollandsche kolonisatie in den Staat Michigan, Noord-Amerika, in het begin van het jaar 1849 medegedeeld in drie brieven van A. C. van Raalte, C. Vander Meulen en S. Bolks aan C. g. Moen, waarachter volgt een brief van G Baay uit Alto.* Amsterdam: Hoogkamer, 1849.
Den Hartogh, G. M. *Het Christelijk Gereformeerd Seminarie te Amsterdam: een poging tot openbaring der Hervormde of Gereformeerde Gezindheid (1850-1852).* Delft: W. D. Meinema, 1939.
De Reformatie. Amsterdam: H. Höveker, 1837-1847. Journal of the Christelijke Gereformeerde Kerk in the Netherlands.
Dosker, Henry E. *Levensschets van Rev. A. C. Van Raalte, D.D.* Nijmegen: C. C. Callenbach, 1893.
Dosker, Nicholas H. *De Hollandsche Gereformeerde Kerk in Amerika.* Nijmegen: P. J. Milborn, 1889. Originally published in *De Hope,* 1888.
Eekhof, A. "De Nederlandsche Kolonisatie in Noord-Amerika." *Haagsch Maandblad* 11, no. 3 (March 1929).
Farnham, Eliza W. *Life in Prairie Land.* New York: 1855.
Flier, A. *Verantwoording tegen de lasteringen van H. P. Scholte.* Zwolle: Rigter, 1838.
Frets, Francois. *De Betrekking van den Staat tot de Godsdienst, volgens de Grondwet: met eene voorafspraak aan Mr. Groen Van Prinsterer.* Rotterdam: M. Wijt & Zonen, 1837.
Gedachten en Beoordeeling bij en na het lezen van het werk van den heer G. Groen van Prinsterer, ten titel voerende: "De Maatregelen tegen de Afgescheidenen aan het Staatsregt getoetst," door een Voorstander van Godsdienstvrijheid en Verdraagzaamheid. Amsterdam: Brave Jr, 1837.
Gedenkboek: uitgegeven bij de herdenking van het eeuwjaar der Afscheiding in opdracht van de Generale Synode der Christelijke Gereformeerde Kerk in Nederland. Dordrecht: D. J. Van Brummen: [1934].
Gefken, J. W. *De Regtsvraag: zijn de bepalingen van het Code Pénal, over ongeoorloofde genootschappen of vergaderingen, toepasselijk op Godsdienstige bijeenkomsten en Godsdienst-oefeningen, in Nederland? In eene pleitrede behandeld.* Amsterdam: Messchert, 1836.
Gilhuis, T. M. *Memorietafel van het Christelijk onderwijs.* Kampen: J. H. Kok, 1974.
Goslinga, A. *Koning Willem I als Verlicht Despoot.* Baarn: E. J. Bosch, 1918.
Groen Van Prinsterer, G. *Brieven aan J. A. Wormser.* Vols. I and II. Amsterdam: Höveker & Zn, 1874-1876.
———. *De maatregelen tegen de Afgescheidenen aan het Staatsregt getoetst.* Leiden: S. & J. Luchtmans, 1837.
———. *Hoe de onderwijswet van 1857 tot stand kwam: historische bijdrage.* Amsterdam:

Höveker & Zn, 1876

———. *Ongeloof en Revolutie: Eene reeks van historische voorlezingen*. Leiden: S. & J. Luchtmans, 1847. At least eight editions.

Groen van Prinsterer's Briefwisseling. 4 vols. The Hague: M. Nijhoff, 1925-1967.

Gunning, J. H. Jr. *H. J. Budding, leven en arbeid*. Goes: A. A. W. Bolland, 1883. 2nd ed. Rhenen: Van Nas, 1909.

Heldring, O. G. *Hoe is ons Nederland zoo rustig? Eene vraag in deze donkere dagen*. Amsterdam: Höveker, 1848.

Herderlijke brief, van de gezamenlijke bedienaren van het Evangelie onzes Heeren en Zaligmakers Jezus Christus in de Nederduitsche Hervormde Gemeente te Amsterdam aan dezelve Gemeente. Amsterdam: J. Van Der Hey and Zn, 1836.

History Seventy-Fifth Anniversary First Reformed Church 1856-1931. Pella, Iowa: 1931.

Holtrop, P. N. *Tussen Piëtisme en Réveil: het 'Deutsche Christentumsgesellschaft' in Nederland, 1784-1833*. Amsterdam: Rodopi N.V., 1975.

Honders, A. C. *Doen en laten in Ernst en Vrede: notities over een Broederkring en een Tijdschrift*. The Hague: Boekencentrum, 1963.

Höveker, H. *Eenige gedachten over den oorsprong, de rechten en de verplichtingen van het ouderlingschap*. Amsterdam: Höveker & Zn, 1870.

Huishoudelijke bepalingen der Christelijke Gereformeerde Gemeente te Amsterdam: benevens het Adres door dezelve ingediend aan Z.M. den Koning in julij 1837. Amsterdam: Höveker, 1837.

Hyma, Albert. *Albertus C. Van Raalte and his Dutch Settlements in the United States*. Grand Rapids, Mich.: Eerdmans, 1947.

Iowa Board of Immigration. *Iowa: the Home for Immigrants: Being a Treatise on the Resources of Iowa*. Des Moines: Mills, 1870.

Iowa Commission of Emigration. *Iowa: het Land voor Emigranten: zijnde een Verslag over de hulpbronnen van Iowa en gevende nuttige informatie met betrekking tot den staat, ten behoeve van landverhuizers en anderen*. Pella: B. Bros, 1870.

Kluit, M. Elisabeth. *Het protestantse Réveil in Nederland en daarbuiten, 1815-1865*. Amsterdam: H. J. Paris, 1970.

Kohlbrügge, H. F. *Het Lidmaatschap bij de Hervormde Gemeente hier te Lande mij willekeurig belet: Voorop gaat mijne afzetting als Luthers Proponent*. Amsterdam: Den Ouden, 1833.

———. *Compleete uitgave van de officieële stulcken betreffende den Uitgang vit het Nederl. Herv. Kerkgenootschap van de leeraren H. P. Scholte, A. Brummelkamp, S. van Velzen, G. F. Gezelle Meerburg en Dr. A. C. Van Raalte*. Kampen. Zalsman, 1863.

Korff, F. W. A. and A. Van Os, eds. *Gods groote daden aan Israël: gedenkboek uitgegeven bij de herdenking van het 50-jarig bestaan der Nederlandsche Vereeniging voor Israël (1861-1911)*. Amsterdam: Van Der Land, 1911.

Kort Verslag van het zoo Geruchtmakend Gedrag des Afgezetten Predikants H. P. Scholte in de Hervormde Gemeenten Doeveren, Genderen en Gansoyen door een vriend der waarheid en des vredes. Utrecht: Bosch, 1835.

Kraan van den Burg, Gerda. *Brandende Harten: de Geschiedenis van Maurits en Suze van Hall*. Kampen: J. H. Kok, 1937.

Kuiper, A. *Varia Americana*. Amsterdam: Höveker and Wormser, 1899.

Le Roy, J. J. *Vrijmoedig Woord over de Geschriften van de Heeren Frets, Van Appeltere en eenen Ongenoemde, betrekkelijk dat van den Heer Groen van Prinsterer, "De Maatregelen tegen de Afgescheidenen aan het Staatsregt getoetst."* Rotterdam: Van Der Meer & Verbruggen, 1837.

Lucas, Henry S. "A Document Relating to Dutch Immigration to Iowa in 1846." *Iowa Journal of History and Politics* 21 (July 1923).

———. *Dutch Immigrant Memoirs and Related Writings*. 2 vols. Assen: Van Gorcum, 1955.

———. *Netherlanders in America: Dutch Immigration to the United States and Canada, 1789-1950*. Ann Arbor, Mich.: London: Oxford Univ. Press, 1955.

Macfarland, Julian E. *The Pioneer Era on the Iowa Prairies*. Lake Mills, Iowa: McFarland, 1969.

Nollen, Jan. *De Afscheiding*. Orange City, Iowa: De Volksvriend Printing House, 1898.

———. *De Hollanders in Iowa: brieven uit Pella, van een Gelderschman*. Arnhem: D. A. Thieme, 1858.

Nye, Russel Blaine. *Society and Culture in America, 1830-1860*. New York: Harper & Row, 1974.

Old Albany: A Picture Book. Albany: Morris Gerber, 1970.

Oostendorp, L. *H. P. Scholte, Leader of the Secession of 1834 and Founder of Pella*. Franeker: T. Wever, 1964.

Over Volksverhuizingen in het algemeen, en die naar Noord-Amerika in het bijzonder: Een ernstig woord aan alle Vrienden des Vaderlands; bijzonder in betrekking tot het geschrift van de Heeren Brummelkamp en Van Raalte. Amsterdam: Fikkert, 1846.

Pape, C. W. *Handelingen van het klassikaal Bestuur van Heusden, omtrent den gewezen predikant H.P. Scholte, en zijne aanhangers*. The Hague: Doorman, 1835.

Petersen, William J. *The Annals of Iowa*. Vol. I. Reprint, Iowa City, Iowa: State Historical Society of Iowa, 1964.

———. *Steamboating on the Upper Mississippi*. Iowa City, Iowa: State Historical Society of Iowa, 1968.

Petrejus, E. W. *Nederlandse zeilschepen in de 19e eeuw*. Bussum: Unieboek, 1974.

Pieters, Aleida J. *A Dutch Settlement in Michigan*. Grand Rapids, Mich.: Eerdmans-Sevensma, 1923.

Ploos van Amstel, J. J. A. Introduction to *Korte Beschrijving van het Leven van en de Wonderbare Leidingen Gods met Bastiaan Broere, in Nederland en in Amerika*. Amsterdam: J. A. Wormser, 1887.

Plowden, David, and John Gunther. *Lincoln and His America, 1809-1865*. New York: Viking Press, 1970.

Ponsteen, A. *Het kerkdorp Hellendoorn in vroeger eeuwen*. Enschede: Stichting Oald Heldern, [1972].

———. *Van Noetsele tot Nijverdal*. Enschede: Twents-Gelderse Uitgever, 1973. Contains a citation by H. Wormser, 1867.

Praamsma, L. *Het dwaze Gods: geschiedenis der Gereformeerde Kerken in Nederland sinds het begin der 19de eeuw*. Wageningen: Zomer & Keuning, 1950.

Prakke, H. J. *Drenthe in Michigan: 'n studie over het Drentse aandeel in de Van Raaltetrek in 1847*. With a foreword by P. J. Bouman. Assen: Van Gorcum, 1948.

Risseeuw, P. J. *Landverhuizers*. 2 vols. Baarn: Bosch en Keuning, 1946. Vol. 3 was added to the 6th condensed ed.

Romein, J. J. "Hollandsche Kolonisatie-arbeid in Amerika herdacht." *Vragen des Tijds* (June 1926).

Rullmann, J. C. *De Afscheiding in de Nederlandsch Hervormde Kerk der 19e eeuw*. Rev. ed. Amsterdam: W. Kirschner, 1916.

———. *Isaac Da Costa's bezwaren tegen den Geest der Eeuw na honderd jaren opnieuw uitgegeven*. Amsterdam: W. Kirchner, 1923.

———. *De strijd voor kerkherstel in de Nederlandsch Hervormde Kerk der 19e eeuw*. Amsterdam: W. Kirchner, 1915.

Sage, Leland L. *A History of Iowa*. Ames: Iowa State Univ. Press, 1974.

Schilder, K. *De dogmatische beteekenis der Afscheiding ook voor onzen tijd*. Kampen: J. H. Kok, 1934.

Scholte, H. P. *Aan de geloovigen in Nederland: Narede tot de stukken betrekkelijk de geschiedenis zijner Afscheiding van het Ned. Herv. Kerkgenootschap.*. Vol. 1. Kampen: 1863.

———. *Aanmerkingen betreffende een Geschrift, getiteld: "Verslag van de Synode der Afgescheidene Gereformeerde Gemeente in Nederland" (17 nov. – 3 dec. 1840 te Amsterdam)*. Amsterdam: Hoogkamer, 1841.

———. *Adressen aan Zijne Majesteit den Koning, aangeboden ter handhaving van Concientie- en Godsdienstvrijheid overeenkomstig de Grondwet door de Bedrukte en Dolerende Gemeenten, welke zich om der Conscientie Wille hebben afgescheiden van het, sedert 1816 opgericht kerkbestuur, en het genootschap hetwelk door dat bestuur wordt geregeerd*. The Hague: Van Golverdingen, 1835.

———. *Eene Stem uit Pella*. Amsterdam: Hoogkamer, 1848.

———. Foreword to *Adres aan de Edelmogende Heeren Staten-Generaal, Tweede Kamer ingediend door Afgescheidene Gereformeerden*. Amsterdam: Höveker, 1838.

———. Foreword to *Formulieren van Eenigheid der Christelijk Gereformeerde kerk in Nederland*. The Hague: J. Van Golverdinge; Amsterdam: Höveker, 1836.

———. Foreword to *Gad, het overwonnen en nogtans overwinnend geslacht*, by Ralph Erskine. Amsterdam: Höveker, 1836.

———. Foreword to *Getuigen, bijgebracht voor God*, by Ralph Erskine. Amsterdam: Höveker, 1836.

———. Foreword to *Handelingen van de Opzieners der Gemeente Jesu Christi vergaderd te Amsterdam den 2den maart en volgende dagen, Anno 1836*. Amsterdam: H. Höveker; The Hague: J. Van Golverdinge, 1836.

———. Foreword to *Opwekking uit Schotland tot het vereenigd gebed....* Amsterdam: Hoogkamer & C., 1842.

———. Foreword to *De tegenwoordige verwachting van de kerk van Christus of de voorspellingen, welke daarvan handelen: Voorgesteld in elf voortelezingen;* by J. N. Darby. Amsterdam: Hoogkamer, 1842

———. Foreward to *Reglement der Christelijke Afgescheidene Gemeente te Utrecht.* Amsterdam: Höveker, 1839..

———. Foreword to *Theologische Bedenkingen over het tegenwoordige bederf der Christenheid in Leer en Leven,* by C. Ziegeuner. Amsterdam: Höveker, 1838.

———. Foreword to *De Vereeniging van Kerk en Staat in Nieuw Engeland: beschouwd in derzelver gevolgen voor de godsdienst in de Vereenigde Staten* 0by anonymous American). Amsterdam: Hoogkamer en C., 1841.

———. *Gods Naam bekend gemaakt door Christus: Leerrede.* Amsterdam: Hoogkamer, 1845.

———. *De Harmonie van het Christelijk Leven en derzelver Vrucht.* Amsterdam: Hoogkamer, 1845. Appeared earlier in *De Reformatie.*

———. *De Heilige Doop, of het teeken in het Vleesch, ook voor de kleine Kinderen der Geloovigen, ter verzegeling van het Eeuwige Verbond.* Amsterdam: Hoogkamer, 1845.

———. *Het Koninklijke Besluit: Predikatie over Lucas 12:32.* Amsterdam: Höveker, 1838.

———. *Iets over de Psalmen: uit het Hoogduitsch vertaald en met een naschrift vermeerderd.* Amsterdam: Messchert & Höveker, 1834.

———. Introduction and postscript to *Merkwaardig Voorbeeld van Hedendaagsche Verdraagzaamheid van het Nederlandsch Hervormd Kerkbestuur, ten opzichte der Gereformeerde Gemeente van Doveren, Genderen en Gansoyen en derzelver herder en leeraar.* The Hague: Van Golverdinge, 1834.

———. *Kerk en Staat.* Amsterdam: Hoogkamer. Appeared earlier in *De Reformatie.*

———. *Laatste Getuigenis tegen de liefdelooze Handelingen van het zoogenaamd Hervormd Kerkbestuur: Benevens eene opwekking aan de geloovigen, tot afzondering van eenen Dank-, Vast- en Bededag.* The Hague: Van Golverdinge, 1835.

———. *Memorie, ingeleverd aan de Hoogen Raad der Nederlanden, ter zake van Godsdienstoefening.* Amsterdam: Höveker, 1839.

———. *Nieuwjaarsgeschenk aan Nederland, een ernstig Woord aan Vorst en Volk.* Amsterdam: Hoogkamer, 1847.

———. *De Roeping der Rijken in Betrekking tot de Armen.* Amsterdam: Hoogkamer, 1846.

———. *Stukken betrekkelijk de Afscheiding der Gereformeerde Gemeente van Doveren, Genderen en Gansoyen, van het Nederlandsch Hervormd Kerkbestuur.* The Hague: Van Golverdinge, 1834.

———. *Tweede Stem uit Pella.* 's-Hertogenbosch: Palier & Zn., 1848. English translation in *Annals of Iowa.* 39, No. 5 (Summer 1968).

———. *Verdediging van Conscientie- en Godsdienstvrijheid: Pleitrede, Arnhem, 10 October, 1835.* The Hague: Van Golverdinge, 1835.

———. *Verdediging van Conscientie- en Godsdienstvrijheid: Pleitrede uitgesproken voor de regtbank van eersten aanleg, te Middelburg.* The Hague: Van Golverdinge, 1836.

———. *Verdediging van Conscientie- en Godsdienstvrijheid: Twee pleitredenen uitgesproken te Utrecht en Amsterdam, met de daarbij behoorende vonnissen.* The Hague: Van Golverdinge, 1836.

———. *Vervolg der liefdelooze handelingen van het zoogenaamd Hervormd Kerkbestuur ten opzigte der Gereformeerde gemeenten van Doeveren, Genderen en Gansoyen benevens derzelver herder en leeraar: met de daarop gegevene antwoorden en verdere aanmerkingen, enz. enz.* The Hague: Van Golverdinge, 1835.

———. *Verzameling van leerstellige stukken hoofdzakelijk gerigt tegen het antichristendom der Groningsche School.* Amsterdam: Hoogkamer & Cie, 1847.

———. *Waarschuwing tegen Geveinsdheid in de Godsdienst: Predikatie over Lucas 21:1.* Amsterdam: Höveker, 1838.

Scholte, H. P., A. Brummelkamp, S. van Velzen, G. F. Gezelle Meerburg and A. C. Van Raalte. *Kompleete uitgave van de officieële stukken betreffende den Uitgang uit het Nederl. Herv. Kerkgenootschap.* Kampen: S. van Velzen, Jr, 1863.

Scholte, H. P., and J. A. Wormser. *Bijdragen ter Bevordering der Regte Kennis aangaande de Leer en Praktijk des Heiligen Doops.* Amsterdam: H. Höveker, 1837.

Scholte, Lenora. *A Stranger in a Strange Land: The Story of a Dutch Settlement in Iowa under the Leadership of H. P. Scholte.* Iowa City, Iowa: State Historical Society of Iowa, 1939.

Schwieder, Dorothy, ed. *Patterns and Perspectives in Iowa History.* Ames: Iowa State Univ. Press, 1973.

Sipma, S. A. *Belangrijke Berigten uit Pella in de Vereenigde Staten van Noord Amerika, of tweede Brief... aan de ingezetenen van Bornwerd....* Dockum: Wed. B. Schaafsma, 1849. English translation in *Annals of Iowa* 38, no. 2 (1965).

———. *Brief aan de ingezetenen van Bornwerd in Westdongeradeel, uit wier midden hij, in het voorjaar van 1847, als landverhuizer is vertrokken naar Pella.* Dockum: Wed. B. Schaafsma, 1848.

Sloane, Eric. *An Age of Barns.* New York: Random House, 1974.

Smits, C. *Classis Dordrecht.* Vol. 2, *De Afscheiding van 1834.* Dordrecht: J. P. Van den Tol, 1974.

———. *Gorichem en "Beneden-Gelderland."* Vol. 1, *De Afscheiding van 1834.* Outkarspel: De Nijverheid, 1971.

Smitskamp, H. *Een keerpunt in de voorgeschiedenis der Vrije Universiteit.* Kampen: J. H. Kok N.V., 1961.

Souvenir History of Pella, Iowa: 1847-1922. Pella: G. A. Stout, 1922.

Swierenga, Robert P. "A Dutch Immigrant's View of Frontier Iowa." *Annals of Iowa* 38, no. 2 (Fall 1965). Includes translation of Sipma 1848.

———. "A Place of Refuge." *Annals of Iowa*. 39, No. 5 (Summer 1968). Includes translation of Scholte's *Tweede Stem Uit Pella*, 1848.

ten Zijthoff, G. J. "Het Reveil en de Christelijke Gereformeerde Amerikaanse Nederlanders. Mythe en Realiteit." *Nederlands Theologisch Tijdschrift* 21, no. 1 (1965).

Tot de prediking van het Woord des geloofs: opstellen ter gelegenheid van de herdenking van de oprichting der Theologische School A.D. 1854 te Kampen. Kampen: Comité van Uitgage, 1954.

Van Appeltere, A. W. *Het Staatsregt in Nederland, vooral met betrekking tot de Kerk, en de Handelingen der Regering ten opzichte der Afgescheidenen, nader toegelicht*. The Hague and Amsterdam: Gebroeders Van Cleef, 1837.

———. *Pleitrede in de zaak van Hendrik Petrus Scholte..., uitgesproken in de teregtzitting van het Hoog Geregtshof te 's-Gravenhage, 2 December 1835*. The Hague and Amsterdam: Gebroeders Van Cleef, 1836.

Van der Groe, Theodorus. *Het Zaligmakende Geloof*. Rotterdam: 1742. Reprint, with a foreword by H. P. Scholte. Amsterdam: Höveker, 1838.

Van Der Kemp, C. M. *Beoordeling van het Geschil over de Maatregelen tegen de Afgescheidenen: eene wederlegging van het geschrift des Heeren van Appeltere*. 2 vols. Rotterdam: Van Der Meer & Verbruggen, 1837, 1838.

Van der Linden, J. *Verzint eer gij begint!: Een hartelijk woord aan mijne landgenooten, over de, in ons vaderland heerschende ziekte, genaamd: Landverhuizing*. Hertogenbosch: J. J. Arkensteyn & Zn., 1846.

Van Der Zee, Jacob. *The Hollanders of Iowa*. Iowa City, Iowa: State Historical Society, 1912.

Van Eerbach, Gerritje. *Mijne Verantwoording en Redenen van Afscheiding opengelegd aan de Kerkeraad van Ulsen*. Amsterdam: Höveker; Zwolle: Rigter, 1837.

Van Hall, A. M. C. *Drie eeuwen: de kroniek van een Nederlandse familie*. Amsterdam: W. Ten Have, 1961.

———. *De Vrijheid van Godsdienst-Oefeningen in Nederland, verdedigd: Pleitrede*. Amsterdam: Messchert, 1835.

———. *De vrijheid der Gereformeerde Gemeenten in Nederland, verdedigd: Pleitrede uitgesproken in de teregtzitting van het Hoog Geregtshof te 's-Gravenhage..., 10 october 1836*. Amsterdam: Messchert, 1836.

Van Hinte, Jacob. *Nederlanders in Amerika: een studie over landverhuizers en volksplanters in de 19e en 20ste eeuw in de Vereenigde Staten van Amerika*. 2 vols. Groningen: P. Noordhoff, 1928. Eng. ed., Robert P. Swierenga, gen. ed., Adriann de Wit, chief trans. Grand Rapids, Mich.: Baker Book House, 1985.

Van Raalte, A. C. Postscript to *Kompleete uitgave van de officieële stukken betreffende den Uitgang uit het Nederl. Herv. Kerkgenootschap, April 1862*. Vol. II. Kampen: 1863.

Van Raalte, J. *Wat was de Gereformeerde Kerk in Nederland?: De geschiedenis van de 'kruisgezinden.'* Goes: Oosterbaan & Le Cointre, 1954.

Van Stigt, Kommer. *Geschiedenis van Pella, Iowa en Omgeving.* 3 Vols. Pella: Weekblad Drukkerij, 1897.

Van Velzen, Simon. Foreword to *Adres aan Zijne Majesteit den Koning, ingediend door de Gemeenten in Vriesland, die wegens de uitoefening der Gereformeerde Godsdienst vervolgd en verdrukt worden.* Leeuwarden: Swartte Van Loon, 1837.

Van Vollenhoven, D. H. Th. "De Afscheiding in de Residentie in het midden der 19e eeuw" In *Bijdragen voor Vaderlandsche Geschiedenis en Oudheidkunde*, edited by Is. Nijhoff, The Hague: M. Nijhoff, 1928.

Veenhof, C. *Kerkgemeenschap en kerkorde: kort overzicht van de strijd, gevoerd in de Afgescheiden kerken tussen 1836 en 1840 over de kerkgemeenschap en kerkorde.* Amsterdam: Buijten & Schipperheijn, 1974.

Verhave, Jan Peter. *Afgescheiden en wedergekeerd: Het leven van J. A. Wormser Sr. en zijn gezin in Amsterdam.* Groen: Uitgeverij Groen, 2000.

Verhave, Jan and Jurriën. *Vier generaties rondom een Boekhandel en Uitgeverij: Gedenkschrift van Boekhandel en uitgeverij W. ten Have N. V. v/h Hövekers Boekhandel: 11 mei 1831-1956.*

White, C. A. *Manual of Physical Geography and Institutions of the State of Iowa.* Davenport: Day, Egbert and Fidlar, 1873.

Wormser, J. A. *"Door kwaad gerucht en goed gerucht": het leven van Hendrik Peter Scholte.* Vol. 2, *Een Schat in aarden Vaten: de Afscheiding in levensbeschrijvingen geschetst.* Nijverdal: E. J. Bosch, 1915.

———. *In twee werelddeelen: het leven van Albertus Christiaan Van Raalte.* Vol. 1, *Een Schat in aarden Vaten: de Afscheiding in levensbeschrijvingen geschetst.* Nijverdal: E. J. Bosch, 1915.

———. *Karakter en Genade: het leven van Simon Van Velzen.* Vol. 4, *Een Schat in aarden vaten: De Afscheiding in levensbeschrijvingen geschetst.* Nijverdal: E. J. Bosch, 1916.

———. *De kinderdoop, beschouwd met betrekking tot het bijzondere, kerkelijke en maatschappelijke leven.* Foreword by G. Groen Van Prinsterer. Amsterdam: Höveker, 1864.

———. *De onkerkelijke rigting, die zich bij vele geloovigen openbaart*, Foreword by G. Groen Van Prinsterer. Amsterdam: Höveker & Zn, 1864.

———. *"Werken zoolang het dag is": let leven van Hendrik de Cock.* Vol. 3, *Een Schat in aarden Vaten: de Afscheiding in levensbeschrijvingen geschetst.* Nijverdal: E. J. Bosch, 1915.

Wyckoff, Isaac N. *Report of a Visit to the Holland Colonies in Michigan and Wisconsin.* In *Dutch Immigrant Memoirs and Related Writings*, ed. Henry S. Lucas. Assen: Van Norkum, 1955. Rev. ed., Grand Rapids, Mich.: Eerdmans, 1997.

Zwaanstra, Henry. *Reformed Thought and Experience in a New World: a Study of the Christian Reformed Church and its American Environment, 1890-1918.* Kampen: J. H. Kok, 1973.

INDEX

Aanen, D.K., 203
Aanen, E. (mayor of Hoornaar), 120, 132, 147, 161, 193, 203, 214; letter of 212-13; wife of, 203
Aanen, Jan, 199
Abrahams (Abrams), Mrs. (member of Amsterdam Christian Seceded Church, married to J.S. Abrahams), 24, 77, 79, 89, 94, 95, 109, 295, 346, 364, 379, 396, 430, 437
Abyssinia, 567
Achterhoek (Netherlands region in eastern Gelderland), 32
Achthoven, Netherlands, 139
Afgescheiden. *See* Seceders of 1834
Afscheiding, De (book), 389
Afscheiding. *See* Secession of 1834
Aglaja (ladies journal), 130
Akkerman, Mr. (husband of Johanna Schellinger), 597
Akkerman, Willie (son of Johanna Akkerman-Schellinger), 597
Akkerman-Schellinger, Johanna (niece of Johanna Schellinger), 597. *See also* Schellinger, Naatje
Albany, N.Y., fires in, 238; as immigrant depot, 35, 43, 47, 51-52, 63, 67, 117, 221, 232, 237-39, 286, 331, 332, 337; population of, 332

Albert, Prince (Queen Victoria's consort), 386
Alcohol, use of, 130, 277
Algemene Handelsblad, Het (Netherlands newspaper), 14
Alsmeer, Netherlands, 579
Alto, Wis., 43
Ameide, Netherlands, 371
America, negative views of, 261, 266, 269, 324, 346, 380; positive views of, 264, 370, 383
"America fever," 134
America letters, xv-xvi, xxiv-xxvi, 64-65, 180, 264, 272-74; criticized, 286-87, 290, 298-300, 308-09, 323, 364; examples of, 92-93; impact of, 121, 165, 197, 206
Americanization, in church, 638; of immigrants, 635
Amerikaansche Boodschappen, De, 86
Amstelveen, Netherlands, 20
Amsterdam, Ia., 110, 178, 182, 192
Amsterdam, Netherlands, 197, 281-82, 339-40; cholera in, 229, 294, 323, 325, 399, 417; Christian Seceded Church in, xviii, 20, 25, 41-42, 408, 418-19, 591-92, 611-12; Christian Seceders in, xv-xix, 2-8, 12-22, 27-28, 225, 342, 333, 355, 472, 625-33; compared to

America, 298-99, compared to Iowa, 72, 107, 251, 271, 276, 294, 322, 455; cost of living in, 487; culture of, 637; destiny of, 634; economy of, 5-6; Evangelical Alliance Conference in, 551, 555-57, 561, 562, 567, 568; evangelists in, 567-568; Hervormde Kerk in, 568-69; living conditions in, 574; measles in, 417; news of, 398; and Pella, xix-xxi, 634-35; plat in 1840s, 8; religious life in, 418-19, 439-40, 444, 469-70, 605-06; remembered, 502, 568; rumors of, 323, 325; Seceder theological school in, 333, 355, 631; Synod of, 85; uprising of 1848 in, 98, 99, 163-65, 192, 305; and Wormser families, xxiii-xxvii, 598-99; mentioned, 7, 9-10, 17, 37, 57, 65, 66, 74, 81, 85, 88, 95, 121, 153, 215, 222, 240, 306, 315, 327, 364, 367, 386, 396, 404, 451, 485, 498, 527, 530, 532, 594

Amsterdam, N.Y., 337

Animal husbandry, 88-89, 139, 154, 290, 315; by Americans, 82; prices, 80, 267, 368-69. *See also* Cattle, Hogs

Anti-Christ, 432. *See also* Babel, Babylon

Antwerp, Belgium, 311

Apeldoorn, Netherlands, 125

Appeltere, A.W., 21

Apple trees, 424

Arends, Magdalena (Mrs. Hendrik Wormser), 7

Arkel, Netherlands, 196

Arnhem, Netherlands, 32, 33, 66, 125, 226, 274, 276, 277; Christian Seceders in, 225, 400; mentioned, 52, 485, 524

Arnoud, Louise, 220, 273

Assen, Netherlands, 444

Axes, 134, 153; described, 258; injuries from, 365

Baambrugge, Netherlands, 223, 553, 557-58, 566, 568, 570, 598

Baay (Baai), Gerrit, 125, 404, 482, 508

Babel, 228-29, 473-74; as America, 637; as Europe, 635-36; as Rome, 637. *See also* Anti-Christ

Babylon, 473-74, 477

Baden, Germany, 41

Bählen, C.D. Louis, 9, 10

Baking, bread, 271

Bakker, 56

Balke, Jan ("Boss," gardener of Judith Zeelt), 17, 92, 105, 109, 416, 557, 566

Baltimore, Md., 45, 64, 123, 143, 199; Dutch in, 78

Banks, 254

Baptism, 27, 42, 529, 562, 599, 628-29; and J.A. Wormser's pamphlets on, 386-87, 392, 412, 420-21, 423, 593; problems in Pella over, 595; refused by H.P. Scholte, 84-85

Baptists, 250, 374, 498, black congregation of, 544; in Pella 211

Barendregt (Barendrecht), Hendrik (carpenter), 38, 42, 43, 69, 78, 93, 142, 143, 144, 170, 171, 172, 209-10, 314, 316, 369, 384, 385; as elder 173

Barger, J., 437

Bavinck, Herman, 228

Baxter family, (London) 555

Beard, Robert (second husband of Maria Krantz-Scholte), 64, 478, 602; character of, 622

Beards, on men, 438

Beatrix, Crown Princess of the Netherlands, 29

Bed bugs, 260, 313

Beer, 52

Beets, Nicolaas, 398, 415, 627

Beijer (Netherlands author), 76

Belgian Revolt, 5, 9, 21

Beltman, Hendrik, 52

Belville, Ill., 317

Bergen-op-Zoom, Netherlands, 11

Berkhout, Gerrit (Amsterdam, brother of Johannes Berkhout), 346

Berkhout (Berkhoud), Johannes (Jan), xvii, xxix, 215, 271, 289, 327, 507, 584; biography, 17; business dealings, 380; buys lots, 356; character of, 221, 249, 250-51, 299,

418, 635; church life, 501; compares Netherlands and Iowa, 572-74, 579; criticizes H.P. Scholte, xx-xxi, 222, 223, 383, 591; and D.A. Budde, 264, 265, 298, 325; death of, 603-04, 622; dislikes in Pella, 602; financial reverses, 109, 281-82, 349-52, 610; hog ventures, 421-22, 424; illnesses of, 569, 599-600; letters of, 260-61, 266, 312-23, 346-53, 359-62, 572-74; owns Pella store, 359-62, 496; as Pella councilman, 389; remigration of, 407, 541, 549-50, 556, 566, 571, 583; mentioned, 79, 89, 339, 364, 509, 515, 518

Berlin, Germany, 41

Betten, Anthony J., 37, 45 (photo), 46, 111, 134, 169-70, 192, 215, 328, 335, 369; as public official, 173, 182; as teaching elder, 132, 146, 173, 384, 385, 389; mentioned, 125, 128, 155, 188

Beurkens, Christoffer, 70, 73, 262, 499

Bible, role of, xxv-xxvi; daily reading of, 149, 192; Dutch and German versions, 451; quoted, 55, 90

Biesheuvel, Johanna, 335

Biezenbroek, Mr., 406, 521

Bilderdijk, Willem, 10

Birks, Rev. (British preacher), 555

Birthing practices, 249

Blaauw & Co. (Amsterdam), 467

Black River, Mich., 80

Blacks, in Netherlands, 567-68; worship of, 544

Blanke, Jan (carpenter), 171, 316

Bleeker, Mrs., 442

Bloemers, Christiana, 53

Bloemers, Johanna, 53

Bloemers, Tobias, 53

Blokland, Netherlands. *See* Hoogblokland

Boderij (Amsterdam tobacco shop), 133

Boekenoogen, Miss, 529

Bolks, Seine, 47-48; and A.C. Van Raalte, 7; called to Milwaukee, 408; carriage accident of, 404-05; criticized, 286-87; as farmer, 288-90; leaves New York, 93; Michigan colony of, 310

Bonnets, 128

Boosterism, 290

Borneo, Netherlands East Indies, 32, 328

Bosch, Mr. (Utrecht), 285

Boston, 45, 143, 273; Dutch in, 53, 220-21

Bot, Dingeman, 335

Bot, Widow, 335

Bouinier, Rev. 431

Bouman (emigrant from Woerden), 215

Bousquet, A.E. Dudok, xvii; business activities, 95-96, 339 (photo), 343-44, 365, 372, 378-79, 380, 408; commends Pella, 373; and D.A. Budde family, 355, 357, 381-82; death of, 422, 501; emigration of, 295; and H.P. Scholte, 285, 391-92; illness of, 410-11; immigration of, 333, 339-42; and Johannes Berkhout, 353, 359, 363-64; lectures of, 340; letters of 340; maid Antje, 341, 378; as teaching elder, 390

Bousquet, Hendrik Lodewyk (Henry, Henri) (born 1841), 340, 365, 499, 595; and Civil War, 506, 508

Bousquet, Herman Frederik (born 1841), 340, 365, 378, 496; and Civil War, 498, 508

Bousquet, J. (Amsterdam, brother of A.E. Dudok Bousquet), 13, 17

Bousquet, Jan (John) Josef (born 1837), 340, 496, 499; fellow Pella volunteer Matthes, 499; wounded in Civil War, 506, 508

Bousquet, Piet Hein (born 1835), 340, 343-44, 365, 473, 489, 502, 506, 509, 512, 595; confession of faith of, 390, 411, 415

Bouw, L., 119, 152, 134

Brand, Mr. (Gorinchem), 124

Brandt, A.H.W. (German Reformed preacher in Amsterdam), 408, 436, 444, 485, 525, 559, 568, 571, 600

Brandt, J.D. (brother-in-law of H.P. Scholte), 12-13, 15, 17, 19

Brandt, Sara Maria (1806-1844), first

wife of H.P. Scholte), 11, 26 (photo) 473; death of, 26-29
Bread, baking of, 271
Breda, Netherlands, 399
Bremen, Germany, 264
Bremer Fellowship, 69
Brighton, Ia., 339
Brouwer, Arie, 208
Brücker, Rev. (Presbyterian cleric in Burlington), 530, 543, 545
Brugmans, H., 16
Brummelkamp, Anthony (Seceder leader in Arnhem, brother-in-law of Carel De Moen, Van Raalte, and Van Velzen), 95, 98, 107, 109, 224, 225 (photo), 225-27, 229, 295, 329, 333, 367, 374, 377, 395, 400, 525, 559-60, 591; biography of, 9-10; character of, 627; criticized, 53, 265; and Evangelical Alliance, 554-55, 556; and Free University, 637; opposed by Hendrik De Cock, 390; preaches in Amsterdam, 426; promotes emigration, 32-35, 273; and Secession of 1834, 6, 12, 14, 15-16, 20, 22, 25, 27-29; and Simon Van Velzen, 430; mentioned, 93, 473
Brummelkamp, Johannes, 559
Bruning (physician), 83
Buchanan, President James, 421
Budde, Anna (daughter of D.A. Budde), 303
Budde, Carlien, 57
Budde, Christina Maria, 489
Budde, Diedrich Arnold, xviii, xxvi-xx; and Amsterdam Seceded Church, 3-4, 6-7, 17-18, 23-25, 26-27; and A.N. Wormser, 237, 241-52, 264-66, 280-82, 298-99, 300, 310, 315, 324-25; biography of, 2, 3, 8; cattle round-up, 266-68; character, 625, 632-33; as churchman, 247, 278-79, 375, 383, 386, 452-54, 535; comments on Civil War, 494-95; death of, 473, 619-21, 622; family of, 271, 333, 340, 341, 342, 364, 496, 570; farm of, 50, 92, 276, 288-89, 262 (map), 544, 584, 585-86; as farmer, 220, 232-33, 244-45, 263, 267-68, 293-94, 310, 354; grave (photo), 626; hardships of, 289-90; and H.P. Scholte, 390-91; illnesses of, 91, 92, 245, 287, 543, 549-50, 553, 556, 562, 569, 586, 613; immigration, 28, 44, 77, 95, 123; and J.A. Wormser, 419, 580-81; and Johannes Berkhout, 264; letters of, xxix-xxx, 54-55, 58-63, 66-75, 78-80, 81-89, 92-94, 101-05, 232-34, 301-03, 306-07, 353-56, 372-75, 392-94, 411-14, 420-22, 452-58, 469-70, 494-95, 513 (photo), 513-14, 535-37, 552, 580-81, 587, 615-19, 625-26; Netherlandic ties, 391; and Pella, 357; piety of, 438, 470; and Simon Van Velzen, 29; views on women, xviii; visited by Cornelius Vander Meulen, 437; mentioned, 94, 231, 379, 397, 431, 509, 515
Budde, Diedrich Christiaan (born 1840, second son of D.A. Budde), 3, 44, 91, 359, 395, 397, 400, 402-03, 429; character of, 242, 422, 425, 452, 489-90, 494, 513; death of, 519-20, 523, 526-28, 534, 538; illnesses of, 61, 106, 243, 303-05; language skills, 73, 77, 451, 491; religious views, 469, 480; mentioned, 96, 98, 105, 357, 368, 375, 414, 431, 445, 460, 486, 487, 515
Budde, Ede (brother of D.A. Budde), 57, 92, 579
Budde, Elena Louisa, 450
Budde, Elizabeth Maria Sophia, 436
Budde, Enno, 57, 92
Budde, Etje (niece of D.A. Budde), 562
Budde, Flora, 480
Budde, Grietje (Mrs. Willem Schaarwächter), 576
Budde, Jansje (daughter of D.A. Budde), 73, 303
Budde, Johan (brother of D.A. Budde), 562, 568
Budde, Johan (nephew of D.A. Budde), 92
Budde, Johan (Jan) Georg, 3, 41, 270, 298-99, 394, 422, 445, 491-92, 526-

28, 543, 546, 595; and Andreas Singer, 602; and A.N. Wormser, 280-82; assists immigrants, 539; cattle round-up by, 267-69; character of, 263, 307, 341, 517-18, 607; as churchman, 375, 505; death of children, 418, 480, 489, 537, 544, 550, 579, 583; describes Civil war, 531; as factory worker, 307, 401-02, 404, 405, 413, 436; as farmer, 73, 246, 354, 357, 401-02, 413, 423-24, 565; illnesses, 79, 81-82, 102, 106, 231, 233, 243, of wife, 613; joins Congregational Church, 469; letters of, 531-32, 602-03, 616, 617, 618, 619-21; marriage, 367-68, 373; relocates to Mount Pleasant, 585-86; teaches Sunday school, 8; unemployed, 304, 450-51; mentioned, 77, 78, 86, 105, 397, 398, 399, 400, 414, 427, 431, 442, 452, 460, 486, 487, 513, 515, 535, 537, 540, 551, 563, 596
Budde, Johanna (daughter of D.A. Budde), 479
Budde, Johanna (daughter of J.G. Budde), 511
Budde, Leentje (Mrs. Schilp), 536
Budde, Maria (Mary)(Mrs. Andreas Singer), 3, 44, 400, 403, 405, 422, 429, 479, 480, 483, 489, 491, 515, 536, 558, 560, 570, 572, 578, 600, 603, 612, 613; children of, 561-62, 563, 564, 586, 587, 594, 596, 618; engagement of, 527, 538, 539, 542-44; illnesses of, 543-44; marriage noted, 556; mother's death, 616, 617; youth, 59, 77, 94, 99, 104, 303, 305, 359, 395; mentioned, 96, 368, 414, 431, 460, 486, 487, 513, 535, 537, 550, 551, 604, 607
Budde, Maria Elizabeth (daughter of D.A. Budde), 414, 423
Budde, Roelf (nephew of D.A. Budde), 403-04, 414, 425, 575, 576, 577, 585
Budde, Sophia, 303
Budde Street (Burlington), 50
Budde, Telem, 303

Budding(h), H.J., 12, 125, 275; and H.P. Scholte, 476-77, theology of, 22, 586, 591
Buffalo, N.Y., Dutch in, 68; as immigrant depot, 51-52, 67-68, 230, 239, 241, 253, 293, 300, 332, 335, 336, 337; population of, 337; Van Raalte in, 51
Bugs, 275, 276
Buiksloot, Netherlands, 54, 56
Buildings, cost of, 243
Buises family, 325
Bunyan, John, 526
Burger, Mrs., 427
Burial customs, 87-88, 252
Burlington Hawk Eye (newspaper), 178
Burlington, Iowa, xviii, 220-21, 253-54, 264, 338-39, 355, 437; and A.N. Wormser, 75, 234-69, 281-82; and Civil War, 488-89; compared favorably to Amsterdam, 93; and D.A. Budde family, 75, 501, 558, 562, 578, 585-86, 594, 626; described, 50, 75-76, 242-43, 245-47, 251, 405; doctors in, 602; Dutch Reformed Church in, 374, 386, 392, 393, 402, 412, 422, 436-37, 450-51, 452-60, 488, 526, 529-30, 539-40, 625; German Evangelical Church in, 357-58, 422; growth of, 104-05, 338, 414; H.P. Scholte family in, 86; life in, 291-93; as market center, 380, 421, 423-24; Mississippi River bridge at, 595; panoramic view of, 401; Presbyterian Church in, 550, 625; railroad travel via, 406, 414, 525, 542; schools in, 298; steamboats at, 257-59; mentioned, 2, 46, 47, 89, 90, 395, 496, 509, 521
Business: ethics, United States and Netherlands compared, 573-74; retail, 348-52, 359-61
Busman, Ben, 403
Butter: churning of, 543; prices of, 369
Buttermilk, 128
Buys, Mr. (Amsterdam), 65

California, and gold rush, 294, 352

Calvin College, xiii, xiv, xxxi
Calvinism, 384
Calvin Theological Seminary, xiii
Camphor, 550
Canada, 337
Canal boats, on Illinois-Michigan Canal, 256-55, 338; *See also* Erie Canal
Canons of Dort. *See* Dort, Canons of
Capadose, Abraham, 10, 17
Carpentry, 137, 204, 261, 316; tools, 257-58
Catechism, 83, 90, 183, 269, 492, 504, 535, 612
Catharina Jackson (ship), 46, 119, 164; sinking of, 202
Catholics. *See* Roman Catholic Church
Cattle: branding, 179-80; care of, 416; lack of stables for, 263; prices, 368-69; raising of, 316, 357, 543; round-up described, 267-69; strays, 179-80
Cemeteries, 391
Central College, xiv, xv, xxxi, 340
Chabot, D. (Utrecht baker), 129
Chabot, Henriette M. (Mrs. A.E. Dudok Bousquet), biography, 339, 391, 415, 418, 571, 621, 622; character of, 518, 535; illnesses of, 95, 99, 109; letters of, 333, 340-45, 364-66, 376-82, 410-11, 495-97, 499-502, 506-09, 512; piety of, 499-500; sons in Civil War, 488-89, 525; visits Netherlands, 529, 530, 541, 595; mentioned, 79, 109, 515, 540, 573, 623
Chabot, M.R., 129
Chamomile, 528
Charlois, Netherlands, 285, 334, 345
Cheating, by immigrant agents, 334. *See also* Swindling
Cheese making, 128, 139, 154, 157, 166, 185, 191, 279, 315; prices of, 369. *See also* Dutch cheese, Rennet
Chester, Captain, 567-68
Chicago, Ill., 36, 46, 221; as "capitol" of Midwest, 2; described, 256-57; fire of 1871 in, 611; as immigrant depot, 241, 253-54, 256-58, 338, 341; population of, 337-38; Reformed church in, 482; mentioned 638

Childbirth: deaths in, 467; troubles in, 311
Children, life styles of, 278
Chiliast, 229
China, 434, 436
Cholera: in Amsterdam, 229, 294, 321, 399, 417, 426; in Iowa, 282, 404; in New Orleans, 300; in United States, 219, 279, 321, 404
Christelijke Gereformeerde Gemeente, De, 22
Christelijke Gereformeerde Seminarie (Amsterdam), 223-24
Christian Church of Pella (Scholte's Church), 155, 339, 369-70, 390; described, 144; divisions in, 376-77
Christian Intelligencer, The, 35, 584
Christian Reformed Church, 390
Christian schools: in Netherlands, 630-33; in Pella, 638
Christian Seceded Church: in America, xxi, 13-16; in Amsterdam, xvi-xviii, xxiiii-xxiv, 3, 12-22, 23-24, 41, 225, 333, 367, 418-19, 426, 444, 573, 625-30; deposes H.P. Scholte, 41-42; dissolution of, 373-74, 505; magazine of, xv; in Netherlands, 55, 115, 125, 172, 225, 328, 333, 534; in Pella, 330; role of, xviii; troubles in, 383, 408
Christians, treatment of: in America, 470; in Europe, 561
Church and state, European model rejected, 474; in Pella, 38
Churches Under the Cross, 591
Cigars, 133, 152, 174, 482
Cincinnati, Ohio, 41, 46, 310, 332
Citizenship, in Pella, 138
Civil War, destruction noted, 494-95; effects on Burlington, 488-89; and H.P. Scholte, 637; and Iowa Dutch, 488-89; letters about, 473; and Pella, 496, 499-97, 506-05; views on, 512-13, 531-32, 533, 538-39, 542; mentioned, 567
Claims, land, 284
Clam River, Mich., 337
Class differences, Netherlands

compared to America, 292
Classis of Illinois (Reformed Church in America), 393
Clements, Walter, 49
Clergymen, criticized, 289
Cleveland, Oh., 337, 580
Clifton (ship), 311
Climate, 266, 293, 294, 296-97; compared to Netherlands, 112, 273, 369, 440-41; Iowa, 88, 137, 267, 277, 281, 304, 312, 343, 357, 363, 365, 410, 421, 424, 451, 606; New York, 332, 337
Clington House, 338
Clothing: American, 128, 150; costs of, 141, 147-48, 292; compared to Netherlands, 298-99; styles of, 150, 291
Coal mines, 158-59, 368
Coevorden, Netherlands, 68
Cohen Stuart, M., 555, 559, 562
Coins ("Willems"), 124, 129, 133
Colic, 411
Colonies, Dutch, rumors about, 278-79
Columbus. Ohio, 47
Communion. *See* Lord's Supper
Communism, 42
Communist Manifesto, 41
Comprie, J.C., 14, 18,
Comrie, A. ("old writer"), 628
Congregationalists, 71, 73, 83, 469; in Burlington, 481
Connecticut, 63, 65
Constantine, Emperor, 383, 636
Constantinianism, 631, 632, 636, 637, 638
Consumption (illness), 431, 504
Conventicles, 98
Cook-Hospers, Hendrieka, 339, 390, 391
Corinth, battle of, 506
Corn, prices, 279-80
Cornbread, 289, 293
Coster family, 442
Courant (ship), 133
Cowper, W. ("old writers"), 24
Craftsmen, 74
Cramer, W.D. (Amsterdam mayor), 17
Crimean War, 386, 393

Crops, 70, 88, 103, 111, 139, 233, 262-63; prices of, 279-78, 354
Curtis, Samuel Ryan (engineer of Des Moines River Improvement at Keokuk), 379, 381
Customs, social, 87, 567-68

da Costa, Isaac, xv, xxiii, 10, 28, 31, 41, 226, 228, 229, 339-40, 367, 396, 477, 557; and Anthony Brummelkamp, 27; and Rèveil, 9
da Costa, Isaac (grandson of Isaac da Costa), 557
da Costa, Mijntje, 481
da Costa, Mrs. Isaac, 509
Dairying, 191. *See also* Animal husbandry
Dam Square (Amsterdam), 98, 99
Daniel, book of, 72, 233
Darby, John N. (British preacher and founder of Plymouth Brethren church), 229
Darbyites, 629; and H.P. Scholte, 42
Darmstadt, Germany, 88
D'Aubigne, Merle, 97
David, King of Israel, 108, 438, 511
Davis, Jefferson (Confederate president), 538
Death: attitudes toward, 30-31, 615-22; in childbirth, 467; of children, 251-52, 269, 303-304, 417; en route, 121, 231, 329-30, 332, 336, 357; in Holland (Mich.) colony, 307-308; of infants, 311, 401, 422, 423, 480, 489, 511, 534, 536, 537, 566, 579, 595; in Netherlands, 395-96, 397-98, 417, 427-28, 430-31, 437, 504-05, 510-11, 536, 612; noted, 405, 413, 523, 593, 595, 598-99, 603, 620-21, 622; spiritual consolation in, 507, 513-15, 516-18, 519-21, 532-33
Deathbed scenes, 523-24, 526-28
de Baai, Hendrika (Mrs. Aart Kool), 180
de Boer, Johan Adam (second son of Johannes M. De Boer), 486, 492, 533
de Boer, Johannes Mattheus (husband of Cato Wormser), 426, 428, 439, 471, 481, 503, 566, 599; alcoholism,

540-41, 557; divorce, 557-58
de Boer family, 452, 513
de Bruin, Rev., 408
Decapolis, 635
Declaration of Independence, 637, 638
de Clercq, Willem (Amsterdam poet), 26, 29
de Cock, Helenius, 224
de Cock, Hendrik, 12, 15, 20, 22, 27, 390, 475, 629, 632
Deference, social, 522-23
de Gelder, Arie, 120, 124, 129, 142, 153-54, 156, 167, 187, 197, 200; mentioned, 161, 173, 188, 192
de Gelder, Betje (Betje-moei) (Mrs. Arie), 120, 156, 166, 197, 200; mentioned, 145, 161, 173, 192, 201
de Gelder, Drieka, 165
de Gelder, Hendrik, 204
de Gelder, Katie, 165, 173
de Gelder, Nicolaas (Klaas), 192, 201
de Gelder, Teunis, 120-21, 153-54, 165, 166, 167, 190, 196, 197, 198, 199, 200, 207; mentioned, 145, 156, 173, 189, 192, 201
de Gelder, Willem, 165
de Gelder family, 202, 207
de Gelder-Steijen (Aunt), 189
de Graaf, N.H. (Hervormde Kerk preacher, Amsterdam), 559, 611
de Groot, Gysbert, 198-99
de Haan, J., 345, 391
de Haas, Aunt, 95
De Havre, Mr., 365
De Heus, Lieutenant, 489
De Hoog, K., 314, 384, 385; as elder, 173
de Jong, Adriaan (of Achthoven), 139, 369
De Jong, Arie, 173
De Jong, Hendrik, 125
De Jong, Koen, 139, 173, 368-70
de Jong, Maria, 208
De Jong, Mie (Mrs. Arie), 173
De Jong, Mrs. Koen, 370-71
De Jong, P., 423-24
De Koning, B. (mayor), 199
de Lamartine, Alphonse, 272
de Liefde, Jan (pastor, Free Evangelical Church, Amsterdam), 447; photo, 222
Delvoa, F. (Reformed Church preacher in Burlington), 386, 436-37, 450, 455
de Mérode, Willem (Netherlands poet), 7
Democrat Party, 638
de Moen, Carel Godefroi (Seceder preacher and brother-in-law of Brummelkamp, Van Raalte, and Van Velzen), 10, 225, 308, 397, 426, 555
de Moen, Christina Johanna (Mrs. A.C. Van Raalte), 10
de Moen, Johanna Christina (Mrs. Simon van Velzen), 10
de Moen, Maria Wilhelmina (Mrs. Anthony Brummelkamp), 10
de Moen, Mrs., 427
de Moen family, 10, 466
den Besten, Gerrit, 189
Den Bosch ('s Hertogenbosch), Netherlands, 285
Den Ham, Netherlands, 225
Den Hartog, Cornelis, 122, 125, 137, 141, 167, 171, 172, 173, 199, 216, 335; mentioned, 128, 155, 189
Den Hartog, Dirk, 149, 188
Den Helder, Netherlands, 44
de Nieve, Dr., 333
Denmark, 100
den Otter, Dirk, 162, 173
den Otter, Grietje, 173
Depression of 1857-1858, 436; in Netherlands, 445
De Roever, Mr., 436, 444
de Ruyter, Aart, 120
Des Moines, Iowa (Fort Des Moines), 177, 283
Des Moines River, 49, 86, 111, 119, 127, 137, 178, 181, 186, 189, 223; flatboats on, 340; land grant for improvement of, 215, 216, 272, 283-86; navigation project of, 283-84, 315; steamboats on, 316, 318, 320
Des Moines school district, 182
Deteleff, Coenraad (Seceder lay preacher in Amsterdam), 12

Detroit, Mich., and A.C. Van Raalte, 36, 51
Deventer, Netherlands, 468
de Vlieg, Arie, 199
de Vos, H.A. (Seceder preacher in Amsterdam), 224-25
De Vries (Buffalo), 300
De Vries, Betje, 231
De Vries, Hein, 230-31
De Vries, Piet, 230-31
De Vries, S., 241, 254, 260, 266; travel troubles of 230-31
de Waal, A.G. (Seceder preacher in Amsterdam), 426, 430, 444
de Winter, Mr., 573
De Witt, Thomas, 35, 43, 52, 62, 328, 385
Diarrhea, 311
Diedam, Netherlands, 389
Diekinga, J.J. (St. Louis immigrant from Amsterdam), 74, 79, 85-86, 89, 222, 223, 260, 264, 364, 431; criticizes H.P. Scholte, 383
Dieman, Netherlands, 20
Dikker, F. S., 166, 209
Dingemans, G. H., 194
Dingemans, Hendrik, 119, 123, 127, 155, 156, 179, 186, 190, 191, 197, 198, 332
Dingemans, Mrs. D.H. (Aafje Overkamp), 194
Doeveren, Netherlands, 11, 328
Dogcarts, 121
Doge & Spaan, 332
Doleantie, 630
Domestics, 53, 379, 403; in Iowa, 606; in Netherlands, 407, 612; in Pella, 410; wages, 271, 358
Donkerdal, N. (friend of Hendrik Hospers), 127
Donkersloot, Netherlands, 161, 173
Donner, Johannes H. (Seceder preacher in Leiden), xx, 7, 389; and Free University, 637; letter from A.C. Van Raalte, 460-66
Doornhouwer family (Amsterdam), 79, 89, 431, 486
Doornhouwer, Truitje, 447
Dorcas Society (Amsterdam), 584

Dordrecht, Netherlands, 37, 146, 206
Dordt College, xxvi
Doremirs, Mr. (New York), 284
Dort: Canons of, 375; Church Order of, 385, 475, 628, 632; Synod of, xxx, 383, 475, 636
Draft (lottery), Civil War, 512
Draymen, 319-20, 423
Drenthe, Province of, 35, 48, 52
Dresel, Rev. (preacher from Basel, Switzerland, in Burlington), 358
Dress, for women, 291
Dropsy, 428
Drought, 436
Drownings, 404-05
Drukker, D.D. (preacher), 628
Drunkenness, 274, 328
Dry goods, prices of, 76
Duin, R.W. (Amsterdam preacher), 438
Dutch. *See* Netherlands
Dutch Americans: in Civil War, 488-89; express satisfaction, 455; warmly received, 78
Dutch cheese, 91, 111. *See also* Cheese making, Rennet
Dutch East Indies, 323
Dutch language: instruction in, 391, 403; usage of, 454, 491, 594, 622, in worship, 393, 527, 550
Dutch Reformed Church. *See* Reformed Church in America
Duwäer, Mr., 99
Duyzen van Almkerk, 149
Dwight, Mr. (headmaster), 379
Dyksterhuis, P.M., 408
Dysentery, 488

Ecumenism, 525, 559
Ede, Netherlands, 95
Education, Netherlands, 328, 386-87; law of 1857, 387; policy, 432-35. *See also* Schools
Eekhout, Mr., 101
Eene Stem uit Pella (H.P. Scholte pamphlet), 163, 189
Eensgezindheid (ship), 6
Eickman, Mr., 320
Elections, 65, 173

Ellis, Stilman (Pella mayor), 389
Elout, Mr., 324
Elwell Mill, Pella, 340
Emigrants, poor language skills of, 393
Emigration, 31-39, 220-21; condemned, 465; cost estimates, 37-38; emotional costs, 48; as escape, 392-93; motives for, 277, 305; rejected, 290-93; satisfaction with, 100-101, 102; societies for, by A.C. Van Raalte, 32, 62, 64-65, societies for, by H.P. Scholte, 330, 384-85; timing of, 51; Utrecht Society for, 37, 158, 216, 223
End times prophecies, 324, 419. *See also* Millenialism
England, 58, 153, 154, 197; postal service via, 124, 202, 215; mentioned, 337, 386, 398
English, 70, 247, 359, 489; manners, 292
English Bible Society (Utrecht), 119
English Channel, 58, 59, 60
English language: study of, 91, 95, 97, 99, 111, 113, 122, 124, 125, 130, 131, 133, 134, 144, 145, 152, 154, 171, 179, 182, 183, 196, 344, 451; usage of, 70, 75, 278, 464, 489, 491; in worship, 275, 456-57, 460, 500, 555, 556, 557, 562
Enlightenment (French), xv
Epilepsy, 414, 415
Episcopal church, 638
Eppens, Rev. (preacher in Burlington), 281, 357-58
Erie Canal, 238-41, 277, 292-93, 332, 337
Erskine, E., 628
Erskine, R., 24, 628
Estreng, J. (Pella immigrant), 389
Europe: as Babel, 635-36; gloomy view of, 285
Eusebius (early church father), 635
Evangelical Alliance: Amsterdam meeting, 541, 553, 555-57, 558-59, 561, 562, 564, 567, 568, 578, 584; New York meeting, 592, 595; 1870 meeting canceled, 600
Evangelist, Der (periodical), 594
Evangelists, in Amsterdam, 567-68

Factories, in Pella, 111, 178
Factory work, 307, 401-02, 404, 405, 413, 436
Fairfield, Ia., 84, 135
Fairview, Ill., 375
Fares: covered wagons, 339; stagecoach, 338
Farming, compared to Netherlands, 111-12, 246; difficulties in, 300, 315; fencing, 179, 267, 310, 315, 316, 379; labor in, 107, 277-78; mechanization in, 73-74; practices, 368-69; profits, 244-45, 279-80; values of farms, 93
Fencing. *See* Farming
Feringa, Mr., 569
Fevers, 79, 102, 106, 130, 233, 519
Fimpton, Rev. 500
Fires, 1871: in cities, 611; on prairies, 85, 140
Fish, as food, 142
Flatboats, 340
Flies, 275
Flooding, in Netherlands, 206, 408
Flörke, Mine, 398
Flörke, Mrs., 57, 92, 94, 398; death of, 95, 97, 99, 106
Fockink Wijnand, Mr. (Amsterdam merchant), 5
Folk medicine. *See* Medicines, folk.
Food, 142, 162; complaints about, 270-71; compared, 235; eating practices, 236-37; prices of, 71, 82, 92, 139, 273-74, 275-76, 314, 490; scarcity of, 321; on shipboard, 52
Forms of Unity, 628, 629
Fort Des Moines. *See* Des Moines, Iowa
Fort Machinaw, Mich.; 337
Fort Sumter, S.C., 538
Fosca Helena (ship), 6, 420, 423
Foundry work, 423
Fourth of July. *See* Independence Day
France, 58, 154, 272, 386, 569-70; and Netherlands, 98; 1848 revolution in, 147, 171, 368
Franciska (ship), 329, 331, 334, 341
Franeker, Netherlands, 186
Freedom: in America, 173, 335, 636;

civil, 72, 87; in education, 35; in Netherlands, 33-35; in religion, 72, 87, 383
Free Scottish Church, 224, 227-28
Free University of Amsterdam, xv, xvi, xxiii, xxv, xxix, 224, 228, 631; founding of, 615; and Pella, 637; mentioned, 473, 477
Freight, shipping rates, 143
French, 70; Huguenots, 340, language study, 179, 183, 327
French Comedy (Amsterdam), 368
Friendship, by women, 407
Friesland, Province of, 23, 337
Frigo, Mr. (Spanish evangelist and partner of Matamoros), 569
Frisians, 48, 410; in Pella, 348, 350
Fruit growing, 416
Fulton Street revivals (New York), 584
Furniture, costs compared to Netherlands, 299; prices of, 274, 281; shoddy workmanship of, 235-36

Galena, Ill., 317
Gameren, Netherlands, 155
Gansoyen, Netherlands, 11
Gardens, 359; English style, 170; in Pella 362-63; produce, 369
Garretson, John, 43, 386, 412-13, 421, 423
Gasteren, Netherlands, 186
Gazelle Meerburg, Georg Frans, 9, 10, 15, 22, 25, 473
Gelderland, Province of, 23, 36, 52, 111, 329, 337, 396, 574, 592; flooding in, 408
Genderen, Netherlands, 11, 328
Geneva, Switzerland, 367
Gereformeerde Kerk Nederland, 475-76, 559
German: doctors, 83; hymns, 499, 565, 568, 571, 594; language, 374, 451, 491-92, 498, 552, 581, language in worship, 393, 418, 456, 460, 526-27, 555; preachers, 68-69, 73, 77, 559
German Evangelical Lutheran Church (Burlington), 82, 90, 91, 278, 357-58, 422

German Reformed Church: in Amsterdam, 600; in Burlington, xvii, 71, 73, 275, 278
Germans, 68, 70, 73, 88, 245, 247, 271, 290, 291, 294, 331, 338, 374, 446, 485, 489, 626; in Burlington, 75, 76, 241; criticized by Dutch, 51; as farmers, 263; as immigrant "material," 300; in Mount Pleasant, 550; as ship passengers, 62
Germantown, Iowa, 405
Germany, 206, 237, 488, 576; and Amsterdam, xviii; emigration, 32; travel in, 491; and Wormser family, 5
Gerritsen, Mr. (Nijmegen), 599
Giessendam, Netherlands, 189
Gildermeester, Rev. (member of Amsterdam society of J.A. Wormser), 611
Gobat, Samuel, Methodist missionary to Abyssinia and Protestant bishop of Jerusalem), 567
God-is-dead theology, 638
Gordon, J., 132
Gorinchem (Gorkum), Netherlands, 46, 115, 120, 124, 132, 133, 173, 190, 192, 199, 206, 208, 212, 285, 314, 327; canal boats at, 196; map of region, 116
Gorkum, Netherlands. *See* Gorinchem, Netherlands
Gouda pipes (tobacco), 154, 179, 194, 197
Graafschap Bentheim, 626
Grafe, E.F., 384
Graham, John Armstrong, 222-23
Graham, Mr. (Keokuk), 338
Grand Haven, Mich., 408, 451
Grand Pierre, Rev. 548, 554
Grand Rapids, Mich., 224-25
Grand River (Mich.), and Dutch, 51
Grant, F.H., 388
Grant, Ulysses S., 567
Graves, Mr. (Pella), 185
Great Lakes, steamboats on, 261
Greenleafton (Preston), Minn., 43
Greve, Mr. (at Leiden), 601-02
Grief, expressions of, 94, 516-18, 519-

20

Groen van Prinsterer, Guallaume, xv, xxiv, 6, 17, 21, 23, 24, 26-27, 31, 220 (photo), 223, 229, 367, 383, 476; characterizes D.A. Budde, 625-27; and education, 386-87, 432; and Evangelical Alliance, 555, 558-59; and H.P. Scholte, 432-33, 630; and J.A. Wormser, 27-28, 516, 517, 583, 626-27; and politics, 41, 420, 630-32, 637, 638; *Stemmen uit Noord Amerika* (pamphlet), 220; photo, 220
Groen van Prinsterer, Mrs. Guallaume, 377
Gruel, groat (food), 128
Guldin, Johannes C. (Reformed Church preacher in New York), 374, 450, 521, 526
Gunsmith, 52-53
Gunther, Mr. (Amsterdam Seceder), 89, 98, 364, 395, 427; death of, 419, 430
Gunther, Sientje, 430

Haagsche Heeren, 367
Haagsche Vrienden, 355, 378
Haarlem, Netherlands, 429-30, 608
Haarlem (Haarlemmer) Oil, 127, 141, 154, 469
Haarlemmermeer, Netherlands, 430
Haefkens, I. (Amsterdam school inspector), 161, 173, 181, 187, 189, 328, 337
Hagedoorn, Captain of *Franciska*, 329
Hagens, G. (Amsterdam emigrant), 216, 314
Hague, The, Netherlands, 15, 17, 65, 456, 516, 556,
Haijen, Mr., 337
Haksteen, Dr. (in Buffalo, N.Y.), 337
Hall, Claiborne (Marion County surveyor), 138
Hall-Pieterse, Widow, 387
Handelsblad, Het (Amsterdam newspaper), 36-37, 123
Hansum, Jan, 173
Hardinxveld, Netherlands, 206
Harrisburg, Pa., 47
Harrison, George, 169, 171
Harrison, John, 188

Hartgerink, Alexander, 32
Hasebroek, Johannes P. (orthodox Hervormde Kerk preacher in Amsterdam), 226, 389, 395, 398, 400, 408, 430, 431, 440, 441, 444, 446, 447, 467, 485, 505, 517, 555, 559; and J.A. Wormser, 28 (photo), 28-29
Haselhof, J. (married Janssen in Milwaukee), 356
Hasselman, Adam P., 171
Hasselman, Antje, 379
Hasselman, W.L., (Mrs. J.D. Brandt), 17
Hazebroek, Herman (Amsterdam jurist, brother-in-law of H.P. Scholte), 49, 140, 378
Head cheese, 134
Heaven, portrayed, 604
Heerenveen, Netherlands, 146
Heerjansdam, Netherlands, 345
Heidelberg Catechism, 86, 402-03, 440, 628
Heinkes (author), 154
Heldring, Rev. Otto G. (Hervormde Kerk preacher), 32, 559, 562, 627; photo, 33
Hellendoorn, Netherlands, 5, 7, 17, 43, 53, 125; and Seine Bolks, 47
Hellenization, 635, 638
Hellevoetsluis, Netherlands, 118, 119, 123
Hemp (crop), 129
Hengeveld, Jan (Pella immigrant), 85, 579
Henriette (ship), 6
Heraut, De (newspaper), 473, 517
Herkimer, N.Y., 337
Hersteld Evangelisch Luthersе Kerk. *See* Restored Evangelical Lutheran Church
Hervormde Kerk Nederland, 475-76, 559
Heukeldam, Netherlands, 149
Heyboer, Mr., 146, 179
Heymans (Amsterdam baker), 148, 202
Hieligje (maid), 208
Hillsdale, Mich., 259
Historische Documentatie Centrum voor Nederlands Protestantisme (Amsterdam), xxv, xxix

Index 677

Hitsert, Netherlands, 172, 187
Hodenpijl (Hodenpeil, Hodenpyl), H (Pieter I.G.), 62
Hoedemaker family (emigrants from Utrecht), 404, 413, 592
Hogs, 280, 315, 424, slaughtering of, 293
Holland, language, 388
Holland Academy (Hope College), xiii, xiv, xxxi, 390, 456, 461, 462
Holland (Mich.) colony, 125, 129; disparaged, 79-80, 174, 178-79, 307-08; founding of, xxvii; rivalry with Pella, 50, 379; sickness in, 80, 264, 307-08; mentioned, 309-10, 390
Hollander, De (Holland, Mich., newspaper), 386, 404
Hollanders, low reputation of, 278-79
Holland Hotel (New York), 62
Holland Iron Railway Company, 45
Holland Reformed Church (Grand Rapids, Mich.), 224-25
Holland Society for the Protection of Immigrants, 62, 64-65
Hoogblokland (Blokland), Netherlands, 46, 116, 121, 123, 155, 163, 166, 174, 198, 200, 203, 327, 328, 330; Hospers family in, 115-17; Seceded Church in, 127, 329. *See also* Van Raalte, colony of
Hoogeveen, Mr. (Pella immigrant), 346, 361
Hoogkamer, B.J. (Amsterdam publisher), 17, 25, 32, 119, 134, 163, 367
Hoorn, Netherlands, 250
Hoornaar, Netherlands, 155, 167, 196
Hope & Co. (Amsterdam banking house), xxiv, 79, 89, 284
Horses, teams, 244
Horst, Mr. (emigration commissioner), 329, 592
Hospers & Harrison lumber yard (Pella), 192
Hospers, Anna Cornelia, 115
Hospers, Cornelia Geertruida (Keetje, Kaatje, Kee), 117, 120, 121, 124, 125, 138, 147, 154-55, 161, 167, 174, 185, 191, 192, 329, 330-31, 332, 333, 334-35; death of, 336
Hospers, Eva Engelina, 117, 119, 130, 142, 166, 191, 192, 332, 334, 335
Hospers, Gelder, 332, 334, 335
Hospers, Gerrit (father of Jan Hospers), 332
Hospers, Gerrit (brother of Jan), 332, 334
Hospers, Gerrit Hendrik, 132, 147, 200-01, 203, 212
Hospers, Gerrit Jan, 132
Hospers, Hanna, 332
Hospers, Hendrik (Henry), xvii-xviii, xxix, 7, 46, 49, 110, 117 (photo), 130, 147, 163, 171, 164, 223, 339, 332, 333, 383, 572; character of, 205; expense accounts of, 151-53; and H.P. Scholte, 162, 217, 384, 477, 478; leads Sioux County settlement, xvii; letters of, 118-19, 126-28, 134-45, 148-53, 157-63, 168-80, 182-86, 193, 204, 208-12, 215-17; lumberyard of, 171, 188; marriage of, 391; and Mrs. G. H. Overkamp; ocean voyage of, 118; as Pella official, xvii, 389; and *Pella's Weekblad*, 390; piety of, 212; sketches Pella lots, 138; studies English, 145; as teacher, 117, 183
Hospers, Hendrik Willem, 120, 166
Hospers, Hendrika, xxviii
Hospers, Hendrika nee Middelkoop (Mrs. Jan), 185-86; letters of, 123-24, 126, 164-66, 191-93
Hospers, Jan (John)("Father"), xvii-xviii, 7, 14-15, 63, 115-17, 122, 172, 185-86, 207, 327 (photo), 332, 345, 355, 357, 391; autobiography, 328-30; and *De Reformatie*, 119; desire to emigrate, 167-68; diary of, xxiii; financial affairs, 132, 147-48, 195-96. 207, 214; and G.H. Overkamp, 194-95; and H.P. Scholte, 156-57, 199, 339; letters of, 120-25, 129-34, 145-48, 153-57, 163-64, 167-68, 180-82, 186-93, 195-208, 212-14; Pella lands of, 140, 189; piety expressed, 126, 130, 180, 188, 191, 198, 200,

201; as teacher, 145, 196; travel account, 331-40, 384
Hospers, Kaatje (Keetje, Kee). See Hospers, Cornelia Geertruida
Hospers, Klaas. See Hospers, Nicholas
Hospers, Maaike, 117, 120, 121, 125, 131, 147, 155, 167, 174, 185, 191, 202, 212, 329-30
Hospers, Miet, 166
Hospers, Nicholas (Klaas, Nikolaas), 117, 121, 122, 130, 148, 155, 166, 185, 190, 192, 200, 201, 204, 332, 334, 335, 339, 380; letters of 131, 166-67
Hospers, Pieter Hendrik, 117, 120, 121, 131, 142, 153, 166, 190, 192, 202, 329-30
Hospers, Sijgje, 332, 334
Hospers, Teunis De Gelder (Gelder), 117, 119, 121, 122, 130, 147, 155, 185, 191, 192, 197, 201
Hospers, Willem Hendrik, 117, 129, 131, 132, 142, 161, 191, 192, 203, 334, 335
Hospitality, by Americans, 76
House churches, xviii, 562
Housekeeping, Dutch, 112
House of Orange, 433
Houses, stone, 240-41, 242
Höveker, Betje (Mrs. Van der Land), 485, 486; marriage of, 486, 487
Höveker, Catharina Johanna (Mrs. Johan Adam Wormser, Jr.), xxii, 471, 569, 582, 587, 592, 594
Höveker, Henricus, xxiii-xxvii, 569, 582, 584, 587, 591, 592, 593, 594, 598, 605, 612; death of, 437; and Secession of 1834, 6, 14, 15, 17, 18, 20 (photo), 23, 24, 25, 27; as publisher, 471, 472-473; wife, 427; mentioned, 603, 607, 613
Höveker, Kaatje. See Höveker, Catharina Johanna
Höveker-van Ommen Bobbendijk, Betsy, 584
Höveker-Wormser Archives, xv, xvi, xxiv, xxvi, xxix
Höweler, Casper Andries, xxv

Höweler, H.A., xv, xxiv
Hudson River, 332, 333
Huet, Rev. (Amsterdam cleric), 556-57, 584
Huidekoper, Peter (Amsterdam mayor, 1842-1848), 380
Hugenholz, Rev. 439-40, 444
Hugens, G., 407
Huguenots, French, 340
Huijding (Huiding, Huyding), Mr. (Amsterdam), 89, 285, 288-89, 294, 379
Huising, Mrs., 299
Hulscher, Jan (friend of Jan Budde), 92
Hulsebosch, Enno, 539
Hulsebosch family (emigrants, relatives of D.A Budde), 539, 544
Huppen, xxv-xxvi
Hymns, German, 249, 505

Illinois, and Dutch, 63-64
Illinois-Michigan Canal, 256-58
Illinois River, 257-59
Illness, 94, 96-97, 335, 344, 381, 401; children, 303-04; in D.A. Budde family, 404; en route, 357; in Holland (Mich.) colony, 307-08; of J.A. Wormser, 366; in Netherlands, 431
Immigrants: cheating of, 264; disappointed, 270-71; ties to homeland, 412
Immigration: aid societies for, 35, 64-65; criticized, 213; factors in, 168; folly of, 264; promoted, 174, 194; return, 264; routes to Pella, 139, 198, 199, 207; of Seceders, 129-30
Independence Day, celebrated, 184, 291-92, 336
India, 386, 434
Indians, 50, 174, 178, 325
Indonesia, 409, 430
Industry, in Pella, 111
Inheritance practices, 516-17
Innkeeper, charges, 423-24
Interest, money lending, 402
Iowa, 2, 36-37; and Civil War, 512-13; conditions in, xvi, xvii, 37; description of, 178; grain fields of, 585; maps of, 163, 175

Iowa City, Iowa, 137, 283, 379
Iowa Farm Advocate (newspaper), 279
Ireland, potato famine in, 41
Isabella (ship), 43, 54
Itjen, Mr., 337

Jaarsma, Elaine, xv
Jaarsma, Ralph, xv
Jannawa, Mr. (married Johanna Teleman), 482
Jansen (Janssen)(Amsterdam Seceder), 79, 89, 101, 395, 430; death of, 485, 505
Janssen, Mr. (Milwaukee, married J. Haselhof), 261, 356, 498
Jaspers, Meitje, 409; death of, 417, 426
Jaspers, Miss (governess), 95
Jaspers, Truitje, 409, 417, 426, 430, 446, 459, 481; death of, 467
Jaspers family (stonemason), 395, 397, 409, 426, 486
Jeremiads, and Civil War, 495, 531-32; about Netherlands, 409
Jerusalem, 411, 635; compared to Pella, 385
Jews: as Christian converts, 10; in Israel, 477; in Jerusalem, 285; mission work among, 367; in Netherlands, 227, 288, 399, 417, 435
Johnstown, Penn., 47
Jordan, Miss (nurse), 329
Journey, ocean; inland. *See* Travel

Kamp, Grietje (Mrs. Bastiaan Vos), 172, 187
Kampen, Netherlands, 113, 444; theological school at, 333, 397, 400, 408, 430
Kamsteeg, Herbert, 189
Kansas, 602
Kars, Albert, 191
Kars, H., 190, 198
Kattenburg Island, Netherlands, 5
Kayser, Captain H.L. (ship), 44, 55, 57, 60
Keables, Dr. B.F. (husband of Sara Scholte), 381, 388, 473, 500-01, 506, 509, 512

Keables, Katie, 622
Keer, J.C. (Amsterdam Seceder), 14
Keesel (Keisel), Jacob, 109, 221, 250, 251, 261, 264, 266-67, 279, 299; letter of, 307, 309, 310
Keitz, Dr. (St. Louis), 69
Keizer (Budde tenant), 270
Keokuk, Iowa, 45, 46, 47, 50, 64, 137, 143, 146, 158, 177, 212, 338, 344; and Civil War, 489, 508; Dutch in, 215, 312, 313, 316, 317-19, 321; as immigrant depot, 151; as market center, 359-60; plank road in 340; Reformed Church in, 482-83
Keosaqua Iowa Democrat, 177
Keppel, Bart, 149, 174
Keppel, Huibert, 129, 133, 135, 155, 188, 189, 197
Keppel, Jan, 174
Keppel, Teunis, 124, 129, 174
Keuning, Jan (school principal in Spijk), 7n
Keuning, Willem Edward (son of Jan), 7n
Kinderdoop, De (pamphlet), 27, 382
King, Don, 362
King, James G. & Sons (New York), 79, 89
King, Mrs. (New York), 284
Klaaswaal, Netherlands, 187
Kliebenstein, Rev. (Presbyterian preacher), 562
Klein, F., 210
Klein, Jan, 180
Klein Heksel, Hendrik, 47
Klein Heksel family, 52
Klyn, Rev. Hendrik G., 437
Knoxville, Ia., 137, 181, 350
Koelman, J., 25
Koeman, H.J., 383
Koffers, J.A., 410
Koffers family, 415
Kohlbrugge, Hermann Friedrich (Seceder preacher), 9
Kok, 332
Kol, Mrs. 380
Kollen, Mr., 554, 566, 572
Kolvoort, Jan, family, 52

Kool, Aart, 180
Koopman, Sara, 15
Koopmans, H.R. (Reformed Church preacher), 390
Koopmans, Rev. (at Heerenveen), 146
Korink, Catharina (Mrs. Georg Adam Wormser), 5
Kortenhof Smit, Rev. (Hervormde Kerk preacher in Amsterdam), 408, 444, 550
Krabbendam-Budde, Betje, 396, 409
Krabbendam-Budde, Grietje, 486
Krantz, Hubertina (Mrs. Herman Hazebroek), 49
Krantz, Jan Willem Daniel, 49
Krantz, Maria (Mariah), Hendrika Elizabeth (second wife of H.P. Scholte), 48-49, 344, 473, 478, 595; gives birth, 366, 509, 512; poor health of, 366; remarriage to Robert Beard, 602; unhappiness of, 385
Krichbaum (Kirschbaum), Mr. (storekeeper in Burlington), 104, 241-42, 300, 303; death of, 530
Kropholder, Heintje, 397
Kruijt, Aafje (Mrs. Isaac Overkamp), 38
Kruijt, Jacobus, 122-23, 189
Kuyper, A.C., xvii, 285, 327, 329, 334, 336, 345, 355, 357; as teaching elder, 332, 333, 337, 339, 385, 389, 434, 585; death of son Jan, 332
Kuyper, Abraham, xxiv, 228, 611, 612; and Free University, 631; newspaper of, 473
Kuyper, Hugo (Pella immigrant), 389
Kuyper, Jan, 332
Kuyper, Peter, 170

Labadism, 629
Labor: child, 278; farm, 277-78
Lagerweij, J., Gz. Hendrik, 131
Lake Erie, 46, 337
Lake Huron, 46, 51, 337
Lake Michigan, 46, 48, 51; *Phoenix* disaster on, 73, 80
Lake Prairie Township, Iowa, 163, plat of 1848, 136
Lake Saint Clair, 337

Land: cessions, 178; clearing, 293; cost of improvements, 309, 316; fertility, 74; H. P. Scholte's dealings in, 158-59; prices, 70, 112, 152, 262, 288-89, 375; purchases, 37-38, 73, 88, 265-66, 287; warrants, 209
Land van Altena, Netherlands, 206
Lankelma, P.C., 573
Lankheet, Gerrit Harmannus (Pella immigrant), 47, 48, 54, 279, 299-300
La Salle, Ill., 64, 338
Laws, and immigrant shipping, 65
Le Cocq, Christina, 482
Le Cocq, Dorus, 306, 414
Le Cocq, Frans (born 1828), 414, 482, 528
Le Cocq, Frans (Jean Francois) (1805-1888), 37, 46, 74, 84, 279, 314, 315 (photo), 316, 353, 356, 384, 407, 411, 495, 497, 528-29, 509; illness of 380; and Johannes Berkhout, 320-21, 363
Le Cocq, Jan, 306, 364-65, 482, 509
Le Cocq, Maria, 482
Le Cocq, Mietje, 365, 414
Leer (Ost Friesland), 2-3, 403, 459, 539, 626
Leerbroek, Netherlands, 122
Leerdam, Netherlands, 37, 133, 190
Leeuwarden, Netherlands, 192
Le Havre, France, 121, 198
Leiden, Netherlands, 10, 66, 601, 607; University of, 16, 38
Lelie, Mr. (harness maker in Gorinchem), 208
Lentz, L.C., 426
Liberalism, theological, 469, 493, 611. *See also* Modernism
Lifestyle, compared to Netherlands, 308-309
Lijsen, Dirk (Amsterdam Seceder, brother-in-law of H. Höveker), 23, 24, 26; remarriage of, 593
Lijsen, Kaatje (Mrs. Van Lent), 395, 426, 446
Lincoln, Abraham, 473; assassination of, 538-39; election of, 538
Liverpool, England, 44-45, 57, 353

Livestock. *See* Animal husbandry
Living conditions, Iowa compared to Netherlands, 287
Lodensteyn ("old writer"), 628
Log cabin, 122, 126, 157, 158, 169, 183, 197, 287, 312, 316, 319, 322; erection of, 136; photo, 127
London, 41, 47
Lord's Day. *See* Sabbath
Lord's Supper, 42, 562; attitudes toward, 402; at Evangelical Alliance, 555
Lothes, Mrs. Peter W., 550
Lothes (Lotthes), Peter W. (elder, Amsterdam Seceded Church), 55, 77, 79, 89, 90, 233, 307, 346, 364, 375, 396, 431, 492; death of, 550
Lots, prices of, in Pella, 137, 138, 146, 356
Lottery, military. *See* Military conscription
Louisiana (ship), 337
Louis Philip, King of France, 272
Lubberden, Martje, 381
Lubberden, Mrs., 85
Lubberden, Mrs. Willem, 381
Lubberden, Piet, 59, 60, 84, 85 (photo)
Lubberden, Willem, 57, 58, 59, 61, 69, 74, 85, 93, 104, 233, 306, 356, 318 (photo), 407
Lubbers, Arend, 415
Lubbers, C.C. (Amsterdam), 164
Lubbers, Herman, 121, 161
Lubbers, Koetje, 121
Lucas, Henry S., xxi
Luther, Martin, 432
Lutherans, xix, 5, 9, 247, 275, 418, 525; in Amsterdam, 426; German, 69; and J.A. Wormser family, 5. *See also* Restored Evangelical Lutheran Church
Luuring (Luring), Jan Willem (Amsterdam colporter), 77, 79, 89, 95, 233, 295, 307, 346, 364, 375, 395, 414, 422, 468, 470; death of, 504, 509, 511, 513, 515, 517
Luuring, Johan (son of Jan Willem), 560
Luuring, Mrs. Jan Willem, 560

Luuring, Saartje (hatmaker, daughter of Jan Willem Luuring), 430, 446, 468, 487, 560
Luuring, Willem (clerk, friend of J.A. Wormser, Jr.), 430, 447, 487, 504, 560
Luuring family (Amsterdam Seceders), 379, 430, 447, 486, 492, 505, 535

Maasdam, Jacob (Pella book dealer), xvii, 66, 119, 129, 153, 165, 181, 197, 198, 206, 207, 214, 285, 323, 327, 329, 339, 345; as teaching elder, 384, 385
Maasstroom, De (ship), 46; ocean voyage of, 115, 116, 119, 121 (photo), 122, 123; rumored sinking of, 133
Maastricht, Netherlands, 26, 96
Mackinaw (Fort), 337
Madoulet, J.B. (first Reformed Church preacher in Burlington, 1853-1855), 374-75, 386, 455
Maids. *See* Domestics
Mail service. *See* Post
Malan, César, 9
Maple syrup, 162
Marion County, Iowa, 78, 129, 137, 138, 169, 177
Marriage, 490; second generation, 473
Marrum, Netherlands, 224
Marryat, Captain, 219
Marxism, 626
Masonic Lodge, 91
Matamoros, Don Manuel (Spanish Protestant evangelist and martyr), 569, 578
Materialism, 626
Mayer, Mr. (New York), 311
Measles, 61, 417
Meat, prices, 275-76
Medicines, folk, 331, 333, 334, 528
Mediterranean Sea, 386
Meerkerk, Netherlands, 121, 187, 189
Memphis, Tenn., 500
Mennonites, 562, 578
Mensink, Mannes (Hellendoorn immigrant to Wisconsin), 43; letter of, 51-54

Merwede (river), 206
Methodists, 71, 90, 91, 106, 247, 250, 278, 405, 482
Mexican War, 64
Meyboom, L.J.P. (liberal preacher in The Hague), 399, 412, 431
Meyer, J. & Son (Amsterdam), 6
Meyer, Jan H. (deacon, Pella), 156, 170, 173, 213, 384
Meyer, R.C., 441
Mice, 270. *See also* Rats
Michigan: and A.C. Van Raalte, 51; compared to Iowa, 112; disparaged by H.P. Scholte, 63-64; fires of 1871, 611; Holland colony in, 36, 289; land prices in, 394; Seceder immigration to, xxx, 2; travel to Pella via, 334; visited by H.P. Scholte, 421
Middel, H. (Amsterdam Seceder), 12
Middelkoop, Floris (Floor), 120, 192
Middelkoop, Gerrit, 117, 123, 128, 141, 190, 198, 200, 202
Middelkoop, Hendrika (Mrs. Jan Hospers), 115-17, 327
Middelkoop, Klaas ("Father," "Grandfather"), 117, 120, 121, 128, 153, 154, 155, 172, 180, 181, 187, 198, 211, 328, 330, 332, 334, 335, 339, 345; financial affairs of, 214; Pella lands of, 140, 146, 160, 189, mentioned, 149, 161
Middelkoop, Mrs. Klaas ("Grandmother"), 117, 156, 211
Middelkoop, Neeltje, 192
Middelkoop, Sijgje (Sijgje-moei), 117, 161, 190, 198, 207
Middelkoop, Willem, 120, 128, 190, 198, 200, 202, 204
Midwifery, 249
Mijdrecht, Netherlands, 13
Milan, Italy, 41
Militaire Willemsorde (Military Williams Order), 5
Military conscription (lottery), in Netherlands, 150, 163, 195, 206
Milking, 425, 489
Millenialism, 229, 629-32, 633; and H.P. Scholte, xx

Mills, 209, 212; grain, 214; grist, 144, 210; saw, 144, 145, 169
Milwaukee, Wis., 35, 79, 338, 498; Dutch in, 261, 310, 356; as immigrant depot, 256
Minkeloos, Netherlands, 129
Mississippi River, 47, 71, 75, 111, 143, 169, 258, 338; crossing of, 273; navigation on, 272; railroad bridge over, 595; steamboats on, 219-18, 314, 317
Modernism, theology, 569, 605, 591. *See also* Liberalism
Mohammedans, 399, 420
Money, 254-55; chest of, 384; interest rates, 243, 250; lending of, 141, 243; worship of, condemned, 308
Monod, Frédéric, 9
Monroe, Iowa, 170
Monster, Aart (Pella immigrant), 172, 320
Mormons, 47, 50
Morphine, 524
Mount Pleasant, Iowa, 50, 345, 379, 403, 405, 442, 564, 565, 579; and D.A. Budde family, 549-50, 558, 561-62, 577-78, 585-86, 616, 625-26; described, 544; Dutch in, 601-02; Presbyterian Church in, 550, 561-62, 595
Mullens, Rev. Dr., 555
Muller, Johan (Reformed Church pastor in Burlington, 1858-1861), 386, 450, 456-57, 459-60, 469-70, 480, 488, 526; and D.A. Budde family, 497-98, 520-21
Muntingh, James (Pella teacher), 110, 122, 152, 170, 171, 182, 183
Muppen, xxv-xxvi

Nagasaki (ship), 46, 119
Nahuis, J.F. (Pella immigrant), 333, 389
Napoleon III (Ludwig Napoleon, Emperor of France), 272, 386
Napoleonic code, 12
Native Americans, 37
Naturalization, in Pella, 173
Nauhuys, J.F. *See* Nahuis, J.F.

Nauvoo, Ill., 47, 50
Neander, John (Reformed Church missionary to the Jews), 62
Nederlander, De (Amsterdam newspaper), 368, 386
Nederlandsche Staatscourant (Amsterdam newspaper), 123
Neede, Netherlands, 32
Negroes. *See* Blacks
Neige, Mr. (Amsterdam society member), 101
Netherlands: agricultural conditions, 120, 125; decadence decried, 392-93; economic troubles in, 297-98, 304-05; emigration fever in, 134; political developments in, 465, 630-33, 635; rejected by emigrants, 53; religious developments, 420, 489; remigration, 115; ruin predicted, 399, 409; return visits by immigrants, 473; taxes in, 108
Netherlands East Indies, 32, 35, 434, 592
Netherlands Reformed Church. *See* Hervormde Kerk Nederland
Netherlands Society for Israel, 228
Netherlands Society for the Protection of Emigrants, 35, 37
Netherlands Trading Company (Nijverdal), 5, 253, 289, 560
New Brunswick Seminary, 365, 404
New Jersey, xxvi, 43
New London, Iowa, 339, 595
New Netherlands Christian Cultural and Social Weekly (periodical), 382
New Orleans, 36, 43, 48; cholera in, 279, 300, 304; as immigrant depot, 64, 65, 70, 139, 143, 149, 160, 198, 199, 257, 264, 281, 311, 312, 404
New Purchase (Iowa land cession), 178
Newspapers, 398, 412
New York City: alcoholism in, 277; cholera in, 279; as commercial center, 424; described, 78-79; H.P. Scholte preaches in, 67; immigrant agents in, 112, 237; as immigrant depot, 44-45, 52, 61-62, 78, 79, 123, 143, 164, 199, 221, 230, 235, 264,

311, 328, 329, 331, 337, 398, 406, 572; immigration protection societies in, 35, 37; Netherlandic interest in, 553; population of, 73; and railroads, 414; Seceder immigration to, xxxi; mentioned, 63, 216, 374, 411, 450, 429, 564
Neyenesch, Herman (Pella immigrant), 478
Niagara (ship), 254-55
Nice, France, 380
Nichteveen, Netherlands, 344
Nicolaas Witsen (ship), 6
Niemeijer, Jan (Netherlands writer and novelist), xiv
Nieuwediep, Netherlands, 54, 55, 56, 62, 340, 610
Nieuwe Rotterdamsche Courant (newspaper), 44, 123
Nieuwkerk, Netherlands, 189
Nieuwland, Netherlands, 122, 129, 132
Nieuwyksche College (La Salle County, Ill.), 64
Nigtevecht, Netherlands, 357
Nijmegen, Netherlands, 192, 374, 420, 599
Nijverdal, Netherlands, 5, 7, 250, 360, 541, 570, 582, 598, 607, 608, 611. *See also* Netherlands Trading Company
Noetele, Netherlands, 5
Nol, Mrs. 344
Nollen, Gerrit H., 389
Nollen, Henry G., 388
Nollen, John (Jan), 388, 389, 473, 573, 622
Nonnebel van Ryn, J.P. (preacher in Hervormde Kerk at Middelburg), 559
Noord Brabant, Province of, 11, 25, 329, 408
Noordbroek family, 446
Noordeloos, Netherlands, 37, 146, 189, 208, 328
Noordhoek, Mr., 417, 516
Noord Holland, Province of, 76, 164, 329
North Sea, 58
Northwestern College Library, 116

Norton, Mr. (Connecticut), 63, 64, 65
Nova Zembla, 391

Obbes, N. (Amsterdam Seceder), 12
Ocean crossing. *See* Travel
Oggel, P.J., 389-92, 390 (photo), 408, 465, 482; death of, 451, 595; illness of, 529; as "Reformer of Pella," 500-01
Ohio River, 46
Old Pella Store, 340
"Old Writers" (*oude schrijvers*), 24-25, 53
Omaha, Neb., 638
Ommen, Netherlands, 7, 17
Ongeloof en Revolutie (book of Groen van Prinsterer), 41
Oostendorp, Lubbertus (Christian Reformed pastor and historian), 222
Oosterzee, J.J. (liberal preacher in Rotterdam and theology professor in Utrecht), 555, 558
Ooyens, Marez G.H. (Amsterdam broker and member of Hervormde Kerk consistory), 468
Ooyens family, 559, 569
Oquawka, Ill., 338
Orthodoxy, theological, 605-06, 611-12
Oskaloosa, Iowa, 86, 170, 381; and Civil War, 499-500, 506
Ost Friesland, Germany, xviii, 2-3, 63, 271, 282, 289, 488, 543; and D.A. Budde family, 626
Otten family (Amsterdam Seceders), 486
Oude Kerk, Amsterdam, 446
Overijssel, Province of, 7, 53, 77, 97, 99, 111, 234, 242, 266, 291, 309, 364, 395; immigration from, 255-56; mentioned, 428, 439, 444, 468
Overisel, Mich., 572, 600
Overkamp, Aafje (Mrs. G.H. Dingemans), 195
Overkamp, G.H., 37, 38 (photo), 38-39, 46, 122, 125, 141, 146, 148-49, 151, 153, 160, 170, 173, 192, 197, 201, 204, 209-10, 334, 369, 384; cemetery of, 391; letter to Jan Hospers, 194-95; as schoolmaster, 49; as teaching elder, 173; mentioned, 128, 189
Overkamp, Isaac (husband of Aafje Kruijt), 37, 38-39, 41, 46, 110, 111, 122, 123, 130, 135, 143, 162, 182, 188, 192, 197, 209, 216, 38 (photo), 328, 335, 369-70; cemetery of, 391; death of, 391; tutors Hendrik Hospers, 115-16, 144, 171; and Jan Hospers, 145; letter of, 139; ocean voyage of, 115, 118, 119; as Pella official, 149, 173, 389; as schoolmaster, 115-16, 144, 171, 390-391; as teaching elder, 173, 384, 385; as *voorzanger*, 130; mentioned, 149, 154
Overkamp, Mrs. (widowed mother of Isaac and G.H. Overkamp), 119
"mothers" Hendrik Hospers, 116, 123, 125, 126, 150, 162, 165-66
Overkamp, Naatje, 143, 193
Ox carts, 318-20
Oxen, as draft animals, 169, 204, 244

Packet boats. *See* Canal boats
Painter, portrait, 389
Palatinate, Germany, 41
Palestine, 285, 567; Jews in, 632
Paris, 41; Commune of, 611; Reformed Church in, 548; Revolution of 1848 in, 171, 194, 296; visits to, 548-49, 553-55, 561, 564; World's Fair of 1867, 551
Pauli (Pouli), C.W.H. (Anglican preacher in Amsterdam), 93
Pawnbrokers, 274
Peaches, cultivated, 416
Peas, cultivated, 157, soup, 155
Pella, accounts of, 602; and Amsterdam, 635-39; architecture of, 170; and Burlington, 83; business opportunities in, 144-45, 204; character of, 638; cheese making in, 157; cholera in, 282; Christian Reformed Church in, 390; church divisions in, 147-48, 355, 372-73, 378, 390; as "city of refuge," 383-84; and Civil War, 496, 499-500, 506-08; climate of, 137; death of Scholte, 586; destiny of,

634; doctors in, 378; excited by Indians, 179; favorable reports on, 306; favorably compared to Holland (Mich.) colony, 369; financial difficulties in, 373; founding of, xxx, 115-17, 120, 129, 135, 339-40; growth of, 379; hires emigration agent, 379; Holland Academy envisioned, 462, 463-64; and Hospers family, 115; housing conditions in, 157-58; and Johannes Berkhout, 573, 604; and Johan A. Wormser, Sr., 628; leaders of, xxx; 66; livestock in, 139; lot prices in, 134, 137, 138, 146, 394; lots in, 140-41, 159, 170, 177; migration to, 157, 186-87, 179, 322-23; mills in, 144, 145, 169, 209, 210, 212, 214; negative reports of, xx, 86, 161, 187, 189, 215, 222-23, 313-14, 325, 355-56; paintings of, 389; panorama, 128; pioneer families of, xviii; plat, 49, 176; political life in, 173; railroad in, 466; reasons for choosing, 312, 316; recommended, 370, 371; Reformed Church in, 383-86, 451, 460-66, 482; region described, 127, 137, 158, 177; religious life of, xix-xx, 132, 193-94, 306, 415, 595; rivalry with Holland (Mich.) colony, 50; roads to, 181; Scholte Church, 93, 209, 330, 345, 355, 370-73, 381, 384-85, 411, 415, 418, 476-77, 482, 508; schools in, 110, 141, 182, 183, 632-33; significance of name, 635-36, 637; situation appraised, 84-85; as "Strawtown," 84, 157; streets surveyed, 138, 170, 177; town described, 138, 170-71; travel to, 317-20, 327; mentioned, 45, 331, 336, 489, 496, 518, 541, 579, 583, 604

Pella (Transjordan), 635-36
Pella cheese, 143
Pella Gazette, xvii, 386, 388, 390, 415, 418, 432, 434
Pella's Maandblad, 390
Pella's Weekblad, 390

Pellikaan, B., 129
Pennsylvania, 88
Peoria, Ill., 338
Peru, Ill., 256-58, 338
Petersen (midwife), 395
Philadelphia, Pa., 109
Phoenix (ship), burning of, 48, 80, 93
Photographs, exchanged, 564, 565, 566, 567, 570, 572, 575, 576, 577, 578
Picard, H., 42, 122, 130, 154, 156, 196
Pierson, Mr., 569, 611
Pieter Floris (ship), 46, 57
Piety, expressions of, 54, 59-60, 96, 102, 126, 129, 194, 233, 344, 365, 367, 369, 371, 438, 470, 481, 490-91, 563, 566, 575-76, 578, 580; by Budde family, 354, 372-73, 394-95, 401-03, 411-12, 470; by Hendrik Hospers, 168-69, 171; by Hendrika Hospers, 164-65; by Henriette Bousquet-Chabot, 499-500; by Jan Hospers, 126; by Johanna Schellinger, 448-49, 478-79
Pigs. *See* Hogs
Pike Slip (Water Street, New York City), 311
Pipes (tobacco), 133, 154, 174, 193, 197, 198, 199, 201, 202. *See also* Gouda pipes
Pittsburgh, as immigrant depot, 45, 47, 64, 104, 300, 310
Plaggemars, Jan (immigrant to Michigan), 52
Plank road, venture of H.P. Scholte, 340
Pleurisy, 243
Plowing, 120, 141, 160, 180, 192
Politics, Christian, 631; G. Groen van Prinsterer, 41, 420, 630-32, 636, 638
Polvliet & Sons, P. (Rotterdam hardware merchants), 141, 154
Pope, 602
Portengen, Carl C.F., 5, 587, 592
Portengen, Jacob (ship captain), 5, 6, 374, 394, 406; and Andries N. Wormser, 252, 282, 295, 310, 311, 312, 324

Portengen, Jacob, Jr., 63
Portengen, K.F.C., 536
Portengen, Leendert, 5, 237, 238, 256, 264
Portengen, Leentje (Mrs. Schilp), 255, 281, 300, 306, 310, 358, 375, 394, 395, 396, 406, 409, 592; birth of daughter, 490
Portengen, Mietje (Maria) (born 1812, married Andries N. Wormser), xxix, 5, 232, 255, 306, 324, 358, 395, 403, 592; illness of, 485, 487; letter of, 269-71
Portengen, Naatje, 324, 430
Portengen, Willem, 5, 592
Port Sheldon, Mich., 404-05
Post, domestic, 255, 281; in Netherlands, 123; transatlantic, 113, 121, 124, 130, 133, 149, 160, 197, 200, 202, 214, 215, 231-32, 286, 346, 353
Post, Moses J., 49, 84, 134, 135
Post office, Pella, 170
Postwijk (Judith Zeelt estate), 246, 426, 558, 566; demolished, 568; photo, 245
Potatoes, 275, 276; blighted, 34, 41
Poverty, in America, 274, 276
Prairies, described, 127, 168; fires on, 140; sod busting of, 141; value of, 122
Prayers, requested, 53
Presbyterian Church, 125, 256; at Mount Pleasant, 550, 561-562, 595
Presbyterians, 64, 278, 333, 375, 412, 456, 530, 621, 625; in Burlington, 451; English, 550; Old School, 539; in St. Louis, 135
Prices: crops, 263; dry goods, 75-76; food, 237; land, 240; livestock, 263
Prins, H., 124
Prooslij, J. (author), 154
Protestant Evangelical Holland Emigrant Society, 35.
Prussia, 100
Psalms, quoted, 59, 60, 452-54, 457-58, 480, 491, 494, 495, 529, 551, 565, 571, 579, 581, 586, 607; singing of, 55, 249, 524

Psalter, Dutch, 491, 564
Public schools. *See* Schools
Public square, Pella, 159
Purmerend, Netherlands, 44, 54, 56

Quilts, 276
Quit claim, 135

Rabbers, Jan (Drenthe immigrant to Holland colony), 52
Radstock, Lord (English missionary), 556, 567, 568
Railroads: at Burlington, 406, 414, 525, 542, 595; at Pella, 340, 466
Raman, W., 586
Raman, W., Jr. (Amsterdam), 101, 586, 591
Rats, 270. *See also* Mice
Red Rocks, Ia., 37
Reformatie, De (Seceder periodical), 20, 22, 23, 24, 25-26, 32-33, 36, 40, 42, 119, 229
Reformation, Protestant, 628, 630
Reformed Church, in Germany, 626. *See also* German Reformed Church
Reformed Church, in Netherlands, 626-33. *See also* Hervormde Kerk Nederland
Reformed Church in America (previously Reformed Protestant Dutch Church), 64, 333; Board of Domestic Missions, 464; Burlington congregation, 374-75, 386, 436-37, 450-54, 455-58, 480-81, 488, 498, 526-28, 529-30, 539-40; in Chicago, 482; Dutch language loss in, 550; in Keokuk, 482; in New York, 450, 458, 481, 526; in Pella, 385-83, 389-90, 451, 482, 500; regulates immigrant pastors, 455-56, 459-60; Secession of 1834, 390; in Silver Creek, Ill., 488
Religion, freedom of, 71-72, 462-63, in Burlington, 269-75, 278; in Pella, 193-94
Religious life, America and Netherlands compared, 574
Remarriage, 413
Remigration, xvi, xxxi, 264, 266, 280-82,

304, 307, 391
Remonstrants (Netherlands), 555, 559, 562
Rennet (lubben), 128, 154, 155, 156-57, 171, 188, 194, 209
Rents, housing, 69, 265
Repadler (ship), 253-54
Republican Party, 638
Restored Evangelical Lutheran Church, xix, 6; changes noted, 408, 568-69; and H.P. Scholte, 475-76; and H.P. Scholte family, 8; and Hervormde Kerk Nederland, xv, 6, 9, 12-13, 21, 55, 224, 226, 328, 367, 390, 444, 525, 556, 592, 605, 630; and J.H.F. Kohlbrugge, 9; Seceders of 1834 return, 505; mentioned, 430. See also Lutherans
Retail trade, Pella, 321-22
Rèveil, xviii, xxi, 9, 16, 477
Revival, religious, in Pella, 306
Revolution of 1848, 41, 171, 194, 228, 229, 635; in Amsterdam, 41, 163-64, 192
Rheinische Hotel (New York City), 311
Rheumatism, 316, 317, 380, 397, 407, 410, 427, 438, 443, 466, 486, 489, 502-03, 512, 530, 534, 536, 537-38, 541, 549, 606
Richland, Oh., 68
Rietveld, Jan (Pella immigrant), 37, 46, 78, 135, 149-50, 165, 189, 202
Rive, Dr. (Wormser family doctor, Amsterdam), 516, 582
Roads, 136
Rochester, N.Y., 253
Roeland, Mr., 127, 161
Roelofsz, Josef (Pella doctor), 113, 378
Roering, Mr. (The Hague), 65
Roman Catholic Church, 71, 229, 275, 405, 429, 473, 516, 626, 635, 638; and American immigration, 1; in Netherlands, 435
Roman Empire, 636
Romanization, 635, 638
Rome, 41, 474
Roozeboom family, 95
Ros (ship officer at Den Helder), 55

Rosier (Roziersz), J. (Pella treasurer), 173
Rossum, Netherlands, 123
Rotterdam, Netherlands, 39, 156, 165, 339, 355, 357; as immigrant depot, 43, 52, 198, 329, 340; harbor sketch, 118; mentioned, 129, 192, 559
Rotterdamsche Courant (newspaper), 86
Russia, 386, 406, 434
Rutgers College, 43
Rynhout van Brederode, Rev. (itinerant preacher), 526-27
Rynsdorp, C., 228

Sabbath, observed, 82-83; on shipboard, 55, 57-58, 337; pamphlets on, 580
Sac and Fox Indians, 178
Saint Clair River, 337
Saint Louis, Mo., 36, 43, 48, 49, 121, 276, 317, 349, 350; and A.C. Van Raalte, 62; and A.N. Wormser, 312; cholera in, 279, 294; described, 259; Dutch in, 67-68, 74, 78, 134, 135, 140, 142, 151, 152, 153, 171, 174, 198, 215, 222, 264, 271, 278, 293, 334, 338, 349, 397; illness in, 85; as immigrant depot, 64, 241, 257-58, 260, 281; as market center, 111, 210, 320-21, 340, 361-62, 372; rapid growth of, 104-05; Scholte family in, 86, 137, 140, 300, 329
Salvatori Building (Amsterdam), 228
Sandbergen family (Amsterdam), 101
Sandusky, Oh., 46, 68
Santje ("Oude" Santje, Amsterdam Seceder), 74, 98
Sarah Sand (ship), 45, 63
Savannah (ship), 45
Saxony, Germany, 450
Scarlet fever, 129, 231, 334, 424
Schaarwächter, Willem (Amsterdam, married to Grietje Budde), 576
Scheepmaker (Amsterdam teacher), 396
Scheer, A., 189
Schellinger, Johanna, letters of, 442-43, 447-49, 478-79, 483-84, 521-23, 532-34, 588-90, 596-97, 614-15; piety of, 448-49, 478, 614

Schellinger, Naatje, 391, 395, 409, 442-43, 483-84, 522-23, 533, 614; marriage, 588, 589-90
Schelluinen, Netherlands, 132
Schijf, Adrianus (Pella blacksmith), 172
Schilp, Mr., 413, 536
Schilp, Mrs. Caroline (Amsterdam Seceder), 587
Schilp, Leentje. *See* Portengen, Leentje
Schilp family, 415, 438
Schladermundt, Joachim (Lutheran pastor at Springfield, Oh.), 69
Schmidt, Rev. (Presbyterian preacher at Burlington and Mount Pleasant), 562, 617
Schnectady, N.Y., 238, 337
Scholte, David (born 1862), 473
Scholte, Hendrik (Henry) Peter, accused of fraud, 86, 133, 249; advises colonists, 153, 197; and A.C. Van Raalte, xxix-xxx, xxx, 50, 63-64, 112, 291; and baptism, 84-85, 376-74; biography, 8-11, 12, 13, 17, 32-39; birthplace, 626; business ventures, 86, 142, 204; children of, 204, 434, 473, 500, 509, 512; characterized, 117, 627-28, 632-33; and Christian schools, 387, 638; and Christian Seceded Church (Netherlands), 628; church polity of, 48, 383-84; considers return to Netherlands, 434; contrasted to D.A. Budde, 632; controversy over church, 384-85; criticized, 6, 133, 209-10, 216-17, 208, 246-47, 251, 264, 265, 278-79, 314-15, 349-52, 361, 362, 366; death of, 473, 477-78, 578, 622, death rumored, 397, 400, 405; deposed in Amsterdam, 383, deposed in Pella, xx, 313-14, 345, 355, 383, 463-65; and *De Reformatie*, xv, xix, 20, 40; as editor of *Pella Gazette*, xvii, 384-85, 386, 388; emigration of, 32-39, 44, 57, 473-76; emigration society of, 328, 330; as entrepreneur, 330, 384, 415, 418; family of, 112-13, 333; family in Burlington, 86, family in Saint Louis, 69, 78, 86, 137, 140; financial dealings of, 158-59, 161, 181-82, 205, 208-09, 215-16, 223, 359-62, 384-85; and G. Groen van Prinsterer, 432-34, 630-33; and H.J. Buddingh, 476-77; and Henry Hospers, 162; house of, xxi, 26 (photo), 49, 84, 134, 158, 170, 208, 342-43, 474 (photo); and Jan Hospers, 156-57, 167, 199; as immigrant leader, xxx, 1-2, 57, 62, 78, 118, 214; independentism of, 629; and Judith Zeelt, 206, 282; as justice of the peace, 147, 171, 173; land dealings, 49, 135, 142, 265, 283, 314, 345, 385-86, 434; land dealings criticized, 153, 286-87, 295, 362, 464; letters of, 63-66, 110-113, 222, 271-72, 282-85, 380, 432-34; loved, 371; millennial views of, 194, 233, 285, 474-75, 477, 636; opposes marriage of daughter Saartje, 381-82; orders rennet, 128, 155, 156-57, 167; pamphlets of, 163, 189, 205; and Pella colony, xx-xxi, 254, 477-78, 635-36; political activities, 65, 209, 421, 432-33; as "Pope of Pella," 157, 208; preacher in Netherlands, 328; preacher in New York; 62, 76; preacher in Pella, 143, 171, 184, 342-43, 345-46, 376-77, 378, 384, 482; predicts fall of Europe, 228-29, 285; as school inspector, 171, 173; and Secession of 1834, 15, 22-23, 24-25, 26-27; sermon sketches of, 132, 133, 134, 182, 192, 195, 196, 197; and slavery, 378; theological views, 39, 475, 629-31; views of America, 636-37; writings, 163, 189, 202, 223, 228; mentioned, 122, 125, 151, 189, 320, 335, 407, 512
Scholte, Henry Peter (born 1848), 285, 378
Scholte, Lenora, 49
Scholte, Maria Isaacs, 38
Scholte, Maria (Mrs. Piet Hein Bousquet), 11, 340, 344, 365, 378, 382, 595
Scholte, Sara (Sarah, Saartje) Johanna

(Mrs. B.F. Keables), xxiii, 11, 110, 272, 285, 306, 344, 365, 509, 512, 595; children of, 500-501; letter of, 621-23; marriage of, 381-82
Scholte, Sarah Johanna Suzanna (Mrs. Jan Nollen), 11, 344, 365, 473, 513, 595
Scholte, Sara Maria (Mrs. P.H. Bousquet), 473
Scholte, Theodora ("Dora") Maria Johanna (1858-1870), 473, 478
Scholte Church, Pella, 93, 142, 168, 171, 184, 330, 345, 355, 372-73, 381, 384-85, 411, 415, 418, 477-78, 482, 508; photo, 437. *See also* Pella, Scholte Church
Scholte Club, 8-11, 15-16, 22
Schools, 274, 276, 278, 305; English, 403; in Burlington, 298; in Netherlands, 432-35; in Pella, 110-11, 145, 182, 183, 633
Schotelmeijer, Naatje (Pella immigrant), 74, 86, 322
Schott, T., 24-25
Schriek family (Amsterdam Seceders), 79, 89, 431, 486
Schulz, Mr., 446
Schut, H. (captain of *De Maasstroom*), 123
Schuurman, J. (preacher in Christian Seceded Church), 468, 487
Schuyt, A.A.W., 63, 206
Schwartz, Carl A.F. (preacher in Free Scottish Church, professor in Scottish Seminary, editor *De Heraut*), 226, 227 (photo) 228, 367, 418, 627
Scotland, Free Church of, 367
Scottish Missionary Church (Amsterdam), 227-28; Seminary of, 236-38; 227 (photo)
Seasickness. *See* Travel
Seceders, 367, 390, 397, 444, 591, 611; discord among, 25-26; emigration of, xv-xvi, xxx-xxxi, 129-30; persecuted, 34-35, 453; Utrecht Emigrant Society of, 133. *See also* Christian Seceded Church, Secession of 1834
Secession: of 1834, xv-xvi, 1-2, 12-22, 223-29, 339, 455, 473, 474-76, 627-28; of 1857, 437, 586; faith of, xxx-xxxi
Second Reformed Church in Albany, N.Y., 43
Seminary, Christian Seceded Church (Amsterdam), 355, 367, 397, 627, 631
's-Graveland, Netherlands, 343
Sheboygan Nieuwsbode, De (newspaper), 224, 386, 404
Sheboygan, Wis., 261, 264
Sherman, John (Civil War Union general), 538
Sherman, Mr., 365
's-Hertogenbosch, Netherlands, 224
Sherwood, Mr., 97
Shipping, freight, 361
Ships, ocean: conditions on, 55-56; and death, 52; and food, 52; rumored sinkings, 133, 400
Shoemaking, 316
Sickness, 267, 334, 341; in Amsterdam, 101; in Burlington, 91; deafness, 270; fevers, 79, 102, 106, 233, 519; in Holland (Mich.), 274; in Pella, 83, 88; sinking, 396, 408
Sielof, J. (coppersmith, Amsterdam Seceder), 443-44
Siemons, Mrs., 444
Silver Creek, Ill., 488, 497, 526
Simons (blacksmith), 430
Singer, Andreas (husband of Maria Budde), 543-44, 561-62, 563, 578, 594, 596, 616, 617; business partner of Johan G. Budde Jr., 585-86, 602; family of, 621; mentioned, 586, 587, 603, 607
Singer, Anna Maria (daughter of Andreas), 562, 564, 578, 586-87, 618
Singer, Elizabeth Christina (daughter of Andreas), 618
Singer, Flora Lydia (daughter of Andreas), 618
Sioux County, Iowa, 117
Sipma, Sjoerd Aukes (Frisian immigrant and palimpsest), 160, 201, 217, 383
Sirius (ship), 45
Skating, ice, 440-41

Skunk River (Pella), 49, 86, 110, 127, 137, 169, 183, 339
Skunk school district, 182
Slavery, views of, 360
Slave trade, and Amsterdam, 8
Sleyster, Mrs. Roelof, 273, 276
Sleyster, Roelof (immigrant to Alto, Wis.), 53
Smallpox, 610
Smeenk (Smink), Jacob (immigrant to Pella), 78
Smeenk, Jan (immigrant to Pella), 46, 210, 211, 216, 222; store of, 340
Smit, G. (Mrs. Johannes Berkhout), xvii, xxix, 342, 379, 381, 411; death of, 609-10, 622; letter of, 362-64; remigration of, 558, 604
Smit, Gerrit, 364
Smit, Lieutenant, 591
Smit, Willem, 323, 332
Smytegeld ("Old Writer"), 53, 628
Snoek, Jan (Pella immigrant), 52
Social class, compared to Netherlands, 112
Society for Emigration to North America, 37, 328
Society for General Welfare (Amsterdam), 399
Sodbusting, 120, 141
Sod houses, described, 157, 179
Sodom, 107
Soils, fertility, of, 51
South, impact of Civil War on, 495
South Africa, 32
Southern (ship), 43
South Holland, Mich., 337
Spain, 569
Spanish flies, 528
Speculators, land, 112, 159, 215, 222-23, 284, 295, 436
Spencer, Rev. 493
Spijk, Netherlands, 215
Sprenger, A. (at Burlington), 374-75
Springfield, Oh., 46, 68-69
Spyker, Rev. 398, 399
Staatscourant (Amsterdam newspaper), 117
Stafford (Captain of *Katharina Jackson*), 164, 202
Stagecoach, 338
Stam, Klaas, 164, 173
Standaard, De (Abraham Kuyper's newspaper), 473
Statenbijbel (official Dutch Bible), xxv
Steamboats, 67, 68, 69, 71, 111, 379; described, 219-20, 255; on Des Moines River, 283, 316, 318, 320, 340; fares, 312, 317; on Great Lakes, 254, 261: on Hudson River, 237, 331, 333, 337: on Illinois River, 257-59, 338; low class of, 277; on Mississippi River, 137, 143, 241, 300, 307, 310, 317
Steenkamp, Crijsje (Amsterdam seamstress), 95, 525, 541
Steijnes, (Steijnis), J., 126, 173, 187
Stomp, Christina Maria (Mrs. Diedrich A. Budde), xvi, xvii, xix, xxix-xxxi, 3, 17, 48, 242; death of, 473, 615-16, 622; grave, 626 (photo); hardships of, 292, 294; hymn verse of, 505; and Johan A. Wormser, Sr., 575-77; letters of, 55-56, 57-58, 75-77, 90-92, 105-09, 303-06, 356-59, 401-06, 414-16, 423-25, 435-38, 449-52, 459-60, 480-83, 487-88, 510-11, 519-20, 526-31, 537-38, 542-45, 549-51, 561-65, 577-79, 585-87, 593-96, 601-03, 606-11, 612-13, 625-26; photo of 510; piety of, 490-91, 495-96, 510-11, 563, 566; problem of overweight, 496; trip to Germany, 491
Stomp, Grandfather, 356
Stores, in Pella, 359-61, 363
Storms, at sea, 59-60, 61, 331
Stowe, Harriet Beecher (American novelist), 436
Strabbers, Jan. See Rabbers, Jan
Strabbink (Strabbing) family, 52
Stranger in a Strange Land (book), 49
Strawtown (Pella), 84, 157
Strikker (brother-in-law of Johannes Berkhout), 346
Stubenraugh, J.K. (Albany immigrant), 332, 333, 334, 335
Sugar industry, Amsterdam, 8, 11, 15

Index 691

Suicide, 614-15
Sunday, observance of, 364
Sunday school, 71-72, 82, 403
Surgery, 304
Surveying, 140, 181, 195; by Hendrik Hospers, 145, 159-60, 177
Swindling, by agents, 334. *See also* Cheating
Synod of Dort. *See* Dort, Synod of
Syracuse, N.Y., 47

Talbeim, Germany, 5
Tannery, 177
Tapeworm, 618
Taverns, 274
Taxes, 274; in Netherlands, 108, 273
Teding van Berkhout, Mr., 367
Teinolen (ship), 338
Teleman, G.H. (Amsterdam Seceder), 17, 466
Teleman, Jansje (Jansi, Jansie, Janse)(married Jannawa, an American), 44, 77, 81, 96, 99, 110, 306, 356, 358, 368, 395, 396, 401, 402, 419, 482, 545; character of, 422; family of, 550; mentioned, 431, 438, 452, 468, 486, 494, 505, 513
Teleman, Johanna (1802-1867), 17, 44, 56, 57, 59, 74-75, 77, 81, 89, 92, 96, 99, 105, 107, 110, 233, 242, 243, 266, 306, 356, 366, 368, 375, 405, 409, 419, 482-83, 528; death of, 550, 558; failing health of, 422, 424-25; midwifery of, 415; mentioned, 399, 414, 431, 438, 452, 474, 486, 490, 494, 505, 513, 545
Temperature. *See* Climate
Tenancy, farm, 92-93, 280, 301, 304, 316, 323, 373, 415
Ter Borg, Rev., 562
Tersteeger, Gerhardt (German poet), 594, 600
Texas, considered by H.P. Scholte, 328
Texel, Netherlands, 123
Theological "parties," 569
Theological School (Amsterdam). *See* Seminary, Christian Seceded Church
Therassom (Island), 60-61

Thiel (Tiel), Netherlands, 430, 559, 560
Tholen, Netherlands, 73
Tholuck, Prof. (Halle, Germany), 555
Thorbecke, J.R. (liberal professor and cabinet minister), 21, 27, 433-34
Thunder Creek, Iowa, 169
Tienhoven, Netherlands, 371
Titus, Roman emperor, 583
't Lam, Adrianus, 173
Tobacco, spitting of, 245
Toekomst, De (H.P. Scholte periodical), 477
Toe Water, Frederick R. (Netherlands consul at St. Louis), 48
Toledo, Ohio, 32
Tollens, Hendrik, 391
Tolsma, Mr. (married widow Van der Veen), 529
Travel, inland, 46-47, 64-65, 67, 68, 69, 93, 104, 253-55, 259-60, 300, 311, 317-21, 331, 335-39, 342-43; costs of, 93, 137, 143, 310; on foot, 52, 313-12; by train, 69, 238-40, 336, 337, 406; troubles in, 230, 334; by wagon, 318-17
Travel, oceanic, 1-2, 43, 52, 54, 56-62, 160, 237-41; deaths, 85, 161; described by A.C. Van Raalte, 80-81; dreaded, 58-59, 290; pleasurable, 61; seasickness in, 58, 232, 341; storms, 286
Train, travel. *See* Travel, inland
Troy, N.Y., 221, 230
True Dutch Reformed Church (later Christian Reformed Church), 638
Tucker, Francis, 568
Tweede Stem uit Pella (H.P. Scholte pamphlet), 205, 223, 228
Typhus (Amsterdam), 397

Uncle Tom's Cabin (book), 386
United States Insurance Company of New York, 330
Utensils, household, 108-09
Utica, N.Y., 337
Utrecht, Netherlands, 9, 11, 119, 122, 132, 181, 189, 196, 413, 550, 573; Christian Seceded Church in, 41, 49,

125, 129; Emigrant Society of, 37, 133, 158, 216; and H.P. Scholte, 33, 35, 629, 632; and Judith Zeelt, 505; Province of, 23, 24, 285, 339, 345; mentioned, 26, 110, 140, 154, 397, 592, 604

van Alphen, Hieronymus, 391
van Alsburg, Claus, 29
van Andel, Kant (member immigration commission), 329, 332, 334
van Andel, Mr. (Gorinchem), 124
van Baaren, Baltus, 189
van Baren, Mr., 335
van Beek, Elena (Lena)(Mrs. Jan G. Budde), 373, 401-02, 414-15, 536, 537, 576, 577, 616; illness of, 618, 621
Van Beek, Mr., 511
van Beekum, Mr., 120
van Bergeijk, Gerrit, 192
van Bergeijk, L. (Pella immigrant), 122, 125, 164, 210, 214, 335; letter of, 205, 211; mentioned, 155, 173, 189
van Beyeren, Jacoba (Countess), 550-51
van Borstelen, Frank, 551
van Citard, Mrs., 381
Van Dam, Herman, 173, 189, 207, 216, 285, 339, financial dispute of, 348-49, 359-62
Van Dam, Jacob (school inspector), 182
van Dam, K., 173
van Dam, Rev. (Hoogblokland pastor), 161, 163
van Dam, Roeland, 163
van de Brugghen, J.J.C., and 1857 education law, 387; and Groen van Prinsterer, 89, 386; and H.P. Scholte, 432-34
van den Berg (writer), 184
Van den Berg, Cornelius, 118, 162, 198
van den Berg, Mr. (Zwolle), 256
van den Berg, P. (Gorinchem), 122, 161, 173
Van den Brugge, Mr., 420
van der Aa, Rev. (lay preacher), 146
van der Basaan, L., 210
van der Bruyn factory, (Amsterdam), 98

van der Groe, T. ("Old Writer"), 25
van der Heim, Mr., 181
Van der Hoeven, Mr., 381
Van der Kamp, 628
Van der Land, Mr., 487
Van der Ley, Pieter M. (Pella immigrant), 122, 132, 133, 156, 173, 197, 198, 213
Van der Linde (doctor and brother-in-law of A.C. Van Raalte), 265, 295
Van der Linden, Klaas (Pella immigrant), 113, 149, 196, 197, 198, 215
Van der Linden, Miss, 467
Van der Linden van Vuuren, 379
Vander Meulen, Rev. Cornelius, 389, 404, 437, 482, 595
Van der Moor, Johanna, 449
Van der Moor, Karel, 409
van der Moor, Matthys, 356, 479, 523, 533; death of, 442-43
van der Moor, Naatje, 403, 405, 480
van de Roovaart, Jan, 336
Van der Pol, G. (Pella immigrant), 135
Van der Pool, H. (Buffalo lawyer), 68, 230, 253-54
Vander Schuur, K.S., 337
Vander Veen, Christian M., 404, 482, 525, 529-27
Vander Veen, Egbertus (Amsterdam coppersmith), 77, 264, 404, 530
van der Ven, Janke (Mrs. Johan Adam Wormser, Sr.), xxiii, xxv, xxiv-xxx, 2, 6, 17, 48, 387, 471, 473, 572, 575; death of, 612-13; death of husband, 516-18; illness of, 608-09; letters of, 94-99, 100-01, 394-96, 407-09, 416-19, 427-29, 443-45, 466-68, 516-18, 557-60, 570-72, 582-84, 591-93, 598-600, 603-05
van der Ven, Riek (Rika)(sister of Janke Wormser-Vander Ven), 77, 92, 93, 94, 96, 97, 99, 101, 109, 260, 267, 282, 295, 306, 359, 402, 424, 416, 419, 425, 426, 428, 431, 437; death of, 439, 443-44, 450
Vander Wilt, Gerrit (school inspector), 182

Van Deventer family (immigrants in St. Louis), 150, 155, 171, 172
Van Dooijen, Jan, 149
Van Driel, P., 165, 189, 369
Van Est, Hendrik (Hendrik Hospers's uncle), 119, 120, 130, 132, 133, 134, 147, 148, 150, 155, 156, 186, 187-88, 189, 191, 195, 199, 200, 202, 213; mentioned, 142, 145, 149, 161, 173, 190, 193
van Golverdinge, J. (Seceder publisher in The Hague), 15
van Gunther, Fientje, 444-45
van Haaften, Mr., 189
van Hall, A.C., 13-17
van Hall, Anne Maurits Cornelis (1808-1838), 16-17, 24
van Hall, Floris Adriaan, Jr., (Amsterdam lawyer), 29, 30, 31, 467
van Hall, Floris Adriaan, Sr. (baron), 5, 21, 472 (photo)
van Hall, Gijsbert (mayor of Amsterdam), 29
Van Hall (grandson of M.C. van Hall), 601, 602, 607, 616
van Hall, Johanna Justina, 29, 30-31
van Hall, Maurits Cornelius, Jr., 29
van Hall, Maurits Cornelius, Sr. (Netherlands Cabinet minister), 21, 29-31, 601, 607
Van Ham, Jacob (Pella immigrant), 170
van Hees (Rotterdam baker and Seceder), 124-25, 129
van Hoorn, Pieter, 189
van Houten, Rev. (Seceder preacher and teacher in Amsterdam), 224, 225, 226, 367, 627
van Houwelingen, Klein, 189
van Kekerik, Antje, 167
van Kleef, Andries, 189, 208
van Klootwyk, Teunis (Pella immigrant), 335
van Lodenstein, J. ("Old Writer"), 25
Van Malsum family (immigrants to Chicago), 338
Van Maurik (minister of justice, Amsterdam), 14
Van Maurik, Gjaje, 167, 169

Van Meveren, Pieter (Pella immigrant), 120, 122, 125, 134, 137, 140, 141, 142, 143, 144, 146, 153, 172, 186, 189, 201
Van Meveren, Pieternella (daughter of Pieter, wife of Jan Klein), 180
Van Nuys, J.J.M.C. (Pella immigrant from Zeeland), 378, 379
van Peursen, Gerrit (Amsterdam book dealer), 6, 17, 221, 604, 609 van Prinsterer, Guillaume Groen. *See* Groen van Prinsterer
van Proosdij, Cornelius (Seceder preacher), 101
Van Raalte, Albertus Christiaan, accused of quackery, 249; as immigrant leader, xvi, 220; biography, 7, 10-11; and Christian politics, 633; colony of, 174, 289, 293, 300, 310, 554; criticized, 6, 53, 63, 79-80, 112, 178-79, 256, 286-87, 307-08, 264, 265, 273, 379; emigration, 31-36, 62, 78; and Evangelical Alliance, 555; and Holland Academy, 390; and H.P. Scholte, xix-xx, 9, 10, 50, 63, 112, 390, 460-66; and Johan A. Wormser, Sr., 628; land dealings, 51-52, 265, 291, 295; letters of, 80-81, 460-66, 545-46; personality of, 11; and P. Zonne, 79-80; photo, 461; and Reformed Church in America, 64; and Reformed church in Burlington, 386; and Reformed church in Pella, 386, 389-90, 421; and Secession of 1834, 12, 14-15, 18-20, 25, 256, 529; Union of 1850, 386; mentioned, 45-46, 62, 68, 473, 482
Van Raalte, Dirk, and Civil War, 500
Van Raalte, Trijntje, 17
van Rennes, H.W., 222
van Rhee, J. (Seceder preacher), 39
Van Schelven, Adriaanus (Pella immigrant), 323
van Schermbeek, Helena Suzanna (Mrs. A.M.C. van Hall), 16, 26, 31, 473
van Siers, Dr. (New York physician), 331
Van Stigt, Corstianus (Pella tanner), 177

Van Stigt, Kommer (Pella historian), 390
van Straten Pinthor, B.A. (Netherlands historian), 42
van Velzen, Simon, character of, 24, 29, 627; criticized, 367; and emigration, 41-42; and Secession of 1834, 9-10, 12, 14, 15-16, 20, 23-24, 333, 390, 397, 400, 408, 444; in Weesp, 584; mentioned, 473, 578
van Vlier, Heintje, 92, 95
Van Vliet, Jacob, 173, 384
Van Waveren family, 330
Van Zante, Mary, xiv
Varsseveld, Netherlands, 53, 80
Veendam, Netherlands, 628
Veenendaal, Netherlands, 592
Vegetables, garden, 170, 245
Veldhorst family (immigrants from Varsseveld), 53
Velp, Netherlands, 608
Vereeningen, De (journal), 367
Verhave, Jan Peter, xvi, xxiii, xxx
Verheij, B., 151
Verheij, G., 151
Verheij, H.C., 17
Verheij, Meintje (Mrs. Jan Balke, maid of Judith Zeelt), 56, 109, 409, 416, 438, 492
Verkerk, Adrianus (Burlington immigrant), 70, 73, 262
Verkerk, Mrs. Adrianus, 528
Vermeer ("Old Writer"), 628
Verseveld, Netherlands. *See* Varrseveld
Versluis, Klaas, 167
Vianen, Netherlands, 120
Victoria, Queen of England, 366
Vienna, Austria, 41
Viersen, H.Y., 46, 135, 216
Viersen, O.H., log cabin photo, 127
Vijn, N., 405
Vink, Jan, 127, 161, 173, 206
Vink, Rev. (Seceder preacher), 559-60
Vis, Mr. 485
Visser, Willem (Pella immigrant), 171
Vonk, 242
Vos, Bastiaan, 172, 187
Vos, Rev. (Pella preacher), 595

Voute, Mrs., 559
Voyage, ocean. *See* Travel, oceanic
Vrije Universiteit. *See* Free University of Amsterdam
Vuren, Netherlands, 113, 196, 197, 198

Waal, De (river), 115, 206
Wächter, Der (periodical), 567, 580
Wagenmaker, 595
Wages, 179, 250, 338
Wagner, John M., 488, 521
Wagon transport, 137, 339
Walloon church (Amsterdam), 441
Walters, Mr. 174
Wambersie, Johan, 65
Wambersie & Crooswijk Agency (Amsterdam shipping company), 65, 155, 329
Wanneperveen, Netherlands, 10
Washing, clothes, 269-70, 299
Washington, D.C., 45, 531
Washington Koffiehuis (Buffalo), 337
Weather. *See* Climate
Weaver, Richard, 568
Weddings, in America, 459; in Netherlands, 445-46, 484-85, 487
Weimer, W., 15
Welle, Cornelia (Mrs. Hendrik Hospers), 391
Welle, Jan, 161
Welle, P., 111, 127, 132, 133, 134, 137, 140, 154, 163, 172, 180, 184, 185, 201, 204, 216, 330, 335; daughter, 314; as deacon, 173, 384; as trustee, 173; mentioned, 128, 189
Welle, Mrs. Pieter, 128
Westerkerke (Hervormde Kerk in Amsterdam), 6
West Leyden, N.Y., 521
Westminster Confession, 550
Wheat, winter, 304
Wheeling, WV, 46
White Cloud (ship), 321
Whooping cough, 423, 466
Wigny, A. (Pella immigrant), 37, 45 (photo), 46, 170
Wildlife, 251
Willem, Alexander F.C.N.M., (brother of

King Willem II), 39
Willem I, King of Netherlands, 12, 13-14, 15-16, 22, 23, 38, 224, 233
Willem II, King of Netherlands, 39, 214, 433, 434
Willem III, King of Netherlands, 39, 433, 434
William and Mary (ship), 48
William (martyred British missionary), 556
Willink family (Amsterdam Seceders), 75, 89, 95, 98, 107, 364, 366, 380
Willink, Mrs. 344, 509
Wilson, J. (Presbyterian preacher at Fairfield), 375
Windjes family, 52
Winterswijk, Netherlands, 53, 80
Wisconsin, 48, 132; and A.C. Van Raalte, 51, 52, 421; land prices, 394
Witchcraft, in Netherlands, 208
Witte, H., 405
Witte Kruis wharf, 44
Woerden, Netherlands, 206, 215
Wolters & Smeenk store, 316, 340
Women, as cheese makers, 154, 157; field work by, 294; as "slaves," 364; social position of, xvi; as submissive wives, 373; work of, 299, 344
Wood, for heating, 288
Woodlots, 244, 288
Wood turner, 82
Work, opportunities for, 72
World culture, 638-39
Wormser, Andries (Dries) Nicolaas (brother of Johan A. Wormser), 2, 8, 17, 77, 79, 97, 109, 115, 324-25, 327, 355-56, 387, 403, 405, 413, 423, 430, 441, 446, 447, 485, 486, 489, 503; biography, 5-6; cattle roundup by, 267; daughters' deaths, 269, 303; death of, 535, 536; disappointments of, 234-35; emigration, 102-104, 108, 221; letters of, 5-6, 231-32, 234-69, 272-82, 286-300, 308-12; negativity of, xvi-xvii, xxiv, xxix-xxxi; recalled, 489-90; rheumatism, 489; views of Holland (Mich. colony), 308-10; mentioned, 28, 46, 530

Wormser, Andries N., Jr., 600
Wormser, Anna (daughter of A.N. Wormser), 5, 231, 234, 251-52, 255, 287-88
Wormser, Catharina (1813-1859, daughter of Georg Adam Wormser), 5
Wormser, Catharina Johanna (Mrs. Caspar Andries Höweler), xxiv-xxv
Wormser, Catharine (Cato, Kaatje, Caatje)(1836-66, daughter of Johan A. Wormser, married Matthys de Boer, divorced), 6, 14, 57, 77, 79, 89, 101, 105, 306, 359, 373, 375, 387, 397, 406, 417, 418, 422, 423, 425, 428, 429, 430, 439, 443, 444, 459, 471, 481, 491, 492, 503, 530, 541, 542, 553, 568, 571, 578, 584, 585, 591, 592, 593, 622, 627; children of, 466-67, 566, 599, 604, 619; death of, 598-99, 601, 602, 603, 604; divorce of, 557-58, 560, 562, 581; learns English, 108, 109; letters of, 99, 400, 425-27, 431-32, 486-87, 514-15, 534-35, 565-67; marriage troubles, 540-41; remembered, 606; mentioned, 391, 395, 396, 414
Wormser, Derkje, 221
Wormser, Elizabeth (Mrs. Jan Keuning), 7
Wormser family, xiv, 5; portrait of, 468
Wormser, Fietje (daughter of A.N. Wormser), death of, 251-52
Wormser, Georg Adam, 5
Wormser, Hendericus (Henricus)(son of Johan A. Wormser, Jr.), 598, 605
Wormser, Hein (Hendrik)(son of A.N. Wormser), 5, 7, 47, 51, 93, 250, 289, 291, 371, 468, 486, 566
Wormser, Henriette, 395, 406, 418, 431, 466, 490, 530, 541, 571, 583, 591, 592, 593, 598, 608, 610; mentioned, 486, 513, 540
Wormser, I., 257
Wormser, Janke. *See* Van der Ven, Janke
Wormser, Jansje (daughter of Hein Wormser, married to Kollen), 554, 565, 566

Wormser, Jansje (Johanna, Jans, Jansi, Jansie)(Mrs. C.M. Wüstenhoff), xxv-xxvi, 6, 77, 79, 89, 97 (photo), 101, 105, 306, 359, 373, 375, 387, 402, 406, 417, 418, 422, 425, 426, 438, 440, 445, 460, 466, 467, 471, 481, 486, 491, 511, 515, 516-517, 518, 535, 541, 557, 558, 561, 571, 578, 597, 591, 593, 596, 598, 608 (photo), 613; bareness of, 583; illness of, 600; learns English, 108, 109; letters of, 95-99, 109-10, 396-98, 429-31, 445-47, 484-86, 502-04, 523-25, 548-49, 556-57, 567-69, 584-85, 608-12; visits Paris World's Fair, 548-49; mentioned, 391, 395, 396, 414, 487, 540, 607

Wormser, Johan Adam (son of Johan Adam Wormser, Jr.,), 605

Wormser, Johan Adam, Jr., xxiv, 395, 406, 429, 438, 439 (photo), 468, 471, 472-73, 481, 490, 503, 505, 510-11, 523, 530, 545, 568, 579, 598; character of, 541; children of, 598, 601, 609; guardianship of, 599, 605; illness of, 438; letters of, 419, 438-42, 605-06; marriage of, 582-83, 587, 591-93; meets A.C. Van Raalte, 11; visits Paris World's Fair, 548-49, 561; mentioned, 391, 486, 540

Wormser, Johan Adam, Sr., xvi, xix, xxiv, xxx, 2, 17, 77, 89, 94, 101, 105, 109, 220, 223, 224, 225, 228, 229, 306, 323, 329, 333, 340, 359, 364, 366, 373, 445, 446, 466, 486, 501, 603, 604; and A.C. Van Raalte, 7; career, xxiv, 6-7, 516; character, 625-27; and Christian politics, 630-33, 636-37, 638; church suspension of, 383; correspondence of, xvii; and D.A. Budde family, 513-14, 606; death of, 472, 507, 510, 514-17, noted, 558, 626; family portrait of, xxv, 471, 530; home and office described, 427-28, 440-41; illnesses of, 28, 466, 502-05, 486; influence of, 559, 580-81; and Judith Zeelt, 471-72; and Free University, 637; and Groen van Prinsterer, 386, 628, 632; and infant baptism, 629-30; and "Old Writers," 628-29; and H.P. Scholte, 50, 628-31; letters of, xiv, xvi,xviii, xxiii, xxix, 323-25, 366-68, 398-99, 493-94; and Netherlands education policy, 387, 435; pamphlets of, 382, 392-93, 411-13, 420-23, 429, 559, 563, 565, 568, 570, 580-81, 583, 592, photo of, 382; petitions of, 387-88, 399; pietism of, xviii; religious views, 493-94; remembered, 601; and Secession of 1834, 16-17, 23-25, 26, 27; photos, 4, 627; mentioned, 391, 538

Wormser, Johanna (born 1838, married to C.W. Wüstenhoff), 487

Wormser, Johanna Christiaan (1804-1820), 5

Wormser, Johannes (nephew of Johan Adam Wormser, Sr., of Nijverdal), 541, 560, 563, 570, 578; wedding of, 585

Wormser, Leentje (eldest daughter of Hein Wormser, married to Rev. J. Schuurman), 403, 486, 489, 494

Wormser, Lena (daughter of Andries N. Wormser), 5, 252, 255, 260, 270, 271

Wormser, Maria (daughter of Johan A. Wormser, Sr.), 560, 570, 578, 585, 593, 598, 599, 609

Wormser, Maria (daughter of Andries N. Wormser), 5, 600

Wormser, Maria Hendrika (daughter of Johan A. Wormser, Sr.), 471

Wormser, Maria Louisa (daughter of Johan A. Wormser, Sr.), 94, 99, 101, 105, 107, 109, 306, 471, 486, 490, 505, 513, 530, 540, 541, 608; marriage of, 544, 582

Wormser, Martinus (Uncle Teunis, brother of Johan A. Wormser, Sr.), 5, 232, 282, 289, 565

Wormser, Meis (daughter of Andries N. Wormser), 255, 260, 270, 271, 395

Wormser, Sophia (daughter of Andries N. Wormser), 5, 231, 255; death of, 287-88

Wormser-Budde Society, 26-27

Wormser Plan, 225, 228
Worship, in Burlington, 82-83, 247, 375; in homes, 401
Wüstenhoff, Carl W., 228, 467, 471, 487, 511, 516-17, 530, 557, 591, 593, 596, 607, 608 (photo), 610, 613; new home of, 582-83; visits Paris World's Fair, 548-49
Wüstenhoff, Carl W., Jr., letter of, 569-70
Wyckoff, Isaac N. (pastor, Second Reformed Church in Albany), 35, 43, 67, 68, 78, 333, 385; church of, 53, 335-36; helps immigrants, 51-52, 332, 339; school of, 332, 337
Wyckoff Cemetery, 336
Wynberger family, 232, 287

Zaltbommel, Netherlands, 339
Zeeland, province of, 70, 73, 154, 163, 337
Zeelanders: in Burlington, 76, 262-63; emigration society of, 36, 405; in Iowa, 249-50
Zeelt, Judith J. (Mrs. Van Ysseldijk, Seceders benefactor), 10, 13, 17, 56,
91, 92, 104, 105, 111, 206, 226-27, 232, 245, 252, 260, 271-72, 360, 373, 397, 409, 428, 431, 438, 444, 445, 451, 452, 471, 472, 525; biography, 222-23; death of, 556-58; home "Postwijk," 282 (photo), 426; and H.P. Scholte, 282-85; illness of, 467-68, 486; and Johan A. Wormser, Sr., 502, 505; mentioned, 312, 416, 483
Zeemeeuw (ship), 44, 54, 55, 56, 57, 58-62, 123
Zeist, Netherlands, 556, 567
Ziegeurer, C. (Netherlands scholar), 25
Zijl, Mr., 341
Zoar (city of refuge for Lot), 107
Zonne, Gertruida (Mrs. Arend Lubbers), 415
Zonne, Peter (Alto, Wis., immigrant leader), 132, 261, 264, 356, 408; colony of, 300, 310; disparages A.C. Van Raalte, 79-80
Zuid Holland, Province of, 115, 329
Zutphen, Netherlands, 211, 221
Zweers, Mr., 332
Zwijndrecht, Netherlands, 13
Zwolle, Netherlands, 113, 256

The Historical Series of the Reformed Church in America
Books in print, William B. Eerdmans, publisher

Dorothy F. Van Ess
Pioneers in the Arab World

James W. Van Hoeven, editor
Piety and Patriotism

Mildred W. Schuppert
Digest and Index of the Minutes of General Synod, 1958-1977

Mildred W. Schuppert
Digest and Index of the Minutes of General Synod, 1906-1957

Gerald F. De Jong
From Strength to Strength

D. Ivan Dykstra
"B. D."

John W. Beardslee III, editor
Vision From the Hill

Howard G. Hageman
Two Centuries Plus

Marvin D. Hoff
Structures for Mission

James I. Cook, editor
The Church Speaks: Papers of the Commission on Theology of the Reformed Church in America, 1959-1984

James W. Van Hoeven, editor
Word and World

Books in Print in the Historical Series of the RCA

Gerrit J. tenZythoff
Sources of Secession: The Netherlands Hervormde Kerk on the Eve of the Dutch Immigration to the Midwest

Gordon J. Van Wylen
Vision for a Christian College

Jack D. Klunder and Russell L. Gasero, editors
Servant Gladly

Jeanette Boersma
Grace in the Gulf

Arie R. Brouwer
Ecumenical Testimony

Gerald F. De Jong
The Reformed Church in China, 1842-1951

Russell L. Gasero
Historical Directory of the Reformed Church in America, 1628-1992

Daniel J. Meeter
Meeting Each Other in Doctrine, Liturgy, and Government

Allan J. Janssen
Gathered at Albany

Elton J. Bruins
The Americanization of a Congregation, 2nd ed., by Elton J. Bruins (1995)

Gregg A. Mast
In Remembrance and Hope: The Ministry and Vision of Howard G. Hageman

Janny Venema, translator & editor
Deacons' Accounts, 1652-1674, First Dutch Reformed Church of Beverwyck/Albany

Morrill F. Swart
The Call of Africa

Lewis R. Scudder III
The Arabian Mission's Story: In Search of Abraham's Other Son

Renée S. House and John W. Coakley, editors
Patterns and Portraits: Women in the History of the Reformed Church in America

Elton J. Bruins & Robert P. Swierenga
Family Quarrels in the Dutch Reformed Churches in the Nineteenth Century

Allan J. Janssen
Constitutional Theology: Notes on the Book of Church Order of the Reformed Church In America

Gregg A. Mast, editor
Raising the Dead: Sermons of Howard G. Hageman

James Hart Brumm, editor
Equipping the Saints: The Synod of New York, 1800-2000

Joel R. Beeke, editor
Forerunner of the Great Awakening

Russell L. Gasero
Historical Directory of the Reformed Church in America, 1628-2000

Eugene Heideman
From Mission to Church: The Reformed Church in America in India

Harry Boonstra
Our School: Calvin College and the Christian Reformed Church

James I. Cook, editor
The Church Speaks, Vol. 2: Papers of the Commission on Theology of the Reformed Church in America, 1985-2000

John W. Coakley
Concord Makes Strength

Robert P. Swierenga
Dutch Chicago: A History of the Hollanders in the Windy City

Paul L. Armerding
Doctors for the Kingdom, The Work of the American Mission Hospitals in the Kingdom of Saudi Arabia

Donald J. Bruggink & Kim N. Baker
By Grace Alone, Stories of the Reformed Church in America

June Potter Durkee
Travels of an American Girl

Mary L. Kansfield
Letters to Hazel, Ministry Within the Women's Board of Foreign Missions of the Reformed Church in America